American Casebook Series
Hornbook Series and Basic Legal Texts
Black Letter Series and Nutshell Series

of

WEST PUBLISHING COMPANY
P.O. Box 64526
St. Paul, Minnesota 55164–0526

Accounting

FARIS' ACCOUNTING AND LAW IN A NUT-SHELL, 377 pages, 1984. Softcover. (Text)

FIFLIS' ACCOUNTING ISSUES FOR LAWYERS, TEACHING MATERIALS, , approximately 750 pages, July, 1991 Pub. (Casebook)

SIEGEL AND SIEGEL'S ACCOUNTING AND FINANCIAL DISCLOSURE: A GUIDE TO BASIC CONCEPTS, 259 pages, 1983. Softcover. (Text)

Administrative Law

BONFIELD AND ASIMOW'S STATE AND FEDERAL ADMINISTRATIVE LAW, 826 pages, 1989. Teacher's Manual available. (Casebook)

GELLHORN AND LEVIN'S ADMINISTRATIVE LAW AND PROCESS IN A NUTSHELL, Third Edition, 479 pages, 1990. Softcover. (Text)

MASHAW AND MERRILL'S CASES AND MATERIALS ON ADMINISTRATIVE LAW—THE AMERICAN PUBLIC LAW SYSTEM, Second Edition, 976 pages, 1985. (Casebook) 1989 Supplement.

ROBINSON, GELLHORN AND BRUFF'S THE ADMINISTRATIVE PROCESS, Third Edition, 978 pages, 1986. (Casebook)

Admiralty

HEALY AND SHARPE'S CASES AND MATERIALS ON ADMIRALTY, Second Edition, 876 pages, 1986. (Casebook)

MARAIST'S ADMIRALTY IN A NUTSHELL, Second Edition, 379 pages, 1988. Softcover. (Text)

SCHOENBAUM'S HORNBOOK ON ADMIRALTY AND MARITIME LAW, Student Edition, 692 pages, 1987 with 1989 pocket part. (Text)

Agency—Partnership

DEMOTT'S FIDUCIARY OBLIGATION, AGENCY AND PARTNERSHIP: DUTIES IN ONGOING BUSINESS RELATIONSHIPS, 740 pages, 1991. Teacher's Manual available. (Casebook)

FESSLER'S ALTERNATIVES TO INCORPORATION FOR PERSONS IN QUEST OF PROFIT, Third Edition, approximately 340 pages, 1991. Softcover. Teacher's Manual available. (Casebook)

HENN'S CASES AND MATERIALS ON AGENCY, PARTNERSHIP AND OTHER UNINCORPORATED BUSINESS ENTERPRISES, Second Edition, 733 pages, 1985. Teacher's Manual available. (Casebook)

REUSCHLEIN AND GREGORY'S HORNBOOK ON THE LAW OF AGENCY AND PARTNERSHIP, Second Edition, 683 pages, 1990. (Text)

SELECTED CORPORATION AND PARTNERSHIP STATUTES, RULES AND FORMS. Softcover. 727 pages, 1989.

STEFFEN AND KERR'S CASES ON AGENCY-PARTNERSHIP, Fourth Edition, 859 pages, 1980. (Casebook)

STEFFEN'S AGENCY-PARTNERSHIP IN A NUTSHELL, 364 pages, 1977. Softcover. (Text)

Agricultural Law

MEYER, PEDERSEN, THORSON AND DAVIDSON'S AGRICULTURAL LAW: CASES AND MATERIALS, 931 pages, 1985. Teacher's Manual available. (Casebook)

Alternative Dispute Resolution

KANOWITZ' CASES AND MATERIALS ON ALTERNATIVE DISPUTE RESOLUTION, 1024 pages, 1986. Teacher's Manual available. (Casebook) 1990 Supplement.

RISKIN AND WESTBROOK'S DISPUTE RESOLUTION AND LAWYERS, 468 pages, 1987. Teacher's Manual available. (Casebook)

RISKIN AND WESTBROOK'S DISPUTE RESOLUTION AND LAWYERS, Abridged Edition, 223 pages, 1987. Softcover. Teacher's Manual available. (Casebook)

American Indian Law

CANBY'S AMERICAN INDIAN LAW IN A NUTSHELL, Second Edition, 336 pages, 1988. Softcover. (Text)

GETCHES AND WILKINSON'S CASES AND MATERIALS ON FEDERAL INDIAN LAW, Second Edition, 880 pages, 1986. (Casebook)

Antitrust—see also Regulated Industries, Trade Regulation

FOX AND SULLIVAN'S CASES AND MATERIALS ON ANTITRUST, 935 pages, 1989. Teacher's Manual available. (Casebook)

GELLHORN'S ANTITRUST LAW AND ECONOMICS IN A NUTSHELL, Third Edition, 472 pages, 1986. Softcover. (Text)

HOVENKAMP'S BLACK LETTER ON ANTITRUST, 323 pages, 1986. Softcover. (Review)

HOVENKAMP'S HORNBOOK ON ECONOMICS AND FEDERAL ANTITRUST LAW, Student Edition, 414 pages, 1985. (Text)

OPPENHEIM, WESTON AND MCCARTHY'S CASES AND COMMENTS ON FEDERAL ANTITRUST LAWS, Fourth Edition, 1168 pages, 1981. (Casebook) 1985 Supplement.

POSNER AND EASTERBROOK'S CASES AND ECONOMIC NOTES ON ANTITRUST, Second Edition, 1077 pages, 1981. (Casebook) 1984–85 Supplement.

SULLIVAN'S HORNBOOK OF THE LAW OF ANTITRUST, 886 pages, 1977. (Text)

Appellate Advocacy—see Trial and Appellate Advocacy

Architecture and Engineering Law

SWEET'S LEGAL ASPECTS OF ARCHITECTURE, ENGINEERING AND THE CONSTRUCTION PROCESS, Fourth Edition, 889 pages, 1989. Teacher's Manual available. (Casebook)

Art Law

DUBOFF'S ART LAW IN A NUTSHELL, 335 pages, 1984. Softcover. (Text)

Banking Law

BANKING LAW: SELECTED STATUTES AND REGULATIONS. Softcover. Approximately 265 pages, 1991.

LOVETT'S BANKING AND FINANCIAL INSTITUTIONS LAW IN A NUTSHELL, Second Edition, 464 pages, 1988. Softcover. (Text)

SYMONS AND WHITE'S BANKING LAW: TEACHING MATERIALS, Third Edition, approximately 775 pages, 1991. Teacher's Manual available. (Casebook)

    Statutory Supplement. *See Banking Law: Selected Statutes*

Business Planning—see also Corporate Finance

PAINTER'S PROBLEMS AND MATERIALS IN BUSINESS PLANNING, Second Edition, 1008 pages, 1984. (Casebook) 1990 Supplement.

    Statutory Supplement. *See Selected Corporation and Partnership*

Civil Procedure—see also Federal Jurisdiction and Procedure

AMERICAN BAR ASSOCIATION SECTION OF LITIGATION—READINGS ON ADVERSARIAL JUSTICE: THE AMERICAN APPROACH TO ADJUDICATION, 217 pages, 1988. Softcover. (Coursebook)

CLERMONT'S BLACK LETTER ON CIVIL PROCEDURE, Second Edition, 332 pages, 1988. Softcover. (Review)

COUND, FRIEDENTHAL, MILLER AND SEXTON'S CASES AND MATERIALS ON CIVIL PROCEDURE, Fifth Edition, 1284 pages, 1989. Teacher's Manual available. (Casebook)

COUND, FRIEDENTHAL, MILLER AND SEXTON'S CIVIL PROCEDURE SUPPLEMENT. 460 pages, 1990. Softcover. (Casebook Supplement)

FEDERAL RULES OF CIVIL PROCEDURE—EDUCATIONAL EDITION. Softcover. 632 pages, 1990.

FRIEDENTHAL, KANE AND MILLER'S HORNBOOK ON CIVIL PROCEDURE, 876 pages, 1985.

Civil Procedure—Cont'd
(Text)

KANE AND LEVINE'S CIVIL PROCEDURE IN CALIFORNIA: STATE AND FEDERAL Approximately 600 pages, July, 1991 Pub. Softcover. (Casebook Supplement)

KANE'S CIVIL PROCEDURE IN A NUTSHELL, Third Edition, approximately 290 pages, 1991. Softcover. (Text)

KOFFLER AND REPPY'S HORNBOOK ON COMMON LAW PLEADING, 663 pages, 1969. (Text)

LEVINE, SLOMANSON AND WINGATE'S CALIFORNIA CIVIL PROCEDURE, CASES AND MATERIALS, . Approximately 550 pages, June, 1991 Pub. (Casebook)

MARCUS, REDISH AND SHERMAN'S CIVIL PROCEDURE: A MODERN APPROACH, 1027 pages, 1989. Teacher's Manual available. (Casebook)

MARCUS AND SHERMAN'S COMPLEX LITIGATION—CASES AND MATERIALS ON ADVANCED CIVIL PROCEDURE, 846 pages, 1985. Teacher's Manual available. (Casebook) 1989 Supplement.

PARK AND McFARLAND'S COMPUTER-AIDED EXERCISES ON CIVIL PROCEDURE, Third Edition, approximately 300 pages, July, 1991 Pub. Softcover. (Coursebook)

SIEGEL'S HORNBOOK ON NEW YORK PRACTICE, Second Edition, Student Edition, 1068 pages, 1991. Softcover. (Text)

Commercial Law

BAILEY AND HAGEDORN'S SECURED TRANSACTIONS IN A NUTSHELL, Third Edition, 390 pages, 1988. Softcover. (Text)

EPSTEIN, MARTIN, HENNING AND NICKLES' BASIC UNIFORM COMMERCIAL CODE TEACHING MATERIALS, Third Edition, 704 pages, 1988. Teacher's Manual available. (Casebook)

HENSON'S HORNBOOK ON SECURED TRANSACTIONS UNDER THE U.C.C., Second Edition, 504 pages, 1979, with 1979 pocket part. (Text)

MURRAY'S COMMERCIAL LAW, PROBLEMS AND MATERIALS, 366 pages, 1975. Teacher's Manual available. Softcover. (Coursebook)

NICKLES' BLACK LETTER ON COMMERCIAL PAPER, 450 pages, 1988. Softcover. (Review)

NICKLES, MATHESON AND DOLAN'S MATERIALS FOR UNDERSTANDING CREDIT AND PAYMENT SYSTEMS, 923 pages, 1987. Teacher's Manual available. (Casebook)

NORDSTROM, MURRAY AND CLOVIS' PROBLEMS AND MATERIALS ON SALES, 515 pages, 1982. (Casebook)

NORDSTROM, MURRAY AND CLOVIS' PROBLEMS AND MATERIALS ON SECURED TRANSACTIONS, 594 pages, 1987. (Casebook)

RUBIN AND COOTER'S THE PAYMENT SYSTEM: CASES, MATERIALS AND ISSUES, 885 pages, 1989. Teacher's Manual Available. (Casebook)

SELECTED COMMERCIAL STATUTES. Softcover. 1776 pages, 1990.

SPEIDEL'S BLACK LETTER ON SALES AND SALES FINANCING, 363 pages, 1984. Softcover. (Review)

SPEIDEL, SUMMERS AND WHITE'S COMMERCIAL LAW: TEACHING MATERIALS, Fourth Edition, 1448 pages, 1987. Teacher's Manual available. (Casebook)

SPEIDEL, SUMMERS AND WHITE'S COMMERCIAL PAPER: TEACHING MATERIALS, Fourth Edition, 578 pages, 1987. Reprint from Speidel et al., Commercial Law, Fourth Edition. Teacher's Manual available. (Casebook)

SPEIDEL, SUMMERS AND WHITE'S SALES: TEACHING MATERIALS, Fourth Edition, 804 pages, 1987. Reprint from Speidel et al., Commercial Law, Fourth Edition. Teacher's Manual available. (Casebook)

SPEIDEL, SUMMERS AND WHITE'S SECURED TRANSACTIONS: TEACHING MATERIALS, Fourth Edition, 485 pages, 1987. Reprint from Speidel et al., Commercial Law, Fourth Edition. Teacher's Manual available. (Casebook)

STOCKTON'S SALES IN A NUTSHELL, Second Edition, 370 pages, 1981. Softcover. (Text)

STONE'S UNIFORM COMMERCIAL CODE IN A NUTSHELL, Third Edition, 580 pages, 1989. Softcover. (Text)

WEBER AND SPEIDEL'S COMMERCIAL PAPER IN

Commercial Law—Cont'd

A NUTSHELL, Third Edition, 404 pages, 1982. Softcover. (Text)

WHITE AND SUMMERS' HORNBOOK ON THE UNIFORM COMMERCIAL CODE, Third Edition, Student Edition, 1386 pages, 1988. (Text)

Community Property

MENNELL AND BOYKOFF'S COMMUNITY PROPERTY IN A NUTSHELL, Second Edition, 432 pages, 1988. Softcover. (Text)

VERRALL AND BIRD'S CASES AND MATERIALS ON CALIFORNIA COMMUNITY PROPERTY, Fifth Edition, 604 pages, 1988. (Casebook)

Comparative Law

BARTON, GIBBS, LI AND MERRYMAN'S LAW IN RADICALLY DIFFERENT CULTURES, 960 pages, 1983. (Casebook)

GLENDON, GORDON AND OSAKWE'S COMPARATIVE LEGAL TRADITIONS: TEXT, MATERIALS AND CASES ON THE CIVIL LAW, COMMON LAW AND SOCIALIST LAW TRADITIONS, 1091 pages, 1985. (Casebook)

GLENDON, GORDON AND OSAKWE'S COMPARATIVE LEGAL TRADITIONS IN A NUTSHELL. 402 pages, 1982. Softcover. (Text)

LANGBEIN'S COMPARATIVE CRIMINAL PROCEDURE: GERMANY, 172 pages, 1977. Softcover. (Casebook)

Computers and Law

MAGGS AND SPROWL'S COMPUTER APPLICATIONS IN THE LAW, 316 pages, 1987. (Coursebook)

MASON'S USING COMPUTERS IN THE LAW: AN INTRODUCTION AND PRACTICAL GUIDE, Second Edition, 288 pages, 1988. Softcover. (Coursebook)

Conflict of Laws

CRAMTON, CURRIE AND KAY'S CASES–COMMENTS–QUESTIONS ON CONFLICT OF LAWS, Fourth Edition, 876 pages, 1987. (Casebook)

HAY'S BLACK LETTER ON CONFLICT OF LAWS, 330 pages, 1989. Softcover. (Review)

SCOLES AND HAY'S HORNBOOK ON CONFLICT OF LAWS, Student Edition, 1085 pages, 1982, with 1988–89 pocket part. (Text)

SIEGEL'S CONFLICTS IN A NUTSHELL, 470 pages, 1982. Softcover. (Text)

Constitutional Law—Civil Rights—see also First Amendment and Foreign Relations and National Security Law

ABERNATHY'S CASES AND MATERIALS ON CIVIL RIGHTS, 660 pages, 1980. (Casebook)

BARRON AND DIENES' BLACK LETTER ON CONSTITUTIONAL LAW, Third Edition, approximately 400 pages, 1991. Softcover. (Review)

BARRON AND DIENES' CONSTITUTIONAL LAW IN A NUTSHELL, Second Edition, approximately 475 pages, 1991. Softcover. (Text)

ENGDAHL'S CONSTITUTIONAL FEDERALISM IN A NUTSHELL, Second Edition, 411 pages, 1987. Softcover. (Text)

FARBER AND SHERRY'S HISTORY OF THE AMERICAN CONSTITUTION, 458 pages, 1990. Softcover. Teacher's Manual available. (Text)

GARVEY AND ALEINIKOFF'S MODERN CONSTITUTIONAL THEORY: A READER, Second Edition, approximately 575 pages, August, 1991 Pub. Softcover. (Reader)

LOCKHART, KAMISAR, CHOPER AND SHIFFRIN'S CONSTITUTIONAL LAW: CASES–COMMENTS–QUESTIONS, Seventh Edition, approximately 1600 pages, 1991. (Casebook) 1991 Supplement.

LOCKHART, KAMISAR, CHOPER AND SHIFFRIN'S THE AMERICAN CONSTITUTION: CASES AND MATERIALS, Seventh Edition, approximately 1250 pages, September, 1991 Pub. Abridged version of Lockhart, et al., Constitutional Law: Cases–Comments–Questions, Seventh Edition. (Casebook) 1991 Supplement.

LOCKHART, KAMISAR, CHOPER AND SHIFFRIN'S CONSTITUTIONAL RIGHTS AND LIBERTIES: CASES AND MATERIALS, Seventh Edition, approximately 1250 pages, September, 1991 Pub. Reprint from Lockhart, et al., Constitutional Law: Cases–Comments–Questions, Seventh Edition. (Casebook) 1991 Supplement.

MARKS AND COOPER'S STATE CONSTITUTIONAL LAW IN A NUTSHELL, 329 pages, 1988. Softcover. (Text)

NOWAK AND ROTUNDA'S HORNBOOK ON CON-

Constitutional Law—Civil Rights—Cont'd

STITUTIONAL LAW, Fourth Edition, approximately 1200 pages, August, 1991 Pub. (Text)

ROTUNDA'S MODERN CONSTITUTIONAL LAW: CASES AND NOTES, Third Edition, 1085 pages, 1989. (Casebook) 1990 Supplement.

VIEIRA'S CONSTITUTIONAL CIVIL RIGHTS IN A NUTSHELL, Second Edition, 322 pages, 1990. Softcover. (Text)

WILLIAMS' CONSTITUTIONAL ANALYSIS IN A NUTSHELL, 388 pages, 1979. Softcover. (Text)

Consumer Law—see also Commercial Law

EPSTEIN AND NICKLES' CONSUMER LAW IN A NUTSHELL, Second Edition, 418 pages, 1981. Softcover. (Text)

SELECTED COMMERCIAL STATUTES. Softcover. 1776 pages, 1990.

SPANOGLE, ROHNER, PRIDGEN AND RASOR'S CASES AND MATERIALS ON CONSUMER LAW, Second Edition, approximately 900 pages, 1991. (Casebook)

Contracts

CALAMARI AND PERILLO'S BLACK LETTER ON CONTRACTS, Second Edition, 462 pages, 1990. Softcover. (Review)

CALAMARI AND PERILLO'S HORNBOOK ON CONTRACTS, Third Edition, 1049 pages, 1987. (Text)

CALAMARI, PERILLO AND BENDER'S CASES AND PROBLEMS ON CONTRACTS, Second Edition, 905 pages, 1989. Teacher's Manual Available. (Casebook)

CORBIN'S TEXT ON CONTRACTS, One Volume Student Edition, 1224 pages, 1952. (Text)

FESSLER AND LOISEAUX'S CASES AND MATERIALS ON CONTRACTS—MORALITY, ECONOMICS AND THE MARKET PLACE, 837 pages, 1982. Teacher's Manual available. (Casebook)

FRIEDMAN'S CONTRACT REMEDIES IN A NUTSHELL, 323 pages, 1981. Softcover. (Text)

FULLER AND EISENBERG'S CASES ON BASIC CONTRACT LAW, Fifth Edition, 1037 pages, 1990. (Casebook)

HAMILTON, RAU AND WEINTRAUB'S CASES AND MATERIALS ON CONTRACTS, 830 pages, 1984. (Casebook)

JACKSON AND BOLLINGER'S CASES ON CONTRACT LAW IN MODERN SOCIETY, Second Edition, 1329 pages, 1980. Teacher's Manual available. (Casebook)

KEYES' GOVERNMENT CONTRACTS IN A NUTSHELL, Second Edition, 557 pages, 1990. Softcover. (Text)

SCHABER AND ROHWER'S CONTRACTS IN A NUTSHELL, Third Edition, 457 pages, 1990. Softcover. (Text)

SUMMERS AND HILLMAN'S CONTRACT AND RELATED OBLIGATION: THEORY, DOCTRINE AND PRACTICE, 1074 pages, 1987. Teacher's Manual available. (Casebook)

Copyright—see Patent and Copyright Law

Corporate Finance—see also Business Planning

HAMILTON'S CASES AND MATERIALS ON CORPORATION FINANCE, Second Edition, 1221 pages, 1989. (Casebook)

OESTERLE'S THE LAW OF MERGERS, ACQUISITIONS AND REORGANIZATIONS, Approximately 1100 pages, June, 1991 Pub. (Casebook)

Corporations

HAMILTON'S BLACK LETTER ON CORPORATIONS, Second Edition, 513 pages, 1986. Softcover. (Review)

HAMILTON'S CASES AND MATERIALS ON CORPORATIONS—INCLUDING PARTNERSHIPS AND LIMITED PARTNERSHIPS, Fourth Edition, 1248 pages, 1990. Teacher's Manual available. (Casebook) 1990 Statutory Supplement.

HAMILTON'S THE LAW OF CORPORATIONS IN A NUTSHELL, Third Edition, approximately 500 pages, 1991. Softcover. (Text)

HENN'S TEACHING MATERIALS ON THE LAW OF CORPORATIONS, Second Edition, 1204 pages, 1986. Teacher's Manual available. (Casebook)

Statutory Supplement. *See Selected Corporation and Partnership*

HENN AND ALEXANDER'S HORNBOOK ON LAWS OF CORPORATIONS, Third Edition, Student Edition, 1371 pages, 1983, with 1986 pocket part. (Text)

Corporations—Cont'd

SELECTED CORPORATION AND PARTNERSHIP STATUTES, RULES AND FORMS. Softcover. 727 pages, 1989.

SOLOMON, SCHWARTZ AND BAUMAN'S MATERIALS AND PROBLEMS ON CORPORATIONS: LAW AND POLICY, Second Edition, 1391 pages, 1988. Teacher's Manual available. (Casebook) 1990 Supplement.

Statutory Supplement. *See Selected Corporation and Partnership*

Corrections

KRANTZ' THE LAW OF CORRECTIONS AND PRISONERS' RIGHTS IN A NUTSHELL, Third Edition, 407 pages, 1988. Softcover. (Text)

KRANTZ AND BRANHAM'S CASES AND MATERIALS ON THE LAW OF SENTENCING, CORRECTIONS AND PRISONERS' RIGHTS, Fourth Edition, approximately 625 pages, 1991. (Casebook)

ROBBINS' CASES AND MATERIALS ON POST-CONVICTION REMEDIES, 506 pages, 1982. (Casebook)

Creditors' Rights

BANKRUPTCY CODE, RULES AND OFFICIAL FORMS, LAW SCHOOL EDITION. 909 pages, 1991. Softcover.

EPSTEIN'S DEBTOR-CREDITOR LAW IN A NUTSHELL, Fourth Edition, approximately 400 pages, 1991. Softcover. (Text)

EPSTEIN, LANDERS AND NICKLES' CASES AND MATERIALS ON DEBTORS AND CREDITORS, Third Edition, 1059 pages, 1987. Teacher's Manual available. (Casebook)

LOPUCKI'S PLAYER'S MANUAL FOR THE DEBTOR-CREDITOR GAME, 123 pages, 1985. Softcover. (Coursebook)

NICKLES AND EPSTEIN'S BLACK LETTER ON CREDITORS' RIGHTS AND BANKRUPTCY, 576 pages, 1989. (Review)

RIESENFELD'S CASES AND MATERIALS ON CREDITORS' REMEDIES AND DEBTORS' PROTECTION, Fourth Edition, 914 pages, 1987. (Casebook) 1990 Supplement.

WHITE'S CASES AND MATERIALS ON BANKRUPTCY AND CREDITORS' RIGHTS, 812 pages, 1985. Teacher's Manual available. (Casebook) 1987 Supplement.

Criminal Law and Criminal Procedure—see also Corrections, Juvenile Justice

ABRAMS' FEDERAL CRIMINAL LAW AND ITS ENFORCEMENT, 866 pages, 1986. (Casebook) 1988 Supplement.

AMERICAN CRIMINAL JUSTICE PROCESS: SELECTED RULES, STATUTES AND GUIDELINES. 723 pages, 1989. Softcover.

CARLSON'S ADJUDICATION OF CRIMINAL JUSTICE: PROBLEMS AND REFERENCES, 130 pages, 1986. Softcover. (Casebook)

DIX AND SHARLOT'S CASES AND MATERIALS ON CRIMINAL LAW, Third Edition, 846 pages, 1987. (Casebook)

GRANO'S PROBLEMS IN CRIMINAL PROCEDURE, Second Edition, 176 pages, 1981. Teacher's Manual available. Softcover. (Coursebook)

HEYMANN AND KENETY'S THE MURDER TRIAL OF WILBUR JACKSON: A HOMICIDE IN THE FAMILY, Second Edition, 347 pages, 1985. (Coursebook)

ISRAEL, KAMISAR AND LAFAVE'S CRIMINAL PROCEDURE AND THE CONSTITUTION: LEADING SUPREME COURT CASES AND INTRODUCTORY TEXT. 747 pages, 1990 Edition. Softcover. (Casebook)

ISRAEL AND LAFAVE'S CRIMINAL PROCEDURE—CONSTITUTIONAL LIMITATIONS IN A NUTSHELL, Fourth Edition, 461 pages, 1988. Softcover. (Text)

JOHNSON'S CASES, MATERIALS AND TEXT ON CRIMINAL LAW, Fourth Edition, 759 pages, 1990. Teacher's Manual available. (Casebook)

JOHNSON'S CASES AND MATERIALS ON CRIMINAL PROCEDURE, 859 pages, 1988. (Casebook) 1990 Supplement.

KAMISAR, LAFAVE AND ISRAEL'S MODERN CRIMINAL PROCEDURE: CASES, COMMENTS AND QUESTIONS, Seventh Edition, 1593 pages, 1990. (Casebook) 1990 Supplement.

KAMISAR, LAFAVE AND ISRAEL'S BASIC CRIMINAL PROCEDURE: CASES, COMMENTS AND QUESTIONS, Seventh Edition, 792 pages, 1990. Softcover reprint from Kamisar, et al., Modern Criminal Procedure: Cases, Comments and Questions, Seventh Edi-

Criminal Law and Criminal Procedure—Cont'd

tion. (Casebook) 1990 Supplement.

LaFave's Modern Criminal Law: Cases, Comments and Questions, Second Edition, 903 pages, 1988. (Casebook)

LaFave and Israel's Hornbook on Criminal Procedure, Second Edition, Student Edition, approximately 1200 pages, December, 1991 Pub. (Text)

LaFave and Scott's Hornbook on Criminal Law, Second Edition, 918 pages, 1986. (Text)

Langbein's Comparative Criminal Procedure: Germany, 172 pages, 1977. Softcover. (Casebook)

Loewy's Criminal Law in a Nutshell, Second Edition, 321 pages, 1987. Softcover. (Text)

Low's Black Letter on Criminal Law, Revised First Edition, 443 pages, 1990. Softcover. (Review)

Saltzburg's Cases and Commentary on American Criminal Procedure, Third Edition, 1302 pages, 1988. Teacher's Manual available. (Casebook) 1990 Supplement.

Uviller's The Processes of Criminal Justice: Investigation and Adjudication, Second Edition, 1384 pages, 1979. (Casebook) 1979 Statutory Supplement. 1986 Update.

Vorenberg's Cases on Criminal Law and Procedure, Second Edition, 1088 pages, 1981. Teacher's Manual available. (Casebook) 1990 Supplement.

Decedents' Estates—see Trusts and Estates

Domestic Relations

Clark's Hornbook on Domestic Relations, Second Edition, Student Edition, 1050 pages, 1988. (Text)

Clark and Glowinsky's Cases and Problems on Domestic Relations, Fourth Edition. 1150 pages, 1990. Teacher's Manual available. (Casebook)

Krause's Black Letter on Family Law, 314 pages, 1988. Softcover. (Review)

Krause's Cases, Comments and Questions on Family Law, Third Edition, 1433 pages,

1990. (Casebook)

Krause's Family Law in a Nutshell, Second Edition, 444 pages, 1986. Softcover. (Text)

Krauskopf's Cases on Property Division at Marriage Dissolution, 250 pages, 1984. Softcover. (Casebook)

Economics, Law and—see also Antitrust, Regulated Industries

Goetz' Cases and Materials on Law and Economics, 547 pages, 1984. (Casebook)

Malloy's Law and Economics: A Comparative Approach to Theory and Practice, 166 pages, 1990. Softcover. (Text)

Education Law

Alexander and Alexander's The Law of Schools, Students and Teachers in a Nutshell, 409 pages, 1984. Softcover. (Text)

Yudof, Kirp and Levin's Educational Policy and the Law, Third Edition, approximately 975 pages, April, 1991 Pub. (Casebook)

Employment Discrimination—see also Women and the Law

Estreicher and Harper's Cases and Materials on the Law Governing the Employment Relationship, 962 pages, 1990. Teacher's Manual available. (Casebook) Statutory Supplement.

Jones, Murphy and Belton's Cases and Materials on Discrimination in Employment, (The Labor Law Group). Fifth Edition, 1116 pages, 1987. (Casebook) 1990 Supplement.

Player's Federal Law of Employment Discrimination in a Nutshell, Second Edition, 402 pages, 1981. Softcover. (Text)

Player's Hornbook on Employment Discrimination Law, Student Edition, 708 pages, 1988. (Text)

Player, Shoben and Lieberwitz' Cases and Materials on Employment Discrimination Law, 827 pages, 1990. Teacher's Manual available. (Casebook)

Energy and Natural Resources Law—see also Oil and Gas

Laitos' Cases and Materials on Natural

Energy and Natural Resources Law—Cont'd

RESOURCES LAW, 938 pages, 1985. Teacher's Manual available. (Casebook)

SELECTED ENVIRONMENTAL LAW STATUTES—EDUCATIONAL EDITION. Softcover. 1020 pages, 1990.

Environmental Law—see also Energy and Natural Resources Law; Sea, Law of

BONINE AND MCGARITY'S THE LAW OF ENVIRONMENTAL PROTECTION: CASES—LEGISLATION—POLICIES, 1076 pages, 1984. Teacher's Manual available. (Casebook)

FINDLEY AND FARBER'S CASES AND MATERIALS ON ENVIRONMENTAL LAW, Third Edition, approximately 750 pages, 1991. (Casebook)

FINDLEY AND FARBER'S ENVIRONMENTAL LAW IN A NUTSHELL, Second Edition, 367 pages, 1988. Softcover. (Text)

RODGERS' HORNBOOK ON ENVIRONMENTAL LAW, 956 pages, 1977, with 1984 pocket part. (Text)

SELECTED ENVIRONMENTAL LAW STATUTES—EDUCATIONAL EDITION. Softcover. 1020 pages, 1990.

Equity—see Remedies

Estate Planning—see also Trusts and Estates; Taxation—Estate and Gift

LYNN'S AN INTRODUCTION TO ESTATE PLANNING IN A NUTSHELL, Third Edition, 370 pages, 1983. Softcover. (Text)

Evidence

BROUN AND BLAKEY'S BLACK LETTER ON EVIDENCE, 269 pages, 1984. Softcover. (Review)

BROUN, MEISENHOLDER, STRONG AND MOSTELLER'S PROBLEMS IN EVIDENCE, Third Edition, 238 pages, 1988. Teacher's Manual available. Softcover. (Coursebook)

CLEARY, STRONG, BROUN AND MOSTELLER'S CASES AND MATERIALS ON EVIDENCE, Fourth Edition, 1060 pages, 1988. (Casebook)

FEDERAL RULES OF EVIDENCE FOR UNITED STATES COURTS AND MAGISTRATES. Softcover. 381 pages, 1990.

FRIEDMAN'S THE ELEMENTS OF EVIDENCE, 310 pages, 1991. Teacher's Manual available.

(Coursebook)

GRAHAM'S FEDERAL RULES OF EVIDENCE IN A NUTSHELL, Second Edition, 473 pages, 1987. Softcover. (Text)

LEMPERT AND SALTZBURG'S A MODERN APPROACH TO EVIDENCE: TEXT, PROBLEMS, TRANSCRIPTS AND CASES, Second Edition, 1232 pages, 1983. Teacher's Manual available. (Casebook)

LILLY'S AN INTRODUCTION TO THE LAW OF EVIDENCE, Second Edition, 585 pages, 1987. (Text)

MCCORMICK, SUTTON AND WELLBORN'S CASES AND MATERIALS ON EVIDENCE, Sixth Edition, 1067 pages, 1987. (Casebook)

MCCORMICK'S HORNBOOK ON EVIDENCE, Third Edition, Student Edition, 1156 pages, 1984, with 1987 pocket part. (Text)

ROTHSTEIN'S EVIDENCE IN A NUTSHELL: STATE AND FEDERAL RULES, Second Edition, 514 pages, 1981. Softcover. (Text)

Federal Jurisdiction and Procedure

CURRIE'S CASES AND MATERIALS ON FEDERAL COURTS, Fourth Edition, 783 pages, 1990. (Casebook)

CURRIE'S FEDERAL JURISDICTION IN A NUTSHELL, Third Edition, 242 pages, 1990. Softcover. (Text)

FEDERAL RULES OF CIVIL PROCEDURE—EDUCATIONAL EDITION. Softcover. 632 pages, 1990.

REDISH'S BLACK LETTER ON FEDERAL JURISDICTION, Second Edition, approximately 230 pages, 1991. Softcover. (Review)

REDISH'S CASES, COMMENTS AND QUESTIONS ON FEDERAL COURTS, Second Edition, 1122 pages, 1989. (Casebook) 1990 Supplement.

VETRI AND MERRILL'S FEDERAL COURTS PROBLEMS AND MATERIALS, Second Edition, 232 pages, 1984. Softcover. (Coursebook)

WRIGHT'S HORNBOOK ON FEDERAL COURTS, Fourth Edition, Student Edition, 870 pages, 1983. (Text)

First Amendment

SHIFFRIN AND CHOPER'S FIRST AMENDMENT, CASES—COMMENTS—QUESTIONS, Approximately 700 pages, 1991. Softcover. (Casebook)

Foreign Relations and National Security Law

FRANCK AND GLENNON'S FOREIGN RELATIONS AND NATIONAL SECURITY LAW, 941 pages, 1987. (Casebook)

Future Interests—see Trusts and Estates

Health Law—see Medicine, Law and

Human Rights—see International Law

Immigration Law

ALEINIKOFF AND MARTIN'S IMMIGRATION: PROCESS AND POLICY, Interim Second Edition, approximately 1075 pages, 1991. (Casebook)

    Statutory Supplement. *See Immigration and Nationality Laws*

IMMIGRATION AND NATIONALITY LAWS OF THE UNITED STATES: SELECTED STATUTES, REGULATIONS AND FORMS. Softcover. 400 pages, 1990.

WEISSBRODT'S IMMIGRATION LAW AND PROCEDURE IN A NUTSHELL, Second Edition, 438 pages, 1989, Softcover. (Text)

Indian Law—see American Indian Law

Insurance Law

DEVINE AND TERRY'S PROBLEMS IN INSURANCE LAW, 240 pages, 1989. Softcover. Teacher's Manual available. (Coursebook)

DOBBYN'S INSURANCE LAW IN A NUTSHELL, Second Edition, 316 pages, 1989. Softcover. (Text)

KEETON'S CASES ON BASIC INSURANCE LAW, Second Edition, 1086 pages, 1977. Teacher's Manual available. (Casebook)

KEETON'S COMPUTER-AIDED AND WORKBOOK EXERCISES ON INSURANCE LAW, 255 pages, 1990. Softcover. (Coursebook)

KEETON AND WIDISS' INSURANCE LAW, Student Edition, 1359 pages, 1988. (Text)

WIDISS AND KEETON'S COURSE SUPPLEMENT TO KEETON AND WIDISS' INSURANCE LAW, 502 pages, 1988. Softcover. Teacher's Manual available. (Casebook)

WIDISS' INSURANCE: MATERIALS ON FUNDAMENTAL PRINCIPLES, LEGAL DOCTRINES AND REGULATORY ACTS, 1186 pages, 1989. Teacher's Manual available. (Casebook)

YORK AND WHELAN'S CASES, MATERIALS AND PROBLEMS ON GENERAL PRACTICE INSURANCE LAW, Second Edition, 787 pages, 1988. Teacher's Manual available. (Casebook)

International Law—see also Sea, Law of

BUERGENTHAL'S INTERNATIONAL HUMAN RIGHTS IN A NUTSHELL, 283 pages, 1988. Softcover. (Text)

BUERGENTHAL AND MAIER'S PUBLIC INTERNATIONAL LAW IN A NUTSHELL, Second Edition, 275 pages, 1990. Softcover. (Text)

FOLSOM, GORDON AND SPANOGLE'S INTERNATIONAL BUSINESS TRANSACTIONS—A PROBLEM-ORIENTED COURSEBOOK, Second Edition, approximately 1150 pages, 1991. Teacher's Manual available. (Casebook) 1991 Documents Supplement.

FOLSOM, GORDON AND SPANOGLE'S INTERNATIONAL BUSINESS TRANSACTIONS IN A NUTSHELL, Third Edition, 509 pages, 1988. Softcover. (Text)

HENKIN, PUGH, SCHACHTER AND SMIT'S CASES AND MATERIALS ON INTERNATIONAL LAW, Second Edition, 1517 pages, 1987. (Casebook) Documents Supplement.

JACKSON AND DAVEY'S CASES, MATERIALS AND TEXT ON LEGAL PROBLEMS OF INTERNATIONAL ECONOMIC RELATIONS, Second Edition, 1269 pages, 1986. (Casebook) 1989 Documents Supplement.

KIRGIS' INTERNATIONAL ORGANIZATIONS IN THEIR LEGAL SETTING, 1016 pages, 1977. Teacher's Manual available. (Casebook) 1981 Supplement.

WESTON, FALK AND D'AMATO'S INTERNATIONAL LAW AND WORLD ORDER—A PROBLEM-ORIENTED COURSEBOOK, Second Edition, 1335 pages, 1990. Teacher's Manual available. (Casebook) Documents Supplement.

Interviewing and Counseling

BINDER AND PRICE'S LEGAL INTERVIEWING AND COUNSELING, 232 pages, 1977. Teacher's Manual available. Softcover. (Coursebook)

BINDER, BERGMAN AND PRICE'S LAWYERS AS COUNSELORS: A CLIENT–CENTERED APPROACH, Approximately 425 pages, 1991. Softcover. (Coursebook)

Interviewing and Counseling—Cont'd

SHAFFER AND ELKINS' LEGAL INTERVIEWING AND COUNSELING IN A NUTSHELL, Second Edition, 487 pages, 1987. Softcover. (Text)

Introduction to Law—see Legal Method and Legal System

Introduction to Law Study

HEGLAND'S INTRODUCTION TO THE STUDY AND PRACTICE OF LAW IN A NUTSHELL, 418 pages, 1983. Softcover. (Text)

KINYON'S INTRODUCTION TO LAW STUDY AND LAW EXAMINATIONS IN A NUTSHELL, 389 pages, 1971. Softcover. (Text)

Judicial Process—see Legal Method and Legal System

Jurisprudence

CHRISTIE'S JURISPRUDENCE—TEXT AND READINGS ON THE PHILOSOPHY OF LAW, 1056 pages, 1973. (Casebook)

Juvenile Justice

FOX'S CASES AND MATERIALS ON MODERN JUVENILE JUSTICE, Second Edition, 960 pages, 1981. (Casebook)

FOX'S JUVENILE COURTS IN A NUTSHELL, Third Edition, 291 pages, 1984. Softcover. (Text)

Labor and Employment Law—see also Employment Discrimination, Social Legislation

FINKIN, GOLDMAN AND SUMMERS' LEGAL PROTECTION OF INDIVIDUAL EMPLOYEES, (The Labor Law Group). 1164 pages, 1989. (Casebook)

GORMAN'S BASIC TEXT ON LABOR LAW—UNIONIZATION AND COLLECTIVE BARGAINING, 914 pages, 1976. (Text)

LESLIE'S LABOR LAW IN A NUTSHELL, Second Edition, 397 pages, 1986. Softcover. (Text)

NOLAN'S LABOR ARBITRATION LAW AND PRACTICE IN A NUTSHELL, 358 pages, 1979. Softcover. (Text)

OBERER, HANSLOWE, ANDERSEN AND HEINSZ' CASES AND MATERIALS ON LABOR LAW—COLLECTIVE BARGAINING IN A FREE SOCIETY, Third Edition, 1163 pages, 1986. Teacher's Manual available. (Casebook) Statutory Supplement.

RABIN, SILVERSTEIN AND SCHATZKI'S LABOR AND EMPLOYMENT LAW: PROBLEMS, CASES AND MATERIALS IN THE LAW OF WORK, (The Labor Law Group). 1014 pages, 1988. Teacher's Manual available. (Casebook) 1988 Statutory Supplement.

Land Finance—Property Security—see Real Estate Transactions

Land Use

CALLIES AND FREILICH'S CASES AND MATERIALS ON LAND USE, 1233 pages, 1986. (Casebook) 1988 Supplement.

HAGMAN AND JUERGENSMEYER'S HORNBOOK ON URBAN PLANNING AND LAND DEVELOPMENT CONTROL LAW, Second Edition, Student Edition, 680 pages, 1986. (Text)

WRIGHT AND GITELMAN'S CASES AND MATERIALS ON LAND USE, Fourth Edition, approximately 1225 pages, 1991. Teacher's Manual available. (Casebook)

WRIGHT AND WRIGHT'S LAND USE IN A NUTSHELL, Second Edition, 356 pages, 1985. Softcover. (Text)

Legal History—see also Legal Method and Legal System

PRESSER AND ZAINALDIN'S CASES AND MATERIALS ON LAW AND JURISPRUDENCE IN AMERICAN HISTORY, Second Edition, 1092 pages, 1989. Teacher's Manual available. (Casebook)

Legal Method and Legal System—see also Legal Research, Legal Writing

ALDISERT'S READINGS, MATERIALS AND CASES IN THE JUDICIAL PROCESS, 948 pages, 1976. (Casebook)

BERCH AND BERCH'S INTRODUCTION TO LEGAL METHOD AND PROCESS, 550 pages, 1985. Teacher's Manual available. (Casebook)

BODENHEIMER, OAKLEY AND LOVE'S READINGS AND CASES ON AN INTRODUCTION TO THE ANGLO-AMERICAN LEGAL SYSTEM, Second Edition, 166 pages, 1988. Softcover. (Casebook)

DAVIES AND LAWRY'S INSTITUTIONS AND METHODS OF THE LAW—INTRODUCTORY

Legal Method and Legal System—Cont'd

TEACHING MATERIALS, 547 pages, 1982. Teacher's Manual available. (Casebook)

DVORKIN, HIMMELSTEIN AND LESNICK'S BECOMING A LAWYER: A HUMANISTIC PERSPECTIVE ON LEGAL EDUCATION AND PROFESSIONALISM, 211 pages, 1981. Softcover. (Text)

KEETON'S JUDGING, 842 pages, 1990. Softcover. (Coursebook)

KELSO AND KELSO'S STUDYING LAW: AN INTRODUCTION, 587 pages, 1984. (Coursebook)

KEMPIN'S HISTORICAL INTRODUCTION TO ANGLO-AMERICAN LAW IN A NUTSHELL, Third Edition, 323 pages, 1990. Softcover. (Text)

MEADOR'S AMERICAN COURTS, Approximately 121 pages, 1991. Softcover. (Text)

REYNOLDS' JUDICIAL PROCESS IN A NUTSHELL, Second Edition, approximately 310 pages, 1991. Softcover. (Text)

Legal Research

COHEN'S LEGAL RESEARCH IN A NUTSHELL, Fourth Edition, 452 pages, 1985. Softcover. (Text)

COHEN, BERRING AND OLSON'S HOW TO FIND THE LAW, Ninth Edition, 716 pages, 1989. (Text)

COHEN, BERRING AND OLSON'S FINDING THE LAW, 570 pages, 1989. Softcover reprint from Cohen, Berring and Olson's How to Find the Law, Ninth Edition. (Coursebook)

   Legal Research Exercises, 3rd Ed., for use with Cohen, Berring and Olson, 229 pages, 1989. Teacher's Manual available.

ROMBAUER'S LEGAL PROBLEM SOLVING—ANALYSIS, RESEARCH AND WRITING, Fifth Edition, approximately 520 pages, 1991. Teacher's Manual with problems available. (Coursebook)

STATSKY'S LEGAL RESEARCH AND WRITING, Third Edition, 257 pages, 1986. Softcover. (Coursebook)

TEPLY'S LEGAL RESEARCH AND CITATION, Third Edition, 472 pages, 1989. Softcover. (Coursebook)

   Student Library Exercises, 3rd ed., 391 pages, 1989. Answer Key available.

Legal Writing

CHILD'S DRAFTING LEGAL DOCUMENTS: MATERIALS AND PROBLEMS, 286 pages, 1988. Softcover. Teacher's Manual available. (Coursebook)

DICKERSON'S MATERIALS ON LEGAL DRAFTING, 425 pages, 1981. Teacher's Manual available. (Coursebook)

FELSENFELD AND SIEGEL'S WRITING CONTRACTS IN PLAIN ENGLISH, 290 pages, 1981. Softcover. (Text)

GOPEN'S WRITING FROM A LEGAL PERSPECTIVE, 225 pages, 1981. (Text)

MELLINKOFF'S LEGAL WRITING—SENSE AND NONSENSE, 242 pages, 1982. Softcover. Teacher's Manual available. (Text)

PRATT'S LEGAL WRITING: A SYSTEMATIC APPROACH, 468 pages, 1990. Teacher's Manual available. (Coursebook)

RAY AND COX'S BEYOND THE BASICS: A TEXT FOR ADVANCED LEGAL WRITING, Approximately 425 pages, 1991. Softcover. (Text)

RAY AND RAMSFIELD'S LEGAL WRITING: GETTING IT RIGHT AND GETTING IT WRITTEN, 250 pages, 1987. Softcover. (Text)

SQUIRES AND ROMBAUER'S LEGAL WRITING IN A NUTSHELL, 294 pages, 1982. Softcover. (Text)

STATSKY AND WERNET'S CASE ANALYSIS AND FUNDAMENTALS OF LEGAL WRITING, Third Edition, 424 pages, 1989. Teacher's Manual available. (Text)

TEPLY'S LEGAL WRITING, ANALYSIS AND ORAL ARGUMENT, 576 pages, 1990. Softcover. Teacher's Manual available. (Coursebook)

WEIHOFEN'S LEGAL WRITING STYLE, Second Edition, 332 pages, 1980. (Text)

Legislation

DAVIES' LEGISLATIVE LAW AND PROCESS IN A NUTSHELL, Second Edition, 346 pages, 1986. Softcover. (Text)

ESKRIDGE AND FRICKEY'S CASES AND MATERIALS ON LEGISLATION: STATUTES AND THE CREATION OF PUBLIC POLICY, 937 pages, 1988. Teacher's Manual available. (Casebook) 1990 Supplement.

Legislation—Cont'd

NUTTING AND DICKERSON'S CASES AND MATERIALS ON LEGISLATION, Fifth Edition, 744 pages, 1978. (Casebook)

STATSKY'S LEGISLATIVE ANALYSIS AND DRAFTING, Second Edition, 217 pages, 1984. Teacher's Manual available. (Text)

Local Government

FRUG'S CASES AND MATERIALS ON LOCAL GOVERNMENT LAW, 1005 pages, 1988. (Casebook)

MCCARTHY'S LOCAL GOVERNMENT LAW IN A NUTSHELL, Third Edition, 435 pages, 1990. Softcover. (Text)

REYNOLDS' HORNBOOK ON LOCAL GOVERNMENT LAW, 860 pages, 1982, with 1990 pocket part. (Text)

VALENTE'S CASES AND MATERIALS ON LOCAL GOVERNMENT LAW, Third Edition, 1010 pages, 1987. Teacher's Manual available. (Casebook) 1989 Supplement.

Mass Communication Law

GILLMOR, BARRON, SIMON AND TERRY'S CASES AND COMMENT ON MASS COMMUNICATION LAW, Fifth Edition, 947 pages, 1990. (Casebook)

GINSBURG, BOTEIN AND DIRECTOR'S REGULATION OF THE ELECTRONIC MASS MEDIA: LAW AND POLICY FOR RADIO, TELEVISION, CABLE AND THE NEW VIDEO TECHNOLOGIES, Second Edition, approximately 650 pages, 1991. (Casebook) 1991 Statutory Supplement.

ZUCKMAN, GAYNES, CARTER AND DEE'S MASS COMMUNICATIONS LAW IN A NUTSHELL, Third Edition, 538 pages, 1988. Softcover. (Text)

Medicine, Law and

FISCINA, BOUMIL, SHARPE AND HEAD'S MEDICAL LIABILITY, 487 pages, 1991. Teacher's Manual available. (Casebook)

FURROW, JOHNSON, JOST AND SCHWARTZ' HEALTH LAW: CASES, MATERIALS AND PROBLEMS, Second Edition, approximately 1200 pages, June, 1991 Pub. Teacher's Manual available. (Casebook)

HALL AND ELLMAN'S HEALTH CARE LAW AND ETHICS IN A NUTSHELL, 401 pages, 1990. Softcover (Text)

JARVIS, CLOSEN, HERMANN AND LEONARD'S AIDS LAW IN A NUTSHELL, Approximately 350 pages, 1991. Softcover. (Text)

KING'S THE LAW OF MEDICAL MALPRACTICE IN A NUTSHELL, Second Edition, 342 pages, 1986. Softcover. (Text)

SHAPIRO AND SPECE'S CASES, MATERIALS AND PROBLEMS ON BIOETHICS AND LAW, 892 pages, 1981. (Casebook)

Military Law

SHANOR AND TERRELL'S MILITARY LAW IN A NUTSHELL, 378 pages, 1980. Softcover. (Text)

Mortgages—see Real Estate Transactions

Natural Resources Law—see Energy and Natural Resources Law, Environmental Law

Negotiation

GIFFORD'S LEGAL NEGOTIATION: THEORY AND APPLICATIONS, 225 pages, 1989. Softcover. (Text)

WILLIAMS' LEGAL NEGOTIATION AND SETTLEMENT, 207 pages, 1983. Softcover. Teacher's Manual available. (Coursebook)

Office Practice—see also Computers and Law, Interviewing and Counseling, Negotiation

HEGLAND'S TRIAL AND PRACTICE SKILLS IN A NUTSHELL, 346 pages, 1978. Softcover (Text)

MUNNEKE'S LAW PRACTICE MANAGEMENT, COURSE MATERIALS, Approximately 630 pages, 1991. (Casebook)

STRONG AND CLARK'S LAW OFFICE MANAGEMENT, 424 pages, 1974. (Casebook)

Oil and Gas—see also Energy and Natural Resources Law

HEMINGWAY'S HORNBOOK ON THE LAW OF OIL AND GAS, Third Edition, Student Edition, approximately 700 pages, Aug., 1991 Pub. (Text)

KUNTZ, LOWE, ANDERSON AND SMITH'S CASES AND MATERIALS ON OIL AND GAS LAW, 857 pages, 1986. Teacher's Manual available. (Casebook) Forms Manual. Revised.

LOWE'S OIL AND GAS LAW IN A NUTSHELL,

Oil and Gas—Cont'd

Second Edition, 465 pages, 1988. Softcover. (Text)

Partnership—see Agency—Partnership

Patent and Copyright Law

CHOATE, FRANCIS AND COLLINS' CASES AND MATERIALS ON PATENT LAW, INCLUDING TRADE SECRETS, COPYRIGHTS, TRADEMARKS, Third Edition, 1009 pages, 1987. (Casebook)

MILLER AND DAVIS' INTELLECTUAL PROPERTY—PATENTS, TRADEMARKS AND COPYRIGHT IN A NUTSHELL, Second Edition, 437 pages, 1990. Softcover. (Text)

NIMMER, MARCUS, MYERS AND NIMMER'S CASES AND MATERIALS ON COPYRIGHT AND OTHER ASPECTS OF ENTERTAINMENT LITIGATION ILLUSTRATED—INCLUDING UNFAIR COMPETITION, DEFAMATION AND PRIVACY, Fourth Edition, Approximately 1175 pages, 1991. (Casebook)

Products Liability

FISCHER AND POWERS' CASES AND MATERIALS ON PRODUCTS LIABILITY, 685 pages, 1988. Teacher's Manual available. (Casebook)

NOEL AND PHILLIPS' CASES ON PRODUCTS LIABILITY, Second Edition, 821 pages, 1982. (Casebook)

PHILLIPS' PRODUCTS LIABILITY IN A NUTSHELL, Third Edition, 307 pages, 1988. Softcover. (Text)

Professional Responsibility

ARONSON, DEVINE AND FISCH'S PROBLEMS, CASES AND MATERIALS IN PROFESSIONAL RESPONSIBILITY, 745 pages, 1985. Teacher's Manual available. (Casebook)

ARONSON AND WECKSTEIN'S PROFESSIONAL RESPONSIBILITY IN A NUTSHELL, Second Edition, approximately 500 pages, 1991. Softcover. (Text)

MELLINKOFF'S THE CONSCIENCE OF A LAWYER, 304 pages, 1973. (Text)

PIRSIG AND KIRWIN'S CASES AND MATERIALS ON PROFESSIONAL RESPONSIBILITY, Fourth Edition, 603 pages, 1984. Teacher's Manual available. (Casebook)

ROTUNDA'S BLACK LETTER ON PROFESSIONAL RESPONSIBILITY, Second Edition, 414 pages, 1988. Softcover. (Review)

SCHWARTZ AND WYDICK'S PROBLEMS IN LEGAL ETHICS, Second Edition, 341 pages, 1988. (Coursebook)

SELECTED STATUTES, RULES AND STANDARDS ON THE LEGAL PROFESSION. Softcover. 678 pages, 1990.

SMITH AND MALLEN'S PREVENTING LEGAL MALPRACTICE, 264 pages, 1989. Reprint from Mallen and Smith's Legal Malpractice, Third Edition. (Text)

SUTTON AND DZIENKOWSKI'S CASES AND MATERIALS ON PROFESSIONAL RESPONSIBILITY FOR LAWYERS, 839 pages, 1989. Teacher's Manual available. (Casebook)

WOLFRAM'S HORNBOOK ON MODERN LEGAL ETHICS, Student Edition, 1120 pages, 1986. (Text)

Property—see also Real Estate Transactions, Land Use, Trusts and Estates

BERNHARDT'S BLACK LETTER ON PROPERTY, Second Edition, approximately 375 pages, June, 1991 Pub. Softcover. (Review)

BERNHARDT'S REAL PROPERTY IN A NUTSHELL, Second Edition, 448 pages, 1981. Softcover. (Text)

BOYER, HOVENKAMP AND KURTZ' THE LAW OF PROPERTY, AN INTRODUCTORY SURVEY, Fourth Edition, approximately 660 pages, 1991. (Text)

BROWDER, CUNNINGHAM, NELSON, STOEBUCK AND WHITMAN'S CASES ON BASIC PROPERTY LAW, Fifth Edition, 1386 pages, 1989. Teacher's Manual available. (Casebook)

BRUCE, ELY AND BOSTICK'S CASES AND MATERIALS ON MODERN PROPERTY LAW, Second Edition, 953 pages, 1989. Teacher's Manual available. (Casebook)

BURKE'S PERSONAL PROPERTY IN A NUTSHELL, 322 pages, 1983. Softcover. (Text)

CUNNINGHAM, STOEBUCK AND WHITMAN'S HORNBOOK ON THE LAW OF PROPERTY, Student Edition, 916 pages, 1984, with 1987 pocket part. (Text)

DONAHUE, KAUPER AND MARTIN'S CASES ON PROPERTY, Second Edition, 1362 pages, 1983. Teacher's Manual available. (Case-

Property—Cont'd
book)

HILL'S LANDLORD AND TENANT LAW IN A NUTSHELL, Second Edition, 311 pages, 1986. Softcover. (Text)

KURTZ AND HOVENKAMP'S CASES AND MATERIALS ON AMERICAN PROPERTY LAW, 1296 pages, 1987. Teacher's Manual available. (Casebook) 1988 Supplement.

MOYNIHAN'S INTRODUCTION TO REAL PROPERTY, Second Edition, 239 pages, 1988. (Text)

Psychiatry, Law and

REISNER AND SLOBOGIN'S LAW AND THE MENTAL HEALTH SYSTEM, CIVIL AND CRIMINAL ASPECTS, Second Edition, 1117 pages, 1990. (Casebook)

Real Estate Transactions

BRUCE'S REAL ESTATE FINANCE IN A NUTSHELL, Third Edition, approximately 270 pages, 1991. Softcover. (Text)

MAXWELL, RIESENFELD, HETLAND AND WARREN'S CASES ON CALIFORNIA SECURITY TRANSACTIONS IN LAND, Third Edition, 728 pages, 1984. (Casebook)

NELSON AND WHITMAN'S BLACK LETTER ON LAND TRANSACTIONS AND FINANCE, Second Edition, 466 pages, 1988. Softcover. (Review)

NELSON AND WHITMAN'S CASES ON REAL ESTATE TRANSFER, FINANCE AND DEVELOPMENT, Third Edition, 1184 pages, 1987. (Casebook)

NELSON AND WHITMAN'S HORNBOOK ON REAL ESTATE FINANCE LAW, Second Edition, 941 pages, 1985 with 1989 pocket part. (Text)

Regulated Industries—see also Mass Communication Law, Banking Law

GELLHORN AND PIERCE'S REGULATED INDUSTRIES IN A NUTSHELL, Second Edition, 389 pages, 1987. Softcover. (Text)

MORGAN, HARRISON AND VERKUIL'S CASES AND MATERIALS ON ECONOMIC REGULATION OF BUSINESS, Second Edition, 666 pages, 1985. (Casebook)

Remedies

DOBBS' HORNBOOK ON REMEDIES, 1067 pages, 1973. (Text)

DOBBS' PROBLEMS IN REMEDIES. 137 pages, 1974. Teacher's Manual available. Softcover. (Coursebook)

DOBBYN'S INJUNCTIONS IN A NUTSHELL, 264 pages, 1974. Softcover. (Text)

FRIEDMAN'S CONTRACT REMEDIES IN A NUTSHELL, 323 pages, 1981. Softcover. (Text)

LEAVELL, LOVE AND NELSON'S CASES AND MATERIALS ON EQUITABLE REMEDIES, RESTITUTION AND DAMAGES, Fourth Edition, 1111 pages, 1986. Teacher's Manual available. (Casebook)

McCORMICK'S HORNBOOK ON DAMAGES, 811 pages, 1935. (Text)

O'CONNELL'S REMEDIES IN A NUTSHELL, Second Edition, 320 pages, 1985. Softcover. (Text)

SCHOENBROD, MACBETH, LEVINE AND JUNG'S CASES AND MATERIALS ON REMEDIES: PUBLIC AND PRIVATE, 848 pages, 1990. Teacher's Manual available. (Casebook)

YORK, BAUMAN AND RENDLEMAN'S CASES AND MATERIALS ON REMEDIES, Fifth Edition, approximately 1050 pages, September, 1991 Pub. Teacher's Manual available. (Casebook)

Sea, Law of

SOHN AND GUSTAFSON'S THE LAW OF THE SEA IN A NUTSHELL, 264 pages, 1984. Softcover. (Text)

Securities Regulation

HAZEN'S HORNBOOK ON THE LAW OF SECURITIES REGULATION, Second Edition, Student Edition, 1082 pages, 1990. (Text)

RATNER'S SECURITIES REGULATION IN A NUTSHELL, Third Edition, 316 pages, 1988. Softcover. (Text)

RATNER AND HAZEN'S SECURITIES REGULATION: CASES AND MATERIALS, Fourth Edition, approximately 1,075 pages, 1991. (Casebook) Problems and Sample Documents Supplement.

Statutory Supplement. *See Securities Regulation, Selected Statutes*

SECURITIES REGULATION, SELECTED STATUTES, RULES, AND FORMS. Softcover. Approximately 1,300 pages, 1991.

Social Legislation—see Workers' Compensation

Sports Law

SCHUBERT, SMITH AND TRENTADUE'S SPORTS LAW, 395 pages, 1986. (Text)

Tax Practice and Procedure

GARBIS, STRUNTZ AND RUBIN'S CASES AND MATERIALS ON TAX PROCEDURE AND TAX FRAUD, Second Edition, 687 pages, 1987. (Casebook)

MORGAN'S TAX PROCEDURE AND TAX FRAUD IN A NUTSHELL, 400 pages, 1990. Softcover. (Text)

Taxation—Corporate

KAHN AND GANN'S CORPORATE TAXATION, Third Edition, 980 pages, 1989. Teacher's Manual available. (Casebook)

SCHWARZ AND LATHROPE'S BLACK LETTER ON CORPORATE AND PARTNERSHIP TAXATION, Approximately 500 pages, September, 1991 Pub. Softcover. (Review)

WEIDENBRUCH AND BURKE'S FEDERAL INCOME TAXATION OF CORPORATIONS AND STOCKHOLDERS IN A NUTSHELL, Third Edition, 309 pages, 1989. Softcover. (Text)

Taxation—Estate & Gift—see also Estate Planning, Trusts and Estates

McNULTY'S FEDERAL ESTATE AND GIFT TAXATION IN A NUTSHELL, Fourth Edition, 496 pages, 1989. Softcover. (Text)

PENNELL'S CASES AND MATERIALS ON INCOME TAXATION OF TRUSTS, ESTATES, GRANTORS AND BENEFICIARIES, 460 pages, 1987. Teacher's Manual available. (Casebook)

Taxation—Individual

DODGE'S THE LOGIC OF TAX, 343 pages, 1989. Softcover. (Text)

GUNN AND WARD'S CASES, TEXT AND PROBLEMS ON FEDERAL INCOME TAXATION, Second Edition, 835 pages, 1988. Teacher's Manual available. (Casebook) 1990 Supplement.

HUDSON AND LIND'S BLACK LETTER ON FEDERAL INCOME TAXATION, Third Edition, 406 pages, 1990. Softcover. (Review)

KRAGEN AND McNULTY'S CASES AND MATERI-ALS ON FEDERAL INCOME TAXATION—INDIVIDUALS, CORPORATIONS, PARTNERSHIPS, Fourth Edition, 1287 pages, 1985. (Casebook)

McNULTY'S FEDERAL INCOME TAXATION OF INDIVIDUALS IN A NUTSHELL, Fourth Edition, 503 pages, 1988. Softcover. (Text)

POSIN'S HORNBOOK ON FEDERAL INCOME TAXATION, Student Edition, 491 pages, 1983, with 1989 pocket part. (Text)

ROSE AND CHOMMIE'S HORNBOOK ON FEDERAL INCOME TAXATION, Third Edition, 923 pages, 1988, with 1989 pocket part. (Text)

SELECTED FEDERAL TAXATION STATUTES AND REGULATIONS. Softcover. Approximately 1560 pages, 1992.

SOLOMON AND HESCH'S PROBLEMS, CASES AND MATERIALS ON FEDERAL INCOME TAXATION OF INDIVIDUALS, 1068 pages, 1987. Teacher's Manual available. (Casebook)

Taxation—International

DOERNBERG'S INTERNATIONAL TAXATION IN A NUTSHELL, 325 pages, 1989. Softcover. (Text)

KAPLAN'S FEDERAL TAXATION OF INTERNATIONAL TRANSACTIONS: PRINCIPLES, PLANNING AND POLICY, 635 pages, 1988. (Casebook)

Taxation—Partnership

BERGER AND WIEDENBECK'S CASES AND MATERIALS ON PARTNERSHIP TAXATION, 788 pages, 1989. Teacher's Manual available. (Casebook)

BISHOP AND BROOKS' FEDERAL PARTNERSHIP TAXATION: A GUIDE TO THE LEADING CASES, STATUTES, AND REGULATIONS, 545 pages, 1990. Softcover. (Text)

SCHWARZ AND LATHROPE'S BLACK LETTER ON CORPORATE AND PARTNERSHIP TAXATION, Approximately 500 pages, September, 1991 Pub. Softcover. (Review)

Taxation—State & Local

GELFAND AND SALSICH'S STATE AND LOCAL TAXATION AND FINANCE IN A NUTSHELL, 309 pages, 1986. Softcover. (Text)

HELLERSTEIN AND HELLERSTEIN'S CASES AND MATERIALS ON STATE AND LOCAL TAXATION, Fifth Edition, 1071 pages, 1988. (Casebook)

Torts—see also Products Liability

CHRISTIE AND MEEKS' CASES AND MATERIALS ON THE LAW OF TORTS, Second Edition, 1264 pages, 1990. (Casebook)

DOBBS' TORTS AND COMPENSATION—PERSONAL ACCOUNTABILITY AND SOCIAL RESPONSIBILITY FOR INJURY, 955 pages, 1985. Teacher's Manual available. (Casebook) 1990 Supplement.

KEETON, KEETON, SARGENTICH AND STEINER'S CASES AND MATERIALS ON TORT AND ACCIDENT LAW, Second Edition, 1318 pages, 1989. (Casebook)

KIONKA'S BLACK LETTER ON TORTS, 339 pages, 1988. Softcover. (Review)

KIONKA'S TORTS IN A NUTSHELL: INJURIES TO PERSONS AND PROPERTY, 434 pages, 1977. Softcover. (Text)

MALONE'S TORTS IN A NUTSHELL: INJURIES TO FAMILY, SOCIAL AND TRADE RELATIONS, 358 pages, 1979. Softcover. (Text)

PROSSER AND KEETON'S HORNBOOK ON TORTS, Fifth Edition, Student Edition, 1286 pages, 1984 with 1988 pocket part. (Text)

ROBERTSON, POWERS AND ANDERSON'S CASES AND MATERIALS ON TORTS, 932 pages, 1989. Teacher's Manual available. (Casebook)

Trade Regulation—see also Antitrust, Regulated Industries

MCMANIS' UNFAIR TRADE PRACTICES IN A NUTSHELL, Second Edition, 464 pages, 1988. Softcover. (Text)

OPPENHEIM, WESTON, MAGGS AND SCHECHTER'S CASES AND MATERIALS ON UNFAIR TRADE PRACTICES AND CONSUMER PROTECTION, Fourth Edition, 1038 pages, 1983. Teacher's Manual available. (Casebook) 1986 Supplement.

SCHECHTER'S BLACK LETTER ON UNFAIR TRADE PRACTICES, 272 pages, 1986. Softcover. (Review)

Trial and Appellate Advocacy—see also Civil Procedure

APPELLATE ADVOCACY, HANDBOOK OF, Second Edition, 182 pages, 1986. Softcover. (Text)

BERGMAN'S TRIAL ADVOCACY IN A NUTSHELL, Second Edition, 354 pages, 1989. Soft-

cover. (Text)

BINDER AND BERGMAN'S FACT INVESTIGATION: FROM HYPOTHESIS TO PROOF, 354 pages, 1984. Teacher's Manual available. (Coursebook)

CARLSON AND IMWINKELRIED'S DYNAMICS OF TRIAL PRACTICE: PROBLEMS AND MATERIALS, 414 pages, 1989. Teacher's Manual available. (Coursebook) 1990 Supplement.

DESSEM'S PRETRIAL LITIGATION: LAW, POLICY AND PRACTICE, Approximately 615 pages, 1991. Softcover. (Coursebook)

DEVINE'S NON-JURY CASE FILES FOR TRIAL ADVOCACY, Approximately 265 pages, 1991. (Coursebook)

GOLDBERG'S THE FIRST TRIAL (WHERE DO I SIT? WHAT DO I SAY?) IN A NUTSHELL, 396 pages, 1982. Softcover. (Text)

HAYDOCK, HERR, AND STEMPEL'S FUNDAMENTALS OF PRE-TRIAL LITIGATION, 768 pages, 1985. Softcover. Teacher's Manual available. (Coursebook)

HAYDOCK AND SONSTENG'S TRIAL: THEORIES, TACTICS, TECHNIQUES, 711 pages, 1991. Softcover. (Text)

HEGLAND'S TRIAL AND PRACTICE SKILLS IN A NUTSHELL, 346 pages, 1978. Softcover. (Text)

HORNSTEIN'S APPELLATE ADVOCACY IN A NUTSHELL, 325 pages, 1984. Softcover. (Text)

JEANS' HANDBOOK ON TRIAL ADVOCACY, Student Edition, 473 pages, 1975. Softcover. (Text)

LISNEK AND KAUFMAN'S DEPOSITIONS: PROCEDURE, STRATEGY AND TECHNIQUE, Law School and CLE Edition. 250 pages, 1990. Softcover. (Text)

MARTINEAU'S CASES AND MATERIALS ON APPELLATE PRACTICE AND PROCEDURE, 565 pages, 1987. (Casebook)

NOLAN'S CASES AND MATERIALS ON TRIAL PRACTICE, 518 pages, 1981. (Casebook)

SONSTENG, HAYDOCK AND BOYD'S THE TRIALBOOK: A TOTAL SYSTEM FOR PREPARATION AND PRESENTATION OF A CASE, 404 pages, 1984. Softcover. (Coursebook)

WHARTON, HAYDOCK AND SONSTENG'S CALI-

Trial and Appellate Advocacy—Cont'd

FORNIA CIVIL TRIALBOOK, Law School and CLE Edition. 148 pages, 1990. Softcover. (Text)

Trusts and Estates

ATKINSON'S HORNBOOK ON WILLS, Second Edition, 975 pages, 1953. (Text)

AVERILL'S UNIFORM PROBATE CODE IN A NUTSHELL, Second Edition, 454 pages, 1987. Softcover. (Text)

BOGERT'S HORNBOOK ON TRUSTS, Sixth Edition, Student Edition, 794 pages, 1987. (Text)

CLARK, LUSKY AND MURPHY'S CASES AND MATERIALS ON GRATUITOUS TRANSFERS, Third Edition, 970 pages, 1985. (Casebook)

DODGE'S WILLS, TRUSTS AND ESTATE PLANNING–LAW AND TAXATION, CASES AND MATERIALS, 665 pages, 1988. (Casebook)

KURTZ' PROBLEMS, CASES AND OTHER MATERIALS ON FAMILY ESTATE PLANNING, 853 pages, 1983. Teacher's Manual available. (Casebook)

MCGOVERN'S CASES AND MATERIALS ON WILLS, TRUSTS AND FUTURE INTERESTS: AN INTRODUCTION TO ESTATE PLANNING, 750 pages, 1983. (Casebook)

MCGOVERN, KURTZ AND REIN'S HORNBOOK ON WILLS, TRUSTS AND ESTATES–INCLUDING TAXATION AND FUTURE INTERESTS, 996 pages, 1988. (Text)

MENNELL'S WILLS AND TRUSTS IN A NUTSHELL, 392 pages, 1979. Softcover. (Text)

SIMES' HORNBOOK ON FUTURE INTERESTS, Second Edition, 355 pages, 1966. (Text)

TURANO AND RADIGAN'S HORNBOOK ON NEW YORK ESTATE ADMINISTRATION, 676 pages, 1986. (Text)

UNIFORM PROBATE CODE, OFFICIAL TEXT WITH COMMENTS. 615 pages, 1989. Softcover.

WAGGONER'S FUTURE INTERESTS IN A NUTSHELL, 361 pages, 1981. Softcover. (Text)

WATERBURY'S MATERIALS ON TRUSTS AND ESTATES, 1039 pages, 1986. Teacher's Manual available. (Casebook)

Water Law—see also Energy and Natural Resources Law, Environmental Law

GETCHES' WATER LAW IN A NUTSHELL, Second Edition, 459 pages, 1990. Softcover. (Text)

SAX, ABRAMS AND THOMPSON'S LEGAL CONTROL OF WATER RESOURCES: CASES AND MATERIALS, Approximately 1030 pages, July, 1991 Pub. (Casebook)

TRELEASE AND GOULD'S CASES AND MATERIALS ON WATER LAW, Fourth Edition, 816 pages, 1986. (Casebook)

Wills—see Trusts and Estates

Women and the Law—see also Employment Discrimination

KAY'S TEXT, CASES AND MATERIALS ON SEX–BASED DISCRIMINATION, Third Edition, 1001 pages, 1988. (Casebook) 1990 Supplement.

THOMAS' SEX DISCRIMINATION IN A NUTSHELL, 399 pages, 1982. Softcover. (Text)

Workers' Compensation

HOOD, HARDY AND LEWIS' WORKERS' COMPENSATION AND EMPLOYEE PROTECTION LAWS IN A NUTSHELL, Second Edition, 361 pages, 1990. Softcover. (Text)

MALONE, PLANT AND LITTLE'S CASES ON WORKERS' COMPENSATION AND EMPLOYMENT RIGHTS, Second Edition, 951 pages, 1980. Teacher's Manual available. (Casebook)

MODERN CONSTITUTIONAL THEORY

A READER

Second Edition

By

John H. Garvey
Ashland Professor of Law
University of Kentucky College of Law

and

T. Alexander Aleinikoff
Professor of Law
University of Michigan Law School

WEST PUBLISHING CO.
ST. PAUL, MINN., 1991

COPYRIGHT © 1989 WEST PUBLISHING CO.
COPYRIGHT © 1991 By WEST PUBLISHING CO.
                    50 West Kellogg Boulevard
                    P.O. Box 64526
                    St. Paul, MN 55164–0526

Library of Congress Cataloging-in-Publication Data

Modern constitutional theory : a reader / [edited] by John H. Garvey
    and T. Alexander Aleinikoff. — 2nd ed.
    p.   cm.
    Includes bibliographical references.
    ISBN 0–314–88368–1
    1. United States—Constitutional law. I. Garvey, John H., 1948–   .
    II. Aleinikoff, Thomas Alexander, 1952–   .
    KF4549.M63   1991
    342.73—dc20
    [347.302]   91–3559
                                                                CIP

ISBN 0–314–88368–1

(G. & A.) Const'l Reader 2d Ed.

∞

Preface

The teaching of Constitutional Law has changed a good deal recently. One cause of the change has been the explosive growth in the dimensions of the subject. Not very long ago, casebooks treated the Bill of Rights as a unitary whole. The Fourth, Fifth, and Sixth Amendments were taught alongside the First Amendment. Now they provide enough material for a course in Criminal Procedure. The same process of fission is evident in other parts of the curriculum. The First Amendment has grown like the tax code, and is generally taught in a separate course. Family Law has absorbed much of the Due Process and Equal Protection Clauses. Federal Courts courses are devoted to Article III problems. Separation of powers provides material for courses in Administrative Law, the Congress, and the Presidency. Taxation of interstate commerce has split off and been ignored.

The reaction to this growth has been to teach less law, not more. That response is not as paradoxical as it seems. There is not enough space for all the details of doctrine, and many of them are more efficiently taught elsewhere in the curriculum. But there is a greater need than before to explore the foundations that support and unify the doctrinal structure. Constitutional Law now tries to go down rather than out.

This emphasis on depth in lieu of breadth has another cause. The enormous growth and change in the coverage of the law have been accompanied by a proliferation of theories about the ideology of law. These include, most prominently, the law and economics movement (and the related development of public choice theory), the critical legal studies movement, and feminist jurisprudence. To these we might add the revival of interest in various philosophical theories (natural rights, utilitarianism, and positivism), in the civic republicanism of the 18th century, and in a liberalism concerned with the political process. We are now more self-consciously concerned with asking whose purposes the law serves, what values it should promote, and even whether law is a meaningful constraint on human behavior. Courses in Constitutional Law cannot ignore this ferment. If there is widespread disagreement about fundamental premises, we cannot make much progress in ironing out doctrinal details.

This book is designed with these problems in mind. It can be used as a supplement to introductory courses in Constitutional Law, or as a text for a course in Constitutional Theory. We have organized it to correspond with the major topics covered in casebooks on Constitutional Law. There are two significant exceptions to this organization. The first is a separate chapter devoted to the problem of interpretation. It is closely allied to the problem of judicial review, and may be addressed in conjunction with those materials. Often, however, the subject is taken up along with a particular substantive problem such as equal protection or privacy. This chapter would fit equally well in that part of a course. The other exception is the First Amendment. It is not addressed in most first-year classes, and is often the subject of a separate upper-level course. For that reason, and because an adequate treatment would require a vast amount of material, we thought it should be covered in a separate volume.

Although the chapters are organized according to doctrinal categories, the readings they contain are not an elaboration (or condensation) of doctrine such as one would find in a hornbook. They seek to go deeper than a restatement of the law, to ask what and whose purposes are served by existing rules, and to inquire whether some other organization is preferable. Not all the readings address these questions from the same point of view. The selections take opposing positions on each subject, in order to make students aware of the existing conflict and to facilitate class discussion of the materials.

Most of the selections have been edited. We have indicated the deletion of sentences and paragraphs by ellipses. We have not drawn attention to omitted footnotes, but have used the original numbering of those retained. Our own footnotes, added for editorial purposes, are numbered alphabetically.

JOHN H. GARVEY
T. ALEXANDER ALEINIKOFF

May, 1991

Acknowledgments

We would like to thank the authors and copyright holders of the following works, who permitted their inclusion in this book:

Morris B. Abram, Affirmative Action: Fair Shakers and Social Engineers. Copyright © 1986 by the Harvard Law Review Association.

Bruce A. Ackerman, Beyond Carolene Products. Reprinted with permission of Bruce A. Ackerman.

T. Alexander Aleinikoff, Constitutional Law in the Age of Balancing. Reprinted by permission of The Yale Law Journal Company and Fred B. Rothman & Company from The Yale Law Journal, Vol. 96, pp. 943 ff.

Raoul Berger, Government By Judiciary. Reprinted by permission of the Harvard University Press. Copyright © 1977 by the President and Fellows of Harvard College.

Charles L. Black, Jr., The People and the Court (1960). Reprinted with permission of Macmillan Publishing Company. Copyright © 1960 by Charles L. Black, Jr.

Alexander M. Bickel, Congress, the President and the Power To Wage War, 48 Chicago-Kent Law Review 131 (1971). Copyright © 1971 by the Illinois Institute of Technology. Reprinted by special permission of the IIT Chicago-Kent College of Law.

Alexander M. Bickel, The Least Dangerous Branch (1962). Reprinted with permission of Josephine A. Bickel.

Robert H. Bork, Neutral Principles and Some First Amendment Problems. Reprinted with permission of the Indiana Law Journal and Fred B. Rothman & Company.

Paul A. Brest, The Misconceived Quest for the Original Understanding. Reprinted with permission of Paul A. Brest and the Boston University Law Review.

Paul Brest, In Defense of the Antidiscrimination Principle. Copyright © 1976 by the Harvard Law Review Association.

Harold H. Bruff, Legislative Formality, Administrative Rationality. Published originally in 63 Texas Law Review 207–250 (1984). Copyright © 1984 by the Texas Law Review. Reprinted by permission.

Stephen L. Carter, The Political Aspects of Judicial Power: Some Notes on the Presidential Immunity Decision, 131 U.Pa.L.Rev. 1341 (1983). Copyright © 1983 by the University of Pennsylvania.

Jesse H. Choper, Judicial Review and the National Political Process (1980). Copyright © 1980 by The University of Chicago. All rights reserved.

Learned Hand, The Bill of Rights. Reprinted by permission of the Harvard University Press. Copyright © 1958 by the President and Fellows of Harvard College.

Lewis B. Kaden, Politics, Money, and State Sovereignty: The Judicial Role. Copyright © 1979 by the Directors of the Columbia Law Review Association, Inc. All rights reserved. This article originally appeared at 54 Colum.L.Rev. 543 (1954). Reprinted by permission.

Yale Kamisar, Final Frontier: Life, Death, and Law: Right to Die or License to Kill? Copyright © 1989 by Legal Times. Reprinted by permission.

Richard S. Kay, Adherence to the Original Intentions in Constitutional Adjudication: Three Objections and Responses. 82 Nw.U.L.Rev. 226 (1988). Copyright © 1988 by Northwestern University.

Randall Kennedy, Persuasion and Distrust: A Comment on the Affirmative Action Debate. Copyright © 1986 by the Harvard Law Review Association.

Charles S. Lawrence, III, The Id, the Ego, and Equal Protection: Reckoning with Unconscious Racism. Copyright © 1987 by the Board of Trustees of the Leland Stanford Junior University.

Sanford Levinson, Law as Literature. Published originally in 60 Texas Law Review 373 (1982). Copyright © 1982 by the Texas Law Review. Reprinted by permission.

Catharine A. MacKinnon, Roe v. Wade: A Study in Male Ideology, from Abortion: Moral and Legal Perspectives, ed. Jay L. Garfield and Patricia Hennessey (Amherst: University of Massachusetts Press, 1984), copyright © 1984 by The University of Massachusetts Press.

Catharine A. MacKinnon, Difference and Dominance: On Sex Discrimination. Reprinted by permission of Rowman & Littlefield Publishers.

Jerry L. Mashaw, The Supreme Court's Due Process Calculus for Administrative Adjudication in Mathews v. Eldridge: Three Factors in Search of a Theory of Value, 44 U.Chi.L.Rev. 28 (1976). Copyright © 1977 by the University of Chicago. All rights reserved.

Robert G. McCloskey, Economic Due Process and the Supreme Court: An Exhumation and Reburial. Reprinted with permission of the University of Chicago Press.

Thomas W. Merrill, The Economics of Public Use, 72 Cornell L.Rev. 61 (1986). Copyright © 1986 by Cornell University. All rights reserved.

Frank I. Michelman, Property, Utility, and Fairness: Comments on the Ethical Foundations of "Just Compensation" Law. Copyright © 1967 by the Harvard Law Review Association.

Robert F. Nagel, The Legislative Veto, the Constitution, and the Courts. Reprinted with permission of Constitutional Commentary.

John T. Noonan, Jr., The Root and Branch of Roe v. Wade. Reprinted with permission of the Nebraska Law Review.

Kathleen Sullivan, Sins of Discrimination: Last Term's Affirmative Action Cases. Copyright © 1986 by the Harvard Law Review Association.

Cass R. Sunstein, **Naked** Preferences and the Constitution. Copyright © 1984 by the Directors of the Columbia Law Review Association, Inc. All rights reserved. This article originally appeared at 84 Colum.L.Rev. 1689 (1984). Reprinted by permission.

Judith Jarvis Thomson, A Defense of Abortion, Philosophy & Public Affairs 1, no. 1 (Fall 1971). Copyright © 1971 by Princeton University Press. Excerpts reprinted with permission of Princeton University Press.

Laurence H. Tribe, "In What Vision of the Constitution Must the Law Be Color-Blind?" Reprinted with permission of the John Marshall Law Review.

Laurence H. Tribe, The Legislative Veto Decision: A Law By Any Other Name? Copyright © 1989 by the President and Fellows of Harvard College. Copied with permission.

Mark V. Tushnet, Following the Rules Laid Down: A Critique of Interpretivism and Neutral Principles. Copyright © 1983 by the Harvard Law Review Association.

William W. Van Alstyne, The Second Death of Federalism. Reprinted with permission of the Michigan Law Review and William W. Van Alstyne.

Richard A. Wasserstrom, Racism and Sexism. From Philosophy and Social Issues by Richard A. Wasserstrom. Copyright © 1980 by University of Notre Dame Press, Notre Dame, IN 46556. Reprinted by permission.

Herbert Wechsler, The Political Safeguards of Federalism: The Role of the States in the Composition and Selection of the National Government. Copyright © 1954 by the Directors of the Columbia Law Review Association, Inc. All rights reserved. This article originally appeared at 54 Colum.L.Rev. 543 (1954). Reprinted by permission.

Herbert Wechsler, Toward Neutral Principles of Constitutional Law. Copyright © 1959 by the Harvard Law Review Association.

Patricia J. Williams, Metro Broadcasting, Inc. v. FCC: Regrouping in Singular Times. Copyright © 1990 by the Harvard Law Review Association.

Wendy W. Williams, The Equality Crisis: Some Reflections On Culture, Courts, and Feminism. Reprinted with permission of the Women's Rights Law Reporter.

*

Summary of Contents

*

Table of Contents

MODERN CONSTITUTIONAL THEORY

A READER

Second Edition

*

Chapter I

BEYOND *MARBURY v. MADISON*: NON–TEXTUAL JUSTIFICATIONS FOR JUDICIAL REVIEW

Marbury v. Madison is a curious case. Although it continues to be viewed as one of the central texts in constitutional law—because of both its result and its style of argumentation—*Marbury* is regularly subjected to scathing criticism in introductory constitutional law classes. It is commonplace to note that alternative interpretations of the Judiciary Act of 1789 and Article III of the Constitution were available to Chief Justice Marshall, interpretations that would have avoided holding the statute unconstitutional. Indeed, some suggest that John Marshall should have recused himself from the case because of his involvement in the underlying events. Finally, it is fairly easy to show that while Marshall's opinion admirably establishes the supremacy of the Constitution, it does not adequately demonstrate that the Supreme Court must be the final interpreter of what the Constitution means. (For an elaboration of these and other familiar criticisms of the opinion in *Marbury*, see Van Alstyne, *A Critical Guide to Marbury v. Madison,* 1969 Duke L.J. 1.)

Poking holes in Supreme Court opinions is the mainstay of scholarly work and classroom discussion. But finding fault with *Marbury v. Madison* is not merely sport or a demonstration of legal acuity. *Marbury* is the fount of the Supreme Court's role in explicating constitutional law. To say that the case rests on unsteady legal foundations is to undermine two centuries of judicial review.

This Chapter explores several attempts by scholars to provide a firmer foundation for judicial review than that supplied by Marshall. These justifications are "non-textual"; that is, they rely not on the specific language of the Constitution (compare Marshall's partial reliance on the Supremacy Clause and the Oath Clause [1]), but rather on the structure of government created by the Constitution, principles and

---

1. Herbert Wechsler also offers a largely textual justification for judicial review in *Toward Neutral Principles of Constitutional Law,* 73 Harv.L.Rev. 1, 2–5 (1959).

purposes that underlie the Constitution, democratic theory, or functional considerations.

Learned Hand argues that the power of judicial review is neither expressly authorized nor implicit in the structure of the Constitution. He suggests that such a power may be interpolated into the text in order "to prevent defeat of the venture at hand"—that is, the successful operation of government.

Charles Black's defense of judicial review derives from the theory of limited powers that underlies our political system. In order to maintain the legitimacy of government, some institution must be authorized to decide whether or not governmental action transgresses constitutional limits. Black suggests that an independent, precedent-respecting, learned tribunal could best carry out this function. Not surprisingly, he views the Supreme Court as such an institution.

Alexander Bickel argues that, due to the counter-majoritarian nature of judicial review, the practice can be justified only if it serves a function distinct from legislative and executive activities that is consistent with the basic democratic principles upon which our system of government is based. He identifies that function as the identification and protection of "enduring values."

Michael Perry, like Bickel, sees the Court playing a crucial role in the promotion of fundamental values. He defends non-interpretive review (that is, the determination of a constitutional issue by reference to a value judgment other than one constitutionalized by the Framers) on functional grounds: it allows us to maintain an accomodation between our democratic commitment and the "possibility that there may be discoverable right answers to fundamental political-moral problems."

As you read the following excerpts, consider not only whether the author's view is sounder than the arguments put forward by Marshall, but also how well each justification stands up against alternative proposals. How, for example, might Charles Black respond to Learned Hand, or Alexander Bickel to Michael Perry?

LEARNED HAND, THE BILL OF RIGHTS
Pp. 3–6, 10–15 (1958).

*   *   * [I begin with the premise] that all political power emanates from the people, and that the Constitution distributed among different "Departments"—as Hamilton called them—the authority of each as it was measured by the grant to it. No provision was expressly made, however, as to how a "Department" was to proceed when in the exercise of one of its own powers it became necessary to consider the validity of some earlier act of another "Department." Should the second accept the decision of the first that the act was within the first's authority, or should it decide the question *de novo* according to its own judgment? A third view prevailed, as you all know: that it was a

function of the courts to decide which "Department" was right, and that all were bound to accept the decision of the Supreme Court.

The arguments of those who, like Jefferson, held that each "Department" was free to decide the issues before it regardless of how any other "Department" had decided it, was, as I understand it, as follows: The exercise of any delegated power presupposes that the grantee believes that the grant extends to the occasion that has arisen; and it is a necessary incident of the grant itself that he shall so decide before he acts at all. He may of course be wrong; and, when he is, he will be accountable to the grantor; but he is accountable to no one else, unless it be an authority paramount to both himself and the grantor.

The federal courts themselves derive all their powers from the "People of the United States" when they "ordain[ed] and establish[ed]" the Constitution, and the same was true, *ceteris paribus,* of the state courts. One cannot find among the powers granted to courts any authority to pass upon the validity of the decisions of another "Department" as to the scope of that "Department's" powers. Indeed, it is to be understood that the three "Departments" were separate and coequal, each being, as it were, a Leibnizian monad, looking up to the Heaven of the Electorate, but without any mutual dependence. What could be better evidence of complete dependence than to subject the validity of the decision of one "Department" as to its authority on a given occasion to review and reversal by another whose own action was conditioned upon the answer to the same issue? Such a doctrine makes supreme the "Department" that has the last word.

Nor can any support for the doctrine of the supremacy of the judiciary be found in the "Supremacy Clause," which, so far as it proves anything, accords rather with the view that, when it was intended to grant courts the power to declare a statute invalid because it was in conflict with the Constitution, some express grant was thought necessary. That clause did indeed require state courts to follow federal laws and the federal constitution when the state laws or the state constitution were "to the contrary"; and that requirement no doubt presupposed that they should have jurisdiction to determine whether a conflict existed. Moreover, we may *arguendo* even admit that when the conflict is between a federal law and a state law or constitution, the state court is to determine the validity of the federal law *quoad* the federal constitution. Furthermore, we may accept Section 25 of the First Judiciary Law as valid, so that on some occasions the Supreme Court might have to decide whether a state court's construction of the Constitution was correct. However, the clause was obviously directed against the states alone to prevent their intruding upon the powers they had delegated or failing to obey limitations on their own powers that they had accepted. Such a grant cannot be stretched into a general authority to pass upon other instances of legislative conflict with the Constitution; rather we should resort to the maxim, *expressio unius, exclusio alterius,* and declare that it indicates the absence of any such authority.

* * *

There was [, then,] nothing in the United States Constitution that gave courts any authority to review the decisions of Congress; and it was a plausible—indeed to my mind an unanswerable—argument that it invaded that "Separation of Powers" which, as so many then believed, was the condition of all free government. That there were other reasons, not only proper but essential, for inferring such a power in the Constitution seems to me certain; but for the moment I am only concerned to show that the reasoning put forward [in *Marbury v. Madison*] to support the inference will not bear scrutiny.

As an approach, let us try to imagine what would have been the result if the power did not exist. There were two alternatives, each prohibitive, I submit. One was that the decision of the first "Department" before which an issue arose should be conclusive whenever it arose later. That doctrine, coupled with its conceded power over the purse, would have made Congress substantially omnipotent, for by far the greater number of issues that could arise would depend upon its prior action.

Hamilton in the 71st number of the Federalist forecast what would probably have been the result. He was speaking of what he called the "tendency of legislative authority to absorb every other." "In governments purely republican, this tendency is almost irresistible. The representatives of the people in a popular assembly seem sometimes to fancy that they are the people themselves, and betray strong symptoms of impatience and disgust at the least sign of opposition from any other quarter; as if the exercise of its rights by either the executive or the judiciary were a breach of their privilege and an outrage on their dignity. They often appear disposed to exert an imperious control over the other departments; and, as they commonly have the people on their side, they always act with such momentum as to make it very difficult for the other members of the government to maintain the balance of the Constitution."

It was unfair to ascribe to a mere lust for power this disposition of legislators to expand their powers. As Hamilton intimated, every legislator is under constant pressure from groups of constituents whom it does not satisfy to say, "Although I think what you want is right and that you ought to have it, I cannot bring myself to believe that it is within my constitutional powers." Such scruples are not convincing to those whose interests are at stake; and the voters at large will not usually care enough about preserving "the balance of the Constitution" to offset the votes of those whose interests will be disappointed.

The issues that arise are often extremely baffling, and the answers are not obvious. They demand, not only a detached approach, but a training in verbal analysis by no means general among legislators, even though they are usually lawyers. The uncertainties that so often arise are shown by the differences in the answers of the judges themselves. Take for instance the power of Congress to levy taxes in order "to pay the debts and provide for the common defense and general Welfare of the United States."

There is indeed no great difficulty in deciding whether a tax is "to pay the debts" of the United States; but at times it is hard to say whether a statute is a tax to "provide for the * * * general Welfare." An excise might be in form a tax and yet not raise enough revenue to pay for the cost of its administration. Furthermore, is the taxing power limited to raising money necessary to the exercise of some of the prescribed powers of Congress, or does it extend to whatever Congress may think beneficial to the "People"?

Again, consider the power "to regulate commerce with foreign nations and among the several States." Are all "regulations" valid so long as they impinge only upon "commerce among the States"? It is constitutional to prevent those who do not pay a minimum wage, or who employ child labor, from sending their wares across state lines; but would it be constitutional to forbid carpenters, plumbers, bakers, or brewers to do so, unless they passed a federal examination and received a federal license? Do the natural resources in land under water below low tide belong to the nation or the abutting states?

What I have called the first alternative would have meant that the interpretation of the Constitution on a given occasion would be left to that "Department" before which the question happened first to come; and such a system would have been so capricious in operation, and so different from that designed, that it could not have endured. Moreover, the second alternative would have been even worse, for under it each "Department" would have been free to decide constitutional issues as it thought right, regardless of any earlier decision of the others. Thus it would have been the President's privilege, and indeed his duty, to execute only those statutes that seemed to him to be constitutional, regardless even of a decision of the Supreme Court. The courts would have entered such judgments as seemed to them consonant with the Constitution; but neither the President, nor Congress, would have been bound to enforce them if he or it disagreed, and without their help the judgments would have been waste paper.

For centuries it has been an accepted canon in interpretation of documents to interpolate into the text such provisions, though not expressed, as are essential to prevent the defeat of the venture at hand; and this applies with especial force to the interpretation of constitutions, which, since they are designed to cover a great multitude of necessarily unforeseen occasions, must be cast in general language, unless they are constantly amended. If so, it was altogether in keeping with established practice for the Supreme Court to assume an authority to keep the states, Congress, and the President within their prescribed powers. Otherwise the government could not proceed as planned; and indeed would almost certainly have foundered, as in fact it almost did over that very issue.

However, since this power is not a logical deduction from the structure of the Constitution but only a practical condition upon its successful operation, it need not be exercised whenever a court sees, or thinks that it sees, an invasion of the Constitution. It is always a preliminary question how importunately the occasion demands an answer. It may be better to leave the issue to be worked out without authoritative solution; or perhaps the only solution available is one that the court has no adequate means to enforce. * * *

CHARLES L. BLACK, JR., THE BUILDING WORK OF JUDICIAL REVIEW

The People and the Court 37–42, 47–53 (1960).

I start with the axiom that a government cannot attain and hold a satisfactorily definite attribution of legitimacy if its actions as a government are not, by and large, received as authorized. Despite its plausibility, this proposition doubtless rests on psychological rather than on purely logical grounds. It is barely possible, as a matter of sheer logic, to conceive of people's feeling that the government under which they lived was a rightful government, but that a great many of its most important governmental acts were usurpative and unempowered. A government, whatever might be the outcome of refined semantic analysis, is actually conceived of by its citizens as more than the sum of its actions. But I suggest that, as a matter of human psychology, it is quite unthinkable that such a tension could long maintain itself unresolved. Immediate and particular actions are what the citizen sees and feels, and if he believes these to be, in great part, unauthorized, lacking the character of authentic governmental acts, mere wrongs committed by persons in power, then I submit that he cannot long retain the feeling that the government itself is legitimate.

If this is true, then one indispensable ingredient in the original and continuing legitimation of a government must be its possession and use of some means for bringing about a consensus on the legitimacy of important governmental measures.

* * *

* * * Whatever else may be said about the intention of the Framers, there can be no question whatever that * * * they intended to found [a government of limited powers]. The powers of the branches of government were enumerated, and it would be pretty hard to see this enumeration as merely playful, or as an elaborate hoax. But if there were any doubt on this score, one might turn to the explicit limitations, worded as such, both in the constitutional text and in some of the Amendments. Perhaps more important (for we are talking about the generation of a conviction of governmental legitimacy among the people) the conception of our government as one of limited powers is and since the beginning has been at the very center of American political

belief. It is an essential part of the picture the American has of his government.

* * *

Now, for a government based on the theory of limited powers the problem of the legitimation of governmental action is one of special difficulty. * * *

First, and perhaps most important, the fact of limitation itself generates doubt and debate on the legitimacy of particular actions. In Britain, no one can argue that a particular measure oversteps the bounds of Parliament's power, for the plain reason that there are no such bounds; an argument of that *form* is impossible. Where, on the other hand, limitations are built into government and into the theory underlying government, it is certain that particular interests will from time to time discern in the limitations a forbidding of some action to which they are about to be subjected. No matter what the nature of the limitations may be, such claims will always arise, for there will be a borderline somewhere. Given the theory of limitation, these claims cannot be brushed aside as political solecisms, but must be met and answered in some fashion.

Secondly, it is to be expected (and certainly is true in the case of our Constitution) that the language in which limitations on government are expressed will be broad, and hence will invite competing constructions, supported in entire good faith. This breadth of language is not accidental. It is inherent in the very concept of limitation, for, paradoxically, a limitation which is specific often fails effectively to limit. Our Bill of Rights, for example, prohibits the imposition of "cruel and unusual" punishments. It would have been possible to omit the general phrase, and to list the punishments specifically forbidden. But it is plain that such a technique would have failed to implement the purpose behind the provision, for if a government were specifically shut off from nose-docking and boiling in oil, it could surely find some punishment equally cruel that was not on the list.

To look at the matter from another side, the affirmative powers of government, to which it is confined, must also be expressed in general, and hence in vague, language. Here again there is no question of intellectual sloppiness; it is impossible to calculate or list, in advance, the concrete and specific measures which a government is to be authorized to take, and if you tried to do so you would unquestionably leave out some that were vital. So constitutional draftsmen, in granting powers as well as in limiting them, are driven, whether they like it or not, to do their work in relatively imprecise language. And it is inevitable that such language will lend itself to conflicting interpretations.

* * *

Thirdly (and this is beyond question the most delicate point), the resolution of doubts as to the legitimacy of governmental action must be undertaken, and bindingly effected, by the government itself. There is no other viable possibility. The alternatives may be briefly stated: judgment by an outsider, and individual judgment by the people and institutions subject to the exercise of the disputed power of government. There is no outsider to judge, and nobody would stand for his judging if there were. The other alternative has been seriously, even passionately put forward, in a limited form, but it seems plain (to cite the classic example) that if South Carolina is to decide whether Congress is empowered to levy a protective tariff, while Massachusetts comes to an opposite decision, we have neither a nation nor a government. Yet there is, in the referral of decision on governmental power to the government itself, a flavor of setting up a party as judge in his own cause. There must always be something of a miracle, as well as much sound political intuition and wisdom, in the overcoming of this difficulty, and what must be looked for is success in satisfactory measure, rather than complete success.

* * *

* * * I have tried to show how a government founded on the theory of limited powers faces and must solve the problem of legitimacy—it must devise some way of bringing about a feeling in the nation that the actions of government, even when disapproved of, are authorized rather than merely usurpative. There are several hopeless ways to go about this, and just one, I think, that has some hope in it.

First, the determinations of Congress and the President could simply have been made final on all questions affecting their own power. I have already indicated the chief objection to that: It is wholly incompatible with the notion of limited power. It might have been acquiesced in, after a while, and a consensus reached on a British-style legitimacy, though conflicts between the President and Congress, and between the nation and the states, would have made that process a highly problematic one. In any case, it is not what happened, and I venture to say there is nothing in the history of this country to indicate it ever could have succeeded.

Trust could have been placed in "appeal to reason"; it could have been tried whether, in the end, people could not be persuaded of the legitimacy of governmental actions by argument alone. This, we can say confidently, would have been doomed. First, there is no finite set of "constitutional questions"; each new period generates new ones, and they are always charged with emotion and tied in with deep political strivings. Secondly, there is no single "reasonable" view of any of the great questions of the Constitution, if by "reasonable" we mean "capable of being held, after mature reflection and study, by an intelligent and relevantly well-informed person." The test of this is objective. Such persons have, in fact, differed on all great constitutional questions—that is what made them questions. But even if we didn't know this as a fact, we'd know it must be so. Words, preeminently the great vague words of the Constitution, have no single fixed meaning, and had no single fixed meaning at the time of adoption.   Difference of private opinion was and is inevitable.

The last expedient, the one that was partly planned and that partly happened, is the one suggested by all of human experience in dealing with disputes.   Where consensus on the *merits* of a question cannot be attained, it is sometimes possible to get consensus on a procedure for submitting the question for decision to an acceptable tribunal.   If this were not true, no baseball game could be played to the end.

The difficulty here, as we have already seen, is that, where the questions concern governmental power in a sovereign nation, it is not possible to select an umpire who is outside government.   Every national government, so long as it is a government, must have the final say on its own power.   The problem, then, is to devise such governmental means of deciding as will (hopefully) reduce to a tolerable minimum the intensity of the objection that government is judge in its own cause.   Having done this, you can only hope that this objection, though theoretically still tenable, will practically lose enough of its force that the legitimating work of the deciding institution can win acceptance.   Reliance here must be on the common sense of the people, who may be expected to see that all has been done that can be done, in the nature of the case, to ensure fair disposition of questions of governmental power.

I would suggest that the first step is to give such a decision-making institution a satisfactory degree of independence from the active policy-making branches of government.   It is in these that controversial exercises of governmental power will originate, and the umpire on questions of power must have such measure of detachment from them as will convince those whose claims are being decided that he is not practically, even though he may be theoretically, deciding his own case.

Secondly, I should want my umpire to be a specialist in tradition— not in sudsy, out-of-focus tradition, but in tradition's concrete minutiae and accurate ground plan.   I would recognize that the decisions I was asking him to make were not open-and-shut arithmetic examples, soluble on the basis of precedent alone.   But I would be sure that wiser and more acceptable work in deciding would be done by someone with respect for precedent, with an instilled feeling of responsibility to precedent, with a trained skill in following precedent—and in discerning when it ought not to be followed.

I would want to assure that my institution would be manned by people who had had training in the orderly presentation of evidence and argument, and who had absorbed the habit, through professional inveteration, of sifting carefully and then deciding firmly.   I would want people who were experienced in the handling of masses of data of all sorts, people who were schooled to deal with little things carefully while keeping big issues clearly in sight.   I should want people who were accustomed enough to the concept of attachment to a cause that it could be expected that, having been assigned the supremely important task of decision that I proposed giving them, they would perceive with clarity that they were now attached to the cause of learned and wise constitutional exposition, in the long-range interest, as best they could see it, of the whole people.

I have been using the plural, and of course we would want more than one man. It would obviously be prudent to reduce the risk of the impact of personal idiosyncracy by composing the tribunal of enough men to check one another, and to provide that institutional continuity through time which is vital to the establishment of independence and a sound tradition of work.

Finally, having set up these requirements, I would not be astounded, or overly disappointed, if the fact fell short sometimes of perfection. No institution can be as perfect, in men or work, as its ideal model, though the very mark of the truly living institution is that it has an ideal model which is always there nudging its elbow.

Now suppose such a body were set up, and given the task of deciding on the constitutional validity of measures taken by the active political departments. What would be the effect on the would-be violator of the navigation laws, when this body, umpiring, told him, "We have concluded that the navigation laws are a valid exercise of a power given to Congress"?

It would be touch and go. He might (like John C. Calhoun) scornfully point to the formal connection of the umpire with one of the parties, saying that nothing new had been added, that it was only proposed to validate the acts of one department of government by the decisions of another department of government. If this view prevailed, the whole device would have come to nothing, and I cannot think of another one so promising. We would have to say, "Very well, we must either give up, in effect, the notion of limited governmental power, or we must give up the thought of being a nation."

But he might, on the other hand, look to the substance and practicalities of the thing. He might say, "I see that you have done all you can to get me a right decision on my claim. I still think the decision is wrong. But the mode of decision was as fair as is humanly possible, under all the circumstances. And that is the most I can ask." Or, if he should still be a little too hot with the exaltation of battle, his friends might counsel with him, "Look, we agreed with you before. You were not getting a square shake. Like us, you were told that this is a government of limited powers, and then they tried to tell you that what that meant was that Congress was limited by its own interpretation of the limits on itself—an insult to the intelligence as well as a breach of faith. But things are different now. This is the real world. There is no way to ascertain, finally and without possibility of error, whether 'commerce' means 'navigation.' The absolute best that any government can do is to choose men learned in our traditions and history, isolated by temperament and placing from the day-by-day flare-up of issues such as this, and dependent on nobody else in government, and then to let them decide. If you ask more than that, you ask the impossible."

What makes the final difference between success and failure of such a legitimating device, between its contemptuous rejection on theoretical grounds and its acceptance as being the substantial best that can be done toward following out in practice the principle of limitation of power? Who can tell? Something clicks into place. When you have done the best you can, it may be good enough. No tree knows whether it will bear fruit; its job is to stand up tall and wait.

In our history, it did work, in sufficient measure. The institution I have described is, as you will have perceived, a court, manned by skillful lawyers steeped in the judicial tradition, and, with the added caveat of imperfection, it is our own Supreme Court. Pretty clearly, it had been foreseen by the Founders that the courts would decide "constitutional" questions where these arose in litigation. Surprising nobody, Congress and the Supreme Court early confirmed this understanding. And the Court took up the umpiring job.

Popular acceptance of this role was not a foregone conclusion. If it had not been forthcoming, no amount of theoretical or historical argument could have enabled the Court to fill this need. But acceptance did come, in sufficient amount and with sufficient reliability.

Now it will have been observed that I have described the function of the Supreme Court in a way which turns the usual account upside down. The role of the Court has usually been conceived as that of *invalidating* "hasty" or "unwise" legislation, of acting as a "check" on the other departments. It has played such a role on occasion, and may play it again in the future.

But a case can be made for believing that the prime and most necessary function of the Court has been that of *validation,* not that of invalidation. What a government of limited powers needs, at the beginning and forever, is some means of satisfying the people that it has taken all steps humanly possible to stay within its powers. That is the condition of its legitimacy, and its legitimacy, in the long run, is the condition of its life. And the Court, through its history, has acted as the legitimator of the government. In a very real sense, the Government of the United States is based on the opinions of the Supreme Court.

* * *

The power to validate is the power to invalidate. If the Court were deprived, by any means, of its real and practical power to set bounds to governmental action, or even of public confidence that the Court itself regards this as its duty and will discharge it in a proper case, then it must certainly cease to perform its central function of unlocking the energies of government by stamping governmental actions as legitimate. If everybody gets a Buck Rogers badge, a Buck Rogers badge imports no distinction. The Court may go thirty or forty years without declaring an Act of Congress unconstitutional; that means nothing, for it is scarcely to be looked for that Congress will pass any given annual or decennial quota of statutes that the Court will regard as invalid. But if it ever so much as became known—even as a matter of tacit understanding in the profession and on the Court, for such a secret could not be kept from the people—that the Court would not seriously ponder the questions of constitutionality presented to it and declare the challenged statute unconstitutional if it believed it to be so, then its usefulness as a legitimatizing institution would be gone.

ALEXANDER M. BICKEL, ESTABLISHMENT AND GENERAL JUSTIFICATION OF JUDICIAL REVIEW
The Least Dangerous Branch 16–26 (1962).

The root difficulty is that judicial review is a counter-majoritarian force in our system. There are various ways of sliding over this ineluctable reality. Marshall did so when he spoke of enforcing, in behalf of "the people," the limits that they have ordained for the institutions of a limited government. And it has been done ever since in much the same fashion by all too many commentators. Marshall himself followed Hamilton, who in the 78th *Federalist* denied that judicial review implied a superiority of the judicial over the legislative power—denied, in other words, that judicial review constituted control by an unrepresentative minority of an elected majority. "It only supposes," Hamilton went on, "that the power of the people is superior to both; and that where the will of the legislature, declared in its statutes, stands in opposition to that of the people, declared in the Constitution, the judges ought to be governed by the latter rather than the former." But the word "people" so used is an abstraction. Not necessarily a meaningless or a pernicious one by any means; always charged with emotion, but nonrepresentational—an abstraction obscuring the reality that when the Supreme Court declares unconstitutional a legislative act or the action of an elected executive, it thwarts the will of representatives of the actual people of the here and now; it exercises control, not in behalf of the prevailing majority, but against it. That, without mystic overtones, is what actually happens. It is an altogether different kettle of fish, and it is the reason the charge can be made that judicial review is undemocratic.

* * *

It is true, of course, that the process of reflecting the will of a popular majority in the legislature is deflected by various inequalities of representation and by all sorts of institutional habits and characteristics, which perhaps tend most often in favor of inertia. Yet it must be remembered that statutes are the product of the legislature and the executive acting in concert, and that the executive represents a very different constituency and thus tends to cure inequities of over- and underrepresentation. Reflecting a balance of forces in society for purposes of stable and effective government is more intricate and less certain than merely assuring each citizen his equal vote. Moreover, impurities and imperfections, if such they be, in one part of the system are no argument for total departure from the desired norm in another part. A much more important complicating factor—first adumbrated by Madison in the 10th *Federalist* and lately emphasized by Professor David B. Truman and others [13]—is the proliferation and power of what Madison foresaw as "faction," what Mr. Truman calls "groups," and what in popular parlance has always been deprecated as the "interests" or the "pressure groups."

No doubt groups operate forcefully on the electoral process, and no doubt they seek and gain access to an effective share in the legislative and executive decisional process. Perhaps they constitute also, in some measure, an impurity or imperfection. But no one has claimed that they have been able to capture the governmental process except by combining in some fashion, and thus capturing or constituting (are not the two verbs synonymous?) a majority. They often tend themselves to be majoritarian in composition and to be subject to broader majoritarian influences. And the price of what they sell or buy in the legislature is determined in the biennial or quadrennial electoral marketplace. It may be, as Professor Robert A. Dahl has written, that elections themselves, and the political competition that renders them meaningful, "do not make for government by majorities in any very significant way," for they do not establish a great many policy preferences. However, "they are a crucial device for controlling leaders." And if the control is exercised by "groups of various types and sizes, all seeking in various ways to advance their goals," so that we have "minorities rule" rather than majority rule, it remains true nevertheless that only those minorities rule which can command the votes of a majority of individuals in the legislature who can command the votes of a majority of individuals in the electorate. In one fashion or another, both in the legislative process and at elections, the minorities must coalesce into a majority. Although, as Mr. Dahl says, "it is fashionable in some quarters to suggest that everything believed about democratic politics prior to World War I, and perhaps World War II, was nonsense," he makes no bones about his own belief that "the radical democrats who, unlike Madison, insist upon the decisive importance of the election process in the whole grand strategy of democracy are essentially correct." [14]

The insights of Professor Truman and other writers into the role that groups play in our society and our politics have a bearing on judicial review. They indicate that there are other means than the electoral process, though subordinate and subsidiary ones, of making institutions of government responsive to the needs and wishes of the governed. Hence one may infer that judicial review, although not responsible, may have ways of being responsive. But nothing can finally depreciate the central function that is assigned in democratic theory and practice to the electoral process; nor can it be denied that

---

13. See D.B. Truman, *The Governmental Process* (New York: Knopf, 1951).

14. R.A. Dahl, *A Preface to Democratic Theory* (Chicago: University of Chicago Press, 1956), pp. 125, 132.

the policy-making power of representative institutions, born of the electoral process, is the distinguishing characteristic of the system. Judicial review works counter to this characteristic.

* * *

* * * Besides being a counter-majoritarian check on the legislature and the executive, judicial review may, in a larger sense, have a tendency over time seriously to weaken the democratic process. Judicial review expresses, of course, a form of distrust of the legislature. "The legislatures," wrote James Bradley Thayer at the turn of the century,

> are growing accustomed to this distrust and more and more readily inclined to justify it, and to shed the considerations of constitutional restraints,—certainly as concerning the exact extent of these restrictions,—turning that subject over to the courts; and what is worse, they insensibly fall into a habit of assuming that whatever they could constitutionally do they may do,—as if honor and fair dealing and common honesty were not relevant to their inquiries. The people, all this while, become careless as to whom they send to the legislature; too often they cheerfully vote for men whom they would not trust with an important private affair, and when these unfit persons are found to pass foolish and bad laws, and the courts step in and disregard them, the people are glad that these few wiser gentlemen on the bench are so ready to protect them against their more immediate representatives. . . . [I]t should be remembered that the exercise of [the power of judicial review], even when unavoidable, is always attended with a serious evil, namely, that the correction of legislative mistakes comes from the outside, and the people thus lose the political experience, and the moral education and stimulus that comes from fighting the question out in the ordinary way, and correcting their own errors. The tendency of a common and easy resort to this great function, now lamentably too common, is to dwarf the political capacity of the people, and to deaden its sense of moral responsibility. It is no light thing to do that.[18]

To this day, in how many hundreds of occasions does Congress enact a measure that it deems expedient, having essayed consideration of its constitutionality (that is to say, of its acceptability on principle), only to abandon the attempt in the declared confidence that the Court will correct errors of principle, if any? It may well be * * * that any lowering of the level of legislative performance is attributable to many factors other than judicial review. Yet there is no doubt that what Thayer observed remains observable. * * *

Finally, another, though related, contention has been put forward. It is that judicial review runs so fundamentally counter to democratic theory that in a society which in all other respects rests on that theory, judicial review cannot ultimately be effective. We pay the price of a

18. [J.B. Thayer, *John Marshall* (Boston: Houghton Mifflin, 1901), pp. 103–04, 106–07.]

grave inner contradiction in the basic principle of our government, which is an inconvenience and a dangerous one; and in the end to no good purpose, for when the great test comes, judicial review will be unequal to it. The most arresting expression of this thought is in a famous passage from a speech of Judge Learned Hand, a passage * * * "of Browningesque passion and obscurity," voicing a "gloomy and apocalyptic view." Absent the institution of judicial review, Judge Hand said:

> I do not think that anyone can say what will be left of those [funda-
> mental principles of equity and fair play which our constitutions
> enshrine]; I do not know whether they will serve only as counsels; but
> this much I think I do know—that a society so riven that the spirit of
> moderation is gone, no court *can* save; that a society where that spirit
> flourishes, no court *need* save; that in a society which evades its
> responsibility by thrusting upon the courts the nurture of that spirit,
> that spirit in the end will perish.[22]

* * *

Such, in outline, are the chief doubts that must be met if the doctrine of judicial review is to be justified on principle. Of course, these doubts will apply with lesser or greater force to various forms of the exercise of the power. For the moment the discussion is at wholesale, and we are seeking a justification on principle, quite aside from supports in history and the continuity of practice. The search must be for a function which might (indeed, must) involve the making of policy, yet which differs from the legislative and executive functions; which is peculiarly suited to the capabilities of the courts; which will not likely be performed elsewhere if the courts do not assume it; which can be so exercised as to be acceptable in a society that generally shares Judge Hand's satisfaction in a "sense of common venture"; which will be effective when needed; and whose discharge by the courts will not lower the quality of the other departments' performance by denuding them of the dignity and burden of their own responsibility. It will not be possible fully to meet all that is said against judicial review. Such is not the way with questions of government. We can only fill the other side of the scales with countervailing judgments on the real needs and the actual workings of our society and, of course, with our own portions of faith and hope. Then we may estimate how far the needle has moved.

The point of departure is a truism; perhaps it even rises to the unassailability of a platitude. It is that many actions of government have two aspects: their immediate, necessarily intended, practical effects, and their perhaps unintended or unappreciated bearing on values we hold to have more general and permanent interest. It is a premise we deduce not merely from the fact of a written constitution but from the history of the race, and ultimately as a moral judgment of the good society, that government should serve not only what we

22. L. Hand, "The Contribution of an Independent Judiciary to Civilization," in I. Dilliard, ed., *The Spirit of Liberty* (New York: Knopf, 1953), pp. 155–65.

conceive from time to time to be our immediate material needs but also certain enduring values. This in part is what is meant by government under law. But such values do not present themselves ready-made. They have a past always, to be sure, but they must be continually derived, enunciated, and seen in relevant application. And it remains to ask which institution of our government—if any single one in particular—should be the pronouncer and guardian of such values.

Men in all walks of public life are able occasionally to perceive this second aspect of public questions. Sometimes they are also able to base their decisions on it; that is one of the things we like to call acting on principle. Often they do not do so, however, particularly when they sit in legislative assemblies. There, when the pressure for immediate results is strong enough and emotions ride high enough, men will ordinarily prefer to act on expediency rather than take the long view. Possibly legislators—everything else being equal—are as capable as other men of following the path of principle, where the path is clear or at any rate discernible. Our system, however, like all secular systems, calls for the evolution of principle in novel circumstances, rather than only for its mechanical application. Not merely respect for the rule of established principles but the creative establishment and renewal of a coherent body of principled rules—that is what our legislatures have proven themselves ill equipped to give us.

Initially, great reliance for principled decision was placed in the Senators and the President, who have more extended terms of office and were meant to be elected only indirectly. Yet the Senate and the President were conceived of as less closely tied to, not as divorced from, electoral responsibility and the political marketplace. And so even then the need might have been felt for an institution which stands altogether aside from the current clash of interests, and which, insofar as is humanly possible, is concerned only with principle. We cannot know whether, as Thayer believed, our legislatures are what they are because we have judicial review, or whether we have judicial review and consider it necessary because legislatures are what they are. Yet it is arguable also that the partial separation of the legislative and judicial functions—and it is not meant to be absolute—is beneficial in any event, because it makes it possible for the desires of various groups and interests concerning immediate results to be heard clearly and unrestrainedly in one place. It may be thought fitting that somewhere in government, at some stage in the process of law-making, such felt needs should find unambiguous expression. Moreover, and more importantly, courts have certain capacities for dealing with matters of principle that legislatures and executives do not possess. Judges have, or should have, the leisure, the training, and the insulation to follow the ways of the scholar in pursuing the ends of government. This is crucial in sorting out the enduring values of a society, and it is not something that institutions can do well occasionally, while operating for the most part with a different set of gears. It calls for a habit of mind, and for undeviating institutional customs. Another advantage that courts have is that questions of principle never carry the same aspect for them as they did for the legislature or the executive. Statutes, after all, deal typically with abstract or dimly foreseen problems. The courts are concerned with the flesh and blood of an actual case. This tends to modify, perhaps to lengthen, everyone's view. It also provides an extremely salutary proving ground for all abstractions; it is conducive, in a phrase of Holmes, to thinking things, not words, and thus to the evolution of principle by a process that tests as it creates.

Their insulation and the marvelous mystery of time give courts the capacity to appeal to men's better natures, to call forth their aspirations, which may have been forgotten in the moment's hue and cry. This is what Justice Stone called the opportunity for "the sober second thought." [26] Hence it is that the courts, although they may somewhat dampen the people's and the legislatures' efforts to educate themselves, are also a great and highly effective educational institution. * * * The educational institution that both takes the observation to correct the dead reckoning and makes it known is the voice of the Constitution: the Supreme Court exercising judicial review. The Justices, in Dean Rostow's phrase, "are inevitably teachers in a vital national seminar." [28] No other branch of the American government is nearly so well equipped to conduct one. And such a seminar can do a great deal to keep our society from becoming so riven that no court will be able to save it. Of course, we have never quite been that society in which the spirit of moderation is so richly in flower that no court need save it.

MICHAEL J. PERRY, NONINTERPRETIVE REVIEW IN HUMAN RIGHTS CASES: A FUNCTIONAL JUSTIFICATION

56 N.Y.U.L.Rev. 278, 278–80, 288–96, 307–310 (1981).

There are two basic sorts of judicial review. Following Tom Grey and John Ely, I will refer to them, respectively, as interpretive review and noninterpretive review.[1] The legitimacy of noninterpretive review is the central problem of contemporary constitutional theory. The distinction between interpretive and noninterpretive review can best be elaborated in terms of a particular conception of the United States Constitution. The Constitution consists of a complex of value judgments the Framers wrote into the text of the Constitution and thereby constitutionalized. The important such judgments fall into two categories. One category defines the structure of American government by specifying the division of authority, first, between the federal government and the governments of the states and, second, among the three

---

26. H.F. Stone, *"The Common Law in the United States,"* 50 Harvard Law Review 4, 25 (1936).

28. See E.V. Rostow, *"The Democratic Character of Judicial Review,"* 66 Harvard Law Review 193, 208 (1952).

1. See J. Ely, DEMOCRACY AND DISTRUST 1 (1980); Grey, *Do We Have An Unwritten Constitution?,* 27 Stan.L.Rev. 703 (1975).

branches of the federal government—legislative, executive, and judicial. The other category defines the limits of governmental authority vis-à-vis the individual; this category of value judgments specifies certain aspects of the relationship that shall exist between the individual and government.

The Supreme Court engages in interpretive review when it ascertains the constitutionality of a given policy choice by reference to one of the value judgments embodied, though not necessarily explicitly, either in some particular provision of the text of the Constitution or in the overall structure of government ordained by the Constitution. Such review is "interpretive" because the Court reaches its decision by interpreting—deciphering—the textual provision (or the aspect of governmental structure) that embodies the determinative value judgment. Interpretive review is a hermeneutical enterprise; the effort is to ascertain, as accurately as available historical materials will permit, the character of a value judgment the Framers constitutionalized at some point in the past. The Court engages in *noninterpretive* review when it makes the determination of constitutionality by reference to a value judgment other than one constitutionalized by the Framers. Such review is "noninterpretive" because the Court reaches its decision without really interpreting, in the hermeneutical sense, any provision of the constitutional text (or any aspect of government structure)—although, to be sure, the Court may explain its decision with rhetoric designed to create the illusion that it is merely "interpreting" or "applying" some constitutional provision.

"Interpretivism" refers to constitutional theory that claims that only interpretive judicial review is legitimate and, in particular, that all noninterpretive review is illegitimate. "Noninterpretivism" describes constitutional theory that claims that at least *some* noninterpretive review—noninterpretive review with respect to at least some categories of constitutional questions, with the categories specified by the noninterpretivist theory in question—is also legitimate. * * *

In this Article I propose to develop a justification for noninterpretive review in human rights cases * * *.

* * * [I] want to isolate a fundamental dimension of our collective American self-understanding that * * * is essential to our comprehension and consequent evaluation of the function of noninterpretive review in human rights cases. Although there are no particular political-moral values supported by either "tradition" or "consensus" sufficiently determinate to be of significant use in resolving the sorts of human rights conflicts that come before the Court, there is a particular conception of the American polity that seems to constitute a basic, irreducible feature of the American people's understanding of themselves. The conception can be described, for want of a better word, as religious.

Before elaborating on the American religious self-understanding I should comment on my use of the word "religious," which undoubtedly risks serious misunderstanding.   Etymologically, "religion" derives from the Latin *"religare, "* which means to bind together that which was once bound but has been broken asunder.   In the following discussion, I use the word "religious" in its etymological sense to refer to a binding vision, a vision that serves as a source of unalienated self-understanding, of "meaning" in the sense of existential orientation or rootedness.   *I do not use the word in any sectarian, theistic, or otherwise metaphysical sense.*

As Robert Bellah has observed, the American people, at least the great bulk of those who have been responsible for establishing, developing, and maintaining the principal institutional constituents of the American political community, have understood themselves to be "chosen" in the biblical sense of that word; they have understood themselves to be charged with a special responsibility, an obligation among the nations of the world.[47]   That responsibility is to realize, if only "partially and fragmentally . . ., a 'higher law.' "[48]   According to this self-understanding, "[t]he will of the people is not itself the criterion of right and wrong.   There is a higher criterion in terms of which this will can be judged; it is possible that the people may be wrong."[49] * * * An integral component of the American people's religious understanding of themselves is the notion of prophecy.   Invariably a people, even a chosen people, fail in their responsibility and need to be called to provisional judgment in the here and now.   That is the task of prophecy.

Today the biblical imagery doubtless seems strange or merely rhetorical to some.   Whereas in less secular times the religious conception I am discussing was expressed in openly and conventionally religious terms, now the expression is more likely than not to take a secular form.   But the cultural cast of the metaphors matters far less than the essential vision those metaphors disclose, and that vision seems not to have changed much over the course of our history.   The American people still see themselves as a nation standing under transcendent judgment: they understand, even if from time to time some members of the intellectual elite have not, that morality is not arbitrary and that justice cannot be reduced to the sum of the preferences of the collectivity.   The United States persists in seeing itself, as did its founders, as a beacon to the world, an American Israel, in regard to human rights.   The American people still value prophecy, although now it might be called, for example, "moral leadership."

The significance of this religious American self-understanding for our purposes is that it supplies the crucial context in which the function of noninterpretive review in human rights cases can be clarified.   Judicial review represents the institutionalization of prophecy.

47. See generally R. Bellah, The Broken Covenant: American Civil Religion in the Time of Trial 36–60 (1975). * * *

48. Bellah, American Civil Religion in the 1970's, Anglican Theological Rev. 8 (Supp.Ser. 1 (July 1973)).

49. Bellah, Civil Religion in America, 96 Daedalus 1, 4 (1967).

The function of noninterpretive review in human rights cases is prophetic; it is to call the American people—actually the government, the representative of the people—to provisional judgment. My point is not that judges in general or members of the Supreme Court in particular are divinely inspired. The Supreme Court is not an American Chair of Peter, such that when a majority of the Justices speak *ex cathedra* on matters of political faith and morals, they speak infallibly. My point is in no sense a metaphysical or supernaturalistic one. In portraying the function of noninterpretive review in human rights cases as prophetic, I invoke no assumptions about any deity or any divinely ordained "natural law." Nor do I suppose that the members of the judiciary are Learned Hand's "bevy of Platonic Guardians."[57] * * * Since I am not suggesting any of that, let me elaborate what my position is.

Our "religious" self-understanding has generally involved a commitment, although not necessarily a fully conscious one, to the notion of moral evolution. In the main, we have avoided the pretense that our current understanding of the moral universe—of ourselves, others, the world we inhabit, and, most fundamentally, of the proper relationship among ourselves, others, and our world—was perfect and complete. Rather, we know that we are fallible and that we must struggle incessantly to achieve a broader and deeper understanding. We also know that we are frail and that our frailty necessitates an ongoing struggle to bring our collective political practice into ever closer harmony with our evolving, deepening moral understanding.

* * *

I will begin explaining my justification for noninterpretive review in human rights cases with some fairly uncontroversial observations about comparative institutional competence. In recent generations, certain political issues have been widely perceived to be fundamental moral issues as well—issues that challenge and unsettle conventional ways of understanding the moral universe and that serve as occasions for forging alternative ways of understanding. In twentieth century America there have been several such issues: distributive justice and the role of government, freedom of political dissent, racism, sexism, the death penalty, and human sexuality. Our electorally accountable policymaking institutions are not well suited to deal with such issues in a way that is faithful to the notion of moral evolution and, therefore, to our religious understanding of ourselves.

Executive and legislative officials tend to deal with fundamental political-moral problems, at least highly controversial ones, when they confront such issues at all, by reflexive reference to the established moral conventions of the greater part of their particular constituencies. They refuse to see in such issues occasions for moral reevaluation and possible moral growth.

* * *

57. L. Hand, The Bill of Rights 73–74 (1958).

* * * Over time, the practice of noninterpretive review has evolved as a way of remedying what would otherwise be a serious defect in American government: the absence of any policymaking institution that regularly deals with fundamental political-moral problems other than by mechanical reference to established moral conventions.

* * * The basic function of noninterpretive review is to deal with those political issues that are also fundamental moral problems in a way that is faithful to the notion of moral evolution and, therefore, to our collective religious self-understanding. That is the sense in which I mean that noninterpretive review in human rights cases represents the institutionalization of prophecy. Such review is an enterprise designed to enable the American polity to live out its commitment to an ever deepening moral understanding and to political practices that harmonize with that understanding. * * *

The justification for noninterpretive review in human rights cases, if anything, is functional. Noninterpretive review has served an important, even indispensable function. It has enabled us, as a people, to keep faith with two of the most basic aspects of our collective self-understanding: our "democratic" understanding of ourselves as a people committed to electorally accountable policymaking and our "religious" understanding of ourselves as a people committed to struggle incessantly to see beyond, and then to live beyond, the imperfections of prevailing moral conventions. My claim is that noninterpretive review in human rights cases enables us to maintain a tolerable accommodation between the two, sometimes seemingly irreconcilable, commitments.

* * * For the reader who suspects that either there is in fact no religious aspect of American self-understanding or that, if there is, I have romanticized it beyond recognition, I will recast my essential claim. Noninterpretive review in human rights cases has enabled us to maintain a tolerable accommodation between, first, our democratic commitment and, second, the possibility that there may indeed be *discoverable* right answers to fundamental political-moral problems.

Regardless of whether there is a religious aspect of American self-understanding resembling what I have suggested, we seem to be open as a society to the possibility that there are right answers to political-moral problems. In any event, we *should be* open to that possibility. * * * I shall not defend the proposition that we should take seriously the possibility that there are right answers since this is not a metaethical treatise. I merely want to emphasize that this proposition is adequate for purposes of the functional justification I develop in this Article. Noninterpretive review enables us to keep faith with a possibility to which we are, or should be, open and enables us to keep faith with that possibility in a manner that accommodates our democratic commitment. As a matter of comparative institutional competence, the politically insulated federal judiciary is likely, when the human rights issue is a deeply controversial one, to move us in the direction of a right answer. It is more likely to do so than is the political process left to its own devices, because that process tends to resolve such issues by reflexive, mechanical reference to established moral conventions. None of this, of course, is to suggest that the Supreme Court, or any other court, necessarily gives right answers.

*   *   *

One clear implication of my argument is that answers to human rights questions are right or wrong independently of what a majority of Americans happens to believe, either in the short term or in the long term. Yet what the majority comes to believe in the long term, after having been rebuffed by the electorally unaccountable Supreme Court in the short term, is more likely to be morally correct than are established but untested, unreflective moral conventions. In adjudicating a person's claim that government has violated his human rights when no value judgment constitutionalized by the Framers is determinative, the Court in effect submits the challenged governmental action to a moral critique. In striking down such action, the Court assumes a prophetic stance, opposing itself to established conventions. But that does not end the matter. The relationship between noninterpretive review and electorally accountable policymaking is dialectical. The electorally accountable political processes generate a policy choice that typically reflects some fairly well established moral conventions. In exercising noninterpretive review, the Court evaluates that choice on political-moral grounds, in the end either accepting or rejecting it. If the Court rejects a given policy choice, the political processes must respond, whether by embracing the Court's decision, by tolerating it, or, if the decision is not accepted or is not accepted fully, by moderating or even by undoing it.

I want to emphasize that I am *not* claiming that the Court always gives right answers, since of course it does not. My basic point is simply that from the constitutional dialogue between the Court and the other agencies of a government—a subtle, dialectical interplay between Court and polity—what emerges is a far more self-critical political morality than would otherwise appear. This morality is therefore likely to be more mature as well—a morality that is moving (inching?) towards, even though it has not always and everywhere arrived at, right answers—rather than a stagnant or even regressive morality.

*   *   *

[Perry next considers whether non-interpretive review can be "reconciled with the principle of electorally accountable policymaking." He concludes that congressional power over the jurisdiction of the Federal courts is an effective and adequate source of political control over non-interpretive review.]

BIBLIOGRAPHY

General Background on the Constitution and Judicial Review

A WORKABLE GOVERNMENT? (B. Marshall ed. 1987).

B. Bailyn, THE IDEOLOGICAL ORIGINS OF THE AMERICAN REVOLUTION (1967).

C. Beard, AN ECONOMIC INTERPRETATION OF THE CONSTITUTION OF THE UNITED STATES (1935).

Bernstein, *Review Essay—Charting the Bicentennial*, 87 Colum.L.Rev. 1565 (1987).

BEYOND CONFEDERATION: ORIGINS OF THE CONSTITUTION AND AMERICAN NATIONAL IDENTITY (R. Beeman, S. Botein & E. Carter II eds. 1987).

E. Corwin, CORWIN ON THE CONSTITUTION (R. Loss ed., 2 vols., 1981, 1987).

A. Cox, THE ROLE OF THE COURT IN AMERICAN GOVERNMENT (1976).

W. Crosskey, POLITICS AND THE CONSTITUTION IN THE HISTORY OF THE UNITED STATES (1953).

D. Currie, THE CONSTITUTION IN THE SUPREME COURT: THE FIRST HUNDRED YEARS, 1789–1888 (1985).

R. Jackson, THE STRUGGLE FOR JUDICIAL SUPREMACY (1941).

M. Kammen, A MACHINE THAT WOULD GO OF ITSELF: THE CONSTITUTION IN AMERICAN CULTURE (1986).

R. McCloskey, THE AMERICAN SUPREME COURT (1960).

F. MacDonald, NOVUS ORDO SECLORUM: THE INTELLECTUAL ORIGINS OF THE CONSTITUTION (1985).

W. Rehnquist, THE SUPREME COURT: HOW IT WAS, HOW IT IS (1987).

H. Storing, THE COMPLETE ANTI–FEDERALIST (1981).

L. Tribe, AMERICAN CONSTITUTIONAL LAW (2d ed. 1988).

C. Warren, THE SUPREME COURT IN UNITED STATES HISTORY, 3 vols. (1922–24).

G. Wills, EXPLAINING AMERICA: THE FEDERALIST (1981).

C. Wolfe, THE RISE OF MODERN JUDICIAL REVIEW: FROM CONSTITUTIONAL INTERPRETATION TO JUDGE–MADE LAW (1986).

G. Wood, THE CREATION OF THE AMERICAN REPUBLIC, 1776–1787 (1969).

Theories of Judicial Review

Ackerman, *The Storrs Lectures: Discovering the Constitution*, 93 Yale L.J. 1013 (1984).

J. Agresto, THE SUPREME COURT AND CONSTITUTIONAL DEMOCRACY (1984).

Attanasio, *Everyman's Constitutional Law: A Theory of the Power of Judicial Review*, 72 Geo.L.J. 1685 (1984).

Ball, *Don't Die Don Quixote: A Response and Alternative to Tushnet, Bobbitt, and the Revised Texas Version of Constitutional Law,* 59 Tex.L.Rev. 787 (1981).

A. Bickel, THE SUPREME COURT AND THE IDEA OF PROGRESS (1970).

Bishin, *Judicial Review in Democratic Theory,* 50 S.Cal.L.Rev. 1099 (1977).

Brest, *The Fundamental Rights Controversy: The Essential Contradictions of Normative Constitutional Scholarship,* 90 Yale L.J. 1063 (1981).

Burt, *Constitutional Law and the Teaching of Parables,* 93 Yale L.J. 455 (1984).

Carter, *Constitutional Adjudication and the Indeterminate Text: A Preliminary Defense of an Imperfect Muddle,* 94 Yale L.J. 821 (1985).

Chemerinsky, *Wrong Questions Get Wrong Answers: An Analysis of Professor Carter's Approach to Judicial Review,* 66 B.U.L.Rev. 47 (1986).

Chemerinsky, *The Price of Asking the Wrong Question: An Essay on Constitutional Scholarship and Judicial Review,* 62 Tex.L.Rev. 1207 (1984).

J. Choper, JUDICIAL REVIEW AND THE NATIONAL POLITICAL PROCESS (1980).

Clor, *Judicial Statesmanship and Constitutional Interpretation,* 26 S.Tex.L.J. 397 (1985).

Corwin, *Marbury v. Madison and the Doctrine of Judicial Review,* 12 Mich.L.Rev. 538 (1914).

Dahl, *Decision–Making in a Democracy: The Supreme Court as National Policy–Maker,* 6 J.Pub.L. 279 (1975).

Deutsch, *Neutrality, Legitimacy, and the Supreme Court: Some Intersections Between Law and Political Science,* 20 Stan.L.Rev. 169 (1968).

J. Ely, DEMOCRACY AND DISTRUST: A THEORY OF JUDICIAL REVIEW (1980).

Fallon, *Of Speakable Ethics and Constitutional Law: A Review Essay* [of Perry, MORALITY, POLITICS, AND LAW], 56 U.Chi.L.Rev. 1523 (1989).

Fiss, *The Supreme Court, 1978 Term—Foreword: The Forms of Justice,* 93 Harv.L.Rev. 1 (1979).

Graglia, *Judicial Review on the Basis of "Regime Principles": A Prescription for Government by Judges,* 26 S.Tex.L.J. 435 (1985).

Leedes, *The Supreme Court Mess,* 57 Tex.L.Rev. 1361 (1979).

Levinson, *"The Constitution" in American Civil Religion,* 1979 Sup.Ct. Rev. 123.

Lindgren, *Beyond Cases: Reconsidering Judicial Review,* 1983 Wis.L. Rev. 583.

Llewellyn, *The Constitution as an Institution,* 34 Colum.L.Rev. 1 (1934).

L. Lusky, BY WHAT RIGHT? (1975).

McCleskey, *Judicial Review in a Democracy: A Dissenting Opinion,* 3 Hous.L.Rev. 354 (1966).

McConnell, *The Role of Democratic Politics in Transforming Moral Convictions into Law,* 98 Yale L.S. 1501 (1989) [review of Perry, MORALITY, POLITICS, AND LAW].

Nelson, *Changing Conceptions of Judicial Review: The Evolution of Constitutional Theory in the United States,* 1790–1860, 120 U.Pa.L. Rev. 1166 (1972).

M. Perry, THE CONSTITUTION, THE COURTS, AND HUMAN RIGHTS (1982).

M. Perry, MORALITY, POLITICS, AND LAW (1988).

Regan, *Community and Justice in Constitutional Theory,* 1985 Wis.L. Rev. 1073.

E. Rostow, THE SOVEREIGN PREROGATIVE (1962).

Rostow, *The Democratic Character of Judicial Review,* 66 Harv.L.Rev. 193 (1952).

Sager, *The Incorrigible Constitution,* 65 N.Y.U.L.Rev. 893 (1990).

Sager, *Rights Skepticism and Process–Based Responses,* 56 N.Y.U.L.Rev. 417 (1980).

Seidman, *Public Principle and Private Choice: The Uneasy Case for a Boundary Maintenance Theory of Constitutional Law,* 96 Yale L.J. 1006 (1987).

Symposium—*Judicial Review versus Democracy,* 42 Ohio St.L.J. 1–434 (1981).

Thayer, *The Origin and Scope of the American Doctrine of Constitutional Law,* 7 Harv.L.Rev. 129 (1893).

Tribe, *The Puzzling Persistence of Process–Based Constitutional Theories,* 89 Yale L.J. 1903 (1980).

M. Tushnet, RED, WHITE, AND BLUE (1988).

Truth, Justice, and the American Way: An Interpretation of Public Law Scholarship in the Seventies, 57 Tex.L.Rev. 1307 (1979).

Tushnet, *Darkness on the Edge of Town: The Contributions of John Hart Ely to Constitutional Theory,* 89 Yale L.J. 1037 (1980).

Wellington, *The Nature of Judicial Review,* 91 Yale L.J. 486 (1982).

Wechsler, *Toward Neutral Principles of Constitutional Law,* 73 Harv.L. Rev. 1 (1959).

Wright, *Professor Bickel, The Scholarly Tradition and the Supreme Court,* 84 Harv.L.Rev. 769 (1971).

Chapter II

METHODS OF CONSTITUTIONAL INTERPRETATION

How ought a court or legislature approach a constitutional question? What counts as a constitutional argument? Traditionally, constitutional law has recognized a range of arguments. Interpreters have consulted the plain or historical meaning of the language in the text; the intent of the drafters of the constitutional provision at issue; the structure of the Constitution as a whole; the purposes sought to be accomplished by the constitutional provision; precedent; and deeply held values or notions of social policy.[1] This Chapter explores the theoretical justifications for some of these interpretive methods.

Interpretivism/Non-interpretivism: Putting to one side the difficult moral issues central to the abortion debate, *Roe v. Wade* poses troubling questions for constitutional interpretation. According to many of *Roe*'s detractors, the Court's opinion (and substantive due process analysis in general) is illegitimate because it is based on norms and values not found in the language or structure of the Constitution. Proponents of the abortion and privacy decisions assert that it is permissible for the Court to rely on values external to the document in interpreting the Constitution. Thomas Grey distinguishes these two views, labelling the four-corners approach "interpretivism" and the external approach "non-interpretivism." Grey contends that throughout our constitutional history, the Court has enforced principles of liberty and justice not traceable to the language of the Constitution. To reject these decisions, he maintains, would be to radically alter prevailing constitutional doctrine. Robert Bork, in an article widely referred to during his (non)confirmation hearing, condemns non-interpretive judicial review. He contends that the Court's identification and imposition of "fundamental values" not found in the document cannot be squared with the presuppositions of a democratic society.

1. See Fallon, *A Constructivist Coherence Theory of Constitutional Interpretation,* 100 Harv.L.Rev. 1189 (1988).

Text: Frederick Schauer suggests that there are far more "easy cases" in constitutional adjudication than one might suppose from reading casebooks and Supreme Court opinions. He contends that language (either from the constitutional text or from a rule in a case or a series of cases) can be a significant, even if unappreciated, constraint on constitutional interpretation. Sanford Levinson turns Schauer's claim on its head. He argues that texts don't constrain interpretation; rather, interpretation creates texts. Drawing on modern literary criticism, Levinson doubts that one can sensibly talk about extracting a "true" or "correct" meaning from a constitutional provision.

In evaluating the arguments of Schauer and Levinson, you may wish to consider the great opinions of Chief Justice Marshall in *Marbury, Gibbons,* and *McCulloch*. In these cases, was the Court substantially limited by the text of the Constitution, or did the Chief Justice "create" the text in the process of writing his opinions? Perhaps it would be fairer to Schauer to think about a case where the textual language looks controlling. Is it possible that the Supreme Court could conclude that a mature 33 year-old is eligible to run for the Presidency?

Original Intent: A familiar claim in constitutional law is that the original intent of the framers ought to control constitutional interpretation. Paul Brest offers both a practical and a normative critique of this view. Richard Kay provides responses to the prevailing criticisms of original intentions adjudication (that is, that it is impossible and that it is normatively objectionable). How would the arguments of Brest and Kay apply in the interpretation of the Equal Protection Clause? Can one reasonably ascertain the "original understanding" of the Clause? Should it be read to cover gender discrimination? Indeed, is the decision in *Brown v. Board of Education* consistent with "original intent"? Does it matter if it is not?

"Neutral Principles": Herbert Wechsler's famous article argues that constitutional decisions, to be legitimate, must be "genuinely principled"—that is, they must rest on reasons that transcend the immediate result of the case and that the judge is willing to apply in similar cases. Mark Tushnet critiques several understandings of "neutral principles." He contends that no version of Wechsler's concept can significantly constrain judicial interpretation of the Constitution.

Wechsler contends at the end of his article that he cannot discover a neutral principle that would justify the *Brown* decision. How might Tushnet think about *Brown?* How would you respond to Wechsler?

Balancing: It is commonplace to think that resolution of a constitutional issue requires a court to "balance" the interests at stake. T. Alexander Aleinikoff identifies "balancing" as a dominant element of modern constitutional reasoning and offers a number of critiques of a balancing methodology. Would it make sense not to balance when considering cases arising under the First Amendment, the Due Process Clause, or the Fourth Amendment? Are there sensible alternatives to balancing, or is all constitutional interpretation, at bottom, an exercise in balancing?

A. INTERPRETIVISM/NON-INTERPRETIVISM

THOMAS C. GREY, DO WE HAVE AN UNWRITTEN CONSTITUTION?

27 Stan.L.Rev. 703, 703–717 (1975).

In reviewing laws for constitutionality, should our judges confine themselves to determining whether those laws conflict with norms derived from the written Constitution? Or may they also enforce principles of liberty and justice when the nomative content of those principles is not to be found within the four corners of our founding document? Excluding the question of the legitimacy of judicial review itself, that is perhaps the most fundamental question we can ask about our fundamental law.

I. THE PURE INTERPRETIVE MODEL

For many years this most basic question has not much engaged the explicit attention of constitutional scholars or of the courts or judges themselves, with at least one important exception. That exception was Mr. Justice Black. Throughout his long and remarkable career on the bench, the most consistently reiterated theme of his constitutional jurisprudence was the need for fidelity to the constitutional text in judicial review, and the illegitimacy of constitutional doctrines based on sources other than the explicit commands of the written Constitution.[1]

It now appears that as a final mark of Mr. Justice Black's achievement, his jurisprudential view of constitutional adjudication may be returning to favor. In the last few years, distinguished commentators on constitutional law have begun to echo Mr. Justice Black's central theme, criticizing constitutional developments in terms that have scarcely been heard in the scholarly community for a generation.

* * *

The truth is that the view of constitutional adjudication that [these commentators] share with Mr. Justice Black is one of great power and compelling simplicity. That view is deeply rooted in our history and in our shared principles of political legitimacy. It has equally deep roots in our formal constitutional law; it is, after all, the theory upon which judicial review was founded in *Marbury v. Madison.*

The chief virtue of this view is that it supports judicial review while answering the charge that the practice is undemocratic. Under the pure interpretive model (as I shall henceforth call the view in question), when a court strikes down a popular statute or practice as

---

1. *See, e.g., In re* Winship, 397 U.S. 358, 377 (1970) (Black, J., dissenting); Griswold v. Connecticut, 381 U.S. 479, 507 (1965) (Black, J., dissenting); Rochin v. Califor- nia, 342 U.S. 165, 174 (1952) (Black, J., concurring); Adamson v. California, 332 U.S. 46, 68 (1947) (Black, J., dissenting).

unconstitutional, it may always reply to the resulting public outcry: "We didn't do it—you did." The people have chosen the principle that the statute or practice violated, have designated it as fundamental, and have written it down in the text of the Constitution for the judges to interpret and apply. The task of interpretation of the people's commands may not always be simple or mechanical; there is no warrant to condemn Mr. Justice Black or his allies with the epithet "mechanical jurisprudence." But the task remains basically one of interpretation, the application of fixed and binding norms to new facts.[9]

II. Beyond Interpretation

The contrary view of judicial review, the one that I espouse and that seems to me implicit in much of the constitutional law developed by the courts, does not deny that the Constitution is a written document, expressing some clear and positive restraints upon governmental power. Nor does it deny that part of the business of judicial review consists of giving effect to these explicit commands.

Where the broader view of judicial review diverges from the pure interpretive model is in its acceptance of the courts' additional role as the expounder of basic national ideals of individual liberty and fair treatment, even when the content of these ideals is not expressed as a matter of positive law in the written Constitution. It must at once be conceded that such a role for our courts is more difficult to justify than is the role assigned by the pure interpretive model. Why, one asks, are the courts better able to discern and articulate basic national ideals than are the people's politically responsible representatives? And one recalls Learned Hand's remark that he would find it "most irksome to be ruled by a bevy of Platonic Guardians, even if I knew how to choose them, which I assuredly do not." [10]

These grave difficulties no doubt explain, although they do not excuse, the tendency of our courts—today as throughout our history—to resort to bad legislative history and strained reading of constitutional language to support results that would be better justified by explication of contemporary moral and political ideals not drawn from the constitutional text. Of course, this tendency of the courts in no way helps to establish the legitimacy of noninterpretive judicial review. Indeed,

---

9. The pure interpretive model should not be confused with *literalism* in constitutional interpretation, particularly with "narrow" or "crabbed" literalism. The interpretive model, at least in the hands of its sophisticated exponents, certainly contemplates that the courts may look through the sometimes opaque text to the purposes behind it in determining constitutional norms. Normative inferences may be drawn from silences and omissions, from structures and relationships, as well as from explicit commands. Thus I do not see the sort of constitutional reasoning described by Professor Charles Black in his

(G. & A.) Const'l Reader 2d Ed.—3

Structure And Relationship In Constitutional Law (1969) as necessarily going beyond the interpretive model.

What distinguishes the exponent of the pure interpretive model is his insistence that the only norms used in constitutional adjudication must be those inferable from the text—that the Constitution must not be seen as licensing courts to articulate and apply contemporary norms not demonstrably expressed or implied by the framers.

10. L. Hand, The Bill of Rights 73 (1958).

standing alone it tends to establish the opposite; for if judges resort to bad interpretation in preference to honest exposition of deeply held but unwritten ideals, it must be because they perceive the latter mode of decisionmaking to be of suspect legitimacy.

However, the tendency to slipshod history and text-parsing does not stand alone. The courts do not only effectuate unwritten ideals and values covertly. Rather, in a very large proportion of their important constitutional decisions, they proceed in a mode that is openly noninterpretive. If this assertion seems at first glance surprising, it may be so partly because of the way in which constitutional law is taught in our law schools.

In the academic teaching of constitutional law, the general question of the legitimacy of judicial review is addressed largely through the vehicle of *Marbury v. Madison.* Students examine the arguments made for judicial review by Chief Justice Marshall, and perhaps contrast them with some of the counterarguments of later judges or commentators. The discussion concludes with the point that, whatever the validity of those arguments as an original matter, history has firmly decided in favor of judicial review. Thereafter, debates about judicial review focus on the question of how "activist" or how "deferential" *it* should be. *It* is always assumed to be the single unitary practice established and justified in *Marbury.*

This seems to me a seriously misleading way of proceeding. *Marbury* defends (and its detractors attack) what I have here called the pure interpretive model of judicial review. The case itself involves the close interpretation of a technical and explicit constitutional provision, which is found, upon conventional linguistic analysis, to conflict with a statute. The argument for judicial review as a general matter is made in terms appropriate to that sort of case. Chief Justice Marshall's stress is on the *writtenness* of the Constitution, and on its supremacy in cases of clear conflict with ordinary law.[11] His heuristic examples all involve obvious conflicts between hypothetical (and unlikely) statutes on the one hand, and particularly explicit constitutional commands on the other.[12]

All this makes *Marbury* a most atypical constitutional case, and an inappropriate paradigm for the sort of judicial review that has been important and controversial throughout our history, from *Dred Scott* [13]

---

11. 5 U.S. (I Cranch) 137, 176–78 (1803). Although the argument proceeds in terms of instances of purely interpretive judicial review, the underlying principle—that the courts must give precedence to constitutional law over ordinary law—is not itself found in or easily inferred from the text. Nevertheless, the argument for that principle still seems to be in the interpretive mode, based as it is on the intentions infer-

able from the framers' adoption of a written constitution.

12. For example, Marshall asks rhetorically whether the courts should enforce a statute generally imposing a duty on exports from a state, or an avowed bill of attainder or ex post facto law. *Id.* at 179.

13. Dred Scott v. Sanford, 60 U.S. (19 How.) 393 (1857).

to the *Legal Tender Cases*[14] to *Lochner*[15] to *Carter Coal*[16] and on to *Brown v. Board of Education*,[17] *Baker v. Carr*,[18] and the Death Penalty[19] and Abortion[20] cases in our own day. In the important cases, reference to and analysis of the constitutional text plays a minor role. The dominant norms of decision are those large conceptions of governmental structure and individual rights that are at best referred to, and whose content is scarcely at all specified, in the written Constitution—dual federalism, vested rights, fair procedure, equality before the law.

The question of the legitimacy of this very different sort of judicial review is scarcely addressed, much less concluded, by the arguments of *Marbury v. Madison.* To approach that question, we might better examine the debate between Justices Chase and Iredell in *Calder v. Bull.*[21] And if exposure to the matchless rhetoric of John Marshall is desired, *Fletcher v. Peck*[22] provides an excellent example. In that case, the Georgia statute is struck down on two alternative grounds. The first is a strained interpretation of the contract clause, comparable in flimsiness to some of the poorer interpretive efforts of the Warren Court. The second ground is expressed in the Court's conclusion that the statute violates "general principles which are common to our free institutions"—in particular, the principle of the inviolability of vested rights. Conspicuously absent is a dissent arguing that this principle is nowhere stated in the constitutional text. Indeed, the other opinion in the case—that of Justice Johnson—expresses agreement with the result on the ground of "general principles," but disavows the strained reading of the contract clause.

The parallel between *Fletcher* and most contemporary judicial review is striking. Today, the Court will formally invoke one of the majestic generalities of the Constitution, typically the due process or equal protection clause, as the textual basis for its decision. Even this much specificity is not always vouchsafed us. Thus we are told of the

14. 79 U.S. (12 Wall.) 457 (1871).

15. Lochner v. New York, 198 U.S. 45 (1905).

16. Carter v. Carter Coal Co., 298 U.S. 238 (1936).

17. 347 U.S. 483 (1954).

18. 369 U.S. 186 (1962).

19. Furman v. Georgia, 408 U.S. 238 (1972).

20. Roe v. Wade, 410 U.S. 113 (1973), Doe v. Bolton, 410 U.S. 179 (1973).

21. 3 U.S. (3 Dall.) 386 (1798). Chase: "I cannot subscribe to the omnipotence of a state legislature, or that it is absolute and without control, although its authority should not be expressly restrained by the constitution, or fundamental law of the State. . . . There are certain vital principles in our free republican governments, which will determine and overrule our ap-

parent and flagrant abuse of legislative power. . . ." *Id.* at 387–88 (majority opinion).

Iredell: "It is true, that some speculative jurists have held, that a legislative act against natural justice must, in itself, be void; but I cannot think, that under such a government, any court of justice would possess a power to declare it so. . . .

"[T]he ideas of natural justice are regulated by no fixed standard; the ablest and the purest men have differed upon the subject; and all that the court could properly say, in such an event, would be, that the legislature, possessed of an equal right of opinion, had passed an act which, in the opinion of the judges, was inconsistent with the abstract principles of natural justice." *Id.* at 398–99 (concurring opinion).

22. 10 U.S. (6 Cranch) 87 (1810).

constitutional "right to travel" that the Court has "no occasion to ascribe the source of this right to * * * a particular constitutional provision." [25] And in the Abortion Cases, the Court's reference to the textual cover for the "right of privacy" is strikingly casual:

> This right of privacy, whether it be founded in the Fourteenth Amendment's concept of personal liberty and restrictions upon state action, as we feel it is, or, as the District Court determined, in the Ninth Amendment's reservation of rights to the people, is broad enough to encompass a woman's decision whether or not to terminate her pregnancy.[26]

It should be clear that in these cases the Court is quite openly *not* relying on constitutional text for the content of the substantive principles it is invoking to invalidate legislation. The parallel reliance on the ninth amendment and the due process clause in the Abortion Cases is instructive on the point. The ninth amendment on its face has no substantive content. It is rather a license to constitutional decisionmakers to look beyond the substantive commands of the constitutional text to protect fundamental rights not expressed therein. In this case at least, the due process clause is being used in the same way.

Much of our substantive constitutional doctrine is of this kind. Where it arises "under" some piece of constitutional text, the text is not invoked as the source of the values or principles that rule the cases. Rather the broad textual provisions are seen as sources of legitimacy for judicial development and explication of basic shared national values. These values may be seen as permanent and universal features of human social arrangements—natural law principles—as they typically were in the 18th and 19th centuries. Or they may be seen as relative to our particular civilization, and subject to growth and change, as they typically are today. Our characteristic contemporary metaphor is "the living Constitution"—a constitution with provisions suggesting restraints on government in the name of basic rights, yet sufficiently unspecific to permit the judiciary to elucidate the development and change in the content of those rights over time.

This view of constitutional adjudication is at war with the pure interpretive model. As Mr. Justice Black said often and forcefully enough, he had no truck with the notion of changing, flexible, "living" constitutional guarantees.[28] The amendment process was the framers' chosen and exclusive method of adopting constitutional values to changing times; the judiciary was to enforce the Constitution's substantive commands as the framers meant them.

25. Shapiro v. Thompson, 394 U.S. 618, 630 (1969) (footnote omitted).

26. Roe v. Wade, 410 U.S. 113, 153 (1973). Students of the aesthetics of pseudo-interpretation may debate whether or not this formulation is preferable to the Court's celebrated shuffle in Griswold v. Connecticut, 381 U.S. 479 (1965), through the "emanations" and "penumbras" of the Bill of Rights.

28. *See, e.g.,* Harper v. Virginia Bd. of Elections, 383 U.S. 663, 670 (1966) (Black, J., dissenting).

This is not to say that the interpretive model is incompatible with one limited sense of the concept of a "living" constitution. The model can contemplate the application of the framers' value judgments and institutional arrangements to new or changed *factual* circumstances. In that sense, its proponents can endorse Chief Justice Marshall's view of the Constitution as "intended to endure for ages to come, and consequently, to be adapted to the various crises of human affairs." [30]

But the interpretive model cannot be reconciled with constitutional doctrines protecting unspecified "essential" or "fundamental" liberties, or "fair procedure," or "decency"—leaving it to the judiciary to give moral content to those conceptions either once and for all or from age to age. That sort of "interpretation" would drain from the interpretive model its animating strength. Once it was adopted, the courts could no longer honestly defend an unpopular decision to a protesting public with the transfer of responsibility: "We didn't do it—you did." No longer would the Court's constitutional role be the technical and professional one of applying *given* norms to changing facts; instead the Court would assume the large and problematic role of discerning a society's most basic contemporary values.

III. The Implications of the Pure Interpretive Model

Let me now give some examples, confined to the area of individual rights, of the numerous and important substantive constitutional doctrines which seem to me unjustified under a consistently applied pure interpretive model of judicial review. First and most obvious is virtually the entire body of doctrine developed under the due process clauses of the 5th and 14th amendments. If those clauses can be seen as having any specific normative content attributable to their framers, it is probably only that given to them by Mr. Justice Black.[31] In his view, due process requires only that deprivations of life, liberty or property be authorized by law duly enacted, rather than carried out by arbitrary executive action. A slightly more ambitious, though highly implausible, narrow interpretation is that adopted by the pre-Civil War Supreme Court—that the clause prohibits departures from the settled course of procedure familiar in the English courts in 1791.[32]

On the interpretive model, then, all the rest of due process doctrine must go. First, what many regard as the core of due process doctrine— its flexible requirement of "fundamentally fair" procedures in criminal and civil proceedings—cannot be reconciled with the interpretive model. These doctrines are developments of the "living constitution"

30. McCulloch v. Maryland, 17 U.S. (4 Wheat.) 415, 427 (1819).

31. *See In re* Winship, 397 U.S. 358, 377–85 (1970) (dissenting opinion). As Mr. Justice Black notes in that opinion, his separate position that the 14th amendment incorporates the Bill of Rights is not based on construction of the due process clause alone, but on "the language of the entire first section of the Fourteenth Amendment, as illuminated by the legislative history surrounding its adoption." *Id.* at 382 n. 11.

32. Murray's Lessee v. Hoboken Land & Improvement Co., 59 U.S. (18 How.) 272, 277 (1856).

concept *par excellence.*[33] In addition, everything that has been labeled "substantive due process" would be eliminated. It is these doctrines on which the proponents of the interpretive model have most often focused their attacks. Much of the force behind their position derives from the deeply felt opposition to the constitutionalization of laissez-faire economics epitomized by *Lochner v. New York,*[34] and they typically unite in opposition to contemporary doctrinal developments that remind them too much of *Lochner.*[35]

A striking point often overlooked by contemporary interpretivists is that the demise of substantive due process must constitutionally free the federal government to engage in explicit racial discrimination. There is no textual warrant for reading into the due process clause of the fifth amendment any of the prohibitions directed against the states by the equal protection clause.[36]

Equally strikingly, the application of the provisions of the Bill of Rights to states cannot be justified under an interpretive model—unless one strains to accept, as the Court clearly has declined to do, the flimsy historical evidence that the framers of the 14th amendment intended this result.[37] Freedom of speech, freedom of religion, and the require-

---

33. *See, e.g., In re* Winship, 397 U.S. 358, 377 (1970) (Black, J., dissenting); Goldberg v. Kelly, 397 U.S. 254 (1970) (Black, J., dissenting).

34. 198 U.S. 45 (1905).

35. It now seems that the ultimate punchline in the criticism of a constitutional decision is to say that it is "like *Lochner.*" Professor Ely has even minted a generic term, "to *Lochner,*" to describe whatever-it-was-so-awful-the-Court-did-in-*Lochner.* Ely, [*The Wages of Crying Wolf: A Comment on* Roe v. Wade, 82 Yale L.J. 920, 944 (1973).]

Lochner is only one of thousands of decisions in the history of the Court that invoke a noninterpretive mode of constitutional adjudication; if it was a bad decision, as I think it was, it by no means follows that the general mode of adjudication it represents is illegitimate. There are many bad decisions in the mode of pure interpretation.

It is an often overlooked point that Mr. Justice Holmes in his classic *Lochner* dissent did not use the case as an occasion to reject noninterpretive adjudication generally, or even substantive due process as such; quite the contrary: "I think that the word liberty in the Fourteenth Amendment is perverted when it is held to prevent the natural outcome of a dominant opinion, *unless it can be said that a rational and fair man necessarily would admit that the statute proposed would infringe fundamental principles as they have been*

understood by the traditions of our people and our law." 198 U.S. at 76 (emphasis added).

36. *See* Bolling v. Sharpe, 347 U.S. 497, 499 (1954). Since *Bolling,* the Court has often applied equal protection doctrine to the federal government "under" the fifth amendment due process clause. *See, e.g.,* Shapiro v. Thompson, 394 U.S. 618 (1969), in which the Court invalidated a District of Columbia statute as a violation of due process, while relying upon the equal protection clause to invalidate similar state statutes. Since *Bolling*—at least as far as I have been able to discover—the Court has never even seriously discussed the possibility that the fifth amendment due process clause might not fully incorporate the requirements progressively imposed on the states under the equal protection clause.

37. The Court's refusal to adopt the "incorporation" theory is clear both from its refusal to apply the requirements of grand jury indictment and civil jury trial to the states, and from its statements in "selective incorporation" cases. *See, e.g.,* Duncan v. Louisiana, 391 U.S. 145, 149 (1968), which held that due process required the states to provide jury trial in serious criminal cases *because* "trial by jury in criminal cases is fundamental to the American scheme of justice. . . ." For the controversy over the intent of the framers, *compare* Fairman, *Does the Fourteenth Amendment Incorporate the Bill of Rights?,* 2 Stan.L.Rev. 5 (1949), *with* Adam-

ment of just compensation in the taking of property, as well as the procedural provisions of the fourth, fifth, sixth, and eighth amendments must then no longer be seen as federal constitutional restraints on state power.

All of the "fundamental interests" that trigger "strict scrutiny" under the equal protection clause would have to be discarded, if the interpretive model were to control constitutional adjudication. Most obviously, the large body of doctrine that has grown up around the interests in the franchise and in participation in the electoral process could not stand. If the values implicit in the equal protection clause are limited only to those that its framers intended at the time of enactment, the clause clearly does not speak to questions of eligibility for the franchise or of legislative apportionment.[38]

Thus far, it seems to me there is little room for disagreement that the premises of the pure interpretive model would require the conclusions I have drawn from it. For those who have not yet had enough, and coming to slightly more doubtful matters, there is serious question how much of the law prohibiting state racial discrimination can survive honest application of the interpretive model. It is clear that the equal protection clause was meant to prohibit *some* forms of state racial discrimination, most obviously those enacted in the Black Codes. It is equally clear from the legislative history that the clause was *not* intended to guarantee equal political rights, such as the right to vote or to run for office, and perhaps including the right to serve on juries.[39]

It is at least doubtful whether the clause can fairly be read as intending to bar any form of state-imposed racial segregation, so long as equal facilities are made available. Professor Bickel's careful study of the legislative history revealed little evidence of intent to prohibit segregation, which at the time was widespread in the North.[40] Professor Bickel did conclude that the original understanding of the amendment was consistent with the decision in the School Segregation Cases, but only in the sense that the general language of the clause *licensed* the courts (and Congress) to enforce evolving ideals of racial justice.[41] Yet this is a classic invocation of the notion of the "living constitution," and as such is not permitted by the interpretive model.

Finally, under the interpretive model, modern applications of the provisions of the Bill of Rights based on their capacity to grow or develop with changing social values would have to be discarded. Prominent among the discarded doctrines would be the prevailing view that the eighth amendment's prohibition of cruel and unusual punishments

---

son v. California, 332 U.S. 46, 68 (1947) (Black, J., dissenting).

38. The numerous dissenting opinions of Mr. Justice Harlan in voting and reapportionment cases put the point beyond doubt. *See, e.g.,* Carrington v. Rash, 380 U.S. 89, 97 (1965) (Harlan, J., dissenting);

Reynolds v. Sims, 377 U.S. 533, 589 (1964) (Harlan, J., dissenting).

39. *See generally* Bickel, *The Original Understanding and the Segregation Decision,* 69 Harv.L.Rev. 1 (1955).

40. *Id.* at 58.

41. *Id.* at 62–65.

must be "interpreted" in light of society's "evolving standards of decency." [42]   It is doubtful that much of modern first amendment doctrine could be defended on the basis of value choices attributable to the framers,[43] and similar doubts must cast a shadow on some of the law of the fourth amendment.[44] The doctrine that the sixth amendment guarantees appointed counsel for indigent defendants [45] is likewise in serious jeopardy, if historically intended meaning must be the only legitimate guide in constitutional adjudication.[46]

While one might disagree with this rough catalogue on points of detail, it should be clear that an extraordinarily radical purge of established constitutional doctrine would be required if we candidly and consistently applied the pure interpretive model. Surely that makes out at least a prima facie practical case against the model. Conservatives ought to be cautious about adopting any abstract premise which requires so drastic a change in accepted practice, and liberals presumably will be dismayed by the prospect of any major diminution in the courts' authority to protect basic human rights.

IV. BEYOND INTERPRETATION: A PROGRAM OF INQUIRY

The uncomfortable results of adopting the interpretive model do not by themselves make a wholly satisfying argument for judicial review that goes beyond interpretation. Constitutional adjudication

42. *See, e.g.,* Trop v. Dulles, 356 U.S. 86, 101 (1958).

43. *See generally* L. Levy, Legacy of Suppression (1960).

44. *See, e.g.,* Katz v. United States, 389 U.S. 347 (1967), in which the Court extended fourth amendment coverage to the recording of oral statements by electronic devices. Justice Black filed a lone dissent arguing—from an interpretive stance— "[s]ince I see no way in which the words of the Fourth Amendment can be construed to apply to eavesdropping, that closes the matter for me. . . . I will not distort the words of the Amendment in order to 'keep the Constitution up to date' or 'to bring it into harmony with the times.' " *Id.* at 373 (dissenting opinion).

45. Johnson v. Zerbst, 304 U.S. 458 (1938).

46. The instances of noninterpretive judicial review I have mentioned fall into three general groups. First are those instances where the courts have created (or found) independent constitutional rights with almost no textual guidance. Examples are the contemporary right of privacy, and the older liberty of contract. Second are those instances where the courts have given general application to norms that the constitutional text explicitly applies in a more limited way. Examples are the application of equal protection and contract clause principles to the federal government, and the application of the Bill of Rights to the states—"under" the conveniently all-embracing due process clauses. The third type is the extension or broadening of principles stated in the Constitution beyond the normative content intended for them by the framers. Examples are the School Segregation Cases, and the extension of the fourth amendment to cover eavesdropping.

Most of the ire of proponents of the pure interpretive model has been directed against the first of these types of noninterpretive review. However the other two types are equally illegitimate, given the logic of the interpretive model. The advantage of placing a controverted case in the third rather than the first grouping is that it is usually possible to argue, with at least a shadow of plausibility, that extension of a specific constitutional prohibition really involves only the application of old norms to changed facts, and not a change in the norms themselves. *See, e.g.,* the majority opinion in Griswold v. Connecticut, 381 U.S. 479 (1965), for an implausible attempt to base a non-textual right of marital privacy on an "interpretation" of various provisions of the Bill of Rights—thus converting a Type 1 case into a "less suspect" Type 3 case.

going beyond the norms implicit in text and original history requires its own affirmative justification. In this short Essay, I can only suggest the several levels on which this inquiry might proceed, and hint at some of the directions it might take.

A. The Question of Practical Wisdom

First, one must consider the question of the wisdom and prudence of putting—or more accurately *leaving*—in the hands of judges the considerable power to define and enforce fundamental human rights without substantial guidance from constitutional text and history. How one views this question depends largely on how one evaluates the practical results, over the long run, of the exercise of this power. Arguments about institutional competence and the general propensities of judges become relevant here. Familiar in this context is the argument made in varying forms by constitutional commentators from Alexander Hamilton to Alexander Bickel that it makes some sense to give the final—or nearly final—say over the barrier between state and individual to the "least dangerous branch," the one that possesses neither purse nor sword.[47] But much can be said the other way, particularly through assignment in the name of popular sovereignty, and through allusion to *Lochner* and its ilk.

B. The Jurisprudential Question

Second, one can ask the jurisprudential question whether as a general matter the defining and enforcing of basic rights without external textual guidance is essentially a judicial task. Judges may be fine folk, but if what they are doing when they engage in judicial review on the basis of changing and unwritten moral principles is not adjudication, then they are sailing under false colors. For they have consistently told us that judicial review is genuinely incident to their traditionally assigned task of deciding litigated cases according to law.

A rigorously positivist jurisprudence would hold that judicial decision not directed by the articulate command of a determinate external sovereign is not truly adjudication. Rather it is a species of legislation. But this sort of positivist also views the entirely traditional judicial task of common law development through case-by-case decision as a form of legislation.[48] If common law development is an appropriate judicial function, falling within the traditionally accepted judicial role, is not the functionally similar case-by-case development of constitutional norms appropriate as well? Granted that the supremacy of constitu-

---

47. *See* The Federalist No. 78, at 504–05 (E. Earle ed.) (A. Hamilton); A. Bickel, The Least Dangerous Branch 23–28 (1962).

48. I do not endorse this positivist analysis. It seems to me that traditional common law decision and constitutional decision according to the noninterpretive mode both can be seen as decision of cases according to law. The law in question consists of the generally accepted social norms applied in the decision of the cases, norms that are—contrary to the positivists' position—best seen as "part of the law," quite independent of their promulgation through defined lawmaking procedures. *See* Dworkin, *The Model of Rules,* 35 U.Chi.L.Rev. 14 (1967); Wellington, *Common Law Rules and Constitutional Double Standards: Some Notes on Adjudication,* 83 Yale L.J. 221 (1973).

tional law over legislation, when contrasted with the formally inferior status of common law, makes a great difference. But the difference is in the hierarchical status of the judicial decision—which turns on a question of *authority*—and not in the intrinsic nature of the task.

C. The Question of Lawful Authority

The question of authority is the third level of inquiry into the justification for noninterpretive judicial review. Even if this mode of judicial review produces good results in the eyes of some beholders, and even if it is not intrinsically unjudicial, there remains the question whether in our Constitution we have actually granted this large power to our judges.

In resolving this issue of legal authority, there seems to me only one plausible method of inquiry. We must apply the conventional and accepted categories of legal argument—original understanding, judicial precedent, subsequent history, and internal consistency—and see if they support judicial review that goes beyond interpretation.

I believe that when these tests are applied, constitutional adjudication of the sort objected to by Mr. Justice Black and the other proponents of the pure interpretive model will be seen to be a lawful and legitimate feature of our system of judicial review. Full development of the argument must await another occasion; it necessarily requires lengthy and detailed historical documentation. But a brief sketch may be useful here.[49]

For the generation that framed the Constitution, the concept of a "higher law," protecting "natural rights," and taking precedence over ordinary positive law as a matter of political obligation, was widely shared and deeply felt. An essential element of American constitutionalism was the reduction to written form—and hence to positive law—of some of the principles of natural rights. But at the same time, it was generally recognized that written constitutions could not completely codify the higher law. Thus in the framing of the original American constitutions it was widely accepted that there remained unwritten but still binding principles of higher law. The ninth amendment is the textual expression of this idea in the federal Constitution.

As it came to be accepted that the judiciary had the power to enforce the commands of the written Constitution when these conflicted with ordinary law, it was also widely assumed that judges would enforce as constitutional restraints the unwritten natural rights as well. The practice of the Marshall Court and of many of its contemporary state courts, and the writings of the leading constitutional com-

---

49. I have set out my sketch as a simple narrative, lacking the detail, the qualifications, and the analysis of conflicting evidence that the full argument requires. I have also left out any documentation, on the theory that incomplete and necessarily misleading citation of sources is worse than none at all. [For a] full-scale development of the historical argument sketched here [, *see* Grey, *Origins of The Unwritten Constitution: Fundamental Law in American Revolutionary Thought*, 30 Stan.L.Rev. 843 (1978)].

mentators through the first generation of our national life, confirm this understanding.

A parallel development during the first half of the 19th century was the frequent attachment of unwritten constitutional principles to the vaguer and more general clauses of the state and federal constitutions. Natural-rights reasoning in constitutional adjudication persisted up to the Civil War, particularly with respect to property and contract rights, and increasingly involving "due process" and "law of the land" clauses in constitutional texts. At the same time, an important wing of the antislavery movement developed a natural-rights constitutional theory, built around the concepts of due process, of national citizenship and its rights, and of the human equality proclaimed in the Declaration of Independence.

Though this latter movement had little direct effect on pre-Civil War judicial decisions, it was the formative theory underlying the due process, equal protection, and privileges and immunities clauses of the 14th amendment. Section 1 of the 14th amendment is thus properly seen as a reaffirmation and reenactment in positive law of the principle that fundamental human rights have constitutional status.

The late 19th century saw the most controversial phase in our history of unwritten constitutional law, with the aggressive development by state and federal judges of constitutional principles protecting "liberty of contract" against labor regulation, and restraining taxation and the regulation of prices charged by private business. The reaction to this tendency marked the beginning of sustained intellectual and political attack on the whole concept of unwritten constitutional principles.

Politically, emergent and eventually dominant social forces continued to press for the legislation that was being invalidated under these constitutional principles. Intellectually, the 18th–century philosophical framework supporting the concept of immutable natural rights was eroded with the growth of legal positivism, ethical relativism, pragmatism, and historicism.

Under the combined assault of these social and intellectual forces, the courts retreated from the doctrines of "economic due process," abandoning them in the 1930's. However, although the more sweeping attack on the whole tradition of unwritten constitutional principles gained some important adherents within the judiciary and still more among academic critics, it did not ultimately prevail.

For at almost the same time as the doctrines protecting the laissez-faire economy were passing out of constitutional law, the judiciary began the active development of new civil libertarian constitutional rights whose protection was deemed "essential to the concept of ordered liberty"—for example, rights against state governments of freedom of speech and religion, rights to "fundamentally fair" proceedings, and rights to familial autonomy in childrearing and education.

The last generation has seen further development of constitutional rights clearly—and sometimes avowedly—not derived by textual interpretation, notably the right of privacy, the right to vote, the right to travel, and generally the rights resulting from application of "equal protection of the laws" to the federal government.   The intellectual framework against which these rights have developed is different from the natural-rights tradition of the founding fathers—its rhetorical reference points are the Anglo–American tradition and basic American ideals, rather than human nature, the social contract, or the rights of man.   But it is the modern offspring, in a direct and traceable line of legitimate descent, of the natural-rights tradition that is so deeply embedded in our constitutional origins.

To summarize, there was an original understanding, both implicit and textually expressed, that unwritten higher law principles had constitutional status.   From the very beginning, and continuously until the Civil War, the courts acted on that understanding and defined and enforced such principles as part of their function of judicial review. Aware of that history, the framers of the 14th amendment reconfirmed the original understanding through the "majestic generalities" of section 1.   And ever since, again without significant break, the courts have openly proclaimed and enforced unwritten constitutional principles.

ROBERT H. BORK, NEUTRAL PRINCIPLES AND SOME FIRST AMENDMENT PROBLEMS
47 Ind.L.J. 1, 1–11 (1971).

The subject of the lengthy and often acrimonious debate about the proper role of the Supreme Court under the Constitution is one that preoccupies many people these days: when is authority legitimate? I find it convenient to discuss that question in the context of the Warren Court and its works simply because the Warren Court posed the issue in acute form.   The issue did not disappear along with the era of the Warren Court majorities, however.   It arises when any court either exercises or declines to exercise the power to invalidate any act of another branch of government.   The Supreme Court is a major power center, and we must ask when its power should be used and when it should be withheld.

Our starting place, inevitably, is Professor Herbert Wechsler's argument that the Court must not be merely a "naked power organ," which means that its decisions must be controlled by principle.[1]   "A principled decision," according to Wechsler, "is one that rests on reasons with respect to all the issues in a case, reasons that in their generality and their neutrality transcend any immediate result that is involved." [2]

1. H. Wechsler, *Toward Neutral Principles of Constitutional Law,* in Principles, Politics, and Fundamental Law 3, 27 (1961)[.]

2. *Id.*

Wechsler chose the term "neutral principles" to capsulate his argument, though he recognizes that the legal principle to be applied is itself never neutral because it embodies a choice of one value rather than another. Wechsler asked for the neutral application of principles, which is a requirement, as Professor Louis L. Jaffe puts it, that the judge "sincerely believe in the principle upon which he purports to rest his decision." "The judge," says Jaffe, "must believe in the validity of the reasons given for the decision at least in the sense that he is prepared to apply them to a later case which he cannot honestly distinguish." [3] He must not, that is, decide lawlessly. But is the demand for neutrality in judges merely another value choice, one that is no more principled than any other? I think not, but to prove it we must rehearse fundamentals. This is familiar terrain but important and still debated.

The requirement that the Court be principled arises from the resolution of the seeming anomaly of judicial supremacy in a democratic society. If the judiciary really is supreme, able to rule when and as it sees fit, the society is not democratic. The anomaly is dissipated, however, by the model of government embodied in the structure of the Constitution, a model upon which popular consent to limited government by the Supreme Court also rests. This model we may for convenience, though perhaps not with total accuracy, call "Madisonian." [4]

A Madisonian system is not completely democratic, if by "democratic" we mean completely majoritarian. It assumes that in wide areas of life majorities are entitled to rule for no better reason [than] that they are majorities. We need not pause here to examine the philosophical underpinnings of that assumption since it is a "given" in our society; nor need we worry that "majority" is a term of art meaning often no more than the shifting combinations of minorities that add up to temporary majorities in the legislature. That majorities are so constituted is inevitable. In any case, one essential premise of the Madisonian model is majoritarianism. The model has also a counter-majoritarian premise, however, for it assumes there are some areas of life a majority should not control. There are some things a majority should not do to us no matter how democratically it decides to do them. These are areas properly left to individual freedom, and coercion by the majority in these aspects of life is tyranny.

Some see the model as containing an inherent, perhaps an insoluble, dilemma.[5] Majority tyranny occurs if legislation invades the areas properly left to individual freedom. Minority tyranny occurs if the majority is prevented from ruling where its power is legitimate. Yet, quite obviously, neither the majority nor the minority can be trusted to

---

3. L. Jaffe, English and American Judges as Lawmakers 38 (1969).

4. *See* R. Dahl, A Preface to Democratic Theory 4–33 (1956).

5. *Id.* at 23–24.

define the freedom of the other. This dilemma is resolved in constitutional theory, and in popular understanding, by the Supreme Court's power to define both majority and minority freedom through the interpretation of the Constitution. Society consents to be ruled undemocratically within defined areas by certain enduring principles believed to be stated in, and placed beyond the reach of majorities by, the Constitution.

But this resolution of the dilemma imposes severe requirements upon the Court. For it follows that the Court's power is legitimate only if it has, and can demonstrate in reasoned opinions that it has, a valid theory, derived from the Constitution, of the respective spheres of majority and minority freedom. If it does not have such a theory but merely imposes its own value choices, or worse if it pretends to have a theory but actually follows its own predilections, the Court violates the postulates of the Madisonian model that alone justifies its power. It then necessarily abets the tyranny either of the majority or of the minority.

This argument is central to the issue of legitimate authority because the Supreme Court's power to govern rests upon popular acceptance of this model. Evidence that this is, in fact, the basis of the Court's power is to be gleaned everywhere in our culture. We need not canvass here such things as high school civics texts and newspaper commentary, for the most telling evidence may be found in the U.S. Reports. The Supreme Court regularly insists that its results, and most particularly its controversial results, do not spring from the mere will of the Justices in the majority but are supported, indeed compelled, by a proper understanding of the Constitution of the United States. Value choices are attributed to the Founding Fathers, not to the Court. The way an institution advertises tells you what it thinks its customers demand.

This is, I think, the ultimate reason the Court must be principled. If it does not have and rigorously adhere to a valid and consistent theory of majority and minority freedoms based upon the Constitution, judicial supremacy, given the axioms of our system, is, precisely to that extent, illegitimate. The root of its illegitimacy is that it opens a chasm between the reality of the Court's performance and the constitutional and popular assumptions that give it power.

I do not mean to rest the argument entirely upon the popular understanding of the Court's function. Even if society generally should ultimately perceive what the Court is in fact doing and, having seen, prove content to have major policies determined by the unguided discretion of judges rather than by elected representatives, a principled judge would, I believe, continue to consider himself bound by an obligation to the document and to the structure of government that it prescribes. At least he would be bound so long as any litigant existed who demanded such adherence of him. I do not understand how, on any other theory of judicial obligation, the Court could, as it does now, protect voting rights if a large majority of the relevant constituency were willing to see some groups or individuals deprived of such rights. But even if I am wrong in that, at the very least an honest judge would owe it to the body politic to cease invoking the authority of the Constitution and to make explicit the imposition of his own will, for only then would we know whether the society understood enough of what is taking place to be said to have consented.

Judge J. Skelly Wright, in an argument resting on different premises, has severely criticized the advocates of principle. He defends the value-choosing role of the Warren Court, setting that Court in opposition to something he refers to as the "scholarly tradition," which criticizes that Court for its lack of principle.[6] A perceptive reader, sensitive to nuance, may suspect that the Judge is rather out of sympathy with that tradition from such hints as his reference to "self-appointed scholastic mandarins." [7]

The "mandarins" of the academy anger the Judge because they engage in "haughty derision of the Court's powers of analysis and reasoning." [8] Yet, curiously enough, Judge Wright makes no attempt to refute the charge but rather seems to adopt the technique of confession and avoidance. He seems to be arguing that a Court engaged in choosing fundamental values for society cannot be expected to produce principled decisions at the same time. Decisions first, principles later. One wonders, however, how the Court or the rest of us are to know that the decisions are correct or what they portend for the future if they are not accompanied by the principles that explain and justify them. And it would not be amiss to point out that quite often the principles required of the Warren Court's decisions never did put in an appearance. But Judge Wright's main point appears to be that value choice is the most important function of the Supreme Court, so that if we must take one or the other, and apparently we must, we should prefer a process of selecting values to one of constructing and articulating principles. His argument, I believe, boils down to a syllogism. I. The Supreme Court should "protect our constitutional rights and liberties." II. The Supreme Court must "make fundamental value choices" in order to "protect our constitutional rights and liberties." III. Therefore, the Supreme Court should "make fundamental value choices."

The argument displays an all too common confusion. If we have constitutional rights and liberties already, rights and liberties specified by the Constitution, the Court need make no fundamental value choices in order to protect them, and it certainly need not have difficulty enunciating principles. If, on the other hand, "constitutional rights and liberties" are not in some real sense specified by the Constitution but are the rights and liberties the Court chooses, on the basis of its

---

6. Wright, *Professor Bickel, The Scholarly Tradition, and the Supreme Court,* 84 Harv.L.Rev. 769 (1971)[.]

7. *Id.* at 777.

8. *Id.* at 777–78.

own values, to give to us, then the conclusion was contained entirely in the major premise, and the Judge's syllogism is no more than an assertion of what it purported to prove.

If I am correct so far, no argument that is both coherent and respectable can be made supporting a Supreme Court that "chooses fundamental values" because a Court that makes rather than implements value choices cannot be squared with the presuppositions of a democratic society. The man who understands the issues and nevertheless insists upon the rightness of the Warren Court's performance ought also, if he is candid, to admit that he is prepared to sacrifice democratic process to his own moral views. He claims for the Supreme Court an institutionalized role as perpetrator of limited coups d'etat.

Such a man occupies an impossible philosophic position. What can he say, for instance, of a Court that does not share his politics or his morality? I can think of nothing except the assertion that he will ignore the Court whenever he can get away with it and overthrow it if he can. In his view the Court has no legitimacy, and there is no reason any of us should obey it. And, this being the case, the advocate of a value-choosing Court must answer another difficult question. Why should the Court, a committee of nine lawyers, be the sole agent of change? The man who prefers results to processes has no reason to say that the Court is more legitimate than any other institution. If the Court will not listen, why not argue the case to some other group, say the Joint Chiefs of Staff, a body with rather better means for implementing its decisions?

*   *   *

It follows that the choice of "fundamental values" by the Court cannot be justified. Where constitutional materials do not clearly specify the value to be preferred, there is no principled way to prefer any claimed human value to any other. The judge must stick close to the text and the history, and their fair implications, and not construct new rights. The [*Griswold* case [a]] illustrates the point. The *Griswold* decision has been acclaimed by legal scholars as a major advance in constitutional law, a salutary demonstration of the Court's ability to protect fundamental human values. I regret to have to disagree, and my regret is all the more sincere because I once took the same position and did so in print.[15] In extenuation I can only say that at the time I thought, quite erroneously, that new basic rights could be derived logically by finding and extrapolating a more general principle of individual autonomy underlying the particular guarantees of the Bill of Rights.

The Court's *Griswold* opinion, by Justice Douglas, and the array of concurring opinions, by Justices Goldberg, White and Harlan, all failed to justify the derivation of any principle used to strike down the

---

a. Griswold v. Connecticut, 381 U.S. 479 (1965).

15. Bork, *The Supreme Court Needs a New Philosophy,* Fortune, Dec., 1968, at 170.

Connecticut anti-contraceptive statute or to define the scope of the principle. Justice Douglas, to whose opinion I must confine myself, began by pointing out that "specific guarantees in the Bill of Rights have penumbras, formed by emanations from those guarantees that help give them life and substance." [16] Nothing is exceptional there. In the case Justice Douglas cited, *NAACP v. Alabama*,[17] the State was held unable to force disclosure of membership lists because of the chilling effect upon the rights of assembly and political action of the NAACP's members. The penumbra was created solely to preserve a value central to the first amendment, applied in this case through the fourteenth amendment. It had no life of its own as a right independent of the value specified by the first amendment.

But Justice Douglas then performed a miracle of transubstantiation. He called the first amendment's penumbra a protection of "privacy" and then asserted that other amendments create "zones of privacy." [18] He had no better reason to use the word "privacy" than that the individual is free within these zones, free to act in public as well as in private. None of these penumbral zones—from the first, third, fourth or fifth amendments, all of which he cited, along with the ninth—covered the case before him. One more leap was required. Justice Douglas asserted that these various "zones of privacy" created an independent right of privacy,[19] a right not lying within the penumbra of any specific amendment. He did not disclose, however, how a series of specified rights combined to create a new and unspecified right.

The *Griswold* opinion fails every test of neutrality. The derivation of the principle was utterly specious, and so was its definition. In fact, we are left with no idea of what the principle really forbids. Derivation and definition are interrelated here. Justice Douglas called the amendments and their penumbras "zones of privacy," though of course they are not that at all. They protect both private and public behavior and so would more properly be labelled "zones of freedom." If we follow Justice Douglas in his next step, these zones would then add up to an independent right of freedom, which is to say, a general constitutional right to be free of legal coercion, a manifest impossibility in any imaginable society.

Griswold, then, is an unprincipled decision, both in the way in which it derives a new constitutional right and in the way it defines that right, or rather fails to define it. We are left with no idea of the sweep of the right of privacy and hence no notion of the cases to which it may or may not be applied in the future. The truth is that the Court could not reach its result in *Griswold* through principle. The reason is obvious. Every clash between a minority claiming freedom and a majority claiming power to regulate involves a choice between the gratifications of the two groups. When the Constitution has not spoken, the Court will be able to find no scale, other than its own value

---

16. 381 U.S. at 484.

17. 357 U.S. 449 (1958).

18. 381 U.S. at 484.

19. *Id.* at 485, 486.

preferences, upon which to weigh the respective claims to pleasure. Compare the facts in *Griswold* with a hypothetical suit by an electric utility company and one of its customers to void a smoke pollution ordinance as unconstitutional. The cases are identical.

In *Griswold* a husband and wife assert that they wish to have sexual relations without fear of unwanted children. The law impairs their sexual gratifications. The State can assert, and at one stage in that litigation did assert, that the majority finds the use of contraceptives immoral. Knowledge that it takes place and that the State makes no effort to inhibit it causes the majority anguish, impairs their gratifications.

The electrical company asserts that it wishes to produce electricity at low cost in order to reach a wide market and make profits. Its customer asserts that he wants a lower cost so that prices can be held low. The smoke pollution regulation impairs his and the company's stockholders' economic gratifications. The State can assert not only that the majority prefer clean air to lower prices, but also that the absence of the regulation impairs the majority's physical and aesthetic gratifications.

Neither case is covered specifically or by obvious implication in the Constitution. Unless we can distinguish forms of gratification, the only course for a principled Court is to let the majority have its way in both cases. It is clear that the Court cannot make the necessary distinction. There is no principled way to decide that one man's gratifications are more deserving of respect than another's or that one form of gratification is more worthy than another.[20] Why is sexual gratification more worthy than moral gratification? Why is sexual gratification nobler than economic gratification? There is no way of deciding these matters other than by reference to some system of moral or ethical values that has no objective or intrinsic validity of its own and about which men can and do differ. Where the Constitution does not embody the moral or ethical choice, the judge has no basis other than his own values upon which to set aside the community judgment embodied in the statute. That, by definition, is an inadequate basis for judicial supremacy. The issue of the community's moral and ethical values, the issue of the degree of pain an activity causes, are matters concluded by the passage and enforcement of the laws in question. The judiciary has no role to play other than that of applying the statutes in a fair and impartial manner.

One of my colleagues refers to this conclusion, not without sarcasm, as the "Equal Gratification Clause." The phrase is apt, and I accept it, though not the sarcasm. Equality of human gratifications, where the document does not impose a hierarchy, is an essential part of constitutional doctrine because of the necessity that judges be principled. To

---

20. The impossibility is related to that of making interpersonal comparisons of utilities. *See* L. Robbins, The Nature and Significance of Economic Science, ch. 4 (2d ed. 1969); P. Samuelson, Foundations of Economic Analysis 243–52 (1965).

be perfectly clear on the subject, I repeat that the principle is not applicable to legislatures. Legislation requires value choice and cannot be principled in the sense under discussion. Courts must accept any value choice the legislature makes unless it clearly runs contrary to a choice made in the framing of the Constitution.

It follows, of course, that broad areas of constitutional law ought to be reformulated. Most obviously, it follows that substantive due process, revived by the *Griswold* case, is and always has been an improper doctrine. Substantive due process requires the Court to say, without guidance from the Constitution, which liberties or gratifications may be infringed by majorities and which may not. This means that *Griswold's* antecedents were also wrongly decided, *e.g., Meyer v. Nebraska,*[21] which struck down a statute forbidding the teaching of subjects in any language other than English; *Pierce v. Society of Sisters,*[22] which set aside a statute compelling all Oregon school children to attend public schools; *Adkins v. Children's Hospital,*[23] which invalidated a statute of Congress authorizing a board to fix minimum wages for women and children in the District of Columbia; and *Lochner v. New York,*[24] which voided a statute fixing maximum hours of work for bakers. With some of these cases I am in political agreement, and perhaps *Pierce's* result could be reached on acceptable grounds, but there is no justification for the Court's methods. In *Lochner,* Justice Peckham, defending liberty from what he conceived as a mere meddlesome interference, asked, "[A]re we all . . . at the mercy of legislative majorities?"[25] The correct answer, where the Constitution does not speak, must be "yes."

B. THE ROLE OF THE TEXT

FREDERICK SCHAUER, EASY CASES

58 S.Cal.L.Rev. 399, 414–423, 430–31 (1985).

* * * [It is] clear that there *are* easy cases in constitutional law— lots of them. The parties concerned know, without litigating and without consulting lawyers, that Ronald Reagan cannot run for a third term; that the junior Senator from Virginia, who was elected in 1982, does not have to run again in 1984 or 1986 even though the Representative from the First Congressional District does; that bills receiving less than a majority of votes in either the House or the Senate are not laws of the United States; that the Equal Rights Amendment, the District of Columbia Representation in the Senate Amendment, and the Balanced Budget Amendment are not now part of the Constitution; and that a twenty-nine year-old is not going to be President of the United States. I have equivalent confidence that I will not receive a notice in the mail informing me that I must house members of the armed forces in my

21. 262 U.S. 390 (1922).

22. 268 U.S. 510 (1925).

23. 261 U.S. 525 (1923).

24. 198 U.S. 45 (1905).

25. *Id.* at 59.

spare bedroom; that criminal defendants in federal courts cannot be denied the right to be represented by a qualified lawyer for whom they are willing to pay; and that the next in line to succeed to the Presidency in the event of the President's death is the Vice–President, and not the Secretary of the Interior, the Congressman from Wyoming, or the quarterback for the Philadelphia Eagles.

The foregoing is only a small sample of the legal events that are "easy" constitutional cases. Once free from the lawyer's preoccupation with close cases—those in which the lawyer *qua* lawyer is a necessary actor in the play [39]—we begin to comprehend the enormous quantity of instances in which the legal results are commonly considered obvious. But why is this? What makes the easy case easy?

In searching for the sources of easiness, it is perhaps best to look for the sources of hardness, and then define easy cases as those without any of the characteristics of hard cases. Such definition by exclusion is not the only approach, but it seems particularly appropriate because it is the exception, the hard case, that most commonly commands our attention.

Prototypically, a vague, ambiguous, or simply opaque linguistic formulation of the relevant rule generates a hard case. Such a linguistic phenomenon may be caused by questions about the result announced by a clearly applicable rule, questions about which rule, if any, is in fact relevant, or both. Regardless of the cause, the result is the same: one cannot find the answer to a question (which is not the same as a controversy) by a straightforward reading of rules.

To the extent that one *can* find an answer to a question by a straightforward reading of rules, other factors may make a case hard. A case that seems linguistically easy may be hard if the result announced by the language is inconsistent with the "purpose" of the rule. In such cases the tension between the plain meaning of the words and the reason for using those words creates a hard case, in much the same way that linguistic imprecision creates a hard case.

Even if a rule seems plainly applicable, and even if that application is consistent with the purpose behind a rule, it may be that two or more rules, dictating different results, will be applicable. If one rule suggests answer *A* to the question, and another suggests answer *B*, then it is as if no answer had been provided. In the calculus of rules, too many rules are no better than none at all.

Finally, and perhaps most importantly, there may be only one relevant rule, it may be quite straightforwardly applicable, and its application would be consistent with its purpose. Yet it may still be morally, socially, or politically hard, however, in the sense of *hard* to swallow. * * *

39. Part of the problem, of course, is that legal theory in general is undertaken largely by those who train lawyers. We will have made considerable strides when we recognize that not only hard cases, but also all litigation and all lawyers, are in important respects epiphenomenal.

There may very well be other sources of hardness, but this sample seems sufficiently large. With these types of hard cases in mind, we can tentatively define an easy case as one having *none* of these characteristics of hardness, one in which a clearly applicable rule noncontroversially generates an answer to the question at hand, and one in which the answer so generated is consistent both with the purpose behind the rule and with the social, political, and moral climate in which the question is answered.

There is clearly more involved than merely describing an easy case. Perhaps easy cases are like unicorns, quite capable of definition and description, but not to be found in the real world. Thus, my list of seemingly easy cases purported to fill this argumentative gap, to show that easy cases not only can be imagined, but in fact exist if we only know where to look. And, as should be apparent from the particular examples offered, my thesis here is that language is a significant and often underappreciated factor in the production of easy cases. I am *not* claiming that only language can generate easy cases. Various other legal, cultural, and historical phenomena can create those shared understandings that will clarify a linguistically vague regulation, statute, or constitutional provision. And, as the foregoing taxonomy of hard cases was designed to demonstrate, language alone is insufficient to generate an easy case. Neither of these qualifications, however, is inconsistent with my central claim that language is significantly important in producing easy cases—that language can and frequently does speak with a sufficiently clear voice such that linguistically articulated norms themselves leave little doubt as to which results are consistent with that command.

One way of supporting the claim that language is important in producing easy cases is to engage in an extended and most likely incomprehensible discussion of numerous theories of meaning, attempting to demonstrate by some collage of philosophical and behavioral arguments the way in which the use of certain artificially created symbols can and does enable us to communicate with each other. In this context, however, and indeed in most others, such an excursus seems to ignore the most significant piece of evidence supporting a claim about meaning, which is that even the discussion of meaning would take place in English. The discussion itself would thus irrefutably prove the very hypothesis at issue, just as this Article is right now doing the same thing.

When Wittgenstein remarked that "[l]anguage must speak for itself," [47] he was not claiming that language existed in a vacuum, or that meaning could be dissociated from context. Rather, he was pointing out that the ability of language to function ought to be self-evident, and that the inability to explain all or even any of the sources of this phenomenon does not detract from the conclusion that language

47. L. Wittgenstein, Philosophical Grammar 40 (1974).

does function. Thus, to demonstrate that language works with a typical-looking argument would be possible only because of the conclusion of that very argument. If language didn't "work," the world would be so different from the world in which we live as to be beyond both description and comprehension. Regardless of how understandable this Article may be, it is certainly more understandable to this audience than it would be if it were written in Hungarian, in Chinese, or in semaphore signals. Whether our ability to understand each other in language is biological, behavioral, sociological, or some combination of these is less important than the fact that we can do it.

This is not meant to be the end of an argument, but only the beginning of one. Because law operates with language, understanding the way in which law works requires starting with the proposition that language works. In many instances, some of which I will deal with presently, it may be important to know *why* or *how* language works. In many other instances, however, it is sufficient to do less thinking and more looking, and at least take certain observable facts about language as a possible starting point in the analysis.

It is thus worthwhile to note that the Constitution is, even if nothing else, a use of language. By virtue of being able to speak the English language, we can differentiate between the Constitution and a nursery rhyme, between the Constitution and a novel, and between the Constitution and the Communist Manifesto. Let us construct a simple thought experiment involving a person who is fluent in English (even the English of 1984, and not necessarily the English of 1787 or 1868), but who knows nothing of the history, politics, law, or culture of the United States. If we were to show this person a copy of the Constitution, would that person glean from that collection of marks on a piece of paper alone at least some rudimentary idea of how *this* government works and of what types of relationships exist between the central government and the states, between the different branches of government, and between individuals and government? Although the understanding would be primitive and significant mistakes would be made, it still seems apparent that the answer to the question would be, "Yes." However sketchy and distorted the understanding might be, it would still exceed the understanding produced by a document written in a language not understood by our hypothetical reader, and surpass as well the understanding gained from no information at all.

This general intelligibility of language enables us to understand immediately the mandate of numerous constitutional provisions without recourse to precedent, original intent, or any of the other standard interpretive supplements. We need not depart from the text to determine the rudiments of how a bill becomes a law, the age and other qualifications for various federal offices, the permissible and impermissible limits on the franchise, the number of terms that may be served by the President, the basic procedure for amending the Constitution, the mechanics of admitting a new state, the number of witnesses necessary in a trial for treason, and the permissibility of calling the defendant as a prosecution witness in a federal criminal case.

In some of these and other instances, some noncontroversial technical knowledge may be necessary for understanding. In order to appreciate the clarity of some of the requirements of the fourth, fifth, and sixth amendments, for example, one must understand what a trial is, how it is conducted, and so on. In order to understand some of the structural provisions, it is useful to have at least some preconstitutional understanding of what a state is. These shared background understandings, however, virtually a part of understanding *this* language, do not make the notion of a clear meaning implausible. Words themselves are nothing other than marks or noises, transformed into vehicles for communication by virtue of those rules of language that make it possible for the listener to understand the speaker in most cases. But these rules are not contained in a set of maroon volumes, the linguistic equivalent to the United States Code. These rules are made and continuously remade by the society that uses the language, and different rules may prevail in different segments of that society at different times.

Thus, language cannot be divorced from its context, because meanings become clear if and only if certain understandings are presupposed. Language cannot and does not transcend completely the culture of which it is a part. It is not something that has been delivered packaged, assembled, and ready-to-use to a previously nonlinguistic culture. Language and society are part and parcel of each other; understanding a language, even at its clearest, requires some understanding of the society that has generated it.

But what does this tell us? Certainly not that the notion of plain meaning is worthless, or that questions of interpreting language collapse completely into questions about a culture. That a rosebush springs from and cannot exist without earth, sun, and water does not mean that the notion of a rosebush is not distinguishable from the concepts earth, sun, and water. Similarly, that language requires context does not mean that language *is* context. Language operates significantly because of and as a system of rules that enable people within a shared context to understand each other. At times these rules may be vague, and thus may produce hard cases, but at other times the rules can and do operate to produce the very kinds of "easy" cases I have been describing.

* * *

I am * * * quite willing to concede that it is impossible to have an entirely clear constitutional clause, for the same reason that it is impossible to have an absolutely airtight legal provision of any kind, or an absolutely airtight definition in any field. This is merely a recasting of the well-known message that all terms and all laws have fringe as well as core applications.[60] That there are fringe meanings of words, or fringe applications of laws, for which one can make a reasonable argument for either inclusion or exclusion, does not mean that there are no core cases in which an argument on one side would be almost universally agreed to be compelling, and an argument on the other side would be almost universally agreed to be specious. That I am unsure whether rafts and floating motorized automobiles are "boats" does not dispel my confidence that rowboats and dories most clearly are boats, and that steam locomotives, hamburgers, and elephants equally clearly are not.

This is not to deny that determining the contents of the core, the fringe, and what is wholly outside are contextually and culturally contingent. I can imagine a world in which "elephant" is a fringe (or core) example of a boat, and I can imagine a set of circumstances in *this* world in which a floating hamburger might legitimately present us with a definitional problem vis-à-vis the class "boats." The mere possibility of such circumstances does not eliminate our ability to make sense out of the words as standardly applied, however. If it did, we would have no way of communicating with each other.

The lesson of open texture, then, is that every use of language is potentially vague * * *. The precision of language is necessarily limited by the lack of omniscience of human beings, and thus any use of language is bounded by the limitations of human foresight. The *non sequitur*, however, is the move from the proposition that language is not perfectly precise to the proposition that language is useless. * * *

Although linguistic nihilism seems scarcely comprehensible as a general statement about language, nihilistic tendencies have had a surprising vitality in legal and constitutional theory. The attractions of nihilism seem to be largely attributable, however, to a crabbed view of the legal world, a view that focuses almost exclusively on those hard cases that wind up in court. If we focus only on the marginal cases, only on the cases that a screening process selects largely because of their very closeness, it should come as no surprise that we would have a skeptical view of the power of language to draw distinctions. The cases that wind up in court are not there solely because they lie at the edge of linguistic distinctions, but this is at least a significant factor. Thus the cases that are in court are hardly a representative sample of the effects of legal language. But if we focus instead on easy as well as hard cases, and thus take into our comprehension the full legal world, we see that the cases at the margin are but a small percentage of the full domain of legal events; the bulk of the remaining cases are those in which we can answer questions by consulting the articulated norm.
* * *

60. *See* Hart, *Scandinavian Realism*, 17 Cambridge L.J. 233, 239 (1959); Williams, *Language and the Law—II*, 61 Law Q.Rev. 179 (1945); *see generally* M. Black, *Reasoning with Loose Concepts*, in Margins of Precision: Essays in Logic and Language 1 (1970); I. Scheffler, Beyond the Letter: A Philosophical Inquiry into Ambiguity, Vagueness, and Metaphor in Language (1979).

* * *

The perspective described above views linguistically articulated rules as excluding wrong answers rather than pointing to right ones. From this perspective, there is no longer any justification to view the specific and the general clauses in the Constitution as fundamentally different in kind. Since no clause can generate a uniquely correct answer, at least in the abstract rather than in the context of a specific question, the best view of the specific clauses is that they are merely less vague than the general clauses. The language of a clause, whether seemingly general or seemingly specific, establishes a boundary, or a frame, albeit a frame with fuzzy edges. Even though the language itself does not tell us what goes within the frame, it does tell us when we have gone outside it.

It is best to view the role of language in setting the size of the frame as presumptive rather than absolute. Factors other than the language of the text, or the language of a specifically articulated rule in a case or series of cases, often influence the size and shape of the frame of permissible argument. The language of the text itself is still, however, commonly not only the starting point, but also a constant check long after leaving the starting point. When we look at an uninterpreted clause (in the sense of a series of authoritative judicial interpretations), we commonly focus quite closely on the text. Even in those cases in which an established body of precedent exists, reference to the text is never considered illegitimate.

The language of the text, therefore, remains perhaps the most significant factor in setting the size of the frame. Those clauses that look quite specific are those where the frame is quite small, and thus the range of permissible alternatives is equivalently small. Those clauses that look much more general are those with a substantially larger frame, giving a much wider range of permissible alternatives. This, however, is a continuum and not a dichotomy. Those clauses that seem specific differ from those that seem general in that the former exclude as wrong a larger number of answers than do the latter.

* * *

* * * If we consider the text to be informative about boundaries, or limits, rather than about centers, or cores, then the text appears far less irrelevant than is commonly assumed. The text presumptively constrains us, or should, from overstepping what are admittedly pretheoretical and almost intuitive linguistic bounds, and thus serves as one constraint on constitutional interpretation.

We can thus view these linguistic frames as telling an interpreter, *for example* the Supreme Court, which areas are legitimately within the province of interpretation, which subjects are properly the business of the interpretation. An interpretation is legitimate (which is not the same as correct) only insofar as it purports to interpret some language of the document, and only insofar as the interpretation is within the boundaries at least suggested by that language.

SANFORD LEVINSON, LAW AS LITERATURE
60 Tex.L.Rev. 373, 376–89 (1982).

I

* * *

Constitutions, of the written variety especially, are usefully viewed as a means of freezing time by controlling the future through the "hardness" of language encoded in a monumental document, which is then left for later interpreters to decipher. The purpose of such control is to preserve the particular vision held by constitutional founders and to prevent its overthrow by future generations. The very existence of written constitutions with substantive limitations on future conduct is evidence of skepticism, if not outright pessimism, about the moral caliber of future citizens; else why not simply enjoin them to "be good" or "do what you think best"? Writers of constitutions must have a very high confidence in the ability of language both to "harden" and to control.

* * *

Any writer, including a framer of constitutions, presumably imagines the following relationship between text and reader: "The reader sets himself to make out what the author has designed and signified through putting into play a linguistic and literary expertise that he shares with the author. By approximating what the author undertook to signify the reader understands what the language of the work means." [14] And, of course, in the case of those particular texts called legal, by understanding the meaning the conscientious adjudicator-reader becomes authorized to enforce it.

The remark just quoted comes from an essay vigorously attacking certain strains of contemporary literary criticism that Abrams finds insufficiently respectful of determinate meanings allegedly generated by disciplined study of texts. The disputes currently raging through literary criticism precisely mirror some of the central problems facing anyone who would take law seriously; the basis of this parallelism is the centrality to law of textual analysis.[15] If we consider law as

14. Abrams, *How to Do Things with Texts,* 46 Partisan Rev. 566 (1979). I owe my familiarity with this comment to Richard Rorty. *See* R. Rorty, *Nineteenth–Century Idealism and Twentieth–Century Textualism,* in Consequences of Pragmatism 139 (1982), *reprinted from* 64 Monist 155 (1981).

15. The best short treatment of these disputes is Culler, *Issues in Contemporary American Critical Debate,* in American Criticism in the Poststructuralist Age 1–18 (I. Konigsberg ed. 1981). A very illuminating book-length study is F. Lentricchia, After the New Criticism (1980). The commonality of some of the problems of law and literary analysis are touched on in Abraham, *Three Fallacies of Interpretation: A Comment on Precedent and Judicial Decision,* 23 Ariz.L.Rev. 771 (1981); Abraham, *Statutory Interpretation and Literary Theory: Some Common Concerns of an Unlikely Pair,* 32 Rutgers L.Rev. 676 (1980); Michaels, *Against Formalism: The Autonomous Text in Legal and Literary Interpretation,* 1 Poetics Today 23 (1979), *reprinted with minor changes as* Michaels, *Against Formalism: Chickens and Rocks,* in The State of the Language 410 (1980); and Yeazell, *Convention, Fiction, and Law,* 13 New Literary Hist. 89 (1981).

literature, then we might better understand the malaise that afflicts all contemporary legal analysis, nowhere more severely than in constitutional theory.

II

* * *

Two classic approaches to understanding a written constitution involve emphasizing either the allegedly plain words of the text or the certain meaning to be given those words through historical reconstruction. I think it fair to say that these particular approaches are increasingly without defenders, at least in the academic legal community. Even so capable an analyst as Professor Monaghan, who is eager to return to the confines of a knowable "originalist" Constitution, admits that he has no way of handling the authority of judicial precedents that (he argues) violate initial understandings.[19]

There is not time in this essay to canvass the problems of originalism. Suffice it to say that the plain meaning approach inevitably breaks down in the face of the reality of disagreement among equally competent speakers of the native language. Intentionality arguments, on the other hand, face not only the problem of explaining why intentions of long-dead people from a different social world should influence us, but also, perhaps more importantly, the problem of extracting intentions from the collectivity of individuals and institutions necessary to give legal validity to the Constitution. Even literary critics most committed to the existence of objective meaning through recovery of authorial intent, like E.D. Hirsch, admit that their approach applies only to individually authored works, and therefore cannot be used to analyze a document like the Constitution.[22]

As Richard Rorty has pointed out, however, there are at least two options open to critics who reject the two approaches outlined above but who, nonetheless, remain interested in interpreting the relevant texts. The first option involves the use of an allegedly more sophisticated method to extract the true meaning of the text. Thus Rorty refers to "the kind of textualist who claims to have gotten the secret of the text, to have broken its code," as a "weak" textualist,[23] where the term is seemingly a metaphor for the power of the individual critic. Whatever pyrotechnics might come from a critic who "prides himself on not being

19. Monaghan, *Our Perfect Constitution,* 56 N.Y.U.L.Rev. 353, 382 (1981). Like Raoul Berger, *see* R. Berger, Government by Judiciary 412–13 (1977), Monaghan does not really counsel turning back the clock by instantly overruling all putatively misdecided cases. Both offer what might uncharitably be regarded as an "adverse possession" approach to constitutional interpretation, whereby precedents that should at one time have been properly overruled (as wrongly decided) become entitled to recognition as authoritative after the passage of enough time and after the citizenry has come to rely on them. Neither offers the slightest guidance for recognizing the terms of such possession. To be fair, no other theorist of precedent does any better. Perhaps the central difference between law and literature is the lack in the latter of the notion of stare decisis.

22. *See* E. Hirsch, Validity in Interpretation 123 & n. 53 (1967); *see also* E. Hirsch, The Aims of Interpretation 1–13 (1976).

23. R. Rorty, *supra* note 14, at 152.

distracted by anything which the text might previously have been thought to be about or anything its author says about it," [24] there remains the infatuation—110 years after Langdell—with the possibility of a science of criticism. A "weak" textualist "is just doing his best to imitate science—he wants a *method* of criticism and he wants everybody to agree that he has cracked the code. He wants all the comforts of consensus, even if only the consensus of readers of the literary quarterlies" (or law reviews).[25]

Perhaps the best current example of such a "weak" textualist is John Hart Ely, whose *Democracy and Distrust,* however radical some of its criticisms of so-called "interpretivism" purport to be, is merely the latest effort to crack the code of the United States Constitution and discover its true essence. As James E. Fleming pointed out in a recent review, Ely is engaged in a "quest for the ultimate constitutional interpretivism" which would in effect foreclose further debate about the genuine meaning of the Constitution.[27]

* * *

No one can read Ely and miss his anger at those who merely read their own views into the Constitution. Indeed, most of Ely's reviewers agree with him at least on this last point, even as they criticize him for reading *his* preferred views into the Constitution. What unites Ely and most of his critics, though, is the continued belief that there is something "in" the Constitution that can be extracted if only we can figure out the best method to mine its meaning.

Against such weak textualists—the decoders, whatever the fanciness of their methods of decoding—Rorty posits "strong" textualists, who reject the whole notion of questing for the essential meanings of a text. "Strong," it should be emphasized, refers to the power of the critic, not the power of the text (or of its author). According to Stanley Fish, one of the leading proponents of this approach, "Interpretation is not the art of construing but the art of constructing. Interpreters do not decode poems; they make them." [30] Fish has argued that "[t]he objectivity of the text is an illusion and, moreover, a dangerous illusion, because it is so physically convincing. The illusion is one of self-sufficiency and completeness. A line of print or a page is so obviously *there* . . . that it seems to be the sole repository of whatever value and meaning we associate with it." [31]

* * *

The view endorsed by Fish regards "human beings as at every moment creating the experimental spaces into which a personal knowledge flows." [35] Meaning is created rather than discovered, though the source of creative energy is the particular community within which one

---

24. *Id.* at 151–52.

25. *Id.* at 152 (emphasis in original).

27. Fleming, *A Critique of John Hart Ely's Quest for the Ultimate Constitutional Interpretivism of Representative Democracy* (Book Review), 80 Mich.L.Rev. 634 (1982).

30. S. Fish, Is There a Text in This Class? 327 (1980) * * *.

31. [*Id.*] at 43. * * *

35. [*Id.*] at 94. * * *

finds him- or herself. Critics more Emersonian in their inspiration, like Harold Bloom, are willing to credit individual acts of creativity, though Bloom's emphasis on the ubiquity of "misreadings," rather than "truthful" renderings of what is inside texts, links him to Rorty's "strong" textualists.[36] All such readers could well join the Whitmanian anthem, where all readings, whether of life or of texts, become songs of oneself.

The patron saint of all strong textualists is Nietzsche:

> [W]hatever exists, having somehow come into being, is again and again reinterpreted to new ends, taken over, transformed, and redirected by some power superior to it; all events in the organic world are a subduing, a *becoming master,* and all subduing and becoming master involves a fresh interpretation, an adaptation through which any previous "meaning" and "purpose" are necessarily obscured or even obliterated.[37]

And the argument of Fish, Bloom, and other strong textualists, whether American or continental, is *not* that they prefer to do their thing as an alternative to the more banal work of "truthseekers" like Abrams or Hirsch, but rather that the project of ultimate truth-seeking is based on philosophical error. At the very least it presumes a privileged foundation for measuring the attainment of truth, and it is precisely this foundation that Nietzsche and most of the more radical literary theorists deny. Like Rorty, they do not substitute a new candidate for a winning method of how to recognize literary truth when one sees it; rather, they reject the very search for finality of interpretation.

To be sure, none of the radical critics defend the position that any interpretation is just as good as any other. Stanley Fish, for example, notes that he genuinely believes in the validity of any given view that he happens to hold, and he can present reasons for rejecting the views of his opponents on the interpretation of a given text.[38] In this regard Fish seems similar to Ronald Dworkin, who views judging as including the phenomenological experience of feeling oneself to have achieved the uniquely correct solution even to a hard case.[39] But Fish, more candid than Dworkin on this point, admits that his own conviction of rightness will provide no answer at all to anyone who happens to disagree with him, and that there is no way to resolve the dispute. It is at this point that he retreats to his Kuhnian [40] emphasis on communities of understanding and shared conventions. It may be true that these communities will share, at any given moment, a sense of what distinguishes "on the wall" from "off the wall" arguments, but Fish is acutely aware of the contingency of such judgments. They describe only our own tempo-

36. *See, e.g.,* H. Bloom, A Map of Misreading (1975).

37. F. Nietzsche, On the Geneology of Morals 77 (W. Kaufmann trans. 1967) (emphasis in original).

38. S. Fish, *supra* note 30, at 338–71.

39. *See* R. Dworkin, Taking Rights Seriously 279–90 (1977) * * *.

40. *See* T. Kuhn, The Structure of Scientific Revolutions (2d ed. 1970)

ral sense of what is currently acceptable, rather than anything genuinely mirroring the essential characteristics of the texts being discussed.

III

Presumably only those professionally interested in literature are forced to wrestle with the issues presented by Abrams * * * and Fish regarding poetics or the interpretation of fiction. But if law is, in some meaningful sense, a branch of literature, then the problems discussed above take on new and bothersome implications. And nowhere is this more true within our own culture than in constitutional interpretation and its emphasis on writtenness.

The role of our Constitution is not only to enable us to pretend that past linguistic acts can control future action. It is also presumably to prevent the rise of Nietzschean "masters." Nietzsche seems to suggest, however, that a massive exercise in social deception is necessary if we are not to recognize the way that "interpretation" inevitably implies a struggle for mastery in the formation of political consciousness. For a Nietzschean reader of constitutions, there is no point in searching for a code that will produce "truthful" or "correct" interpretations; instead, the interpreter, in Rorty's words, "simply beats the text into a shape which will serve his own purpose." [43]

* * * If one takes seriously the views articulated by Nietzsche, Rorty, and Fish (among others), one must give up the search for principles and methods of constitutional interpretation. Instead, one assesses the results of an interpretive effort by something other than the criterion of adherence to an inner essence of the text being interpreted * * *.

To put it mildly, there is something disconcerting about accepting the Nietzschean interpreter into the house of constitutional analysts, but I increasingly find it impossible to imagine any other way of making sense of our own constitutional universe. For some years I have organized my own courses in constitutional interpretation around the central question, "But did the Court get it right?", as if one could grade any given opinion by whether or not it measured up to the genuine command of the Constitution. Answering such a question, of course, requires the development of a full set of "principles and methods of correct interpretation," and my courses have involved a search for such principles and methods.

I still spend a great deal of time examining various approaches, ranging from the linguistic to the historical, from the structural to what my colleague Philip Bobbitt calls the "ethical," [46] but I have less and less confidence that this is a sensible enterprise. At the very least there is no reason to believe that the community of persons interested in constitutional interpretation will coalesce around one or another of these approaches. Moreover, insofar as one accepts the plausibility of

43. R. Rorty, *supra* note 14, at 151.   **46.** See P. Bobbitt, Constitutional Fate (1982) * * *.

an analysis like Rorty's, there is no reason to regret this, for it is the result of a genuine plurality of ways of seeing the world, rather than of the obdurate recalcitrance of those who refuse to bend to superior argument.

Yet there are obvious difficulties in adopting Rorty's metaphor of the conversation (rather than the argument), for the principal social reality of law is its coercive force vis-à-vis those who prefer to behave other than as the law "requires." As Chairman Mao pointed out, a revolution is not a tea party, and the massive disruption in lives that can be triggered by a legal case is not a conversation. The legal system presents a conversation from which there may be no exit, and there are certainly those who would define hell as the vision of their least favorite constitutional interpreter, whether the Court or a benighted law professor.

What does one do, then, when studying opinions, if one gives up the enterprise of determining whether or not they are "correct"? Are cases simply historical fragments which should be studied for insight into the ideology of the time? [48] One no longer would say, for example, that *Dred Scott* [49] or *Lochner v. New York,* [50] or any other case, was "wrongly" decided, for that use of language presupposes belief in the knowability of constitutional essence. One *can* obviously show that constitutional tastes and styles shift over time, but this retreat into historicism has nothing to do with the legal science so desperately sought by Langdell and his successors.

* * *

Consider * * * the way we treat the innovative judges of our legal tradition, particularly as they appear in law school courses. Do we really wish to argue that John Marshall or Earl Warren (or the most recent dynamic innovator, William Rehnquist) got the essence right in their interpretations of the Constitution, or do we recognize instead the extent to which we have been subdued by their political visions?

Perhaps the most significant example of this dilemma is John Marshall himself, or rather I should say our response to Marshall. I have little trouble stating that I consider his major opinions to run the gamut from the intellectually dishonest [60] to the majestically visiona-

---

48. This seems to be the approach taken by some of the most fruitful practitioners of "critical legal studies." *See, e.g.,* M. Horwitz, The Transformation of American Law, 1780–1860 (1977); M. Tushnet, The American Law of Slavery 1810–1860 (1981).

49. Dred Scott v. Sandford, 60 U.S. (19 How.) 393 (1856).

50. 198 U.S. 45 (1905). There is obviously not space here to consider in depth the complexity of our responses to these two cases. One might begin, though, by asking whether Taney's or Peckham's arguments in the two cases are really "off-the-wall" in terms of the conventions of American legal discourse; it seems clear that the answer is no.

60. *See* Marbury v. Madison, 5 U.S. (1 Cranch) 137 (1803) (presentation and construction of § 13 of the Judiciary Act of 1789).

ry,[61] and rarely to contain the only (or even the most) plausible rendering of the Constitution. Yet there is also a profound irrelevance to such a criticism. Not only does it assume the existence of a privileged discourse that allows me to dismiss Marshall as "untruthful" rather than merely different, it also ignores the fundamental fact that John Marshall is as much a "founder" of the American legal system as those who wrote the Constitution he purported to interpret. He is, perhaps, the great Nietzschean judge of our tradition.

C. ORIGINAL INTENT

PAUL BREST, THE MISCONCEIVED QUEST FOR THE ORIGINAL UNDERSTANDING

60 B.U.L.Rev. 204, 204–09, 214–24, 231–34 (1980).

By "originalism" I mean the familiar approach to constitutional adjudication that accords binding authority to the text of the Constitution or the intentions of its adopters.[1] At least since *Marbury,* in which Chief Justice Marshall emphasized the significance of our Constitution's being a written document, originalism in one form or another has been a major theme in the American constitutional tradition. The most widely accepted justification for originalism is simply that the Constitution is the supreme law of the land. The Constitution manifests the will of the sovereign citizens of the United States—"we the people" assembled in the conventions and legislatures that ratified the Constitution and its amendments. The interpreter's task is to ascertain their will. Originalism may be supported by more instrumental rationales as well: Adherence to the text and original understanding arguably constrains the discretion of decisionmakers and assures that the Constitution will be interpreted consistently over time.

The most extreme forms of originalism are "strict textualism" (or literalism) and "strict intentionalism." A strict textualist purports to construe words and phrases very narrowly and precisely. For the strict intentionalist, "the whole aim of construction, as applied to a provision of the Constitution, is . . . to ascertain and give effect to the intent of its framers and the people who adopted it." [2]

Much of American constitutional interpretation rejects strict originalism in favor of what I shall call "moderate originalism." The

61. *See* McCulloch v. Maryland, 17 U.S. (4 Wheat.) 316 (1819) (invocation of American nationalism).

1. John Ely uses the term "interpretivism" to describe essentially the same concept. J.H. Ely, Democracy and Distrust: A Theory of Judicial Review, chs. 1–2 (1980). At the cost of proliferating neologisms I have decided to stick with "originalism." Virtually all modes of constitutional decisionmaking, including those endorsed by Professor Ely, require interpretation. The differences lie in what is being interpreted, and I use the term "originalism" to describe the interpretation of text and original history as distinguished, for example, from the interpretation of precedents and social values.

2. Home Bldg. & Loan Ass'n v. Blaisdell, 290 U.S. 398, 453 (1934) (Sutherland, J., dissenting).

text of the Constitution is authoritative, but many of its provisions are treated as inherently open-textured. The original understanding is also important, but judges are more concerned with the adopters' general purposes than with their intentions in a very precise sense.

Some central doctrines of American constitutional law cannot be derived even by moderate originalist interpretation, but depend, instead, on what I shall call "nonoriginalism." The modes of nonoriginalist adjudication defended in this article accord the text and original history presumptive weight, but do not treat them as authoritative or binding. The presumption is defeasible over time in the light of changing experiences and perceptions.

* * *

PART ONE: THE CONCEPTS AND METHODS OF ORIGINALISM

* * *

I. Textualism

Textualism takes the language of a legal provision as the primary or exclusive source of law (a) because of some definitional or supralegal principle that only a written text can impose constitutional obligations, or (b) because the adopters intended that the Constitution be interpreted according to a textualist canon, or (c) because the text of a provision is the surest guide to the adopters' intentions. The last of these, probably the central rationale for an originalist-based textualism, is sometimes stated as a preamble to textualist canons. For example:

> It is a cardinal rule in the interpretation of constitutions that the instrument must be so construed as to give effect to the intention of the people, who adopted it. This intention is to be sought in the Constitution itself, and the apparent meaning of the words employed is to be taken as expressing it, except in cases where that assumption would lead to absurdity, ambiguity, or contradiction.[8]

Implicit in the preceding quotation is a canon of interpretation paradigmatic of textualism—the so-called "plain meaning rule." Chief Justice Marshall invoked this canon in *Sturges v. Crowningshield:*

> [A]lthough the spirit of an instrument, especially of a constitution, is to be respected not less than its letter, yet the spirit is to be collected chiefly from its words. . . . [I]f, in any case, the plain meaning of a provision, not contradicted by any other provision in the same instrument, is to be disregarded, because we believe the framers of that instrument could not intend what they say, it must be one in which the absurdity and injustice of applying the provision to the case, would be so monstrous that all mankind would, without hesitation, unite in rejecting the application.[9]

The plain meaning of a text is the meaning that it would have for a "normal speaker of English" under the circumstances in which it is used. Two kinds of circumstances seem relevant: the linguistic and the

---

8. H. Black, Handbook on the Construction and Interpretation of the Laws 20 (1911).

9. 17 U.S. (4 Wheat.) 202–03 (1819).

social contexts. The linguistic context refers to vocabulary and syntax. The social context refers to a shared understanding of the purposes the provision might plausibly serve.

A tenable version of the plain meaning rule must take account of both of these contexts. The alternative, of applying a provision according to the literal meanings of its component words, misconceives the conventions that govern the use of language. Chief Justice Marshall argued this point eloquently and, I think, persuasively, in *McCulloch v. Maryland*,[13] decided the same year that he invoked the plain meaning rule in *Sturges*. The state had argued that the necessary and proper clause authorized only legislation "indispensable" to executing the enumerated powers. Marshall responded with the observation that the word "necessary," as used "in the common affairs of the world, or in approved authors, . . . frequently imports no more than that one thing is convenient, or useful, or essential to another."[14] He continued:

> Such is the character of human language, that no word conveys to the mind, in all situations, one single definite idea; and nothing is more common than to use words in a figurative sense. Almost all compositions contain words, which, taken in their rigorous sense, would convey a meaning different from that which is obviously intended. It is essential to just construction that many words which import something excessive, should be understood in a more mitigated sense—in that sense which common usage justifies. . . . This word, then, like others, is used in various senses; and, in its construction, the subject, the context, the intention of the person using them, are all to be taken into view.[15]

As Marshall implied, to attempt to read a provision without regard to its linguistic and social contexts will either yield unresolvable indeterminacies of language or just nonsense. Without taking account of the possible purposes of the provisions, an interpreter could not, for example, decide whether singing, flag-waving, flag-burning, picketing, and criminal conspiracy are within the protected ambit of the first amendment's "freedom of speech," or whether the "writings" protected by the copyright clause include photographs, paintings, sculptures, performances, and the contents of phonograph records. She would not know whether the phrase, "No person except a natural born Citizen . . . shall be eligible to the Office of President," disqualified persons born abroad or those born by Caesarian section. We understand the range of plausible meanings of provisions only because we know that some interpretations respond to the kinds of concerns that the adopters' society might have while others do not.

That an interpreter must read a text in the light of its social as well as linguistic context does not destroy the boundary between textualism and intentionalism. Just as the textualist is not concerned with the adopters' idiosyncratic use of language, she is not concerned

13. 17 U.S. (4 Wheat.) 316 (1819).   **15.** *Id.* at 414–15.

14. *Id.* at 413.

with their subjective purposes. Rather, she seeks to discern the purposes that a member of the adopters' society would understand the provision to encompass.

Suppose that phrases such as "commerce among the several states," or "freedom of speech," or "equal protection of the laws," have quite different meanings today than when they were adopted. An originalist would hold that, because interpretation is designed to capture the original understanding, the text must be understood in the contexts of the society that adopted it: "The meaning of the constitution is fixed when it is adopted, and it is not different at any subsequent time when a court has occasion to pass upon it." [21]

When a provision is interpreted roughly contemporaneously with its adoption, an interpreter unconsciously places the provision in its linguistic and social contexts, which she has internalized simply because she is of that society. But she cannot assume that a provision adopted one or two hundred years ago has the same meaning as it had for the adopters' society today. She must immerse herself in their society to understand the text as they understood it. Although many provisions of the Constitution may pose no serious interpretive problems in this respect, the textualist interpreter cannot be sure of this without first understanding the ordinary usage at the time of adoption. Did "commerce" include manufacture as well as trade? Did the power to "regulate" commerce imply the power to prohibit it? Did the power to "regulate commerce among the several states" include the power to regulate intrastate transactions which affected interstate commerce? With what absoluteness did 18th century Americans understand the prohibitions against "impairing" contractual obligations and "abridging the freedom of speech?" What did the words "privileges," "immunities," "due process," "equal protection of the laws," "citizen," and "person" mean to those who adopted the fourteenth amendment in 1868?

Despite the differences between textualism and intentionalism, placing a constitutional provision in its original contexts calls for a historical inquiry quite similar to the intentionalist interpreter's.
* * *

II. Intentionalism

By contrast to the textualist, the intentionalist interprets a provision by ascertaining the intentions of those who adopted it. The text of the provision is often a useful guide to the adopters' intentions, but the text does not enjoy a favored status over other sources. * * *

* * *

21. T.M. Cooley, A Treatise on the Constitutional Limitations Which Rest Upon the Legislative Power of the States of The American Union 124 (Carrington's 8th ed. 1927) (n.p. 1868). * * *

1. Who Are the Adopters?

The adopters of the Constitution of 1787 were some portion of the delegates to the Philadelphia Convention and majorities or supermajorities of the participants in the ratifying conventions in nine states. For all but one amendment to the Constitution,[35] the adopters were two-thirds or more of the members of each House of Congress and at least a majority of the legislators in two-thirds of the state legislatures.

For a textual provision to become part of the Constitution, the requisite number of persons in each of these bodies must have assented to it. Likewise, an intention can only become binding—only become an institutional intention—when it is shared by at least the same number and distribution of adopters. (Hereafter, I shall refer to this number and distribution as the "adopters.")

If the only way a judge could ascertain institutional intent were to count individual intention-votes, her task would be impossible even with respect to a single multimember law-making body, and a fortiori where the assent of several such bodies were required. Therefore, an intentionalist must necessarily use circumstantial evidence to educe a collective or general intent.

Interpreters often treat the writings or statements of the framers of a provision as evidence of the adopters' intent. This is a justifiable strategy for the moderate originalist who is concerned with the framers' intent on a relatively abstract level of generality—abstract enough to permit the inference that it reflects a broad social consensus rather than notions peculiar to a handful of the adopters. It is a problematic strategy for the strict originalist.

As the process of adoption moves from the actual framers of a constitutional amendment to the members of Congress who proposed it to the state legislators who ratified it, the amount of thought given the provision surely diminishes—especially if it is relatively technical or uncontroversial, or one of several of disparate provisions (e.g., the Bill of Rights) adopted simultaneously. This suggests that there may be instances where a framer had a determinate intent but other adopters had no intent or an indeterminate intent. For example, suppose that the framers of the commerce clause considered the possibility that economic transactions taking place within the confines of a state might nonetheless affect interstate commerce in such a way as to come within the clause, and that they intended the clause to cover such transactions. But suppose that most of the delegates to the ratifying conventions did not conceive of this possibility and that either they "did not intend" that the clause encompass such transactions or else their intentions were indeterminate. Under these circumstances, what is the institutional intent, i.e., the intent of the provision?

---

35. The twenty-first amendment was ratified by state conventions.

If the intent of the framers is to be attributed to the provision, it must be because the other adopters have in effect delegated their intention-votes to the framers. Leaving aside the question whether the adopters-at-large had any thoughts at all concerning this issue of delegation, consider what they might have desired if they had thought about it. Would they have wanted the framers' intentions to govern without knowing what those intentions were? The answers might well differ depending on whether the adopters had "no intent" or "indeterminate intent."

A delegate to a ratifying convention might well want his absence of intention (*i.e.,* "no-intent") regarding wholly intrastate transactions to be treated as a vote against the clause's encompassing such transactions (*i.e.,* "intent-not"): Since no-intent is the intentionalist equivalent of no-text, to accede to the framers' unknown intentions would be tantamount to blindly delegating to them the authority to insert textual provisions in the Constitution.

Where the framers intend that the activity be covered by the clause, and the adopters' intentions are merely indeterminate, the institutional intent is ambiguous. One adopter might wish his indeterminate intent to be treated as "no intent." Another adopter might wish to delegate his intention-vote to those whose intent is determinate. Yet another might wish to delegate authority to decisionmakers charged with applying the provision in the future. Without knowing more about the mind-sets of the actual adopters of particular constitutional provisions, one would be hard-pressed to choose among these.

2. The Adopters' Interpretive Intent

The intentionalist interpreter's first task must be to determine the interpretive intentions of the adopters of the provision before her—that is the canons by which the adopters intended their provisions to be interpreted. The practice of statutory interpretation from the 18th through at least the mid–19th century suggests that the adopters assumed—if they assumed anything at all—a mode of interpretation that was more textualist than intentionalist. The plain meaning rule was frequently invoked: judicial recourse to legislative debates was virtually unknown and generally considered improper. Even after references to extrinsic sources became common, courts and commentators frequently asserted that the plain meaning of the text was the surest guide to the intent of the adopters.

This poses obvious difficulties for an intentionalist whose very enterprise is premised on fidelity to the original understanding.

3. The Intended Specificity of a Provision

I now turn to an issue that lies at the intersection of what I have called interpretive and substantive intent: How much discretion did an adopter intend to delegate to those charged with applying a provision? Consider, for example, the possible intentions of the adopters of the cruel and unusual punishment clause of the eighth amendment. They might have intended that the language serve only as a shorthand for the Stuart tortures which were their exemplary applications of the clause. Somewhat more broadly, they might have intended the clause to be understood to incorporate the principle of *ejusdem generis* —to include their exemplary applications and other punishments that they found or would have found equally repugnant.[41]

What of instances where the adopters' substantive intent was indeterminate—where even if they had adverted to a proposed application they would not have been certain how the clause should apply? Here it is plausible that—if they *had* a determinate interpretive intent—they intended to delegate to future decisionmakers the authority to apply the clause in light of the general principles underlying it. To use Ronald Dworkin's terms, the adopters would have intended future interpreters to develop their own "conceptions" of cruel and unusual punishment within the framework of the adopters' general "concept" of such punishments.[42]

What of a case where the adopters viewed a certain punishment as not cruel and unusual? This is not the same as saying that the adopters "intended not to prohibit the punishment." For even if they expected their laws to be interpreted by intentionalist canons, the adopters may have intended that their own views not always govern. Like parents who attempt to instill values in their child by both articulating and applying a moral principle, they may have accepted, or even invited, the eventuality that the principle would be applied in ways that diverge from their own views.[43] The adopters may have understood that, even as to instances to which they believe the clause ought or ought not to apply, further thought by themselves or others committed to its underlying principle might lead them to change their minds. Not believing in their own omniscience or infallibility, they delegated the decision to those charged with interpreting the provision. If such a motivation is plausible with respect to applications of the clause in the adopters' contemporary society, it is even more likely with respect to its application by future interpreters, whose understanding of the clause will be affected by changing knowledge, technology, and forms of society.

The extent to which a clause may be properly interpreted to reach outcomes different from those actually contemplated by the adopters depends on the relationship between a general principle and its exemplary applications. A principle does not exist wholly independently of its author's subjective, or his society's conventional exemplary applications, and is always limited to some extent by the applications they

---

41. On a rather restrictive view, "would have found" means that, although the adopters did not advert to a punishment, they nonetheless intended that it be prohibited.

42. R. Dworkin, Taking Rights Seriously 135 (1977).

43. See id. at 134.

found conceivable. Within these fairly broad limits, however, the adopters may have intended their examples to constrain more or less. To the intentionalist interpreter falls the unenviable task of ascertaining, for each provision, how much more or less.

* * *

IV. *The Interpreter–Historian's Task*

The interpreter's task as historian can be divided into three stages or categories. First, she must immerse herself in the world of the adopters to try to understand constitutional concepts and values from their perspective. Second, at least the intentionalist must ascertain the adopters' interpretive intent and the intended scope of the provision in question. Third, she must often "translate" the adopters' concepts and intentions into our time and apply them to situations that the adopters did not foresee.

The first stage is common to originalists of all persuasions. Although the textualist's aim is to understand and apply the language of a constitutional provision, she must locate the text in the linguistic and social contexts in which it was adopted. * * * The intentionalist would ideally count the intention-votes of the individual adopters. In practice, she can at best hope to discover a consensus of the adopters as manifested in the text of the provision itself, the history surrounding its adoption, and the ideologies and practices of the time.

The essential difficulty posed by the distance that separates the modern interpreter from the objects of her interpretation has been succinctly stated by Quentin Skinner in addressing the analogous problem facing historians of political theory: [52]

> [I]t will never in fact be possible simply to study what any given classic writer has *said* . . . without bringing to bear some of one's own expectations about what he must have been saying. . . . [T]hese models and preconceptions in terms of which we unavoidably organize and adjust our perceptions and thoughts will themselves tend to act as determinants of what we think or perceive. We must classify in order to understand, and we can only classify the unfamiliar in terms of the familiar. The perpetual danger, in our attempts to enlarge our historical understanding, is thus that our expectations about what someone must be saying or doing will themselves determine that we understand the agent to be doing something which he would not—or even could not—himself have accepted as an account of what he *was* doing.

To illustrate the problem of doing original history with even a single example would consume more space than I wish to here. Instead, I suggest that a reader who wants to get a sense of the elusiveness of the original understanding study some specific areas of constitu-

52. Skinner, *Meaning and Understanding in the History of Ideas,* 8 Hist. & Theory 3[, 6] (1969). * * *

tional history, reading both works that have been well received,[54] and also the controversy surrounding some of those that have not.[55]

The intentionalist interpreter must next ascertain the adopters' interpretive intent and the intended breadth of their provisions. That is, she must determine what the adopters intended future interpreters to make of their substantive views. Even if she can learn how the adopters intended contemporary interpreters to construe the Constitution, she cannot assume they intended the same canons to apply one or two hundred years later. Perhaps they wanted to bind the future as closely as possible to their own notions. Perhaps they intended a particular provision to be interpreted with increasing breadth as time went on. Or—more likely than not—the adopters may have had no intentions at all concerning these matters.[57]

For purposes of analytic clarity I have distinguished between (1) the adopters' interpretive intent and the intended scope of a provision and (2) their substantive intent concerning the application of the provision. If interpretive intent and intended scope can be ascertained at all, they may instruct the interpreter to adopt different canons of interpretation than she would prefer. Under these circumstances, the intentionalist interpreter may wish to ignore these intentions and limit her inquiry to the adopters' substantive intentions. Leaving aside the normative difficulty of such selective infidelity, this is a problematic strategy: To be a coherent theory of interpretation, intentionalism must distinguish between the adopters' personal *views* about an issue and their *intentions* concerning its constitutional resolution. And it is only by reference to their interpretive intent and the intended scope of a provision that this distinction can be drawn.

The interpreter's final task is to translate the adopters' intentions into the present in order to apply them to the question at issue. Consider, for example, whether the cruel and unusual punishment clause of the eighth amendment prohibits the imposition of the death penalty today. The adopters of the clause apparently never doubted that the death penalty was constitutional. But was death the same event for inhabitants of the American colonies in the late 18th century as it is two centuries later? Death was not only a much more routine

54. *See, e.g.,* C. Fairman, Reconstruction and Reunion, 1864–88, Pt. 1 (1971); L. Levy, Origins of the Fifth Amendment (1968); L. Levy, Legacy of Suppression (1960). *See also* I. Brandt, The Life of James Madison (1941–61); G. Wood, The Creation of the American Republic, 1776–87 (1969).

55. A recent example is Raoul Berger's Government by Judiciary: The Transformation of the Fourteenth Amendment (1977), which argues that almost of all the Supreme Court's decisions under the fourteenth amendment are incorrect. *See, e.g.,* Kutler, *Raoul Berger's Fourteenth Amend-*

ment: A History or Ahistorical, 6 Hastings Const.L.Q. 511 (1979); Murphy, Book Review, 87 Yale L.J. 1752 (1978); Soifer, Review Essay, 54 N.Y.U.L.Rev. 651 (1979). *But see* Perry, Book Review, 78 Colum.L. Rev. 685 (1978).

57. In any case, the adopters' sense of time and change—of the relationship between present and future—was almost certainly not the same as ours, which has been affected by such phenomena as the industrial revolution, theories of evolution, relativity and quantum mechanics, and the possibility of annihilation.

and public phenomenon then, but the fear of death was more effectively contained within a system of religious belief.[60]   Twentieth-century Americans have a more secular cast of mind and seem less willing to accept this dreadful, forbidden, solitary, and shameful event.[61]   The interpreter must therefore determine whether we view the death penalty with the same attitude—whether of disgust or ambivalence—that the adopters viewed their core examples of cruel and unusual punishment.[62]

Intentionalist interpretation frequently requires translations of this sort.   For example, to determine whether the commerce clause applies to transactions taking place wholly within the boundaries of one state, or whether the first amendment protects the mass media, the interpreter must abstract the adopters' concepts of federalism and freedom of expression in order to find their analogue in our contemporary society with its different technology, economy, and systems of communication.   The alternative would be to limit the application of constitutional provisions to the particular events and transactions with which the adopters were familiar.   Even if such an approach were coherent, however, it would produce results that even a strict intentionalist would likely reject: Congress could not regulate any item of commerce or any mode of transportation that did not exist in 1789; the first amendment would not protect any means of communication not then known.

However difficult the earlier stages of her work, the interpreter was only trying to understand the past.   The act of translation required here is different in kind, for it involves the counterfactual and imaginary act of projecting the adopters' concepts and attitudes into a future they probably could not have envisioned.   When the interpreter engages in this sort of projection, she is in a fantasy world more of her own than of the adopters' making.

* * *

Even when the interpreter performs the more conventional historian's role, one may wonder whether the task is possible.   There is a hermeneutic tradition, of which Hans–Georg Gadamar is the leading modern proponent, which holds that we can never understand the past in its own terms, free from our prejudices or preconceptions.[65]   We are hopelessly imprisoned in our own world-views; we can shed some preconceptions only to adopt others, with no reason to believe that they are the conceptions of the different society that we are trying to understand.   One need not embrace this essentially solipsistic view of

60. *See* P. Aries, Western Attitudes Toward Death 11–13 (1974); D. Stannard, The Puritan Way of Death 93 (1977).

61. *See* Death in American Experience 102 (A. Mack ed. 1973); P. Aries, *supra* note 60, at 85–86.

62. *See* Granucci, *"Nor Cruel and Unusual Punishment Inflicted": The Original Meaning,* 57 Calif.L.Rev. 839 (1969).

65. *See* Hans–Georg Gadamer, Truth and Method (Eng. trans. 1975). *See also* P. Winch, The Idea of a Social Science and its Relation to Philosophy (1958); Taylor, *Interpretation and the Sciences of Man,* 25 Rev. of Metaphysics 3 (1971). For a sharply critical review of Gadamer's work, see E.D. Hirsch, Validity in Interpretation 245 (1967).

historical knowledge to appreciate the indeterminate and contingent nature of the historical understanding that an originalist historian seeks to achieve.

None of this is to disparage doing history and other interpretive social science. It suggests, however, that the originalist constitutional historian may be questing after a chimera. The defense that "We're doing the best we can" is no less available to constitutional interpreters than to anyone else. But the best is not always good enough. The interpreter's understanding of the original understanding may be so indeterminate as to undermine the rationale for originalism. Although the origins of some constitutional doctrines are almost certainly established, the historical grounding of many others is quite controversial. It seems peculiar, to say the least, that the legitimacy of a current doctrine should turn on the historian's judgment that it seems "more likely than not," or even "rather likely," that the adopters intended it some one or two centuries ago.

V. Two Types of Originalism

The originalist interpreter can approach her task with different attitudes about the precision with which the object of interpretation—the text [or] intentions * * *—should be understood. In this section I describe the attitudes of "strict" and "moderate" originalism—two areas, not points, on a spectrum—and briefly survey the practices of American constitutional decisionmaking in terms of them.

I have devoted very little attention to the most extreme form of strict textualism—literalism. A thorough-going literalist understands a text to encompass all those and only those instances that come within its words read without regard to its social or perhaps even its linguistic context. Because literalism poorly matches the ways in which we speak and write, it is unable to handle the ambiguity, vagueness, and figurative usage that pervade natural languages, and produces embarrassingly silly results.

Strict intentionalism requires the interpreter to determine how the adopters would have applied a provision to a given situation, and to apply it accordingly. The enterprise rests on the questionable assumption that the adopters of constitutional provisions intended them to be applied in this manner. But even if this were true, the interpreter confronts historiographic difficulties of such magnitude as to make the aim practicably unattainable.

Strict textualism and intentionalism are not synergistic, but rather mutually antagonistic approaches to interpretation. The reader need only consider the strict textualist's and intentionalist's views of the first amendment protection of pornographic literature. By contrast, moderate textualism and intentionalism closely resemble each other in methodology and results.

A moderate textualist takes account of the open-textured quality of language and reads the language of provisions in their social and linguistic contexts. A moderate intentionalist applies a provision consistent with the adopters' intent at a relatively high level of generality, consistent with what is sometimes called the "purpose of the provision." Where the strict intentionalist tries to determine the adopters' actual subjective purposes, the moderate intentionalist attempts to understand what the adopters' purposes might plausibly have been, an aim far more readily achieved than a precise understanding of the adopters' intentions.

* * *

Strict originalism cannot accommodate most modern decisions under the Bill of Rights and the fourteenth amendment, or the virtually plenary scope of congressional power under the commerce clause. Although moderate originalism is far more expansive, some major constitutional doctrines lie beyond its pale as well.

A moderate textualist would treat almost all contemporary free speech and equal protection decisions as within the permissible ambit of these clauses, though not necessarily entailed by them. Because of our uncertainty about the original understanding, it is harder to assess the legitimacy of these doctrines from the viewpoint of a moderate intentionalist. For example, the proper scope of the first amendment depends on whether its adopters were only pursuing "representation reinforcing" goals,[70] or were more broadly concerned to promote a free marketplace of ideas or individual autonomy.[71] The level of generality on which the adopters conceived of the equal protection clause presents a similar uncertainty, but whether or not a moderate intentionalist could accept all of the "new" or "newer" equal protection,[72] she could read the clause to protect "discrete and insular minorities" besides blacks.

On the other hand, a moderate originalist, whether of textualist or intentionalist persuasion, would have serious difficulties justifying (1) the incorporation of the principle of equal protection into the fifth amendment,[73] (2) the incorporation of provisions of the Bill of Rights into the fourteenth amendment,[74] (3) the more general notion of sub-

---

70. See J.H. Ely, supra note 1, at chs. 4–6. See also Mills v. Alabama, 384 U.S. 214, 218–20 (1966) * * *.

71. See, e.g., J.S. Mill, On Liberty (1859); Richards, Free Speech and Obscenity Law: Toward a Moral Theory of the First Amendment, 123 U.Pa.L.Rev. 45 (1974); Scanlon, A Theory of Free Expression, 1 Phil. & Pub. Affairs 204 (1972).

72. See generally, [P. Brest, Processes of Constitutional Decisionmaking 809–93 (1975)]; Gunther, In Search of Evolving Doctrine on a Changing Court: A Model for a Newer Equal Protection, 86 Harv.L.Rev. 1 (1972).

73. See, e.g., Frontiero v. Richardson, 411 U.S. 677 (1973); Bolling v. Sharpe, 347 U.S. 497 (1954); Linde, Judges, Critics, and the Realist Tradition, 82 Yale L.J. 227, 233–34 (1972).

74. Compare Justice Black's and Justice Frankfurter's views in Adamson v. California, 332 U.S. 46 (1947). See also L. Levy, The Fourteenth Amendment and the Bill of Rights in Judgements: Essay on American Constitutional History 64 (1972); Fairman, Does the Fourteenth Amendment Incorporate the Bill of Rights? The Original Understanding, 2 Stan.L.Rev. 5 (1949); Morrison, Does the Fourteenth Amendment Incorporate the Bill of Rights? The Judicial Interpretation, 2 Stan.L.Rev. 140 (1949).

stantive due process, including the minimal rational relationship standard,[75] and (4) the practice of judicial review of congressional legislation established by *Marbury v. Madison.*[76] * * *

* * *

Moderate originalism is a perfectly sensible strategy of constitutional decisionmaking. But its constraints are illusory and counterproductive. Contrary to the moderate originalist's faith, the text and original understanding have contributed little to the development of many doctrines she accepts as legitimate. Consider the relationship between the original understanding of the fourteenth amendment and current doctrines prohibiting gender-based classifications [103] and discriminations in the political process.[104] For the moderate originalist these may be legitimately premised on the equal protection clause. But to what extent have originalist sources *guided* the evolution of these doctrines? The text is wholly open-ended; and if the adopters had any intentions at all about these issues, their resolution was probably contrary to the Court's. At most, the Court can claim guidance from the general notion of equal treatment reflected in the provision. I use the word "reflected" advisedly, however, for the equal protection clause does not establish a principle of equality; it only articulates and symbolizes a principle defined by our conventional public morality. Indeed, because of its indeterminacy, the clause does not offer much guidance even in resolving particular issues of discrimination based on race.[105]

* * *

In sum, if you consider the evolution of doctrines in just about any extensively-adjudicated area of constitutional law—whether "under" the commerce, free speech, due process, or equal protection clauses—explicit reliance on originalist sources has played a very small role compared to the elaboration of the Court's own precedents. It is rather like having a remote ancestor who came over on the Mayflower.

---

75. *See, e.g.,* R. Berger, *supra* note 55; C. Fairman, *supra,* note 54, at 1207 * * *.

76. *See* L. Boudin, Government by Judiciary (1932); A. Westin, Introduction and Historical Bibliography to C. Beard, The Supreme Court and the Constitution (1912); Judicial Review and the Supreme Court 1–12 (Levy ed. 1967). *But see* R. Berger, Congress v. The Supreme Court (1969); E. Corwin, Court Over Constitution (1938); Corwin, *Marbury v. Madison and the Doctrine of Judicial Review,* 12 Mich.L. Rev. 538 (1914) * * *.

103. *E.g.,* Craig v. Boren, 429 U.S. 190 (1976).

104. *E.g.,* Harper v. Virginia Bd. of Elections, 383 U.S. 663 (1966).

105. *See* Brown v. Board of Educ., 347 U.S. 483, 489–91 (1954); Bickel, *The Original Understanding and the Segregation Decision,* 69 Harv.L.Rev. 1 (1955); Kelly, *The Fourteenth Amendment Reconsidered: The Segregation Question,* 54 Mich.L.Rev. 1049 (1956).

RICHARD S. KAY, ADHERENCE TO THE ORIGINAL INTENTIONS IN CONSTITUTIONAL ADJUDICATION: THREE OBJECTIONS AND RESPONSES

82 Nw.U.L.Rev. 226, 228–30, 236, 242–57, 259, 284–92 (1988).

This essay will critically examine the reasons given by modern scholars for rejecting the conventional norm of judicial review—adherence to the original intentions of the Constitution's enactors. While variously phrased, their reasons may be subsumed under three general objections: 1) Adherence to the original intentions is impossible; 2) It is self-contradictory; and 3) It is wrong.

While there is some force in each of these objections, I conclude that the first two are unconvincing and the third depends on personal judgments ultimately not susceptible to rational resolution. My objective is to provide responses to these objections and not to make a complete affirmative case for original intentions adjudication. * * *

I also do not intend to argue that, historically, adjudicated constitutional law is in any significant way an actual reflection of the original intentions. Clearly it is not. Rather my goal is to clarify the arguments for one or another approach to constitutional adjudication as an abstract matter. Moreover, the practical consequences of accepting the propriety of original intentions adjudication may be extremely limited. The legal, social and economic impacts of judicial review cannot be wished away, nor may we want them to be. An abrupt and complete adoption of original intentions adjudication might inflict injuries that far transcend the kinds of specifically legal considerations I discuss here. I am convinced, however, that we cannot intelligently discuss these practical matters until we have a clear sense of the underlying theoretical positions and disagreements.

* * *

* * * Adherence to the conventional view of constitutional adjudication is sometimes associated with the idea that judges should be tethered to the intentions of those who enacted the relevant constitutional provisions, and sometimes with the idea that judges should be restrained by the *text itself,* independent of the particular historical intentions of those who created it. The model I discuss will require further elaboration, but, briefly put, it calls for judges to apply the rules of the written constitution *in the sense in which those rules were understood by the people who enacted them.* Probably the purest judicial exposition and application of this understanding can be found in Justice Sutherland's dissenting opinion in the Minnesota Mortgage Moratorium case.[17] He said the "aim of construction" is to "discover the meaning," that is to "ascertain and give effect to the intent of its

17. Home Building & Loan Ass'n v. Blaisdell, 290 U.S. 398, 448 (1934) (Sutherland, J., dissenting).

framers and the people who adopted it." [18]   The view discussed here, therefore, rejects the idea that judicial allegiance is owed only to the mere words of the Constitution.

* * *

III.   First Objection: It's Impossible

* * *

A.   It's Really Impossible

The objection that original intentions adjudication is really impossible is founded on an extreme and general proposition about the capacity of human beings to communicate a determinate meaning through the medium of language.   The argument suggests that because linguistic communication is impossible, it is futile for judges to attempt to learn the intentions of the constitution-makers by studying what they said or what other people said about them.

Some legal scholars have taken positions similar to this by adopting the views of writers in the fields of philosophy and literary criticism.[50] * * *

* * *

The most glaring problem with the extreme position that interpretation according to original intentions is impossible, when applied to the use of language in general, is that it is wildly counterintuitive.   It is inconsistent with the way people carry on their lives every day.   We all confidently proceed on the assumption that we are capable of communicating through words a single determinate intention and that we are capable of understanding the single, determinate intentions of others.   Most of the time our confidence is well-founded.   We arrive at the right place for the right meetings at more or less the right time.   We read and discuss articles with the impression that we are talking about the same thing.   We stop at stop signs, file our tax returns, and obey subpoenas.   All these commonplace experiences testify powerfully against the claim that the inference of a determinate meaning from a sequence of words uttered in a particular context is essentially, and always, impossible. * * *

The most telling response to this objection is simply that no one really believes it, not even the writers who make the objection.   If they did, they would not use language to advance the argument. * * *

B.   It's Too Hard

The more moderate form of the impossibility objection to original intentions adjudication—It's too hard—appears much more plausible. It concedes that language is sometimes capable of communicating a speaker's or writer's intentions, but holds that interpretation of the

---

18. *Id.* at 453.

50. *See, e.g.,* Garet, *Comparative Normative Hermeneutics: Scripture, Literature, Constitution,* 58 S.Cal.L.Rev. 35

(1985); Levinson, *Law As Literature,* 60 Tex.L.Rev. 373 (1982); Peller, *The Metaphysics of American Law,* 73 Calif.L.Rev. 1151 (1985).

American Constitution creates peculiar problems which make the relevant original intentions inaccessible.

* * *

Before addressing [this criticism], it is necessary to explain precisely what original intentions adjudication requires of judges in the context of actual litigation. No judge is ever required to answer the abstract question: "What did the enactors intend by the phrase 'due process of law'?" Rather, judges must decide in a specific case whether or not, given the original intentions of the constitution-makers, a particular governmental action deprives someone of liberty or property without due process of law. The difference between the two questions is critically important. It is much easier to answer the second than the first because the alternatives are binary. The question can and can only be answered "yes" or "no," and since the judge must give some answer, it follows that he need not answer with certainty. All he needs to do is decide which of the two possible answers in that case is *more likely* correct.

Defining the judge's task as that of choosing which of two outcomes is more likely consistent with original intentions is particularly important in light of criticisms that stress the impossibility of ascertaining those intentions with sufficient certainty. It is true that we can never know the original intentions with certainty, but then we can never know any speaker's or writer's intent with certainty. Nevertheless, it is almost always possible to examine the constitutional text and other evidence of intent associated with it and make a reasonable, good faith judgment about which result is more likely consistent with that intent. Of course confidence in these judgments will be different in different situations, but one answer will almost always appear better than the other. Indeed, one of the two possible responses may be obviously incorrect because, while it is theoretically possible that the lawmakers held such an intention, the available historical evidence will be overwhelmingly against it. Thus, we can be uncertain about the intended meaning of a constitutional provision at the same time we are convinced that it is not consistent with one of the two contesting positions in a lawsuit. And, given that we have only two options, that conviction will decide the case.

There is nothing extraordinary in making important decisions this way. Almost every decision we make and action we take is based on a judgment of probabilities, often as to the probable intended meaning of what we read or hear. To insist on certainty would lead to paralysis. In asking judges to make decisions in this way we demand nothing more or less than the same kinds of decisions everyone makes everyday.

1. *The Problem of Multiple Intentions.* * * * The first problem concerns the difficulty of discerning a single intention when there are multiple constitution-makers.[82]

---

82. *See* R. Dworkin, [Law's Empire] 315–21 [(1986)]; Brennan, [The Constitu- *tion of the United States: Contemporary Ratification*, 27 S.Tex.L.J. 433, 435 (1986)];

In one sense this argument is a variant of the more extreme claim discussed above. To speak of an intention is to speak of a human mind. A joint intention cannot be the simple analog of an individual intention because we cannot easily conceive of a joint or group mind. But intent can be attributed to a group without positing the idea of a group mind. When we speak of such an intention we usually mean that each member of the group holds an identical individual intention. If a husband and wife discuss and settle on a list of invitations to a dinner party it seems perfectly proper to say that they have "an intention" about who their guests will be. This phenomenon would only be impossible if the couple could not articulate and communicate their intentions to each other in a way that let each one know those intentions coincided. I have alrady discussed why I believe such communication is not only possible but common.

Nevertheless, ascertaining the intention of a group is more complicated than discovering the intention of a single person. Many individuals in different capacities were involved in making the Constitution. In investigating the original intentions of these individuals, one problem lies in identifying those people whose coincident intentions created the relevant original intent. This problem is two-fold. First, every constitutional provision is the product of consideration and approval by different groups; therefore, we must identify which groups should be counted in defining the original intention. Second, within a specific group, there will be a variety of individual intentions and we will have to decide whose intentions define the intention of the group. Each of these aspects will be considered in turn.

a. *Which groups?*—In answering the first question, it is useful to recall the reason for being concerned with intention in the first place. * * * Recourse to intention is necessary because only certain people have the authority to make law. Thus, in constitutional law, we must identify which groups could, by their approval, give the Constitution the sanction of law.

It is necessary at this point to distinguish between the original Constitution of 1787 and subsequent amendments. We ordinarily treat amendments as law because they were created in accordance with Article V. An amendment becomes law when it is ratified by the legislatures of three-fourths of the States. The intentions of these legislatures is, thus, essential. But knowing those intentions is not sufficient. According to Article V, state legislatures may only ratify amendments that have been proposed by Congress with a two-thirds majority in each House. Thus, the Senate and House of Representatives are indispensable actors in the law-making process. In sum,

Brest, [*The Misconceived Quest for the Original Understanding,* 60 B.U.L.Rev. 204, 212–13 (1980)]; Dworkin, *The Forum of Principle,* 56 N.Y.U.L.Rev. 469, 480–81, 487–88 (1981); Radin, [*Statutory Interpreta-* *tion,* 43 Harv.L.Rev. 863, 870–71 (1930)]; Saphire, *Judicial Review in the Name of the Constitution,* 8 U.Dayton L.Rev. 745, 772–80 (1983); Hancher, *Dead Letters: Wills and Poems,* 60 Tex.L.Rev. 507 (1982).

constitutional amendments require identical intentions in the two Houses of Congress and in thirty-eight state legislatures.

When we consider the Constitution of 1787, of course, there is no governing law analogous to Article V that informs us who must agree before the Constitution acquires the force of law. The Constitution was a clean break with prior existing law. This does not mean, however, that we have no idea whose judgments and approval gave the Constitution authority. Like any supreme law, the legal character of the Constitution will depend on political beliefs and attitudes in a society about who has the final right to make law. This is a complex matter I have addressed at some length elsewhere.[89] It is sufficient here to note that the authority of the Constitution is conventionally and popularly premised on the understanding that it was the work of "the People" in their original, sovereign capacity. Actually, the role of "the People" was played by the special ratifying conventions in the individual states. The drafters at the Philadelphia Convention could claim no such mandate from "the people." Some supporters of the Constitution went so far as to disparage the importance of the Convention, except insofar as it was able to place a proposal before the state conventions.[91] The inquiry into original intent, therefore, should focus on the intentions of the various ratifying bodies who possessed the constituent authority.

With regard to both the body of the Constitution and its amendments, then, the only valid original intentions will be those held in common by a number of legislative bodies. This conclusion raises an obvious problem: What if we discover that, though they approved the same texts, different groups held different intentions so that no single intention can be applied to a particular question of interpretation? I will return to this question shortly.

b. *Which individuals within groups?*—The very same problem arises in answering the second question. Once we have found the authoritative groups, we must find a single intention for each group. Which individuals' intentions in, say, the Senate or in the Virginia Ratifying Convention should be considered?

The reasoning employed above can be applied to this problem. We wish to obtain the group intention because we deem it capable of establishing an authoritative rule. A given body acts when some number of its members agree to act. In the ordinary course that number is a majority. In the case of the Houses of Congress proposing amendments it is—by virtue of prior governing law—a two-thirds majority. The intention of the body, therefore, is embodied in the shared intentions of the appropriate majority of its members.

---

89. *See* Kay, [*Preconstitutional Rules,* 42 Ohio St.L.J. 187 (1981)]; Kay, *The Creation of Constitutions in Canada and the United States,* 7 Can.–U.S.L.J. 111 (1984).

91. *See* 1 M. Farrand, Records of the Federal Convention of 1787 295 (remarks of A. Hamilton), 253 (remarks of J. Wilson) (1966); The Federalist No. 40 at 247–48 (J. Madison) (C. Rossiter ed. 1961) * * *.

One consequence of this reasoning is that only the intentions of those voting in favor of the constitutional provision at issue will be relevant. The intentions of dissenters may be useful in illuminating the intention of the proponents, but they are not a part of the authoritative intention. Dissenters neither contributed nor were necessary to the event which made the text law and, for reasons already discussed, our concern is with the intentions of the lawmakers. Proper inquiry, therefore, is restricted to the members of the majority.

As we saw earlier when there were numerous law-making bodies, however, there may be more than one intention in the majority that approves the very same act of legislation. The difficulty will be even greater here because the number of potential intentions will be larger. When we multiply the number of possible intentions in a legislature by the number of possible intentions among legislative bodies the task of determining one original intention might appear hopeless.

 c. *Summing different intentions.*—The possibility of multiple, varying intentions is not, however, fatal to the enterprise of original intentions adjudication. The difficulty is intractable only if there are multiple and totally *contradictory* intentions. This could happen if, for example, a constitutional provision was created with some constitution-makers intending it to mean X and only X, while other constitution-makers intended it to mean not-X and only not-X. Such contradiction is extremely unlikely, however, because though the intentions involved are held by different people, those intentions are associated with the adoption of identical language. The use of the same language suggests a common core of meaning shared by all. Any different intentions are, therefore, likely to be overlapping not contradictory. Thus, if an ordinance prohibits "vehicles in the park," it is safe to assume that all of the enactors intended it apply to ordinary automobiles. Similarly, in a constitutional context, probably all of the enactors of the fifth and fourteenth amendments understood that incarceration would be a deprivation of liberty requiring due process of law. The differences in intention will arise in cases beyond the obvious situations suggested by the language, as that language was ordinarily used and understood. Where there is disagreement it will be with respect to the outer reach or scope of the rule. To use the terminology of some modern philosophers of language, these differences will be attributable to the vagueness, not the ambiguity, of the words adopted.[95]

Originally, I stated the problem in this section to be the combination of disparate intentions into one authoritative intention of the group with authority to make law. But, given the kind of differences likely to occur, we should be able to accumulate enough *identical* intentions to compose an authoritative lawmaker. By discerning the language's central paradigm, we can define an area of application that was intended by virtually all the relevant individuals who together

---

95. *See* W. Quine, Word and Object 125–34 (1960); Young, *Equivocation in the*   *Making of Agreements,* 64 Colum.L.Rev. 619, 626–32, 646–47 (1964).   * * *

constitute the lawmaker. As we move out from this core idea to somewhat less obvious applications, we can expect to find fewer individuals who intend the law to extend so far. Still, as long as it is probable that a necessary law-making majority shared a particular understanding it will be appropriate to so interpret the provision. This approach, therefore, requires the judge to ask whether the challenged action falls within a meaning intended by an authoritative lawmaker. Idiosyncratic meanings held by individuals within the majority (or by individual law-making bodies) falling outside that shared, core intention will not have the force of law because they lack such an authoritative source. They may be ignored for the same reasons that we ignore the intentions of the dissenters.

This argument assumes that individuals do not employ the same words to mean entirely opposite things, especially in circumstances where they discuss and debate the meaning of those words before adopting them. Therefore, there will almost always be some core meaning that reflects the intentions of the constitution-makers. This is true even when there is no controlling intention with respect to other, fringe meanings.

* * *

2. *The Problem of Historical Understanding.*—Another argument against original intentions adjudication suggests that it is very difficult, if not impossible, to understand intentions formed and expressed a very long time ago.[103] * * * This claim is based on a "fatal" gap between the moment of expression and the moment of understanding. But all interpretation—contemporary as well as ancient—is historical in this sense. And, if it is conceded that some immediate communication is possible, then the difficulty is not different in kind simply because the time between speaking and listening or writing and reading is changed from minutes or days to decades or centuries.

* * *

The very breadth of this claim makes it implausible. It is essentially an attack on the possibility and validity of historical investigation. While some students of history deny the possibility of objectively correct historical conclusions, the contrary view is also widely and firmly held. Indeed, the force of the latter position is strengthened by the fact that history is a well-established discipline to which thousands of sensible people have devoted and continue to devote their energy and intelligence. These scholars proceed on the assumption that, with varying degrees of effort, it *is* possible to ascertain and adopt the viewpoint of another person, even if that other person is remote in place, culture or time.

* * *

Finally, as I noted when considering the problem of multiple intentions, original intentions adjudication only calls for decisions re-

---

103. *See* Brennan, *supra* note 82, at 435; Powell, *Rules for Originalists*, 73 Va. L.Rev. 659, 673–74 (1987); Tushnet, *Fol-* *lowing the Rules Laid Down: A Critique of Interpretivism and Neutral Principles*, 96 Harv.L.Rev. 781, 793–804 (1983).

garding which of two proposed interpretations is more likely to be
consistent with those original intentions. In most cases, it should be
possible to recapture enough of the past to make that choice.

3. *The Probabilities in Balance.*—The discussion thus far has
omitted one significant possibility. A judge, after considering the
evidence of the relevant intentions, could decide that neither of the
contesting propositions about the original intention is more likely than
the other—that is, he might conclude that the evidence exactly balances. In such cases, we might have a supplemental rule that, for
example, places the burden of proof on the party claiming that constitutional rules have been violated.[115] But unless such a rule itself could be
inferred from the original intentions of the enactors, this would result
in cases being decided on grounds independent of the original intentions. There may exist, therefore, certain cases in which original
intentions adjudication will yield no answer.

In practice, however, these "ties" will be exceedingly rare. This is
because the available information about the creators of the constitutional rules is so plentiful. Given the usual denseness of the historical
record, a competent person is unlikely to come across many cases where
the evidence that the original intentions did and the evidence that it
did not extend to the act in question is precisely equal. The strength of
an interpreter's convictions may depend on the relative strength of the
two cases, but he will almost always be able to say that one is better
than the other.

*   *   *

 *   *   * [S]ome things may fall outside the categories established by
the constitution-makers *   *   * because they are so different from
those the enactors knew about. In such cases, we cannot assume they
made any provision for them at all. But do such cases really result in a
0–0 tie with original intentions adjudication providing no solution? I
believe the Constitution, as intended by its creators, provides a decision
on constitutionality for every possible action no matter how different it
is from the things and circumstances the constitution-makers had in
mind. Implicit in the Constitution are "back-up rules" which cover all
things not provided for in the explicit rules. It must be stressed these
back-up rules are *not* new constructs created in order to make original
intentions adjudication feasible. Rather, they are legitimate inferences
from the enactment of the constitutional text. They are an inherent
part of what the constitution-makers did when they created the Constitution.

These back-up rules are a necessary consequence of the federal
system of granted and residual powers established by the Constitution.
The Constitution created a national government against a background
of pre-existing states. That government exists *only* by virtue of the

---

115. *See, e.g.,* Metropolitan Cas. Ins. Co.
v. Brownell, 294 U.S. 580, 584 (1935) (heavy
burden of proof rests on party claiming
unconstitutionality of statutes); Brown v.
Maryland, 25 U.S. (12 Wheat.) 419, 436
(1827) (same).

enactment of the Constitution. Therefore, we must find in the Constitution all of its features and all of its powers. There is nowhere else to look. Consequently, any action of the federal government not traceable to the enumerated institutions and powers is an exercise of power not granted to it and is contrary to the Constitution. Any truly *new* thing done by the federal government is unauthorized and therefore void.

On the other hand, the United States Constitution was enacted on the assumption that the existing states would continue to exist. The states necessarily derived their governmental institutions and powers from sources outside the new Constitution. Therefore, the absence of a reference to a state power is not equivalent to a lack of authorization. The Constitution declares itself to be and was, no doubt, intended to be supreme over the states, but only insofar as it specifically limited state powers. Any truly *new* thing done by a state must be outside of those prohibitions, and must, therefore, be constitutional.

This conclusion is itself an interpretation of the Constitution. It is, therefore, subject to rebuttal by persuasive historical evidence to the contrary. The case for it, however, is very strong. The constitution-makers differed among themselves about the appropriate scope of the powers of the new national government, but there is no serious evidence that these powers (whatever their extent) were not entirely granted by the new constitution or that state power was altered except insofar as affirmatively limited by the Constitution. The Tenth Amendment makes this explicit. The Civil War amendments significantly altered the constitutional allocation of national and state powers by enlarging federal legislative authority and especially by placing new and broad limits on state power. But it did not alter the underlying scheme of granted and residuary powers. Debate about power in the federal system, therefore, must turn on what the Constitution gave to the federal government and what it took away from the States. So long as that is true, there is an answer to the validity of every new thing. There are no omitted cases.

* * *

* * * Original intentions adjudication may not achieve [its] goals perfectly, but to conclude that it is, therefore, useless "is like saying that as a perfectly aseptic environment is impossible, one might as well conduct surgery in a sewer." [137] When honestly applied, original intentions adjudication seems to reduce the influence of the personal and idiosyncratic aspects of a judge's personality or ideology more than do alternative theories that rely on ill-defined standards of one kind or another. Such rule-governed adjudication may or may not be appealing, but, for the reasons suggested, it is possible.

* * *

137. C. Geertz, the Interpretation of Cultures 30 (1973) (attributed to Robert Solow). * * *

IV. Second Objection: It's Self–Contradictory

The second principal objection to original intentions adjudication is that the enactors themselves did not want their intentions to govern judicial exposition on the lawfulness of certain governmental action. Proponents of this argument suggest that the constitution-makers intended judges to look elsewhere for guides to decision and (depending on the proponent) wanted judges to possess varying degrees of discretion.

* * *

[This] * * * objection assumes that the interpretative intentions of the enactors ought to control constitutional interpretation and that those intentions were that substantive intentions should not control. The latter can be reduced to a mere (although certainly difficult) question of historical fact. We know that the constitution-makers thought it was important to enact written constitutional rules. We know they took great pains to choose the terms they did and that they argued about the best language and about the merits of the proposals before them as if their decisions on these things would make a difference. We would not expect such deliberation from people who wanted their intentions to be ignored or to play a minor role in the future application of the rules they made. A strong case would seem in order from those who would impute such a desire to them. I do not contend that such a claim could never be proven. But [for reasons not included in these excerpts] it does not seem to me to have been proven yet.

V. Third Objection: It's Wrong

* * * [E]ven if [original intentions] adjudication is both possible and coherent, it must face a final objection: that [it] makes for bad government and bad law. While rarely put so bluntly, this is the most potent of the three objections that I have listed. Its power derives from the fact that, unlike the first two, refuting it requires more than simply an appeal to facts, history, or ordinary experience. This objection is the expression of a political and moral judgment about the best way for people to live in society. As such, conventional argument can take us only so far.

To evaluate this objection, we cannot consider original intentions adjudication in isolation, as we were able to do with the first two objections. The judgment here is necessarily relative: original intentions adjudication must be worse than *some other* system in which constitutional decisions are made according to some standards or processes other than fidelity to the original intentions.

* * *

* * * [This] third objection to original intentions adjudication might be put this way: limiting government by fixed rules intended by people in the more or less distant past will yield less satisfactory political and social consequences than will some other limiting technique. The exact nature of the objection depends on the proffered alternative, but most versions find similar problems with submission to the original intentions. These problems involve the incapacity of set, abstract rules to respond over time to our collective and individual well-being. * * *

* * *

* * * [A fair] response is to affirm the values inherent in "inflexibility"—the values of stability and clarity. Constitutional government exists to limit the sphere of appropriate government activity. It rests on the premise that there should be a realm of action and private decision-making immune from public coercion. The value of dividing human activity into exclusively private and potentially public zones would be severely diminished if the boundary between the two areas could be frequently and unpredictably altered. It is not merely the ability to contest, and sometimes successfully resist, government impositions that benefit those living under a constitutional government. It is, at least as much, the ability to "count on" government being constrained by certain procedures and within certain limits. Such stability permits us confidently to plan our lives, a freedom which is at the core of our capacity for self-definition. The opposite kind of existence, where we live in perpetual dread of the secret decree and the surprise order becomes, at the extreme, totalitarianism—the opposite of government under law.

This characteristic of government under law is not the only important value in the relationship of government and the individual, but it is difficult to overestimate its importance. * * * When life-plans are at stake, we are "risk-averse." Indeed, it may be the securing of a class of expectations from undefined and unpredictable interferences that is the peculiar contribution of law to society, a contribution particularly important when it is applied to the potential dangers of abuse by government.

* * *

But recognition of this value does not rebut the initial objection to original intentions adjudication that static constitutional rules are unsuitable for a constantly changing society. It is merely a counterweight. Whether it is sufficient depends on an evaluation of the relative importance of the competing values: the value of flexibility and adaptability on the one hand, and the value of predictability and stability on the other.

Moreover, in specific cases, these concerns cannot be considered in isolation. How we view their competing advantages will be influenced by the substantive content of the constitutional rules at issue, and our regard for the individuals who, as judges, will undertake whatever revisions are allowed. Our enthusiasm for stable rules will be reduced if we think the rules protected are oppressive and unfair. Our taste for responsive and up-to-date rules will be diminished if we know they will be "improved" by people we regard as ignorant or immoral. Thus the preconstitutional decision must be largely empirical, depending on facts that may be disputed and it must, therefore, be only provisional.

Even if we could agree about the quality of the substantive rules and the credentials of the judges who would supervise their evolution, we would probably still disagree on the desirability of adhering to the original intentions because the weights we assign these competing sets of values are different. Those preferences, in turn, would depend on our confidence in the capacity of government officials, including judges, to discover and act on the public good without well-defined prior rules and on the risk that, without strict prior limits, such officials might cause suffering, unrest, and injury. Our choice of the governing norm of constitutional adjudication, then, will turn on the kinds of chances we are willing to take in living together in society, and, what comes to the same thing, on our judgment as to the kind of people we are.

D. NEUTRAL PRINCIPLES

HERBERT WECHSLER, TOWARD NEUTRAL PRINCIPLES OF CONSTITUTIONAL LAW
73 Harv.L.Rev. 9, 11–20, 31–35 (1959).

* * * [Are there] any criteria that both the Supreme Court and those who undertake to praise or to condemn its judgments are morally and intellectually obligated to support?

Whatever you may think to be the answer, surely you agree with me that I am right to state the question as the same one for the Court and for its critics. An attack upon a judgment involves an assertion that a court should have decided otherwise than as it did. Is it not clear that the validity of an assertion of this kind depends upon assigning reasons that should have prevailed with the tribunal; and that any other reasons are irrelevant? That is, of course, not only true of a critique of a decision of the courts; it applies whenever a determination is in question, a determination that it is essential to make either way. Is it the irritation of advancing years that leads me to lament that our culture is not rich with critics who respect these limitations of the enterprise in which they are engaged?

You may remind me that, as someone in the ancient world observed—perhaps it was Josephus—history has little tolerance for any of those reasonable judgments that have turned out to be wrong. But history, in this sense, is inscrutable, concealing all its verdicts in the bosom of the future; it is never a contemporary critic.

I revert then to the problem of criteria as it arises for both courts and critics—by which I mean criteria that can be framed and tested as an exercise of reason and not merely as an act of willfulness or will. Even to put the problem is, of course, to raise an issue no less old than our culture. Those who perceive in law only the element of fiat, in whose conception of the legal cosmos reason has no meaning or no place, will not join gladly in the search for standards of the kind I have in mind. I must, in short, expect dissent *in limine* from anyone whose view of the judicial process leaves no room for the antinomy Professor Fuller has so gracefully explored.[38] So too must I anticipate dissent from those more numerous among us who, vouching no philosophy to warranty, frankly or covertly make the test of virtue in interpretation whether its result in the immediate decision seems to hinder or advance the interests or the values they support.

I shall not try to overcome the philosophic doubt that I have mentioned, although to use a phrase that Holmes so often used—"it hits me where I live." That battle must be fought on wider fronts than that of constitutional interpretation; and I do not delude myself that I can qualify for a command, great as is my wish to render service. The man who simply lets his judgment turn on the immediate result may not, however, realize that his position implies that the courts are free to function as a naked power organ, that it is an empty affirmation to regard them, as ambivalently he so often does, as courts of law. If he may know he disapproves of a decision when all he knows is that it has sustained a claim put forward by a labor union or a taxpayer, a Negro or a segregationist, a corporation or a Communist—he acquiesces in the proposition that a man of different sympathy but equal information may no less properly conclude that he approves.

You will not charge me with exaggeration if I say that this type of *ad hoc* evaluation is, as it has always been, the deepest problem of our constitutionalism, not only with respect to judgments of the courts but also in the wider realm in which conflicting constitutional positions have played a part in our politics.

* * *

* * * [W]hether you are tolerant, perhaps more tolerant than I, of the *ad hoc* in politics, with principle reduced to a manipulative tool, are you not also ready to agree that something else is called for from the courts? I put it to you that the main constituent of the judicial process is precisely that it must be genuinely principled, resting with respect to every step that is involved in reaching judgment on analysis and reasons quite transcending the immediate result that is achieved. To be sure, the courts decide, or should decide, only the case they have before them. But must they not decide on grounds of adequate neutrality and generality, tested not only by the instant application but by others that the principles imply? Is it not the very essence of judicial method to insist upon attending to such other cases, preferably those involving an opposing interest, in evaluating any principle avowed?

Here too I do not think that I am stating any novel or momentous insight. But now, as Holmes said long ago in speaking of "the unrest which seems to wonder vaguely whether law and order pay," we "need education in the obvious." [46] We need it more particularly now respect-

---

38. See Fuller, *Reason and Fiat in Case Law,* 59 Harv.L.Rev. 376 (1946).

46. Holmes, Law and the Court, in Collected Legal Papers 291, 292 (1920).

ing constitutional interpretation, since it has become a commonplace to grant what many for so long denied: that courts in constitutional determinations face issues that are inescapably "political" * * * in that they involve a choice among competing values or desires, a choice reflected in the legislative or executive action in question, which the court must either condemn or condone.

* * * [W]hat is crucial, I submit, is not the nature of the question but the nature of the answer that may validly be given by the courts. No legislature or executive is obligated by the nature of its function to support its choice of values by the type of reasoned explanation that I have suggested is intrinsic to judicial action—however much we may admire such a reasoned exposition when we find it in those other realms.

Does not the special duty of the courts to judge by neutral principles addressed to all the issues make it inapposite to contend, as Judge Hand does, that no court can review the legislative choice—by any standard other than a fixed "historical meaning" of constitutional provisions [48]—without becoming "a third legislative chamber"? [49] Is there not, in short, a vital difference between legislative freedom to appraise the gains and losses in projected measures and the kind of principled appraisal, in respect of values that can reasonably be asserted to have constitutional dimension, that alone is in the province of the courts? Does not the difference yield a middle ground between a judicial House of Lords and the abandonment of any limitation on the other branches—a middle ground consisting of judicial action that embodies what are surely the main qualities of law, its generality and its neutrality? This must, it seems to me, have been in Mr. Justice Jackson's mind when in his chapter on the Supreme Court "as a political institution" he wrote [50] in words that I find stirring, "Liberty is not the mere absence of restraint, it is not a spontaneous product of majority rule, it is not achieved merely by lifting underprivileged classes to power, nor is it the inevitable by-product of technological expansion. It is achieved only by a rule of law." Is it not also what Mr. Justice Frankfurter must mean in calling upon judges for "allegiance to nothing except the effort, amid tangled words and limited insights, to find the path through precedent, through policy, through history, to the best judgment that fallible creatures can reach in that most difficult of all tasks: the achievement of justice between man and man, between man and state, through reason called law"? [51]

You will not understand my emphasis upon the role of reason and of principle in the judicial, as distinguished from the legislative or executive, appraisal of conflicting values to imply that I depreciate the

---

48. [L. Hand, The Bill of Rights 65 (1958).]

49. *Id.* at 42.

50. Jackson, The Supreme Court in the American System of Government 76 (1955).

51. Frankfurter, Chief Justices I Have Known, in Of Law and Men 138 (Elman ed. 1956).

duty of fidelity to the text of the Constitution, when its words may be decisive—though I would certainly remind you of the caution stated by Chief Justice Hughes: "Behind the words of the constitutional provisions are postulates which limit and control." [52] Nor will you take me to deny that history has weight in the elucidation of the text, though it is surely subtle business to appraise it as a guide. Nor will you even think that I deem precedent without importance, for we surely must agree with Holmes that "imitation of the past, until we have a clear reason for change, no more needs justification than appetite." [53] But after all, it was Chief Justice Taney who declared his willingness "that it be regarded hereafter as the law of this court, that its opinion upon the construction of the Constitution is always open to discussion when it is supposed to have been founded in error, and that its judicial authority should hereafter depend altogether on the force of the reasoning by which it is supported." [54] Would any of us have it otherwise, given the nature of the problems that confront the courts?

At all events, is not the relative compulsion of the language of the Constitution, of history and precedent—where they do not combine to make an answer clear—itself a matter to be judged, so far as possible, by neutral principles—by standards that transcend the case at hand? I know, of course, that it is common to distinguish, as Judge Hand did, clauses like "due process," cast "in such sweeping terms that their history does not elucidate their contents," [55] from other provisions of the Bill of Rights addressed to more specific problems. But the contrast, as it seems to me, often implies an overstatement of the specificity or the immutability these other clauses really have—at least when problems under them arise.

No one would argue, for example, that there need not be indictment and a jury trial in prosecutions for a felony in district courts. What made a question of some difficulty was the issue whether service wives charged with the murders of their husbands overseas could be tried there before a military court. [56] Does the language of the double-jeopardy clause or its preconstitutional history actually help to decide whether a defendant tried for murder in the first degree and convicted of murder in the second, who wins a reversal of the judgment on appeal, may be tried again for murder in the first or only murder in the second? [57] Is there significance in the fact that it is "jeopardy of life or limb" that is forbidden, now that no one is in jeopardy of limb but only of imprisonment or fine? The right to "have the assistance of counsel" was considered, I am sure, when the sixth amendment was proposed, a right to defend by counsel if you have one, contrary to what was then

---

52. Principality of Monaco v. Mississippi, 292 U.S. 313, 322 (1934).

53. Holmes, Holdsworth's English Law, in Collected Legal Papers 285, 290 (1920).

54. Passenger Cases, 48 U.S. (7 How.) 283, 470 (1849).

55. Hand, [*supra* note 48], at 30.

56. See Reid v. Covert, 354 U.S. 1 (1957), *reversing on rehearing* 351 U.S. 487 (1956).

57. See Green v. United States, 355 U.S. 184 (1957).

the English law.[58] That does not seem to me sufficient to avert extension of its meaning to imply a right to court-appointed counsel when the defendant is too poor to find such aid [59]—though I admit that I once urged the point sincerely as a lawyer for the Government.[60] It is difficult for me to think the fourth amendment freezes for all time the common law of search and of arrest as it prevailed when the amendment was adopted, whatever the exigencies of police problems may now be or may become. Nor should we, in my view, lament the fact that "the" freedom of speech or press that Congress is forbidden by the first amendment to impair is not determined only by the scope such freedom had in the late eighteenth century, though the word "the" might have been taken to impose a limitation to the concept of that time—a time when, President Wright has recently reminded us, there was remarkable consensus about matters of this kind.[61]

Even "due process," on the other hand, might have been confined, as Mr. Justice Brandeis urged originally,[62] to a guarantee of fair procedure, coupled perhaps with prohibition of executive displacement of established law—the analogue for us of what the barons meant in Magna Carta. Equal protection could be taken as no more than an assurance that no one may be placed beyond the safeguards of the law, outlawing, as it were, the possibility of outlawry, but nothing else. Here too I cannot find it in my heart to regret that interpretation did not ground itself in ancient history but rather has perceived in these provisions a compendious affirmation of the basic values of a free society, values that must be given weight in legislation and administration at the risk of courting trouble in the courts.

So far as possible, to finish with my point, I argue that we should prefer to see the other clauses of the Bill of Rights read as an affirmation of the special values they embody rather than as statements of a finite rule of law, its limits fixed by the consensus of a century long past, with problems very different from our own. To read them in the former way is to leave room for adaptation and adjustment if and when competing values, also having constitutional dimension, enter on the scene.

Let me repeat what I have thus far tried to say. The courts have both the title and the duty when a case is properly before them to review the actions of the other branches in the light of constitutional provisions, even though the action involves value choices, as invariably action does. In doing so, however, they are bound to function otherwise

---

58. "Throughout the eighteenth century counsel were allowed to speak in cases of treason and misdemeanour only." 1 Stephen, A History of the Criminal Law of England 453 (1883).   *   *   *

59. See Johnson v. Zerbst, 304 U.S. 458 (1938).

60. Walker v. Johnston, 312 U.S. 275 (1941).

61. Wright, Consensus and Continuity, 1776–1787 *passim* (1958).   *   *   *

62. "Despite arguments to the contrary which had seemed to me persuasive, it is settled that the due process clause of the Fourteenth Amendment applies to matters of substantive law as well as to matters of procedure." Whitney v. California, 274 U.S. 357, 373 (1927) (concurring opinion).

than as a naked power organ; they participate as courts of law. This calls for facing how determinations of this kind can be asserted to have any legal quality. The answer, I suggest, inheres primarily in that they are—or are obliged to be—entirely principled. A principled decision, in the sense I have in mind, is one that rests on reasons with respect to all the issues in the case, reasons that in their generality and their neutrality transcend any immediate result that is involved. When no sufficient reasons of this kind can be assigned for overturning value choices of the other branches of the Government or of a state, those choices must, of course, survive. Otherwise, as Holmes said in his first opinion for the Court, "a constitution, instead of embodying only relatively fundamental rules of right, as generally understood by all English-speaking communities, would become the partisan of a particular set of ethical or economical opinions. . . ." [63]

The virtue or demerit of a judgment turns, therefore, entirely on the reasons that support it and their adequacy to maintain any choice of values it decrees, or, it is vital that we add, to maintain the rejection of a claim that any given choice should be decreed. The critic's role, as T.R. Powell showed throughout so many fruitful years, is the sustained, disinterested, merciless examination of the reasons that the courts advance, measured by standards of the kind I have attempted to describe. I wish that more of us today could imitate his dedication to that task.

III. SOME APPRAISALS OF REVIEW

One who has ventured to advance such generalities about the courts and constitutional interpretation is surely challenged to apply them to some concrete problems—if only to make clear that he believes in what he says. A lecture, to be sure, is a poor medium for such an undertaking, for the statement and analysis of cases inescapably takes time. Nonetheless, I feel obliged to make the effort and I trust that I can do so without trespassing on the indulgence you already have displayed.

* * *

[Consider] the school decision, which for one of my persuasion stirs the deepest conflict I experience in testing the thesis I propose. Yet I would surely be engaged in playing Hamlet without Hamlet if I did not try to state the problems that appear to me to be involved.

The problem for me, I hardly need to say, is not that the Court departed from its earlier decisions holding or implying that the equality of public educational facilities demanded by the Constitution could be met by separate schools. I stand with the long tradition of the Court that previous decisions must be subject to reexamination when a case against their reasoning is made. Nor is the problem that the Court disturbed the settled patterns of a portion of the country; even that must be accepted as a lesser evil than nullification of the Constitution.

63. Otis v. Parker, 187 U.S. 606, 609 (1903).

Nor is it that history does not confirm that an agreed purpose of the fourteenth amendment was to forbid separate schools or that there is important evidence that many thought the contrary; [111] the words are general and leave room for expanding content as time passes and conditions change. Nor is it that the Court may have miscalculated the extent to which its judgment would be honored or accepted; it is not a prophet of the strength of our national commitment to respect the judgments of the courts. Nor is it even that the Court did not remit the issue to the Congress, acting under the enforcement clause of the amendment. That was a possible solution, to be sure, but certainly Professor Freund is right [112] that it would merely have evaded the claims made.

The problem inheres strictly in the reasoning of the opinion, an opinion which is often read with less fidelity by those who praise it than by those by whom it is condemned. The Court did not declare, as many wish it had, that the fourteenth amendment forbids all racial lines in legislation, though subsequent per curiam decisions may, as I have said, now go that far. Rather, as Judge Hand observed,[113] the separate-but-equal formula was not overruled "in form" but was held to have "no place" in public education on the ground that segregated schools are "inherently unequal," with deleterious effects upon the colored children in implying their inferiority, effects which retard their educational and mental development. So, indeed, the district court had found as a fact in the Kansas case, a finding which the Supreme Court embraced, citing some further "modern authority" in its support.

Does the validity of the decision turn then on the sufficiency of evidence or of judicial notice to sustain a finding that the separation harms the Negro children who may be involved? There were, indeed, some witnesses who expressed that opinion in the Kansas case, as there were also witnesses in the companion Virginia case * * *, whose view was to the contrary. Much depended on the question that the witness had in mind, which rarely was explicit. Was he comparing the position of the Negro child in a segregated school with his position in an integrated school where he was happily accepted and regarded by the whites; or was he comparing his position under separation with that under integration where the whites were hostile to his presence and found ways to make their feelings known? And if the harm that segregation worked was relevant, what of the benefits that it entailed: sense of security, the absence of hostility? Were they irrelevant? Moreover, was the finding in Topeka applicable without more to Clarendon County, South Carolina, with 2,799 colored students and only 295 whites? Suppose that more Negroes in a community preferred separation than opposed it? Would that be relevant to whether they were hurt or aided by segregation as opposed to integration? Their fates

---

111. See Bickel, *The Original Understanding and the Segregation Decision,* 69 Harv.L.Rev. 1 (1955).

112. See Freund, *Storm Over the American Supreme Court,* 21 Modern L.Rev. 345, 351 (1958).

113. Hand, [*supra* note 48], at 54.

would be governed by the change of system quite as fully as those of the students who complained.

I find it hard to think the judgment really turned upon the facts. Rather, it seems to me, it must have rested on the view that racial segregation is, in principle, a denial of equality to the minority against whom it is directed; that is, the group that is not dominant politically and, therefore, does not make the choice involved. For many who support the Court's decision this assuredly is the decisive ground. But this position also presents problems. Does it not involve an inquiry into the motive of the legislature, which is generally foreclosed to the courts? [117] Is it alternatively defensible to make the measure of validity of legislation the way it is interpreted by those who are affected by it? In the context of a charge that segregation *with equal facilities* is a denial of equality, is there not a point in *Plessy* in the statement that if "enforced separation stamps the colored race with a badge of inferiority" it is solely because its members choose "to put that construction upon it"? [118] Does enforced separation of the sexes discriminate against females merely because it may be the females who resent it and it is imposed by judgments predominantly male? Is a prohibition of miscegenation a discrimination against the colored member of the couple who would like to marry?

For me, assuming equal facilities, the question posed by state-enforced segregation is not one of discrimination at all. Its human and its constitutional dimensions lie entirely elsewhere, in the denial by the state of freedom to associate, a denial that impinges in the same way on any groups or races that may be involved. I think, and I hope not without foundation, that the Southern white also pays heavily for segregation, not only in the sense of guilt that he must carry but also in the benefits he is denied. In the days when I was joined with Charles H. Houston in a litigation in the Supreme Court, before the present building was constructed, he did not suffer more than I in knowing that we had to go to Union Station to lunch together during the recess. Does not the problem of miscegenation show most clearly that it is the freedom of association that at bottom is involved, the only case, I may add, where it is implicit in the situation that association is desired by the only individuals involved? I take no pride in knowing that in 1956 the Supreme Court dismissed an appeal in a case in which Virginia nullified a marriage on this ground, a case in which the statute had been squarely challenged by the defendant, and the Court, after remanding once, dismissed per curiam on procedural grounds that I make bold to say are wholly without basis in the law.[119]

117. Motive is open to examination when executive action is challenged as discriminatory, but there the purpose is to show that an admitted inequality of treatment was not inadvertent. See, *e.g.*, Snowden v. Hughes, 321 U.S. 1 (1944). Even in such a case, invidious motivation alone has not been held to establish the inequality.

118. Plessy v. Ferguson, 163 U.S. 537, 551 (1896).

119. See Ham Say Naim v. Naim, 197 Va. 80, 87 S.E.2d 749, *vacated,* 350 U.S. 891

But if the freedom of association is denied by segregation, integration forces an association upon those for whom it is unpleasant or repugnant. Is this not the heart of the issue involved, a conflict in human claims of high dimension, not unlike many others that involve the highest freedoms—conflicts that Professor Sutherland has recently described.[120] Given a situation where the state must practically choose between denying the association to those individuals who wish it or imposing it on those who would avoid it, is there a basis in neutral principles for holding that the Constitution demands that the claims for association should prevail? I should like to think there is, but I confess that I have not yet written the opinion. To write it is for me the challenge of the school-segregation cases.

MARK V. TUSHNET, FOLLOWING THE RULES LAID DOWN: A CRITIQUE OF INTERPRETIVISM AND NEUTRAL PRINCIPLES

96 Harv.L.Rev. 781, 805–24 (1983).

The rule of law, according to the liberal conception, is meant to protect us against the exercise of arbitrary power. The theory of neutral principles asserts that a requirement of consistency, the core of the ideal of the rule of law, places sufficient bounds on judges to reduce the risk of arbitrariness to an acceptable level. The question is whether the concepts of neutrality and consistency can be developed in ways that are adequate for the task. My discussion examines various candidates for a definition of neutrality, beginning with a crude definition and moving toward more sophisticated ones. Yet each candidate suffers from similar defects: each fails to provide the kinds of constraints on judges that liberalism requires. Some candidates seek to limit the results judges might reach, others the methods they may use. The supposed substantive bounds that consistency imposes on judges, however, are either empty or parasitic on other substantive theories of constitutional law, and the methodological bounds are either empty or dependent on a sociology of law that undermines liberalism's assumptions about society.

A. Neutral Content

Robert Bork's version of neutral principles theory would require that decisions rest on principles that are neutral in content and in application.[65] Bork's formulation may be an attempt to generalize Wechsler's definition, which characterizes neutrality as judicial indifference to who the winner is. For Wechsler, such indifference was a matter of judicial willingness to apply the present case's rule in the next case as well, regardless whether the beneficiary in the later case was less attractive than the earlier winner in ways not made relevant

(1955), *on remand,* 197 Va. 734, 90 S.E.2d 849, *appeal dismissed,* 350 U.S. 985 (1956).

120. See Sutherland, The Law and One Man Among Many 35–62 (1956).

65. Bork, *Neutral Principles and Some First Amendment Problems,* 47 Ind.L.J. 1, 6–7 (1971).

by the rule itself.[66]   Neutral content for Bork might mean a similar indifference, but now within the case: the principle governing the case should be developed in a form that employs only general terms and that avoids any express preference for any named groups.   This outcome, however, is impossible.   We might coherently require that rules not use proper names, but there is no principled way to distinguish between the general terms that in effect pick out specific groups or individuals and those that are "truly" general.   Any general term serves to identify some specific group; hence if the notion of content neutrality is to make any sense, it must depend on a prior understanding of which kinds of distinctions are legitimately "neutral" and which are not.   The demand for neutrality in content thus cannot provide an independent criterion for acceptable decisions.

Standing alone, the theory that principles must be neutral in content cannot constrain judicial discretion.   But it could be coupled with some other theory—such as interpretivism, Ely's reinforcement of representation,[a] or a moral philosophy.   When coordinated with some such substantive theory, the demand for neutral principles stipulates that a decision is justified only if the principles derived from the other theory are neutrally applied.   Yet to require neutral application of the principles of the other theory is merely to apply those principles in given cases; the requirement of content neutrality adds nothing.[68]

B.   Neutral Method

If neutrality is to serve as a meaningful guide, it must be understood not as a standard for the content of principles, but rather as a constraint on the process by which principles are selected, justified, and applied.   Thus, the remaining candidate explications of neutrality all focus on the judicial process and the need for "neutral *application.*"   This focus transfers our attention from the principles themselves to the judges who purport to use them.

* * *

1.   Prospective Application.—What then are methodologically neutral principles?   To Wechsler, such principles are identified primarily by a forward-looking aspect: a judge who invokes a principle in a specific instance commits himself or herself to invoking it in future cases that are relevantly identical.   For example, a judge who justifies the holding in *Brown v. Board of Education* that segregated schools are unconstitutional by invoking the principle that the state may not take race into account in any significant policy decision is thereby also committed to holding state-developed affirmative action programs unconstitutional.   The judge's interior monologue involves specifying the

66. Wechsler, *Toward Neutral Principles of Constitutional Law,* 73 Harv.L.Rev. 1, 11–12, 15 (1959).

a. J. Ely, Democracy and Distrust (1980).

68. In the larger work of which this Article will be a part, I argue that the other, substantive theories are all internally contradictory, at least beyond a narrow range of applications.   If that argument is correct, neutral application is again an empty concept, for anything can be derived from a contradiction.

principle about to be invoked, imagining future cases and their proper resolution, determining whether those cases are different from the present one in any ways that the proposed principle itself says are relevant, and asking whether the principle yields the proper results.

There are two levels of problems with the idea that commitment to prospective neutral application constrains judicial choices. First, there are two features of our judicial institutions that dissipate any constraining force that the demand for prospective neutrality may impose. Second, there is a conceptual problem that robs the very idea of prospective neutrality of any normative force.

(a) Institutional Problems.—The first institutional problem is that Supreme Court decisions are made by a collective body, which is constrained by a norm of compromise and cooperation. Suppose that in case 1 Justices *M, N,* and *O* have taken neutral principles theory to heart and believe that the correct result is justified by principle *A.* Justices *P, Q, R,* and *S* have done likewise but believe that the same result is justified by principle *B.* Justices *T* and *V,* who also accept principle *A* but believe it inapplicable to case 1, dissent. The four-person group gains control of the writing of the opinion, and the three others who agree with the result accede to the institutional pressure for majority decisions and join an opinion that invokes principle *B.* Now case 2 arises. Justices *T* and *V* are convinced that, because case 2 is relevantly different from case 1, principle *A* should be used. They join with Justices *M, N,* and *O* and produce a majority opinion invoking principle *A.* If principle *B* were used, the result would be different; thus, there are four dissenters.

Kent Greenawalt has argued that neutral principles theory is required to acknowledge that neutrality sometimes must yield to other considerations, such as the institutional pressure for majority decisions.[78] If the norm of compromise is thought to authorize submersion of individual views in the selection of principles, we could not charge anyone with prospective nonneutrality in the handling of case 1. When case 2 subsequently arises, however, it would be odd—and ultimately destructive of the willingness to compromise—to demand that Justices *M, N,* and *O* follow principle *B* to a result that they, on principled grounds, believe wrong. But at the same time, to allow a judge criticized for nonneutrality to reply that in the particular situation neutrality had to yield to more pressing circumstances is to give the game of theory away. If we allow neutrality to yield to the institutional need here (a need that is quite weak—we all can live with fragmented Courts and decisions), a sufficiently pressing need will likely be available to justify virtually any deviation from neutrality.

A second institutional problem is that prospective neutrality involves unreasonable expectations concerning the capacities of judges.

78. Greenawalt, *The Enduring Significance of Neutral Principles,* 78 Colum.L. Rev. 982, 1007–08 (1978).

Every present case is connected to every conceivable future case, in the sense that a skilled lawyer can demonstrate how the earlier case's principles ought to affect (although perhaps not determine) the outcome in any later case. In these circumstances, neutral application means that each decision constrains a judge in every future decision; the import of the prospective approach is that, the first time a judge decides a case, he or she is to some extent committed to particular decisions for the rest of his or her career.

There are two difficulties here. First, even if we confine our attention to cases in the same general area as the present one, this formulation of the neutrality requirement is obviously too stringent. We cannot and should not expect judges to have fully elaborated theories of race discrimination in their first cases, much less theories of gender, illegitimacy, and other modes of discrimination as well. Second, to the extent that perceptions of connections vary with skill, the theory has the curious effect of constraining only the better judges. The less skilled judge will not think to test a principle developed in a race-discrimination case against gender-discrimination or abortion cases; a more skilled judge will.

Wechsler responded to these difficulties by relaxing the requirement: the judge must test the principle against "applications that are now foreseeable," and must either agree with the result in such applications or be able to specify a relevant difference between the cases.[83] But now the judge charged with nonneutrality will often be able to defend by saying that he or she simply had not foreseen the case at hand when the prior one was decided. That defense may lead us to conclude that the judge is not terribly competent, but it defeats the charge of nonneutrality.

(b) Conceptual Difficulty.—The third, largely conceptual difficulty with the theory of neutral principles was foreshadowed by the example of a case whose result could be justified by either of two principles. Neutral application requires that we be able to identify *the* principle that justified the result in case 1 in order to be sure that it is neutrally applied in case 2. This requirement, however, cannot be fulfilled, because there are always a number of justificatory principles available to make sense of case 1 and a number of techniques to select the "true" basis of case 1. Of course, the opinion in case 1 will articulate a principle that purports to support the result. But the thrust of introductory law courses is to show that the principles offered in opinions are never good enough. And this indefiniteness bedevils—and liberates—not only the commentators and the lawyers and judges subsequently dealing with the decision; it equally affects the author of the opinion.

---

83. Wechsler, *The Nature of Judicial Reasoning,* in Law and Philosophy 290, 298 (S. Hook ed. 1964).

* * * At the moment a decision is announced, we cannot identify the principle that it embodies. Even when we take account of the language of the opinion, each decision can be traced to many different possible principles, and we often learn the justifying principle of case 1 only when a court in case 2 states it * * *. The theory of neutral principles thus loses almost all of its constraining force when neutrality has a prospective meaning. What is left is something like a counsel to judges that they be sincere within the limits of their ability. But this formulation hardly provides a reassuring constraint on judicial willfulness.

2. Retrospective Application.—Although Wechsler framed the neutral principles theory in prospective terms, it might be saved by recasting it in retrospective terms. The theory would then impose as a necessary condition for justification the requirement that a decision be consistent with the relevant precedents.[98] This tack links the theory to general approaches to precedent-based judicial decisionmaking in non-constitutional areas. It also captures the natural way in which we raise questions about neutrality. The prospective theory requires that we pose hypothetical future cases, apply the principle, and ask whether the judges really meant to resolve the hypothetical cases as the principle seems to require. Because the hypothetical cases have not arisen, we cannot know the answer; we can do little more than raise our eyebrows, as Wechsler surely did, and emphasize the ''really'' as we ask the question in a skeptical tone.

In contrast, the retrospective theory encourages concrete criticism * * *. We need only compare case 2, which is now decided, with case 1 to see if a principle from case 1 has been neutrally applied in case 2. But if the retrospective demand is merely that the opinion in case 2 deploy some reading of the earlier case from which the holding in case 2 follows, the openness of the precedents means that the demand can always be satisfied. And if the demand is rather that the holding be derived from the principles actually articulated in the relevant precedents, differences between case 2 and the precedents will inevitably demand a degree of reinterpretation of the old principles. New cases always present issues different from those settled by prior cases. Thus, to decide a new case, a judge must take some liberties with the old principles, if they are to be applied at all. There is, however, no principled way to determine how many liberties can be taken; hence this second reading of the retrospective approach likewise provides no meaningful constraints.

The central problem here is that, given the difficulty of isolating a single principle for which a given precedent stands, we lack any criteria for distinguishing between cases that depart from and those that conform to the principles of their precedents. In fact, any case can

98. *But cf.* Wechsler, *supra* note 66, at 31 (stipulating that neutrality is not a matter of adhering to precedents).

compellingly be placed in either category. Although such a universal claim cannot be validated by example, examples can at least make the claim plausible. Therefore, the following paragraphs present several instances of cases that simultaneously depart from and conform to their precedents.

The first is *Griswold v. Connecticut,* in which the Supreme Court held that a state could not constitutionally prohibit the dissemination of contraceptive information or devices to married people.[100] *Griswold* relied in part on *Pierce v. Society of Sisters,*[101] which held unconstitutional a requirement that children attend public rather than private schools, and *Meyer v. Nebraska,*[102] which held that a state could not prohibit the teaching of foreign languages to young children. In *Griswold,* the Court said that these cases relied on a constitutionally protected interest, conveniently labeled "privacy," that was identical to the interest implicated in the contraceptive case.

On one view, *Griswold* tortures these precedents. Both were old-fashioned due process cases, which emphasized interference "with the calling of modern language teachers . . . and with the power of parents to control the education of their own." [103] On this view, the most one can fairly find in *Meyer* and *Pierce* is a principle about freedom of inquiry that is rather narrower than a principle of privacy. Yet of course one can say with equal force that *Griswold* identifies for us the true privacy principle of *Meyer* and *Pierce,* in the same way that the abortion funding cases identify the true principle of *Roe v. Wade.* * * * [T]he retrospective approach to neutral principles must recognize the extensive creativity exercised by a judge when he or she imputes to a precedent "the" principle that justifies both the precedent and the judge's present holding. [Other examples omitted—eds.]

3. The Craft Interpretation.—This critique of the retrospective-application interpretation points the way to a more refined version— what I will term the craft interpretation—of the calls of the neutral principles theorists for retrospective consistency. The failings of this final alternative bring out the underlying reasons that the demand for consistency cannot do the job expected of it.

The preceding discussion has reminded us that each decision re-works its precedents. A decision picks up some threads that received little emphasis before, and places great stress on them. It deprecates what seemed important before by emphasizing the factual setting of the precedents. The techniques are well known; indeed, learning them is at the core of a good legal education. But they are techniques. This recognition suggests that we attempt to define consistency as a matter of craft. When push comes to shove, in fact, adherents of neutral principles simply offer us lyrical descriptions of the sense of professionalism in lieu of sharper characterizations of the constraints on judges. Charles Black, for example, attempts to resolve the question whether

---

100. 381 U.S. 479 (1965).   **102.** 262 U.S. 390 (1923).
101. 268 U.S. 510 (1925).   **103.** *Id.* at 401.

law can rely on neutral principles by depicting "the art of law" living between the two poles of subjective preference and objective validation in much the same way that "the art of music has its life somewhere between traffic noise and a tuning fork—more disciplined by far than the one, with an unfathomably complex inner discipline of its own, far richer than the other, with inexhaustible variety of resource." [116] The difficulty then is to specify the limits to permissible craftiness. One limit may be that a judge cannot lie about the precedents—for example, by grossly mischaracterizing the facts. And Black adds that "decision [must] be taken in knowledge of and with consideration of certainly known facts of public life," such as the fact that segregation necessarily degrades blacks.[118] But these limits are clearly not terribly restrictive, and no one has suggested helpful others.

If the craft interpretation cannot specify limits to craftiness, another alternative is to identify some decisions that are within and some that are outside the limits in order to provide the basis for an inductive and intuitive generalization. As the following discussion indicates, however, it turns out that the limits of craft are so broad that in any interesting case any reasonably skilled lawyer can reach whatever result he or she wants. The craft interpretation thus fails to constrain the results that a reasonably skilled judge can reach, and leaves the judge free to enforce his or her personal values, as long as the opinions enforcing those values are well written. Such an outcome is inconsistent with the requirements of liberalism in that, once again, the demand for neutral principles fails in any appreciable way to limit the possibility of judicial tyranny.

The debate over the propriety of the result in *Roe v. Wade* [120] illustrates this problem. It seems to be generally agreed that, as a matter of simple craft, Justice Blackmun's opinion for the Court was dreadful.[121] The central issue before the Court was whether a pregnant woman had a constitutionally protected interest in terminating her pregnancy. When his opinion reached that issue, Justice Blackmun simply listed a number of cases in which "a right of personal privacy, or a guarantee of certain areas or zones of privacy," had been recognized. Then he said, "This right of privacy, whether it be founded in the Fourteenth Amendment's concept of personal liberty . . . or . . . in the Ninth Amendment's reservation of rights to the people, is broad enough to encompass a woman's decision whether or not to terminate

116. C. Black, Decision According to Law 81 (1981); *see also id.* at 21–24 (metaphorical evocation of delicate logic of law); *see* Sandalow, *Constitutional Interpretation,* 79 Mich.L.Rev. 1033 (1981) (tracing delicate balance between faithfulness to the constitutional text and accommodation to the needs of the time).

118. C. Black, *supra* note 116, at 82.

120. 410 U.S. 113 (1973).

121. *See, e.g.,* Ely, *The Wages of Crying Wolf: A Comment on* Roe v. Wade, 82 Yale L.J. 920 (1973); Epstein, *Substantive Due Process by Any Other Name: The Abortion Cases,* 1973 Sup.Ct.Rev. 159; Tribe, *The Supreme Court, 1972 Term—Foreword: Toward a Model of Roles in the Due Process of Life and Law,* 87 Harv.L.Rev. 1, 2–5 (1973).

her pregnancy."[122] And that was it. I will provisionally concede that this "argument" does not satisfy the requirements of the craft.

But the conclusion that we are to draw faces two challenges: it is either uninteresting or irrelevant to constitutional theory. Insofar as *Roe* gives us evidence, we can conclude that Justice Blackmun is a terrible judge. The point of constitutional theory, though, would seem to be to keep judges in line. If the result in *Roe* can be defended by judges more skilled than Justice Blackmun, the requirements of the craft would mean only that good judges can do things that bad judges cannot without subjecting themselves to professional criticism. For example, John Ely argues that, although *Roe* is beyond acceptable limits, *Griswold* is within them, though perhaps near the edge.[125] Justice Douglas' opinion for the Court in *Griswold* identified a number of constitutional provisions that in his view explicitly protected one or another aspect of personal privacy. The opinion then noted that the Court had in the past protected other interests closely related to those expressly protected. By arguing that those "penumbral" interests overlapped in the area of marital use of contraceptives, Justice Douglas could hold the challenged statute unconstitutional.

If *Griswold* is acceptable, we need only repeat its method in *Roe*. Indeed, Justice Douglas followed just that course in a brilliant concurring opinion.[126] And even if *Griswold*'s logic is rejected, skilled lawyers could still rewrite *Roe* to defend Justice Blackmun's outcome.[127] There is in fact a cottage industry of constitutional law scholars who concoct revised opinions for controversial decisions.[128] Thus, the craft interpretation of neutrality in application is ultimately uninteresting for reasons that we have already seen. At most it provides a standard to measure the competence of judges, a standard that by itself is insufficient to constrain adequately the risk of tyranny.

The other difficulty with the craft interpretation runs deeper. Craft limitations make sense only if we can agree what the craft is. But consider the craft of "writing novels." Its practice includes Trollope writing *The Eustace Diamonds,* Joyce writing *Finnegan's Wake,* and Mailer writing *The Executioner's Song.* We might think of Justice Blackmun's opinion in *Roe* as an innovation akin to Joyce's or Mailer's. It is the totally unreasoned judicial opinion. To say that it does not look like Justice Powell's decision in some other case is like saying that a Cubist "portrait" does not look like its subject as a member of the Academy would paint it. The observation is true, but irrelevant both to the enterprise in which the artist or judge was engaged and to our ultimate assessment of his product.

---

122. Roe v. Wade, 410 U.S. at 153.

125. Ely, *supra* note 121, at 929–30.

126. Roe v. Wade, 410 U.S. at 209 (Douglas, J., concurring).

127. *See, e.g.,* Regan, [*Rewriting* Roe v. Wade, 77 Mich.L.Rev. 1569 (1979).]

128. *See, e.g.,* Henkin, Shelley v. Kraemer: *Notes for a Revised Opinion,* 110 U.Pa.L.Rev. 473 (1962); Pollak, *Racial Discrimination and Judicial Integrity,* 108 U.Pa.L.Rev. 1 (1959).

C. Rules and Institutions

We can now survey our progress in the attempt to define "neutral principles." Each proposed definition left us with judges who could enforce their personal values unconstrained by the suggested version of the neutrality requirement. Some of the more sophisticated candidates, such as the craft interpretation, seemed plausible because they appealed to an intuitive sense that the institution of judging involves people who are guided by and committed to general rules applied consistently. But the very notions of generality and consistency can be specified only by reference to an established institutional setting. We can know what we mean by "acting consistently" only if we understand the institution of judging in our society. Thus, neutral principles theory proves unable to satisfy its demand for rule-guided judicial decisionmaking in a way that can constrain or define the judicial institution; in the final analysis, it is the institution—or our conception of it—that constrains the concept of rule-guidedness.

Consider the following multiple choice question: "Which pair of numbers comes next in the series 1, 3, 5, 7? (a) 9, 11; (b) 11, 13; (c) 25, 18." It is easy to show that any of the answers is correct. The first is correct if the rule generating the series is "list the odd numbers"; the second is correct if the rule is "list the odd prime numbers"; and the third is correct if a more complex rule generates the series.[131] Thus, if asked to follow the underlying rule—the "principle" of the series—we can justify a tremendous range of divergent answers by constructing the rule so that it generates the answer that we want. As the legal realists showed, this result obtains for legal as well as mathematical rules.[132] The situation in law might be thought to differ, because judges try to articulate the rules they use. But even when an earlier case identifies the rule that it invokes, only a vision of the contours of the judicial role constrains judges' understanding of what counts as applying the rule. Without such a vision, there will always be a diversity of subsequent uses of the rule that could fairly be called consistent applications of it.

There is, however, something askew in this anarchic conclusion. After all, we know that no test maker would accept (c) as an answer to the mathematical problem; and indeed we can be fairly confident that test makers would not include both (a) and (b) as possible answers, because the underlying rules that generate them are so obvious that they make the question fatally ambiguous. Another example may sharpen the point. The examination for those seeking driver's licenses in the District of Columbia includes this question: "What is responsible

---

131. One possible rule is the following: $f(1) = 1$; for n greater than 1, if n is divisible by 5, $f(n) = n^2$; if $(n - 1)$ is divisible by 5, $f(n) = f(n - 1) - f(n - 2)$; if neither n nor $(n - 1)$ is divisible by 5, $f(n) = 2n - 1$.

132. Although I believe that the realists demonstrated this point, I acknowledge that most of them refused to press their arguments all the way to the conclusion drawn in the text. For overviews of the realist movement, see E. Purcell, The Crisis of Democratic Theory 74–94, 159–78 (1973); W. Rumble, American Legal Realism (1968).

for most automobile accidents?   (a) The car; (b) the driver; (c) road conditions."   Anyone who does not know immediately that the answer is (b) does not understand what the testing enterprise is all about.

In these examples, we know something about the rule to follow only because we are familiar with the social practices of intelligence testing and drivers' education.   That is, the answer does not follow from a rule that can be uniquely identified without specifying something about the substantive practices.   Similarly, although we can, as I have argued elsewhere, use standard techniques of legal argument to draw from the decided cases the conclusion that the Constitution requires socialism,[134] we know that no judge will in the near future draw that conclusion.   But the failure to reach that result is not ensured because the practice of "following rules" or neutral application of the principles inherent in the decided cases precludes a judge from doing so.   Rather, it is ensured because judges in contemporary America are selected in a way that keeps them from thinking that such arguments make sense.   This branch of the argument thus makes a sociological point about neutral principles.   Neither the principles nor any reconstructed version of a theory that takes following rules as its focus can be neutral in the sense that liberalism requires, because taken by itself, an injunction to follow the rules tells us nothing of substance.   If such a theory constrains judges, it does so only because judges, before they turn to the task of finding neutral principles for the case at hand, have implicitly accepted some image of what their role in shaping and applying rules in controverted cases ought to be.

There is something both odd and important here.   The theory of neutral principles is initially attractive because it affirms the openness of the courts to all reasonable arguments drawn from decided cases. But if the courts are indeed open to such arguments, the theory allows judges to do whatever they want.   If it is only in consequence of the pressures exerted by a highly developed, deeply entrenched, homeostatic social structure that judges seem to eschew conclusions grossly at odds with the values of liberal capitalism, sociological analysis ought to destroy the attraction of neutral principles theory.   Principles are "neutral" only in the sense that they are, as a matter of contingent fact, unchallenged, and the contingencies have obvious historical limits.

At the same time, however, the theory shows us an institution at the heart of liberalism that contains the potential for destroying liberalism by revealing the institution's inconsistencies and its dialectical instability.   The neutral rule of law was Locke's solution to the Hobbesian problem of order.   But the rule of law requires that preexisting rules be followed.   If we accept substantive limitations on the rules that courts can adopt, we abandon the notion of rule-following as a neutral enterprise with no social content; yet if we truly allow all reasonable arguments to be made and possibly accepted, we abandon

134. Tushnet, Book Review, 78 Mich.L.
Rev. 694, 696–98 (1980).

the notion of rule-following entirely, and with it we abandon the ideal of the rule of law. What is odd is that liberalism has generated an institution that reveals these irresolvable tensions.

E. BALANCING

T. ALEXANDER ALEINIKOFF, CONSTITUTIONAL LAW IN THE AGE OF BALANCING

96 Yale L.J. 943, 945–46, 972–92 (1987).

I. THE DEFINITION AND FORMS OF BALANCING

A. Definition

The metaphor of balancing refers to theories of constitutional interpretation that are based on the identification, valuation, and comparison of competing interests. By a "balancing opinion," I mean a judicial opinion that analyzes a constitutional question by identifying interests implicated by the case and reaches a decision or constructs a rule of constitutional law by explicitly or implicitly assigning values to the identified interests. * * * [T]his definition captures most of the work that the Supreme Court does under the name of balancing.

Some commentators see balancing as any method of resolving conflicts among values.[7] * * * [But] choices may be made among values in ways that are not based on an assessment of the "weights" of the values at stake. Similarly, balancing, as I define it, differs from methods of adjudication that look at a variety of factors in reaching a decision. These would include some of the familiar multi-pronged tests[8] and "totality of the circumstances" approaches.[9] These standards ask questions about how one ought to characterize particular events. Was the confession voluntary or involuntary? Did the government action constitute a "taking"? In answering such questions, one starts with some conception of what constitutes voluntariness and involuntariness and then asks whether the particular situation shares more of the voluntary elements or the involuntary elements. Or one begins with a checklist of factors that have been used in the past to determine whether a "taking" has occurred. The reasoning is thus primarily analogical. Balancing represents a different kind of thinking. The focus is directly on the interests or factors themselves. Each interest seeks recognition on its own and forces a head-to-head comparison with competing interests.

7. See, e.g., Shiffrin, [The First Amendment and Economic Regulation: Away from a General Theory of the First Amendment, 78 Nw.U.L.Rev. 1212, 1249 (1983).] ("[B]alancing is nothing more than a metaphor for the accommodation of values.").

8. See, e.g., Lemon v. Kurtzman, 403 U.S. 602 (1971). See generally Nagel, The Formulaic Constitution, 84 Mich.L.Rev. 165 (1985) (examining constitutional formulas).

9. See, e.g., Connolly v. Pension Benefit Guar. Corp., 106 S.Ct. 1018, 1026 (1986) (takings claim); Cleavinger v. Saxner, 106 S.Ct. 496, 501 (1985) (immunity from suit); Illinois v. Gates, 462 U.S. 213, 230–31 (1983) (probable cause under Fourth Amendment).

B. Metaphorical Forms

The balancing metaphor takes two distinct forms. Sometimes the Court talks about one interest *outweighing* another. Under this view, the Court places the interests on a set of scales and rules the way the scales tip. For example, in *New York v. Ferber,*[10] the Court upheld a statute criminalizing the distribution of child pornography because "the evil . . . restricted [by the statute] so overwhelmingly outweighs the expressive interests, if any, at stake."[11] Constitutional standards requiring "compelling" or "important" state interests also exemplify this form of the balancing metaphor.[12]

The Court employs a different version of balancing when it speaks of "striking a balance" between or among competing interests. The image is one of balanced scales with constitutional doctrine calibrated according to the relative weights of the interests. One interest does not override another; each survives and is given its due. Thus, in *Tennessee v. Garner,*[13] which considered the constitutionality of a state statute permitting the use of deadly force against fleeing felons, the Court ruled neither that the state interest in preventing the escape of criminals outweighed an individual's interest in life nor that the individual's interest outweighed the state's. The "balancing process"[14] recognized both interests: The Court ruled that an officer may not use deadly force unless such force is necessary to prevent escape and the officer has probable cause to believe that the suspect poses a threat of serious physical harm.[15] What unites these two types of balancing—and the reason they will be considered together—is their shared conception of constitutional law as a battleground of competing interests and their claimed ability to identify and place a value on those interests.

* * *

IV. AN INTERNAL CRITIQUE OF BALANCING

Despite the widespread use of balancing, the Supreme Court has spent surprisingly little time exploring the difficult analytic and operational problems the method presents. The following sections highlight a number of these issues. The first set of problems takes the balancing metaphor seriously and examines how interests are identified, valued and compared. The second set of problems raises the question of whether balancing—even if adequately performed—is a justifiable or sensible method of constitutional interpretation.

A. The Problem of Evaluation and Comparison

A frequent criticism of balancing is that the Court has no objective criteria for valuing or comparing the interests at stake. As Laurent

10. 458 U.S. 747 (1982).

11. *Id.* at 763–64.

12. *See, e.g.,* Trimble v. Gordon, 430 U.S. 762 (1977); Craig v. Boren, 429 U.S. 190 (1976).

13. 471 U.S. 1 (1985).

14. *Id.* at 9.

15. *Id.* at 11.

Frantz has nicely put it, the judge's task is to "measur[e] the un-measurable . . . [and] compare the incomparable." [189]

* * *

Competing interests are not, by definition, incomparable. Apples and oranges can be placed on a fruit scale or assigned a price in dollars per pound. The problem for constitutional balancing is the derivation of the scale needed to translate the value of interests into a common currency for comparison. The balancer's scale cannot simply represent the personal preferences of the balancer, lest constitutional law become the arbitrary act of will today characterized as "lochnering." Moreover, a personal scale would undermine a system of precedent and provide little guidance to lower courts, legislators, administrators, and lawyers and clients.

* * *

In the search for an external scale—for weights "out there"—the modern Court has relied upon several sources that seem sensible. It may turn to history [196] or search for a current "social consensus" [197] on the importance of an interest. Interests may also be assigned weight based on their contribution to the achievement of constitutional or non-constitutional goals. This instrumental valuation (often expressed in quasi-empirical terms) is evident in dormant commerce clause opinions (measuring, for example, the burden a state's regulation places on interstate commerce and the safety benefits afforded by the regulation),[198] First Amendment libel cases (evaluating the impact on the news media occasioned by various sets of liability rules),[199] procedural due process cases (examining the financial burden that procedural requirements would impose on the government),[200] and exclusionary rule cases (considering the benefit of deterring unlawful police conduct against the cost of excluding probative evidence).[201] Sometimes the Court looks at actual numbers, but frequently it adopts a seat-of-the-pants approach, freely speculating on the real world consequences of particular rules.[202]

189. Frantz, [*Is the First Amendment Law? A Reply to Professor Mendelson*, 51 Calif.L.Rev. 729, 748 (1963).]

196. *Compare* Zablocki v. Redhail, 434 U.S. 374, 383–86 (1978) (right to marriage deeply rooted in our society) *with* Bowers v. Hardwick, 106 S.Ct. 2841, 2844–46 (1986) (right to homosexual relations never recognized by society).

197. *See, e.g.,* Hudson v. Palmer, 468 U.S. 517, 528 (1984) ("[S]ociety would insist that [privacy interests] always yield to . . . the paramount interest in institutional security.").

198. *See, e.g.,* Kassel v. Consolidated Freightways Corp., 450 U.S. 662, 670 (1981) (plurality opinion).

199. *See, e.g.,* Dun & Bradstreet, Inc. v. Greenmoss Builders, Inc., 472 U.S. 749 (1985); Gertz v. Robert Welch, Inc., 418 U.S. 323, 343–48 (1974).

200. *See, e.g.,* Lassiter v. Department of Social Servs., 452 U.S. 18 (1981); Mathews v. Eldridge, 424 U.S. 319, 334–35 (1976).

201. *See, e.g.,* INS v. Lopez–Mendoza, 468 U.S. 1032, 1041–50 (1984); United States v. Leon, 468 U.S. 897, 915–22 (1984); United States v. Janis, 428 U.S. 433, 447–60 (1976).

202. *See, e.g.,* Plyler v. Doe, 457 U.S. 202, 230 (1982) (speculating on how class of illiterate illegal aliens would affect unemployment, welfare, and crime).

Whether or not these potentially conflicting sources of value are defensible (and no balancer has developed a theory explaining which should prevail and why), they do not solve the "external scale" problem unless the same scale is applied to all the interests at stake in the case. It is here that the "apples and oranges" critique has real bite. We may know with a fair degree of certainty that society places a high value on procedural fairness in the deprivation of property and that the cost of providing welfare recipients pre-termination hearings is (let's say) $500 per case. But what follows? Nothing in the "external" sources offers a clue about how to compare differently derived values.

* * *

B. The Problem of a Universe of Interests

* * *

While, in theory, balancing takes an expansive view of what should count as a constitutional interest, in practice, the Court never makes a full inventory of the relevant interests. In *Goldberg v. Kelly*,[219] for example, the Court did not consider a huge range of interests that ought to bear on the question of whether there should be a hearing before welfare benefits are terminated. These might include broader societal notions of fairness; the willingness of society to continue funding the welfare program and other entitlement programs; the ripple effect of wrongful terminations on poor communities, housing stock and crime rates; the morale of the welfare bureaucracy and its views of its clients; the weakening or strengthening of political groups pressing for welfare reform. The Court no doubt recognized that including these considerations would have turned the opinion into a monograph on the welfare system. But on what basis (other than convenience) does the Court restrict its balance to just a few of the relevant interests? The point may be generalized. Taking balancing seriously would seem to demand the kind of investigation of the world that courts are unable or unwilling to undertake.

C. The Problem of Cumulation

Even if a balancer has properly identified the relevant interests and has an objective scale for their valuation, there is still the problem of *which* holders of the relevant interests should be counted. * * * [C]onsider *Youngberg v. Romeo*,[220] the case involving treatment of a mentally retarded person involuntarily committed to a state hospital. There the Court purported to weigh the individual's interest in safety and freedom from restraint against the hospital's interest in confining his movements.[221]

* * *

* * * [But] the Court did not survey other institutions in the state or around the country. It did not estimate whether the conditions

---

219. 397 U.S. 254 (1970).

220. 457 U.S. 307 (1982).

221. *Id.* at 320–21. The Court never defines the state interests, although it does

give the example of protecting patients from violence. *Id.* at 320.

in the defendant hospital were typical or whether the cost of fewer restrictions would be less burdensome in other institutions. It did not "sum up" the individual weights of all Romeos or ask whether other similarly situated persons might have greater or lesser interests in freedom from restraint. Romeo stood for all patients and Pennhurst State Hospital for all institutions.

This problem is endemic to the balancing methodology; the alternative is an unwieldy litigation process in which the trial court would have to make a complete survey of similar institutions. Every case would demand Brandeis briefs of extraordinary complexity, and the costs of constitutional litigation would skyrocket. It is no wonder that the Justices are content to see Romeo as "all patients." However, in making balancing work, the Court has adopted a truncated form that ought not to be acceptable to the conscientious balancer.

* * *

E.   The Problem of the Individual/State Dichotomy

Balancing opinions typically pit individual against governmental interests. This characterization, however, is arbitrary. Interests may be conceived of in both public and private terms. The *individual* interest in communicating one's ideas to others may also be stated as a *societal* interest in a diverse marketplace of ideas. Time, place, and manner limitations on expressive behavior may be based on a *governmental* interest in public safety or a *private* interest in unencumbered access to public facilities.

Consider *Hudson v. Palmer*,[232] in which the Court described a search of a prisoner's cell as posing a conflict between the prisoner's Fourth Amendment interest in privacy and the government's interest in jail security. In that case, the prisoner's interest could also have been stated as a public interest. Society has a general interest in preventing unwarranted governmental intrusions. Extending the Fourth Amendment's protection of privacy in one context may contribute to, and reinforce, a social sense of personal freedom and liberty. As a collective body, we are in the cell with Palmer; the interests at stake are not his alone. Similarly, the government's interest in prison security may also be stated as a private interest. Both prisoners and guards have an individualized interest in being free from assaults and in having a governmental authority protect them. Because public and private interests appear on both sides, there is little sense in seeing the balance in terms of individual versus governmental interests.

To answer these problems, Roscoe Pound recommended that interests be compared "on the same plane,"[234] and occasionally the Court does so. But this "solution" reintroduces the incompleteness objection discussed above. In *Hudson v. Palmer,* one *could* state the conflict as the social interest in freedom from unreasonable searches versus the

232.   468 U.S. 517 (1985).   **234.**   Pound, [*A Survey of Social Interests,* 57 Harv.L.Rev. 1, 2 (1943).]

social interest in prison security. But this eliminates from the balance the very real private interests at stake.

* * *

V. THE EXTERNAL CRITIQUE OF BALANCING

Perhaps a Hercules of a judge (or a well-programmed computer) could balance in a manner that overcomes the preceding "internal" critique. But balancing also implicates deeper questions about the role of the Court and the nature of judicial review. This section links these concerns with the earlier discussion to argue that balancing builds upon, and fosters, an inappropriate conception of constitutional law.

A. The Role of the Court

A common objection to balancing as a method of constitutional adjudication is that it appears to replicate the job that a democratic society demands of its legislature. The legislative aspect of balancing has become quite pronounced in a number of recent opinions that have openly explored the "costs" and "benefits" of constitutional rules and appealed to empirical evidence of the effect of constitutional doctrine on societal interests. Such a methodology may be an appropriate model for common law adjudication. But balancing needs to be defended in constitutional interpretation where the decision of a court supplants a legislative decision.

What defense might be offered for an understanding of the role of the Court as replicating the legislative task? Some may view judicial balancing as a way to catch errors in the legislative calculations. Just as we do sums twice to check our addition, so we might want to rebalance interests through judicial review. But normally when our second sum is not the same as the first, we add again. Thus this defense must develop a theory that explains why we always accept the judiciary's calculation. Moreover, the structure established by the Constitution explicitly provides for an "addition-checker" in the form of bicameralism.

A better argument for the balancer is that the Court improves the balancing process by giving weight to interests that the legislature tends to ignore or undervalue. Under this view, the Court plays two important roles. First, it reinforces representation, ensuring that the interests of unpopular or underrepresented groups are counted and counted fairly. Second, it protects constitutional rights and interests that are sometimes forgotten in the hurly-burly of politics.

Both of these "thumb-on-the-scales" claims are plausible. Legislators may have difficulty crediting the interests of minority groups to which they do not belong. We might also be justifiably suspicious of the legislature's evaluation of constitutional interests that conflict with popular governmental conduct. Thus the balancer may claim that her form of constitutional interpretation provides a procedural and a substantive justification for judicial review.

While these arguments may point to troubling flaws in the legislative process, they do not alone establish a justification for the judiciary's performance of the legislative task. The argument from undervalued interests might support a model of judicial review analogous to court review of administrative decisions: If a court determines that an agency has ignored or misevaluated relevant interests, it may order the agency to go through the decisionmaking process again. Similarly, a conclusion that the legislature has wrongfully ignored certain interests might justify judicial review in the form of a "suspensive veto" [247] and a "remand." [248] But it does not warrant an evaluation and balancing of the interests by the court. Once the legislature has openly considered the values that the court tells it are at stake, what grounds are there for preferring a court's subsequent determination of the balance?

A balancer might respond that it is improper to portray judicial balancing as duplicating legislative balancing. According to this view, a balancing approach attempts not to maximize social welfare or represent voters. Its primary focus is the Constitution. It simply insists that the Constitution not be interpreted in a vacuum and that courts be aware of the social context and impact of constitutional doctrine. The court that balances, the argument might run, is really searching for a reasonable understanding of the Constitution—one that harmonizes constitutional provisions and values with important governmental interests. The balancing court does not *replicate* the legislative function or *supplant* legislative judgments of good social policy. It *uses* the legislative act as a measure of social importance and thus as a basis for calculating the degree to which the constitutional interest should be "softened." [249]

I think that this is the balancer's best case, and it does indeed supply a role for the court distinct from those of the other branches of government. The judicial role might be described as: Protect and preserve all constitutional interests, taking into account the value that the other branches place on achieving other legitimate ends. But this description raises a deep, and generally unaddressed, problem. Even if the balancing court purports to accept the value that the legislature places on its own output, it cannot simply factor the legislature's determination into a constitutional calculus. It must first convert the constitutional value and the legislative value into a common currency. How does a court decide how "important" a legislative or administrative policy is? For example, why are a "city's aesthetic interests" sufficiently "substantial" to sustain a city ordinance prohibiting political posters on utility poles,[250] but "administrative convenience" not an

---

247. *See* Sandalow, [*Judicial Protection of Minorities,* 75 Mich.L.Rev. 1162, 1183–93 (1977).]

248. *See* G. Calabresi, A Common Law for the Age of Statutes 17 (1982); Bickel & Wellington, *Legislative Purpose and the Judicial Process: The* Lincoln Mills *Case,* 71 Harv.L.Rev. 1, 14–35 (1957).

249. *See* C. Ducat, Modes of Constitutional Interpretation 133–34 (1978) (contrasting legislative and judicial balancing).

250. Members of the City Council v. Taxpayers for Vincent, 466 U.S. 789 (1984).

adequate justification for requiring servicewomen (but not servicemen) to prove the dependency of their spouses to receive housing allowances? [251]   At work here is some undisclosed scale of social value, one not obviously derived from the Constitution.   Balancers must defend this inevitable aspect of balancing. They must suggest reasons why judgments assigning a social value to legislation are within the province and capacity of the courts.

B.   The Conception of Constitutional Law

For the balancer, constitutional law is comprised of principles discovered by weighing interests relevant to resolution of a particular constitutional problem.   These interests may be traceable to the Constitution itself (free speech, federal regulation of commerce) or discoverable elsewhere (clean streets, law enforcement).   Some interests are accorded great weight because society generally recognizes their importance, others because they are located in the Constitution.   Indeed, one may understand the Constitution, from the balancer's point of view, as a document intended to ensure that judges (among others) treat particular interests with respect.   It is an honor roll of interests.

Although this conception of law may have brought realism to the common law, it threatens to do real damage to constitutional law. Early critics of balancing were largely concerned about the impact of the methodology on the protection of constitutional rights.   And, as Ronald Dworkin has tirelessly argued, viewing constitutional rights simply as "interests" that may be overcome by other non-constitutional interests does not accord with common understandings of the meaning of a "right." [253]

But the implications of balancing for constitutional law go far beyond strategic discussions about the best way to protect constitutional rights. (In fact, since the original critiques, balancing has proven to be a robust methodology for the creation and extension of rights). Balancing is undermining our usual understanding of constitutional law as an interpretive enterprise.   In so doing, it is transforming constitutional discourse into a general discussion of the reasonableness of governmental conduct.

One can see this trend most clearly in opinions that define or describe a constitutional right and then weigh the right against competing state interests.   Here, balancing appears as an extra step in constitutional interpretation.   Once a court has done the hard work of explicating a constitutional provision through the usual methods of textual, precedential, and consequentialist reasoning, the result is subjected to another test—the weight of competing interests.

* * *

Not all balancing opinions add the balance at the end. Many view the underlying constitutional principle itself in balancing terms.   Thus,

251. Frontiero v. Richardson, 411 U.S. 677 (1973) (plurality opinion).

253. See R. Dworkin, Taking Rights Seriously 194, 269 (1977) * * *.

in procedural due process cases, the constitutional requirement is determined by comparing the weights of three interests.[262]   Here the problem is that balancing does not require the Court to develop and defend a theoretical understanding of a constitutional provision.   Under a balancing approach, the Court searches the landscape for interests implicated by the case, identifies a few, and reaches a reasonable accommodation among them.   In so doing, the Court largely ignores the usual stuff of constitutional interpretation—the investigation and manipulation of texts (such as constitutional language, prior cases, even—perhaps—our "ethical tradition").   Balancing at its bleakest, to use Justice Brennan's phrase, is "doctrinally destructive nihilism." [264]

This revolt against theory is most troubling in cases that balance constitutional and non-constitutional interests.   In these cases, the Constitution is viewed as a broom closet in which constitutional interests are stored and taken out when appropriate to be considered with other social values.   Because the weight of the constitutional interest is usually assumed to be substantial, most of the Court's attention is focused on the competing state interests: How strong are they?   Can they be achieved with less of an impact on the constitutional interest?   In a curious way, constitutional law goes on *next to* the Constitution.

* * *

Does this transformation of constitutional law matter?   Some might argue that balancing has made constitutional law more reasonable and accessible.   But I believe that the transformation has important and troubling consequences.   Constitutional law provides a set of peremptory norms—a checking power—that is basic to the American notion of a government of limited powers.   Equally important, although less frequently noted, is constitutional law's validating function.   As Charles Black noted long ago, "one indispensable ingredient in the original and continuing legitimation of a government must be its possession and use of some means for bringing about a consensus on the legitimacy of important governmental measures." [271]   Constitutional cases provide a forum for the affirmation of background principles and for ratification of changes in those principles—changes the amendment process could only sporadically produce.

Balancing undermines the checking and validating functions of constitutional law.   This is most apparent in opinions that adopt a legislative voice, openly weighing costs and benefits in order to maximize social welfare.   If constitutional decisions and normal political decisions examine similar variables in similar ways, then constitutional answers ought not to "trump" non-constitutional answers; the constitutional process simply serves as an arithmetic "check" on the non-constitutional process.   Nor can constitutional law perform its validation function if constitutional judgment is reached in the same manner

---

262. Mathews v. Eldridge, 424 U.S. 319, 335 (1976).

264. New Jersey v. T.L.O., 469 U.S. 325, 369 (1985).

271. C. Black, The People and the Court 38 (1960).

as the legislative judgment.   The Court's agreement might only show that the Court and the legislature used the same calculator.   These concerns are not alleviated even under the best account of balancing offered above (that a court does not replicate the legislative task but simply accommodates constitutional values with other social interests). That account supplies no basis for the authority or ability of a court to assign a value to the legislative output.

Claims that an interpretive strategy threatens the legitimacy of constitutional review are easy to make but hard to prove.   More easily seen is the devastating impact that balancing has had on constitutional theory.   Balancing opinions give one the eerie sense that constitutional law as a distinct form of discourse is slipping away.   The balancing drum beats the rhythm of reasonableness, and we march to it because the cadence seems so familiar, so sensible.   But our eyes are no longer focused on the Constitution.   If each constitutional provision, every constitutional value, is understood simply as an invitation for a discussion of good social policy, it means little to talk of constitutional "theory."

Ultimately, the notion of constitutional supremacy hangs in the balance.   For under a regime of balancing, a constitutional judgment no longer looks like a trump.   It seems merely to be a card of a higher value in the same suit.

BIBLIOGRAPHY

Interpreting the Constitution: General

Bandes, *The Negative Constitution: A Critique,* 88 Mich.L.Rev. 2271 (1990).

Bennett, *Objectivity in Constitutional Law,* 132 U.Pa.L.Rev. 445 (1984).

C. Black, STRUCTURE AND RELATIONSHIP IN CONSTITUTIONAL LAW (1969).

P. Bobbitt, CONSTITUTIONAL FATE (1982).

Bork, *Styles in Constitutional Theory,* 26 S.Tex.L.J. 383 (1985).

E. Chemerinsky, INTERPRETING THE CONSTITUTION (1987).

Dworkin, *Hard Cases,* 88 Harv.L.Rev. 1057 (1957), reprinted in TAKING RIGHTS SERIOUSLY 81 (1978).

Dworkin, *The Jurisprudence of Richard Nixon,* New York Rev.Books, May 4, 1972, at 17, reprinted as Constitutional Cases, in TAKING RIGHTS SERIOUSLY 131 (1978).

Ely, DEMOCRACY AND DISTRUST: A THEORY OF JUDICIAL REVIEW (1980).

Fallon, *A Constructivist Coherence Theory of Constitutional Interpretation,* 100 Harv.L.Rev. 1189 (1987).

Fletcher, *Principlist Models in the Analysis of Constitutional and Statutory Texts,* 72 Iowa L.Rev. 891 (1987).

Greenawalt, *The Enduring Significance of Neutral Principles*, 78 Colum.L.Rev. 982 (1978).

Komesar, *Back to the Future—An Institutional View of Making and Interpreting Constitutions*, 81 Nw.U.L.Rev. 191 (1987).

Komesar, *Taking Institutions Seriously: Introduction to a Strategy for Constitutional Analysis*, 51 U.Chi.L.Rev. 366 (1984).

Lipkin, *Conventionalism, Pragmatism, and Constitutional Revolutions*, 21 U.C.Davis L.Rev. 645 (1988).

Michelman, *The Supreme Court, 1985 Term—Foreword: Traces of Self-Government*, 100 Harv.L.Rev. 4 (1986).

Munzer & Nickel, *Does the Constitution Mean What It Always Meant?*, 77 Colum.L.Rev. 1029 (1977).

Nagel, *The Formulaic Constitution*, 84 Mich.L.Rev. 165 (1985).

Post, *Theories of Constitutional Interpretation*, 30 Representations 13 (Spring 1990).

D. Richards, TOLERATION AND THE CONSTITUTION (1986).

Sager, *Review Essay: What's A Nice Court Like You Doing in a Democracy Like This?* [reviewing M. Perry, THE CONSTITUTION, THE COURTS, AND HUMAN RIGHTS], 36 Stan.L.Rev. 1087 (1984).

Sandalow, *Constitutional Interpretation*, 79 Mich.L.Rev. 1033 (1981).

Schauer, *An Essay on Constitutional Language*, 29 U.C.L.A.L.Rev. 797 (1982).

Symposium, *Interpretation*, 58 S.Cal.L.Rev. (1985).

Symposium, 6 Const.Comm. 19 (1989).

Wellington, *Common Law Rules and Constitutional Double Standards: Some Notes on Adjudication*, 83 Yale L.J. 221 (1973).

West, *Progressive and Conservative Constitutionalism*, 88 Mich.L.Rev. 641 (1990).

The Original Intent Debate

Alfange, *On Judicial Policymaking and Constitutional Change: Another Look at the "Original Intent" Theory of Constitutional Interpretation*, 5 Hastings Const.L.Q. 603 (1978).

R. Berger, GOVERNMENT BY JUDICIARY (1977).

Berger, *New Theories of "Interpretation": The Activist Flight from the Constitution*, 47 Ohio St.L.J. 1 (1986).

Dworkin, *The Forum of Principle*, 56 N.Y.U.L.Rev. 469 (1981).

Farber, *The Originalism Debate: A Guide for the Perplexed*, 49 Ohio St. L.J. 1085 (1989).

Maltz, *Some New Thoughts on an Old Problem—The Role of the Intent of the Framers in Constitutional Theory*, 63 B.U.L.Rev. 811 (1983).

Monaghan, *Our Perfect Constitution*, 56 N.Y.U.L.Rev. 353 (1981).

Nelson, *History and Neutrality in Constitutional Adjudication,* 72 Va.L. Rev. 1237 (1986).

Powell, *The Original Understanding of Original Intent,* 98 Harv.L.Rev. 885 (1985).

Powell, *Rules for Originalists,* 73 Va.L.Rev. 659 (1987).

Rotunda, *Original Intent, the View of the Framers, and the Role of the Ratifiers,* 41 Vand.L.Rev. 507 (1988).

Simon, *The Authority of the Framers of the Constitution: Can Originalist Interpretation Be Justified?,* 73 Calif.L.Rev. 1482 (1985).

Solum, *Originalism as Transformative Politics,* 63 Tulane L.Rev. 1599 (1989).

The Non–Interpretivism/Interpretivism Debate

Brest, *The Fundamental Rights Controversy: The Essential Contradictions of Normative Constitutional Scholarship,* 90 Yale L.J. 1063 (1981).

Corwin, *The "Higher Law" Background of American Constitutional Law,* 42 Harv.L.Rev. 149, 365 (1928–29).

Grano, *Judicial Review and a Written Constitution in a Democratic Society,* 28 Wayne L.Rev. 1 (1981).

Grey, *Origins of the Unwritten Constitution: Fundamental Law in American Revolutionary Thought,* 30 Stan.L.Rev. 843 (1978).

MacArthur, *Abandoning the Constitution: The New Wave in Constitutional Theory,* 59 Tul.L.Rev. 280 (1984).

Nichol, *Children of Distant Fathers: Sketching an Ethos of Constitutional Liberty,* 1985 Wis.L.Rev. 1305.

M. Perry, THE CONSTITUTION, THE COURTS, AND HUMAN RIGHTS (1982).

Rehnquist, *The Notion of a Living Constitution,* 54 Tex.L.Rev. 693 (1976).

Richards, *Human Rights as the Unwritten Constitution: The Problem of Change and Stability in Constitutional Interpretation,* 4 U.Dayton L.Rev. 295 (1979).

Sherry, *The Founders' Unwritten Constitution,* 54 U.Chi.L.Rev. 1127 (1987).

Symposium—*Judicial Review and the Constitution—The Text and Beyond [marking the publication of M. Perry,* THE CONSTITUTION, THE COURTS, AND HUMAN RIGHTS], 4 U.Dayton L.Rev. 443–831 (1983).

Chapter III

FEDERALISM

Students of constitutional law look at federalism through a different lens than political scientists and politicians do. The latter ask what is wise and prudent in the allocation of lawmaking, enforcement, and interpretive authority between national and state governments. The former ask only what is permitted and what forbidden. Many of these constitutional questions are less important today than they once were, because the limits on permissible federal action have receded almost out of view. The readings in this Chapter are devoted to two areas where controversy is still lively. The first concerns permitted federal action. The question here is whether there are limits to national power when it is aimed at state governments themselves, rather than at private actors. The second concerns forbidden state action. Here the question is what lawmaking authority the Constitution takes away from the states—an issue most extravagantly litigated in connection with the Commerce Clause.

A. NATIONAL POWER: REGULATION OF STATE GOVERNMENTS

The character of federal-state relations has changed greatly since the New Deal. The proximate cause of the change has been the vast increase in regulation and spending by the federal government. It is sometimes assumed that this growth has been accompanied by a corresponding diminution in the power of state governments, as though lawmaking were a zero-sum game in which losses must always offset gains. This is not so. State and local governments too have grown enormously in absolute terms, in response to the same social and economic conditions that the federal government has tried to deal with.

But there has been a change in the locus of initiative, funding, and control of the business of government. Congress (and federal agencies) can now act whenever it is convenient to do so, and use the federal income tax to pay the bills. This authority, coupled with the Supremacy Clause, means that much of the legislative agenda is written in Washington rather than the state capitals. State governments are

114

then asked to administer federal benefit programs (for education, welfare, health, small business), carry out federal regulation of private conduct (the environment), and comply with federal standards in their own behavior (wages, hours, safety, nondiscrimination). We can no longer think of our political system as a 'dual federalism,' with exclusive authority over particular subjects allocated to different levels of government. The appropriate metaphor is not a layer cake but a marble cake.[1]

This arrangement is still controversial. It is one thing for the federal government to preempt state law in the regulation of private conduct. It may be another for the federal government to control state governments themselves. Some fear that the assimilation of states into a predominantly federal confection will undermine important values traditionally associated with state sovereignty. These concerns have inevitably been brought to the courts. The states' role in executing federal benefit programs was reviewed in *Steward Machine Co. v. Davis*[2] and *South Dakota v. Dole*.[3] Their role in carrying out federal regulation of private conduct was an issue in *FERC v. Mississippi*[4] and *Hodel v. Virginia Surface Mining & Reclamation Ass'n*.[5] Their duty to comply with federal standards in their own behavior was denied in *National League of Cities v. Usery*[6] and then upheld in *Garcia v. San Antonio Metropolitan Transit Authority*.[7] Each case asked whether there was some limit to Congress's authority to enlist (conscript?) state governments to carry out its own projects. That question in turn requires thought about a more fundamental one: what functions are served by a federal system and threatened by these uses of national power?

The readings in this Section explore these issues from several angles. Herbert Wechsler's influential article on *The Political Safeguards of Federalism*, written in the 1950's, contends that the fear of state assimilation is unfounded because of the role the states play in the composition and selection of the central government. Jesse Choper carries this a step further. He argues that political safeguards are the *only* defense we should rely on to protect state sovereignty. Judicial review of such issues is unnecessary, and depletes the store of good will that courts should preserve for individual rights cases. The Supreme Court's opinion in *Garcia* was greatly influenced by both these pieces.

Lewis Kaden and William Van Alstyne disagree. Kaden claims that Wechsler's assumptions are obsolete, and that it is unrealistic to suppose the states can look out for themselves in the political process at

---

1. Grodzins, *Centralization and Decentralization in the American Federal System*, in A NATION OF STATES 1 (R. Goldwin, ed. 1963).

2. 301 U.S. 548, 57 S.Ct. 883, 81 L.Ed. 1279 (1937).

3. 483 U.S. 203, 107 S.Ct. 2793, 97 L.Ed. 2d 171 (1987).

4. 456 U.S. 742, 102 S.Ct. 2126, 72 L.Ed. 2d 532 (1982).

5. 452 U.S. 264, 101 S.Ct. 2352, 69 L.Ed. 2d 1 (1981).

6. 426 U.S. 833, 96 S.Ct. 2465, 49 L.Ed. 2d 245 (1976).

7. 469 U.S. 528, 105 S.Ct. 1005, 83 L.Ed. 2d 1016 (1985).

the federal level. Van Alstyne argues that Choper's thesis is inconsistent with *Marbury v. Madison*: it abandons the courts' function of judicial review.

Kaden also spells out the values that he thinks are served by state sovereignty within a federal system. These include both improved governmental processes and enhanced individual liberty. The article by Andrzej Rapaczynski complements Kaden in a variety of ways. Rapaczynski urges that even after *Garcia* courts should review federalism cases to make sure that states are represented in the political process. Like Kaden, but with a different emphasis, Rapaczynski sees real contemporary values in federalism. These include providing a space for participatory politics, and acting as a counterweight to a powerful central government.

HERBERT WECHSLER, THE POLITICAL SAFEGUARDS OF FEDERALISM: THE ROLE OF THE STATES IN THE COMPOSITION AND SELECTION OF THE NATIONAL GOVERNMENT

54 Colum.L.Rev. 543–552, 557–560 (1954).

I

Our constitution makers established a central government authorized to act directly upon individuals through its own agencies—and thus they formed a nation capable of function and of growth. To serve the ends of federalism they employed three main devices:

They preserved the states as separate sources of authority and organs of administration—a point on which they hardly had a choice.

They gave the states a role of great importance in the composition and selection of the central government.

They undertook to formulate a distribution of authority between the nation and the states, in terms which gave some scope at least to legal processes for its enforcement.

Scholarship—not only legal scholarship—has given most attention to the last of these enumerated mechanisms, perhaps because it has been fascinated by the Supreme Court and its interpretations of the power distribution clauses of the Constitution. The continuous existence of the states as governmental entities and their strategic role in the selection of the Congress and the President are so immutable a feature of the system that their importance tends to be ignored. Of the Framers' mechanisms, however, they have had and have today the larger influence upon the working balance of our federalism. The actual extent of central intervention in the governance of our affairs is determined far less by the formal power distribution than by the sheer existence of the states and their political power to influence the action of the national authority.

The fact of the continuous existence of the states, with general governmental competence unless excluded by the Constitution or valid

Act of Congress, set the mood of our federalism from the start. The first Congress did not face the problem of building a legal system from the ground up; it started with the premise that the standing *corpus juris* of the country was provided by the states.   *   *   *

National action has thus always been regarded as exceptional in our polity, an intrusion to be justified by some necessity, the special rather than the ordinary case. This point of view cuts even deeper than the concept of the central government as one of granted, limited authority, articulated in the Tenth Amendment. National power may be quite unquestioned in a given situation; those who would advocate its exercise must none the less answer the preliminary question why the matter should not be left to the states. Even when Congress acts, its tendency has been to frame enactments on an *ad hoc* basis to accomplish limited objectives, supplanting state-created norms only so far as may be necessary for the purpose. Indeed, with all the centralizing growth throughout the years, federal law is still a largely interstitial product, rarely occupying any field completely, building normally upon legal relationships established by the states.   *   *   *

*   *   *

II

If I have drawn too much significance from the mere fact of the existence of the states, the error surely will be rectified by pointing also to their crucial role in the selection and the composition of the national authority.   *   *   *

Despite the rise of national parties, the shift to popular election of the Senate and the difficulty of appraising the precise impact of such provisions on the legislative process, Madison's analysis has never lost its thrust:

> The State governments may be regarded as constituent and essential parts of the federal government; whilst the latter is nowise essential to the operation or organization of the former.[7]

> A local spirit will infallibly prevail much more in the members of Congress, than a national spirit will prevail in the legislatures of the particular States.[8]

> Even the House of Representatives, though drawn immediately from the people, will be chosen very much under the influence of that class of men, whose influence over the people obtains for themselves an election into the State legislatures.[9]

To the extent that federalist values have real significance they must give rise to local sensitivity to central intervention; to the extent that such a local sensitivity exists, it cannot fail to find reflection in the Congress. Indeed, the problem of the Congress is and always has been to attune itself to national opinion and produce majorities for action

---

7. The Federalist, No. 45 at 288 (Lodge ed. 1888).

8. *Id.*, No. 46 at 294.

9. *Id.*, No. 45 at 288–89.

called for by the voice of the entire nation. It is remarkable that it should function thus as well as it does, given its intrinsic sensitivity to any insular opinion that is dominant in a substantial number of the states.

III

The point is so clear in the Senate that, as Madison observed of the equality accorded to the states, it "does not call for much discussion." [11] The forty-nine votes that will determine Senate action,[a] even with full voting, could theoretically be drawn from twenty-five states, of which the combined population does not reach twenty-nine millions, a bare 19% of all state residents. The one-third plus one that will defeat a treaty or a resolution of amendment could, equally theoretically, be drawn from seventeen states with a total population little over twelve millions, less than that of New York. I say theoretically since, short of a combination to resist an effort to impair state equality within the Senate (which the Constitution purports to place beyond amendment) or to diminish the political power of the smaller states in other ways, a coalition in these terms is quite unthinkable. The fact remains that in more subtle ways the Senate cannot fail to function as the guardian of state interests as such, when they are real enough to have political support or even to be instrumental in attaining other ends. And if account is taken of the operation of seniority within the Senate, of the opportunity of Senators to marshal individual authority, not to speak of the possibility of filibuster, this power of negation, vested in the states without regard to population, multiplies in many ways. Given a controversy that has any sectional dimension, it is not long before the impact of this power is perceived.

*   *   *

IV

Even the House is slanted somewhat in the same direction, though the incidence is less severe. *   *   * [Here it stems from] the states' control of voters' qualifications, on the one hand, and of districting, on the other.

The position with respect to voters' qualifications derives from the constitutional provision that fixes the electorate of Representatives (and of Senators as well since the Seventeenth Amendment) as those persons who "have the qualifications requisite for electors of the most numerous branch of the State Legislature." Subject, then, to the prohibition of the denial of franchise because of color, race or sex, embodied in the Fifteenth and Nineteenth Amendments and the radiations of the equal protection clause of the Fourteenth, the states determine—indirectly it is true—the electorate that chooses Representatives. The consequences of contracting the electorate by such devices as a poll-tax are, of course, incalculable, but they tend to buttress what

11. The Federalist, No. 62, at 385   a. Alaska and Hawaii were admitted as
(Lodge ed. 1888).   states in 1959.

traditionally dominant state interests conceive to be their special state position; that is the point of the contraction. This sentiment, reflected in the Representatives that these constituencies send to Congress, is not ordinarily conducive to support for an adventurous expansion of the national authority, though there have been exceptions, to be sure.

* * *

State control of congressional districting derives from the constitutional provision that the "times, places and manner of holding elections for Senators and Representatives, shall be prescribed in each State by the Legislature thereof." * * *

It is well known that there are great discrepancies in district size in many multi-district states, paralleling for Congress the discrepancies, to forego harsher terms, that prevail in districting for the state legislatures. A recent study estimates that in the spring of 1952, 115 of the 435 congressional districts showed variation as to size larger than 15% above or below the state average, the maximum above the average being 129.8% in Texas and, below the average, 51.3% in South Dakota (where there are only two districts). * * *

* * *

It may be said, and perhaps rightly, that the situation with respect to districting, while detracting from the equality of popular representation in the House, has little bearing on the role of Congress in preserving federalist values. I am not so sure. It is significant, for one thing, that it is the states that draw the districts; one can hardly think the district lines would be the same had they been drawn from the beginning by Congress. Beyond this, however, the general motive and tendency of district deviations has quite clearly been to reduce urban power, not in the meaning of the census classification but in the sense of the substantial cities. The tendency is so appreciable that a recent article assures the readers of a small town magazine that while cities or towns of under 10,000 coupled with the farms account for only 51% of the entire population, residents of such areas are numerically dominant in 265 of the 435 congressional districts, accounting for the choice of 61% of the House (including 18 of the 21 committee chairmen) in addition to their numerical dominance in the choice of 75% of the Senate. Traditionally, at least, a more active localism and resistance to new federal intrusion centers in this 51% of Americans than in the other 49% . I should suppose that this is likely to continue; and that the figures, therefore, have some relevancy to an understanding of why presidential programs calling for the extension of national activity, and seemingly supported by the country in a presidential election, may come a cropper notwithstanding in the House. Such hostility to Washington may rest far less on pure devotion to the principle of local government than on opposition to specific measures which Washington proposes to put forth. This explanation does not make the sentiment the less centrifugal in its effects. Federalism would have few adherents were it not, like other elements of government, a means and not an end.

V

If Congress, from its composition and the mode of its selection, tends to reflect the "local spirit" predicted by Madison, the prime organ of a compensating "national spirit" is, of course, the President—both as the Chief Executive and as the leader of his party. Without the unifying power of the highest office, derived from the fixed tenure gained by his election and the sense that the President speaks for and represents the full national constituency, it would be difficult to develop the centripetal momentum so essential to the total federal scheme.

*   *   *

*   *   *

Federalist considerations *   *   * play an important part even in the selection of the President, although a lesser part than many of the Framers must have contemplated. A presidential candidacy must be pointed towards the states of largest population in so far as they are doubtful. It must balance this direction by attention to the other elements of the full coalition that is looked to for an electoral majority. Both major parties have a strong incentive to absorb protest movements of such sectional significance that their development in strength would throw elections to the House. Both must give some attention to the organized minorities that may approach balance of power status in important states, without, however, making promises that will outrun the tolerance of other necessary elements of their required strength. Both parties recognize that they must appeal to some total combination of allegiance, choice or interest that will yield sufficient nation-wide support to win elections and make possible effective government.

The most important element of party competition in this framework is the similarity of the appeal that each must make. This is a constant affront to those who seek purity of ideology in politics; it is the clue, however, to the success of our politics in the elimination of extremists—and to the tolerance and basic unity that is essential if our system is to work.

The President must be, as I have said above, the main repository of "national spirit" in the central government. But both the mode of his selection and the future of his party require that he also be responsive to local values that have large support within the states. And since his programs must, in any case, achieve support in Congress—in so far as they involve new action—he must surmount the greater local sensitivity of Congress before anything is done.

VI

If this analysis is correct, the national political process in the United States—and especially the role of the states in the composition and selection of the central government—is intrinsically well adapted to retarding or restraining new intrusions by the center on the domain of the states. Far from a national authority that is expansionist by nature, the inherent tendency in our system is precisely the reverse, necessitating the widest support before intrusive measures of importance can receive significant consideration, reacting readily to opposition grounded in resistance within the states. Nor is this tendency effectively denied by pointing to the size or scope of the existing national establishment. However useful it may be to explore possible contractions in specific areas, such evidence points mainly to the magnitude of unavoidable responsibility under the circumstances of our time.

It is in light of this inherent tendency, reflected most importantly in Congress, that the governmental power distribution clauses of the Constitution gain their largest meaning as an instrument for the protection of the states. Those clauses, as is well known, have served far more to qualify or stop intrusive legislative measures in the Congress than to invalidate enacted legislation in the Supreme Court.

* * *

The prime function envisaged for judicial review—in relation to federalism—was the maintenance of national supremacy against nullification or usurpation by the individual states, the national government having no part in their composition or their councils. This is made clear by the fact that reliance on the courts was substituted, apparently on Jefferson's suggestion, for the earlier proposal to give Congress a veto of state enactments deemed to trespass on the national domain. And except for the brief interlude that ended with the crisis of the thirties, it is mainly in the realm of such policing of the states that the Supreme Court has in fact participated in determining the balances of federalism.[56] This is not to say that the Court can decline to measure national enactments by the Constitution when it is called upon to face the question in the course of ordinary litigation; the supremacy clause governs there as well. It is rather to say that the Court is on weakest ground when it opposes its interpretation of the Constitution to that of Congress in the interest of the states, whose representatives control the legislative process and, by hypothesis, have broadly acquiesced in sanctioning the challenged Act of Congress.

Federal intervention as against the states is thus primarily a matter for congressional determination in our system as it stands. So too, moreover, is the question whether state enactments shall be stricken down as an infringement on the national authority. For while the Court has an important function in this area, as I have noted, the crucial point is that its judgments here are subject to reversal by

56. Of the great controversies with respect to national power before the Civil War, only the Bank and slavery within the territories were carried to the Court and its participation with respect to slavery was probably its greatest failure. The question of internal improvements, for example, which raised the most acute problem of constitutional construction, was fought out politically and in Congress. After the War only the Civil Rights Cases and income tax decisions were important in setting limits on national power—until the Child Labor Case and the New Deal decisions. The recasting of constitutional positions since the crisis acknowledges much broader power in the Congress—as against the states—than it is likely soon or ever to employ.

Congress, which can consent to action by the states that otherwise would be invalidated. The familiar illustrations in commerce and in state taxation of federal instrumentalities do not by any means exhaust the field. The Court makes the decisive judgment only when—and to the extent that—Congress has not laid down the resolving rule.[59]

JESSE H. CHOPER, THE SCOPE OF NATIONAL POWER VIS–A–VIS THE STATES: THE DISPENSABILITY OF JUDICIAL REVIEW

Judicial Review and the National Political Process 175–176, 201–203, 211, 215–218, 222–223, 244, 246–256 (1980).

THE FEDERALISM PROPOSAL

* * * [T]he major thesis of this chapter—hereafter referred to as the Federalism Proposal—may be briefly stated: The federal judiciary should not decide constitutional questions respecting the ultimate power of the national government vis-à-vis the states; rather, the constitutional issue of whether federal action is beyond the authority of the central government and thus violates "states' rights" should be treated as nonjusticiable, final resolution being relegated to the political branches—i.e., Congress and the President. It should be emphasized that neither this proposal nor the discussion that follows speaks to the substantive question of whether, in any given instance, the national government has overreached its delegated authority. Rather, the Federalism Proposal is addressed solely to the question of which branch of government should decide this constitutional issue.

* * *

There is a distinctive qualitative difference separating constitutional issues of federalism from those of individual liberty, a dissimilarity that augurs for the variant judicial role proposed herein. * * * [T]he difference may be described as one between issues of practicality and issues of principle.

When government action abridges constitutionally ordained personal liberties, it seems likely that, at least in view of short run concerns for efficient public administration and businesslike accomplishment of laudable public objectives, the commonwealth would usually be better served by compromising the interests seeking judicial protection. Thus, one of the major reasons for Federalist opposition to a bill of rights was the fear that it would inhibit effective government. In the main, it is only our historic ideals and special regard for the

---

59. The judicial function in relation to federalism thus differs markedly from that performed in the application of those constitutional restraints on Congress or the states that are designed to safeguard individuals. In this latter area of the constitutional protection of the individual against the government, both federal and state, subordination of the Court to Congress would defeat the purpose of judicial mediation. For this is where the political processes cannot be relied upon to introduce their own correctives—except to the limited extent that individuals or small minorities may find a champion in some important faction. See Stone, J., in United States v. Carolene Products Co., 304 U.S. 144, 152–53 n. 4 (1938).

dignity of the individual that compel the collective will to subjugate its more immediate needs to the preservation of designated individual rights. In short, it is government according to principle.

Constitutional issues of federalism, on the other hand, are a distinguishable species. One of the principal purposes behind the abandonment of the Articles of Confederation and the adoption of the Constitution—if not *the* major purpose—was to establish a workable central government, one whose authority was unquestionably limited but one nonetheless with sufficient power to cope with problems which prior experience had shown the states incompetent to resolve separately and for which national action was desperately needed. Assessment of the relative capabilities of the different levels of government, then, is a key step in determining whether a particular exercise of federal power exceeds the assigned boundaries. * * * [The] constitutional issue is not whether there is *any* government power to fulfill the public need; it is whether the goal may be accomplished only through action of the individual states. As between the two levels of government, Madison originally saw the "impossibility of dividing powers of legislation, in such a manner, as to be free from different constructions by different interests, or even from ambiguity in the judgment of the impartial." As Woodrow Wilson stated over half a century ago, the matter "cannot . . . be settled by the opinion of any one generation, because it is a question of growth, and every successive stage of our political and economic development gives it a new aspect, makes it a new question." Inherent in this inquiry is whether, as a functional matter, the states are separately capable of effecting the desired result. The pragmatic, almost literally borderline question posed is thus one of comparative skill and utility—in a word, an issue of practicability.

Whatever the judiciary's purported or self-professed special competence in articulating the values and defining the scope of those constitutional clauses that declare individual rights, when the fundamental issue turns in large measure on the relative competence of different levels of government to deal with societal problems, the Court is no more inherently capable of correct judgment than its companion federal branches. Indeed, the judiciary may well be less capable, given both the highly pragmatic nature of federal-state questions and the forceful representation of the states (which are most directly affected by their resolution) in the national process of political decisionmaking. * * *

Lest there be any misunderstanding, I am not arguing that constitutional decisions of federalism should rest with the political branches because they (especially the Congress) are better equipped than the Court to gather the underlying factual data necessary for intelligent judgment or more adept at fashioning the broad evaluations required to make wise public policy. A great many of the personal liberties questions that the Court decides—such as the nature of the threat posed by political "subversives," the ability of the accused criminal to defend without the assistance of counsel, the need for an abortion to be performed in a licensed hospital—similarly subsume large policy issues with complex and debatable factual considerations. Rather, the point is that constitutional questions of federalism differ from those of individual liberty both in terms of their distinctive, pragmatic quality and in the likelihood of their fair resolution within the national political chambers. When democratic processes may be generally trusted to produce a fair constitutional judgment, it advances the democratic tradition to vest that judgment with popularly responsible institutions.

* * *

OBJECTIONS TO THE FEDERALISM PROPOSAL

* * *

Efficacy of Judicial Review for Preserving Federalism

* * *

Frequently heard and often coupled with specific hypothetical illustrations is the argument that if judicial review of alleged federal usurpation of states' rights were unavailable, Congress would not merely be able to regulate all aspects of human affairs but would also possess the unrestrained power to swallow the states whole and thus destroy federalism. * * * But the argument cannot withstand realistic analysis.

* * * [T]he Court's definitions of the nation's powers have afforded the political branches exceedingly loose reins. Many of the constitutional grants of authority to Congress and the President, especially the most important ones, are phrased in expansive and expandable language—as are many of the crucial constitutional limitations on government power. And, if anything, the Court's pronouncements have enhanced their flexibility, suggesting only the slightest restrictions on federal power vis-à-vis the states. Thus, * * * under historic and modern judicial interpretations of the commerce clause—gilded by the Court's lavish construction of the necessary and proper clause—Congress may not only regulate every person or commodity involved in intercourse among the states but may also reach all details of commercial transactions (and, indeed, virtually every facet of human conduct) that radiate beyond the borders of a single state. Pursuant to its taxing power, Congress is capable of effectively governing a myriad of activities even though they may be totally confined within each state's boundaries, if such confinement is really possible. In furtherance of the authority to spend—augmented rather than qualified by the fertile phrase "for the general welfare"—the Court has awarded Congress a seemingly unrestrained opportunity to work its will within the states. And, in passing upon the power to enter treaties—a power held jointly by the President and Senate—the Court similarly appears to have handed the political branches a potent weapon to regulate intrastate behavior.

* * *

These Supreme Court decisions, and others, demonstrate that the absence of pervasive federal control over all conduct within the states has been more the product of political than of judicial restraint. Nor should this be surprising. In contrast to the state and local orientation of the members of the political branches, the Justices—appointed with no specific regard for their geographic origins and without the tradition of senatorial courtesy—are much more inclined to view matters from a national perspective. Congress, on the other hand, has not only refrained from using its powers to anything approaching their fullest extent, but has also left virtually untapped such potentially fruitful sources as the full faith and credit and guarantee clauses. Indeed, on a number of occasions—involving such varied subjects as intoxicants and insurance—Congress has reacted to judicial denials of state authority vis-à-vis the national government by restoring the power withheld by the Court. It would thus appear that, despite seemingly casual dicta to the contrary, if the Court's expansive pronouncements as to the scope of national authority under its delegated powers—again, particularly the commerce clause—were to be taken seriously, even the most extreme exercises of national power hypothesized above might well have been upheld.

* * *

Thus, * * * the presence of judicial review would appear to afford mean solace to those who fear the national government's ability to "devour the essentials of state sovereignty." * * *

* * *

The Federalism Proposal, it should be made clear, does not depend on the assumption that the states' position in the councils of national government provides an ironclad guarantee that no violations of states' rights will ever occur. If the federalism question is a close one, as virtually all real world ones are, then, irrespective of its "correct" answer, the political branches should be trusted to produce a reasonable and fair judgment. But should a true constitutional crisis arise, with Congress and the President joining forces in ignoring clear constitutional mandates—and these it must be remembered are the operative agencies in this regard, not minor federal bureaucrats or even state legislatures—it is probably futile to rely on the Court to right the matter.

Learned Hand's observation "that a society so riven that the spirit of moderation is gone, no court can save," echoed James Bradley Thayer's sound conclusion sixty-five years earlier that "under no system can the power of courts go far to save a people from ruin." Thayer, in turn, drew on Justice Gibson's early nineteenth-century wisdom that "once let public opinion be so corrupt as to sanction every misconstruction of the Constitution and abuse of power which the temptation of the moment may dictate, and the party which may happen to be predominant will laugh at the puny efforts of a dependent power [the judiciary] to arrest it in its course."

In the best of times, the people, viewing the Court as a nonrepresentative institution, ordinarily accord its invalidations of popular action an ambivalent respect. In the worst of times—and that is surely the situation when the elected representatives of the states and the people in the federal political branches determine to transgress plainly established constitutional boundaries—the Court is practically helpless. There is scant reason to believe that a people in social upheaval will heed the Court's pronouncements of the obvious. As evidenced by our own Civil War and the continued experience of constitutional republics throughout much of the rest of the world, the game of constitutional checks and balances, no matter how bold the lettering and durable the paper, works only if the players respect the rules. For clear constitutional violations, it is only the societal checks of popular conscience and responsibility that can finally preserve American federalism by demanding that the political branches return to course.

*   *   *

Federalism as a Guarantor of Individual Liberty

Perhaps the most deeply rooted argument for rejecting the Federalism Proposal is that the federal system, the scheme of territorial division of power within the United States * * * was designed to preserve individual freedom and prevent government tyranny. The framers believed, the argument continues, that a powerful central monolith would become arrogant and despotic; fragmentation of authority would avoid suppression of disagreement and dissent. Years later, Lord Acton found that "the distribution of power among several States is the best check on democracy. . . . It is the protectorate of minorities and the consecration of self-government." And, as stated tersely by Justice Frankfurter, "Time has not lessened the concern of the Founders in devising a federal system which would . . . be a safeguard against arbitrary government."

* * * But the assertion that federalism was meant to protect or does in fact protect, individual constitutional freedoms akin to those conventionally so defined has no solid historical or logical basis.

*   *   *

* * * [T]he federalism principle was conceived—in phrases of those at the Philadelphia Convention—because of the persisting "passion for separate sovereignty" of the states, and * * * this precept was reaffirmed in the tenth amendment. But, the argument [goes,] the reason for this historic concern for "state governments" was that they were to be relied on for the preservation of individual liberty. Decentralized decisionmaking units would assure greater individual participation in the political process and better opportunity for the selection of officials whose views reflected those of their constituents. Thus, the lower the level of effective government, the closer to the people, the greater the control each individual would have of his own destiny. Especially because of the wide religious, political, and cultural diversity of the people who were spread over the large territory of the former colonies, small groups of like-minded persons would be much more disposed than would a distant national government to impose laws that

were locally desired and in harmony with local values. Through these means, freedom would be maintained.

* * *

This rationale merits serious attention. To begin from the perspective of history: as is unfortunately true of many assertions concerning the intentions that motivated the framers, the record in regard to *the* reason for the sanctification of the states is cloudy. Indeed, what appears to emerge most clearly is that a primary purpose (if not *the* reason) for the desire to sustain the vitality of the state governments was not so much to assure personal freedom but rather to promote the efficiency of government administration. * * *

This conclusion—that "the issue, then, in controversy over 'States' Rights' . . . [was] not an issue of liberty" but rather "an issue solely of effective government"—may be seen most lucidly in Madison's unqualified statement to the Philadelphia Convention: "The great objection made [against] an abolition of the State [governments] was that the [general government] could not extend its care to all the minute objects which fall under the cognizance of the local jurisdictions. The objection as stated lay not [against] the probable abuse of the general power but [against] the imperfect use that could be made of it throughout so great an extent of country, and over so great a variety of objects. . . . Were it practicable for the [general government] to extend its care to every requisite object without the cooperation of the State [governments] the people would not be less free as members of one great Republic than as members of thirteen small ones." * * *

* * *

* * * [A]part from the strongly held belief that the states were necessary for effective administration, freedom—at least of a kind—was also comprehended within the federalism ideal in the minds of many who advocated limited power for the national government. * * *

But the freedom that the framers hoped would be furthered by curtailing the authority of the central government so as to assure the continued vitality of the states is of a special genre, quite different from the individual rights designated in Art. I, §§ 9 and 10 of the original Constitution and then supplemented by the first series of amendments. It is "freedom" somewhat elusive to define in traditional terms of "personal liberty." The purpose was not to guard the "sovereignty of the individual" from an all powerful national monolith but rather to preserve the sovereignty of states as political units. The "right of the people" was not to have some area carved out in which they would be shielded from all government incursions, but rather the right to have this area of their affairs governed only by the states. This was a collective rather than a personal right—a right that was intended not for the ultimate security of defined liberties but to insure the people's ability to choose in political units smaller than the national legislature whether and how certain of their activities would be regulated. Recalling the oppressive decisions made for them from across the Atlantic where their voices were barely heard and even less heeded, the former colonists rested their faith in the process of local government to secure their "freedom" and guard against the arbitrariness of uninformed and unresponsive majorities of strangers.   *   *   *

                    *   *   *

   *   *   * [W]hatever the reason for the framers' concern over centralism at the expense of states' rights, they were also at least equally fearful of a national despotism—of the threat to traditionally defined rights of individuals posed by an unrestrained federal legislative authority.   *   *   * [But] there is little reason to believe that the local government process secured by the federalism precept was relied on to insure these rights.   For one thing, the fear of legislative tyranny was in large measure engendered by the tendency at that time of the state lawmaking bodies to assume what was thought to be undue power.   For another, both Hamilton and Madison, the framers' most knowledgeable spokesmen, explicitly recognized that greater dangers to personal freedom were posed by the states than by the national government.   Madison stated that "the smaller the number of individuals composing a majority, and the smaller the compass within which they are placed, the more easily will they concert and execute their plans of oppression. Extend the sphere, and you take in a greater variety of parties and interests, you make it less probable that a majority of the whole will have a common motive to invade the rights of other citizens; or if such a common motive exists, it will be more difficult for all who feel it to discover their own strength and to act in unison with each other."
*   *   *

   *   *   * The insight of Madison *   *   * has been confirmed by subsequent events.   For our history has demonstrated that the smaller the population and geographic area, the greater the likelihood of dominance by a single political party or machine with a single set of mores and the greater the opportunity for aggregations of economic power to overshadow the political scene.   This in turn imposes stronger pressures toward conformity, lesser incentives and larger difficulties for minorities to obtain influence, and narrower community tolerance for deviant beliefs and behavior.   Even the most casual survey of the *United States Reports* reveals that in every area of constitutionally designated individual liberties—whether it be speech, race, religion, the rights of the accused, or any other—the record of state and local governments has been far inferior to that of the nation.   *   *   *

                    *   *   *

   But what of that special brand of "freedom" that is afforded by federalism: that "liberty" that is achieved through decisionmaking in small political units by locally elected officials who are peculiarly sensitive to local concerns?   Should the Court not also exercise its power of judicial review in regard to allegations that the constitutional provisions protecting this feature of American political life have been abridged?

                    *   *   *

It may be that the peculiar qualitative nature of constitutional issues of federalism—discussed earlier—should excuse the Court from participation because the national political forum, which is highly responsive to states' rights and the general interest in localism, has decided that no constitutional violation has occurred. But this answer may not be found to be wholly satisfactory by the complainants because, no matter how large the state majority favoring the federal action, different states and the people within them may be affected by it in very different ways—in their lives, their pocketbooks, or simply in their attitudes about national intervention. Nor is the answer strengthened by the fact that the Court's current standard for reviewing federalism contentions, one that virtually abdicates to the national political process rather than carefully scrutinizing its product, implies that the judiciary's considered view is that the "freedoms" affected are not comparable to conventionally defined individual rights. No matter how accurately this may portray the Court's judgment, it assumes the conclusion being debated.

At a different level, it may be forthrightly urged that the federalism principle has simply outlived its usefulness. Along with the concept of separation of powers among the federal branches, federalism was originally designed to diffuse power in order to make national action difficult—to enfeeble the central lawmaking system through built-in requirements of negotiation and compromise. But, the argument may proceed, the advantages to the country of having a sluggish national government have long since passed. Whatever the virtues of state and local administration may earlier have been—and Woodrow Wilson observed their deterioration as viable instruments of government almost a century ago—the growth of the nation and of the complex nature of its problems, its transformation from a relatively stable agrarian society to one that is highly mobile and integrated, has rendered the states incapable of effectively functioning as laboratories of social experimentation. Furthermore, whereas the states may be seen as having neglected the task of furthering progressive and libertarian values, the record of the national government, although far from perfect, is much better, not only in substance but in terms of its political responsiveness as well, as evidenced by increasing extensions of the franchise. It is no longer the size of government per se that threatens freedom but rather the risk that its operation will fail to abide with the constitutional mandates of liberty. To safeguard against such abuse, the Court sits.

* * * [But] one need not rely on [this argument] to justify the Court's refusal to review constitutional challenges to the scope of national power. On balance, two principal factors * * * support the Federalism Proposal. First, whatever the precise quality of the special type of "freedom" that is nourished by a restrained exercise of national power, it is equally likely that the withdrawal of judicial review will result in a more fastidious concern for states' rights by the federal political branches which will assume the mantle of final decision,

rather than in diminished political awareness of the virtues of limited national authority.

Second, and more important, if the ultimate question is how best to further individual constitutional liberties of *all* kinds, then removing the burden of reviewing federalism issues from the Court's shoulders is the wiser course.   *   *   * [T]he record of time discloses that the Court's ability to defend the personal rights of minorities who have fared poorly in the political process is a fragile one, ultimately dependent on the willingness of the people to abide by the Court's antimajoritarian rulings.   *   *   * [J]udicial validations of federal power as against states' rights have often placed the Court at the center of a storm of controversy, thus endangering its authority in unrelated areas of constitutional adjudication.   So, too, have the Court's rulings invalidating such national action expended its institutional credit and prestige.

LEWIS B. KADEN, POLITICS, MONEY, AND STATE SOVEREIGNTY: THE JUDICIAL ROLE

79 Colum.L.Rev. 847–858, 860–863, 865–868 (1979).

From 1936 to 1976 Congress determined the allocation of governmental power in the federal system virtually without judicial interference.   The vast array of domestic programs initiated during this period signaled an expanding national attempt to promote social and economic activity, protect public health and welfare, redistribute resources, and facilitate participation in public decisionmaking.   Many of these programs involved transfers of authority from the states to the national government and imposed new obligations on subnational governments to share in the costs and administrative burdens of mandated public services.   The expansion of federal domestic spending has been accompanied, therefore, by even more dramatic growth in state and local government activity, much of it attributable to the requirements of federal policies.   The result has been not only a sizeable expansion of the public sector, but also a vastly more complicated system of federalism characterized by shared costs, complex bureaucratic arrangements, and intersecting regulatory authority.

Except in the area of protection of individual rights, the expansion of the public sector and the attendant changes in the face of our federalism have occurred with substantial judicial approval.   First anticipating and then adhering to Professor Herbert Wechsler's admonition that "the Court is on weakest ground when it opposes its interpretation of the Constitution to that of Congress in the interest of the states," the Supreme Court regularly rejected challenges to the exercise of federal legislative power under the spending, commerce, and war clauses of the Constitution when those challenges were based upon an asserted interest in state autonomy.   So long as the Constitution conferred upon Congress the power to regulate the underlying subject, the Court deemed it irrelevant whether the regulated object involved public or private activity.   The courts and the country grew comfortable with the nationalization of public policy, and the states were obliged to seek vindication of their interest in autonomy through the political process. * * *

* * *

* * * [T]he proliferation of federal legislation imposing significant obligations on the states—"federalizing" the machinery of state government to serve the ends of national policy—warrants some broader measure of judicial supervision than the courts have recently supplied. The political branches in 1979 may no longer be as well suited as they once were to the task of safeguarding the role of the states in the federal system and protecting the fundamental values of federalism. Changes in both political practices and the direction and breadth of national initiatives suggest a new basis for judicial intervention. The task is to determine at what point the allocation of authority effected by Congress so imperils these values as to warrant the extraordinary intervention of the courts against the judgments of the political branches. * * *

I. STATE SOVEREIGNTY—ITS NATURE AND IMPORTANCE

A. *The Constitutional Concept of Sovereignty*

As Professor Wechsler observed, the framers of the Constitution were compelled to accept and protect the separate existence of the states—as their autonomy was the "means and the price" of forming the nation. * * *

The historical materials supply little guidance, however, about the nature of the state sovereignty that was to be preserved. Neither the concept of a state nor its intended functions were described in the Constitution. A geographic entity with a discrete territory was no doubt an element of the conception, but not a sufficient definition, since boundaries could be modified and nonstates shared the quality of territorial administration. Then, too, the framers must have assumed that states would have their separate governments, since they allocated responsibilities to the state legislatures and presupposed the existence of state executive and judicial authorities. But the pertinent sources belie a simple equation of a state with its government in eighteenth-century political theory, tending more often to center the concept of sovereignty in the ancient notion of the body politic: the community, or the aggregate of all inhabitants of the specific territory. * * *

* * *

Though the records of the Constitutional Convention and the nineteenth-century opinions by the Court supply shadowy suggestions of an original conception, they furnish little aid in defining the contemporary role of the state. As a starting point, however, it is not difficult to describe some of the attributes of sovereignty related to separate existence in the twentieth century. To function as a state, the body politic must have at least a minimum of its powers protected against outside interference, including control over the structure of government, the distribution of administrative responsibilities, the process of selecting popular agents, and the capacity to tax and spend. This is but another way to say that the characteristic integral to separate identity in contemporary terms is a power to make choices—about how to use public monies and direct public attention, and about how to vary the choices as the needs of the community change. Though the range of choices available to a state—the range of needs to which it may respond or services it may choose to provide—also varies over time, within the zone of its sovereign authority its assessments and elections as to public wants and needs must control. In short, sovereignty can have little modern significance unless within its domain a state is free to prefer health services over highways or public colleges over correctional facilities and to use its sovereign powers to effectuate those preferences. Similarly, to the extent it is not preempted by federal institutions, the state must be free to determine what kinds of constraints it will impose on private activity and what business activities it will regulate, as well as how it will regulate them and structure its regulatory agencies to implement the decisions it has made.

* * *

B. The Importance of State Sovereignty

The search for a point at which limitation of a state's freedom of choice jeopardizes its integrity or separate existence must begin with some identification of the basic goals or values that support a federal system. * * *

1. *Improved Governmental Processes.* One clear value of the federal form resides in its potential to provide maximum opportunities for participation in government. Inevitably, governmental choices must be made through representatives, but decisionmaking in smaller units makes possible more direct public participation in both the process of representative selection and the process of policy determination by the delegates chosen. This participation is critical to any viable notion of accountability. Representative government depends upon the maintenance of the connection between the governors and the governed, not merely in the sense that elected officials will then reflect the popular will, but also because there is then some assurance that public preferences are communicated to the public officials whose own expressions help shape popular opinion. A fundamental advantage of local government is the opportunity it affords for this kind of communication. Simply put, proximity increases accountability by increasing access.

Experience also supports the traditional claim that federalism promotes variety in political choice and counters the impulse toward social and ideological homogeneity by allowing cultural differences to find expression in different places. Despite the homogenizing effects of media and mobility on twentieth-century American life, the existence of separate state and local governmental units still provides avenues for expression of the variations in style in different parts of the country. Tax burdens, public services, habits of living, and patterns of tolerance do vary as one moves from Maine to Alabama or New York to New Mexico, reflecting in part the differences in the political choices made by subnational governmental authorities. Thus one state opts for an elaborate system of subsidized postsecondary education while another spends far less on this service; one state chooses to permit the use of marijuana while others continue to prosecute for possession; and one state appeals to retired persons by supplementing the natural advantage of climate with tax preferences, while another discourages this type of migration.

The aphorism that a federal system permits the states to serve as laboratories for experimentation has also been borne out in our experience. * * * [S]tate experiments in matters as diverse as public financing of political campaigns, regulation of hospital facilities, protection of health and safety on the job, and requirements for open meetings by public agencies and public access to official records have laid the foundation for similar national legislative actions. * * *

2. *Individual Liberty.* Beyond these values of participation, accountability, diversity, and experimentation in government, however, the case for a federal form rests most fundamentally on the capacity of a federal system to enhance and protect individual liberty. * * *

The concept of liberty here at issue requires some greater specification. In one sense, of course, individual liberty is merely the absence of public or official constraint on individual action. This kind of personal liberty—liberty as license—looks not to social order, but rather to the freedom available to an individual to think and act as he pleases. The kind of liberty more pertinent to the values inherent in a federal system of government, however, is not the freedom to be left alone but the freedom to become involved in the public life of a polity. Political liberty—the freedom to participate in the community's political life—is the core of democratic government. This distinction, a staple of political philosophy since Aristotle, remains vital. * * *

The political liberty of the individual secured by our Constitution is a freedom to influence that same process of political choice that defines the essence of sovereignty. As discussed above, the effectiveness of this political participation turns on accountability, the connection between the representative and the represented. In our system, the connection is reinforced by rights that need not be absolute to be fundamental to democratic government, such as access to the voting booth and ballot, rights of expression through lobbying, and contributions of time and money. But beyond such guarantees, political liberty requires a level of awareness in the electorate. Information about the process of choice, including the range of alternatives and their probable effects, is a critical means of assuring accountability. Realistically, a legislator who supports a bill is accountable to the people he serves, both individually and through their association with others of like interest, to the extent that they know the options he discarded as well as the decision he adopted. In the press, the campaign fund, or the ballot box, the voter may or may not view the particular matter as critical to his ongoing support for the representative; he may judge an unwelcome decision outweighed by other decisions that he supports, or by the shortcomings of the available alternatives. The critical point, however, is that he must at least know whom to hold responsible.

To the extent accountability is diminished by reason of the electorate's lack of knowledge or understanding of the lines of authority, the value or effectiveness of participation is necessarily reduced, and the protection of political liberty is necessarily jeopardized. By fostering participation and accountability in the political process, a state's autonomy thus serves a primary constitutional value, and judicial protection of state sovereignty in circumstances where the political branches fail to safeguard it adequately is thus seen as an essential part of the traditional judicial assignment to protect the individual's right to liberty against majoritarian abuse.

These are some of the benefits of our federal system. In the contemporary political process, however, many factors combine to undermine the capacity of the separate states to realize these advantages. The following section illuminates some of these factors.

II. THE DECLINE OF STATES' INFLUENCE UPON THE FEDERAL GOVERNMENT

Congressional sensitivity to the states' autonomy turns not only on the external relationships between state officials and the federal government, but also on various internal factors, such as the structure of government as defined by the Constitution and the rules of procedure developed by the Congress for its own governance. Thus, the method of selecting members of Congress, the standards of voter eligibility, and the design of boundaries for election districts, as well as the rules governing selection of legislative leaders, all affect the state role in the selection and composition of the national legislature. Congressional representation of state interests is also influenced by political factors that contribute to legislative choice, including the effects of the media, campaign expenditures, seniority, incumbency, and party loyalty. In addition, the values and aspirations of the individuals who comprise the expanding bureaucracies in both the federal and state governments exert a significant influence upon federal actions.

Any examination of the extent to which a particular concern for state sovereignty is reflected in the Congress requires some examination of the impact of these forces. My argument, admittedly based more on impressions than the results of systematic empirical testing, is that recent changes in this internal political process have also diminished the likelihood that congressional action will be guided by special sensitivity to state autonomy.

* * *

In the last quarter century, many of the structural and political factors affecting sensitivity to localism in the Congress have changed dramatically, with the result that opposition to "federalization" of the state governmental process in the name of state sovereignty is less likely to prove compelling in congressional debates.

1. *The Structural Elements.* Some of the changes in the structural elements of federalism are by now familiar. Commencing with *Wesberry v. Sanders* in 1964, the Supreme Court began to limit the states' ability to control the process of congressional election districting. District lines must now be drawn to approach numerical equality among the constituencies. Neither municipal boundaries nor attempts to avoid political gerrymandering will excuse even slight deviations from mathematical equality. The courts have also scrutinized state plans to ensure contiguity and prevent use of the districting power to exclude minorities from political representation. At a minimum, the political effect of the decisions mandating substantial equality of congressional districting has been to diminish the influence of state parties on the composition of the Congress, and to shift a measure of political power from the previously overrepresented rural areas to the cities and, more recently, to the increasingly populous suburbs.

Next, the Court, the Congress, and the constitutional amendment process combined to limit state control over the qualifications of voters in elections for Congress. The first recent blow to state efforts to restrict electoral participation through this means was the decision in *Harper v. Virginia State Board of Elections,* an event that ended, in one swoop, years of fruitless congressional debate over proposals to abolish the poll tax. Soon after the *Harper* decision, the Congress widened the electorate even more drastically through the Voting Rights Act of 1965, facilitating the registration of black voters and the creation of new black voting strength throughout the South. * * * [In 1971] the twenty-sixth amendment [was ratified], guaranteeing for the eighteen-year-old the right to vote in all elections.

* * * Other changes at the state level facilitating participation in a party's primary elections without regard to a voter's prior membership or involvement in party affairs have further contributed to the decline of party control and the development of personal constituencies by successful candidates for Congress.

2. *The Political Forces.* The effects of the various structural modifications tending to erode sensitivity to state interests have been intensified by more subtle changes in the political process affecting national election campaigns and the internal workings of Congress. The last twenty-five years have brought enormous changes in the types of persons elected to the Senate and House, and in the techniques used in their successful campaigns. The core element in this transformation has been the decline in importance of state party organizations, itself a product of several related forces—the effect of money on politics, the changing use of media in campaigns, the phenomenon of celebrity success in politics, and the substitution of welfare state programs for the community service functions of the neighborhood political organiza-

tion. The consequences are varied, but clearly point in one direction. As Senators and Members of the House develop independent constituencies among groups such as farmers, businessmen, laborers, environmentalists, and the poor, each of which generally supports certain national initiatives, their tendency to identify with state interests and the positions of state officials is reduced. * * *

* * * The result is evident in the class of new Senators elected in 1978, which includes many first-time officeholders. As legislators, these persons seem less likely than their counterparts in the 1950's to respond to state concerns merely because voiced by state officials or state parties and significantly more likely to pursue an independent course. * * * Indeed, while prior state government service is still common to many members of Congress, the proportion with this background has declined significantly. In the Eightieth Congress, twenty-eight Senators had served formerly as Governor of their states, while only sixteen former Governors sat in the Ninety-fifth Senate. * * *

Once in Washington, the same characteristics that have distinguished the new Congressman from his predecessors have also contributed to changes in the internal procedures of the national legislature. These modifications in congressional rules and practices also tend to reduce the force of the proposition that the separate states generally acquiesce in acts of Congress interfering with their sovereignty. On the desirability of reelection, there is little to distinguish the contemporary Congressman. Most want to stay and their wish is seldom denied. But the same strains of independence that mark their election have also characterized the Congressmen's service in Washington. The old rule that "to get along in the House, you go along," while still of some importance, belies the increasing assertiveness of junior Members. The most notable consequence has been the rising influence of the party caucus in the House and the consequent decline of strict seniority in the selection of major committee chairmen. In 1974, three senior committee chairmen were defeated, in each case following the negative response of freshman Members to their appearances before the newcomers' caucus. In part as a result of the changes in seniority rules, there has been a trend away from southern states'-rights oriented domination of committee leadership positions. In the Ninety-fifth Congress, only five of twenty major House committee chairmen and five of fifteen Senate committee chairmen were from the South; not many years before, the ratio of southern to nonsouthern representatives in the leadership was significantly higher.

* * * The combined effects of incumbency, direct access to the electorate, and declining adherence to seniority in the Congress contribute to the relative independence of Congressmen from the state party and state officials.

3. *The Expansion of the Federal Government.* * * * The vast expansion in the scope of federal domestic programs has produced a new class of public administrators, in both Washington and state

regional offices of federal agencies, commissioned to monitor state activities. The enlarged requirements of federal law and federal largesse have in turn expanded and altered the roles of the states, and stimulated a corresponding growth of state bureaucracies responsible for program implementation. As a result of the pervasive intermingling of functions and responsibilities among the different levels of government in the federal system, the "layer cake" of federalism has become increasingly "marbled," with local, state, and federal governments sharing responsibility for a multitude of public services. * * *

From these developments there has emerged a new system of representation and mutual influence in the federal system, comprised of two classes of public administrators who work closely with the interest groups and constituencies affected by the programs they administer as well as with individual legislators and committee staff. Collectively, they shape and implement legislation that imposes administrative obligations and fiscal burdens on the states in return for increased federal aid. Individuals in the federal and state administrative bureaucracies often move back and forth between them, and share common backgrounds and ambitions, most particularly the commitment to maintain and expand the public services they supervise. * * *

4. *Summary.* Taken together, the new relationship of the states and state administrators to the federal government and the new politics of congressional representation have dramatically changed the workings of the process of federalism. It is now far less likely that the states' interest in their continuing autonomy will consistently receive expression within the political branches of the federal government, or that the political process will yield dependable lines of accountability between the governed and the government. As Congress increasingly implements national policy by directing the governmental activity of the states, the people in whom sovereignty ultimately resides are left without a clear sense of the persons they may call to account—the national legislators who conceived and ordered a program, or the state officials charged with its implementation. And as the states find their resources and energies increasingly consumed in meeting obligations imposed by the national government, they confront a system of federalism more coopting than cooperative, in which the basic values of pluralism, creativity, participation, and liberty are progressively undermined.

[In the latter part of his article Kaden argues that state autonomy may need judicial as well as political protection. He offers several examples of cases where this may be true. One is the case of direct commands to the states. Congress would be justified in applying Clean Air Act standards to state activities in common with the activities of private groups. But it would go too far if it commanded the state legislature to establish a new agency to regulate labor relations in local government according to congressional standards. A second type of case involves conditions attached to federal grants. Given the pervasive nature of federal aid to state governments in the modern federal system, Congress could bring about almost any state behavior it wanted by making compliance a condition of assistance. Kaden would have courts apply a kind of intermediate scrutiny to such conditions, insisting that they be related to important federal objectives.]

WILLIAM W. VAN ALSTYNE, THE SECOND DEATH OF FEDERALISM

83 Mich.L.Rev. 1709, 1720–1725 (1985).

The *Garcia* case, with its overruling of *Usery,* attracted a fair amount of journalistic comment. Much of that comment was interesting but predictably limited to *Garcia's* immediate practical implications. *The (London) Economist,* however, was more discerning. It reported an appropriate sense of English puzzlement. It appeared to *The Economist* that the Supreme Court had partly repudiated *Marbury v. Madison,* in favor of a rule of parliamentary supremacy in respect to the boundaries of federalism. "[I]t is curious," *The Economist* observed, "that in the San Antonio case the justices explicitly overruled a decision they had made only nine years before." It then went on to note something even "more startling":

> Even more startling, though, was the view of federalism that the majority put forward to support its decision. The court could have made its ruling on a narrow technical ground. It did not. Justice Harry Blackmun, whose change of heart since 1976 was enough to shift the court, wrote in the majority opinion that the protection of the states from federal power "inhered principally in the workings of the national government itself," rather than in the constitution as interpreted by the Supreme Court. In other words, the states have some influence on congress and the president; if they do not succeed in using it to keep Washington from encroaching unduly on their powers, they should not expect the court to do the job for them by declaring federal laws unconstitutional. This view, said one of the dissenting justices, Mr. Lewis Powell, "rejects almost 200 years of the understanding of the constitutional status of federalism."

> [The Blackmun opinion] also called into question a central principle of the Supreme Court's own constitutional position. Since 1803 the court has claimed the authority . . . to invalidate actions of the federal government if they conflict with the constitution. *The San Antonio decision seems to suggest that the principle of judicial review does not apply to questions of federalism when congress acts under the commerce clause.*

> [T]he Supreme Court seems to have declared that judicial enforcement of the constitutional position on federalism is at an end.[56]

56. *Nine for the Seesaw,* [The Economist, Mar. 2, 1985,] at 21 (emphasis added).

Is the "judicial enforcement of the constitutional position on federalism at an end" and, if it is, why? Is it because the general approach of the Court in *Usery* was improper and, if it was, what made it so? Or does *Garcia* actually insinuate a different sort of answer altogether, even as *The Economist* suggests it does—that federalism questions in general (and not merely in *Garcia*-type cases) are not for the Court, but fundamentally for *Congress,* finally to determine?

* * *

The constitutional clauses examined in *Usery* [58] and reexamined in *Garcia* have borne more of the burden of federalism litigation than any other clauses, including the spending clause. From the beginning, moreover, there has been a blurriness in their scope and an admitted uncertainty in measuring their margins, even as reflected in the tumultuous reactions to the Court's earliest decisions.

Even so, with all the ups and downs of judicial vagary, the commerce clause and the tenth amendment have not until now been read as though they declared that it was not for the Court, but rather for Congress, to determine the extent to which enumerated powers permit the displacement of state laws or the command of state governments. Rather, each has been a staple of substantive judicial review. It has been for Congress to decide what to do. It has been for the Court to say whether it was within Congress' power to do it.

The results of that judicial review have not always been consistent, but perfect consistency is not to be expected insofar as judicial attitudes must themselves vary and none is particularly entitled to control all the rest. Usually, however, even in close cases when the federalism claim has failed (as most often it has indeed failed), it has failed because the Court has yielded to an assertion of some overriding federal interest it deemed adequate to rationalize the exceptional intrusiveness of the challenged act. In *Garcia,* * * * the majority identified no such overriding interest. Rather, it deemed itself excused from this element of judicial review. It then weakly explained that it regarded the political safeguards of federalism to be the appropriate check against unconstitutional excesses by Congress.

By itself, this may do no more than to overrule *Usery,* i.e., to eliminate any requirement of justification even when Congress presumes to command the states themselves and even when it is not asserted that the states are engaging in commerce. Writ large, however, as the sources relied upon by Justice Blackmun would have us do,[62] such alleged political safeguards of federalism may excuse the Court

---

58. I.e., the commerce clause, the necessary and proper clause, and the tenth amendment.

62. *See, e.g.,* J. Choper, Judicial Review and the National Political Process 175–84 (1980), *cited in* Garcia v. San Antonio Metro. Transit Auth., 105 S.Ct. 1005, 1018 n. 11 (1985). (The same footnote also cites

to an article by Wechsler, urging extreme deference to Congress although not outright abdication of the judicial function. *See* Wechsler, *The Political Safeguards of Federalism: The Role of the States in the Composition and Selection of the National Government,* 54 Colum.L.Rev. 543 (1954).)

from answering any other question of a like kind as well. The practical choice between state action and national action generally, indeed always, in this view, is not to be judicially constrained but only politically constrained. To be sure, the Constitution may appear to have made an allocation (enumerating what may be national and homogeneous, reserving the rest to the states and protecting them in some measure from being commanded as well as preempted), but it is best not for the judiciary to say whether the constitutional plan is being adhered to. The determinations to be made are more appropriately resolved in Congress where the respective interests are able to work out the appropriate accommodations, rather than in the courts. The constitutional plan is thus not checked by an impacted litigant's standing to object as a sore loser in court; it is checked, rather, by the structural representation already amply afforded the states by the Constitution.

If, then, "the states" or "the people" do not appear to keep Congress to the plan, it may be because they do not see any real departure from that plan; alternatively, supposing they do, presumably they do not regard the departure as an undesirable rearrangement. Under these circumstances, it is scarcely for the courts to say that the Emperor, i.e., Congress, has no clothes. For the Constitution itself (under this view) relies upon the finality of federal politics, rather than judicial review, to determine the sufficiency of the national wardrobe. It is the role of the judiciary to uphold and enforce the majoritarian verdict on these questions and not to oppose it with a perception of its own.

Generally, the argument to this effect (which the *Garcia* case suggests the Court now flirts with), has been opposed principally in terms of the alleged naiveté of its political science.[63] Unquestionably that objection is well taken but, ironically, to press one's objection in such terms is in one sense to miss the point of what is being said. It puts the real objection on quite the wrong ground. Even to participate in that debate is in one sense to lose it. It implies that if, as, or when (in the Court's view) such structural safeguards *might* reasonably be seen as adequate, at least then and to that extent it would be inappropriate not to defer to them. Alternatively, it may concede even more, namely, that if it is true that the Constitution deems such safeguards adequate, the Court should not set up its opposing opinion, even if the Court finds those safeguards inadequate. In brief, if it is part of the constitutional plan that the constitutional boundaries of federalism are to be politically settled, rather than judicially maintained until altered by amendment, then the Court should, in decency, respect its assigned (non)role in such matters.

This is the strong form of what Justice Blackmun seems to have implied in the critical part of *Garcia*. And it is exactly *this* implication

63. [*See, e.g.,* Kaden, *Politics, Money, and State Sovereignty: The Judicial Role,* 79 Colum.L.Rev. 847 (1979).]

that raised an English eyebrow in surprise, as well it should. Stripped of its elegance, *Garcia* proposes the piecemeal repeal of judicial review. It also involves a double counting of what are in fact merely *pre*-judicial and *post*-judicial "safeguards" of the American constitutional plan, safeguards (such as they are) merely additional to, *and not in substitution of,* substantive judicial review.

The Constitution does of course notice the states other than through article III, i.e., other than in the duty of article III judges to hold an act of Congress invalid when, in an appropriate case, the government is unable to demonstrate the consistency of the act with the federalism provisions of the Constitution. It notices them in the representation formula of the Senate, with its assurance of two senators per state irrespective of size. It notices them in the Electoral College. It notices them in article V, with regard to the states' power to initiate and ratify proposed amendments, etc. How well (or ill) these constitutive provisions contrive to keep Congress and the President in check, one may measure for oneself. Unless, however, they are designed not as merely additive to the safeguards of substantive judicial review but rather as partial or whole substitutes for that review, their speculative efficacy or inefficacy is utterly without relevance in constitutional litigation. They are, with all respect, not the proper concern of the Supreme Court in the adjudication of a particular case.

Concretely, if in the Court's view the bare bones of the commerce clause are insufficient as against the particular objections fielded in the *Garcia* case, then the Court must say so. As to that question, moreover, *nothing* can be derived from references to constitutive processes. The Court may not appropriately uphold an act of Congress based on reasoning that relies even partly on some theory of renvoi to what are, at best, altogether separate possible sources of constraint. Those constraints either worked or did not work (to hold Congress within the boundaries laid down), and it is for the Court now to answer whether they did. The inputs of those features of the Constitution are now concluded. The product is at hand. The special "safeguard" of the Court's independent view of constitutional consistency is now requested. The litigant asks for the *Court's* answer.

ANDRZEJ RAPACZYNSKI, FROM SOVEREIGNTY TO PROCESS: THE JURISPRUDENCE OF FEDERALISM AFTER GARCIA

1985 Sup.Ct.Rev. 341–346, 359–360, 364–366, 380, 382, 385–390, 395–401, 404, 408–412, 414–418.

The position of federalism in our constitutional law is peculiar. On the one hand, next to separation of powers and individual rights, federalism is clearly one of the three main branches of our constitutional structure. On the other hand, judicial enforcement of any limits on national power that the concept of federalism might entail has a rather unfortunate history and, at least insofar as the limitations on national commerce power are concerned, seems to have been abandoned in the *Garcia* case in favor of what Professor Wechsler has called "the political safeguards of federalism."

More than in any other area of constitutional adjudication, the Court's attempts to impose federalism-related limitations on the national government have been, throughout history, frustrated by the political process, resulting three times in constitutional amendments. The Court's decision in the *Dred Scott* case that slavery was a municipal institution outside federal control, was "overruled" by the Civil War Amendments. The decision in *Pollock v. Farmers' Loan and Trust Co.* that "the boundary between the Nation and the States . . . would have disappeared" if the national taxing power had been extended to taxing income from real estate, led to the enactment of the Sixteenth Amendment. The Court's attempts to give meaning to the Tenth Amendment by limiting national regulation of private activities under the Commerce Clause were instrumental in precipitating the "constitutional crisis" of 1937 and led to a wholesale judicial retreat. As recently as 1970, the Court's decision in *Oregon v. Mitchell,* holding that Congress lacked the power to enfranchise eighteen-year-olds in state elections, resulted in passing the Twenty–Sixth Amendment, which it took the country only three months to ratify.

It is important to inquire into the reasons for this rather dismal record of judicial intervention. The most common explanation, seemingly adopted by the *Garcia* Court, is that federalism is essentially a political arrangement and that the policing of it is, for one reason or another, unsuited to the *modus operandi* of the judicial department. The extreme version of this argument is exemplified by Professor Choper's claim that the Court is most needed and most effective in protecting individual rights against governmental encroachments and that its reservoir of legitimacy is only dissipated if the Court intervenes in the distribution of institutional competences among governmental entities. Whatever merit this view may have, it is clearly not shared by the Court, which has not shied away from highly charged, controversial issues of institutional competence in the area of separation of powers, most recently in *Immigration and Naturalization Service v. Chadha.* Instead, the Court's reasoning in *Garcia* singles out the federalism-related limitations on the national power as peculiarly unsuitable for judicial resolution. We are not really told, however, what distinguishes federalism from the separation of powers in this respect: it is certainly not the absence of the "political safeguards" of the latter, for the Constitution abounds in provisions guaranteeing that at least the Congress and the President have ample means to protect themselves in the political arena. * * *

* * *

The most plausible explanation of the repeated frustration of judicial intervention in the area of state-national relations is the failure of judges and scholars to produce a viable theory of federalism that would help to develop workable principles for the judicial resolution of federalism-related disputes. To begin with, rather than focusing on a functional analysis of the role of the states in the federal system—an analysis that would parallel the Court's jurisprudence in the area of separation of powers—the basic intellectual inquiry has been concentrated on the concept of state sovereignty and its implications for the limitation of national authority. * * *

It is also possible that a political disinclination toward the state-rights doctrine, stemming from the Civil War divisions and the intellectual ascendancy of the New Deal, further contributed to the neglect of a theory of federalism. But the past failures should not be taken to preclude the possibility of future success. Indeed, even if the protection of the federal structure of the United States is to rest ultimately with the political process, and not the courts, the actors in that process, no less than judges, must have some idea of the basic purposes of federalism and the reasons behind their constitutional protection. A new theory of federalism is thus necessary to allow us a more comprehensive understanding of the American institutions. * * *

* * *

PROCESS JURISPRUDENCE: AN ALTERNATIVE APPROACH

* * *

Garcia stresses the fact that the Constitution "divested" the states of "their original powers" and that it is futile to try to "identify principled constitutional limitations on the scope of Congress' Commerce Clause powers over the States merely by relying on *a priori* definitions of state sovereignty." Instead, the decision proposes to rely primarily on the political safeguards of federalism and to ground any future judicial intervention not in a defense of state sovereignty but in the idea of compensating for possible failings in the national political process.[56]

* * *

Viewed from this perspective, the gist of *Garcia's* holding lies not in ruling out as nonjusticiable all matters of federalism-related limitations on national power, but rather in formulating an approach to the elaboration of the judicial standards of review. This approach has much in common with the "process jurisprudence" originating in the famous footnote four of the *Carolene Products* decision[69] and subsequently elaborated in the scholarly literature.[70] The assumption of this approach is that the Constitution largely confines the outcomes of governmental action to the political process and that judicial review should, with a few exceptions related to very concrete substantive

---

56. Garcia v. San Antonio MTA, 105 S.Ct. at 1019–20: "[A]ny substantive restraint on the exercise of Commerce Clause powers must find its justification in the procedural nature of [the] basic limitation [the Constitution imposes to protect the states], and it must be tailored to compensate for possible failings in the national political process rather than to dictate a 'sacred province of state autonomy.'"

69. United States v. Carolene Products Co., 304 U.S. 144, 152–53 n. 4 (1938).

70. See, above all, Ely, Democracy and Distrust (1980) * * *.

provisions in the Constitution, be directed toward preserving the integrity of the political process, keeping open the channels of political change, and so on. In elaborating this theory of judicial review, however, process jurisprudence does not limit the scope of judicial intervention to explicitly procedural remedies or to the enforcement of specifically procedural principles. * * * Thus, for example, in reviewing governmental actions that may inhibit free speech or discriminate against certain minorities, a court sympathetic to the tenets of process jurisprudence will feel free to elaborate the standards of review that will directly address the substantive issues of free speech or minority rights, but it will justify them not so much in terms of the autonomous values of speech or equality as in terms of their role in the properly functioning democratic process and will attempt to identify some distortions in that process that account for its presumably abnormal results. * * *

In the context of federalism, the process jurisprudence endorsed by *Garcia*, if I interpret it correctly, does not imply, therefore, an unconditional rejection of even the specific principle of the protection of the integrity of state governmental operations put forth by the *National League of Cities* so long as this principle is not rooted in the assumption of state sovereignty. Should it turn out, for example, on the basis of a well-grounded analysis of the significance of local politics for the proper functioning of the national political process, that certain systemic characteristics of the national government make it prone to fail to recognize the interdependence between its own health and the robustness of political life in the states, the Court might view with suspicion federal interference with the integrity of some vital governmental operations of the states, in much the same way as it applied its "strict scrutiny" analysis to governmental actions involving race-based classifications.

* * *

The Function of the States Within the Federal System

* * *

A. Tyranny Prevention

* * * Perhaps the most frequently mentioned function of the federal system is the one it shares to a large extent with the separation of powers, namely, the protection of the citizen against governmental oppression—the "tyranny" that the Framers were so concerned about.

* * *

There are three somewhat different scenarios of governmental oppression that the Framers seem to have had in mind when they spoke of the danger of "tyranny." First, they were clearly concerned that a small minority might be oppressed by a sufficiently homogeneous majority. Second, they were concerned with the danger that a few powerful minority interests might gain ascendancy over the political process and exploit the rest of society. And third, they were afraid that a powerful central government may itself develop its own separate interest and oppress the citizenry.

* * *

How is federalism related to the Framers' objection of preventing the three-headed specter of tyranny? Many American liberals tend to look with skepticism on the states as the protectors of individual freedom and they point to a whole host of situations in which the states, much more than the federal government, have engaged in practices violative of individual rights. Quite apart from the special problem of racial discrimination, which is historically tied to the regional character of slavery in the United States, there are in fact good reasons to believe that the states represent a more direct threat than the national authorities to the rights of small minorities and that the states have only a secondary role to play in protecting such minorities—so long as these minorities are not geographically defined. The explanation for this lies in the fact that local constituencies are much more homogenous and cohesive than the national one, both because their members share more common interests and values and because, the constituencies being less numerous, stable majoritarian interests are more likely to exist within them and to be easier to organize. Consequently, at least insofar as the first of the Framers' scenarios of governmental oppression is concerned, state governments are more likely than the national one to be captured by powerful majoritarian interests and to oppress small minorities with little power to resist. * * *

* * * [W]hile the states are more easily captured by relatively undifferentiated majoritarian interests intent on suppressing small minorities, the federal government may be a more likely subject of capture by a set of special minoritarian interests, precisely because the majority interest of the national constituency is so large, diffuse, and enormously difficult to organize. * * *

It is quite easy to see how a system weighted in favor of local interests (either through the importance of state institutions or through a regional representation on the national level) will provide an institutional support to geographically defined groups that may be subject to exclusion or exploitation by the more powerful regions. But it is no less important to see that the existence of a strong system of local government may also modify those divisions between the potential ins and outs that are essentially social in nature (such as between the traditional and new industries, organized and unorganized labor, producers and consumers, and so on) rather than primarily geographically determined. * * * [T]he very scale on which an organization must succeed before it gains meaningful access to the political process and can use the machine of the government to improve its position vis à vis other groups is very often decisive with respect to whether an effective collective action takes place. It is thus quite likely that an effort to exclude certain groups may be more successful on the federal than on the state level and that maintaining the domination of an already existing power elite is much more difficult on the local level. Insofar, then, as a large proportion of governmental benefits is dispensed on an independent local level or as the constellation of forces on the local level determines the influence on the national level, the danger of minoritarian oppression is significantly diminished.

* * *

But the most influential protection that the states offer against tyranny is the protection against the special interest of the government itself. For the fact that the federal government may be less likely than the states, in what we may call "normal times," to oppress small minorities whose mode of life offends a homogeneous majority does not mean that it is never likely to oppress them as well as to deprive the citizenry as a whole of their legitimate voice in running the national affairs. Should the federal government ever be captured by an authoritarian movement or assert itself as a special cohesive interest, the resulting oppression would almost certainly be much more severe and durable than that of which any state would be capable. In such a situation, both private individuals and private-interest groups prepared to defend their rights would face very grave organizational obstacles and could not provide anything even approaching in effectiveness the resistance that may be offered by a governmental institution, endowed with the power of coercing those who may lack a sufficient individual motivation to contribute (if even only financially) to the common good. It is precisely because the states are governmental bodies that break the national authorities' monopoly on coercion that they constitute the most fundamental bastion against a successful conversion of the federal government into a vehicle of the worst kind of oppression.

Viewed from this perspective, freedom from federal interference enjoyed by state governmental machinery, and especially by those of its organs that potentially provide the easiest means by which the citizenry can organize itself against a tyrannical movement on the national level, turns out to be a value quite independent from any limitation of the federal power to regulate any substantive field of private activity. While traditional liberal doctrine relied quite heavily on the exclusion of government from most private activities and hoped to guard us in this way from tyrannical overreaching, the realization of the pervasiveness of market failures in a complex, advanced society has made the doctrine of *laissez-faire* of less use under modern conditions. Similarly, the increasing interdependence of social and economic problems on the national scale makes it unrealistic to expect that the federal government can be kept away from regulating the ever increasing details of what had previously been thought to be essentially local activities. In this situation, when it is no longer an option simply to resist most forms of federal involvement in the private sector, the federalist idea of the separation of the national and local governmental institutions acquires more, and not less, significance for the prevention of governmental oppression. For the independence of the very process of state government, without seriously hampering the national authorities in regulating most private activities, assures the existence of an organizational framework, more efficient than any private institution could provide, that may always be used as an effective tool for bringing together otherwise defenseless individuals with some stakes in resisting the overreaching of the national government. The value of this organizational apparatus thus lies not so much in any of its concrete regulatory activities that the national government could not do as well (or better), as in the very fact that it eliminates the national monopoly on the power to coerce. * * *

* * *

B. Providing a Space for Participatory Politics

The value of citizen participation in governmental operations has often been stressed in legal literature and its enhancement has often been viewed as one of the most important purposes of federalism. But the objectives of citizen participation are usually seen as clustered around such things as the facilitation of the flow of information between the citizens and the government, improving the efficiency of governmental decisions, and the enhancement of the accountability of public officials or of the public acceptance of governmental decisions. Viewed in this way, citizen participation appears, above all, as a means of strengthening the representativeness of governmental institutions and enhancing the perception of its legitimacy. * * *

* * *

* * * [T]here is much truth in these observations but also much that is problematic. Even if we do not question the assumption that the interest of the "people" is ultimately identical to the interest of individuals, it is by no means clear that individuals themselves are best able to articulate the types of considerations that will most affect their interests or identify the decisions that will maximize them. In fact, one of the basic tenets of the classical theory of representation is that it is both wasteful and dangerous for the masses to busy themselves with the complex matters of policy making that may be better handled by professional politicians who choose this as their full-time occupation. * * * There are also persuasive arguments that too much electoral control may in some situations unproductively divert the efforts of the legislators or make them systematically ignore those issues that do not provide an immediate payoff at the polls—even though they may have an ultimately greater impact on the electorate's welfare. * * * Finally, it is not difficult to conceive of situations in which a competent bureaucrat, operating in a clear hierarchical structure in which he expects to make his career, may do a much better job at serving the public than a politician directly responsible to the electorate.[141]

* * *

141. Lawyers often make arguments of this kind against the elective judiciary. But the problem is equally apparent in other areas and does not depend only on the need for expertise. * * *

The model of representative politics rests on the idea that the main task of political institutions consists in providing a method of selecting a social policy that reflects in a fair and acceptable manner the preferences and interests of those groups or individuals who are members of a given political society. What is distinctive in this model is its essentially atomistic conception of society in which the basic interests of social actors do not derive from their being members of the political community and in which the government serves an essentially instrumental function of aggregating the actors' primary preferences into social policies.

Against this representative model, the model of participatory government, which goes as far back as Aristotle, views political activity not as instrumental toward achieving a proportionate share in the distribution of available resources, to be used in a variety of private pursuits, but rather as a good in itself, something essentially implicated in the very concept of human freedom. This way of thinking, which stresses the role of the community in the very shaping of the "interests" of its members and in infusing their lives with a sense of purpose, was by no means absent from the thought of the Founding Fathers. * * * [T]heir ever present concern with what they called public, civic, or "republican" virtue testifies clearly to their belief that the "good life," as Aristotle would have termed it, involves a commitment to a political community and participation in a process by which individuals shape in common the mode of life they are going to share. * * *

* * * [I]f there is some genuine room for noninstrumental participation in American political life, it can realistically exist only on the local level. There have been some efforts to devise new means, using modern communications technology, of reviewing participatory politics on a large scale, but the dominant view is that the optimum size of a political body that can afford significant citizen participation is nowhere near the size of the modern nation state or even of its main provincial subdivisions. * * *

* * *

If one of the primary functions, within the federalist framework, of state-run institutions is to provide the public space for participatory politics, then from this point of view federalism does not conceive the division between the state and national governments as a way of parceling out "sovereignty"—the control over substantive fields of regulation—but rather as a way of preserving alternative modes of decision making. Naturally, the vitality of the participatory state institutions depends in part on the types of substantive decisions that are left for the states. Should the federal government preempt them from most fields that touch directly on the life of local communities, the states would become but empty shells within which no meaningful political activity could take place. But whatever the effect of preemption, the principles of federalism provide an important and independent reason for protecting the autonomy of the political processes of local governments, and this not just in the name of democratic control (for the federal government is also subject to such control), but also in the name of protecting a different form of political space that the national government is very unlikely to provide.

* * *

C. Laboratories of Experiment

Courts as well as commentators are very fond of repeating Justice Brandeis's dictum that "[i]t is one of the happy incidents of the federal system that a single courageous state may, if its citizens choose, serve as a laboratory; and try novel social and economic experiments without risk to the rest of the country." While the context of Justice Brandeis's remark had nothing to do with protecting the states from Congressional interference and while his point concerned only an "incident" of the federal system, the claim that the states constitute "national laboratories of experiment" came to be viewed by many as a cornerstone of the federalist thinking and has quickly become one of the least examined verities of constitutional theory. Only recently has there been some scholarly effort to assess the accuracy of this claim, and the most that can be said is that the jury is still out.

The importance attached by many to the states' function as laboratories of experiment is at least in part exaggerated and, in any case, of little significance for constitutional adjudication. This is true for three reasons. First, whether a strong protection of the states' autonomy would actually contribute to the efficiency of the American government is a very complex question that does not admit of an easy answer. In fact, there are many arguments to the contrary. Second, insofar as there is something to the laboratory-of-experiment argument, a unitary government could avail itself of the same advantages by a partial delegation of authority to its local branches, so that there may be nothing in the laboratory rationale that is peculiarly related to the federal structure of American government. Finally, even if it turns out that decentralization does contribute to governmental efficiency, the analysis necessary to determine which aspects of local governance should be protected from central interference is of a very complex and largely pragmatic nature and thus unsuitable either for elevation to the constitutional level or for judicial assessment. In sum, then, in developing their federalist jurisprudence, the courts should concentrate on the other, more fundamental state functions within the federal framework: the protection against tyranny and the provision of a space for participatory politics.

We should begin with the observation that if the laboratory-of-experiment argument were fully accepted, it would be hard to limit its conclusions to the protection of the internal mode of state governmental operations, as proposed by *National League of Cities,* and not to apply them to the states' control over the private sector. After all, to take the facts of *National League of Cities* as an example, the imposition of minimum-wage requirements for private hospitals reduces the possibility of state experimentation (to say nothing of private experimentation) in this area no less than in the case of public hospitals. Indeed, the very possibility of federal preemption of the regulation of any field of private activity decreases the possibility of state-introduced innovation. Thus, unless we are seriously prepared to consider reversing the long tradition of the Commerce Clause jurisprudence and go back to the idea of preserving some areas of exclusive state regulation, the laboratory-of-experiment argument proves too much.

On closer scrutiny, however, the laboratory-of-experiment argument may turn out to prove not too much but too little. * * * There are, in fact, a number of different considerations that have only rarely been taken into account in assessing the laboratory-of-experiment argument but without which its validity cannot be ascertained. The following list is probably incomplete, but it may suffice to force a reconsideration:

a). If, as has been argued, the states are political units that may have their justification in history but do not necessarily correspond to the economic and social realities of contemporary America, then the forces that determine the direction of local policies may be much less than ideally suited to foster the most efficient governmental solutions. A central government possessed of a power to reshuffle the boundaries and powers of its territorial subdivisions could perhaps produce much better (more efficient) local administration.

b). State regulation is often likely to have spillover effects on other states and produce inefficient solutions by ignoring the costs borne by outsiders. Again, a central government may tailor its delegations of regulatory powers to jurisdictions designed to minimize such externalities.

c). States will often compete with one another for various resources, such as capital, which can move relatively easily to those jurisdictions that offer them the most favorable conditions. As a by-product of this rivalry, however, states may have to forego many redistributive and social programs that make the cost of doing business higher. * * * A central government capable of devising national solutions can afford to be much more innovative in such situations.

d). The costs involved in certain types of innovative regulatory activity (such as the costs of collecting and transmitting information or administering a program) may be too high for a local government to bear, but economies of scale on the national level may make regulations more cost effective. * * *

e). Related to the previous point is the question of incentives that local elective politicians may have, as compared to a professional looking to improve his career prospects in a national bureaucratic hierarchy. * * * First, unlike a competitive economic market, the federal system does not allow a local official to "sell" his product (i.e., to gain additional votes) outside his jurisdiction, and this limits his incentive to innovate. Second, the fact that beneficiaries of governmental innovation do not, as a rule, move from one jurisdiction to another, so as to find the one in which the government's willingness to take risks matches their own preferences, the politician's "portfolio" of governmental projects will tend to cater to the risk preferences of those around the population median (rather than gravitating toward more risky innovations).   Third, the possibility of free riding on the innovative solutions of other jurisdictions further reduces a politician's incentive to take new and more risky paths.   Compared to that, a career bureaucrat, looking to the approval of his superiors and the effects of his work in a well-designed national hierarchy of administrators may (though, of course, only may) have a system of incentives more favorable to innovation.

f).   Finally, the advantages of uniformity may often outweigh the benefits of local innovation, even if some local solutions may have more intrinsic merit.   Thus, for example, all states, except for Louisiana, have recognized the advantages of adopting the Uniform Commercial Code.   But similar advantages to commerce could perhaps accrue from a uniformity in at least parts of tort or insurance law.   Again, a central government, not subject to local political or constitutional constraints, could probably be much more efficient in this respect.

The considerations just listed do not, of course, mean that the function of the states as the laboratories of experiment is entirely illusory.   They do mean, however, that the question of how to structure the division of competences among different levels of government to achieve the most desirable degree of innovation and efficiency is a very complex one and that the answer to it hinges on a variety of empirical and constantly shifting factors.   It is thus quite likely that some forms of unitary government, with a flexible system of delegation that would not be limited by constitutional provisions concerning the structure of local authorities, could accommodate much better the demands of governmental efficiency than our own federal system.   *   *   *

*   *   *

FUTURE DOCTRINAL DEVELOPMENTS

The outcome of my discussion is that the process-oriented analysis of the constitutional functions of federalism, endorsed but not really carried out in the *Garcia* decision, leads to a more affirmative procedural role of the states within the federal system than suggested on the face of Justice Blackmun's opinion.   Also, two important functions of the states—tyranny prevention and the provision of a space for participatory politics—are likely to be endangered by the national government and warrant a close judicial scrutiny of federal interference with state and local governmental operations.   To some extent, then, my analysis confirms the accuracy of the insights implicit in *National League of Cities* by showing that its insistence on the protection of the political process of local governments, rather than on a guarantee of some exclusive state controls over the private sector, responded to the most fundamental desiderata of federalism, while also showing that some of these insights need not be viewed as incompatible with the *Garcia* approach.

Nevertheless, developing a constitutional theory of federalism does not automatically translate into a clear judicial doctrine specifying a set of genuinely manageable standards of review. In fact, it is the problematic character of such standards that occupies the bulk of the Court's opinion in *Garcia* and the unmanageability of the "traditional governmental functions" test laid down by *National League of Cities* seems to have been one of the main reasons for its overruling. What needs to be seen is whether the theory of federalism I have articulated can provide more reliable guidance for judicial application.

* * * *Garcia*'s merciless critique of the criterion of tradition seems to evince a desire for watertight, mechanical tests of protected governmental functions that simply cannot be had in an area as complex as that of federalism. Constitutional adjudication is not, after all, a field in which simple standards predominate, and there can be no substitute for a painful case-by-case refinement and elaboration. Still, there are a number of ways in which the concerns of federalism may be intelligibly used as a guide for judicial review.

First, there are some state governmental functions so directly related to the federalist concern with preventing tyranny that they present rather easy cases for judicial intervention (though perhaps they are also, at this moment, the least likely to meet with serious interference). Under any approach, for example, federal interference with the agenda of the highest state legislative and executive organs is likely to undermine the overall autonomy of the political processes in the states and eliminate their constitutional role within the federal system. Similarly, an interference with the state electoral processes, insofar as it is not clearly related to the protection of individual rights but threatens to gerrymander the local districts in order to change the configuration of political forces in favor of the nationally powerful interests, would be clearly beyond the pale. A gradual subordination of state police forces to a federal command structure would cripple the states' ability to enforce their basic choices and resist tyrannical pressures from above. A radical limitation of the states' ability to tax would make their fiscal solvency a matter of federal grace and ultimately make a mockery of the federalist concerns.

It may be a little harder to come up with equally clearly unconstitutional instances of federal interference with the states' function of enhancing participation, especially since, as I have noted, it is mostly not the state governments themselves but rather their local emanations that provide the primary locus of direct citizen involvement in the political life in America. Even here, though, there may be clear enough cases. For example, given the special participatory mode in which school boards operate in most states, a federal education law that would attempt to transform those boards into an extension of the federal bureaucratic machinery would strike at the very core of participatory politics in the United States.

Furthermore, it would be a mistake to think that cordoning off some areas of state governments from federal interference is the only possible method of implementing the principles of federalism. After all, if it is not the protection of state sovereignty that is at stake here but rather the basic functions of the states within the federal system, it is quite likely that the nature of the central intervention itself should be more determinative of its constitutionality than the local activity interfered with. Thus, for example, many federal laws that depend on state governmental machinery for their implementation attempt, though usually with only very modest success, to assure that the states open the administrative process to citizen involvement. Insofar as such programs attempt to open up state politics to citizen participation, without undermining those aspects of local representative systems that may be important to preventing tyranny, they may be subject to a looser form of control than laws that have the opposite effect. Similarly, federal laws that provide reimbursements for costs imposed on local governments may be more acceptable than those that constitute a serious drain on state fiscal resources.

Finally, although *National League of Cities* concentrated exclusively on federal interference through a system of direct commands to local governments, federalist concerns also have some implications with respect to national action under the spending power. The common issue that is bound to arise in both contexts, but which was left unanalyzed by *National League of Cities* and its progeny, is the question of when the states are unconstitutionally induced by the national government into something that may impair their ability to fulfill their constitutional functions. In the context of the Commerce Clause, the question arose in *FERC v. Mississippi* as a result of Justice Blackmun's intimation that if the federal government had the power to preempt the states from the field of utility regulation, it could also condition its permission for the states to engage in the regulation of utilities on their acceptance of federally mandated standards and procedures. The ostensible explanation was that since the states were free to withdraw from the field altogether, they were not coerced by the federal requirements. Justice O'Connor's dissent in *FERC* disputed this approach but gave no real criteria for distinguishing incentives from coercion. It is this issue that becomes central when *National League of Cities'* concern with the federal coercion of the states is carried over to spending power legislation, which constitutes the national government's main tool of securing state compliance with its demands. The reason why federalist concerns are usually ignored in the judicial review of spending power legislation is primarily related to the claim that the states are free to refuse to participate in the federal spending programs and thus are not really coerced into anything.[187] Nevertheless, while emphasis on the

---

187. This doctrine was spelled out in Steward Machine Co. v. Davis, 301 U.S. 548 (1937). Somewhat paradoxically, the Court elaborated its doctrine concerning the states' unconditional freedom at about the same time as it started to doubt the old *Lochner* wisdom that regulating hours of work was an abridgement of the workers' freedom of contract.

consent given by the states to the various conditions in federal grants (often quite unrelated to the purposes of the grant itself) may comport quite well with the idea of state sovereignty, the states' consent is often likely to be free in a rather Pickwickian sense. Even apart from coercion, the emphasis on consent may sometimes raise serious questions under the process analysis developed here. Even if the states should "consent" to measures that weaken their organizational capacity to resist tryrannical pressures from the national government or their ability to protect local participatory institutions, it is not clear that the Constitution allows the federal government to undermine its own democratic character by proposing such measures.

BIBLIOGRAPHY

Background Reading on the American Federal System

Beer, *Federalism, Nationalism, and Democracy in America,* 72 Am.Pol. Sci.Rev. 9 (1978).

S. Davis, THE FEDERAL PRINCIPLE, A JOURNEY THROUGH TIME IN QUEST OF A MEANING (1978).

Diamond, *The Federalist's View of Federalism,* in ESSAYS IN FEDERALISM 21 (Institute for Studies in Federalism, 1961).

D. Elazar, THE AMERICAN PARTNERSHIP (1962).

McConnell, *Federalism: Evaluating the Founders' Design,* 54 U.Chi.L. Rev. 1484 (1987).

W. Riker, FEDERALISM (1964).

Rose–Ackerman, *Does Federalism Matter? Political Choice in a Federal Republic,* 89 J. of Pol.Econ. 152 (1981).

Scheiber, *Federalism and the Constitution: The Original Understanding,* in L. Friedman & H. Scheiber, AMERICAN LAW AND THE CONSTITUTIONAL ORDER 85 (1978).

Storing, *What the Anti–Federalists Were For,* in H Storing, ed., THE COMPLETE ANTI–FEDERALIST (1981).

THE FEDERALIST, Nos. 10, 14, 39, 44–46, 51.

Tullock, *Federalism: Problems of Scale,* 6 Pub.Choice 19 (1969).

Tushnet, *Federalism and the Traditions of American Political Theory,* 19 Ga.L.Rev. 981 (1985).

Federal Regulatory and Fiscal Control of State Governments

Advisory Commission on Intergovernmental Relations, REGULATORY FEDERALISM: POLICY, PROCESS, IMPACT AND REFORM (1984).

Field, Garcia v. San Antonio Metropolitan Transit Authority: *The Demise of a Misguided Doctrine,* 99 Harv.L.Rev. 84 (1985).

Grodzins, *Centralization and Decentralization in the American Federal System,* in R. Goldwin, ed., A NATION OF STATES 1 (1963).

Heineman, *The Law Schools' Failing Grade on Federalism,* 92 Yale L.J. 1349 (1983).

D. Kettl, THE REGULATION OF AMERICAN FEDERALISM (1983).

LaPierre, *The Political Safeguards of Federalism Redux: Intergovernmental Immunity and the States as Agents of the Nation,* 60 Wash. U.L.Q. 779 (1982).

Nagel, *Federalism As A Fundamental Value: National League Of Cities In Perspective,* 1981 Sup.Ct.Rev. 81.

M. Reagan, THE NEW FEDERALISM (1972).

Soifer, *Truisms That Never Will Be True: The Tenth Amendment and the Spending Power,* 57 Colo.L.Rev. 793 (1986).

Stewart, *Federalism and Rights,* 19 Ga.L.Rev. 917 (1985).

B. STATE POWER: REGULATION OF COMMERCE

Questions about the extent of national and state power in our federal system have been most thoroughly explored in the context of commercial regulation. The Commerce Clause gives Congress power

> To regulate Commerce with foreign Nations, and among the several States, and with the Indian Tribes[.] (Art. I, § 8, cl. 3)

The Clause is silent about state power. The traditional question here has been whether it somehow limits state authority, even in its 'dormant' state (when Congress has not acted). During the past decade this problem has engaged the Court's attention as keenly as at any other period in our history.

The issue of state power has many facets. One is the source of the constitutional restraint (if there is one) on state action. How does the silence of the Commerce Clause speak to the issue of state power? Noel Dowling's article contends that it actually doesn't—that restraints flow from Congress's failure to act—a proposition disputed by Daniel Farber and Donald Regan. This issue is related to another curious facet of Commerce Clause jurisprudence which Dowling is at pains to explain: the fact that Congress can 'overrule' Supreme Court decisions about the commerce power of the states.[1] A third problem that has arisen with increasing frequency in recent years is the proper treatment of states when they act as participants in the market.[2] And a fourth is the proper role of the Article IV Privileges and Immunities Clause, which the Court has said shares the same "vision of federalism" as the Commerce Clause.[3]

1. See, e.g., Prudential Insurance Co. v. Benjamin, 328 U.S. 408, 66 S.Ct. 1142, 90 L.Ed. 1342 (1946); *In re* Rahrer, 140 U.S. 545, 11 S.Ct. 865, 35 L.Ed. 572 (1891).

2. See, e.g., South–Central Timber Development v. Wunnicke, 467 U.S. 82, 104 S.Ct. 2237, 81 L.Ed.2d 71 (1984); Reeves, Inc. v. Stake, 447 U.S. 429, 100 S.Ct. 2271, 65 L.Ed.2d 244 (1980).

3. Hicklin v. Orbeck, 437 U.S. 518, 98 S.Ct. 2482, 57 L.Ed.2d 397 (1978).

These questions are important and difficult, but in the big picture of Commerce Clause litigation they are peripheral rather than central. The most significant issue still remains: what standards do (or should) the courts use to test constitutional claims about state regulation of commerce? The readings in this section are primarily about this issue. They suggest three different approaches. Dowling proposes a balancing test, and his argument has had great influence on the Supreme Court's decisions during the past half century. The Court now balances local benefits against burdens on commerce even when local and foreign trade are treated alike.[4] But more recent scholarship evinces great dissatisfaction with both the theory and the practice of balancing. Farber and Regan both reject that approach, and propose instead that we focus on intentional discrimination. Their reasons for this shift in focus differ, though. Farber believes that the courts should intervene when the political process is not working, and discrimination against unrepresented foreign interests is a signal that that is happening. Regan argues that a process approach is overbroad, and worse, inconsistent with fundamental assumptions about our federal system. He suggests instead an anti-protectionism principle.

NOEL T. DOWLING, INTERSTATE COMMERCE AND STATE POWER

27 Va.L.Rev. 1–6, 19–24 (1940).

PRIOR THEORIES

The views which have been entertained as to the effect of the commerce clause on state power may be summarized under four heads. Each of them has been held by the Court, or a number of Justices, at one time or another, and one of them contains in substance, as I will try to show, the desirable doctrine for the future. They are:

1. That the clause impliedly prohibits all state regulation or taxation of interstate commerce;

2. That the clause itself prohibits nothing, the states being free to regulate and tax as they see fit unless and until they are stopped by Congressional action;

3. That the clause prohibits some, but not all, state regulation and taxation—that is, sometimes it prohibits and sometimes it does not;

4. That though the clause itself prohibits nothing an impediment may arise from the express or implied will of Congress.

The first is of historical interest as that to which the Court inclined at the beginning. In *Gibbons v. Ogden*, counsel contended that "as the word 'to regulate' implies in its nature full power over the thing to be regulated, it excludes, necessarily, the action of all others that would perform the same operation on the same thing," and further that "regulation is designed for the entire result, applying to those parts

4. Pike v. Bruce Church, Inc., 397 U.S. 137, 90 S.Ct. 844, 25 L.Ed.2d 174 (1970).

which remain as they were, as well as to those which are altered."
"Great force" was conceded to this argument by Chief Justice Marshall,
and the Court was "not satisfied that it has been refuted." But it was
unnecessary in that case to decide whether the power of the states was
surrendered by the mere grant to Congress, or is retained until Congress shall exercise the power, for the reason that the power had been
exercised, and the regulations which Congress deemed it proper to
make were in full operation. And the narrow holding was that the Act
of Congress prevailed over the inconsistent regulation of the New York
statute. As to taxation, *Brown v. Maryland* all but committed the
Court to the first view. * * *

The second view is, in substance, the one expounded by Chief
Justice Taney, particularly in the *License* cases. Though his opinion
did not win the support of a full majority of the Court, there was
agreement in the conclusion to which it led. In general, this view
would remove the commerce clause from judicial consideration.
* * *

The third view, a compromise between the two earlier views,
represents the first definite position taken by the Court on the commerce clause; and this occurred in *Cooley v. The Board of Wardens,* in
1851. In the course of the opinion the Court undertook to explain the
cause of its prior diversities of opinion, saying that they arose "from the
different views taken of the nature of the power." But when, the Court
added, the nature of a power like this is spoken of, when it is said that
the nature of the power requires that it should be exercised exclusively
by Congress, "it must be intended to refer to the subjects of that power,
and to say they are of such a nature as to require exclusive legislation
by Congress." For the power to regulate commerce, the Court observed, embraces a vast field, containing not only many, but exceedingly various subjects, quite unlike in their nature; some imperatively
demanding a single uniform rule, and some as imperatively demanding
that diversity which alone can meet local necessities. * * *

The fourth view may be described as a composite of the second and
third, and a limited version of it was announced by the Court in 1890.
It originally covered only interstate commerce in intoxicating liquors,
though it was later enlarged. This view squares with the second in the
sense that no prohibition inheres in the commerce clause itself, and it
preserves the results of the third in that some state action would be
upheld—*e.g.,* where "matters of local concern" are involved—and some
overturned. Also it calls for the same kind of inquiry as under *Cooley
v. The Board,* but with this difference in result: if the subject were held
"national," a congressional negative would be presumed rather than a
constitutional prohibition applied. This view admitted the power of
Congress to exercise complete control in both fields: to supersede state
action in local matters, to permit it in national. The significant and
salutary effect was to take constitutional rigidity out of the commerce
clause problem and substitute the flexible and adaptable will of Con-

gress. At the same time it recognized a definite function for the courts in the ascertainment of that will. * * *

In the intervening period up to 1938 no distinctive theory appears to have been formulated or urged. New terminology crept into the opinions, and the Court talked increasingly of "direct" and "indirect" effects or burdens on interstate commerce, the former being held invalid and the latter valid. The "direct-indirect" test had this much at least in common with *Cooley v. The Board,* that it upheld some and overturned other state action; but it was far from satisfying since it offered so little of a criterion for determining on which side a case would fall. Quarantine laws, for example, which hit interstate commerce head-on and stopped it dead in its tracks at the border, surely would have to be classed as "direct," yet they were sustained. The oleomargarine laws of Massachusetts had a no less direct impact on traffic than did Iowa's liquor laws, but Massachusetts won and Iowa lost. * * *

* * *

WHAT OF THE FUTURE?

From what has gone before, a doctrine can be drawn which offers, I believe, desirable and helpful guidance for the Court in the future. It is, that in the absence of affirmative consent a Congressional negative will be presumed in the courts against state action which in its effect upon interstate commerce constitutes an unreasonable interference with national interests, the presumption being rebuttable at the pleasure of Congress. Such a doctrine would free the states from any constitutional disability but at the same time would not give them license to take such action as they see fit irrespective of its effect upon interstate commerce. With respect to such commerce, the question whether the states may act upon it would depend upon the will of Congress expressed in such form as it may choose. State action falling short of such interference would prevail unless and until superseded or otherwise nullified by Congressional action.

[Several] reasons support the foregoing:

1. The congressional consent aspect of the doctrine would entail no sharp break with the past, and its adoption would constitute the acceptance of some of the best efforts of the Court. * * * I have always thought that it was implicit in *Cooley v. The Board* [.] * * * [The] doctrine was slow in taking form and did not acquire definite proportions until *Leisy v. Hardin* in 1890. The fact that the Court's arrival at this position culminated a long consideration accentuates the burden upon those who would depart from it. * * *

2. The substantive standard embodied in the doctrine, "unreasonable interference with national interests," would commit the Court to no new or untried principle. It would, to be sure, involve an avowal that the Court is deliberately balancing national and local interests and making a choice as to which of the two *should* prevail. That, as I see

the matter, is a policy judgment. But the test of reasonableness in interstate commerce cases is not the same as, for example, in due process cases. Additional factors are involved. In a sense, a state law must take the hurdle of due process before it comes to the interstate barrier. The blow post law case from Georgia affords a striking illustration. The requirement that trains slow down at crossings was deemed, as well as it can be gleaned from the report and with regard to the situation in Georgia, an appropriate and permissible means for securing safety of life and property notwithstanding the inconvenience to local traffic and to the companies. At that stage the judicial scales tipped in favor of the statute. But other factors thrown into the other side of the scales—*e.g.*, convenience and economy of time in through traffic, more efficient and less expensive operation of railway systems— tipped them back against the statute.[35]

As already indicated, *Cooley v. The Board* comprehended a certain balancing of state and national interests, though the Court did not go into the subject in detail. And it was just there, in an effort to discover the relevant considerations for answering the question whether the "national interest in maintaining freedom of commerce across state lines" has been infringed, that Mr. Justice Stone tackled the problem in his *Di Santo* dissent.[a] His approach in that opinion appears to be well calculated to produce a "realistic" judgment whether any given state action constitutes an unreasonable interference with national interests. * * * He essayed no exhaustive list, nor would he exclude such factors as the desirability of uniform regulation (the principal point of *Cooley v. The Board*); or the consequences to the state if its action were disallowed—how serious and widespread the evil and what the prospect for national action; or the intangible but nevertheless real benefits to be had from giving the people of the states the satisfaction of, and stimulus to responsibility from, home government as against distant government. And in order to bring all such considerations into the judicial forum, could not the rules of evidence be made more generous and elastic? It is true that the litigation is between private parties, but the issue touches the relative jurisdictions of nation and state. After all, this is statecraft in which the courts are engaged.

3. This doctrine would provide flexibility in the adjustment and accommodation of national and state interests, at the same time preserving the judicial and amplifying the legislative function. From the judicial point of view it would preserve a role which the Court, beginning with the leadership of Marshall, has worked out for itself and which has conspicuously contributed to the functioning of the federal system. That role brings to constitutional cases the best of the common law methods in the building up of principles from specific decisions. The trial courts would operate out on the front line, where the impact of state action on interstate commerce is first felt, and they could

35. Seaboard Air Line R.R. v. Blackwell, 244 U.S. 319 (1917).

a. Di Santo v. Pennsylvania, 273 U.S. 34, 43 (1927).

appraise at close range the conflicting state and national interests. Furthermore, the judicial sifting of the facts would have the manifest merit of sharpening the issues and facilitating legislative efforts in the event that Congress, dissatisfied with the judicial results, should desire to take corrective action of its own.

* * *

There is no assurance that the commerce problem would be as well handled by Congress alone as where both Congress and the courts participate in its solution. I say "would", drawing a distinction between what seems likely and what is theoretically possible. Congress is a big and heavy machine to set in motion, and its progress is sometimes impeded even when national interests of the highest order are at stake. Meanwhile much damage to interstate commerce, to say nothing of the otherwise amicable relationships among the states, might be caused by unrestrained state action. * * *

Even if Congress should accept the task it would not find it an easy one. It would have to labor with much of the same evidence that would be offered in the courts, as well as other matters bearing upon various phases of policy (including sheer political pressures); and perhaps more often than not the solution would have to be stated in general terms. And then, after all that were done, it is not at all unlikely that the whole thing would be thrown into the courts for final settlement, but with this difference, that whereas formerly the courts could turn to the judicially developed principles and feel their way along, henceforth they would have to interpret and apply new and general formulas from Congress.

DANIEL A. FARBER, STATE REGULATION AND THE DORMANT COMMERCE CLAUSE
3 Con.Comm. 395–406, 410–414 (1986).

The Court's current view of the so-called "dormant" commerce clause, in a nutshell, is as follows. State regulations having a discriminatory effect on interstate commerce are subject to stringent judicial scrutiny even if the discrimination was inadvertent. On the other hand, regulations that burden interstate commerce without discriminating against it are subject to a less rigorous balancing test: a state law that burdens local and interstate commerce equally will be upheld if the law's local benefits outweigh the burden on commerce.

This doctrine is said to serve two purposes: preventing discrimination against outsiders who are not represented in the state's political process, and furthering the national interest in free trade among the states.[8] In the last decade, the Court has become increasingly aggressive in its pursuit of these goals. * * *

* * *

8. Another rationale sometimes used is that the Court is implementing what it believes to be the unexpressed will of Congress. That is, congressional silence is assumed to demonstrate an intention to place restrictions on the states. *See* Dow-

The Court's Current Approach

In understanding the Supreme Court's current approach, it is useful to distinguish among three types of cases. The first type involves intentional discrimination against interstate commerce. *City of Philadelphia v. New Jersey* illustrates the Court's approach to such statutes. New Jersey faced a serious shortage of landfill space. To conserve existing space as long as possible, the legislature prohibited the importation of waste from other states for disposal in New Jersey. The Supreme Court found this legislation unconstitutional on its face. "[W]hatever New Jersey's ultimate purpose, it may not be accomplished by discriminating against articles of commerce coming from outside the State unless there is some reason, apart from their origin, to treat them differently." Thus, intentional discrimination against interstate commerce is generally prohibited.

Even when discrimination is unintentional, state laws are subject to substantial scrutiny, as illustrated by *Hunt v. Washington State Apple Advertising Commission*. Federal law provided a system of grades to be used in labeling apples. North Carolina prohibited the use of any other grades on labels. The suit was brought by Washington apple growers, who contended that the Washington grading system was superior and that the ban on use of these grades impaired the marketability of their apples. The law did not on its face discriminate against interstate commerce. The discriminatory effect on Washington apples was enough, however, to subject the law to heightened scrutiny. Given this discriminatory effect, the state had the burden to "justify it both in terms of the local benefits flowing from the statute and the unavailability of nondiscriminatory alternatives adequate to preserve the local interests at stake." The state was unable to carry this burden.

Even a statute with neither a discriminatory purpose nor a discriminatory effect may be unconstitutional. The leading case on commerce clause review of non-discriminatory statutes is *Pike v. Bruce Church, Inc.* *Pike* involved an Arizona statute governing cantaloupe packing. A state official claimed that enforcement of this law required that the cantaloupes be packed inside the state, which would have required the company to build an expensive new packing shed. The Court began its constitutional analysis with a synthesis of the previous case law:

> Although the criteria for determining the validity of state statutes affecting interstate commerce have been variously stated, the general rule that emerges can be phrased as follows: Where the statute regulates evenhandedly to effectuate a legitimate local public interest, and its effects on interstate commerce are only incidental, it will be upheld unless the burden imposed on such commerce is clearly excessive in relation to the putative local benefits. If a legitimate local

ling, [*Interstate Commerce and State Power,* 27 Va.L.Rev. 1 (1940).] The obvious flaw in this concept is that congressional silence, in the end, means only that Congress has not decided to legislate. Interpreting what Congress means when it has spoken is often difficult enough; to determine what Congress means when it has said nothing at all is impossible.

purpose is found, then the question becomes one of degree. And the extent of the burden that will be tolerated will of course depend on the nature of the local interest involved, and on whether it could be promoted as well with a lesser impact on interstate activities. Occasionally the Court has candidly undertaken a balancing approach in resolving these issues, but more frequently it has spoken in terms of "direct" and "indirect" effects and burdens.

The state requirement under consideration in *Pike* did not survive this balancing test. Since *Pike,* the balancing test has been applied to a variety of subjects ranging from state corporation laws to highway safety regulations.

The *Pike* test is to some extent rigged against the state. A state law may create benefits as well as burdens for outsiders. The burdens are weighed against the state, but any beneficial effect on interstate commerce is not weighed. *Pike,* in other words, establishes a judicial cost-benefit analysis in which all of the costs of a state law are counted, but only some of the benefits.

The Court's current approach has been subjected to strong scholarly criticism. To begin with, results in dormant commerce clause cases are notoriously unpredictable. This is particularly true of the *Pike* test, which requires an ad hoc balancing based on the trial record in each case. For example, even after a Wisconsin truck regulation was struck down, no one could be sure of the validity of a similar Iowa regulation until the Court ruled, since the records in the two cases differed.[29]

The more fundamental flaw in the current approach is that it places the Court in the position of evaluating economic policy. Under *Pike,* as Professor Kitch has observed,

> The question, in other words, is not whether the regulation or tax is or is not on interstate commerce. The question is whether, all things considered—including the national interest—the tax or regulation of commerce, interstate or not, is good or bad. This approach, of course, has a close kinship with the now discredited substantive due process of cases like *Lochner v. New York,* 198 U.S. 45 (1905). The Court abandoned substantive due process in the 1930s, but the method has lived on in Commerce Clause matters. . . .

In one recent case, for example, the Court heavily stressed the virtues of the unregulated free market in allocating resources to their best use. The Court may be right, but many people share Justice Holmes's skepticism about assertions that the Constitution embodies particular economic theories. * * * Justices Black and Douglas argued cogently against a predecessor of the *Pike* test on just this ground.[34]

*   *   *

29. *See* [Kassel v. Consolidated Freightways Corp.], 450 U.S. 662 (1981); [Raymond Motor Transp., Inc. v. Rice], 434 U.S. [429 (1978).]

34. Southern Pacific Co. v. Arizona, 325 U.S. 761, 784, 795 (1945). * * *

REFORMULATING THE JUDICIAL ROLE

* * *

Establishing the proper standard for judicial review under the dormant commerce clause requires first that the purposes of judicial review be determined. At various times, the Supreme Court has relied on two quite different justifications for judicial review under the commerce clause. One justification relates to the political process; the other relates to substantive constitutional values.

The process rationale is based on the lack of representation for non-residents in the political process. At least since *Carolene Products* [43] it has been a commonplace that judicial review is most defensible when it compensates for a defect in the political process. The paradigm is judicial protection of minority groups under the equal protection clause. Like racial minorities during much of our history, out-of-state residents lack political representation and thus the democratic process may fail fully to safeguard their interests.

This process rationale does provide some justification for reviewing at least some state legislation. In particular, it may justify review of state legislation that discriminates against interstate commerce. But it falls well short of justifying the extent of judicial review allowed under current doctrine. In particular, lack of political representation hardly justifies the *Pike* test. Under *Pike*, completely non-discriminatory legislation that burdens non-residents is subject to judicial review. Since the burden on non-residents is the same as that on residents, however, the state's political process seems to offer adequate protection.

Therefore, any justification for the Court's current approach must rely on substance rather than process. The Court has often referred to the important constitutional value of free trade. On close examination, however, this value does not justify expansive judicial review. Admittedly, concern about discriminatory state trade barriers was important in motivating the adoption of the Constitution in general and the commerce clause in particular. But no evidence exists that the clause was intended of its own force to institute free trade, or that the courts were authorized to supervise state legislation. Indeed, two strong arguments can be made against finding a judicially enforceable value of "free trade" in the clause.

First, to paraphrase Justice Stevens, "there is only one commerce clause." It is well settled that Congress may not only erect trade barriers of its own, but may also freely authorize the states to do so. If the clause embodied a constitutional preference for free trade, then allowing Congress to use the commerce power to restrict trade would be as perverse as using the first amendment as a basis for censorship. The breadth of congressional power long recognized by the Court seems to be in tension with the view that the clause established free trade as a substantive constitutional goal.

43. United States v. Carolene Products Co., 304 U.S. 144 (1938).

Second, even finding a free-trade value in the clause would not in itself justify a judicial role in enforcing that value. Various portions of article I seem directed at achieving a wide variety of goals, from national security to technological progress. Yet no one thinks these clauses create any warrant for a judge-made body of law directed at these goals. Thus, justifying current doctrine requires an explanation of why a grant of power to Congress has the effect of authorizing judicial review of state legislation, when Congress has not acted. One traditional justification is that Congress simply cannot keep up with the myriad of relatively insignificant state barriers to free trade. Even if the dubious factual premise of this argument is granted, its logic is flawed. The limitations of the other branches do not necessarily imply a correlative judicial power to fill the need. The Constitution places several express limitations on forms of state economic regulation that the framers found undesirable. Rather than place such a limitation on state incursions into free trade, the framers simply made free trade one of the many aspects of "general welfare" entrusted to Congress.

The process approach has recently received strong support from the Supreme Court in another federalism-related context. In *National League of Cities v. Usery,* the Court had taken upon itself the duty of protecting a substantive value (state sovereignty) without any express textual basis. In *Garcia v. San Antonio Metropolitan Transit Authority,* the Court overruled *National League of Cities.* As the *Garcia* Court explained, judicial intervention is proper only when the federal legislative process is inadequate to protect the interests of the states. The Court found no such flaw in the legislative process behind the extension of the federal minimum wage to state employees. If process theory is to determine the extent of judicial protection of the states, it seems equally applicable when determining judicial limitations on state powers. The teaching of *Garcia* is that, absent a textual limitation, protection for federalism-related values is to be found in the political process, with judicial intervention only when that process has broken down. By the same reasoning, the dormant commerce clause should be limited to its process rationale.

Under this interpretation, the dormant commerce clause serves a function much like that of the equal protection clause. Both protect politically disenfranchised groups. Yet the scope of protection under the two existing doctrines is quite different. Under current law, interstate businesses receive far more protection from state legislation than do racial minorities. A business can establish a prima facie claim under the commerce clause by showing either discriminatory intent, a disparate impact, or a substantial burden. But a law imposing a substantial burden on a racial minority is not considered suspect; even a disparate impact on the minority is not enough. Instead, minority groups must prove discriminatory intent.

Is this radical difference in doctrine justifiable? Since judicial action under the commerce clause is subject to congressional override, it is less undemocratic than judicial action under the equal protection clause. Arguably, therefore, a more freewheeling form of review is appropriate under the commerce clause.

While in isolation this argument may sound strong, powerful arguments can be made that review under the commerce clause is much *less* needed than protection of minorities. Typically, government actions that burden interstate commerce also adversely affect many state residents. For example, if outside firms are barred from entering a state market, consumers lose the benefit of the competition and pay higher prices. These consumers may not be as well organized politically as local business lobbies, but they are not completely lacking in political power. Furthermore, multistate firms may often be important in a state's domestic economy, giving them the opportunity to exert pressure on the government. Finally, even if they lack votes, interstate businesses have the other vital ingredient of political influence: money.

Thus, while the harm done to the democratic process by judicial review under the commerce clause is perhaps less, the justification for judicial review is also weaker. On balance, it is hard to see any justification for providing substantially greater judicial protection to interstate businesses than to racial minorities.

* * *

The contrast between equal protection law and commerce clause law is illustrated by two cases. In one, *Dean Milk v. City of Madison*, Madison passed a law forbidding the sale of milk imported from more than twenty-five miles away, and requiring pasteurization plants to be located within five miles of town. Obviously, the burden fell on Wisconsin farmers outside the Madison area as much as on out-of-state farmers. Yet the Court struck down the law as facially discriminatory. In contrast, *Personnel Administrator v. Feeney* involved a Massachusetts law giving an employment preference to veterans, who were, with few exceptions, men. Just as the Wisconsin law excluded many in-state farmers and all out-of-state farmers, the Massachusetts law excluded many men and virtually all women. But in *Feeney* the Court found no reason to subject the law to heightened scrutiny as a form of gender discrimination. After all, there was no demonstrated intent to discriminate against women, and the impact on a large group of men provided a political check on the legislature.

In *Dean*, the existence of discrimination was considered so serious as to create almost a per se finding of invalidity, while in *Feeney* there was not even enough discrimination to subject the legislation to serious judicial scrutiny. Under the approach suggested in this section, *Dean* would be decided differently. In the absence of a finding of intent to exclude non-residents from the market, the mere existence of an exclusionary effect would be irrelevant.

* * *

OVERCOMING DOCTRINAL INERTIA

* * *

* * * Even if current doctrine is weak as a matter of legal theory, it still might be worth retaining if it served an important practical function. The Court has often proclaimed the importance of the dormant commerce clause in maintaining the national economy. If indeed current doctrine were important to the health of the economy, conceptual purity might have to give way to practical necessity.

In reality, however, vigorous judicial review is probably not needed to keep states from blockading the national economy. Other powerful safeguards exist. Historically, state legislation has been judicially reviewed under the commerce clause on the basis that Congress cannot be expected to trouble itself with minor matters. This argument has lost whatever validity it may once have had, as Congress has shown itself willing and able to preempt burdensome state legislation.

Although Congress formerly met only for short sessions, and therefore may have had time only for the most pressing matters of national concern, clearly that is no longer true. In particular, burdens on commerce that are important enough to justify action by the Court are also likely to be important enough to prompt congressional action. For instance, after the Court's repeated bouts with the issue of truck length on interstate highways, Congress acted to settle the issue.[103]

Since Congress can correct judicial mistakes, what is ultimately at stake under the dormant commerce clause is the burden of inertia. Should the states or interstate businesses have the burden of getting congressional action? In allocating this burden, it is useful to consider which party is more likely to get judicial mistakes corrected. The very reason for giving the power to regulate interstate commerce to Congress, rather than to state legislatures, is that Congress is more responsive to the national interest and less responsive to parochial interests. If so, those claiming to represent the national interest should be better able to secure congressional action than their opponents. Hence, the burden of overcoming congressional inertia should be on them.

* * *

[There are other safeguards against improper state legislation.] The market exacts its own inexorable penalties for needlessly burdensome regulations. For example, in *Pike*, Arizona imposed an apparently senseless and expensive requirement that its farmers build packing sheds inside the state. A state that makes a practice of doing such things will soon find that multistate firms like the plaintiff in *Pike* are making their investments elsewhere. Those farmers remaining in the state will suffer a competitive disadvantage compared with farmers in neighboring states. Similarly, laws that protect in-state firms from

103. *See Kassel,* 450 U.S. 662 (1981); *Rice,* 434 U.S. 429 (1978); *Surface Transportation Assistance Act of 1982,* Pub.L. No. 97–424, 96 Stat. 2097 (1982); *Depart-* *ment of Transportation and Related Agencies Appropriations Act, 1983,* Pub.L. No. 97–369, 96 Stat. 1965 (1982). * * *

competition in local markets have the effect of raising prices, so the ultimate burden is borne by local consumers. These consumers may not be able to organize as effectively as business lobbies, but they should not be dismissed as a political force. * * *

* * *

In summary, the Court's current approach to the dormant commerce clause is badly in need of reform. The disparate impact and undue burden phases of current doctrine give the federal courts an undesirable policymaking role. Under current doctrine, courts are asked to decide whether laissez-faire is better national policy than state regulation. Such policy determinations are better left with more democratic institutions.

This article suggests [a more limited] judicial role in dormant commerce clause cases. * * * [T]he Court should only intervene when an intent to discriminate against interstate commerce can be proved. As in equal protection law, disparate impacts or undue burdens should not be enough in themselves to trigger judicial review.

DONALD H. REGAN, THE SUPREME COURT AND STATE PROTECTIONISM: MAKING SENSE OF THE DORMANT COMMERCE CLAUSE

84 Mich.L.Rev. 1091, 1094–1095, 1112–1118, 1124–1125, 1160–1166 (1986).

WHAT IS "PROTECTIONISM"?

* * *

I shall say that a state statute (or administrative regulation, or local ordinance, or whatever) is protectionist if and only if:

(a) the statute (or whatever) was adopted for the purpose of improving the competitive position of local (in-state) economic actors, just because they are local, vis-à-vis their foreign (by which I mean simply out-of-state) competitors; and

(b) the statute (or whatever) is analogous in form to the traditional instruments of protectionism—the tariff, the quota, or the outright embargo (all of which can be on imports or exports).[a]

The doctrine that states may not engage in protectionism (may not adopt protectionist legislation as I have defined it) I shall refer to as the "anti-protectionism principle."

* * *

There are three objections to state protectionism, which I shall call the "concept-of-union" objection, the "resentment/retaliation" objection, and the "efficiency" objection.

a. Regan states that part (b) of the definition "is necessary in part to account for the Court's recent decisions on the state-as-market-participant; but it is necessary for other reasons as well, and it has its own theoretical justification * * *. As it happens, all the state laws involved in what the reader would think of as standard cases under the dormant commerce clause satisfy part (b) of the definition * * *." Regan's full discussion of part (b) is omitted.

The concept-of-union objection is so obvious that it is easily over-looked. State protectionism is unacceptable because it is inconsistent with the very idea of political union, even a limited federal union. Protectionist legislation is the economic equivalent of war. It is hostile in its essence.

In saying protectionist legislation is hostile, I do not mean that the harm to the foreign victims is necessarily valued for itself. The ultimate goal may be only promotion of local well-being. But the harm to foreign interests is also not merely incidental. The immediate intended means to improvement of local well-being is the transfer of certain profitable activities from foreign to local hands. Protectionism does not merely harm some foreign interests in the process of confer-ring an independent local benefit. Rather, it takes away from the foreigners in order to give to local residents exactly what has been taken away. Nations under arms are often no more hostilely disposed to their enemies than this. Such behavior has no place in a genuine political union of any kind.

Notice I have not said that all legislation that distinguishes be-tween locals and foreigners is objectionable. A state does have a special relationship to its own citizens. Alaska may provide that only Alaskans can run for governor or share in the distribution of the state's oil royalties. Such legislation is not hostile to non-Alaskans in the way protectionism is hostile. It takes nothing away from non-Alaskans that we would normally think they have as much right to as Alaskans have.

The reader might wonder whether protectionist legislation is any more hostile than ordinary competitive economic behavior. When the Coca–Cola Company introduced its new flavor of Coke, it was trying to take business away from Pepsi–Cola and transfer that business to itself. We would not normally characterize Coca–Cola's behavior as hostile. We even tend to assume behavior like this is socially valuable.

Now, states do not ordinarily compete with each other for custom-ers in the way Coca–Cola and Pepsi–Cola compete, but states do sometimes try to help local businesses compete by what we would think of as normal marketing techniques. Thus, the State of Michigan advertises Michigan as a vacation paradise for boaters and fishermen, hoping thereby to benefit the Michigan tourist industry, and recogniz-ing that any benefit will come at least in part at the expense of other states' tourist industries.

Such behavior by Michigan is perfectly permissible. * * * [D]eveloping our war analogy, we might say that protectionism takes over a market share by force; it is like acquiring territory by armed conquest. Advertising, like product improvement and other standard market ploys, uses no force; it encourages a free transfer of allegiance. It is like acquiring territory by plebiscite of the inhabitants.

The next objection to protectionism is the resentment/retaliation objection. If protectionism is conceptually inconsistent with political union, it is also practically inconsistent. Protectionist impositions cause resentment and invite protectionist retaliation. If protectionist legislation is permitted at all, it is likely to generate a cycle of escalating animosity and isolation (and even of hostility in the strongest sense, where the harm to foreign interests *is* valued as such), eventually imperiling the political viability of the union itself.

* * *

The third objection to protectionism is that it is inefficient. Now, "efficiency" is a treacherous notion. Let us pause to be sure we know what we are saying. Why exactly is protectionism inefficient? The obvious answer is that tariffs, embargoes, quotas, and the like interfere with efficiency in the production of goods; they divert business from low-cost (foreign) to high-cost (local) producers.

For some purposes, the statement that protectionism is inefficient because it diverts business from low-cost (foreign) to high-cost (local) producers would be perfectly adequate. But for our purposes, it is inadequate. It tells part of the story, but not the whole story, of why classical protectionist measures seem so self-evidently objectionable on efficiency-related grounds.

The first problem with the statement as it stands is this: It suggests that *every* law which diverts business away from the producers who currently have it is necessarily diverting business from low-cost to high-cost producers and impairing efficiency. But that need not be so.

Consider the Oregon bottle law.[b] That law diverted business from can manufacturers to bottle manufacturers and, because of the increased transportation cost associated with heavier containers, from out-of-state bottlers to in-state bottlers. But there is no reason to think the Oregon bottle law impaired productive efficiency. The object of the law was to discourage a mode of production, the packaging of beverages in nonreusable and nonreturnable cans, that created costs (in the form of litter) not accounted for by market mechanisms. In other words, the object of the law was to improve productive efficiency by correcting an inefficiency that resulted from an external cost of the existing productive process.

* * *

Our discussion of the Oregon bottle law makes it clear that we cannot be satisfied with a statement of the efficiency objection to protectionism that suggests that every law that diverts business away from (foreign) producers who currently have it impairs productive efficiency and thus shares the evil of protectionism. How shall we reformulate the efficiency objection in order to avoid this suggestion?

We could say that protectionism is inefficient because it diverts business from producers who are the low-cost producers under the cost-assignment scheme implicit in the legal status quo, without the state's even claiming the justification, which Oregon claimed for its bottle law,

b. In 1971 Oregon passed a law to protect the environment by discouraging the use of nonreturnable cans.

that that cost-assignment scheme is defective. Or, compressing what we have just said: protectionism is inefficient because it diverts business away from presumptively low-cost producers without any colorable cost-based justification.

This reformulation of the efficiency objection is an improvement, but it is still not fully acceptable. The change we have made, focusing as it does on cost-based justification, responds too exclusively to the Oregon bottle law. We can see the need for further reformulation by considering a somewhat different case, *Exxon Corp. v. Maryland.* If we give the Maryland legislature the benefit of any doubts about its purpose, the object of the Maryland law forbidding ownership of retail service stations by producers or refiners of petroleum was to secure fairer treatment of independent service station operators. Is that a "cost-based justification" for the diversion of retail business away from vertically integrated oil refiners? There may be room for someone to argue that this fairness justification for the Maryland law is not cost-based; but if there is room, that merely shows that a formulation of the efficiency objection in terms of cost-based justification is still not the right formulation. Whether or not we regard the claimed justification for the Maryland law as cost-based, the justification prevents the law from being self-evidently and unambiguously objectionable in the way a classical tariff is. (Remember we are assuming innocent purpose.) To be certain we exclude the Maryland law from the scope of the efficiency objection, we need to state the efficiency objection to protectionism more narrowly still, if we can find a way to do so.

Here is the proper formulation: protectionism is inefficient because it diverts business away from presumptively low-cost producers without any colorable justification in terms of a benefit that deserves approval from the point of view of the nation as a whole. Or, again compressing slightly: protectionism is inefficient because it diverts business away from presumptively low-cost producers without any colorable justification in terms of a "federally cognizable benefit."

Consider once more the classical tariff, and see how this reformulated efficiency objection fits it. The classical protectionist tariff diverts business away from those producers who currently have it, and the only benefit sought by the state imposing the tariff is a transfer of welfare from foreign producers (firms or workers) to their local counterparts. This transfer is a benefit from the narrowly self-interested viewpoint of the state imposing the tariff; but by its very nature this benefit to the imposing state is balanced by an equal loss to some other state or states. From the point of view of the nation as a whole, such a bare transfer of welfare between similarly situated parties in different states creates no benefit at all.

It is clear, then, that a classical tariff aims at no federally cognizable benefit, no benefit that deserves approval from the point of view of the nation as a whole. But what about the Oregon bottle law, or the Maryland law about service stations? Must there be a national policy in favor of reducing the litter in Oregon's parks and highways, or must we be able to say there should be such a national policy, before we can say the Oregon law seeks a federally cognizable benefit? No. The states are independent entities. Part of the point of federalism is to allow states to make their own decisions about such matters as what sort of an environment they value and want to maintain. So long as there is no constitutionally stipulated policy against minimizing litter (that is, no constitutionally stipulated policy in favor of litter *as such*), the elimination of litter from Oregon's parks and highways is a good thing from the federal viewpoint if Oregon says it is. Similarly, so long as there is no constitutional policy against fairer treatment (or what Maryland views as fairer treatment) for independent service stations, securing fairer treatment for independent service stations in Maryland is a good thing from the federal viewpoint if Maryland says it is.

*   *   *

I have put the efficiency objection last, even though it would occur first to many constitutional scholars, because it deserves to be down-played. The relevant sense of "efficiency" turns out to be much weaker than one might at first assume; and the objection also was not primary in the framers' thinking. The people who wrote our Constitution were by no means thoroughgoing free traders. They envisaged a mercantil-ist foreign trade policy for the United States as a whole. One reason they wanted to locate the power to regulate commerce with foreign nations in Congress was that independent regulation of such commerce by the states prevented the implementation of an optimal national mercantilist policy. The framers did have some efficiency-related objec-tion to interstate protectionism. They argued that eliminating prefer-ential state regulation of trade would encourage agriculture and indus-try. But that is a much narrower claim than is suggested by modern apostles of efficiency, who operate with a strong presumption in favor of total economic *laissez-faire.* The framers would have recognized many good reasons for state economic regulation, and they would have recognized that the states must be the primary judges of what are good reasons. To the extent the framers were concerned with efficiency, it seems reasonable to think of their objection as being the objection I have formulated.

The structural argument against state protectionism is now com-plete. It remains only to consider whether there is a textual argument as well. In my opinion, the structural argument does not need to be supported by an argument from any single short bit of text (which is what lawyers normally mean by a "textual" argument), so long as there is no short bit of text that contradicts the structural argument (and there is none). Even so, let us see what we make of the text in bits.

Does the constitutional text include any bit that prohibits state protectionism? That depends, not surprisingly, on how the bits are approached. If we ask whether there is any bit of text that, taken by itself, naturally suggests to a modern reader that the states are forbidden to engage in protectionism against other states, the answer is easy: No, there is not. But there is another question, still about bits of text, that may be of interest. Is there any bit of text that might have suggested to a reader in 1787 that state protectionism was forbidden? Or, what is almost the same question, is there any bit of text that we could reasonably take to embody a final intention of the framers to forbid state protectionism, if we have independent reason to think the framers intended to forbid it and intended the text to say so? Here, the answer is: Yes. The relevant bit of text is the words, "The Congress shall have power . . . to regulate commerce . . . among the several states. . . ."

There is much evidence that the main point of this grant (unlike the grant of power over foreign commerce) was not to empower Congress, but rather to disable the states from regulating commerce among themselves. The type of commercial regulation uppermost in the framers' minds was what we might categorize generally as mercantile regulation—regulation of navigation, customs regulation, and the like. The framers wanted commerce among the states to be free of state-originated mercantilist impositions. Giving Congress the power to regulate internal commerce was one way of denying states that power, under the view, much more natural to the framers than to us, that granted regulatory powers were exclusive. I have remarked previously that as Congress' power over interstate commerce is now understood, we cannot treat that power as exclusive. But that does not mean the framers could not have regarded as exclusive the much narrower power they were thinking of. There is considerable evidence that they did so regard it.[68]

Against the Carolene Products Theory of the Dormant Commerce Clause and Open–Ended Private Interest Balancing

The basic idea of the Carolene Products theory of the dormant commerce clause is simple enough: When states adopt economic regulations that affect out-of-state interests, those out-of-state interests are likely to be shortchanged because they are not represented in the political process that produces the regulations. But everyone who is affected ought to be represented. Therefore we have judicial review of state economic regulation that affects out-of-state interests in order to give those interests "virtual representation."

* * *

68. * * * Of course, if the commerce clause forbids state mercantilist legislation, then it also provides a ground for judicial review to prevent such legislation. But notice that this argument for judicial review extends only so far as state legislation is flatly prohibited, which is to say, only so far as Congress' power is exclusive. This argument provides no ground for judicial review of all state legislation which is "commercial" in the sense that it duplicates what Congress might do under its (largely nonexclusive) commerce power as presently interpreted. (It is a very natural extension of the mercantilist exclusion, however, to say the Court may suppress what is superficially ordinary commercial legislation if that legislation has a protectionist purpose.)

Now, in discussing the *Carolene Products* theory of the dormant commerce clause (which I shall refer to hereafter as just the "*Carolene Products* theory," leaving the limitation to the dormant commerce clause understood), the first thing we need to do is to be clear about the scope of judicial review that the theory is supposed to justify.

The *Carolene Products* theorist might argue only for judicial application of the anti-protectionism principle as I have developed it. This would put him on solid ground, but it would rob his theory of any interest. Certainly the *Carolene Products* theory entails the anti-protectionism principle as a consequence. There would be no protectionist legislation (in my sense) if foreign interests were represented equally with the local interests they compete against. However, the idea of virtual representation is not necessary to justify the anti-protectionism principle. My own argument for the anti-protectionism principle made no use of the idea of virtual representation. (The idea that one state may not behave hostilely to another is a much more limited idea, as is the idea that state regulation producing protectionist effect must aim at some federally cognizable benefit.) If virtual representation is the central idea of the *Carolene Products* theory, then the *Carolene Products* theory is not necessary to ground the anti-protectionism principle, and acceptance of the anti-protectionism principle does not commit us to the *Carolene Products* theory.

The *Carolene Products* theory is interesting only if it entails more than the anti-protectionism principle—specifically, if it entails that economic regulation that affects foreign interests should be reviewed by courts applying a balancing methodology. Open-ended private interest balancing is what virtual representation requires, and it is what most *Carolene Products* theorists have argued for.[c] (The balancing that is required is private interest balancing because it is private interests that are supposed to deserve virtual representation.)

Now, one problem with the *Carolene Products* theory is that if it justifies balancing at all, it requires balancing over a much broader range of cases than its proponents usually recognize. Justice Stone, the original *Carolene Products* theorist (in the dormant commerce clause area as elsewhere), suggested that judicial review would not be necessary if there were in-state interests functionally equivalent to the damaged out-of-state interests. * * * But if any foreigners are harmed, then representation of those foreigners in the political process of the enacting state might have shifted the political balance and prevented the adoption of the regulation. This is true even if there are already similarly burdened local interests, and even if these local interests are more heavily burdened than the foreign. * * *

c. "Open-ended private interest balancing," Regan explains elsewhere, is the view "that any cost imposed by a statute on a private party can be advanced as an argument against the constitutionality of the statute[.]" Not every such cost will invalidate a law, but every cost counts in the scale used to measure validity.

This means the *Carolene Products* theory requires review of laws no one would normally think of as requiring judicial scrutiny. If Minnesota adopts an advertising campaign to try to discourage smoking among its population, or if it forbids smoking in enough stores, offices, and places of public assembly to affect significantly the total number of cigarettes smoked, then the law should be judicially inspected to see that it does not unjustly harm tobacco growers in North Carolina. If a major city adopts a rent control ordinance, judicial review is required to protect the interests of people living elsewhere who might have moved to the city except for the increased difficulty of securing housing.[131] If a state has a stingy workmen's compensation program that attracts employers, the courts must stand ready to consider whether representation in that state's legislature of foreign workers might not have produced a program that was more generous.

My last example might elicit the response that review is not required because the foreign workers are not objecting to the program as it exists so much as they are objecting to the state's failure to have a more generous program. This raises an interesting question about what counts as action by a state and what is a mere omission. But even if we could make that distinction perfectly clear, it would not help the *Carolene Products* theorist. On his theory, the courts ought to review legislative omissions as freely as they review positive legislative action. After all, representation of foreign interests would not result only in blocking legislation. Sometimes it would tip the balance in favor of legislation where none was otherwise forthcoming. * * *

Overbreadth, however, is not the most fundamental problem with the *Carolene Products* theory of the dormant commerce clause. The *Carolene Products* theory assumes that out-of-state interests really ought to be represented—the theory assumes it is a defect in our system that the system denies foreigners representation, as it is a defect if racial minorities or women are unrepresented or represented ineffectively. But that assumption is not warranted. Nonrepresentation of foreign interests follows from the simple fact that there are separate states; and the existence of separate states, while it might be a defect in an ideal political system, can hardly be treated as a defect in ours.

I suggest that with regard to treatment by the states of out-of-state interests, our system embodies the following compromise between unlimited state autonomy and perfect national unity. The states may not single out foreigners for disadvantageous treatment just because of their foreignness. But, provided they do not single out foreigners, the states need not attend positively to the foreign effects of laws they adopt nor to the distribution between locals and foreigners of the benefits and burdens of those laws. "Singling out" foreigners does not necessarily involve explicitness. It does involve purpose. The state

---

131. This example is borrowed from Kitch [*Regulation and the American Common Market*, in Regulation, Federalism, and Interstate Commerce 31 (A. Tarlock, ed. 1981).]

legislature that simply fails to attend to foreign interests or to any local/foreign distinction may do as it pleases. This is the message of the dormant commerce clause, as it is the general message of the privileges and immunities clause of article IV.

Clearly, this is a compromise. If the states were perfectly autonomous, they would be free to single out foreigners for disadvantageous treatment. If, on the other hand, we had perfect national unity, there would be no states at all, except perhaps as administrative departments, and all interests throughout the nation would be taken into account in any significant legislative decision. Giving foreign interests virtual representation in the actual independent state legislatures may be thought of as an attempt to mimic a regime of perfect national unity. But in view of the compromise I have described, such "virtual" perfect unity is not required.

The autonomy interest of the states that we protect by not requiring virtual representation may seem like just a freedom to harm foreigners with impunity so long as it is done by inadvertence. This is not an interest one can feel much enthusiasm for. But in fact, there is more at stake.

By not requiring state lawmakers to be always looking over their shoulders for foreign interests and always calculating the proportionate incidence of benefits and burdens, we make legislation a possible task for lawmakers with less expertise and less administrative support available to them than Congress has. We also avoid a massive transfer of power to the courts, federal and state. And we avoid the tendency to homogenization of values that commitment of economic regulation to the courts, under the general supervision of the Supreme Court, would tend to bring about. It is worth remembering that states can disagree about issues with significant interstate aspects for reasons having nothing to do with hostility to, or even indifference to, foreigners as such.

BIBLIOGRAPHY

Article IV Privileges and Immunities Clause

Eule, *Laying the Dormant Commerce Clause to Rest,* 91 Yale L.J. 425 (1982).

Varat, *State "Citizenship" and Interstate Equality,* 48 U.Chi.L.Rev. 487 (1981).

Congressional Silence; Consent to State Laws

Abel, *The Commerce Clause in the Constitutional Convention and in Contemporary Comment,* 25 Minn.L.Rev. 432 (1941).

Cohen, *Congressional Power to Validate Unconstitutional State Laws,* 35 Stan.L.Rev. 387 (1983).

Powell, *The Still Small Voice of the Commerce Clause,* Proceedings Nat. Tax Ass'n 337 (1938).

States as Market Participants

Anson & Schenkkan, *Federalism, the Dormant Commerce Clause, and State–Owned Resources,* 59 Tex.L.Rev. 71 (1980).

Gergen, *The Selfish State and the Market,* 66 Tex.L.Rev. 1097 (1988).

Gillen, *A Proposed Model of the Sovereign/Proprietary Distinction,* 133 U.Pa.L.Rev. 661 (1985).

State Taxation of Interstate Commerce

Brown, *The Open Economy: Justice Frankfurter and the Position of the Judiciary,* 67 Yale L.J. 219 (1957).

J. Hellerstein, STATE TAXATION (1983).

Hellerstein, *Is "Internal Consistency" Foolish?: Reflections on an Emerging Commerce Clauase Restraint on State Taxation,* 87 Mich. L.Rev. 138 (1988).

Hellerstein, *State Taxation and the Supreme Court: Toward a More Unified Approach to Constitutional Adjudication?,* 75 Mich.L.Rev. 1426 (1977).

Hunter, *Federalism and State Taxation of Multistate Enterprises,* 32 Emory L.J. 89 (1983).

Lockhart, *A Revolution in State Taxation of Commerce?,* 65 Minn.L.Rev. 1025 (1981).

Theory and Practice of State Commerce Regulation

Black, *Perspectives on the American Common Market,* in REGULA-TION, FEDERALISM, AND INTERSTATE COMMERCE 59 (Tarlock ed. 1981).

Collins, *Economic Union as a Constitutional Value,* 63 N.Y.U.L.Rev. 43 (1988).

Dowling, *Interstate Commerce and State Power—Revised Version,* 47 Colum.L.Rev. 547 (1947).

F. Frankfurter, THE COMMERCE CLAUSE (1937).

Kitch, *Regulation and the American Common Market,* in REGULA-TION, FEDERALISM, AND INTERSTATE COMMERCE 9 (Tarlock ed. 1981).

Maltz, *How Much Regulation Is Too Much—An Examination of Commerce Clause Jurisprudence,* 50 Geo.Wash.L.Rev. 47 (1981).

O'Fallon, *The Commerce Clause: A Theoretical Comment,* 61 Ore.L.Rev. 395 (1982).

Regan, *Siamese Essays: (I) CTS Corp. v. Dynamics Corp. of America and Dormant Commerce Clause Doctrine; (ii) Extraterritorial State Legislation,* 85 Mich.L.Rev. 1865 (1987).

T. Sandalow and E. Stein, eds., COURTS AND FREE MARKETS (1982).

Sedler, *The Negative Commerce Clause As A Restriction On State Regulation And Taxation: An Analysis In Terms Of Constitutional Structure,* 31 Wayne L.Rev. 885 (1985).

Smith, *State Discriminations Against Interstate Commerce,* 74 Calif.L. Rev. 1203 (1986).

Tushnet, *Rethinking the Dormant Commerce Clause,* 1979 Wis.L.Rev. 125.

Chapter IV

SEPARATION OF POWERS

Like federalism, separation of powers doctrine deals with relations among the institutions of American government. The former is sometimes said to address the "vertical" division of authority between national and state governments, the latter a "horizontal" division among the national executive, legislature, and judiciary. Lately the Supreme Court has decided to entrust many federalism issues to the political branches, on the theory that they are capable of protecting their own interests.[1] The Court seems to have made a different assumption about separation of powers: the area is one in which it now plays an unusually active supervisory role.

A. GENERAL THEORETICAL APPROACHES

We cannot deal intelligently with separation issues without first thinking about the purposes served by a division of authority within the national government. One reason ("efficiency") for creating a strong executive was that the Framers viewed legislative government—with which they had some experience under the Articles of Confederation—as too fragmented and episodic. They thought that the national government would be more efficient if they separated executive from legislative functions. A second reason for dividing power—one mentioned prominently by Madison[2]—is the prevention of tyranny. Lest one institution become too powerful the Constitution confers on others the ability to check and balance its authority. So, for example, the President can veto legislation, the Congress can impeach the President and cut his budget, and the courts can invalidate executive and legislative actions. But the objectives of tyranny-prevention and efficiency may conflict with one another (checks and balances will weaken a strong executive), and with still other functions served by separation. How they should best be reconciled is one theme taken up in the articles by David Currie and Peter Strauss.

1. Garcia v. San Antonio Metropolitan Transit Authority, 469 U.S. 528, 405 S.Ct. 1005, 83 L.Ed.2d 1016 (1985).

2. The Federalist No. 47.

The controversy over purposes is entwined with a second theme that is important today in all areas of constitutional law—the conflict over methods of interpreting the Constitution. One approach, labelled "formal" by its opponents, urges that the text and structures of the Constitution and the intentions of its authors provide clear answers to many conflicts about separation of powers. Currie argues that Articles I and II create separate categories of legislative and executive power that have edges sharp enough for drawing lines. Strauss takes a position that might be called "functional," by way of contrast. He contends that the categories of legislative and executive power overlap, especially in a complex administrative state. Strauss urges us to think about keeping institutional powers practically in balance rather than categorically separate.

DAVID P. CURRIE, THE DISTRIBUTION OF POWERS AFTER BOWSHER

1986 Sup.Ct.Rev. 19–36.

Article I of the Constitution entrusts the legislative power of the United States to Congress, so that democratically elected representatives will determine national policy. Article II vests the executive power in the President, in the interest of unified administration by an elected officer. Article III places the judicial power in judges appointed for life and removable only for high crimes and misdemeanors, so that cases may be decided without fear of reprisal. Above all, the distribution of these powers among three separate branches serves as a powerful check against arbitrary action, for it means that three distinct bodies must concur before the individual is effectively deprived of his liberty or property: Congress must pass a law, the President must seek to enforce it, and the courts must find a violation.

One would scarcely suspect all this from observing the current operations of the national government. Executive departments as well as independent agencies promulgate regulations that look for all the world like statutes. Violations of law are prosecuted by officials independent of presidential control. Administrators and "non-Article III judges" decide cases within the federal judicial power. Most strikingly, sometimes all three functions are combined in a single agency largely independent of all three branches and enjoying none of their attributes. The Federal Trade Commission, whose members are appointed for seven years and removable for "inefficiency, neglect of duty, or malfeasance in office," adopts regulations defining unfair methods of competition, institutes proceedings against purported offenders, and passes on the merits of its own complaints in a "quasi-judicial" proceeding.

* * *

In the last few years, however, the Court has displayed increasing concern for the distribution of powers. Despite its permissive precedents, the Court made clear in *INS v. Chadha* that Congress could not delegate lawmaking authority to one of its Houses, and there have been hints that delegations to administrators may also be scrutinized more closely. * * * [T]he Court held in *Buckley v. Valeo* that Congress could not appoint officers with executive duties. Last Term, in *Bowsher v. Synar*, the Court took another step in the same direction: Congress cannot remove such officers either.

The individual decisions have been dissected in detail elsewhere. My aim is to be neither bibliographic nor repetitive but to present a concise general view of the distribution of powers.

I. LEGISLATIVE POWER

"All legislative powers herein granted," says Article I, "shall be vested in a Congress of the United States. . . ."

Historically the transfer of legislative power from monarch to representative assembly was, as Montesquieu observed, an important step toward self-government. It was also a significant means of protecting liberty and property. Long before there were limitations on the power of the state as a whole, liberty and property were safeguarded by requiring the consent of the people themselves, through their representatives, before their interests could be invaded.

* * *

* * * [T]he debate on the Constitution was replete with explanations why it was desirable to place legislative powers in a representative assembly. First was the conviction that, notwithstanding ultimate popular control of other organs of government, it was important to give some substantial role in lawmaking to a body directly elected by the people. * * *

Gerry appeared to suggest that self-government was an end in itself: "It is a maxim that the people ought to hold the purse strings." [18] Franklin and Madison saw it as a means of protecting the interests of the people, the former insisting that "those who feel, can best judge," [19] the latter that without a direct role in selection of the House "the people would be lost sight of altogether." [20] Wilson saw direct election of the House as contributing to "the confidence of the people," without which [n]o government could long subsist." [21]

Apart from the democratic nature of the House, a second pervasive theme of the debates was the value of having legislative decisions made by a collective body in which various interests were represented. "[A] numerous legislature," wrote Hamilton, was "best adapted to deliberation and wisdom, and best calculated to conciliate the confidence of the people and to secure their privileges and interests." [22] * * *

The final theme, independent of the virtues of a particular lawmaking body, was the more general one of separation of powers: It was important to liberty that the legislative power not be in the same hands

18. [1 Farrand] 233.
19. *Id.* at 546.
20. *Id.* at 50.
21. *Id.* at 49. * * *
22. The Federalist, No. 70.

as the executive. This of course had been a central point for Montes-quieu, whom Madison explicitly invoked during the Convention. "The accumulation of all powers legislative, executive, and judiciary in the same hands," Madison repeated in the Federalist Papers, "whether few or many, and whether hereditary, self appointed, or elective, may justly be pronounced the very definition of tyranny." [26]

In short, despite the fact that the new Constitution provided for indirect popular control of the executive, the Framers were insistent that it was important to entrust the legislative power to Congress. For the more democratic nature of the House, the sheer numbers and representative nature of an assembly, and the mere separation of legislative from executive power were seen as important means of strengthening self-government, protecting against ill-founded or oppressive legislation, and securing the confidence of the people.[27]

A.   The Supremacy of Statutes

The first and most obvious consequence of vesting legislative authority in Congress is the supremacy of statutes validly enacted.

That congressional enactments bind the public at large is implicit in the concept of law and confirmed by history: The Framers meant to create not a debating society but a maker of public policy. * * * [T]he binding effect of statutes on other branches is indispensable to effectuation of the expressed purpose of parliamentary control of public policy and thus implicit in the grants of legislative power in Article I, reinforced by the declaration of Article VI that "laws of the United States . . . shall be the supreme law of the land" and by Article II's command that the President "take care that the laws be faithfully executed."

* * *

B.   The Necessity for Legislation

The second implication of vesting legislative authority in Congress is that no other branch may legislate. With rare exceptions, moreover, the executive may act only on the basis of law.

It is clear enough that executive officers cannot make laws, and in general federal courts cannot either. The common law tradition in both England and the states does show that interstitial lawmaking by other branches subject to legislative correction is not wholly incompatible with the ultimate policymaking authority of the legislature. That tradition, however, is based on necessity; judges must decide cases whether or not the legislature has laid down a rule of decision. To extend such authority to the executive branch would poorly serve the goals of the Framers, for to require affirmative congressional action to

26. The Federalist, No. 47. * * *

27. Illustrative of the prevailing attitude was Hamilton's response to the objection that the proposed Constitution did not forbid standing armies: The interests of the people were adequately safeguarded by lodging the authority to raise them not in the executive but in "a popular body, consisting of the representatives of the people." The Federalist, Nos. 24, 26, 28.

undo bad laws made by others combines the weight of inertia with the certainty of interim harm.

Hamilton's insistence that placing the power to raise armies in Congress was adequate protection against its arbitrary exercise [34] makes clear the understanding that the executive could not raise them; legislative powers were given to Congress because the Framers did not want other federal officers exercising them. The absence of lawmaking power in executive officers is thus implicit both in the grant of that authority to Congress and in the limited enumeration of executive powers, as Justice Black suggested in *Youngstown:* "[T]he Constitution is neither silent nor equivocal as to who shall make laws which the President is to execute."

Apart from the Constitution's independent grants of Presidential authority in such fields as foreign affairs and defense, it follows that executive officers can act only on the basis of legislation. An undeclared executive war undermines the purposes of the Framers just as seriously as a declared one. The lesson of Hamilton's essay on armies was not only that the President could not pass laws raising them, but that he could not raise them at all. This was likewise the purport of Justice Black's opinion for the Court in the *Youngstown* case, for the executive had not professed to pass a law seizing the steel mills; he was forbidden to act without congressional authorization. Since its purpose was to assure legislative control of policy, the congressional monopoly of federal legislative power inherent in Articles I and II implies a monopoly of policymaking with respect to the subjects confided to congressional care.

C. The Nondelegation Doctrine

The third consequence of the vesting of legislative power in Congress is that it cannot be further delegated.   *   *   *

*   *   * This does not preclude Congress from leaving details to another agency, for filling gaps in applying inevitably imprecise legislation is inseparable from the executive function. But the purposes of the Framers in granting legislative power to a representative assembly cannot be attained unless the lawmakers themselves lay down, as the Supreme Court has said, a "primary standard" or an "intelligible principle."

Fifty years ago, in *Panama Refining Co. v. Ryan* and in *Schechter Poultry Corp. v. United States,* the Supreme Court found two instances in which Congress had failed to heed this important limitation. These decisions were no reactionary aberrations. Both were joined by such respected liberals as Brandeis and Stone, the second—rendered without dissent—also by Cardozo. It was obviously inconsistent with the constitutional plan to authorize the President, in *Schechter,* to require whatever was good for the economy.   *   *   *

---

34. See note 27 *supra.*

Later decisions seemed lenient in reviewing claims that legislative power had been invalidly delegated. During the 1940s, for example, the Court upheld grants of authority to set "fair and equitable" maximum prices, to appoint receivers for national banks, and to recapture "excessive profits" from government contractors.[50] Such decisions have led some observers to the unsettling conclusion that the nondelegation doctrine is dead.

In no case, however, has the Court repudiated the principle. In the decisions just noted, for example, the Justices emphasized that there was no absence of standards to guide the exercise of delegated authority. * * * In two [recent] cases Justice Rehnquist argued that the not very sweeping authority to carry out a congressional policy of all feasible protection from certain workplace health hazards went too far.[54]

In sum, individual decisions over the years may have stretched the nondelegation doctrine; but it remains the law that delegated authority must be confined in order to preserve the responsibility of the legislature to make basic policy.

D. The Legislative Veto

It is clear enough that the directly elected House of Representatives was meant to play a central role in the lawmaking process. It is equally clear, however, that the House was not to make law on its own; Article I, § 7 provides for the enactment of laws by the concurrence of both Houses, subject to an overridable Presidential veto. Apart from the obvious safeguard against ill-considered action provided by any bicameral legislature, the history reveals a deliberate decision to give the states equal voices in one chamber and to require the consent of a body partly insulated by a six-year term from the fickle popular will. The President's veto was designed both to protect the executive from legislative encroachments and as an additional safeguard "against the enaction of improper laws."

When Congress began passing laws authorizing one or both of its Houses to block executive action, it undermined these provisions. Nowhere is Congress given power to reverse executive policy except by legislation; and Congress has only the powers given it by the Constitution. The Supreme Court recognized this in *INS v. Chadha* in 1983. It was not really a hard case.

II. Executive Power

"The executive Power," says Article II, "shall be vested in a President of the United States of America."

---

50. Yakus v. United States, 321 U.S. 414 (1944); Fahey v. Mallonee, 332 U.S. 245 (1947); Lichter v. United States, 334 U.S. 742 (1948).

54. Industrial Union Dept. v. American Petroleum Inst., 448 U.S. 607, 671–88 (1980) (concurring); American Textile Manufacturers Inst. v. Donovan, 452 U.S. 490, 543–48 (1981) (dissenting).

Three critical concerns underlie this provision. The first is the democratic principle that the executive should be elected and thus responsive to the people: "It was desirable, that the sense of the people should operate in the choice of the person to whom so important a trust was to be confided." [62] The second was once again the desire to separate the executive and legislative powers in order to reduce the risk of invasions of liberty. * * * The third was the need to concentrate executive power in the hands of a single person. Rutledge argued that "[a] single man would feel the greatest responsibility and administer the public affairs best"; Wilson "preferred a single magistrate, as giving most energy dispatch and responsibility to the office." [64] "The persons . . . to whose immediate management [the administration of government is] committed," wrote Hamilton, "ought to be considered as the assistants or deputies of the chief magistrate; and, on this account, they ought to derive their offices from his appointment, or at least from his nomination, and ought to be subject to his superintendence." [65]

The consequences of vesting the executive power in a single, independent, elected President are several.

A. Congress May Not Execute the Laws

Apart from such matters as impeachment and consent to appointments, where it functions as a check on other branches, Congress has been given only legislative powers. The debates show that the withholding of executive authority from Congress was, among other things, a deliberate means of protecting against the dangers that arise when the same persons both make and carry out the laws. The limited enumeration of congressional powers and the explicit vesting of the executive power in the President preclude Congress from administering spending programs, prosecuting offenses, or giving orders to armies in the field.

It follows that Congress cannot effectively control the exercise of executive power by making the tenure of those who administer the laws dependent upon congressional whim. * * * To grant executive power to an officer removable at the discretion of Congress would undermine all the reasons for creating an independent executive. For, as Hamilton wrote in connection with judges, "A power over a man's subsistence amounts to a power over his will." [68]

This unsurprising conclusion informs the decision in *Bowsher v. Synar* that Congress could not empower the Comptroller General to administer the Gramm–Rudman law requiring a balanced federal budget. As the dissenters noted, Congress could discharge that official only upon a finding of "disability, . . . inefficiency, . . . neglect of duty, . . . malfeasance, . . . felony or . . . moral turpitude"; but that is

62. The Federalist, No. 68 (Hamilton).

64. 1 Farrand at 65. See also The Federalist, Nos. 70, 74. * * *

65. The Federalist, No. 72.

68. The Federalist, No. 79.

a far cry from the degree of control the Framers grudgingly afforded Congress in the impeachment clauses.

Finally, for similar reasons, Congress may not appoint those who execute the laws. As *Buckley v. Valeo* held, Article II makes this plain by authorizing Congress to vest appointing power in almost anybody except itself; and in any event the default provision for nomination by the President and confirmation by the Senate marks the degree of intended legislative control over appointments. * * *

In short, congressional execution of the laws and congressional appointment or removal of executive officers would make the executive more dependent upon the legislature than is consistent with the constitutional plan.

B. *The President Must Control Execution of the Laws*

Although the Court properly refrained from so deciding in *Bowsher,* it should be equally plain that Congress cannot deprive the President of the executive power. For the Constitution not only denies executive authority to Congress, in the interest of separation of powers; it also vests that authority in the democratically elected President, in order to concentrate executive authority in a single responsive official.

Thus the Court was plainly right in *Myers v. United States* that Congress could not forbid the President to discharge a postmaster. The aggravating circumstance that Congress had purported to give one of its Houses a veto power over removal played a minor role in the decision; the essence of the argument was that the President could not fulfill his duty to see that the laws were faithfully executed if he could not control those executing them. *Myers* was the converse of *Bowsher:* as one with power to discharge can control, one without that power cannot.

This does not mean that ordinary civil service limitations on groundless discharges are invalid; so long as the President retains authority to give orders, their disobedience will be cause for discharge. But the President has no such authority over Federal Trade Commissioners; a central purpose of the legislation was to create a body independent of Presidential control. Thus the 1935 decision in *Humphrey's Executor v. United States,* upholding the statute forbidding dismissal of such a Commissioner without cause, was grievously wrong. The filing of complaints, as the Court emphasized in *Buckley,* is an executive function; and the Constitution requires the President to control the execution of the laws.

It is no answer that, as the Court argued in *Humphrey's,* the Commission's prosecuting function is in some sense incidental to other activities that may be characterized as "quasi-legislative" or "quasi-judicial." *Buckley* makes that clear as to appointments, and it is no less true as to removal. The Constitution recognizes only three kinds of federal powers: legislative, executive, and judicial. If the power either to "fill[ ] in . . . the details" of the congressionally prescribed prohibitions or to adjudicate disputes arising under federal law can properly be lodged outside Congress and the courts, it is only on the theory that they pertain to the implementation of law; and this means that they too must be subject to Presidential control. To uphold the Commission's independence on the ground that these powers are not executive, on the other hand, is to argue that Congress may violate Article II whenever it is willing to violate Articles I and III as well. *Bowsher* should therefore have come out the same way if authority to administer the budget law had been given to an officer independent of congressional as well as Presidential control.

Finally, an examination of the reasons for lodging executive power in the President supports the Court's 1839 dictum that the clause of Article II empowering Congress to provide for the appointment of inferior officers by "the President alone, . . . the Courts of law, or . . . the Heads of Departments" permitted appointments only by "the department of the government to which the officer to be appointed most appropriately belonged." [85] For judges to appoint their own clerks makes obvious sense; for them to appoint State Department officials would seem quite inconsistent with the Framers' notions of unified executive power. For them to appoint prosecutors, as they were authorized to do in the wake of the Nixon Administration scandals, offends the separation of powers as well by giving judges too much influence over the prosecution.[a]

PETER L. STRAUSS, THE PLACE OF AGENCIES IN GOVERNMENT: SEPARATION OF POWERS AND THE FOURTH BRANCH

84 Colum.L.Rev. 573, 577–580, 596–605, 609–620, 622–623, 625–626, 633–635, 637–639 (1984).

Three differing approaches have been used in the effort to understand issues [about the place of agencies in government]. The first, "separation of powers," supposes that what government does can be characterized in terms of the kind of act performed—legislating, enforcing, and determining the particular application of law—and that for the safety of the citizenry from tyrannous government these three functions must be kept in distinct places. Congress legislates, and it only legislates; the President sees to the faithful execution of those laws and, in the domestic context at least, that is all he does; the courts decide specific cases of law-application, and that is their sole function. These three powers of government are kept radically separate, because if the same body exercised all three of them, or even two, it might no longer be possible to keep it within the constraints of law.

---

85. U.S. Const. Art. II, § 2; In re Hennen, 13 Pet. 230, 257–59 (1839). Later Justices in Ex parte Siebold, 100 U.S. 371, 397–98 (1880), disputed this conclusion on the basis of the language of the Clause, but the Court added that no branch was more appropriate than the courts to appoint federal election supervisors.

a. This article was written before the Supreme Court's decision in Morrison v. Olson, 108 S.Ct. 2597 (1988).

"Separation of functions" suggests a somewhat different idea, grounded more in considerations of individual fairness in particular proceedings than in the need for structural protection against tryannical government generally. It admits that for agencies (as distinct from the constitutionally named heads of government) the same body often does exercise all three of the characteristic governmental powers, albeit in a web of other controls—judicial review and legislative and executive oversight. As these controls are thought to give reasonable assurance against systemic lawlessness, the separation-of-functions inquiry asks to what extent constitutional due process for the particular individual(s) who may be involved with an agency in a given proceeding requires special measures to assure the objectivity or impartiality of that proceeding. The powers are not kept separate, at least in general, but certain procedural protections—for example, the requirement of an on-the-record hearing before an "impartial" trier—may be afforded.

"Checks and balances" is the third idea, one that to a degree bridges the gap between these two domains. Like separation of powers, it seeks to protect the citizens from the emergence of tyrannical government by establishing multiple heads of authority in government, which are then pitted one against another in a continuous struggle; the intent of that struggle is to deny to any one (or two) of them the capacity ever to consolidate all governmental authority in itself, while permitting the whole effectively to carry forward the work of government. Unlike separation of powers, however, the checks-and-balances idea does not suppose a radical division of government into three parts, with particular functions neatly parceled out among them. Rather, the focus is on relationships and interconnections, on maintaining the conditions in which the intended struggle at the apex may continue. From this perspective, as from the perspective of separation of functions, it is not important how powers below the apex are treated; the important question is whether the relationship of each of the three named actors of the Constitution to the exercise of those powers is such as to promise a continuation of their effective independence and interdependence.

In the pages following I argue that, for any consideration of the structure given law-administration below the very apex of the governmental structure, the rigid separation-of-powers compartmentalization of governmental functions should be abandoned in favor of analysis in terms of separation of functions and checks and balances. * * * A shorthand way of putting the argument is that we should stop pretending that all our government (as distinct from its highest levels) can be allocated into three neat parts. The theory of separation-of-powers breaks down when attempting to locate administrative and regulatory agencies within one of the three branches; its vitality, rather, lies in the formulation and specification of the controls that Congress, the Supreme Court and the President may exercise over administration and regulation.

* * *

From the perspective suggested here, the important fact is that an agency is neither Congress nor President nor Court, but an inferior part of government. Each agency is subject to control relationships with some or all of the three constitutionally named branches, and those relationships give an assurance—functionally similar to that provided by the separation-of-powers notion for the constitutionally named bodies—that they will not pass out of control.[18] Powerful and potentially arbitrary as they may be, the Secretary of Agriculture and the Chairman of the SEC for this reason do not present the threat that led the framers to insist on a splitting of the authority of government at its very top. What we have, then, are three named repositories of authorizing power and control, and an infinity of institutions to which parts of the authority of each may be lent. The three must share the reins of control; means must be found of assuring that no one of them becomes dominant. But it is not terribly important to number or allocate the horses that pull the carriage of government.

* * *

[This essay advances] three general propositions about the three theoretical approaches to understanding the place of agencies in government identified [above.] The first is that, as a textual and interpretational matter, the separation-of-powers model need and probably should be taken no further than its use for understanding the interrelationships of the three named actors (Congress, President, Court) at the very pinnacle of government. * * *

Although agencies certainly might be assigned to one or another of the executive, legislative, or judicial branches (but not more than one, if we are rigorously to pursue the separation idea), that signifies little for the functions they perform. No compelling textual or interpretive mandate requires such a formal placement to be effected.

A second proposition emerging from the cases is that considerations of individual fairness more closely associated with the idea of separation of functions often underlie the cases in which the idea of separation of powers appears to have played a significant role. * * *

Finally and perhaps most importantly, the text and particularly the context suggest a series of postulates about necessary relationships between the President and administrative agencies—relationships readily understood in checks-and-balances terms. The important constraint on Congress's ability to structure the work of law-administration lies in the need to perpetuate the tensions and interactions among the three named heads of the Constitution. Whatever arrangements are made, one must remain able to characterize the President as the unitary,

18. For example, one may understand the delegation doctrine in this functional way, rather than as an indication "where" in government rulemaking occurs. That doctrine requires both statutory authorization (a relationship with Congress) and a capacity on the part of the courts to assure legality (a relationship with the courts). The availability of at least limited judicial review, indeed, appears to be identified with increasing frequency as an essential element of the grant of rulemaking authority.

politically accountable head of all law-administration, sufficiently potent in his own relationships with those who actually perform it to serve as an effective counter to a feared Congress. * * *

A. THE TEXT AND CONTEXT OF THE CONSTITUTION

The text and structure of the Constitution impose few limits on Congress's ability to structure administrative government. One scanning the Constitution for a sense of the overall structure of the federal government is immediately struck by its silences. Save for some aspects of the legislative process, it says little about how those it names as necessary elements of government—Congress, President, and Supreme Court—will perform their sanctions, and it says almost nothing at all about the unelected officials who, even in 1789, would necessarily perform the bulk of the government's work. Thus, article I describes in some detail the makeup of the House and Senate, the subjects on which they might act, and the manner in which they may effectively legislate; but even this relatively full description talks only to the authority and actions of elected officials. One finds no mention there of important aspects of Congress's work, or of most persons who now work on its behalf—committees and their staffs, the General Accounting Office, the Congressional Budget Office, the Library of Congress.

* * * Article II speaks directly only about elected officials, chiefly the President and his powers; it describes those powers in the most summary of terms. He is vested generally with "the executive Power," but what that is in the domestic context does not readily appear. Putting aside foreign relations and military authority—a very large part of the Presidency, but not the focus of this essay—he has the following powers and/or responsibilities:

> to appoint those "Officers of the United States . . . which shall be established by Law," subject to the requirement of senatorial confirmation and to the possibility that Congress might effectively limit this power to appointing "the Heads of Departments"; [90]

> to "require the Opinion, in writing, of the principal Officer in each of the executive Departments, upon any Subject relating to the Duties of their respective Offices"; [91]

> "from time to time give to the Congress Information of the State of the Union, and recommend to their Consideration" proposed legislation; [92]

> to "take Care that the Laws be faithfully executed." [93]

These provisions suggest a supervisory, perhaps even caretaker presidential role, in relationship to shadowy "executive departments" from which opinions might be sought. One is left to infer that there would be other officers possessing legal authority to act for the government, and one simply is not told whether the President or those officers are to act on those opinions.

---

90. U.S. Const. art. II, § 2, cl. 2.

91. U.S. Const. art. II, § 2, cl. 1.

92. U.S. Const. art. II, § 3.

93. Id.

* * * In almost all significant respects, then, the job of creating and altering the shape of the federal government was left to the future—to the congressional processes suggested by Congress's authority to adopt any law "necessary and proper for carrying into Execution the foregoing Powers, and all other Powers vested by this Constitution in the Government of the United States, or in any Department or Officer thereof." [94]

If one moves outward from the text to its structure, the context in which it was drafted, the records and debates of the constitutional convention, and its initial implementation by the first Congress, one can identify a number of fundamental underlying judgments. * * *

1. *The President is to be a Unitary, Politically Accountable Head of Government.*—Of the decisions clearly taken, perhaps none was as important as the judgment to vest the executive power in a single, elected official, the President. * * * While it was understood that there would be departments responsible for daily administration, the Convention clearly and consciously chose a single and independent executive over a collegial body subject to legislative direction.[100]

* * *

If the Convention was clear in its choice of a single executive—and its associated beliefs that such a person might bear focused political accountability for the work of law-execution and serve as an effective political counter-weight to Congress—it was ambivalent in its expectations about the President's relations with those who would actually do the work of law-administration and desirous of the advantages of congressional flexibility in defining the structure of government within the constraints of this choice. * * * Thus, the shadowy references to executive departments and, in particular, the opinions in writing clause, seem to be residues of propositions such as Gouvernour Morris's proposal in the final days of the Convention for a council of state composed of the Chief Justice and Secretaries of Domestic Affairs, State, Foreign Affairs, War, Marine, and Commerce and Finance.

* * *

Certainly one consideration underlying rejection of the Morris proposal was the wish to leave to successive Congresses, through the medium of the necessary and proper clause, the flexibility required for shaping the government to the demands of changing circumstances. Another consideration was to enhance the accountability—and thus the power—of the President by denying him the chance to hide behind a council's approval of his acts. * * *

One ought not, however, mistake the drafters' possible ambivalance about presidential role and their willingness to trust the issue of governmental superstructure to future Congresses for a willingness to

94. U.S. Const. art. I, § 8, cl. 18.

100. The Federalist No. 70 (A. Hamilton), the first of the *Federalist* papers addressing the requisites of the presidency, is given over entirely to this choice, as the most important of the choices made, in its tendency to promote decisiveness and responsibility.

see the President assigned a role distinctly subordinate to Congress. In providing that Congress need not be convened until December of each year, the draftsmen plainly anticipated a substantial executive function. Congress's articulated functions lay in the passage of legislation to create the framework of government and then to set the standards and appropriate the funds by which the business of government would be carried on. Inevitably that legislation would be episodic—enacted without necessary care for its relationship to existing law and having to be applied to future events, not foreseen, in light of the then existing corpus of law and the exigencies of the moment. Executive authority had to provide correctives for these inherent difficulties, and it was important that the chief executive have a body of individuals, held in his confidence, with whom to consult. The responsibility of government was to be focally his; but day-to-day administration and decision, of necessity, was to be entrusted to the hands of others.

2. *The Maintenance of Tension Among the Named Bodies.*—A central, coordinating and overseeing role for the President in relation to all government "officers" is required, also, to permit that office to serve as an effective check on the otherwise to be feared authority of Congress. The framers sought both to create a more effective national government than they had previously experienced, and to make it resistant to domination by transitory majorities or those who for the moment might be the public's political representatives. To those ends, the governmental structure they created embodies both separated powers and interlocking responsibilities; the purpose was to prevent both majoritarian rashness and the governmental tyranny that could result from the conjoining of power in a single source. Maintaining conditions that would sustain the resulting tension between executive and legislature was to be the central constraint on any proposed structure for government.

The Constitutional Convention arose out of dissatisfaction with a government dominated by the legislature, a dissatisfaction on both practical and theoretical grounds. In practice, legislative government did not work; legislatures were fragmented and episodic in their attention to the affairs of state, diffusing and defeating responsibility. In theory, the joining of all government functions in one authority, unchecked by others, was an invitation to tyranny. Interpenetration of function and competition among the branches would protect liberty by preventing the irreversible accretion of ultimate power in any one. As Madison wrote in the *Federalist* papers, the essence lay in "giving to those who administer each department the necessary constitutional means and personal motives to resist encroachments of the others." [117] Madison's strategy was given form in the veto power and in Congress's authority to create the infrastructure of executive government and to

117. The Federalist No. 51 * * * (J. Madison).

exercise plenary control over the President's expenditure of funds (and thus over the size and power of the executive establishment).

*   *   *

Thus, while the actual text of the Constitution says little about the structure of the federal government beneath the apex, the structure and history of the Constitution make clear the framers' decisions concerning the interdependence of the three branches and the place of the agencies as subsidiary to all three. One may see the issue of balance of power among the three named branches of government as reflecting a process not an institution, with impermanence of resolution not only inevitable but desirable as an outcome. *   *   *

B. INTERPRETATIONS OF THE CONSTITUTIONAL CONSTRAINTS

In addition to constitutional text and context, the interpretations given the President's place in government by courts and others during the past two hundred years influence contemporary understandings of his relationship to the agencies and Congress's power to structure that relationship. *   *   *

*   *   * Congress is free to choose between placing ultimate responsibility for decision with the President and giving that responsibility to those to whom it has initially assigned the work of administration. Even within what is undoubtedly the sphere of executive influence—for example, the conduct of law enforcement—that proposition finds support in the Constitutional Convention's failure to adopt measures such as the Morris plan. The proposition seems undebatable where Congress can find circumstances, such as a need for objective decision, that warrant placing administration beyond the sphere of its own as well as the President's political influence. Yet note that neither choice effects or is a justification for presidential *exclusion.* However unserviceable rigid separation-of-powers arguments have become beneath the very top levels of government, the checks-and-balances idea retains force: congressional arrangements that threaten the viability of an independent, unitary executive capable of opposing the Congress's own assertions of power are, for that reason, suspect.

*   *   *

[1. *The*] *Formal Approach to the Place of Administration*[.]

*   *   *

Understanding of the relation between the Presidency and administration was shaped by two cases of the 1920's and 30's, *Myers v. United States* [142] and *Humphrey's Executor v. United States.* [143] Both tested the President's claim of inherent executive authority to remove presidential appointees from office in the face of statutory limitations on removal; both appeared to use a strictly formal, separation-of-powers approach to the place of agencies in government. The seemingly opposite conclusions to which they came are usually understood in terms of that approach as denying the independent regulatory commis-

---

142. 272 U.S. 52 (1926).   **143.** 295 U.S. 602 (1935).

sions any determinate place in the tripartite structure of government. Yet their conclusions can also be understood in light of the checks-and-balances approach, and so understood the opinions are both readily reconciled and consistent with the constitutional scheme.

Myers concerned a postmaster appointed to a four-year term under a statute which for fifty years had required senatorial assent to both appointment and removal of these officials. The President sought to remove him before the expiration of his term, without obtaining senatorial concurrence. * * * A divided Court found that reserving congressional participation in the removal of an executive officer unconstitutionally invaded the President's executive function. The Court's opinion, written by a former President, suggested that the President enjoyed an inherent authority to remove every officer of government he was empowered to appoint (other than a judge protected by article III). It appeared to eradicate the executive/administrative distinction by establishing the President's disciplinary control as universally available. * * *

Humphrey's Executor resulted from President Roosevelt's effort, on the authority of *Myers,* to remove a commissioner of the Federal Trade Commission before the expiration of his seven-year statutory term. Here, a statute enacted before *Myers* required specification of cause for removal, but did not require senatorial concurrence. The President suggested no "cause" for Humphrey's removal beyond political incompatibility—a reason plainly insufficient under the statute. This challenge arose, however, at a time when presidential rather than congressional hegemony may have seemed the more palpable threat; it was decided on the same day that the Court invalidated the National Industrial Recovery Act, once the centerpiece of the New Deal, on the ground of excessive delegation to the President. * * * Acting scant weeks after argument, the Court unanimously repudiated the *Myers* dicta and found that Congress could validly impose a "cause" requirement on the discharge of a Federal Trade Commissioner; given the circumstances, the Court did not have to say what cause could be.

Reading both opinions, one is struck by their emphasis on a radical separation of powers within government, with a concomitant need to place agencies *in* one or another branch, maximally free from intrusion by the others. For the *Myers* Court, "the reasonable construction of the Constitution must be that the branches should be kept separate in all cases in which they were not expressly blended, and the Constitution should be expounded to blend them no more than it affirmatively requires." From placement of the Post Office Department in the executive branch and the absence of any constitutional provision for congressional participation in removal, all else followed. For the *Humphrey's Executor* Court, "[t]he fundamental necessity of maintaining each of the three general departments of government entirely free from the control or coercive influence, direct or indirect, of either of the others, has often been stressed, and is hardly open to serious question."

* * * [T]he Court said the President could exercise no authority over [Federal Trade Commission] members beyond the constitutionally explicit one of appointment. Viewing both the unquestioned congressional purpose to remove the FTC from politics and the agency's particular functions, the Court described it as "an agency of the legislative or judicial department of the government," exercising in those contexts only an "executive function—as distinguished from executive power in the constitutional sense."

More than *Myers,* but perhaps in consequence of that decision, the reasoning of the *Humphrey's Executor* Court seems open to question. * * * [T]he opinion tells us that the agency is in *both* the legislative *and* the judicial branches, because of the functions it performs, but not how an agency can at the same moment reside in both the legislative and the judicial branches, consistent with the "fundamental necessity of maintaining each of the three general departments of government entirely free from the control or coercive influence . . . of either of the others." * * *

If the formal question where in government to place the agency is put aside, however, it is not hard to understand the Court's result. It described the FTC's functions as follows:

(1) The FTC could direct cessation of unfair methods of competition in commerce, *after* full-dress adjudicatory hearings;

(2) It could conduct investigations culminating in a report to the Congress with recommendations for legislation; and

(3) It could act 'as a master in chancery' in antitrust suits brought by the Attorney General and referred to it by a district court.

Assurance of impartiality and the absence of political controls of any character are centrally important to two parts of the statutory scheme as thus described; providing information-gathering service to Congress (not the President) characterizes the remainder. So far as the Court was educated to the Commission's functions, the FTC did little as to which unified policy direction was even arguably relevant. Thus, the need to maintain tension between the named branches was not implicated. The Court was acutely conscious, however, of the extent to which the Commission acted in circumstances calling for judicial impartiality and the removal from politics that might tend to protect it. * * *

Once fairness considerations are taken into account, these cases can be seen as explained by the difference between * * * presidential power that implicates a struggle between the branches and one that does not. *Myers* can readily be limited to the issue * * * [of] senatorial concurrence in removal[.] * * * Reservation of senatorial approval for removals suggests political power struggles between President and Senate that are not connoted by a judgment that fixed tenure in office, with limitations on discharge, will be useful for the ends of public policy. * * * [Congress] has not only limited the President's ordinary political authority by imposing a "for cause" requirement, but also greatly expanded its own political authority by insisting on a voice in that determination. The latter measure defeats any claim that the measure has an apolitical end such as assuring objectivity.

Humphrey's Executor, in turn, could be understood as having turned on precisely this distinction between those limitations on removal where Congress has retained some role and those in which it has not. * * * The FTC Act imposes no congressional intrusion analogous to that presented to the Court in *Myers;* on its facts, it does not even foreclose some presidential involvement in FTC policy formation. * * * [T]he Court found only that Congress could legitimately insist that one holding the office of Federal Trade Commissioner serve on terms other than those of a personal adviser. It did not have to say whether the President could give the FTC Commissioners binding directives, or if so of what sort, or what might be the consequences of any failure of theirs to honor them.

* * *

[2.] *The Checks-and-Balances Approach to the Place of Administration*[.] [In the 1970's the Court indicated that it] might be ready to abandon the pigeonholing of agencies as "executive," "legislative" or "judicial" in favor of considering the impact of particular challenged provisions respecting them on the balance of authority among the institutions defined in articles I, II and III. * * *

* * *

This more functional inquiry assumed particular importance in *Buckley v. Valeo,*[177] a case concerning the necessary character of presidential and congressional relationships to an administrative agency. *Buckley* presented a series of challenges to the Federal Election Act and to the Federal Election Commission (the Commission) the Act created and empowered; significant for our purposes was a separation-of-powers challenge to a provision for direct legislative appointment of some members of the Commission. The Commission was authorized, inter alia, both to conduct investigations—the quasi-legislative activity considered in *Humphrey's Executor* —and to engage in rulemaking, [a] quasi-legislative activity which had not been at issue in that case. Were the FEC only empowered to conduct investigations, the Court reasoned, the appointment provisions would not have been objectionable; such powers are "in the same general category as . . . Congress might delegate to one of its own committees." But rulemaking "represents the performance of a significant governmental duty exercised pursuant to a public law," and is *therefore* to be exercised only by officers of the United States—by persons subject to appointment by the President (with or without senatorial assent) or by a head of one of "the executive Departments."

* * *

When one is playing a shell game, however, it is important to maintain the observer's confidence that one of the shells does contain

177. 424 U.S. 1 (1976).

the pea, even if it is not the shell currently under examination. By characterizing as a function having to be exercised outside the legislature just that quasi-legislative activity (rulemaking) that previously had been described with some uniformity as the result of a delegation of *legislative* power, the Court destroyed that illusion, breaking through any separation-of-powers notion that the powers of government generally could be neatly parcelled into three uniquely empowered entities. The Court insisted that the central issue was to be the character of the relationships between that agency and the named heads of government, and not the formal structure of the agency in question. Those conclusions could be reached without having to "put" the FEC anywhere; the claim to that power and relationship does not depend on where the agency "is," so much as the necessity of maintaining the desired sharing of authority among the named actors of the Constitution.

* * *

* * *

The checks-and-balances concerns with relationship and effective functioning thus suggested seem to be paralleled by analytic developments in other contexts in which the structural constraints of the Constitution are the central issue. Debate over the tenth amendment, for example, revived by *National League of Cities v. Usery*,[190] resolved into near unanimity in formulating the relevant inquiry (if not its application): whether a challenged measure threatens the integrity of the states in the constitutional scheme. Allocation of authority between state and nation, like that between executive and legislature, can be understood as a means of protecting individuals from overwhelming governmental power; deciding what is required to preserve that protection for citizens has characterized the recent judicial debates more than a cataloguing of activities inherently for the states qua states. The same may also be suggested for the public debate—not yet captured in litigation—whether the Constitution constrains Congress's authority to make exceptions to the appellate jurisdiction of the Supreme Court. What would "prevent the [Judicial] Branch from accomplishing its constitutionally assigned functions"[192] is widely accepted as the appropriate inquiry to be made.

Inquiry along these lines has substantial advantages. It permits the judiciary to recognize the inescapable merger of some governmental functions, and permits it, as well, to tolerate periodic changes in relative political effectiveness as between President and Congress, Congress and Court, Nation and States. Our political history has been characterized by the emergence of first one and then the other as the more forceful national political presence; even if it were desirable, it seems unlikely that courts could sustain the constant intervention that would be required to maintain a fixed relationship. Rigid molds are

---

190. 426 U.S. 833 (1976). [This article was written a year before the Court's decision in Garcia v. San Antonio Metropolitan Transit Authority, 469 U.S. 528 (1985), overruling National League of Cities v. Usery—eds.note.]

192. Nixon v. Administrator of General Services, 433 U.S. 425, 445 (1977).

more easily broken; permitting growth and change makes more likely the enduring of the essential form.

* * *

C. SEPARATION OF FUNCTIONS AND CONSIDERATIONS OF INDIVIDUAL FAIRNESS

Much of the force apparently attached to the issue of "place" in the cases separating the President from the agencies has its source in considerations of fairness—notions more readily ascribed to the idea of separation of *functions* than separation of *powers*. Separation of powers, as a theoretical concern, has to do with the general tendency of certain governmental structures to result in (or prevent) tyrannical government—that is, a government no longer under the control of the people. Separation of functions suggests a much more atomistic inquiry, asking what combinations of functions or impacts of external influence will interfere with fair resolution of a particular proceeding. [T]he *Humphrey's Executor* Court [expressed horror] at the idea that a judge of the "legislative" Court of Claims might be subject to presidential discipline in "exercising judicial power." That the Court accepted her sitting on a *legislative* court suggests that the issue for the Court was not (or not only) one of place but one of function. Wherever she is located in government, a judge ought not to be connected with the controversy or the parties, ought not to be interested in the outcome, must learn from the parties only what they convey in the presence of each other, and—above all—ought not to be called upon to explain her decision in the political forum. External or political intervention in on-the-record decisionmaking would be regarded as inappropriate, whether done by the President or any other political figure (e.g., a legislator) * * *. These are judgments we reach wholly without regard to the balance of advantage between Congress and the White House in overseeing the day-to-day functioning of political government. Within agencies themselves * * * these judgments are reflected in the creation of officials (administrative law judges, appeal bodies, judicial officers) remarkably free of organizational responsibilities or political supervision, who perform on-the-record judging functions.

This separation-of-functions rationale provides, in effect, a politically neutral basis for supporting congressional judgments about governmental structure that might otherwise appear to threaten presidential function. Legislative judgments that certain types of decisions are preferably made in the absence of *any* political intervention tend to defeat arguments that statutory provisions for agency independence reflect the outcome of competition between Congress and President for political dominance. Acquiescing in such judgments has no strong implications for the allocation of authority between the political branches, and raises few threats to the scheme of checks and balances. The very judgment made requires that the relationship between Congress and the agency be affected equally with that between the President and the agency; where these considerations come into play, it

would be inappropriate for either to intervene unless as a party.
*   *   *

*   *   *

D. CONFLICT BETWEEN THE MODELS OR A RETURN TO FORMALISM?
*   *   *

The preceding pages should suggest that of the three approaches commonly used to describe our government's structure, the checks-and-balances model, understood in light of the fairness aspirations of the separation-of-functions principle, best describes the complexity of contemporary government in terms that permit adherence, as well, to the framers' vision. The seeming bright-line simplicity of separation of powers, never in fact fully embraced by those who wrote the Constitution, is neither necessary as a matter of text, context or past interpretation for those parts of government not named in the Constitution itself, nor possibly successful in describing that bulk of government as it is. Courts have been able to reconcile the reality of modern administrative government and the strict separation-of-powers model, as in *Humphrey's Executor,* only by blind fears of definition—internally inconsistent while at the same time effectively negating the ability of a unitary, competent President to serve as an essential check against legislative hegemony.

Yet an analysis framed in terms of interference with the capacity to maintain one's core function is more effective as a means of organizing debate than as a rule for deciding cases. It leaves more room for judicial fact-finding and the operation of judicial discretion than "bright-line" formulae such as those employed in *Humphrey's Executor* appear to. To one who takes from constitutional history, above all, a sense that the framers both intended effective government and placed our protection from overwhelming government in continuing struggle among its parts rather than rigid demarcation of function, that is not troublesome. However, the bright line has its allure for justices faced with the responsibility to decide particular cases in ways that will guide the future conduct of others, future justices included. *   *   *

*   *   *

[Consider the effect this allure had on the Court in *INS v. Chadha.*[257]] [T]he majority opinion strikingly returns to the formalities of *Humphrey's Executor* at the same time as it repudiates the particular use to which they were put in that case. Although denying any purpose to suggest that the three branches of government are "hermetically sealed," the opinion makes its dominant metaphor an expression of fear lest the "hydraulic pressures" of power-seeking burst the boundaries of each branch's appropriate function—a palpable evocation of the "air-tightness" of the *Myers–Humphrey's Executor* approach. Where the *Humphrey's Executor* Court accomplished its ends by placing "quasi-adjudication" and "quasi-legislation" outside the executive branch, however, the *Chadha* majority identifies both as executive branch

257. [462 U.S. 919] (1983).

activities—a characterization consistent with *Buckley v. Valeo*—and thus finds a significant question whether Congress has usurped the President's power.

Note that the decision here subjected to congressional review cannot easily be characterized as the President's: it was made in the first instance by a civil servant strongly protected against political interference in his judgment and required by statute to decide the case before him "on the record." The difference between decisions that are explicitly presidential and those that are not is that the compartmentalization inherent in the separation-of-powers idea is an essential element of the framer's plan only for the former. * * *

* * *

Suppose the Court had been willing to dissociate the agency from the President and had focused primarily on the question of the relationships between the agency and the three named heads of constitutional authority. From that perspective the legislative veto issue might have looked rather different. The question would then be what impact the legislative veto could be expected to have on the President's own relationship with the agency and, in particular, on his claim to function as the sole head of government. A veto mechanism need not defeat such a claim; indeed, the more it seemed that the action being taken was fairly to be characterized as the President's own, the less objectionable the veto might be. From a checks-and-balances perspective, the need for cross-checking institutions of control is the more urgent where authority is to be exercised by one of the named heads of government. For example, in the reorganization context it might readily be argued that Congress could afford to confer the authority to initiate restructuring of government on the President only if it reserved the counterbalancing possibility of "legislative veto" disapproval. The President, gaining the initiative through the authorizing legislation, would hardly lose in the exchange.

Where the action clearly is not the President's, on the other hand, the legislative veto begins to appear, not as a device for sharing enlarged responsibility within government, but as a means for enhancing congressional political controls at the expense of presidential ones. At least within a certain range, we have seen that Congress readily can exclude the President from political control of regulatory outcomes. Yet the rationale for these measures, and for the apparent offense they give to the President's claim to serve as the unitary head of executive government, equally requires that Congress exclude itself from such controls. A measure that enhances Congress's political controls while isolating the President would threaten both his position as unitary head of government, and his continuing capacity to function as a political counterweight to Congress. Thus, in *Chadha*, Congress's reserved power to disapprove a proposed suspension is made even more problematic by the "on-the-record" regime within the Department that impairs direct presidential control. If the President is excluded from directing that a given rule be adopted, amended, or rejected while Congress is able to assert that authority, one has lost the intended focus of responsibility and balance.

How would Currie and Strauss deal with the problems presented in the independent counsel case, *Morrison v. Olson*, 487 U.S. 654 (1988)?

BIBLIOGRAPHY

Bruff, *On the Constitutional Status of the Administrative Agencies*, 36 Am.U.L.Rev. 491 (1987).

Chemerinsky, *A Paradox Without a Principle: A Comment on the Burger Court's Jurisprudence in Separation of Powers Cases*, 60 S.Cal.L.Rev. 1083 (1987).

J. Choper, JUDICIAL REVIEW AND THE NATIONAL POLITICAL PROCESS ch. 5 (1980).

Devins, *Budget Reform and the Balance of Powers*, 31 Wm. & Mary L.Rev. 993 (1990).

THE FEDERALIST Nos. 47–48, 51 (Madison).

Feld, *Separation of Political Powers: Boundaries or Balance?*, 21 Ga.L. Rev. 171 (1986).

L. Fisher, CONSTITUTIONAL CONFLICTS BETWEEN CONGRESS AND THE PRESIDENT (1985).

L. Fisher, THE POLITICS OF SHARED POWER (1981).

W. Gwyn, THE MEANING OF THE SEPARATION OF POWERS (1965).

Krent, *Separating the Strands in Separation of Powers Controversies*, 74 Va.L.Rev. 1253 (1988).

Levi, *Some Aspects of Separation of Powers*, 76 Colum.L.Rev. 371 (1976).

Osgood, *Governmental Functions and Constitutional Doctrine: The Historical Constitution*, 72 Cornell L.Rev. 553 (1987).

Sargentich, *The Contemporary Debate About Legislative–Executive Separation of Powers*, 72 Cornell L.Rev. 430 (1987).

Sharp, *The Classical American Doctrine of "The Separation of Powers"*, 2 U.Chi.L.Rev. 385 (1935).

Stith, *Congress' Power of the Purse*, 97 Yale L.J. 1343 (1988).

Stith, *Rewriting the Fiscal Constitution: The Case of Gramm–Rudman–Hollings*, 76 Calif.L.Rev. 595 (1988).

Strauss, *Formal and Functional Approaches to Separation-of-Powers Questions—A Foolish Inconsistency?*, 72 Cornell L.Rev. 488 (1987).

M.J.C. Vile, CONSTITUTIONALISM AND THE SEPARATION OF POWERS (1967).

B. THE EXECUTIVE POWER: DOMESTIC AFFAIRS

Courses in constitutional law usually deal with issues of value and method, like those discussed in Section A, in the context of particular substantive problems. For the sake of simplicity we group these problems in four categories. The first two focus on the scope of executive power. Unlike Article I of the Constitution, which states in some detail the powers given to Congress, Article II is fairly laconic about the President's authority. This generates frequent conflict about the limits of executive power in domestic affairs [1] (which we address in this Section) and foreign affairs [2] (which we take up in Section C).

Edward Corwin discusses the scope of the President's inherent authority in domestic affairs—an issue raised by President Truman's seizure of the nation's steel mills during the Korean War. Corwin takes a fairly broad view of that authority. If we wish to control the President, he argues, we should rely on congressional action, rather than on judicial enforcement of such ideas as "executive power."

EDWARD S. CORWIN, THE STEEL SEIZURE CASE: A JUDICIAL BRICK WITHOUT STRAW
53 Colum.L.Rev. 53–61, 66 (1953).

President Truman's seizure of the steel industry without specific statutory warrant [1] brings to a new pitch a developing reliance on the "Executive Power" which began almost at the inception of the Federal Government. True, this development has not always proceeded at the same pace; while at times it has seemed to be arrested, during the last fifty years its maturation has been virtually uninterrupted. Moreover, the forces, interests and events which have energized the development are today more potent than ever.

The opening clause of Article II of the Constitution reads: "The executive Power shall be vested in a President of the United States of America." The records of the Constitutional Convention make it clear that the purposes of this clause were simply to settle the question whether the executive branch should be plural or single and to give the executive a title. [2] Yet, in the very first Congress to assemble under the Constitution, the opening clause of Article II was invoked by James Madison and others in order to endow the President with power to remove officers whose appointments had been made with the advice and consent of the Senate. Madison's view prevailed, and was finally ratified by the Supreme Court in 1926. [4] The same theory was invoked

1. Youngstown Sheet & Tube Co. v. Sawyer, 343 U.S. 579, 72 S.Ct. 863, 96 L.Ed. 1153 (1952).

2. Dames & Moore v. Regan, 453 U.S. 654, 101 S.Ct. 2972, 69 L.Ed.2d 918 (1981); United States v. Curtiss-Wright Corp., 299 U.S. 304, 57 S.Ct. 216, 81 L.Ed. 255 (1936).

1. Youngstown Sheet & Tube Co. v. Sawyer, 343 U.S. 579 (1952).

2. 2 Farrand, Records of the Federal Convention 171, 185 (rev. ed. 1937).

4. Myers v. United States, 272 U.S. 52 (1926).

by Hamilton in support of President Washington's Proclamation of Neutrality upon the outbreak of war between France and Great Britain. This time the Court's acquiescence was not long delayed. Even in the act of asserting the power of the Court to pass upon the constitutionality of acts of Congress, Chief Justice Marshall said: "By the Constitution of the United States the President is invested with certain important political powers, in the exercise of which he is to use his own discretion, and is accountable only to his country in his political character, and to his own conscience." [6] Even Thomas Jefferson, cousin and congenital enemy of Marshall, had said of the executive power in an official opinion as Secretary of State in 1790: "The Executive [branch of the government], possessing the rights of self-government from nature, cannot be controlled in the exercise of them but by a law, passed in the forms of the Constitution." [7]

Throughout the last half century the theory of presidential power has recruited strength from a succession of "strong" presidents, from an economic crisis, from our participation in two world wars and a "cold" war, and finally from organization of the labor movement. Moreover, the constitutional basis of the doctrine has shifted somewhat since the early nineteenth century. It no longer relies exclusively, or even chiefly, on the opening clause of Article II. To the terminology of political disputation in the Jacksonian period it is indebted for such concepts as "residual," "resultant" and "inherent" powers. Thanks to Lincoln, it is able to invoke the president's duty to "take care that the laws," i.e., all the laws, "be faithfully executed," and his power as commander-in-chief of the armed forces. * * *

* * *

The Facts of the Youngstown Case. To avert a nation-wide strike of steel workers which he believed would jeopardize the national defense, President Truman, on April 8th, 1952, issued Executive Order 10340 directing the Secretary of Commerce to seize and operate most of the country's steel mills. The order cited no specific statutory authorization, but invoked generally the powers vested in the president by the Constitution and laws of the United States. Secretary Sawyer forthwith issued an order seizing the mills and directing their presidents to operate them as managers for the United States in accordance with his regulations and directions. The President promptly reported these events to Congress, conceding Congress' power to supersede his order; but Congress failed to take action either then or a fortnight later, when the President again raised the problem in a special letter. Of course, in the Defense Production Act of 1950, the Labor Management Relations (Taft–Hartley) Act of 1947 and the Selective Service Act of 1948, Congress had in fact provided other procedures for dealing with such situations; and in the elaboration of these statutory schemes it had repeatedly declined to authorize governmental seizures of property to settle labor disputes. The steel companies sued the Secretary in a

---

6. Marbury v. Madison, 1 Cranch 137, 166 (U.S. 1803).

7. 5 Writings of Jefferson 209 (Ford ed. 1895).

federal district court, praying for a declaratory judgment and injunctive relief. The district judge issued a preliminary injunction, which the court of appeals stayed. On certiorari to the court of appeals, the Supreme Court affirmed the district court's order by a vote of six to three. Justice Black delivered the opinion of the Court in which Justices Frankfurter, Douglas, Jackson and Burton concurred * * *. The Chief Justice, speaking for himself and Justices Reed and Minton, dissented.

The Doctrine of the Opinion of the Court. The chief point urged in Justice Black's opinion is that there was no statute which expressly or impliedly authorized the President to take possession of the steel mills. On the contrary, in its consideration of the Taft–Hartley Act in 1947, Congress refused to authorize governmental seizures of property as a method of preventing work stoppages and settling labor disputes. Authority to issue such an order in the circumstances of the case was not deducible from the aggregate of the executive powers under Article II of the Constitution; nor was the Order maintainable as an exercise of the president's powers as commander-in-chief of the armed forces. The power sought to be exercised was the lawmaking power. * * *

The pivotal proposition of the opinion is, in brief, that inasmuch as Congress could have ordered the seizure of the steel mills, there was a total absence of power in the president to do so without prior congressional authorization. To support this thesis no proof in the way of past opinion, practice or adjudication is offered. * * *

The somewhat different truth of the matter is that the framers of the Constitution were compelled to defend their handiwork against the charge that it violated "the political maxim that the legislative, executive, and judicial departments ought to be separate and distinct." [27] To meet this charge Madison sought to show in the *Federalist* that the three departments ought not to be so far separated as to have no control over each other.[28] In his opinion for the Court in *Ex parte Grossman,*[29] decided 137 years later, Chief Justice Taft adopted the same point of view: the fact that when two departments both operate upon the same subject matter the action of one may cancel that of the other *affords no criterion of the constitutional powers of either.* Rather the question is what does *the pertinent historical record* show with regard to presidential action in the field of congressional power?

The Historical Record. Our history contains numerous instances in which, contrary to the pattern of departmental relationship assumed in the Black opinion, presidential action has occurred within a recognized field of congressional power and has, furthermore, fully maintained its tenancy until Congress adopted superseding legislation. And Congress' right to supersede was not contested. In brief, the mere existence in Congress of power to do something has not, of itself,

27. The Federalist, No. 47 at 245 (Everyman's ed. 1929).

28. The Federalist, No. 48 (Madison).

29. 267 U.S. 87 (1925). * * *

excluded the president from the same field of power until Congress finally acted. But once this happened, its legislation was forthwith recognized as governing the subject and as controlling presidential action in the area.

* * *

[One] field which the President and Congress have occupied successively is extradition. In 1799 President Adams, in order to execute the extradition provisions of the Jay Treaty, issued a warrant for the arrest of one Jonathan Robbins. As Chief Justice Vinson recites in his opinion:

> This action was challenged in Congress on the ground that no specific statute prescribed the method to be used in executing the treaty. John Marshall, then a member of the House of Representatives, in the course of his successful defense of the President's action, said: "Congress, unquestionably, may prescribe the mode, and Congress may devolve on others the whole execution of the contract; but, till this be done, it seems the duty of the Executive department to execute the contract by any means it possesses." [32]

Not until 1848 did Congress enact a statute governing extradition cases and conferring on the courts, both State and Federal, the duty of handling them.

The power of the president to act until Congress acts in the same field is also shown in these instances. The first Neutrality Proclamation, issued by President Washington in 1793, was also without congressional authorization. The following year Congress enacted the first neutrality statute, and subsequent proclamations of neutrality have been based on an act of Congress governing the matter. The president may, in the absence of legislation by Congress, control the landing of foreign cables in the United States and the passage of foreign troops through American territory, and has done so repeatedly. Likewise, until Congress acts, he may govern conquered territory [37] and, "in the absence of attempts by Congress to limit his power," may set up military commissions in territory occupied by the armed forces of the United States.[38] He may determine in a manner binding on the courts whether a treaty is still in force as law of the land, although again the final power in the field rests with Congress.[39] One of the president's most ordinary powers and duties is that of ordering the prosecution of supposed offenders against the laws of the United States. Yet Congress may do the same thing under the "necessary and proper" clause.[40] On September 22, 1862, President Lincoln issued a proclamation suspending the privilege of the writ of habeas corpus throughout the

32. Youngstown Sheet & Tube Co. v. Sawyer, 343 U.S. 579, 684 (1952), citing 10 Annals of Congress 619 (1948).

37. Santiago v. Nagueras, 214 U.S. 260 (1909).

38. Madsen v. Kinsella, 343 U.S. 341 (1952).

39. Charlton v. Kelly, 229 U.S. 447 (1913). See also Botiller v. Dominquez, 130 U.S. 238 (1889).

40. See Sinclair v. United States, 279 U.S. 263, 289, 297 (1929).

Union in certain classes of cases. By an act passed March 3, 1863, Congress ratified his action and at the same time brought the whole subject of military arrests in the United States under statutory control. Conversely, when President Wilson failed in March, 1917, to obtain Congress' consent to his arming American merchant vessels with defensive arms, he went ahead and did it anyway, "fortified not only by the known sentiments of the majority in Congress but also by the advice of his Secretary of State and Attorney General." [42]

* * *

The doctrine dictated by the above considerations as regards the exercise of executive power in the field of legislative power was well stated by Mr. John W. Davis, principal counsel on the present occasion for the steel companies, in a brief which he filed nearly forty years ago as Solicitor General. The brief defended the action of the president in withdrawing certain lands from public entry, although his doing so was at the time contrary to express statute. "Ours," the brief reads, is a self-sufficient Government within its sphere. (*Ex parte Siebold*, 100 U.S. 371, 395; *in re Debs*, 158 U.S. 56, 564, 578.) "Its means are adequate to its ends" (*McCulloch v. Maryland*, 4 Wheat. 316, 424), and it is rational to assume that its active forces will be found equal in most things to the emergencies that confront it. While perfect flexibility is not to be expected in a Government of divided powers, and while division of power is one of the principal features of the Constitution, it is the plain duty of those who are called upon to draw the dividing lines to ascertain the essential, recognize the practical, and avoid a slavish formalism which can only serve to ossify the Government and reduce its efficiency without any compensating good. The function of making laws is peculiar to Congress, and the Executive can not exercise that function to any degree. But this is not to say that all of the *subjects* concerning which laws might be made are perforce removed from the possibility of Executive influence. The Executive may act upon things and upon men in many relations which have not, though they might have, been actually regulated by Congress. In other words, just as there are fields which are peculiar to Congress and fields which are peculiar to the Executive, so there are fields which are common to both, in the sense that the Executive may move within them until they shall have been occupied by legislative action. These are not the fields of legislative prerogative, but fields within which the lawmaking power may enter and dominate whenever it chooses. This situation results from the fact that the President is the active agent, not of Congress, but of the Nation. As such he performs the duties which the Constitution lays upon him immediately, and as such, also, he executes the laws and regulations adopted by Congress. He is the agent of the people of the United States, deriving all his powers from them and responsible directly to them. In no sense is he the agent of Congress. He obeys

42. Berdahl, War Powers of the Executive in the United States 69 (1921).

and executes the laws of Congress, not because Congress is enthroned in authority over him, but because the Constitution directs him to do so.

Therefore it follows that in ways short of making laws or disobeying them, the Executive may be under a grave constitutional duty to act for the national protection in situations not covered by the acts of Congress, and in which, even, it may not be said that his action is the direct expression of any particular one of the independent powers which are granted to him specifically by the Constitution. Instances wherein the President has felt and fulfilled such a duty have not been rare in our history, though, being for the public benefit and approved by all, his acts have seldom been challenged in the courts.

* * *

* * * [T]he moral from all this is plain: namely, that escape must be sought from "presidential autocracy" by resort not to the judicial power, but to the legislative power—in other words, by resort to timely action by Congress and to procedures for the meeting of emergency situations so far as these can be intelligently anticipated.

And—not to give the thing too fine a point—what seems to be required at the present juncture is a new Labor Disputes Act which ordains procedures for the handling of industry-wide strikes in terms so comprehensive and explicit that the most headstrong president cannot sidestep them without manifest attaint to the law, the Constitution and his own oath of office. "Presidential autocracy," when it is justified, is an inrush of power to fill a power vacuum. Nature abhors a vacuum; so does an age of emergency. Let Congress see to it that no such vacuum occurs.

BIBLIOGRAPHY

Presidential Power

Abascal & Kramer, *Presidential Impoundment Part I: Historical Genesis and Constitutional Framework,* 62 Geo.L.J. 1549 (1974); *Part II: Judicial and Legislative Responses,* 63 Geo.L.J. 149 (1974).

Black, *Some Thoughts on the Veto,* 40 L. & Contemp.Probs. 87 (1976).

Bruff, *Judicial Review and the President's Statutory Powers,* 68 Va.L. Rev. 1 (1982).

Easterbrook, *Presidential Review,* 40 Case W.Res.L.Rev. 905 (1990).

THE FEDERALIST Nos. 67–77 (Hamilton).

Fleishman & Aufses, *Law and Orders: The Problem of Presidential Legislation,* 40 L. & Contemp.Probs. 1 (1976).

Ledewitz, *The Uncertain Power of the President to Execute the Laws,* 46 Tenn.L.Rev. 757 (1979).

P. Shane & H. Bruff, THE LAW OF PRESIDENTIAL POWER (1988).

Sidak, *The President's Power of the Purse,* 1989 Duke L.J. 1162 (1989).

A. Westin, THE ANATOMY OF A CONSTITUTIONAL CASE (1958).

C. The Executive Power: Waging War

Iraq's invasion of Kuwait in August, 1990 recalled the public's attention to an issue that has never really receded from view since the Viet Nam War. The Constitution makes the President Commander in Chief of the armed forces. But it also grants Congress the authority to declare war, to raise, support, and regulate the army and navy, and a number of related powers. Suppose, as is generally the case, that the President is more willing to commit forces to combat than Congress is. What independent authority does he have? When must he get Congress's permission before acting? And how may Congress rein him in if he acts in ways that it finds objectionable?

Alexander Bickel and Eugene Rostow debated these questions in the context of the Viet Nam War, and their pieces have a remarkably contemporary cast. Bickel contends that the framers intended Congress to play the dominant role. They wanted to make it easier to get out of war than into it, and the way to ensure that was to require the approval of the most broadly representative branch of government. Bickel makes two important claims about this approval. One is that it is required for conflicts falling short of declared war. The other is that it must be given at the time hostilities begin—not by an advance delegation or a belated ratification.

Rostow makes the familiar claim that the intentions of the framers are difficult to discern, and that the original meaning of the text has been substantially modified by two centuries of practice. Presidents have deployed the armed forces without Congress's explicit approval throughout the nineteenth and twentieth centuries. Bickel's rule against delegation would make it impossible for the United States to sign military treaties, and for the President to engage in deterrent diplomacy.[1]

1. The pieces by Bickel and Rostow discuss constitutional aspects of the warmaking power. Since 1973 this controversy has also had a statutory aspect. In that year, as a kind of climax to the debate over the war in Viet Nam, Congress passed the War Powers Resolution over President Nixon's veto. 50 U.S.C. §§ 1541–1548. The Resolution tries to encourage consultation between the President and Congress when hostilities are imminent. It is also designed to require Congressional approval within 60 (or 90) days any time the President commits armed forces to real or imminent hostilities.

The Resolution has not succeeded in either aim. It is difficult to legislate a requirement of consultation. And the mechanism designed to trigger congressional approval has malfunctioned. Congress is required to act within 60 days after the President files a report under § 1543(a)(1). But Presidents Ford, Carter, Reagan, and Bush have simply avoided filing such reports, so the 60–day clock never starts running. The Resolution also authorizes Congress to direct the removal of forces by concurrent resolution. But the validity of that provision has been in doubt since the Supreme Court held the legislative veto invalid in INS v. Chadha, 462 U.S. 919, 103 S.Ct. 2764, 77 L.Ed.2d 317 (1983).

The upshot is that constitutional questions still take precedence over statutory questions in war power debates. We must first decide when Congress can stay the President's hand. Only then will we get compliance with rules about consultation, reporting, and termination of hostilities.

ALEXANDER M. BICKEL, CONGRESS, THE
PRESIDENT AND THE POWER TO WAGE WAR

48 Chi.–Kent L. Rev. 131–140, 143–144 (1971).

When the Constitutional Convention was debating allocation of the war power within the federal government George Mason of Virginia said that he "was against giving the power of war to the Executive, because not safely to be trusted with it; or to the Senate, because not so constructed as to be entitled to it. He was for clogging rather than facilitating war; but for facilitating peace." Oliver Ellsworth of Connecticut, later the third Chief Justice of the United States, expressed the same thought. "It should be more easy to get out of war," said Ellsworth, "than into it."

We have managed, over the years, to reverse the proper order of things. We have managed to clog peace and facilitate war.

The Founding Fathers were no visionaries. They did not believe that in terms of formulating and executing the policy of a great nation, it is in fact easier to make peace than to make war. It is in fact, as Ellsworth was careful to say, harder to make peace and simpler to make war. But the Framers of the Constitution intended that our nation's institutions and processes should be so arranged as to make it harder to do the easy thing, and easier to achieve the difficult. For this reason, they insisted that the declaration of war not be an executive prerogative, as it had been under the British Crown. They insisted also that it not be left to the Senate, a single, less numerous chamber which they viewed as capable of more expeditious action than the House or than Congress as a whole. Rather they provided that Congress, acting through both Houses, should have the power to declare war.

The Convention earlier had thought of using another, more comprehensive word, and empowering Congress to *make* war. But this term seemed to vest in the Congress the function of conducting a war once it had started, and also possibly to deny the power of the Commander-in-Chief to repel attacks against the United States. Hence the Framers said, "declare," not "make." The President was to be Commander-in-Chief, exercise independent tactical control over the armed forces, and see to their safety. Congress, as the Framers knew and as Congress itself has on occasion discovered—for example during the Civil War—cannot well exercise command, and should not attempt to do so. The President was to have power also to repel attacks, and we must say in modern times, to respond to the threat of attacks against the United States or against our forces, when instant action is of the essence.

Yet the Framers were extraordinarily wary of standing armies and of their use by the Executive. They authorized Congress to "raise and support Armies," and then tried to ensure that the exclusive power of Congress would be jealously guarded, by providing that no appropriation of money to raise and support armies "shall be for a longer Term than two Years." Moreover, Congress was given the overall, comprehensive "necessary-and-proper" power.

The "necessary-and-proper" clause of article I of the Constitution authorizes Congress to make "all Laws which shall be necessary and proper for carrying into Execution the foregoing Powers. . . ." The reference is to the previously enumerated powers of Congress. But there is another portion of the necessary-and-proper clause, not so often cited, which is of the greatest consequence. The clause also charges Congress to make all laws which shall be necessary and proper for carrying into execution "all other Powers vested by this Constitution in the Government of the United States, or in any Department or Officer thereof"—a phrase that includes the President! The implied powers of the federal government, most of the unstated powers that inhere in nationhood, most everything that went without saying or that is residual—all that belongs to Congress.

Against this roster of congressional functions stand the summary provisions of article II of the Constitution, vesting the executive power in the President, declaring that he shall be Commander-in-Chief, and authorizing him, with the advice and consent of the Senate, to make treaties and appoint ambassadors.

The text of the Constitution and its history thus plainly limit the President. Yet the law of the Constitution under our system is not only defined by the text, but influenced by usage long indulged. The earliest practice conformed to the division of war-making powers intended by the Framers. Later practice, however, in this century, and on occasion in the nineteenth, has tended to enlarge the scope of independent presidential initiatives.

* * *

Prior presidential initiatives have been fitted—at least the variously plausible attempt was made to fit them—into theories that fall short of complete repudiation of the constitutional division of war-making power between Congress and the President. Essentially the President's power has been justified as necessitated by, and arising in, emergencies. The President has been viewed as entrusted with a reactive, not a self-starting function; as possessing the power to respond to an emergency, not the affirmative, ultimate power to commit the material and moral resources of the nation to full-scale war.

The decisions and actions of 1965 outran such theories. There was no sudden attack aimed at or endangering forces of the United States of the sort that can be deemed to require instant response and thus to make resort to Congress impossible if effective action is to be taken. Nor were we in any sense, as in some of our Latin American ventures, interposing our forces in a foreign country to protect American citizens and property, while remaining neutral with respect to conflicts there.

The Korean action, no doubt, stretched presidential emergency power to a prior extreme. But the invasion of South Korea from the North was sudden, and it did threaten to succeed quite rapidly and irrevocably, thus affecting the position of our own forces in neighboring Japan. * * * But no such [justification is] possible for the round-the-clock bombing of North Vietnam, which began in February, 1965, or for the sending of 50,000 troops to fight in South Vietnam, by a single decision that President Johnson announced on July 28, 1965, commenting, "this is really war."

It was really war. It raised the American troop level to over 100,000, soon of course to be multiplied five times over, and it committed, as President Johnson had said some two weeks earlier, on July 9, "our power and our national honor"—by a deliberate decision, considered over an extended period of time, not forced by sudden events; a decision functionally and in every other way amounting to an initiative for war. If this decision was not for Congress under the Constitution, then no decision of any consequence in matters of war and peace is left to Congress. * * *

* * *

President Johnson relied heavily on the Tonkin Gulf resolution of August, 1964, as a source of authority, although the Nixon Administration abandoned it, and Congress repealed it in December, 1970. The language of that resolution is so extraordinarily broad that it can be read to have given away anything and everything. * * * Yet the first wisdom in the construction of statutes is that the intent of the legislature is to be understood against the background of facts and circumstances existing at the time of enactment, to which the legislature was addressing itself. Congress addressed itself immediately to the relatively trivial Tonkin Gulf incident. * * *

If the resolution is read to have done more, the question arises whether it is within the power of Congress to give prospective approval to actions that would not, without such approval, conform to the Constitution. If without the Tonkin Gulf resolution the President had no constitutional authority to commit the nation to war in circumstances then undefined and unforeseen, could Congress prospectively, by blank check, give him that authority? In other contexts, the Supreme Court has held that Congress has no power to give away its power by delegating it to the President without standards for use in the future in indefinite circumstances. The relevant, well-known cases— not in the least shaken or rendered obsolete—are *Schechter Poultry Corp. v. United States, Panama Refining Co. v. Ryan,* and more recent and most relevant, *Kent v. Dulles.* The doctrine that delegation without standards is unconstitutional, which was decisive of these cases, is no mere technical teaching. It is concerned * * * with the sources of policy, with the crucial joinder between power and broadly based democratic responsibility, bestowed and discharged after the fashion of representative government. Delegation without standards short-circuits the lines of responsibility that make the political process meaningful.

United States v. Curtiss–Wright Corp. is often cited as indicating a modern development of independent presidential power, which cuts across, it is said, what would otherwise be the requirements of the doctrine of delegation. * * * But it is really quite a limited holding. Congress had, by joint resolution, authorized the President to prohibit sales of arms and munitions to countries then engaged in a specific armed conflict in the Chaco, whenever the President found that such a prohibition would contribute to the reestablishment of peace between those countries. The President used this authority, and the joint resolution was attacked as void for excessive delegation. The Court assumed without deciding that the delegation would have been excessive if applicable to internal affairs. But this assumption was probably not valid even at that time. Little more was delegated to the President than the power to establish a necessary factual condition precedent. The joint resolution closely defined what the President was to do, and where he was to do it—a far cry from the Tonkin Gulf resolution. This was hardly delegation running riot.

Having assumed *arguendo,* without deciding, that as applied to domestic affairs the delegation would be unconstitutional, the Court declared that "within the international field [Congress] must often accord to the President a degree of discretion and freedom from statutory restriction which would not be admissible were domestic affairs alone involved." Hence the delegation was held valid. There followed some eloquent assertions of independent presidential power in the "vast external realm," which were largely *dicta,* and were restricted to statements that the President alone can "speak or listen as a representative of the nation;" that he alone negotiates treaties and that the Senate cannot intrude, although it must give advice and consent; that the President has "plenary and exclusive power . . . as the sole organ of the federal government in the field of international relations," which in context must be taken as a restatement of his role as sole spokesman and listener, especially since the Court added that presidential powers "must be exercised in subordination to the applicable provisions of the Constitution;" and that the President, and not Congress, has the better opportunity of knowing conditions in foreign countries, because the President has his agents, and is better able to maintain secrecy. That was all. Nothing about powers to go to war or to use the armed forces without restriction. So far as broad delegation without standards of legislative power to the President is concerned, *Kent v. Dulles,* decided a generation later, has made clear that it will no more be tolerated in the "vast external realm" than domestically. Not that *United States v. Curtiss–Wright Corp.,* on its facts, ever held to the contrary.

* * *

It is asserted also in defense of independent presidential action that Congress is authorized by the Constitution only to declare war; and in modern circumstances, that is, after all, often not what is wanted. It is too much, and since too much is all that Congress has authority to do, it must be for the President to do anything somewhat less, which in present world conditions is generally what is required. The argument is altogether fallacious. There may actually be some sort of difference between the war we have waged in Vietnam and a war that Congress might have declared, although the difference, if any, is metaphysical. But there is utterly no reason to think that Congress has only the mega-power to declare war in the exact terms of the constitutional clause that authorizes declarations of war and no mini- or intermediate power to commit the country to something less than a declared war. Congress, as I have emphasized, has the necessary-and-proper power, the power to do anything that is necessary and proper to carry out the functions conferred upon it and upon any other department or officer of the government. If in the conditions of our day it is necessary to carry out the power to declare war by taking measures short of a declaration of war, everything in the scheme of government set up by the Constitution indicates that Congress has the needed authority.

* * *

The President represents a distinct constituency, of course, and ought properly, therefore, to speak with an independent voice and to have considerable leverage. But the President is a single official, in many ways a distant and regal personage. The discipline of the democratic process plays on him only grossly, at wholesale. He commands attention and he communicates with greater impact than any other institution of government, but he is not equally communicated with. His policy-making process is necessarily private, almost like that of a court. The large results become known, and on these he can be judged and held to account. But the process by which he reaches them is seldom open to much scrutiny and, consequently, little open to influence.

Congress, on the other hand, is institutionalized communication, access. Congress reflects in its very membership varieties of views and represents most groupings of opinion, to each of which it parcels out a share of power, at least negative power. It is subject, therefore, to being disabled by a minority of its membership from deciding too much, too soon, or even at all. Congress, in short, is the institution where we do not merely hold our government to account, but take part in it. It isn't always, but it can be. The Presidency by its nature rarely is.

The Presidency can speak for an existing broad consensus, and its genius is action. But its antennae are blunt, and it can mistake silence for consensus. Its errors are active ones, like the Indochina war—sins of commission. The genius of Congress lies precisely in its antennae, in its differentiated sensitivity. Its errors generally are those of irresolution, sins of omission; and we have learned, I trust, that these are, by and large, the less grave sins—in government, at any rate.

EUGENE V. ROSTOW, GREAT CASES MAKE BAD LAW: THE WAR POWERS ACT

50 Texas L.Rev. 833, 843–844, 849–851, 863–866, 885–886, 890, 892 (1972).

The most serious illusion of legal positivism is the notion that "the original intention" of those who drafted and voted for a law is thereafter knowable, save as a guideline of broad purpose or principle. The debates of judges and scholars about the legitimacy of *Marbury v. Madison,* the scope of the commerce power, or the true import of the Fourteenth Amendment are evidence enough of the limited value of such inquests as a guide to later decisions. It is psychologically impossible for a man of the twentieth century, however learned and sensitive, to perceive the world as the men of 1787 did. There is no way for him to reproduce the structure and climate of their universe— to understand as they did the relation of the several parts to each other and the weight which various fears, concerns and ambitions had in their minds. The most important words John Marshall ever wrote were that we should never forget it is a *constitution* we are expounding—a constitution intended to endure for ages to come, and capable of adaptation to the various crises of human affairs—but a *constitution* nonetheless, assuring continuity as well as flexibility, boundaries of power, coupled with a wide freedom of democratic choice.

* * *

In what is probably his finest opinion, Justice Jackson commented on the exercise of their war powers by President and Congress in these terms:

> Just what our forefathers did envision, or would have envisioned had they foreseen modern conditions, must be divined from materials almost as enigmatic as the dreams Joseph was called upon to interpret for Pharaoh. A century and a half of partisan debate and scholarly speculation yields no net result but only supplies more or less apt quotations from respected sources on each side of any question. They largely cancel each other. And court decisions are indecisive because of the judicial practice of dealing with the largest questions in the most narrow way.
>
> The actual art of governing under our Constitution does not and cannot conform to judicial definitions of the power of any of its branches based on isolated clauses or even single Articles torn from context. While the Constitution diffuses power the better to secure liberty, it also contemplates that practice will integrate the dispersed powers into a workable government. It enjoins upon its branches separateness but interdependence, autonomy but reciprocity.[26]

The early years of the nation under the new constitution were a period of acute turbulence which tested the parchment rules of the document in the crucible of intense and sustained experience. The

26. Youngstown Sheet & Tube Co. v. Sawyer, 343 U.S. 579, 634–35 (1952) (Jackson, J., concurring).

respective authority of Congress and the President with regard to the use of the armed forces was a matter of active controversy. Several issues of principle were settled * * * by the pattern of practice[.] * * *

With regard to the actual employment of the armed forces, it is apparent that the term "declare war" in the Constitution referred to the classifications of the law of nations, which makes a sharp distinction between the law of war and the law of peace. The law of nations was an intimate familiar to the men of the revolutionary generation in America. So far as international law is concerned, nations were then, and are now, free to use force in time of peace by way of self-help against acts or policies of other nations which they deem contrary to international law, and which have remained unredressed after a demand for amends. Different words are used to describe various categories of self-help: retorsion; reprisal; pacific embargoes or blockades; limited intervention to protect nationals; humanitarian intervention to restore order in situations of massacre, natural disaster, or extreme civil disturbance; and others. They are all subsumed under the inherent and sovereign right of self-defense, which has been reenacted in Article 51 of the Charter of the United Nations. * * *

It is tempting, but would be incorrect, to suggest, as Hamilton did, that the constitutional allocation of power between President and Congress with respect to the use of the armed forces corresponds to the categories of international law, with the President authorized to use the armed forces as head of state and commander-in-chief in those situations in which international law would acknowledge the use of armed force as permissible self-help in time of peace, while only Congress could move the nation into the juridical world of a state of war, within the meaning of international law. The constitutional pattern is, and should be, more complex than any such formula.

In the formative years of the Republic, Presidents and Congress alike found that the exigencies of diplomacy in a world at war required many uses and threats to use military power which defied simplified classification. When in office, Jefferson, Madison, and Hamilton all discovered that they could not quite live according to the brave rules they had pronounced as theorists of the Constitution. Then, and since, the invocation of force as a tool of national policy ranged from the purely Presidential to the full declaration of war, the latter as rare in the eighteenth century and the early days of the nation as it has been in this century.

* * *

The United States has used its armed forces abroad more than 150 times since 1789, and on many more occasions the President has threatened to use force. A declaration of "solemn war," fully invoking the international law of war, has been issued on only five occasions. Some of the remaining uses of force or the threat of force were undertaken pursuant to Congressional authority, although the experts debate about how many were actually responsive to prior Congressional action. In the rest, including some costly and extended campaigns, the President acted, formally at least, on his own constitutional authority.

A number of lists have been compiled, reaching different conclusions as to the number of episodes of hostilities in time of peace actually authorized in any meaningful sense by statute. * * * In the most recent compilation of this kind, Senator Goldwater lists 153 military actions taken by the United States abroad without a declaration of war, of which he claims 63 were "arguably" initiated under prior legislative authority, 34 under a treaty, 26 under legislation, and, in the case of Samoa in 1888–89 and 1899, Lebanon in 1958, and Vietnam, both under a treaty and under legislation implementing it.[70]   Arguably, one could count the Cuban Missile Crisis of 1962 in this final category as well, although it is more realistic to classify that incident as an example of a use of force by the President alone.

These lists include major events: Commodore Perry's expedition to Japan and those which followed it; the array of 50,000 troops in Texas during 1865 and 1866 to support our diplomatic suggestion that France withdraw from Mexico; the participation of American forces in the hostilities following the Boxer Rebellion in China in 1900–01; the suppression of revolt in the Philippines between 1899 and 1901; the hostilities with Mexico, between 1914 and 1917; the deployments and uses of force by Wilson and Franklin Roosevelt before both World Wars; and the occupations of Haiti, the Dominican Republic, and Nicaragua, to note only the more conspicuous.

This brief evocation of history suggests two conclusions.

First, the pattern * * * is old, familiar, and rooted in the nature of things.   There is nothing constitutionally illegitimate or even dubious about "undeclared" wars.   We and other nations fought them frequently in the eighteenth and nineteenth centuries, as well as in the twentieth.   The charge that the practice is an unconstitutional invention of this century, or of Presidents McKinley, Wilson, Franklin Roosevelt, Truman, Kennedy, and Johnson is a myth.

* * *

Congress has the last word on matters of peace and war, but the President's authority goes far beyond that to repel sudden attacks, the example Madison gave to illustrate the desirability of changing the language in Article I Section 8 from "make war" to "declare war."   As Professor Ratner says:

> But preeminent war-peace authority is not necessarily exclusive war-peace authority, although that congruence has been suggested by some executive and judicial statements.   The ultimate decider should not always be the initial decider.   Congressional action takes time. Invariably, the President confronts the problem first;   may he as

---

70. [*War Powers Legislation: Hearings on S. 731, S.J.Res. 18, and S.J.Res. 59 Be-* fore the S. Comm. on Foreign Relations, 92d Cong., 1st Sess. 359–379 (1972).]

commander-in-chief order American forces to fight without waiting for congressional authorization?

The Constitutional Convention suggested the answer by approving the motion of Madison and Gerry to amend the congressional power by "insert[ing] *'declare,'* striking out *'make'* war; leaving to the Executive the power to repel sudden attacks"—though the explanatory clause was not included in the constitutional text nor given the scrutiny of proposed inclusion. That clause thus recognized, but did not authoritatively delineate, the war-making authority of the President, implied by his role as executive and commander-in-chief and by congressional power to declare, but not make, war.

In 1787, "repel sudden attack" probably meant "resist invasion or rebellion." But constitutional policy for ensuing epochs is not congealed in the mold of 1787 referants. Such policy is derived from the long-range goals that underlie the constitutional language as illuminated by the Convention proceedings, from the implications of the language disclosed by resolution of subsequent problems, and from its function in the context of altered social needs. Aggression beyond the seas could not threaten Americans in the eighteenth century as it can in the twentieth. Underlying the constitutional language and the explanatory clause is a long-range purpose that authorizes the President to protect Americans from external force in an emergency.

* * *

The amorphous distinction between offense and defense does not effectively delineate the scope of the President's emergency war power. In a world where increasingly mobile weapons enhance the advantage of military initiative, the distinction turns, for the most part, on an appraisal of motives and intentions. With his heavy load of responsibility, the President may sometimes conclude that offense is the best defense. As the foregoing examples indicate, presidentially-authorized hostilities are always ostensibly "defensive." And, though his characterization may be debatable, the President must necessarily be accorded a broad discretion.[72]

As to sustained hostilities in the absence of a declaration of war, the pattern of constitutional practice offers no sharp and formal lines. There are instances of Congressional action to authorize undeclared wars, and instances in which, nominally at least, Congress was silent. The practice, however, does justify a second general conclusion: It is an illusion to suppose, in the nature of our political system, that the formal silence of Congress on some of these occasions when force was used extensively represents a genuine opposition between Congress and the Presidency. The power of the United States to employ force or to carry on any other sustained policy can be exercised in fact only when Congress and the President cooperate, however unwillingly. The silences and the tacit arrangements of American politics are often more important than its nominal dispositions and documents.

* * *

72. Ratner, [*The Coordinated Warmaking Power—Legislative Executive, and Judicial Roles,* 44 S.Cal.L.Rev. 461, 466–469 (1971).]

UNDUE DELEGATION OF LEGISLATIVE AUTHORITY

Professor * * * Bickel advance[s] another contention in [his] effort to exorcise the Tonkin Gulf Resolution and other legislation supporting the war in Vietnam. To [him], the cycle of Presidential, Senatorial, and Congressional decisions with regard to Vietnam, regularly renewed over a period of more than sixteen years, is insufficient to satisfy * * * the unambiguous requirements of constitutional orthodoxy. [He argues that] hostilities can be authorized only by Congressional action *at the time they begin,* and then by delegations narrowly limited in scope. In [his] opinion, neither a treaty nor a congressional resolution can authorize a President to use force *in advance of the event.* Such provisions, [he] argue[s,] unconstitutionally delegate legislative power to the President, because they are not suitably limited to the circumstances of the event which gave rise to the resolution—in the case of the Tonkin Gulf Resolution, the attack on American naval vessels in the Gulf of Tonkin.

* * *

* * * Bickel discover[s] the source of [his] rule in * * * the original intent of the men who gave Congress the power "to declare war," despite 182 years of opinion and practice to the contrary. The principle of full legislative control of the military power, [he] argue[s], precludes much Presidential discretion, and requires Congressional action only at the ritual moment, and then only in terms addressed to defined circumstances. Advance approval for the use of force [is] a transfer to the President of a power Congress cannot yield even for a moment, even though it retains full authority to change the course of the nation thereafter by repealing, modifying, or reversing its policy, and the President's.

* * *

Actually, the Tonkin Gulf Resolution would appear to be beyond censure even under Bickel's extraordinary rule, since there had been some use of force by the United States in Vietnam, and Congress knew more was being considered at the time the Resolution was passed. Furthermore, the Tonkin Gulf Resolution would seem to contain suitably practical and defined standards to channel and confine the President's authority: it was addressed to what Congress and the President had found to be an "armed attack" by North Vietnam on South Vietnam within the meaning of the SEATO Treaty; and it could be terminated by Congress through a concurrent resolution, that is, without risk of veto. It is hard to conceive of a more precise or controlled "delegation" than one to help defeat a particular attack by one named state against another, pursuant to a policy already embodied in a Treaty.

* * *

The argument of undue delegation fails for a deeper reason. It is at war with the "nature of things," those stubborn exigencies of the external world that Montesquieu rightly saw as the true source of law, the nature of things in the late eighteenth century and the nature of things now. The necessities of circumstance in dealing with the hurly-burly of the real world have produced a quite different pattern of practice since 1789, not less democratic than the model in the mind[ ] of Professor[ ] Bickel * * * but far more flexible, resourceful, and effective. To treat Resolutions like the Tonkin Gulf Resolution as nullities would make it nearly impossible to associate Congress with the President in the articulation of an effective deterrent diplomacy. Such a rule would make foreign affairs even more exclusively the province of the President than is the case today.

* * *

The delegation theory of Professor * * * Bickel would deny the President and the Congress the most ordinary and elementary tools for protecting the nation in a time of international turbulence. Under [this] rule, we should be the only nation on earth incapable of making a credible military treaty. [The] rule would make it impossible firmly to delineate American interests in advance, and thus to deter and contain processes of expansion which Congress and the President deem threatening to national security. It would emasculate both Congress and the Presidency, and deprive even treaties like NATO of their weight and credibility.

The Constitution, Justice Goldberg once said, is not "a suicide pact." [114] The war power, the Supreme Court has remarked, is the power to wage war successfully. So too, the power of the President and of the Congress over foreign relations is the power to wage peace successfully. There is nothing in the history of the war power and the foreign relations power, since President Washington's first term, to suggest that the United States may not seek to avert the danger of war by giving potential enemies of the nation a credible and effective warning in advance. *McCulloch v. Maryland* teaches that those who oppose the presumptive constitutional validity of the means Congress and the President together select as appropriate to protect the security of the nation face a nearly insuperable burden of proof.

BIBLIOGRAPHY

Foreign Affairs

Bestor, *Separation of Powers in the Domain of Foreign Affairs: The Original Intent of the Constitution Historically Examined,* 5 Seton Hall L.Rev. 527 (1974).

Casper, *Constitutional Constraints on the Conduct of Foreign and Defense Policy: A Nonjudicial Model,* 43 U.Chi.L.Rev. 463 (1976).

M. Glennon, CONSTITUTIONAL DIPLOMACY (1990).

R. Goldwin & R. Licht, FOREIGN POLICY AND THE CONSTITUTION (1990).

114. Aptheker v. Secretary of State, 378 U.S. 500, 509 (1964).

L. Henkin, CONSTITUTIONALISM, DEMOCRACY, AND FOREIGN AFFAIRS (1990).

L. Henkin, FOREIGN AFFAIRS AND THE CONSTITUTION (1972).

H. Koh, THE NATIONAL SECURITY CONSTITUTION (1990).

Koh, *Why the President (Almost) Always Wins in Foreign Affairs: Lessons of the Iran–Contra Affair,* 97 Yale L.J. 1255 (1988).

Symposium, *The United States Constitution in Its Third Century: Foreign Affairs,* 83 Am.J.Int'l L. 713 (1989).

War Powers

Adler, *The Constitution and Presidential Warmaking: The Enduring Debate,* 103 Pol.Sci.Q. 1 (1988).

Berger, *War–Making by the President,* 121 U.Pa.L.Rev. 29 (1972).

Biden, *The War Power at a Constitutional Impasse: A "Joint Decision" Solution,* 77 Geo.L.J. 367 (1988).

Ely, *The American War in Indochina (Parts I & II),* 42 Stan.L.Rev. 876, 1092 (1990).

Lobel, *Covert War and Congressional Authority: Hidden War and Forgotten Power,* 134 U.Pa.L.Rev. 1035 (1986).

Lofgren, *On War–Making, Original Intent, and Ultra–Whiggery,* 21 Val. U.L.Rev. 53 (1986).

Lofgren, *War–Making Under the Constitution: The Original Understanding,* 81 Yale L.J. 672 (1972).

Note, *Congress, the President, and the Power to Commit Forces to Combat,* 81 Harv.L.Rev. 1771 (1968).

Note, *The Failure of Constitutional Controls Over War Powers in the Nuclear Age: The Argument for a Constitutional Amendment,* 40 Stan.L.Rev. 1543 (1988).

Ratner, *The Coordinated Warmaking Power—Legislative, Executive, and Judicial Roles,* 44 S.Cal.L.Rev. 461 (1971).

Reveley, *Presidential War–Making: Constitutional Prerogative or Usurpation?,* 55 Va.L.Rev. 1243 (1969).

W.T. Reveley, WAR POWERS OF THE PRESIDENT AND CONGRESS (1981).

A. Sofaer, WAR, FOREIGN AFFAIRS AND CONSTITUTIONAL POWER (1976).

Van Alstyne, *Congress, the President, and the Power to Declare War: A Requiem for Vietnam,* 121 U.Pa.L.Rev. 1 (1972).

F. Wormuth & E. Firmage, TO CHAIN THE DOG OF WAR: THE WAR POWER OF CONGRESS IN HISTORY AND LAW (1986).

War Powers Resolution

Carter, *The Constitutionality of the War Powers Resolution,* 70 Va.L. Rev. 101 (1984).

Ely, *Suppose Congress Wanted a War Powers Act That Worked,* 88 Colum.L.Rev. 1379 (1988).

Emerson, *The War Powers Resolution Tested: The President's Independent Defense Power,* 51 N.D. Lawyer 187 (1975).

Glennon, *The War Powers Resolution: Sad Record, Dismal Promise,* 17 Loyola L.A.L.Rev. 657 (1984).

Lungren & Krotoski, *The War Powers Resolution After the Chadha Decision,* 17 Loy.L.A.L.Rev. 767 (1984).

Rostow, *"Once More Into the Breach:" The War Powers Resolution Revisited,* 21 Val.U.L.Rev. 1 (1986).

Rubner, *The Reagan Administration, the 1974 War Powers Resolution, and the Invasion of Grenada,* 100 Pol.Sci.Q. 627 (1986).

Scigliano, *The War Powers Resolution and the War Powers,* in THE PRESIDENCY IN THE CONSTITUTIONAL ORDER 124 (J. Bessette & J. Tulis eds. 1981).

Vance, *Striking the Balance: Congress and the President Under the War Powers Resolution,* 133 U.Pa.L.Rev. 79 (1984).

D. CONGRESSIONAL AND PRESIDENTIAL CONTROL OF ADMINISTRATIVE AGENCIES

What roles should the President and Congress play in directing administrative agencies? This is the common thread in the third set of substantive separation-of-power problems. Up until the New Deal courts were preoccupied with reconciling the delegation of power to this fourth branch of government with the institutional structure created by the Constitution.[1] Today it is generally agreed that agencies may make policy judgments—even very important ones—in the first instance. The important issue now is how to allocate control over them between Congress and the executive (and the courts). Many of the modern cases have arisen out of Congress's efforts to control the federal bureaucracy through such devices as appointment,[2] removal,[3] and the legislative veto.[4]

---

1. A.L.A. Schechter Poultry Corp. v. United States, 295 U.S. 495, 55 S.Ct. 837, 79 L.Ed. 1570 (1935). See Mistretta v. United States, 488 U.S. 361, 109 S.Ct. 647, 102 L.Ed.2d 714 (1989).

2. Morrison v. Olson, 487 U.S. 654, 108 S.Ct. 2597, 101 L.Ed.2d 569 (1988); Buckley v. Valeo, 424 U.S. 1, 96 S.Ct. 612, 46 L.Ed. 2d 659 (1976).

3. Morrison v. Olson, *supra* note 2; Bowsher v. Synar, 478 U.S. 714, 106 S.Ct.

3181, 92 L.Ed.2d 583 (1986); Wiener v. United States, 357 U.S. 349, 78 S.Ct. 1275, 2 L.Ed.2d 1377 (1958); Humphrey's Executor v. United States, 295 U.S. 602, 55 S.Ct. 869, 79 L.Ed. 1611 (1935); Myers v. United States, 272 U.S. 52, 47 S.Ct. 21, 71 L.Ed. 160 (1926).

4. INS v. Chadha, 462 U.S. 919, 103 S.Ct. 2764, 77 L.Ed.2d 317 (1983).

In both *Morrison v. Olson* and *Bowsher v. Synar* the major doctrinal issue was whether Congress could limit or displace the President's power to remove federal officials (the special prosecutor, the Comptroller General). The excerpt from Louis Fisher outlines some of the historical background of this controversy. It also suggests that we will find no clear answers in the text of the Constitution, the specific intentions of the Founders, or precedent. For a proper resolution we may have to look instead to the larger questions of purpose and method discussed in Section A.

The legislative veto procedure held unconstitutional in *INS v. Chadha* was a different kind of legislative response to the growth of the federal bureaucracy. It permitted Congress to give agencies broad and general statutory directives and then, when laws were implemented through orders and rules, to use the veto device to weed out agency action that it viewed as inconsistent with its mandates. Whether this procedure created more serious problems than the ones it solved, and whether its invalidation will prove to be a healthy tonic for Congress, are questions addressed by Laurence Tribe, Harold Bruff, Robert Nagel (and to some degree by Currie and Strauss in Section A).

LOUIS FISHER, THEORY IN A CRUCIBLE: THE REMOVAL POWER

Constitutional Conflicts Between Congress and the President 60–70 (1985).

Occasionally a statement in the *Federalist Papers* is so wide of the mark, at such odds with events to come, that it has an abrupt and startling effect. So it is with the breezy claim of Alexander Hamilton, in Federalist 77, that the consent of the Senate "would be necessary to displace [public officials] as well as to approve."

The issue that Hamilton disposed of so nonchalantly produced deep divisions among the members of the First Congress. It overshadowed most of the matters that pressed upon the fledgling legislative body in 1789. From May 19 through June 24 the House of Representatives explored the removal power in all its nuances. The debate, occupying almost two hundred pages of the record, represents one of the most thorough expositions on the nature of implied powers. In contrast to many members of Congress today, who let constitutional issues slide by to be disposed of by the courts (if at all), the members of the First Congress faced the constitutional issue with a deep sense of responsibility.

For more than a century it has been the custom of attorneys and scholars, when discussing the removal issue in the First Congress, to write of four schools of thought: (1) the Senate, because of its role in appointments, must have equal participation; (2) removals may be made only by the constitutional process of impeachment; (3) Congress, since it creates an office, may attach to it any condition it decides proper for tenure and removal; (4) the power of removal belongs exclusively to the President as an incident of the executive power.

(G. & A.) Const'l Reader 2d Ed.—9

Those four categories, although convenient for simplicity and tidiness, fail to do justice to the wide-ranging nature of the debate, the complexity of the issues, or the shifting tide of opinion that advanced and receded each day as the deliberation continued. The debate merits close attention because of its instruction on constitutional power.[2]

THE "DECISION OF 1789"

James Madison began the debate by proposing three executive departments: Foreign Affairs, Treasury, and War. At the head of each department would be a Secretary appointed by the President with the advice and consent of the Senate "and to be removable by the President." William Smith of South Carolina immediately objected to giving the President sole power of removal. * * * If a department head were found unfit for his office "the person must remain there," Smith said, just like a member of Congress, unless guilty of some crime. * * * As the first day's debate drew to a close, the House by a "considerable majority" declared that the removal power lay with the President.

Two days later the House considered a resolution to make the heads of the three executive departments "removable by the President." Eleven members, Madison among them, were appointed to draw up a bill. When the House took up the topic on June 16, William Smith clarified his position by identifying two choices: either the Constitution gave the President the power of removal (in which case it was nugatory for Congress to repeat it) or else it was not given to him (and therefore improper for Congress to confer). He also cautioned that competent people would be reluctant to accept a position and risk their reputation if the President could remove them at will. Smith wanted the language eliminated and the question left to the judiciary. This represents a fifth school of thought on the removal issue and an early inclination, long before *Marbury v. Madison* (1803), of judicial review.

Madison, after taking a few days to reexamine the Constitution, conceded that it did not "perfectly correspond with the ideas I entertained of it from the first glance." Precisely how he had adjusted his opinion is not evident from his remarks. The Constitution, he said, vested the executive power in the President, subject to certain exceptions, such as the Senate's participation in the appointment process. He believed that Congress could not extend the exceptions or modify in any way the President's authority. Therefore it was improper to associate the Senate with the President in the removal process. Yet to strike the clause might imply that Congress doubted whether the President had the removal power. It was better, Madison concluded, to retain the language.

2. The House debate in 1789, on all three executive departments, appears in the Annals of Congress, I, 368–83 (May 19), 384–96 (May 20), 396 (May 21), 455–79 (June 16), 479–512 (June 17), 512–52 (June 18), 552–77 (June 19), 578–85 (June 22), 590–92 (June 24), 592–607 (June 25), 611–14 (June 27), 614–15 (June 30), and 615 (July 1).

Other delegates objected to letting Congress amend the Constitution by statutory construction whenever the document was silent on a question. Congressman Samuel Livermore acknowledged that Congress had authority to create an office and to attach to it whatever limitations and restrictions it thought appropriate, but he thought it very improper to say that the power of giving birth to a creature permitted Congress to "bring forth a monster." Since he feared that a President might remove someone on mere caprice to make room for a favorite, he wanted every person "to have a hearing before he is punished." Here we have a sixth school; procedural due process.

On June 17 the House resumed debate on the motion to make the Secretary of Foreign Affairs "removable by the President." Thomas Hartley from Pennsylvania denied that officials had a property in their office and could be removed only for criminal conduct. That doctrine "may suit a nation which is strong in proportion to the number of dependents upon the Crown, but will be very pernicious in a Republic like ours." Some officers held their commissions during good behavior; others, like the Secretary, served at the pleasure of the President.

George Clymer of Pennsylvania had no doubt that the removal power belonged to the executive. Even if the Constitution had been silent on the power of appointment, he reasoned, the executive would have had that power as well. The Constitution mentioned appointment only to "give some further security against the introduction of improper men into office. But in cases of removal there is not such necessity for this check." One of the more active participants in the debate, Roger Sherman of Connecticut, said that an officer existed as a creature of Congress. Depending upon the statute creating the office, the person might hold office during good behavior, be elected every year, displaced for negligence of duty, or subjected to any other provision without calling upon the President or the Senate.

Madison abhorred this theory of government. He considered it fundamental that the Constitution vested the executive power in the President and required him to take care that the laws be faithfully executed. If the President wantonly removed a meritorious officer, that would "subject him to impeachment and removal from his own high trust." Madison wanted to protect the responsibility of the President: "Vest this power in the Senate jointly with the President, and you abolish at once that great principle of unity and responsibility in the Executive department, which was intended for the security of liberty and the public good."

Debate continued on June 18. The idea of deriving the removal power from the general nature of "executive power," as Madison had suggested, elicited a challenge from Alexander White of Virginia, who said that such a doctrine could be supported only by examples "brought from beyond the Atlantic." *   *   *

Still another Virginian, John Page, objected to joining the Senate with the President in the removal power. In nine cases out of ten, he predicted, where the President was confident that someone must be removed, it would be impossible to produce the necessary evidence. Could the Senate proceed without evidence? If not, should such a man "be saddled upon the President, who has been appointed for no other purpose but to aid the President in performing certain duties?" James Jackson denied that the heads of departments were necessarily dependent upon the President. The Constitution itself "specifically points them out." Benjamin Goodhue blunted the force of that argument. He explained that while Senators played an important role in confirming an officer, since they might be better acquainted with the nominee than the President, the man's *performance in office* could be judged better by the President. He would more likely learn of improper conduct by subordinates. To Livermore, Congress should not interfere with the executive departments by including language on removals: "Leave them to do their duty, and let us do ours."

June 19 arrived and the House still did not know whether to strike the words "to be removable by the President." Peter Silvester of New York helped crystallize the issue: Congress had to give its opinion either by declaration or by implication. If the Constitution lodged the removal power in the President it was useless for Congress to interfere by making an express declaration. If the Constitution did *not* leave the power with the President, could Congress give it? Although the Constitution did not expressly grant the power, neither was there anything "in contradiction to it." The problem was compounded, Sherman added, by the fact that the words "to be removable by the President" might imply that the President lacked the removal power and had to have it granted by law. The motion to strike the language was rejected, 20 to 34.

By June 22 the House was headed in the direction of treating the removal power by implication, not declaration. Benson moved that the bill provide that the chief clerk (second in command in the Foreign Affairs Department) take charge of all records whenever the Secretary "shall be removed from office" by the President. His motion avoided the problem in the phrase "to be removable by the President," which appeared to be a grant of power by Congress. The new language displeased Smith, who preferred that Congress express itself in "more candid and manly" terms by declaration, not implication, but Benson's motion carried, 30 to 18. Benson then moved to strike the phrase "to be removable by the President," to which the House agreed, 31 to 19.

When the Senate took up the bill and someone proposed to delete the President's power to remove the Secretary of Foreign Affairs, a tie vote (nine to nine) resulted. Vice President Adams broke the tie by voting against the motion. A few days later, during House action on the bill to establish a War Department, Benson offered language to give the President removal power by implication. Although the identical principle and language were at issue, his motion carried by the smaller margin of 24 to 22. On a motion in the Senate to strike the President's power to remove the Secretary of War, the effort failed by the close vote of nine to ten.

The Foreign Affairs and War Departments had been regarded as "executive departments," largely because of their origin and evolution during the Continental Congress. No such concession was made for Treasury. One would have expected Congress, jealous of its control over finances during the preceding decade, to contest the President's power to remove the Secretary of the Treasury. The challenge came from the Senate, not the House. The Senate deleted the President's power to remove the Secretary. Later on a motion that the Senate recede from its position and accept the House language, another tie vote occurred, ten to ten. Vice President Adams cast the deciding vote for the motion.

As a result of these actions, Congress passed legislation to adopt the same approach for the Departments of Foreign Affairs, War, and Treasury. The subordinate officers would have charge and custody of all records whenever the Secretary "shall be removed from office by the President of the United States."

The fact that Congress recognized the President's freedom to remove department heads did not mean that the President could remove *all* administrative officials. Congress did not vest the entire removal power with him. When Madison turned his attention to the tenure of the Comptroller of the Treasury, he said that it was necessary "to consider the nature of this office." Its properties were not "purely of an Executive nature," he said. "It seems to me that they partake of a Judiciary quality as well as Executive; perhaps the latter obtains in the greatest degree." Because of the mixed nature of the office, "there may be strong reasons why an officer of this kind should not hold his office at the pleasure of the Executive branch of the Government." Madison's insight would hold the attention of scholars and the courts more than a century later.

* * *

CONTROVERSIES FROM JACKSON TO CLEVELAND

Congress has authority to create an office and specify the term of office. May it also specify the manner in which an incumbent is removed? This issue, offered here as an academic riddle, assumed solid form with Andrew Jackson in the White House.

Jackson's predecessors had used the removal power with restraint. The opportunity for removals, however, expanded considerably in 1820 when Congress passed legislation that limited a large number of federal officers to a term of four years, stipulating that they would be "removable from office at pleasure." Supported by this legislative authority and by his own philosophy favoring rotation of federal personnel, Jackson removed more officers than all of the Presidents who preceded him (252 for Jackson compared to 193 for his predecessors). These numbers, though large, are less impressive as a proportion of the growing bureaucracy and do not constitute anything near the "clean sweep" suggested by some historians.

Congressional opposition to Jackson's policy came to a head in 1833 when he removed the Secretary of the Treasury for refusing to carry out his policy toward the national bank. At issue was more than the removal power. Congress regarded Treasury with proprietary interest, often treating the Secretary as *its* agent. It had, for example, delegated to the Secretary—not the President—the responsibility for placing government funds either in national banks or state banks. The Senate responded to Jackson's action by passing a resolution of censure: "*Resolved,* That the President, in the late Executive proceedings in relation to the public revenue, has assumed upon himself authority and power not conferred by the Constitution and laws, but in derogation of both."

Jackson, outraged that the Senate should censure him on the basis of unspecified charges, without an opportunity to be heard and in circumvention of the formal constitutional procedure for impeachment, prepared a lengthy and impassioned protest. With great force he argued that the Constitution vested in the President the executive power, requiring him to take care that the laws be faithfully executed. That made him, he said, "responsible for the entire action of the executive department." Following this logic, the President had a right to employ agents of his own choice to aid him. When no longer willing to be responsible for their acts, he could remove them. Jackson regarded the Secretary of the Treasury as "wholly an executive officer." Three years later the Senate ordered its resolution of censure expunged from the record. * * *

The removal power ripened into a poisonous dispute during the administration of Andrew Johnson. Even before he took office, Congress had begun to trench upon the President's removal power. Legislation in 1863 created a Comptroller of the Currency to hold office for the term of five years "unless sooner removed by the President, by and with the advice and consent of the Senate." Two years later Congress passed legislation to permit military and naval officers, upon dismissal by the President, to apply for a trial.

Congress continued this policy in 1867 by passing the Tenure of Office Act. Every person holding civil office with the advice and consent of the Senate became entitled to hold office until the President appointed a successor, with the advice and consent of the Senate. The bill further provided that the Secretaries of State, Treasury, War, Navy, and Interior, the Postmaster General, and the Attorney General should hold office during the term of the President who appointed them, and for one month thereafter, "subject to removal by and with the advice and consent of the Senate." During Senate recess the President could suspend an official but would have to report to the Senate, upon its return, the evidence and reasons for the suspension. If the Senate concurred in his action the suspended officer would be removed. If the Senate refused to concur, the suspended officer would resume the functions of his office.

Here was a frontal challenge to presidential control over his own officers. Johnson vetoed the bill, claiming that it violated the Constitution and the construction placed upon it by the debate of 1789. His message was well reasoned and fully documented. But Congress, caught up in the fierce politics of that time, was not receptive to facts or argument. Both Houses promptly overrode his veto.

Johnson had hoped that the disruptive voice in his Cabinet, Secretary of War Edwin M. Stanton, would resign. He did not. As the months rolled by and the political crisis deepened, Johnson decided to suspend Stanton. The Senate returned from its recess and refused to concur in the suspension. Johnson upped the ante by *removing* Stanton, with the expectation that the constitutionality of the Tenure of Office Act would be tested in the courts. Yet because of the actions of Ulysses S. Grant, whom Johnson had installed as War Secretary ad interim, and Lorenzo Thomas, Grant's successor, the tactic backfired. Stanton was able to regain his office. Johnson's strategy merely fanned the fire of impeachment that had been smoldering for a year, a movement that fell one vote short in the Senate.

The political extravagance of Congress did not go unnoticed. President Grant, in his first annual message in 1869, recommended that Congress repeal the Tenure of Office Act. To him the law was inconsistent with efficient administration: "What faith can an Executive put in officials forced upon him, and those, too, whom he has suspended for reason?" Congress revised the act that year, softening the suspension section but retaining the Senate's involvement in the removal process.

Congress continued to expand the Senate's role. Legislation in 1872 required the Postmaster General and his three assistants to be appointed by the President, by and with the advice and consent of the Senate, and provided that they might be "removed in the same manner." In 1876 Congress required the Senate's advice and consent for the removal of all first-, second-, and third-class postmasters.

A new confrontation between President and Congress occurred from 1885 to 1886, after Grover Cleveland suspended several hundred officials and refused to deliver certain papers and documents to the Senate. Cleveland declared that the power to remove or suspend executive officials was vested solely in the President by the Constitution, particularly by the "executive power" and "take care" clauses. He also noted that the law governing suspensions, as amended in 1869, did not justify the Senate's request for documents. Because of this dispute, Congress repealed the Tenure of Office Act in 1887.

LAURENCE H. TRIBE, THE LEGISLATIVE VETO DECISION: A LAW BY ANY OTHER NAME?

21 Harv.J.Legis. 7–10, 12–15, 17 (1984).

[Jagdish Rai Chadha came to the United States under a student visa. When his authorized stay expired an immigration judge, acting on behalf of the Attorney General, suspended his deportation under § 244 of the Immigration and Nationality Act, which allowed suspension in cases of extreme hardship. Section 244 also permitted one house of Congress to override a suspension (a "legislative veto"), and in Chadha's case the House of Representatives did so.]

Much, although far from all, of the controversy over the legislative veto was resolved when the Supreme Court held in *INS v. Chadha* that the one-House legislative veto provision in section 244(c)(2) was unconstitutional.[35] In an opinion by Chief Justice Burger, the Court held that *all* action by Congress that is "legislative" in "character" must be taken in accord with the "single, finely wrought and exhaustively considered, procedure" set out in the "explicit and unambiguous provisions" of Article I. Those provisions expressly mandate both *bicamerality* (passage by a majority of both Houses)[40] and *presentment* to the President for possible veto (with a requirement of two-thirds of each House to override),[41] not simply when Congress *purports* to be legislating but whenever it takes action that must be *regarded* as "legislative."

* * *

According to a majority of the Court, the House veto of Chadha's status as a permanent resident alien *had* to be viewed as "an exercise of legislative power." Thus, since it was neither approved by both Houses nor presented to the President for signature or veto—two independently fatal flaws—the House's action was doubly unconstitutional.

That "a law is a law is a law" is hard to refute. But that statement sheds little light on *why* the veto at issue in *Chadha was* so "law-like" an action that it "had" to be deemed legislative. * * *

* * * The Chief Justice explained that the veto of Chadha's suspension of deportation was "essentially legislative" because it "had the purpose and effect of altering the legal rights, duties and relations of persons . . . outside the legislative branch." Absent the veto, after all, Chadha would remain in the United States. * * *

* * * [But] as Justice White stressed in his thoughtful dissent, we live in a sprawling administrative state in which "legislative" power, in the exact sense employed by the *Chadha* majority, is *routinely* exercised by the federal executive branch, by the headless "fourth branch of the government," and even by private individuals and groups. These exercises of power all occur without any of the structural checks

---

35. 103 S.Ct. 2764 (1983).　　　　**41.** U.S. Const. art. I, § 7, cl. 2 * * *.

40. U.S. Const. art. I, §§ 1, 7 * * *.

the *Chadha* Court held indispensable when similar power is wielded by legislators pursuant to otherwise indistinguishable statutory delegations of authority to Congress or to one of its parts. Yet the absence of those checks is evidently deemed immaterial in these many cases.

* * *

The only imaginable justification for what Justice White called "this odd result" lies in a principle never expressly articulated by the majority: "that the legislature can delegate authority to others *but not to itself.*" * * *

* * *

[It is not clear why this should be so.] [T]he *only* objection peculiarly applicable to the exercise of statutorily delegated power by all or part of Congress itself—as opposed to such exercise of delegated power by an agent or agency *external* to Congress—must be the proposition that entrusting members of Congress with such power ipso facto confers upon federal lawmakers the mantle of "officers" of the United States government, in violation of the Appointments Clause [66] and of the Incompatibility Clause.[67] It is noteworthy that the *Chadha* majority not only failed to mention but also seems not to have envisioned any such rationale for its holding. * * *

One must, nonetheless, ask whether this rationale that "Congressmen cannot be officers" could be put forward to declare the veto unconstitutional. Its key premise would, of course, have to be that the delegation of legislative veto authority to Congress (or to part of that body) automatically makes the members of Congress who are entrusted with such veto power into "officers of the United States." The objection would then have to be made that these officers were not appointed by the executive branch in the manner required by Article II, Section 2, Clause 2. To add the final blow, it would be stressed that the very membership of these officers in Congress violates the Incompatibility Clause of Article I, Section 6, Clause 2.

The argument is a tidy one—but it confronts at least one major problem. Neither is there, nor could there be, any general principle that anyone to whom a federal statute delegates a significant decision-making role on which the rights or duties of persons outside Congress may depend becomes, by virtue of such delegation, an "Officer of the United States" within the meaning of the Appointments Clause and the Incompatibility Clause. If such a principle existed, then Congress could

---

66. [The President] shall nominate, and by and with the Advice and Consent of the Senate, shall appoint Ambassadors, other public Ministers and Consuls, Judges of the supreme Court, and all other Officers of the United States, whose Appointments are not herein otherwise provided for, and which shall be established by Law; but the Congress may by Law vest the Appointment of such inferior Officers, as they think proper, in the President alone, in the Courts of Law, or in the Heads of Departments.

U.S. Const. art. II, § 2, cl. 2, *applied in* Buckley v. Valeo, 424 U.S. 1, 40–41 (1976) (per curiam).

67. U.S. Const. art. I, § 6, cl. 2 ("[N]o Person holding any Office under the United States, shall be a Member of either House during his Continuance in Office.").

not "confer upon the *States*"—which are surely not United States "Officers"—"an ability to restrict the flow of interstate commerce that they would not otherwise enjoy." And the private individuals and groups to whom decisionmaking roles were delegated in *Currin v. Wallace* [74] and *United States v. Rock Royal Co–Operative,* [75] for example, would have been United States officers whose failure to be appointed in accord with Article II would have constituted fatal constitutional flaws in the statutory schemes upheld in those two landmark decisions.

What made the members of the Federal Election Commission (FEC) United States "officers" in *Buckley v. Valeo* was the significant executive responsibility those FEC members exercised under the Federal Election Campaign Act of 1971. The responsibility exercised by the House and Senate under the reservation of legislative veto authority struck down in *Chadha* seems profoundly different. Whether viewed as the *unicameral rejection* of an action taken by the Attorney General in those instances where a veto is cast by one House, or viewed as the *bicameral acceptance* of a legislative proposal made by the Attorney General in those instances where neither House vetoes the Attorney General's suspension of deportation, what Congress does in cases like *Chadha* hardly seems to involve congressional interference with the "execution" of any enacted law. Indeed, it bears repeating here that the *Chadha* majority itself was at pains to insist that the power at issue in the veto is "legislative" in nature.

Whatever classification scheme one may adopt for other purposes, the core concern of the Appointments and Incompatibility Clauses hardly seems to be activated by legislative vetoes of the sort involved in *Chadha*. That concern, which is tied closely to the Constitution's rejection of parliamentary government, is to ensure that federal executive power is located under the ultimate direction of a single President chosen by and responsive to a national electorate. Such power is not to be dispersed among a series of ministries selected from the National Legislature, each headed by a congressman answerable only to a local constituency.

Giving Congress a legislative veto over certain intrinsically executive functions, such as the initiation of criminal prosecutions, or entrusting a legislative veto to a congressional committee or committee head, might significantly implicate this antiparliamentary concern. But treating *all* legislative vetoes—or even all vetoes in situations analogous to that in *Chadha*—as a threat to the Constitution's choice of a presidential over a parliamentary system seems altogether implausible, particularly in an era when presidential politics may be no less sectional than congressional politics often is.

* * *

74. 306 U.S. 1 (1939) (marketing restrictions effective only upon approval by majority of affected farmers).

75. 307 U.S. 533 (1939) (marketing orders issued by Secretary of Agriculture subject to veto by certain affected producers).

Chadha thus seems remarkable particularly because it is so *transparently* perplexing. The gaps in the Court's argument are almost too obvious, leaving one with the strange feeling that comes from confronting an edifice in which the flaws seem too conspicuous to be accidental, rather like approaching a building with windows but no door. Surely the architect knew that the omission would strike others as a defect in design. But if the architect knew, then are we perhaps overlooking something?

Two speculations suggest themselves. The first is that *Chadha* represents a return to a form of constitutional exegesis that simply proclaims intelligible essences more than it purports to explain or to justify philosophical or practical premises. "The legislative veto simply *is* a perversion of the Constitution's design," the *Chadha* Court seems to announce; "those who cannot 'see' it that way are just out of touch." The second, and more plausible, possibility is that *Chadha* represents only a transition to a more thoroughgoing repudiation of the constitutional upheaval that led to the approval, beginning in the mid–1930's, of the modern administrative state. Even if *Chadha* makes little sense against a backdrop of nearly limitless judicial tolerance for delegations of lawmaking authority to federal agencies and commissions, the decision would at least be of a piece with a significant judicial tightening of the limits within which Congress may entrust *anyone* with lawmaking power.[a]

HAROLD H. BRUFF, LEGISLATIVE FORMALITY, ADMINISTRATIVE RATIONALITY

63 Texas L.Rev. 207, 211–222 (1984).

III. LEGISLATIVE FORMALITY

A. *The Demise of the Legislative Veto*

The most prominent recent controversy over the limits of congressional power to oversee the executive concerned the legislative veto. Statutes delegating power to the executive often retained authority to invalidate executive implementation by vote of one or both houses of Congress. This technique markedly increased the power of Congress to control execution; the alternative, statutory override of executive action, requires both bicameral concurrence in Congress and presentation to the President for his possible veto.

The Supreme Court's landmark legislative veto case, *INS v. Chadha*,[27] was rigidly formalist in effect. The Court's sweeping opinion appeared to invalidate every version of the legislative veto. It began by identifying two pertinent purposes of the bicameral structure of Congress and the presentation requirement. The first, instrumental to maintaining a balance of power within government, is to restrict the

---

a. For a more recent statement of Prof. Tribe's views, see American Constitutional Law 216, n. 19, 245–246 (2d ed. 1988).

27. [462 U.S. 919] (1983).

power of Congress compared to that of the President. The second, instrumental to limiting the power of government as a whole, is to avoid unwise legislation, in part by dampening the effects of faction in the legislative process.

After alluding to the central importance of these structural controls on legislation, the Court turned to the question whether the legislative veto should be considered legislation. In a conclusory passage, the Court defined the legislative action that must be passed by both houses of Congress and presented to the President to include any action altering the legal rights and duties of persons outside the legislative branch. Any attempt by Congress to compel the executive branch to exercise its delegated statutory authority in a particular way falls within this definition of legislative action. In consequence, Congress may now compel executive compliance "in only one way; bicameral passage followed by presentment to the President. Congress must abide by its delegation of authority until that delegation is legislatively altered or revoked." [32]

It is not clear why the Court decided to restrict Congress to the traditional form for legislation. The purposes of that form, accurately described in *Chadha*, are surely pertinent, yet the Court failed to say how the legislative veto contravened them. The majority opinion's opacity suggests that the Court may not understand why it is requiring adherence to forms. [Nevertheless, in the context of regulation there is reason to believe that] confining Congress to the formal legislative process can be defended on a rationale that the Court hinted at in *Chadha*. It stems from the second purpose of the Constitution's form for legislation, that of controlling the influence of faction in the national political process.

B. A Rationale for Formalism

Because regulation has direct effects on the people, it is the political purposes underlying the Constitution's structure that engender the strongest arguments for formal controls on legislative action in the regulatory context. Control of the agencies has not so shifted from Congress to the President that the advantages of formal controls on Congress should be foregone in order to redress a serious imbalance of power between the branches.

In *Chadha*, the Court mentioned the hopes of the Framers that the Constitution's institutional safeguards would foster legislation advancing the general public interest. The Framers saw human nature as both rational and self-interested; they relied on competition among officeholders to neutralize these characteristics. In addition, they thought that the political process would reinforce the Constitution's structural controls. In his famous argument in the *Federalist No. 10*, Madison relied on the size and diversity of the new nation to offset the effects of faction. * * *

32. *Id.* at [954–55.]

To assess how well the Framers' hopes for a political process that would embody the public interest have been realized, I turn to modern theories that explore the nature of our political process and its relationship with the Constitution's structure. This analysis aids an appraisal of how the constitutional requisites should be interpreted today.

1. Public Choice Theory.[41] * * *

*   *   *

In relying on the diversity of the polity to negate the effects of faction, Madison did not sufficiently reckon with the advantages that factions receive from the incentives in our system. Public choice theory has systematically explored these advantages. I summarize them here not to argue that all legislation serves narrow interests, but only to show that there is a sufficient tendency for it to do so to justify giving full effect to the formal controls on the legislative process that do dampen faction.

*   *   *

Interest groups tend to demand private goods benefiting their members. If they spent their time and money seeking public goods,[44] much of the benefit would escape to others. It is rational for any group to seek goods whose benefits to them exceed the costs they bear, even if the program is inefficient from a broader point of view. Thus, if the benefits of a program are significantly more concentrated than the costs, the beneficiaries will find it rational to support the program even if the total costs exceed the benefits. When groups compete for legislation, each has an incentive to demand its private benefits, even though the net result of the process is a welfare loss to all. Similarly, these groups do not have sufficient incentives to oppose the activity of other groups, because that opposition would create a public good.

Congressmen also have significant incentives to support private goods legislation. Because relatively small interest groups possess distinct advantages in organizing their constituencies, congressmen can ordinarily build constituent support more effectively through response to interest groups than by appeal to the general public. In doing so, legislators have ample opportunity to overstate the benefits of a program to its beneficiaries while discounting the costs to those disadvan-

41. *See* D. Mueller, Public Choice 1–2 (1979). The intellectual link between the Framers' views and public choice theory is the economic and political theory of Adam Smith. Public choice theory assumes that political actors pursue their self-interest in a rational fashion and analyzes how legal rules can be expected to affect human behavior under those conditions. But much behavior is not explained by these assumptions. Thus, the theory is perforce limited; it identifies tendencies that occur a significant proportion of the time and that archi-

tects of legal rules should consider. [Relocated footnote.]

44. Public goods are characterized by jointness of supply (so that one person's consumption of the good does not lessen that of another) and the impracticability of excluding anyone from enjoying the good once it is supplied generally (so that "free riders" can obtain the good for free unless payment is coerced). Common examples are national defense and law enforcement. [Relocated footnote.]

taged.[53] The resulting tendency of our factional politics to redistribute wealth from large groups to small ones has produced the opposite of the oppressive majorities that the Framers feared.

Territorial representation creates pressure on congressmen to support legislation that has divisible local benefits not enjoyed by other districts. It is easier for a legislator to claim credit for introduction and passage of legislation with localized benefits than for other public or private goods legislation, because of the more diffused responsibility in Congress for the latter.

Interest groups using political action committees can direct their contributions where they will have the most effect—usually to influential members of the pertinent committees. The effect is partially to transform territorial representation into interest representation. The outcome can be regulation that distributes benefits and burdens on both territorial and interest group bases.

Thus, the incentives affecting both citizens and legislators have defeated Madison's hope that faction would be self-neutralizing. Instead, faction is powerfully self-reinforcing within both houses of Congress. * * *

                              * * *

2. *Structural Checks on Faction.*—In designing structural controls on legislation, the Framers confronted dilemmas that are inherent in any collective decisionmaking process. There are two important stages of collective choice. The first, or constitutional, stage authorizes the future government to decide certain issues and specifies the pertinent decision rule, such as a majority, to be used for each issue. The second, or operational, stage consists of public choice under the governing decision rules, as in ordinary legislation. Selecting a decision rule requires a prospective—and necessarily rough—judgment about which rule will produce the lowest sum of two kinds of costs: the decision costs of obtaining assent from the requisite number of participants and the external costs of decisions that disfavor a given participant. A rule requiring unanimous decision eliminates external costs but imposes high and perhaps insuperable decision costs. Redistribution inheres in any collective choice process that does not require unanimity.

(a) *The structure of congressional decisionmaking.*—Majority rule, the primary decision rule within Congress, has the lowest decision cost of any rule that can produce a stable outcome. Thus, it greatly facilitates policymaking, but it necessarily imposes substantial external costs. The incentives that foster private goods legislation ensure relatively high externalities under majority rule. Indeed, with territorial representation and simple majority rule, the smallest coalition needed for victory can approach one quarter of the voters (just over half in half the districts). If interest groups are more randomly scattered, decision costs rise and external costs diminish. This means that under pure

53. In public finance, this is known as the "fiscal illusion." * * *

majority rule, interest groups that are present in substantial numbers in many districts have an advantage over equally numerous groups that are concentrated in a few districts. Farmers may be a group possessing such an advantage.

The response of the Framers to the problem of faction was to condition legislation on the concurrence of three institutions with differing bases of representation, or supermajorities of two of them. Their choice was apt; the price, however, was sharply increased decision costs. Thus, the addition of a second house in our bicameral system shifts the decision rule toward unanimity and reduces the power of factions. The amount of the reduction depends on the degree of interest group overlap in the two chambers. The partial district overlap between the House and Senate reduces, but does not eliminate, the efficacy of bicameralism in controlling faction.

In addition to the Constitution's structural checks, Congress itself has developed a set of formal and informal controls that promote the stability of legislation and dilute the influence of faction. For private goods to be collectively produced, coalitions must form around a package of benefits in both houses of Congress. Theoretically, a bill with benefits barely over half its costs can succeed. Such a coalition, however, would be unstable—votes in its favor would be subject to reversal by a competing coalition at the next opportunity. The primary formal response to this problem is an array of agenda control devices, such as the functions of the House Rules Committee. More informally, the need for stable coalitions often leads to bills that distribute benefits much more widely, if inefficiently, than would measures supported by only bare majority coalitions. Congressmen can cooperate in this way without threatening one another's capacity to serve constituents. These arrangements within Congress, together with the aspects of our constitutional structure that raise decision costs, promote the stability of legislation. Regulatory legislation is relatively stable because, unlike continuing subsidies, it does not require substantial later appropriations. Because such legislation may not be evaluated carefully each session, the coalition need not maintain a firm hold on a majority of supporters.

(b) The President's veto power.—The President's participation in the legislative process, both in proposing and supporting legislation and in exercising the veto power, dampens faction and increases the stability of legislation. The President's veto power is a more potent check on faction than is the bicameral structure of Congress, because the President's national constituency makes his calculus of the merits of a bill different from that of any congressman. He lacks the territorial representative's incentive to favor divisible local benefits. Also, because his constituency is an amalgam of all interest groups, he must weigh the benefits and costs of a bill directly against each other; Congress avoids doing so by combining provisions that benefit particular members but that are not justifiable in the aggregate. The coali-

tions that support the President may differ enough from the one promoting a particular bill to make a veto attractive; the smaller the coalition supporting a bill, the more likely is this disparity. Moreover, the mere threat of a veto can raise the size of the coalition necessary to push a bill through Congress and can affect the bill's substance.

    3. The Legislative Veto.—When Congress passed statutes reserving legislative veto authority in one or both of its houses, the effect was to lower congressional decision costs on particular issues, while necessarily increasing externalities both for members of Congress and ultimately for society as a whole. Decision costs were lowered in two ways. First, the statutes excluded the President (and often one of the two houses of Congress) from the consensus needed to override a regulation. Second, because veto resolutions were limited to invalidating regulations, it was easier to form a coalition of those opposed to a rule for various reasons than it would have been to enact a substitute policy. The external costs burdened those congressmen and citizens who stood to benefit from regulations that were either invalidated by a veto resolution or altered in response to more informal congressional pressures.

    It is easy to see why Congress was tempted to replace the ordinary process of legislation with the legislative veto—Congress suffers all of the decision costs of legislation but only a portion of the external costs produced by more informal processes.[88] The less formal process subverted primary controls on the fairness of legislation in two ways. The first was to vitiate the effectiveness of the bicameralism and presentation requirements in raising the size of coalitions needed for collective choice. Retention of veto authority systematically favored interest groups having advantages in one or both houses of Congress because of their distribution throughout the nation. Second, the veto device allowed Congress to select its decision rule at the operational stage of policymaking rather than at the constitutional stage. A check on the fairness of selecting decision rules is the difficulty of determining who will profit from their later use in specific cases. Yet at the operational stage it is much easier to predict the winners and losers from a change in the decision rules. In some cases, it might be possible to predict which particular faction would be aided by legislative veto authority.

    The Framers expected that our constitutional structure, which makes it easier to block than to effect legislative change, would restrict the amount of legislation to which the people would be subject. The legislative veto, by circumventing the usual structure and creating an incentive for Congress to lower its decision costs by delegating power, tended to increase the size of government as a whole.

    Agencies taking actions subject to legislative veto could avoid a veto by building at least the minimum necessary coalition in Congress.

---

88. External costs within Congress from legislative vetoes would have been due to both frustrated expectations of the members who favored a vetoed regulation and complaints from constituents.

Drafting a regulation in a way that would neutralize opposition in Congress increased the chance that relatively narrow factions would benefit from regulation if they were especially powerful in one or both houses. Congress, placed in a more reactive stance than in drafting legislation, lost agenda control and the opportunity to amend the agency regulation in ways that would broaden support for it. A collateral effect was to destabilize policy, because of the possibility of conflict between the agency and one or both houses of Congress. All might differ on appropriate policy; no part of the veto mechanism led out of the impasse.

The legislative veto thus stripped away some central advantages of our legislative structure, but left some central disadvantages. In *Chadha,* the Court restored the role of legislative formality in ensuring the fairness of legislation, but with only the most oblique references to its reasons for doing so.

ROBERT F. NAGEL, THE LEGISLATIVE VETO, THE CONSTITUTION, AND THE COURTS
3 Const. Comm. 61, 65–66, 69–72 (1986).

In recent years * * * the Court's general willingness to use its power has included a growing inclination to monopolize questions of power definition at the national level. In 1969, for example, the Court overturned the exclusion of Adam Clayton Powell from the House of Representatives despite the apparent constitutional commitment of questions regarding "the qualifications of its own members" to each House of Congress.[7] The Court thus assumed for itself the power to define Congress's constitutional authority over its own operations, blandly insisting that this sort of determination "falls within the traditional role accorded courts. . . ." The *Powell* decision raises the serious possibility that the Court may invade the clear authority of Congress over the impeachment process.

In 1974 the Justices rushed to judgment in the famous case involving the power of the judiciary to subpoena President Nixon's Watergate tapes. In sober second light it is now clear that this was a case for judicial caution. No specific constitutional provision was involved; the issues of whether to read a presidential power of immunity into the Constitution and how to balance such an implied power against the judiciary's authority were exceedingly difficult, certainly issues on which "human reason may pause." Nevertheless, the Supreme Court not only acted, but acted in enormous haste, deciding the case before the Court of Appeals could even hear arguments on the propriety of Judge Sirica's ruling. Meanwhile the appropriate committee of Congress was responsibly exercising its undoubted constitutional authority to investigate the possible impeachment and removal of the

7. Art. I, § 5 states, "Each House shall be the Judge of the Elections, Returns and Qualifications of its own Members. . . ."

President. The Court's action in *Nixon* effectively aborted the investigation, further reducing the credibility of the constitutional sanction for presidential misconduct.

* * *

The *Chadha* decision must be understood within the context of the modern Court's tendency to monopolize the resolution of constitutional issues of power distribution. The Court's willingness—indeed, eagerness—to strike down the legislative veto is a powerful illustration of the recent tendency to sweep within "the judicial power" the authority to decide organizational issues, even those that involve the operations of another branch and are apparently committed by the Constitution to that other branch. A decision that so profoundly trivializes the constitutional responsibilities of Congress is, to say the least, an unlikely vehicle for injecting new vigor and integrity into the lawmaking process.

* * *

The *Chadha* opinion repeatedly invoked "the Constitutional design for separation of powers." The theory of separation of powers came to America from the seventeenth century Levellers, who opposed the British King's participation in lawmaking. The theory was passed through Montesquieu, and contributed to the Jeffersonians' opposition to aristocracy and their extreme commitment to popular control over lawmaking. As the Court noted in *Chadha,* separation of powers in its pure form involves differentiation by function. Power is to be checked by dividing it; each branch exercises a distinctive type of power, and none shares or interferes with the power exercised by the others.

In the American Constitution separation of powers was combined with a different principle—balance. Constitutional balance has its antecedents in the mixed government of Great Britain, where royalty shared some of the lawmaking function and where the aristocracy was given both the power to judge and the power to make laws in the House of Lords. Balance involves sharing of power among the branches of government and active checking of one branch by another; its functions have been to block popular control over lawmaking and to assure representation of class interests.

It is elementary that these opposite principles, separation and balance, were strangely and successfully combined by the framers. The Constitution divides government into three distinct branches, and the lawmaking power is given to a popularly accountable branch. However, the President shares the judicial function through, for instance, his pardon power; and he shares the legislative function through his veto power. The Senate shares the executive function, for example, by its power to confirm appointments. And the doctrine of judicial review permits courts to share (and check) the power of both the legislative and executive branches.

Now, despite the Court's emphatic reliance on the theory of separation of powers, it should be plain that the legislative veto considered in

Chadha did not threaten the principle of separation. Insofar as it violated the bicameralism requirement, the veto threatened only the principle of balance, raising the possibility that class or regional interests would not be adequately represented in a deportation decision accomplished by a vote of only one House of Congress. Insofar as the veto violated the presentment requirement, it did threaten the authority of the executive branch. But authority of what kind? The executive authority at risk was, first, the authority of the President to veto a specific decision to suspend a deportation (the President having already had the opportunity to veto the general scheme setting up the system of legislative vetoes in deportation cases). The veto power, again, is a part of the principle of balance whereby the legislative power is shared and checked by the Executive. The second kind of presidential authority at risk was the authority to make the suspension decision itself, for the Attorney General's determination under the Immigration Act could be, and was, reversed by one House of Congress. *But this is the very decision that the Court described at length as legislative in nature.* In this respect also, then, the kind of executive authority threatened was the President's authority to share (through exceedingly broad delegation) the power of lawmaking.

The Court invalidated a device found in over 200 federal statutory provisions by invoking separation of powers when it meant, if anything, the opposite principle of constitutional balance. That the Court could misname a fundamental principle is in itself disturbing in a country where vast judicial power is justified by reference to the capacity of judges to understand and apply legal principles. More important, understanding the principle that *Chadha* does implement helps to remove the last shadows from around the decision. Although the Court spoke in terms of separation of powers and emphasized the protection of the integrity of legislative procedures, the decision in fact protected a principle, traceable to the British royalty and House of Lords, that has long been at war with popularly accountable legislatures. *Chadha* is a striking expansion of the judicial assault on the democratic values associated with the principle of separation of powers, which allocates the lawmaking function to Congress and not to the executive or judicial branch.

Once the real issue in *Chadha* is properly named, some small but bewildering aspects of the Court's opinion become understandable. Not only in its major contours but also in its detail, the opinion expresses repugnance at the legislative process. The decision is permeated by a hostility to the Congress that, once perceived, makes it obvious that the possibility of a judicially-led reinvigoration of the political process is fanciful.

In its description of the facts, the Court observed that in Chadha's case Congress waited "for reasons not disclosed" for a full year and a half to decide about his deportation. Similarly, the Court mentioned the precise date of the House's action and the termination date of the statutory time period for vetoing the suspension, making plain that if the House had waited seven more days, "Chadha's deportation proceedings would have been cancelled." Although it was relevant to nothing in the case, the Court stated that the House resolution was "not printed" and "was not made available to other members of the House [besides those in the relevant committee] prior to the vote." The Court also noted, for no apparent reason, that Chadha's case was one of a group of some 340 and that the resolution in his case passed without debate or recorded vote. And it opined (in a footnote) that "[i]t is not at all clear whether the House generally or Chairman Eilberg in particular . . . understood the relationship between the Resolution and the Attorney General's decision. . . ."

In short, much of the Court's statement of the facts of the case bears little if any relationship to the legal issues involved; the Court's purpose, obviously, was to paint a grim picture of the quality of the legislative process. Whether or not this process worked as badly in Chadha's case as the Court implied, there is no doubt that legislative decisionmaking can be uninformed, cruel, and messy. This is no doubt true as well for many decisions that issue from the bowels of the bureaucracy or judiciary. The more rational procedures, often presumed to be generally available from administrators or judges, are, at any rate, a reflection of their distinct functions. To perform *their* functions, legislators must respond to felt constituent concerns and must trade across issues; the legislature's role in a democracy requires it to operate differently (and perhaps more untidily) than the other branches. If responsibilities are to be removed from the Congress whenever legislative techniques look different from judicial or administrative processes, there will be little of importance left for the Congress to contribute.

If there remains any doubt about whether *Chadha* portends a reinvigoration of the legislative process, consider that the decision also contained a long and approving discussion of congressional experience with the impracticality of special deportation bills. Thus the only congressional judgment given credence in the Court's opinion is the admission that Congress could not hope to legislate well on the individual suspension issues that much of the Court's opinion defined as inherently legislative in nature. With the legislative veto invalidated and special bills declared too cumbersome, Congress has left only the option of delegating its lawmaking authority to the other branches of government.

Chadha is justifiable, if at all, only on the ground that the judiciary, not the legislature, is the appropriate forum for deciding the practical questions that arise in the difficult, complicated effort to make the modern regulatory state democratically accountable. The significance of the decision is not that it protects the principle of separation of powers or that it offers new hope for the integrity or importance of the legislative process. Its significance is that it confirms and accelerates the drive, which until *Chadha* could be discerned but not fully appreciated, toward the judicial monopolization of crucial questions of power definition and distribution.

BIBLIOGRAPHY

Delegation

S. Barber, THE CONSTITUTION AND THE DELEGATION OF CONGRESSIONAL POWER (1975).

Brooks, *Gramm–Rudman: Can Congress and the President Pass This Buck?*, 64 Tex.L.Rev. 131 (1985).

Krent, *Fragmenting the Unitary Executive: Congressional Delegations of Administrative Authority Outside the Federal Government*, 85 Nw.U.L.Rev. 62 (1990).

T. Lowi, THE END OF LIBERALISM ch. 5 (2d ed. 1979).

Pierce, *The Role of Constitutional and Political Theory in Administrative Law*, 64 Tex.L.Rev. 469 (1985).

Schoenbrod, *The Delegation Doctrine: Could the Court Give It Substance?*, 83 Mich.L.Rev. 1223 (1985).

Appointment and Removal

Carter, *The Independent Counsel Mess*, 102 Harv.L.Rev. 105 (1988).

Corwin, *Tenure of Office and the Removal Power Under the Constitution*, 27 Colum.L.Rev. 353 (1927).

Entin, *The Removal Power and the Federal Deficit: Form, Substance, and Administrative Independence*, 75 Ky.L.J. 699 (1987).

Glitzenstein & Morrison, *The Supreme Court's Decision in* Morrison v. Olson: *A Common Sense Application of the Constitution to a Practical Problem*, 38 Amer.U.L.Rev. 359 (1989).

Kahn, *Gramm–Rudman and the Capacity of Congress To Control the Future*, 13 Hastings Const.L.Q. 185 (1986).

Miller, *Independent Agencies*, 1986 Sup.Ct.Rev. 41.

Shane, *Independent Policymaking and Presidential Power: A Constitutional Analysis*, 57 Geo.Wash.L.Rev. 596 (1989).

Verkuil, *The Status of Independent Agencies After* Bowsher v. Synar, 1986 Duke L.J. 779.

The Legislative Veto

Bruff & Gellhorn, *Congressional Control of Administrative Regulation: A Study of Legislative Vetoes*, 90 Harv.L.Rev. 1369 (1977).

Elliott, INS v. Chadha: *The Administrative Constitution, the Constitution, and the Legislative Veto*, 1983 Sup.Ct.Rev. 125.

Javits & Klein, *Congressional Oversight and the Legislative Veto: A Constitutional Analysis*, 52 N.Y.U.L.Rev. 455 (1977).

Martin, *The Legislative Veto and the Responsible Exercise of Congressional Power,* 68 Va.L.Rev. 253 (1982).

Smolla, *Bring Back the Legislative Veto: A Proposal for a Constitutional Amendment,* 37 Ark.L.Rev. 509 (1984).

Spann, *Deconstructing the Legislative Veto,* 68 Minn.L.Rev. 473 (1984).

Strauss, *Was There a Baby in the Bathwater? A Comment on the Supreme Court's Legislative Veto Decision,* 1983 Duke L.J. 789.

L. Tribe, CONSTITUTIONAL CHOICES ch. 6 (1985).

Watson, *Congress Steps Out: A Look at Congressional Control of the Executive,* 63 Calif.L.Rev. 983 (1975).

E. EXECUTIVE PRIVILEGES AND IMMUNITIES

The fourth set of separation of powers problems concerns efforts by one branch of government to interfere in the internal affairs of another. Sometimes Congress or the courts will thrust themselves into executive affairs. Impeachment is one (serious) example; lawsuits and congressional demands for information are more typical. Sometimes the judiciary and the executive will pry into the affairs of Congress. Here the Constitution offers some explicit protection—in the Speech or Debate Clause—though its scope is uncertain.[1]

Stephen Carter and Gerald Gunther discuss interference in executive affairs, in the context of actions against former president Nixon. Does the President, like Congress, have some protection against such action? In particular, may he assert executive privileges (against production)[2] and immunities (from suit)?[3]

We sometimes forget that in these cases the proper role of the judiciary is a separation of powers question. The political question doctrine states that there are times when the courts should allow the other branches to resolve their own differences.[4] But that doctrine may be honored more in the breach than in the observance. Carter and Gunther both argue that the Supreme Court should intervene less often than it has of late. (Nagel, in Section D, makes the same point.) It is worth considering whether they are correct.

1. Hutchinson v. Proxmire, 443 U.S. 111, 99 S.Ct. 2675, 61 L.Ed.2d 411 (1979); Eastland v. United States Servicemen's Fund, 421 U.S. 491, 95 S.Ct. 1813, 44 L.Ed. 2d 324 (1975); Doe v. McMillan, 412 U.S. 306, 93 S.Ct. 2018, 36 L.Ed.2d 912 (1973); Gravel v. United States, 408 U.S. 606, 92 S.Ct. 2614, 33 L.Ed.2d 583 (1972); United States v. Brewster, 408 U.S. 501, 92 S.Ct. 2531, 33 L.Ed.2d 507 (1972).

2. Nixon v. Administrator of General Services, 433 U.S. 425, 97 S.Ct. 2777, 53 L.Ed.2d 867 (1977); United States v. Nixon, 418 U.S. 683, 94 S.Ct. 3090, 41 L.Ed.2d 1039 (1973).

3. Nixon v. Fitzgerald, 457 U.S. 731, 102 S.Ct. 2690, 73 L.Ed.2d 349 (1982); Mississippi v. Johnson, 71 U.S. (4 Wall.) 475, 18 L.Ed. 437 (1866).

4. Baker v. Carr, 369 U.S. 186, 82 S.Ct. 691, 7 L.Ed.2d 663 (1962).

STEPHEN L. CARTER, THE POLITICAL ASPECTS OF JUDICIAL POWER: SOME NOTES ON THE PRESIDENTIAL IMMUNITY DECISION

131 U.Pa.L.Rev. 1341, 1353–1371 (1983).

[In the first part of his article Carter reviews the Supreme Court's decision in *Nixon v. Fitzgerald*.[a] The plaintiff in that case sued President Nixon for damages, claiming that he had been fired for exercising his right to freedom of speech. The Court held, 5–4, that the President was immune from suit for damages.]

The conclusion that the federal courts lack authority to punish the President of the United States may at first seem somewhat startling, but after a little thought, it makes more sense. One may begin by hypothesizing the contrary. Suppose a court did try to hold the President of the United States in contempt for disobeying an order addressed to him. Would federal marshals arrive at the White House, demanding that the Secret Service agents let them seize the President? Suppose the President—with the assistance of the security personnel— decided to resist arrest. Aside from a definite air of lese majesty about the whole thing, there is also the undeniable fact that should matters come to a showdown, the President has more guns at his command than a federal court does. The Supreme Court has never pretended other- wise. During the Reconstruction Era, the Court in *Mississippi v. Johnson*,[53] took explicit note of the difficulties it would encounter in trying to "force" a President to comply with an order, and dismissed a complaint against President Andrew Johnson. Earlier opinions includ- ed dicta to similar effect.[56]

The mere fact that forcing the President to pay damages might not be easy does not by itself justify a constitutional rule against trying. After all, President Nixon did turn over the Watergate tapes, even though the federal courts probably could not have enforced a contempt citation against him. Besides, resistance to judicial decrees is hardly new. Had the President not decided to send troops to Little Rock in the wake of *Cooper v. Aaron*,[60] the schools in that city might be segregated to this day. The Court's inability to enforce its order without the assistance of the executive branch did not mean that the Justices had no power to issue the order. Thus the claim that the Court lacks power to punish the President must be defended on some ground other than the Court's lack of enforcement power.

In supporting its conclusion in *Nixon v. Fitzgerald*, the majority focused on what it considered the public policy reasons militating in favor of an immunity rule. Justice White's dissent at least showed that these arguments have two sides. The malleability of public policy

a. 457 U.S. 731 (1982).

53. 71 U.S. (4 Wall.) 475 (1867).

56. *Cf.* Chisholm v. Georgia, 2 U.S. (2 Dall.) 419, 476–78 (1793) (dictum) (sover- eign immunity derives from ability to re- sist judicial process).

60. 358 U.S. 1 (1958).

arguments makes the majority's reasoning suspect, but need not vitiate the result. In order to tie its decision more closely to the Constitution, the Court could have relied on something other than public policy.

Before suggesting some justifications that, although available, were absent from the majority opinion, it is useful to pause and recall what the case did not involve. The Court was not required to construe the Constitution's "open-ended" provisions protecting individual rights against government abuse. The dilemma whether to read those clauses as though the Constitution were a statute—or perhaps a contract—or to take them as invitations to import extra-constitutional values motivates much contemporary scholarship on constitutional theory.

Happily, determining whether a reasoned constitutional basis exists for the presidential immunity decision does not require wading into the midst of that scholarly battle. Whatever the best approach to the adjudication of claims under the clauses protecting individual rights (and it is not at all clear that there need be only one), there is no apparent reason to believe that the same interpretive approach ought to apply to other constitutional provisions. Different sections of the document have different purposes and interpreting each in light of its purpose will probably lead to drastically different approaches. Thus, it is one thing to look to extra-constitutional sources in deciding what rights are "retained by the People" or incorporated in the phrase "Privileges or Immunities;" it is something else altogether to do so when considering whether federal courts can, for example, review a presidential decision to cast a veto—or whether the President is a proper defendant in a suit seeking civil damages.

Provisions describing the functions and powers of the government may demand a different interpretive approach from provisions describing the rights of the people. A strict textual approach, focusing on the understanding of the Framers, may be a more sensible method to use in interpreting the structural clauses of the Constitution. * * *

1. THE ORIGINAL UNDERSTANDING APPROACH

* * * The original understanding—when one can be discerned— is more likely to be important in a case involving the system of checks and balances than it is in a case involving individual rights. The reason should be obvious. In protecting individuals against government mistreatment, those who drafted the 1787 Constitution and its amendments took pains to use language so broad as fairly to beg to be filled with substantive content from external sources. They used words sparingly, an approach that makes sense when one begins with a conception of rights as broad and government power as narrow. In structuring the government, however, the drafters set themselves rather a different task and used dramatically different language.

The 1787 Constitution set forth with painstaking attention to detail the powers and functions of the federal government. Despite a few glaring errors,[72] the document reflects an obsessive concern for the minutiae of government operation. Words were used cautiously so as to leave little room for interpretation. Thus although some wanted to make the President impeachable for any reason, the delegates in Philadelphia finally voted to limit impeachable offenses to "Treason, Bribery, or other high Crimes and Misdemeanors," in the hope of limiting congressional power over him. The Constitution also does not include a requirement that members of the House of Representatives be "mature"—although maturity emerged as a major concern in the debates—but only that they be at least twenty-five years old. One can imagine a Constitution providing that elected representatives be "mature" or "of good character," but there is something disturbing, perhaps counterintuitive, about such provisions, as there would be about a provision for congressional overriding of the President's veto "by an extraordinary majority," unless the provision specified what the majority must be. These hypothetical provisions seem counterintuitive for a good reason, and that good reason probably explains their absence from the Constitution: in determining such matters as the qualifications for elected officials, the Framers were structuring a government, not setting forth rights. In the Framers' view, the former called for more precise language than did the latter. The precise wording of the structural provisions reflects an effort to define the structure of government carefully and circumscribe the powers of government narrowly. This purpose should not be ignored when construing the structural provisions of the Constitution.

It therefore makes sense to try to determine the way that the Framers hoped that the Presidency would be controlled. * * * The great weight of the historical evidence suggests the existence of a consensus at the time of ratification to the effect that those checks on presidential abuse of power expressly set forth in the document were the only checks available.

This consensus emerges from the nature of the disputes among the drafters and ratifiers over the proper functions and powers of the President. The intense debate surrounding the Presidency induced the Framers to define their views with rare precision. Those who favored a loose confederation of quasi-independent states argued that the President was too strong and not sufficiently accountable for wrongdoing; those who thought the central government should be strong argued that the President was too weak, that he was subject to too many

---

72. A good example concerns the role of the Vice President. The Vice President serves as President of the Senate. U.S. Const. art. I, § 3. When the President of the United States is tried in the Senate following impeachment by the House of Representatives, the Chief Justice of the United States presides. *Id.* That is the only provision in the Constitution requiring the Vice President to turn over the gavel to another individual. Yet the Vice President himself is also impeachable, and if impeached by the House, he would be tried in the Senate. It appears, therefore, that the Vice President could preside at his own impeachment trial, should he choose to do so.

controls and potential punishments to be able to do his job properly. Supporters of the Constitution had ready responses to each objection.

The President was not too strong, supporters contended, because he was subject to several specific checks on abuses of his authority. The supporters always listed the checks appearing in the document: the power of the purse rested with Congress, the President could be impeached, his veto could be overridden, he could make no appointments or treaties without Senate consent, he was subject to reelection every four years. Hamilton went to great lengths in *The Federalist* to assure the worried public that these provisions were adequate to control presidential misconduct.[97] At the same time, Hamilton and other supporters of ratification repeatedly warned that no additional checks should be permitted, lest the President become too weak.

The Constitution's supporters made, with slightly different emphasis, the same argument to those who thought the Constitution made the executive too weak. In reassuring those who feared presidential weakness, supporters emphasized that the limitations actually stated in the Constitution were the only limitations placed on the President, and these, the opponents were assured, would not impair the President's ability to do his job. Some provision had to be made against the possibility of presidential tyranny, supporters pointed out, and the drafters had done the best they could without limiting the Chief Executive's powers too greatly.

There is no reason to belabor this; attempts to piece together an original "understanding" from the fragments of history tend to end up looking silly. What is rather startling in this instance is that the same questions and answers occur again and again in the surviving records. That is why it may be safe to assume that a consensus existed. At the very least, it cannot fairly be asserted that the history points in some other direction.

2. THE STRUCTURAL APPROACH

The Constitution's relatively precise clauses describing the operation of the federal government are designed to fit together to form a coherent structure. This purpose distinguishes them from the open-ended clauses, many of which were designed to address particular problems and bear little relation to the other parts of the document. * * *

The system of checks and balances is a delicate one, and the Constitution sets forth with some degree of care the checks that each branch may apply to the others. Thus the President may nominate and, if the Senate consents, appoint Justices to the Supreme Court and judges to the lower federal courts, but only Congress, through impeachment and conviction, may remove them. Congress may propose legisla-

97. * * * The Federalist No. 69 at 444–45 (A. Hamilton) (B. Wright ed. 1961)[.]

tion (including legislation channeling the President's discretion), but absent extraordinary majorities in both Houses, the proposals do not become law if the President objects. Congress may go through the motions of enacting legislation that violates the Constitution, but the federal courts, in a case properly brought, may strike those statutes down. Congress holds exclusive power of the purse, and Congress alone can impeach the President and remove him from office. A few other checks, mostly in the form of congressional powers, are scattered through the document. In addition, because all members of Congress as well as the President are elected, popular sentiment provides a powerful and constant check on the operation of the entire system. Outside the interplay of these powers, the Constitution provides no further express controls on misconduct.

As American society has evolved, powerful arguments have arisen that other checks—checks for which the Constitution makes no apparent provision—ought to be applied against any one of the three branches in order to control its growing power. New remedies instituted by Congress included statutes restricting the President's power to remove executive branch functionaries. The first such statutes were struck down, but later versions were sustained. A more recent example of an attempt to restrict the presidency was the congressional creation of the "legislative veto," through which Congress attempted to influence day-to-day policymaking in the executive branch and in the administrative agencies without affording the President an opportunity to exercise his constitutional prerogative by casting a veto. If the presidency has become "imperial" and if none of the existing restraints seems sufficient to rein in whatever maniac might then be occupying the Oval Office, the idea of creating a new remedy has a certain appeal. But in entrusting to any one branch of government the authority to create new checks on one or both of the others, the proponent of the new check is inviting one branch to act unilaterally to alter the delicate balance that the Constitution creates. At the risk of sounding melodramatic, those who advocate the creation of new checks are, however unintentionally, ultimately seeking to subvert the balance of powers in order to save it. It is difficult to see how the checks built into the structural provisions of the Constitution will retain their intended force if they are not tempered by a continuing balance.

The balance of powers among the three branches of the federal government is a delicate construct, and if any one of the branches is empowered to create new checks on the others that branch will be in the position to upset the very balance that it purports to protect. Thus the system requires placing the narrowest possible reading on the authority of each branch of government to act in the name of preserving that system. Attention to the original understanding and a strict view of constitutional language are both merely means to the end of maintaining the balance of power among the branches of the federal government.

*   *   *

The arguments set out above are arguments that the majority could have made, but failed to make in any detail, in support of the theory that the decision is constitutionally based. The arguments share a simple conclusion: in determining the role that each branch should play in the system of checks and balances, all judgments on proper policy must be subordinated to the most important policy, preserving that selfsame system of checks and balances. Permitting one branch to create fresh remedies will upset the balance. Anything that upsets the balance is wrong. That is why the federal courts cannot create a cause of action for damages running against a President or former President on the basis of misconduct in office.

Had it explained *Nixon v. Fitzgerald* that way, the Court would presumably have gone on to explain why the theory that all other interests must be subordinated to the need to preserve the system of checks and balances does not do violence to precedent. A distinction must be drawn between the two very different roles the federal courts play in the system of checks and balances. To paraphrase Felix Frankfurter, when the courts settle a dispute between the two more overtly political branches, they act as "referees at prize fights;" but when they act affirmatively to vindicate an individual claim of right against a representative of another branch, they act as "functionaries of justice." In *Nixon v. Fitzgerald*, an individual asked the Court to make him whole, and the Justices hesitated. The majority's reasoning suggests constitutional limitations on the judicial power to act as functionaries of justice by creating fresh remedies. Nothing in the decision is inconsistent with the cases in which the Court has acted as a referee.

United States v. Nixon [109] does not fall squarely into either category, but it is probably best viewed as a "court-as-referee" decision. The Justices were not settling a dispute between the other two branches, but they were also not protecting the rights of any individual against government excess. The Court was called upon instead to act as referee *within* a particular branch of government.[110] The Court accepted the task, and its resolution of the dispute required the President to comply with an order. The result in *Nixon v. Fitzgerald* suggests that had the President defied the Court's order in *United States v. Nixon*, the Justices would not have created a fresh remedy through which to try and punish him. The risk of presidential defiance, however, although much bandied-about at the time, was probably close to nil. President Nixon was politically helpless and the Justices must have known that. Had he refused to comply with the Court's "definitive" decision, he would almost certainly have been impeached and removed from office. The federal court could not, under the logic of the

---

109. 418 U.S. 683 (1974).

110. Acting as a referee *within* a particular branch is a power that the Court exercised previously in 1969 when it issued its controversial decision in Powell v. Mc-

Cormack, 395 U.S. 486 (1969), invalidating a congressional attempt to exclude a member on grounds other than the "Qualifications" that the Court said are set forth expressly in the Constitution. * * *

presidential immunity decision, have acted against him directly, but a punishment for disobedience would have been imposed all the same. The order would simply have been enforced by a branch other than the one that issued it.

That inability to act against the President directly is hardly inconsistent with other cases in which the federal courts have, in evaluating the legitimacy of presidential actions, evinced reluctance to deal with the President directly. With rare exception, the courts have reviewed presidential activities through suits naming as a defendant not the President himself, but some lower executive functionary. The same theory—that no punishment question was involved and the courts were merely acting as referees—may explain these results, but another theory fits them even better. The President was not a defendant, and it is only to the President himself, with his special place in the constitutional scheme and history, that immunity attaches. The Supreme Court acknowledged as much when, on the same day that it decided the presidential immunity case, it ruled in *Harlow v. Fitzgerald* that no similar immunity attaches to the President's aides.[116] Because the President almost always acts through his subordinates, a non-immune defendant will generally be available in any case brought to contest the validity of a presidential directive.

If the President's aides are not immune from suit as he is, they may be placed in an uncomfortable position when he orders them to do something that they believe to be wrong. There is a temptation to say flippantly that an executive functionary placed in that position may resign, tell his story to the *Washington Post,* and write a bestselling book. More seriously, the position may be uncomfortable, but the choice should not be difficult. The employees of the executive branch work for the United States of America, not for the person who happens to occupy the office of President. Faced with an order they believe to be illegitimate, executive functionaries should state their belief and refuse to carry the order out. They may be dismissed for that refusal, but they will have acted in accord with the requirements of the Constitution.

GERALD GUNTHER, JUDICIAL HEGEMONY AND LEGISLATIVE AUTONOMY: THE NIXON CASE AND THE IMPEACHMENT PROCESS

22 U.C.L.A.L.Rev. 30, 31–35 (1974).

To me, the most admirable feature of our recent constitutional history lies in the demonstration that the House of Representatives is capable of taking its impeachment responsibilities seriously. Despite the impatience with the slowness of the House Judiciary Committee and the deliberateness of the Doar–Jenner staff, despite the cynicism about the capacities of the supposed mediocrities in the House, the

116. * * * 457 U.S. 800 (1982)
* * *.

Committee proceedings moved forward thoughtfully and conscientiously, culminating in that impressive debate on the articles of impeachment.

To a regrettable extent, the triumph of the legislative branch was diminished by the Supreme Court's performance. For most of the first half of 1974, the Judiciary Committee proceedings were at center stage. That is where they belonged. The impeachment route is the most appropriate one in our Constitution for the pursuit of problems such as those raised by Watergate. The Court's action tended to push the Committee off center stage. With *United States v. Nixon,* the Supreme Court managed to overshadow the impeachment process which had been, and should have continued to be, primary. That impact stemmed from two sources: the Court's timing and the Court's reasoning.

Though I think the timing to be the less important one, I find it a troublesome aspect nevertheless. The Court granted certiorari soon after review was sought in the intermediate appellate court from Judge Sirica's decision, before judgment, or indeed argument and opinions, in the Court of Appeals for the District of Columbia. Plainly, the Supreme Court took the case much earlier than it had to, and the decision came down on the very day the Judiciary Committee's public debate on proposed articles of impeachment got under way. The practical impact of the decision is clear: the impeachment process was soon aborted. Twelve days after the July 24 decision, President Nixon made public the transcript of the fateful and fatal June 23, 1972 tapes. Three days after that, he resigned. The interval between Court decision and presidential response afforded just enough time for the completion of the House Judiciary Committee debate and for the adoption of three articles of impeachment. But the turnover of the tapes compelled by the Court made floor debate in the House and trial in the Senate unnecessary; instead of running its full course, the impeachment process was short-circuited.

*   *   *

But was not the Court compelled to intervene? I think not—certainly not at the time it chose. I do not argue that the Court should have found itself powerless to adjudicate the case: Special Prosecutor Jaworski's subpoena claim came in a criminal proceeding; his demand was appropriately adjudicable by the courts. To me, the critical question was timing. Were there truly compelling arguments to have the Supreme Court enter the dispute as early as it did? The Special Prosecutor's claim was that the subpoena issue was an urgent one because the evidence he sought was needed for the Watergate trial then scheduled for early September. For effective relief, he argued, the Court had to act before its summer recess. Yet the scheduling of the Watergate trial and of a Senate impeachment trial were surely interdependent variables. If the impeachment process had run its normal course, and if a Senate trial had been scheduled for the fall, it seems most unlikely that the Watergate trial would have come on in September. If Watergate witnesses had been needed before the jurors in the Senate, assembling of the jurors in the courthouse would presumably have been postponed by the trial judge. A Supreme Court refusal to grant the Special Prosecutor's petition for extraordinarily expeditious review of the subpoena case would not have been the primary cause for delay of the Watergate trial. More probably, the criminal trial would have been delayed in any event because of the pendency of the Senate impeachment trial. Permitting the subpoena case to go to the court of appeals and to the Supreme Court in the normal course, in short, would have permitted the orderly progress of the impeachment process with no significant practical costs to the criminal proceedings.

Nevertheless, the Supreme Court granted certiorari before judgment in the court of appeals. Why, if the formal argument for such extraordinary speed—the criminal trial schedule—is so thin? I have no doubt that the Justices granted expeditious review in entire good faith; I suspect that they simply concluded that any other course, any consideration of the case under a more normal time schedule, would have been irresponsible. But that good faith judgment seems to me precisely the rub: it is a judgment of a Court that is more imbued than it may realize with a view that flourished in the Warren years, that somehow it is the Court's special obligation to save the nation in episodes of constitutional crisis. It is a Court response not only to that lingering self-image, but also to the concomitant public expectations generated by recent Courts' behavior. That makes it perhaps antiquarian to suggest that the nation would be better off with a somewhat diminished appetite for the judicial *deus ex machina*. That admonition seems especially appropriate in a context in which a parallel, indeed preeminent, constitutional process was in motion. The Court did not claim to decide issues of impeachment directly, to be sure. Yet its timing made an indirect impact on the impeachment process inevitable. It was an avoidable impact. And in speculating as to why it was not avoided, the aptest analogies may lie in Nevada or in medieval Europe. May it be appropriate to think of compulsive gamblers unable to resist a piece of the action, or of knights in shining armor tempted to ride to the rescue in every situation of distress?

But the Court's reasoning seems to me even more troubling than its timing. * * *

Two quite separate issues ran through the lower court proceedings in the Jaworski subpoena case, as they had in the Cox subpoena litigation in 1973. The first was presidential amenability to the judicial process. The second was the scope of executive privilege. It was possible to decide against President Nixon's claim as to the first issue and yet support his argument as to the second: it was possible to say that in subpoena efforts incident to a criminal case there is no presidential immunity from judicial process and yet conclude that the President, as a matter of constitutional interpretation of article II powers, had absolute discretion to determine the scope of executive privilege.

Marbury v. Madison is an especially relevant source in deciding the first issue. It is far more tenuously related to the second. Respectable arguments after all have been made, and not only by President Nixon's counsel, that absolute executive immunity is a legitimate constitutional inference.

The opinion in *United States v. Nixon* tended to merge and blur those separate issues. And the linchpin in intertwining them was the excessive use of *Marbury v. Madison.* As Chief Justice Burger stated at one point:

> The President's counsel, as we have noted, reads the Constitution as providing an absolute privilege of confidentiality for all presidential communications. Many decisions of this Court, however, have un-equivocally reaffirmed the holding of [*Marbury v. Madison*] that "it is emphatically the province and duty of the judicial department to say what the law is."

That "however" suggests that the *Marbury* passage helps answer the executive privilege contention: Chief Justice Burger's handling of the issue suggests that recognizing absolute executive privilege as a matter of constitutional interpretation would somehow be contrary to *Marbury v. Madison*'s view of the proper judicial role. But there is nothing in *Marbury v. Madison* that precludes a constitutional interpretation which gives final authority to another branch.

I do not believe that the Court intended to announce that every constitutional issue requires final adjudication on the merits by the judiciary. As in the past, there are likely to be issues in the future which the Court will find to have been "committed by the Constitution to another branch of government. . . ." [10] For example, I would think (and hope) that a conviction on impeachment would be found unreviewable in the courts. Nor do I mean to suggest that the Court's result was wrong on the merits: I think checks and balances arguments make a non-absolute view of executive privilege appropriate. I simply suggest that the argument for absolute executive privilege deserved a more focused, careful, separable answer than the Court's invocation of *Marbury v. Madison* provides.

BIBLIOGRAPHY

Impeachment

R. Berger, IMPEACHMENT: THE CONSTITUTIONAL PROBLEMS (1973).

C. Black, IMPEACHMENT: A HANDBOOK (1974).

I. Brant, IMPEACHMENT: TRIALS AND ERRORS (1972).

10. Baker v. Carr, 369 U.S. 186, 211 (1962).

Committee on Federal Legislation of the Bar Association of the City of New York, THE LAW OF PRESIDENTIAL IMPEACHMENT (1974).

Fenton, *The Scope of the Impeachment Power,* 65 Nw.U.L.Rev. 719 (1971).

Firmage & Mangrum, *Removal of the President: Resignation and the Procedural Law of Impeachment,* 1974 Duke L.J. 1023.

Garvey, *Foreword: Judicial Discipline and Impeachment,* 76 Ky.L.J. 633 (1988).

Gerhardt, *The Constitutional Limits to Impeachment and Its Alternatives,* 68 Texas L.Rev. 1 (1989).

HIGH CRIMES AND MISDEMEANORS (Funk & Wagnalls 1973).

Privileges, Immunities

R. Berger, EXECUTIVE PRIVILEGE: A CONSTITUTIONAL MYTH (1974).

Cox, *Executive Privilege,* 122 U.Pa.L.Rev. 1383 (1974).

Ervin, *The Gravel and Brewster Cases: An Assault on Congressional Independence,* 59 Va.L.Rev. 175 (1973).

Freund, *Foreword: On Presidential Privilege,* 88 Harv.L.Rev. 13 (1974).

Mishkin, *Great Cases and Soft Law: A Comment on United States v. Nixon,* 22 UCLA L.Rev. 76 (1974).

Separation and the Judicial Power

Fallon, *Of Legislative Courts, Administrative Agencies, and Article III,* 101 Harv.L.Rev. 916 (1988).

Redish, *Legislative Courts, Administrative Agencies, and the* Northern Pipeline *Decision,* 1983 Duke L.J. 197.

Young, *Public Rights and the Federal Judicial Power: From* Murray's Lessee *Through* Crowell *To* Schor, 35 Buffalo L.Rev. 765 (1986).

Chapter V

PROPERTY

A significant number of provisions in the Constitution protect "property." The list includes the Eminent Domain Clause, the Due Process Clauses, the Contract Clause, and the Equal Protection Clause, to name only the most obvious. This Chapter focuses on eminent domain and due process, since these clauses are, in modern times, the most energetically enforced.

A. THE EMINENT DOMAIN CLAUSE

The Fifth Amendment decrees that "private property [shall not] be taken for public use, without just compensation." [1] This is an important statement about the significance of property rights under our Constitution, but it says less than it seems to. Read literally it appears to mean that the government must not disturb the distribution of wealth arrived at in people's private dealings with one another. Whenever the government takes something from A it must give A equivalent compensation.[2] It also appears to forbid even equivalent exchanges unless the government is acting for a "public use."

But we cannot understand the clause so literally. First, "Government hardly could go on if to some extent values incident to property could not be diminished without paying for every such change in the general law." [3] Traffic lights divert customers away from some merchants; the placement of fire hydrants affects home insurance premiums. The government cannot be required to readjust the distribution of private wealth whenever it decides to provide such amenities. Second, and more fundamentally, the existing distribution of private

---

1. The Fifth Amendment applies only to the federal government. Its 'takings' requirements have been read into the Fourteenth Amendment Due Process Clause, which applies to the states. *Missouri Pac. Ry. v. Nebraska,* 164 U.S. 403, 17 S.Ct. 130, 41 L.Ed. 489 (1896) (public use); *Chicago, B. & Q. R.R. Co. v. Chicago,* 166 U.S. 226, 17 S.Ct. 581, 41 L.Ed. 979 (1897) (just compensation).

2. This is in fact the reading given the clause in R. Epstein, Takings: Private Property and the Law of Eminent Domain (1985). Epstein's thesis is criticized in Grey, *The Malthusian Constitution,* 41 U.Miami L.Rev. 21 (1986).

3. *Pennsylvania Coal Co. v. Mahon,* 260 U.S. 393, 413, 43 S.Ct. 158, 159, 67 L.Ed. 322 (1922).

property is shaped by common law rules of acquisition and exchange. There is no pre-legal arrangement of goods which the Fifth Amendment freezes in place. But if the government gave yesterday what it takes away today, why should it have to pay compensation? Third, in order to make sense of the requirement that government can acquire property only for "public use," we must have a theory of the proper ends for which government can act. But the courts have all but abandoned hope of formulating such a theory in other areas of the law (*e.g.*, in establishing limits on the enumerated powers of Congress or legislative power under the Due Process Clauses), and there is little reason to think they will be more successful here.

The readings in this Section focus on these issues for the light they shed on the constitutional significance of property rights. The first three selections deal in general with the distinction between compensable takings and noncompensable regulations. This has been a most fruitful cause of litigation; in the past decade the Supreme Court has revisited the problem almost annually. Most agree that its efforts have not been crowned with success. Finding the appropriate dividing line "may be the lawyer's equivalent of the physicist's hunt for the quark." [4] Joseph Sax's article reviews the most common ways of drawing that line and concludes that each is inadequate at best.

Perhaps we have gone astray in our attempts to solve the compensation problem by focusing too much on the ideas of "taking" and "regulation." Those concepts may not be fundamental here. Morris R. Cohen once suggested that we need "[a]n adequate theory of private property [to] enable us to draw the line between justifiable and unjustifiable cases of confiscation." [5] Instead of chasing quarks we might do better to think about what property is, why we should protect it, and how.

Frank Michelman's article outlines a utilitarian approach to these issues. What the utilitarian most values is maximizing the output of satisfactions (wealth). Settled expectations about the distribution of resources (property) help produce wealth by giving people an incentive to labor and invest. Redistribution, on the other hand, reduces wealth because it is demoralizing. We can avoid this cost by compensating people when it occurs. But sometimes we can maximize wealth by not compensating. In the case of the traffic light it may cost more to identify the losers and measure their losses than it would to accept their demoralization. Here is a principle (though a very general one) for distinguishing between compensable and noncompensable takings: we should compensate when demoralization costs exceed the administrative costs of settling claims. Michelman makes this idea more specific by applying it to the test (diminution of value) most often used by the Supreme Court in takings cases.

4. C. Haar, Land–Use Planning 766 (3d ed. 1976).

5. Cohen, *Property and Sovereignty,* 13 Cornell L.Q. 8, 26 (1927).

This utilitarian account assumes that our system of private property has as its primary purpose encouraging the production of wealth. Carol Rose suggests that that may not be so. She points to a conflicting tradition in our history—one that subordinates the acquisition of wealth to the promotion of virtue. In this tradition, property is valued for its contribution to certain qualities of character. But since too much property can be corrupting, redistribution may sometimes be a good thing. Rose believes that the perennial muddle over the takings issue can be traced to the conflict between these two deep-rooted traditions.

The fourth selection in this Section deals with the "public use" limitation on takings. Up until the time of the New Deal the courts viewed this restriction as one they were capable of enforcing against too activist legislatures.[6] Since then it has become a dead letter.[7] There is an obvious parallel between this development and the Court's treatment of legislative powers under Article I and the Due Process Clause. Thomas Merrill explains the reasons for this similarity. He goes on to argue that the judiciary can enforce the 'public use' requirement, not (as Michelman's article suggests) by forbidding inefficient takings altogether, but by supervising the ways in which the government acquires property.

JOSEPH L. SAX, TAKINGS AND THE POLICE POWER

74 Yale L.J. 36, 37, 46–53, 60 (1964).

Two basic approaches have been developed by the courts to distinguish takings from police power regulations. The earlier theory, articulated in the main by the first Justice Harlan, drew on traditional legal concepts for its rules. Notions such as appropriation of a proprietary interest, physical invasion giving rise to a prescriptive easement, and nuisance were its basic tools. The second approach originated with Justice Holmes in the first quarter of this century, when the expansion of governmental regulation yielded a proliferation of claims for compensation by aggrieved owners of private property. Holmes' approach denied the utility of artificial legalisms such as Harlan employed. Holmes proposed reliance on a pragmatic, case-by-case resolution of the policy-conflict which he perceived to lie at the heart of the problem— the conflict between public need and private loss. Neither of these two approaches has proved able to produce satisfactory results. Harlan's theory reduces the constitutional issue to a formalistic quibble; an airport noise case, for example, may turn on whether the planes have

---

6. *Cincinnati v. Vester,* 281 U.S. 439, 446, 50 S.Ct. 360, 362, 74 L.Ed. 950 (1930) ("It is well established that in considering the application of the Fourteenth Amendment to cases of expropriation of private property, the question what is a public use is a judicial one.").

7. The tide turned in *United States ex rel. TVA v. Welch,* 327 U.S. 546, 551, 66 S.Ct. 715, 717, 90 L.Ed. 843 (1946) ("it is the function of Congress to decide what type of taking is for a public use").

physically penetrated that segment of air directly above the claimant's land. The Holmesian approach has equal failings. Its central premise—that the right to compensation depends on the magnitude of loss suffered—is historically unsound, has never in fact been acceptable to the Court, and wasn't even followed by Holmes himself.

* * *

THE INVASION THEORY

* * * [I]t is obvious that whether the government takes title or possession of the subject property is merely a matter of the form in which it chooses to proceed. One of the oldest tricks of capitalizing on form is to try to depreciate the value or inhibit the development of property through zoning, so that it has a much reduced market value when the government gets around to buying it. Thus the government gets most of the value of the property without any formal "taking." New Jersey cities seem to have pioneered this technique. The city of Plainfield once zoned plaintiff's property exclusively for school, park, and playground use.[63] * * * The state courts have quite uniformly rejected these guises and required the payment of compensation.

But a similar device slipped by the U.S. Supreme Court, at least in part, because the Court applied the old invasion theory. In *United States v. Central Eureka Mining Company*,[68] the War Production Board shut down privately owned gold mines for the purpose of inducing experienced miners, who were in very short supply, to go into more essential war work. In essence what the government was doing was improving the labor situation by putting the competition out of business. In the private realm this is ordinarily done by buying the competitor. And in the ordinary situation this is what would have been done. But instead of buying the right to operate the business in question, and thus the economic power to induce a shift of labor to other industries, the government merely "regulated" the gold mines out of business without invoking the magic talisman of a physical invasion. Form prevailed over substance; the Court's opinion turned in at least some degree on its finding that "the Government did not occupy, use or in any manner take physical possession of the gold mines or of the equipment connected with them." Compensation was denied.

For constitutional questions to depend on such formalities is, as these cases demonstrate, preposterous. The formal appropriation or physical invasion theory should be rejected once and for all.

THE NOXIOUS USE THEORY

Analysis will show the noxious use test to be no more adequate than the invasion test, although it has a beguiling simplicity and a perpetual appeal. Since the taking provision is undoubtedly an attempt to find some fair balance between the forces of change and the security of established interests, it has seemed particularly appropriate

63. Joint Meeting v. Borough of Middle-
sex, 69 N.J.Super. 136, 173 A.2d 785 (1961).

68. 357 U.S. 155 (1958).

to believe that the compensation problem could be solved by saying that the uses which could be destroyed without compensation were those that were noxious, or wrongful, or harmful in some sense.

Of course it has long been obvious that all non-compensable uses could not be described in terms of moral obloquy such as might be appropriate for the regulation of prostitution or liquor. But a more modern version of the noxious use test has had considerable popularity, and it is this version which must be discussed. This is the "creation of the harm" test, based on the argument that while in general established economic interests cannot be diminished merely because of a resulting public benefit, that rule does not apply where the individual whose interest is to be diminished himself created the need for public regulation by his conduct. The test has been most explicitly articulated in the series of grade-separation cases which have come before the Court. In those situations a railroad track crosses a highway at street level. As highway traffic increases, the legislature determines that in the interests of safety, a grade separation is necessary. The cost of providing the improvement is usually assessed in large part against the railroad. It has been almost universally the rule that the railroad must pay, and the justification has been that:

> Having brought about the problem, the railroads are in no position to complain because their share of the cost of alleviating it is not based solely on the special benefits accruing to them from the improvements.[72]

* * *

This test is, however, insufficient to explain a great number of other very important cases. Perhaps nuisance abatement is the best example. Zoning out of nuisances is perhaps the classic example of the non-compensable exercise of the police power. The typical nuisance situation is one in which a perfectly lawful industrial enterprise located on the outskirts of the city suddenly finds itself in the midst of a new and unforeseen residential development.[74] It can hardly be said that the industrial user created this evil which is now sought to be remedied: the patent fact is that the evil was created by the unfortunate juxtaposition of two lawful activities. Indeed that is precisely the situation in the grade crossing cases. If all we mean by "creation of the evil" is that one has located himself in a place which subsequently turns out to be inconsistent with the public interest—and that is all that can be said of the nuisance and grade crossing cases—then we must also say that the farmer who buys land in a place which is subsequently needed for a state highway has "created" the harm to be remedied and need not be given compensation.

Actually the problem is not one of noxiousness or harm-creating activity at all; rather it is a problem of inconsistency between perfectly innocent and independently desirable uses. And what is true of the

---

72. Atchison, T. & S.F. Ry. v. Public Utilities Comm'rs, 346 U.S. 346, 353 (1953).

74. Hadacheck v. Sebastian, 239 U.S. 394 (1915).

nuisance and grade crossing cases is equally true of a great many cases in which the Court denies compensation.

For example, incompatibility is the essence of the famous decision in *Miller v. Schoene*.[76] There the complainant was required to destroy his red cedar trees because they produced cedar rust which was fatal to apple trees which happened to be cultivated nearby. To say that the cedar tree owner caused the harm is no more accurate than to say that the apple growers caused the harm by locating near cedar groves. If we are talking about blameworthiness, some moral wrongdoing or conscious act of dangerous risk-taking which induces us to shift the cost to a partricular individual, it simply does not exist in these cases.

Of course the same is true of cases like * * * *Goldblatt* [v. *Town of Hempstead*].[78] The users there created the harm only in the sense that they decided to mine sand and gravel in a place which subsequently became desirable for residential homesites. * * *

THE DIMINUTION OF VALUE THEORY

Since emphasis on the diminution of value is probably the most popular current approach to the taking problem, it is important to understand precisely what it comprehends: Essentially the theory appears to express two interrelated ideas: (1) that all legally acquired existing economic values are property, and (2) that while such values may be diminished somewhat without compensation, they may not be excessively diminished: the meaning of "excessive" is necessarily imprecise, but it is fairly clear under the theory that it would be unconstitutional to deprive a property of all or substantially all its economic value.

This approach, too, has tremendous appeal. It seems to bear out the oft-repeated observation that "the political ethics reflected in the fifth amendment reject confiscation as a measure of justice." This is a strong and attractive sentiment, but it has unfortunately been used to obscure the real problems of the compensation clause. The problem is much more complicated than merely identifying existing economic values, denominating them property, and providing a rule that those values may not be wholly or substantially destroyed.

The Test Presupposes a False Definition of Property

The first complication is presented by the fact that we very often permit total destruction of established values; in so doing we circumvent the diminution of value approach by an alternative analysis, which simply says that the interest affected was not property and thus not entitled to constitutional protection. This is a very common approach, used by Holmes himself on several occasions.[81] The classic

---

76. 276 U.S. 272 (1928).

78. 369 U.S. 590 (1962). [In this case the Court upheld a town "safety regulation" that banned mining at Goldblatt's sand and gravel pit in a suburban area.]

81. * * * It was Holmes who pointed out that "there are many things which a man might do at common law that the states may forbid" and which have never been thought to be property entitled to constitutional protection. "He might em-

formulation of the "no-compensation because no-property" approach was provided by Justice Jackson in the *Willow River Power* case:

> Only those economic advantages are "rights" which have the law back of them . . . whether it is a property right is really the question to be answered.[82]

The significance of this is that it shows the erroneous and delusive simplicity of the diminution of value approach. For every time we deny compensation on the ground that the interest affected was not really a property right, we repudiate in some measure the essence of the diminution of value test—the proposition that established economic values as such are entitled to constitutional protection.

In fact there are so many of these non-property situations that one must be irrevocably led to the conclusion that whatever it is that the compensation clause is preventing, it is something other than the destruction of established economic values. Changes in the common law are frequently made, and they are changes which may have very substantial economic import; yet we invariably deny compensation on the ground that there was no property interest in maintenance of the status quo. In the field of tort law, for example, such changes as abolition of the privity rule, imposition of the doctrine of products liability, or the extinguishment of charitable immunity are well known instances. The constitutionality of such laws is assumed on the ground that the economic advantage affected—like the common law right to embezzle—is not property. Similarly in the law of real property, it seems never to have been suggested that a compensable taking was involved when the courts first "took away" an easement by necessity from an unwilling grantor, although we today clearly treat an easement as a kind of interest which can give rise to a taking problem.

Similarly the legislatures are permitted to prohibit the continuance of businesses, lawful when established, with ensuing total or near total destruction of values. As that practice formerly affected lotteries, or the manufacture of liquor,[86] it proceeds apace today against debt adjustment,[87] and whatever other businesses which once "were thought useful adjuncts of the state" but have since fallen into popular disfavor. Of these crushing economic dislocations for the affected persons we merely say that there was no property interest involved.

When the legislature destroys 90% of value by prohibiting continuance of a brickyard,[89] it contents itself with saying the activity was a nuisance, and everyone knows that there is no property in a nuisance; when it imposes heavy regulation on the oil industry,[90] it says it is

bezzle until a statute cut down his liberty." Noble State Bank v. Haskell, 219 U.S. 104, 113 (1911).

82. United States v. Willow River Power Co., 324 U.S. 499, 502 (1945).

86. Mugler v. Kansas, 123 U.S. 623 (1887).

87. Ferguson v. Skrupa, 372 U.S. 726 (1963).

89. Hadacheck v. Sebastian, 239 U.S. 394, 408–09 (1915).

90. Champlin Refining Co. v. Corporation Comm'n, 286 U.S. 210 (1932).

preventing waste, and so too, there is plainly no property interest in waste. Zoning, with losses of 75% or more of value, is similarly treated.[91]

* * *

The conclusion to be drawn from these examples, just a few among many, is clear. The diminution of value test gives a highly unreal view of the actual working of the compensation rule in American law. Destruction of recognized economic interests, on the ground that there is no property interest, is so widespread and pervasive that the policy of preventing individual economic loss as such, can hardly be said to have been given significant recognition by the courts. Nor can it be seriously argued that the foregoing examples are part of a special limited class of noxious or harmful uses; they are, like the typical taking cases, merely uses which have become inconsistent with the legislatively declared public interest. Thus, the question naturally arises as to whether or not we have been misled in thinking that the function of the compensation clause is essentially to protect and maintain established values. Certainly if we look to what the Court has done, the answer must be that in fact and in result the Court has not treated protection of values as its primary goal.

* * *

The Test Imports an Unworkable Problem of Definition

Because the diminution test turns on the degree of quantitative diminution of value, it is necessary that the property at issue be precisely defined, so that we can determine how great the impairment of value is. But this is no easy task. If the government floods 80 acres of a 640 acre farm, is that a total destruction of 80 acres, or a mere 12½ percent loss? In a case of compulsory dedication of real property by a land subdivider, the acreage given up can be treated as a total loss, or merely as a loss of a small portion of the entire tract, in which case the end result might even be seen as an increase in the value of the property because of the prospect of municipal services. In the famous *Pennsylvania Coal* case is the loss to be treated as a total taking of that quantum of coal left in the ground, or as a small fraction of the total productivity of the mine? These definitional problems are difficult; they have never been seriously treated in opinions which invariably solve them by flat and unsupported assertions as to the identity of "the" property at issue. Since degree of loss is the very essence of the test, this is a central problem. The failure to deal with the issue, and the terrible complexities of trying to do so are further evidence of the unsatisfactory nature of the diminution of value test.

* * *

[Sax goes on to propose that we solve the takings riddle by distinguishing between "enterprise" and "arbitral" functions of government. Compensation should be required when the government takes property

---

91. Euclid v. Ambler Realty Co., 272 U.S. 365, 384 (1926).

in furtherance of its own interests as an enterprise—to maintain an army, build highways, run schools, etc. It is not due when the government decides disputes between private parties. This rule, Sax argues, would protect us against "arbitrary, unfair or tyrannical government" behavior—a real danger only in "enterprise" cases.]

Seven years later Sax changed his mind and proposed an even more permissive rule: the government need not pay compensation when it acts to prevent "spillover" effects (external costs of property use). These he defined to include uses of private property that affect the health or well-being of others. *Takings, Private Property and Public Rights,* 81 Yale L.J. 149 (1971).

FRANK I. MICHELMAN, PROPERTY, UTILITY, AND FAIRNESS: COMMENTS ON THE ETHICAL FOUNDATIONS OF "JUST COMPENSATION" LAW

80 Harv.L.Rev. 1165, 1211–1218, 1224, 1229–1234 (1967).

[In the first part of this article Michelman reviews the rules of decision typically used to identify compensable takings and concludes, as Sax does, that they rest in general on illusory distinctions. He then turns to an examination of the purposes of the compensation requirement. The discussion excerpted here deals with a utilitarian justification for property rights and compensation. In the concluding portion of this excerpt that theory is applied to the diminution-of-value test announced by Justice Holmes in *Pennsylvania Coal Co. v. Mahon.*]

SOME THEORIES OF PROPERTY

A number of pre-utilitarian property theories rested * * * on behavioral premises indicating that productivity will be enhanced by pride and responsibility of office; or that productivity will be frustrated and consumption voided of satisfaction by the discord which only clear and simple rules of control can forestall; or that productivity demands planning and organization. Assumptions such as these stand independent of, though they perhaps suggest, the further assumption that a high level of productivity depends on arrangements which assure to every person who invests or labors that he will share in the fruits of his investment or labor to a predictable extent. This additional assumption * * * seems to have been definitively clarified and elaborated by Bentham. It was he who stimulated emphasis on the relevance of appearance and suggestion to the intensity of productive activity, as well as to the maintenance of that state of association which itself lifts productivity to a new plateau. Bentham's emphasis is of peculiar importance for present purposes because it * * * furnish[es] the germ of a theoretically satisfying approach to compensation questions.

Property, according to Bentham, is most aptly regarded as the collection of rules which are presently accepted as governing the exploitation and enjoyment of resources.[96]   So regarded, property becomes "a basis of expectations" founded on existing rules; that is to say, property is the institutionally established understanding that extant rules governing the relationships among men with respect to resources will continue in existence.   The justification—Bentham regards it as a practical necessity—for adherence to such an understanding is that only through such adherence can we hope for a minimally acceptable level of productivity.   The human motivations which result in production are, he believes, such that they will not operate in the absence of secure expectations about future enjoyment of product.   It is supposed that men will not labor diligently or invest freely unless they know they can depend on rules which assure them that they will indeed be permitted to enjoy a substantial share of the product as the price of their labor or their risk of savings.

If one agrees with Bentham that the will to labor and the will to invest depend upon reliable assurances about the future enjoyment of any product, he must agree also that any unpredictable redistribution is potentially destructive of society's material wellbeing.   For a newly conceived redistribution, no matter how accomplished or to what end, is always something of a disappointment to the expectations which Bentham regards as the essence of property.   And the very act of redistributing implies that society will not scruple to effect like redistributions in the future.   It is this implication or suggestion—this disavowal of perfect security of expectation—which utilitarian property theory chiefly deprecates.

We thus receive from Bentham a theory of social utility which can explain why collective allocational decision making, deemed unobjectionable in and of itself, *might* be deemed impermissible if attended by capricious redistributions.   And we may be encouraged to try to derive from that theory some criteria for determining which collective allocational decisions, attended by what particular distributional impacts, should be deemed impermissible unless those impacts are offset by compensation payments.   Still we must recognize that, despite its obvious and direct relevance to the general compensation problem, the utilitarian theory will not show us how to discriminate among capricious redistribution cases—will not, that is, show us how to perfect our general practice, certain to be retained, of compensating in some but not all of such cases—if its only implication is a general one militating broadly against *all* capricious redistributions.   Given the framework of practices within which the compensation problem actually arises in our society, the practical relevance of the utilitarian theory will [not be great] until it has been shown that the utilitarian theory * * * is translatable into pertinent questions of degree.

The problem, then, is to show that utilitarian property theory, applied with utmost consistency, does *not* require payment of compen-

---

96. The statement which is usually accepted as definitive of Bentham's position is J. Bentham, Theory of Legislation chs. 7–10 (6th ed. 1890). * * *

sation in every case of social action which is disappointing to justified, investment-backed expectations. * * *

The utilitarian * * * will probably be unable to avoid the conclusion that it is sometimes right for society to adopt a measure which cannot practically be purged of a capriciously redistributive effect frustrating to justified expectations: he could avoid that conclusion only if he were of the implausible view that no social measure which is visibly disappointing to expectations can possibly improve the allocational picture enough to outweigh resultant losses in productive effort.

* * * [W]e must remember that the utilitarian's solicitude for security is instrumental and subordinate to his goal of maximizing the output of satisfactions. Security of expectation is cherished, not for its own sake, but only as a shield for morale. Once admit that not all capricious redistributive effects are totally demoralizing, and utilitarian theory can tell us where to draw the line between compensable and noncompensable collective impositions. An imposition is compensable if not to compensate would be critically demoralizing; otherwise, not.

UTILITY * * * AND COMPENSATION

* * *

A strictly utilitarian argument leading to the specific identification of "compensable" occasions would have a quasi-mathematical structure. Let us define three quantities to be known as "efficiency gains," "demoralization costs," and "settlement costs." "Efficiency gains" we define as the excess of benefits produced by a measure over losses inflicted by it, where benefits are measured by the total number of dollars which prospective gainers would be willing to pay to secure adoption, and losses are measured by the total number of dollars which prospective losers would insist on as the price of agreeing to adoption. "Demoralization costs" are defined as the total of (1) the dollar value necessary to offset disutilities which accrue to losers and their sympathizers specifically from the realization that no compensation is offered, and (2) the present capitalized dollar value of lost future production (reflecting either impaired incentives or social unrest) caused by demoralization of uncompensated losers, their sympathizers, and other observers disturbed by the thought that they themselves may be subjected to similar treatment on some other occasion. "Settlement costs" are measured by the dollar value of the time, effort, and resources which would be required in order to reach compensation settlements adequate to avoid demoralization costs. Included are the costs of settling not only the particular compensation claims presented, but also those of all persons so affected by the measure in question or similar measures as to have claims not obviously distinguishable by the available settlement apparatus.

A measure attended by positive efficiency gains is, under utilitarian ethics, prima facie desirable. But felicific calculation under the definition given for efficiency gains is imperfect because it takes no account of demoralization costs caused by a capricious redistribution, or alternatively, of the settlement costs necessary to avoid such demoralization costs. When pursuit of efficiency gains entails capricious redistribution, either demoralization costs or settlement costs must be incurred. It follows that if, for any measure, both demoralization costs and settlement costs (whichever were chosen) would exceed efficiency gains, the measure is to be rejected; but that otherwise, since either demoralization costs or settlement costs must be paid, it is the lower of these two costs which should be paid. The compensation rule which then clearly emerges is that compensation is to be paid whenever settlement costs are lower than both demoralization costs and efficiency gains. * * *

Let us now focus on the problem of appraising demoralization costs. Since we are looking ultimately to the specification of practical methods for identifying compensable occasions, we may begin by saying that it obviously will not do to interview every potential compensation claimant and ask him how demoralized he expects to be if a given measure is adopted without provision for compensation. The objections to such a solution run far deeper than the obvious one about the costs of conducting such interviews. The interviewee probably will not himself know the answer to the question (putting aside the difficulty of his attaching a dollar value to his outrage and his loss of incentive even if he could appraise those subjectively) and, for strategic reasons, would not reveal the true answer if he knew it.

We are compelled, then, to frame the question about demoralization costs in terms of responses we must impute to ordinarily cognizant and sensitive members of society. Utilitarian algebra, it appears, cannot specify a sound compensation practice—the equation cannot be solved for that "value" of compensation which yields a maximum excess of efficiency gains over demoralization or settlement costs—until supposed facts about human psychology and behavior have been plugged into the equation as independent variables.

If we hypothesize a utilitarian defense of currently observable social practices pertaining to compensation, we can make some interesting deductions about the behavioral assumptions which must have entered into the utilitarian calculation. One clear characteristic of current practices is their reflection of a special urgency in the demand for publicly financed compensation when a loss has evidently been occasioned by deliberate social action. Society has not yet placed itself under any systematic discipline designed to assure people of compensation for all economic losses inflicted by forces regarded as beyond social control, such as earthquake or plague. * * *

We are thus led to inquire whether there is any reason to suppose that a visible risk of majoritarian exploitation should have any greater disincentive effect than the ever-present risk that accidents may happen, this being the only supposition which seems, on utilitarian premises, to justify a constitutional guaranty aimed specially against the former sort of risk. If I am able to mobilize my productive faculties under the general conditions of uncertainty which prevail in the universe, why should I be paralyzed by a realization that I am at the mercy of majorities?

There seems only one possible way to defend this behavioral supposition. The defense must begin with an imputation to human actors of a perception that the force of a majority is self-determining and purposive, as compared with other loss-producing forces which seem to be randomly generated. The argument must then proceed to the effect that even though people can adjust satisfactorily to random uncertainty, which can be dealt with through insurance, including self-insurance, they will remain on edge when contemplating the possibility of strategically determined losses. For when the bearing of strategy is evident, one faces the risk of being *systematically* imposed upon, which seems a risk of a very different order from the risk of occasional, accidental injury. One faces also the rational necessity of devoting a large proportion of his energies and resources to counter-strategy aimed at fending off the risk; where the possibility of loss will visibly be determined by strategy, that possibility cannot be conveniently dismissed from consciousness on the ground that, being uncontrollable, it is not worth thinking about.

Whatever the empirical verity of this behavioral picture, it does seem implicit in any attempt to rationalize current compensation practices in utilitarian (product-maximizing) terms. Accordingly, it seems in order to ask what criteria of compensability will emerge if the practice of compensating is taken to have the purpose of quieting people's unease about the possibility of being strategically exploited.

It seems obvious, to begin with, that this unease will be stirred by any spectacle of capricious redistribution which could easily have been avoided. Capricious redistributions will not be tolerated, even as accidental adjuncts of efficiency-dictated measures, when compensation settlements can be reached without much trouble, that is, when settlement costs are low. The clearer it is that the claimant has sustained an injury distinct from those sustained by the generality of persons in society, and the more obviously there appears to be some objectively satisfactory measure of his disproportionate or distinctive injury, the more compelling will his claim to compensation become.

Society, moreover, will have to avoid not only those capricious redistributions which a compensation payment could easily offset, but also those practically noncompensable ones which cannot plausibly be said to be necessitated by the pursuit of efficiency. Thus, measures whose efficiency is open to grave question will have to be rejected unless attended by compensation even though their arguable efficiency is enough to justify their adoption in some form. Payment of compensation in such cases may furnish a necessary assurance that the measure is not simply a disguised attempt to redistribute deliberately, by confirming the hypothesis that society deems the measure a "gainful" (efficient) one in the only ethically sure sense. Therefore, as the collective allocational measure approaches the limit of doubtful efficiency, the claim for compensation will become more compelling.

Other intertwined branches of a compensability inquiry could grow out of a utilitarian purpose to cater to the sense of security by preserving an illusion of long-run indiscriminateness in the distribution of social burdens and benefits. Thus the magnitude of the imposition would plainly be relevant: is it of quotidian variety, or is it once in a lifetime mayhem? But magnitude of individual burden, no matter how purposively conceived, reveals only a fragment, meaningless by itself, of the whole picture. We need additional information. For example, is the burden for which compensation is sought a rare or peculiar one, or do like burdens seem to have been widely, even though not uniformly, scattered about the community? Is there implicit in the measure some reciprocity of burdens coupled with benefits (as, for example, in a measure restricting a large area to residential development) or does it channel benefits and burdens to different persons? How likely does it seem that members of the class burdened by the measure were able to wield enough effective influence in the process leading to its adoption to have extracted some compensatory concession "in kind"?

* * *

THE RULES OF DECISION REVISITED

* * *

Diminution of Value

[Many people have] found it hard to understand why compensability should be thought to turn on a comparison of the size of the claimant's loss with the preexisting value of that spatially defined piece of property to which the loss in value seems to be specifically attached. It can now be suggested that judicial reliance on such comparisons reflects a utilitarian approach to compensability, as qualified by some special behavioral assumptions.

* * * [The] purpose of compensation is to prevent a special kind of suffering on the part of people who have grounds for feeling themselves the victims of unprincipled exploitation. [The appeal of the diminution of value test] rests ultimately in administrative expediency[: it defines a class] of cases whose numbers will (a) usually be easy to identify and (b) usually, under certain behavioral suppositions, present a particularly strong subjective need for compensation.

* * * [T]hese statements require explanation. We may begin by noticing a refinement, not mentioned earlier, which might initially seem only to deepen the mystery. It will be recalled that Justice Holmes, writing for the Court in the famous *Pennsylvania Coal* case,[111] held that a restriction on the extraction of coal, which effectively prevented the petitioner from exercising certain mining rights which it owned, was a taking of property and so could be enforced only upon

111. Pennsylvania Coal Co. v. Mahon, 260 U.S. 393 (1922).

payment of compensation. Holmes intimated strongly that the separation in ownership of the mining rights from the balance of the fee, prior to enactment of the restriction, was critically important to the petitioner's victory. But why should this be so? We can see that if one owns mining rights only, but not the residue of the fee, then a regulation forbidding mining totally devalues the owner's stake in "that" land. But is there any reason why it should matter whether one owns, in addition to mining rights, residuary rights in the same parcel (which may be added to the denominator so as probably to reduce the fraction of value destroyed below what is necessary for compensability) or residuary rights in some other parcel (which will not be added to the denominator)?

The significance of this question is confirmed by its pertinency to many comparable judicial performances. There is, for example, the widespread rule requiring compensation to the owner of an equitable servitude (such as a residential building restriction) when the government destroys the servitude's value by acquiring the burdened land and then using that land in violation of the private restriction embodied in the servitude. Vis-à-vis the servitude owner, the government cannot be said in the narrow sense to have "taken" any property. It has not * * * engaged in an activity which would be an actionable eviction if privately instigated. It is not affirmatively exploiting any prerogative formerly held by the owner of the servitude. It is simply engaging in activity which, absent the servitude, might have been a nuisance; but government does not usually come under an automatic obligation to compensate whenever it maintains a nuisance. Yet many courts award compensation to persons deprived by government action of the benefits of private building restrictions, without asking any questions about how much value, or what fraction of some value, has been destroyed. Thus, government activity, on land adjacent to the complainant's, which would otherwise give rise to no claim to compensation, may support such a claim if it violates a building restriction of which the complainant is a beneficiary. If a justification exists for such a difference in treatment, it would seem to be that one's psychological commitment to his explicit, formally carved out, appurtenant rights in another's land is much more sharply focused and intense, and much nearer the surface of his consciousness, than any reliance he places on his general claim to be safeguarded against nuisances. This proposition, if valid, would not affect the "fairness" of noncompensation, but it means that a utilitarian, with his eye on the actual long term psychological effects of his decisions, will be wary of denying compensation to the affronted servitude owner.

* * *

The "fraction of value destroyed" test, to recapitulate, appears to proceed by first trying to isolate some "thing" owned by the person complaining which is affected by the imposition. Ideally, it seems, one traces the incidence of the imposition and then asks what "thing" is likely to be identified by the owner as "the thing" affected by this measure? Once having thus found the denominator of the fraction, the test proceeds to ask what proportion of the value or prerogatives formerly attributed by the claimant to that thing has been destroyed by the measure. If practically all, compensation is to be paid.

All this suggests that the common way of stating the test under discussion—in terms of a vaguely located critical point on a sliding scale—is misleading (though certainly a true representation of the language repeatedly used by Holmes). The customary labels—magnitude of the harm test, or diminution of value test—obscure the test's foundations by conveying the idea that it calls for an arbitrary pinpointing of a critical proportion (probably lying somewhere between fifty and one hundred percent). More sympathetically perceived, however, the test poses not nearly so loose a question of degree; it does not ask "how much," but rather (like the physical-occupation test) it asks "whether or not": whether or not the measure in question can easily be seen to have practically deprived the claimant of some distinctly perceived, sharply crystallized, investment-backed expectation.

The nature and relevance of this inquiry may emerge more clearly if we notice one other familiar line of doctrine—that which enjoins special solicitude, when a new zoning scheme is instituted, for "established" uses which would be violations were the scheme applied with full retrospective vigor. The standard practice of granting dispensations for such "nonconforming uses" seems to imply an understanding that simply to ban them without payment of compensation, thus seriously reducing the property's market value, would be wrong and perhaps unconstitutional. But a ban on potential uses not yet established may destroy market value as effectively as does a ban on activity already in progress. The ban does not shed its retrospective quality simply because it affects only prospective uses. What explains, then, the universal understanding that only those nonconforming uses are protected which were demonstrably afoot by the time the regulation was adopted? The answer seems to be that actual establishment of the use demonstrates that the prospect of continuing it is a discrete twig out of his fee simple bundle to which the owner makes explicit reference in his own thinking, so that enforcement of the restriction would, as he looks at the matter, totally defeat a distinctly crystallized expectation. Here, then, is a case in which functional division of spatially unitary property makes the same kind of difference it made in *Pennsylvania Coal* * *, although the division here exists only within the eye of the beholder whose feelings we are concerned about, and is not reflected in any title papers.

The worth of this kind of analysis in a utilitarian compensation program depends on a number of assumptions which, while not void of plausibility, are surely debatable. The assumptions are (1) that one thinks of himself not just as owning a total amount of wealth or income, but also as owning several discrete "things" whose destinies he controls; (2) that deprivation of one of these mentally circumscribed things is an event attended by pain of a specially acute or demoralizing kind, as compared with what one experiences in response to the different kind of event consisting of a general decline in one's net worth; and (3) that events of the specially painful kind can usually be identified by compensation tribunals with relative ease.

* * * Of the three propositions, the second surely is the most suspect. The first seems self-evident, and the third seems probably true. Thus, the claimant in *Pennsylvania Coal,* which supposed itself to own a mining interest before the incidence of the regulation, owned nothing of consequence afterward, but a residential owner in the regulated district still had essentially what he had before (though its market value may have been reduced). * * * The zoned-out apartment house owner no longer has the apartment investment he depended on, whereas the nearby land speculator who is unable to show that he has yet formed any specific plans for his vacant land still has a package of possibilities with its value, though lessened, still unspecified—which is what he had before.

CAROL M. ROSE, *MAHON* RECONSTRUCTED: WHY THE TAKINGS ISSUE IS STILL A MUDDLE
57 S.Cal.L.Rev. 561, 582, 586–595 (1984).

[Rose reviews the Supreme Court's decision in *Pennsylvania Coal Co. v. Mahon,*[a] where Justice Holmes held unconstitutional a law forbidding the mining of anthracite coal beneath someone else's property if that would cause a subsidence of the surface. Before the law was enacted Pennsylvania Coal had conveyed the surface above its property to Mahon's father, expressly reserving the right to remove all underlying coal. Rose asserts that the Court struck the law down because it was seen as a naked redistribution of property from one group to another, without any net social gain.]

* * * This conclusion, however, only moves the problem to a different level: what is wrong with redistribution? Why condemn a law because it transfers property from the Company to the Mahons?

* * *

Some of Holmes' remarks suggest [that] transfer is undesirable [because it] might disrupt what Holmes called the "stream of products."[126] This reasoning reflects Madison's views, as set forth in his famous statement that the "first object of government" is the protection of "[t]he diversity in the faculties of men, from which the rights of property originate."[127] Bentham's theories add a gloss to the argument: a country will accumulate wealth if it protects the ability to acquire, but that ability flourishes only where the laws assure some

---

a. 260 U.S. 393 (1922).

126. Letter from Holmes to Harold Laski (May 8, 1917), in Holmes–Laski Letters 84 (M. Howe ed.1953).

127. The Federalist No. 10, at 78 (J. Madison) (C. Rossiter ed. 1961).

continuity in property expectations.[128] Acquisition of wealth requires planning, investment of time and effort, and secure knowledge of return on the investment. Continuous property transfers, though they may all eventually even out, will not encourage wealth production. In John Locke's language, "industrious and rational" persons cannot get a foothold if legislatures transfer their property rights, and force them to pool their labors with the "quarrelsom[e] and contentious." [130] Hence pure transfers should be restrained in the political market, * * * because they cause too much turmoil for wealth producing enterprise.

* * *

The Fundamental Tension: Wealth Versus Virtue

Despite the familiarity of the stability argument, a deeper question remains: why encourage wealth? Is encouraging the production of wealth the primary purpose of our system of private property? A careful look at the American property tradition reveals that other views of the purpose of private property have coexisted with the wealth maximizing view since at least the framing of the Constitution.

Wealth, Virtue, And The American Property Tradition

Aristotle related property acquisition and spending to the virtue of generosity. On this account, one needs a certain amount of wealth in order to be magnanimous, but it does not necessarily follow that more is better. The ethical ends of generosity and magnanimity constrain wealth accumulation; pure acquisitiveness has no claim for protection unless it also promotes those virtues. Some theorists of the Middle Ages went far beyond Aristotle, arguing that true virtue required the renunciation of material possessions. In general, the premodern philosophic theorists saw wealth acquisition at best as subordinate to the promotion of the virtue of generosity, and at worst as a highly suspicious and dangerous passion.

Madison rejected this theory, as had Hobbes and Locke before him. According to Madison, human virtues are notoriously unstable and reliance upon them may easily lead to outrage, despoliation, and bloodshed.[140] Madison felt it safer to rely not on virtues, but on self-interest. Among self-interested motives, avarice, though perhaps the homeliest, is also the most constant and reliable. By splitting society into a multiplicity of property interests, avarice distracts persons from the perhaps more majestic, but certainly more predatory, endeavors of our forebears. Businesspersons slit each other's throats only symbolically; they fight no duels and make no great point of honor. Yet their successes encourage others to make money instead of strife, and may produce a surplus that strengthens the nation against outsiders. Thus,

128. J. Bentham, [The Theory of Legislation 70–73 (Oceana Publications, Inc., ed. 1975)].

130. J. Locke, Second Treatise of Government § 34 (P. Laslett ed.1963).

140. *See* The Federalist No. 10, at 81 (J. Madison) (C. Rossiter ed. 1961) (neither religious nor moral motives are reliable as checks upon oppression).

protecting acquisitive interests increases both productivity and national strength.

On this reasoning, the protection of settled expectations promotes acquisition which in turn brings internal peace as well as strength vis-à-vis outsiders. Thus, in the classic triad of life, liberty, and property, the element of property ultimately serves life by reducing strife at home and presenting the image of strength abroad.

* * *

Familiar as the wealth maximizing argument for protecting expectations may be, American governing institutions have frequently acted as if protecting acquisition does not really deliver wealth and its supposed derivatives of peace and strength. More importantly, one strand in American political thinking has consistently rejected the argument's underlying assumptions that the *res publica* has no meaning aside from the sum of individual satisfactions, and no functions aside from smoothing over the transaction costs encountered by self-interested humans.

J.G.A. Pocock has brilliantly illustrated the manner in which thinkers from the sixteenth through the eighteenth centuries revived and transformed the Aristotelian idea that human excellence is linked with participation in the polity and that the polity in turn depends on the character or "virtue" of its members.[148] In the early years of the republic, this view coexisted with the antithetical Lockean conception of government based on and serving the desires of only discrete individuals. For those who looked to civic virtue as the safeguard of the republic (and vice versa), property functioned to foster the independence and civic participation of a morally committed citizenry. The protection of property was necessarily subordinate to that function, even at the cost of substantial redistribution.

Thus could Jefferson argue for wide distribution of agricultural property as conducive to civic character, and maintain that extreme inequalities in property would corrupt the republic.[151] Thus could the Antifederalists argue that riches and power were neither the exclusive nor the most important goals for American government. To the Antifederalists, the important issues related to the nature of the regime and the qualities that it produced in the people.[152] * * *

This eighteenth and early nineteenth century "propertarianism" sought to foster civic virtue through property—property that would encourage sturdy independence and liberty. Beyond that point of citizen independence, however, the widely espoused civic property doc-

---

148. For an exposition of the development of this civic virtue school of thought, *see* J. Pocock, [The Machiavellian Moment: Florentine Political Thought and the Atlantic Republican Tradition 423–505 (1975).]

151. *See* Katz [*Thomas Jefferson and the Right to Property in Revolutionary*

America, 19 J.L. & Econ. 467, 470–74, 480–81 (1975)].

152. *See* 1 The Complete Anti-Federalist 20–23 (H. Storing ed. 1981) (republican government depends on civic virtue and devotion to fellow citizens). * * *

trine had a strong egalitarian element, and might tolerate or even encourage redistribution.

* * *

The Continuing Tension in the American Property Tradition

Neither of these traditions has vanished. The Lockean/Madisonian/Benthamite argument for acquisition, with its concomitant denial of a polity founded on any civic qualities beyond individual satisfactions, has found an exuberant revival in neoclassical economics. On the other hand, the civic conception of property as a means of developing character and promoting republican participation also persists * * *. The constant (and, according to economists, hopeless) efforts to restrain landlords and fast talking merchants are outgrowths of the tradition that subordinated property protection to civic virtue, requiring the "haves" to treat the "have-nots" more generously—just as the medieval prohibitions on regraters, forestallers, and engrossers attempted to suppress the exploitation of commercial advantage by some to the detriment of others.

In takings doctrine, the tradition of property's civic responsibility is embodied in a test that balances public benefits against private losses from a particular measure. This test baffles legal commentators who take a neoclassical economic approach. From a Benthamite point of view, this test might be relevant to the utility of the proposed measure, but would have no bearing at all on the issue of compensation: if the public needs property, it may acquire it, but must still pay for it. The premise of this takings test, however, is quite the reverse; that is, that citizens may be required to sacrifice and bear private losses in the face of a substantially greater public need.

Thus, the arguments about disturbing established expectations take two very different directions: one would protect the acquisitive faculties which bring wealth and strength; the other would protect the citizen independence and participation which enhance the community, but would thereafter raise no principled objections to redistribution.

Why the Takings Problem Remains

This tension between the two arguments helps explain why the takings problem is so intractable. Our traditional discourse envisions property as serving quite divergent purposes. Although these purposes frequently overlap, the two views of property ultimately suggest different characters and limits for public protection of property ownership; the disagreements over purposes are manifested in disagreements about the circumstances under which the public may regulate property without compensation.

The proacquisitive position is that individuals should be able to act on numerous fixed property expectations, and thus any involuntary and uncompensated disruption of those expectations is a wrongful taking. This view clearly has a rhetorical advantage. One of our prominent political metaphors includes a prepolitical right to property: humans supposedly bring property into the social contract, and consent to government in order to protect individual property, not diminish it.[170] This metaphor rejects redistribution of property and effectively precludes all but acquisitive abilities as appropriate objects of protection. The vocabulary of Locke, Madison, and Bentham, and not that of Aristotle, dominates the takings discourse, blurring the notion of a prepolitical property right with the political goals of strength and internal peace.

The concept of a prepolitical property right is problematic, primarily because it fails to address the question of what it means to "own" anything in the absence of the community's protection. For this and other reasons, courts have seldom recognized such a prepolitical right. Justice Chase, at a time when the Supreme Court still discussed seriously application of natural law in civil matters, denied that property existed prior to the social contract.[173] Aside from such an open reference to political theory, in takings litigation courts always veer noticeably away from the directions in which this antiredistributive theory should drive. Powerful as the theory is in many areas of American social thought, it has historically been rather frail in takings jurisprudence. *Mahon* is, after all, an exceptional case. The usual practice in takings jurisprudence is to allow political communities wide latitude in defining citizens' obligations, similar to the practice in the jurisprudence of obligation of contract. The rhetoric of protecting expectations of gain does appear in takings jurisprudence, but so does the rhetoric of civic duty.

THOMAS W. MERRILL, THE ECONOMICS OF PUBLIC USE

72 Cornell L.Rev. 61, 66–78, 80–81 (1986).

THE MEANS–ENDS PROBLEM

Drawing on Calabresi and Melamed's model,[a] one may isolate four possible rights that a citizen might have when faced with an attempted government taking. At one extreme, the citizen would have no entitlement; the government could take his property without his consent and without compensation. This is a citizen's plight when the government legitimately exercises its power to tax or its police power. A second possibility is that a liability rule would protect a citizen's property; the government could take the property without his consent, but would have to pay compensation. This describes a taking by eminent domain. A third possibility is that a property rule would protect a citizen's

---

170. J. Locke, *supra* note 130, at §§ 25–51, 87.

173. Calder v. Bull, 3 U.S. (3 Dall.) 386, 394 (1798).

a. Calabresi & Melamed, *Property Rules, Liability Rules, and Inalienability: One View of the Cathedral*, 83 Harv.L.Rev.

1089 (1972). "Property rules," as defined by Calabresi and Melamed, allow an owner to protect a right or entitlement from an unconsented taking by securing injunctive relief. "Liability rules" afford protection only through an ex post award of damages.

property; the government could take the property only with the citizen's consent, i.e., if he agreed to sell it to the government. This is the rule generally followed when government acquires chattels or employment services. Finally, a fourth possibility is that the government could not acquire a citizen's property by any means. This situation occurs if the proposed acquisition serves a purpose or end not permitted by the Constitution, for example, the purchase of votes or the services of a slave.

A clear distinction exists between the first three of these rules—no entitlement, liability rule, and property rule—and the fourth, which completely bars government acquisitions of property. The first three rules define different means of achieving permissible government ends. The fourth, however, effectively demarcates a sphere of impermissible government ends. In fact, the means-ends distinction inherent in the Calabresi–Melamed framework suggests that judges may ask two questions of any proposed government acquisition. First, the ends question: is the government acquiring the resources for a constitutionally permissible purpose? Second, the means question: if the purpose is permissible, should the government proceed by police power regulation, eminent domain, or voluntary exchange in the marketplace?

The two questions present sharply different inquiries. The ends question asks what the government plans to do once the property is obtained. This inquiry, in turn, requires a clear conception of the legitimate functions or purposes of the state. May the state promote employment by subsidizing the construction of a privately owned factory? May it own a professional football team or undertake land reform? The answers to such questions demand an exercise in high political theory that most courts today are unwilling (or unable) to undertake. The means question, by contrast, is narrower. It asks where and how the government should get property, not what it may do with it. For example, the means approach accepts that a state may own a professional football team. It then asks: how should the state acquire the team? Must it purchase the team through voluntary negotiations? Or may the state coerce a transfer by condemning the team? Or may it simply commandeer the team under its police power? The means approach, of course, is also "political" in that it concerns state actions that will advance or retard conflicting interests. Nevertheless, the means approach demands a more narrowly focused and judicially manageable inquiry than the ends approach.

In deciding public use cases, courts nearly always pose the issue in terms of ends rather than in terms of means. Perhaps the constitutional language is responsible for this focus. The fifth amendment provides, "nor shall private property be taken *for public use,* without just compensation." This phrasing suggests that the government may exercise the power of eminent domain, but only if it puts the property acquired to a public use, that is, an end that is sufficiently "public" in nature.

The focus on ends also figures into the two judicial tests most often relied upon to define "public use." Under the narrower test, public use means literal use by the public. Under this test, a taking must yield a facility physically accessible to some segment of the public. By contrast, the broader test requires only that the taking produce a public benefit or advantage. This test roughly equates public use with "public interest." Although courts have almost unanimously resolved this interpretive dispute in favor of the broader public interest view, the main point for present purposes is that both tests look to the ends of the taking, not whether eminent domain is an appropriate means to achieve those ends.

The distinction between ends and means clarifies several developments associated with the jurisprudence of public use. First, it helps explain the emergence of language of extreme judicial deference in the last thirty years. Given that courts have understood the public use doctrine to refer to the ends of government, the question naturally arises: which institution is better suited to determine permissible ends—the courts or the legislature? In a society committed to majoritarian rule, not surprisingly the answer has been the legislature.

Here, as elsewhere, the crisis in democratic theory generated by judicial opposition to the New Deal provided the critical event. As late as 1930 the Supreme Court still clung to the position that legislative declarations of public use were subject to de novo judicial review. After a change in Court personnel produced a fundamental shift in judicial attitudes, however, the Court did an abrupt about-face and implied that the public use determination is exclusively for the legislature. This reversal ultimately produced Justice Douglas's formulation in *Berman v. Parker:* "Subject to specific constitutional limitations, when the legislature has spoken, the public interest has been declared in terms well-nigh conclusive." [29] As long as courts regard the public use doctrine as a limitation upon permissible government ends, this extreme rhetoric of deference to legislative judgments will no doubt persist.

*   *   *

[T]he distinction between ends and means [also] helps to explain the Supreme Court's statements equating the public use doctrine with the police power. The association originated with Justice Douglas's opinion in *Berman.* Deciding a public use challenge to a Washington, D.C., urban renewal project, Justice Douglas wrote, "We deal . . . with what traditionally has been known as the police power." In recent decisions, including [*Hawaii Housing Authority v.*] *Midkiff,* the Supreme Court has reiterated this theme, declaring that "the 'public use' requirement of the Taking Clause is 'coterminous with the scope of a sovereign's police powers.' " [35] This pronouncement has dismayed

29. 348 U.S. 26, 32 (1954).

35. Ruckelshaus v. Monsanto Co., 467 U.S. 986, 1014 (1984) (quoting [Hawaii Housing Authority v. Midkiff, 467 U.S. 229, 240 (1984)]).

commentators because the outer limit of the police power has traditionally marked the line between *noncompensable* regulation and compensable takings of property, not the line between compensable takings and the area where the constitution bars government from engaging in any sort of exchange whatever. Legitimately exercised, the police power requires no compensation. Thus, if public use is truly coterminous with the police power, a state could freely choose between compensation and noncompensation any time its actions served a "public use." This approach would seemingly overrule the entire takings doctrine in a single stroke.

The illogic of the Court's statements disappears, however, once one recognizes that the police power, like eminent domain, can also refer to the question of proper governmental ends, rather than means. This is clearly what Justice Douglas meant in *Berman* when he said that the police power "is essentially the product of legislative determinations addressed to the purposes of government, purposes neither abstractly nor historically capable of complete definition." He was not saying that government could freely employ any means of achieving slum clearance, and with it choose either compensation or noncompensation. Instead, he was saying that slum clearance is a permissible end of government. The Court's recent decisions echo this notion. "Police power" is here synonymous with the extent to which government may constitutionally regulate private activity. It defines those issues with which government may properly concern itself. The Court's statements again indicate that the permissible ends principle cuts across all means of resource acquisition, and that one should, for the sake of analytical clarity, keep questions of ends and means distinct.

The most important insight to be gained from the distinction between ends and means, however, is that the public use limitation might be recast or reinterpreted to perform a different role. Rather than concerning itself with government ends, the public use limitation might serve to restrict a legislature's choice of means. I am not suggesting that it is somehow wrong, as a matter of first principles, to inquire about the ends to which government will put condemned property. Rather, the point is that the American judiciary is unlikely soon to assume the task of closely scrutinizing legislative judgments about the legitimate ends of government. Given also that the choice of means question is an analytically distinct and important inquiry, it is worth asking whether the public use limitation can be reformulated as a choice of means doctrine, and if so, whether the judiciary should have a role in reviewing the exercise of eminent domain from this perspective.

* * *

EMINENT DOMAIN AS A MEANS: AN ECONOMIC APPROACH

The literature addressing the public use issue from an economic perspective suggests three possible analytical models. I will briefly consider the first two, only to set them aside in favor of the third.

Elements of the first two, however, ultimately reappear, "through the back door" as it were, under my "refined" version of the third approach.

The first economic model of public use, endorsed by Frank Michelman,[43] involves a straightforward comparison of costs and benefits. This model would have a court calculate all costs associated with an exercise of eminent domain, including the costs of compensation, and compare them with the taking's expected benefits. If the benefits exceed the costs, the court would deem the taking to serve public use; conversely, if the costs exceed the benefits, it would deem the taking to serve an unconstitutional private use.

The cost-benefit model of public use raises several problems. The first relates to measurement. How can courts accurately measure a taking's projected benefits, many of which will be intangible and speculative? A second problem involves the question of proper institutional roles. Presumably, the legislature has concluded that a taking's benefits exceed its costs. Are courts somehow better suited to make such a determination? Finally, the most telling problem, from this article's perspective, is that the cost-benefit calculus demands an inquiry into the ends of the taking rather than the choice of means. The cost-benefit approach explicitly adopts wealth maximization as the proper end, or at least one proper end, of government. Once again, I do not argue that the cost-benefit model is necessarily wrong. The problem is simply that the American judiciary, for reasons related to democratic theory, is not presently inclined to enforce directly any conception of limited government ends.

A second economic model of public use, recently advocated by Richard Epstein,[44] involves the public goods concept. Public goods, in their pure form, possess two properties: jointness in supply and impossibility of exclusion.[45] In particular, because of the latter attribute, the market generates fewer public goods than generally thought desirable. Hence, theorists have long viewed public goods as an appropriate object of governmental action. Under the public goods model, a court would ask whether an exercise of eminent domain is designed to procure a public good. If so, the court would deem the taking to serve a public use; if not, the court would deem the exercise an unconstitutional taking for a private use.

As with the cost-benefit approach, the public goods model presents several difficulties. First, a definitional problem: there are very few "pure" public goods—goods of a kind that consumption by one does not

43. Michelman, [*Property, Utility, and Fairness: Comments on the Ethical Foundations of "Just Compensation" Law,* 80 Harv.L.Rev. 1165, 1241 (1967).]

44. R. Epstein, [Takings: Private Property and the Power of Eminent Domain 166–169 (1985).]

45. * * * Jointness in supply means that consumption by one person does not diminish or otherwise affect consumption by others. Impossibility of exclusion means that once the good is supplied, no one can be prevented from consuming it. Classic examples of public goods are national defense and environmental controls.

diminish in some measure consumption by others. With most goods, consumption by one necessarily excludes, at least partially, consumption by someone else. Moreover, one can say that any activity that generates positive externalities—keeping one's lawn mowed, for example—shares the quality of public goods. Thus, the public goods analysis can be either very restrictive or very broad, depending on how the term is defined. Again, however, the main failing of the public goods model, at least for present purposes, is that it directs attention to ends rather than means. It asks whether government will use acquired property to provide a public good, not whether nonconsensual means are necessary to acquire the property.

The third economic model of public use derives from the property rule/liability rule distinction introduced by Calabresi and Melamed. From this perspective, eminent domain provides a mechanism that allows government to convert property rules into liability rules. This model presumes that property rules work well where low transaction costs make consensual exchange of resources practical. Liability rules, on the other hand, are necessary where high transaction costs render consensual exchange difficult. Applied to eminent domain, this analysis suggests that where a functioning market for a resource exists, the public use doctrine should require that government use that market. In contrast, where barriers to market exchange render such acquisition problematic, the doctrine should permit government to use its power of eminent domain. Importantly, the property rule/liability rule model of public use has the virtue of addressing eminent domain as a means. The distinction focuses on the conditions of the market in which property is acquired, not on its postacquisition use.

In the remainder of this section, I use the property rule/liability rule distinction to develop a basic model of the role of courts in determining eminent domain's proper scope. I then qualify the basic model in light of three persuasive economic objections. Taken together, these qualifications yield what I call the refined economic model of the judicial role in public use cases.

A. The Basic Model

The purpose of eminent domain is analogous to that of other liability rules, in that eminent domain applies where market exchange, if not impossible to achieve, is nevertheless subject to imperfections. To illustrate the point, consider the most common situation in which we see the exercise of eminent domain: a public or private project requiring the assembly of numerous parcels of land. Suppose, for example, that an oil refining company wants to construct an underground pipeline to transport crude oil from a producing field to a refinery several hundred miles away. Suppose further that only one feasible pipeline route exists. Without an exercise of eminent domain, the company must obtain an easement from each of hundreds of contiguous property owners. Each owner would have the power to hold out, should he choose to exercise it. If even a few owners held out, others might do the same. In this way, assembly of the needed parcels could become prohibitively expensive; in the end, the costs might well exceed the project's potential gains.

* * *

The oil pipeline hypothetical illustrates the potential for rent seeking.[b] The opportunity cost of any one landowner's interest is near zero.[54] But when this interest combines with other similar interests to form a right of way for a pipeline, its potential value becomes considerable. The difference between these two sums—the property's negligible opportunity cost and its value as part of the pipeline project represents a potential economic rent to the seller.

Assembly projects, however, do not exhaust a seller's rent-seeking opportunities. For example, rent seeking can occur when a buyer wants access to land that he already owns, but which is surrounded by the seller's land. It can also arise when a buyer needs to expand an existing site by acquiring adjacent land; when the buyer will lose undepreciated improvements if he does not acquire certain property from the seller; or when the seller owns property uniquely suited for some undertaking by the buyer, such as promontory for a lighthouse or a narrows for a bridge. I will hereinafter refer to any situation where a seller can extract economic rents from a buyer as a "thin market." Conversely, I will call any situation where market conditions do not allow a seller to extract economic rents from a buyer a "thick market."

Whatever a thin market's source, its potential for engendering rent seeking may make it economically efficient to confer the power of eminent domain on a buyer. On the one hand, we know that eminent domain would transfer the resource to a higher-valued use, because its value in the new use exceeds its value in every existing possible use (its opportunity cost); otherwise the seller could not extract an economic rent. On the other hand, if this transaction were left to the market, monopoly pricing (or strategic bargaining) could lead to a suboptimal quantity of the resource being acquired, or could even prevent the transaction from taking place at all.

Before completing discussion of the basic model, however, we must consider another important factor. So far we have focused exclusively on what might broadly be termed the transaction costs of market exchange. But we must also consider the administrative costs of eminent domain, and compare these costs with the costs of market exchange in either thick or thin market settings.

* * *

b. A seller gets economic rents when she is able to charge a price higher than her property's opportunity cost. This may happen in the oil pipeline case because each property owner is a monopolist who controls a resource needed to complete the project.

54. Each individual property interest—the right to use a small underground tunnel—almost certainly has little or no market value if offered for sale for any other use.

Given what might collectively be called the "due process" costs of eminent domain—obtaining legislative authority, drafting and filing the complaint, serving process, securing a formal appraisal, the possibility of a trial and appeal, and so forth—it is safe to conclude that, in a thick market setting, eminent domain is a more expensive way of acquiring resources than market exchange. This conclusion has important implications for the basic model. In effect, it means that the decision whether to use eminent domain should be, from an economic perspective, self-regulating. In thick markets, where the model initially suggests that eminent domain is inappropriate, the acquiring party should in fact utilize market exchange because eminent domain would consume more resources. Conversely, in thin market settings, where the model suggests that it is appropriate to use eminent domain, the acquiring party should in fact use eminent domain, so long as the administrative costs are less than the costs of market exchange.

* * *

If, as the basic model suggests, the decision to use the power of eminent domain is essentially self-regulating, this holds important implications for judicial review of public use issues. Most obviously, there would seem to be little point in courts second-guessing legislative and executive determinations of public use.   * * *

B.   The Refined Model

Despite the basic model's appealing simplicity, with its thick market/thin market distinction and its modest conception of the judicial role, the model raises a number of troubling economic and noneconomic questions. To avoid unduly complicating the argument, I will discuss only the economic objections.

[Merrill goes on to describe several situations where the self-regulating character of eminent domain breaks down and where courts should consequently review decisions to condemn more carefully. One is the case where the condemnee suffers large subjective losses. (She has a sentimental attachment to the property or has modified it to accommodate her unique needs.) Because these are not compensated through an award of fair market value, the government will be tempted to eschew purchase in favor of eminent domain. A second is the case where a few private parties capture the political process and employ eminent domain for their own gain. Stricter application of the public use test in these cases (a tilt toward a "property" rather than a "liability" standard) would offer greater protection to condemnees.]

BIBLIOGRAPHY

In General

B. Ackerman, PRIVATE PROPERTY AND THE CONSTITUTION (1977).

Berger, *A Policy Analysis of the Taking Problem,* 49 N.Y.U.L.Rev. 165 (1974).

F. Bosselman, D. Callies, & J. Banta, THE TAKING ISSUE: AN ANALYSIS OF THE CONSTITUTIONAL LIMITS OF LAND USE CONTROL (1973).

Dunham, *Griggs v. Allegheny County in Perspective: Thirty Years of Supreme Court Expropriation Law,* 1962 Sup.Ct.Rev. 63.

R. Epstein, TAKINGS: PRIVATE PROPERTY AND THE LAW OF EMINENT DOMAIN (1985).

Grey, *The Malthusian Constitution,* 41 U. Miami L.Rev. 21 (1986).

Levmore, *Just Compensation and Just Politics,* 22 Conn.L.Rev. 285 (1990).

J. Pennock & J. Chapman, NOMOS XXII: PROPERTY (1980).

Peterson, *The Takings Clause: In Search of Underlying Principles, Part I,* 77 Calif.L.Rev. 1299 (1989); *Part II,* 78 Calif.L.Rev. 53 (1990).

Symposium, *The Jurisprudence of Takings,* 88 Colum.L.Rev. 1581 (1988).

What Is Property

Baker, *Property and Its Relation to Constitutionally Protected Liberty,* 134 U.Pa.L.Rev. 741 (1986).

Demsetz, *Toward A Theory of Property Rights,* 57 Am.Econ.Rev. 347 (1967).

Note, *The Origins and Original Significance of the Just Compensation Clause of the Fifth Amendment,* 94 Yale L.J. 694 (1985).

Radin, *Property and "Personhood",* 34 Stan.L.Rev. 957 (1982).

The Taking/Regulation Distinction

Krier, *The Regulation Machine,* 1 Sup.Ct.Econ.Rev. 1 (1982).

Mandelker, *Investment–Backed Expectations: Is There a Taking?,* 31 Wash.U.J.Urb. & Contemp.L. 3 (1987).

Sax, *Takings, Private Property and Public Rights,* 81 Yale L.J. 149 (1971).

Symposium, *Constitutional Issues in Land Use Regulation,* 8 Hastings Const.L.Q. 449 (1981).

Public Use

Berger, *The Public Use Requirement in Eminent Domain,* 57 Or.L.Rev. 203 (1978).

Comment, *The Public Use Limitation on Eminent Domain: An Advance Requiem,* 58 Yale L.J. 599 (1949).

Just Compensation

Blume & Rubinfeld, *Compensation for Takings: An Economic Analysis,* 72 Calif.L.Rev. 569 (1984).

Costonis, *"Fair" Compensation and the Accommodation Power: Antidotes for the Taking Impasse in Land Use Controversies,* 75 Colum. L.Rev. 1021 (1975).

Kaplow, *An Economic Analysis of Legal Transitions,* 99 Harv.L.Rev. 509 (1986).

R. Posner, ECONOMIC ANALYSIS OF LAW § 3.6 (1986).

Williams, Smith, Siemon, Mandelker & Babcock, *The White River Junction Manifesto,* 9 Vt.L.Rev. 193 (1984).

B. PROPERTY AND DUE PROCESS

The Fifth and Fourteenth Amendments provide that no person shall be deprived of "life, liberty, or property, without due process." Under current doctrine, application of the Due Process Clause requires a two-step analysis. First a court must determine whether the interest being denied or impinged upon constitutes "life," "liberty," or "property" within the meaning of the Due Process Clause. If it does, the court then must determine what process the individual is entitled to.[1]

Common usage tells us much about the meaning of "property." Certainly an individual's home, land, or television set ought to constitute "property" for due process purposes. But the Supreme Court has recognized that "the property interests protected by procedural due process extend well beyond actual ownership of real estate, chattels or money."[2] Influenced by Charles Reich's classic article *The New Property,*[3] the Court has defined "property" to include "entitlements" such as government benefits and public employment.

The extension of due process protections to the deprivation of entitlements demolished the so-called "right/privilege distinction" which had characterized public benefits as "gratuities" that could be conditioned as the sovereign saw fit. Following the Supreme Court's lead in *Goldberg v. Kelly*[4] and *Board of Regents v. Roth,* courts found the Due Process Clause applicable to the termination or denial of a wide range of government benefits and jobs.

But lurking within entitlement theory is a "positivist trap."[5] Since, as the Court stated in *Roth,* property interests "are created and their dimensions are defined by existing rules or understandings that stem from an independent source such as state law,"[6] the government can virtually nullify due process protection by defining benefits and jobs in ways that don't create entitlements. For example, if a state makes contracts that can be terminated at will, a court could conclude

---

1. To determine this, the courts use a balancing test formulated in Mathews v. Eldridge, 424 U.S. 319, 96 S.Ct. 893, 47 L.Ed.2d 18 (1976).

2. Board of Regents v. Roth, 408 U.S. 564, 572, 92 S.Ct. 2701, 2706, 33 L.Ed.2d 548 (1972).

3. 73 Yale L.J. 733 (1964).

4. 397 U.S. 254, 90 S.Ct. 1011, 25 L.Ed. 2d 287 (1970).

5. See Mashaw, *Administrative Due Process: The Quest for a Dignitary Theory,* 61 B.U.L.Rev. 885, 888–93 (1981).

6. 408 U.S. at 577, 92 S.Ct. at 2709.

that the employee with whom it has contracted has no entitlement to continuation in the job. Similarly, it can be argued that the "property interest" created by state statute ought to be deemed to include the procedures provided by the state for the interest's vindication. This is the "bitter with the sweet" analysis pressed by Justice Rehnquist in *Arnett v. Kennedy*.[7]

In *Cleveland Board of Education v. Loudermill*,[8] the Court refused to be caught in the "positivist trap." It announced that under due process analysis "[t]he categories of substance and procedure are distinct. Were the rule otherwise, the [Due Process] Clause would be reduced to a mere tautology. 'Property' cannot be defined by the procedures provided for its deprivation any more than can life or liberty." While *Loudermill* firmly rejects the "bitter with the sweet" approach, it does so more by assertion than argument. This Section explores the implications of entitlement theory. Frank Easterbrook asserts that the process/substance distinction adopted by the Court in due process cases cannot be sustained. Accordingly, "[a] court that protects the legislative power to define substantive entitlements ought to give it control of process as well."

Rodney Smolla disagrees. While he concedes that the Court's definition of "property" has, in effect, reintroduced the rights/privilege distinction in due process analysis, he suggests that a way out of the positivist trap would be to require that conditions placed on government largess pass a "minimum rationality test"—even if the legislature has attempted to create a program without procedural protections.

Assuming we can identify a "property interest" that triggers application of the Due Process Clause, the next question is what process is due. Jerry Mashaw offers a critique of the prevailing approach announced by the Court in *Mathews v. Eldridge*.

FRANK H. EASTERBROOK, SUBSTANCE AND DUE PROCESS

1982 Sup.Ct.Rev. 85, 85–90, 109–119.

The Supreme Court keeps saying that it is entitled under the Due Process Clause of the Constitution to determine what process is "due" when governmental action affects a liberty or property interest. Although the Court gives legislatures the utmost deference in specifying the particulars of a substantive right, it retains the privilege of determining what procedures must be used to evaluate claims of entitlement arising under the substantive rule.

I propose to examine the rationale of the peculiar constitutional dichotomy between substance and process in cases in which legislatures are given free rein in defining substance. It is peculiar, not only because there is no immediately apparent warrant for the distinction in

---

7. 416 U.S. 134, 148–58, 94 S.Ct. 1633, 1641–46, 40 L.Ed.2d 15 (1974) (Rehnquist, J., dissenting).

8. 470 U.S. 532, 105 S.Ct. 1487, 84 L.Ed. 2d 494 (1985).

the structure or history of the Constitution, but also because substance and process are two aspects of the same phenomenon. The process a legislature describes for vindicating the entitlements that it creates is a way of indicating how effective its plan should be. The more process it affords, the more the legislature values the entitlements and thus is willing to sacrifice to avoid mistakes. A court that protects the legislative power to define substantive entitlements ought to give it control of process as well.

I. INTRODUCTION: THE SUBSTANCE–PROCESS DICHOTOMY

* * *

Under *Logan v. Zimmerman Brush Co.*,[a] *Arnett v. Kennedy*,[b] and *Vitek v. Jones*,[c] due process analysis is a two-step routine. First the Court determines whether by statute or regulation the State has created an entitlement ("liberty or property") the existence or extent of which turns on some determinable facts. It also is enough that there is an antecedent interest in personal liberty, one the government may not extinguish except for cause. * * * Many cases stop here with a finding that the claim involves neither liberty nor property. If nothing turns on determinable facts, there is no need for a hearing, because the state's officer need not pay attention to the claimant's demands; the state may do what it pleases. A claimant turned away without either hearing or substance has lost nothing to which his claim was better than anyone else's.

Except in the case [where there is an antecedent interest in personal] liberty (or the rare case in which the Court finds the substantive rules unconstitutional), the definition of the entitlement is a question wholly within the power of the political branches to answer. Any political unit dissatisfied with the Court's resolution of entitlement questions may amend its statutes or regulations so that the decision no longer is controlled by determinable facts. No entitlement, no process. And the Supreme Court reviews substantive law under the most lenient standards. Legislation affecting economic interests, and most other interests as well, will be sustained as long as the Court can conceive of a set of facts under which the legislation would be rational.[10] If, however, the constitution, statute, or regulation creates a liberty or property interest, then the second step—determining "what process is due"—comes into play. At this step the legislative disposition gets some, but not very much, deference.

The most important of the recent cases in this line is *Mathews v. Eldridge*.[11] The Court explained that [12]

> identification of the specific dictates of due process generally requires consideration of three distinct factors: First, the private interest that

a. 455 U.S. 422 (1982).

b. 416 U.S. 134 (1974).

c. 455 U.S. 480 (1980).

10. Schweiker v. Hogan, 102 S.Ct. 2597 (1982); Railroad Retirement Board v. Fritz,

449 U.S. 166 (1980); Vance v. Bradley, 440 U.S. 93 (1979); Usery v. Turner Elkhorn Mining Co., 428 U.S. 1 (1976). * * *

11. 424 U.S. 319 (1976).

12. *Id.* at 335.

will be affected by the official action; second, the risk of an erroneous deprivation of such interest through the procedures used, and the probable value, if any, of additional or substitute procedural safeguards; and finally, the Government's interest, including the function involved and the fiscal or administrative burdens that the additional or substitute procedural requirement would entail.

The Court made it clear that it would conduct the balancing itself, assigning its own weights and assessing the probabilities and interests. To be sure, it would listen to the legislature's views on these subjects, embodied in the statutes, with interest and respect, but with no need to accept the views as binding.

In cases since *Eldridge* the Court has conducted an essentially unrestrained interest balancing. In two cases it has held that judicial damages remedies for administrative error were sufficient process,[13] but in the others it has insisted on hearings, more or less elaborate, as part of an administrative procedure. The administrative procedure itself must afford an opportunity for a hearing "at a meaningful time and in a meaningful manner," [14] which sometimes varies with the identity of the affected party and the nature of his problem.[15]

* * *

The Court approaches its due process question much as an ideal legislature would, asking statute by statute, and sometimes case by case, what is the optimal amount of process. The Court does not treat substantive entitlements in anything like that manner.

* * *

III. Modern Justifications of the Substance–Process Dichotomy

There are two modern justifications of the substance-process dichotomy, one that the Court offers for its decisions and one that scholars offer. The Court's justification is largely instrumental, the scholars' justification largely noninstrumental.

A. *The Instrumental Justification*

The Court's justification for specifying process once the statute has specified substance is that "any other conclusion would allow the State to destroy at will virtually any state-created property interest." [80] This would be a good argument if the Court could explain why a state may

---

13. Ingraham v. Wright, 430 U.S. 651 (1977); Parratt v. Taylor, 451 U.S. 527 (1981).

14. Armstrong v. Manzo, 380 U.S. 545, 552 (1965), a question-begging formula quoted most recently in Logan v. Zimmerman Brush Co., 455 U.S. 422, 437 (1982).

15. Lassiter v. Department of Social Services, 452 U.S. 18 (1981) (due process entitlement to counsel in parental rights termination matters must be evaluated case by case); Greene v. Lindsey, 102 S.Ct.

1874, 1879 (1982) (in circumstances of a particular case, notice of eviction by posting on a tenant's door is unconstitutional). More commonly, however, "procedural due process rules are shaped by the risk of error inherent in the truthfinding process as applied to the generality of cases, not the rare exceptions." Mathews v. Eldridge, 424 U.S. 319, 344 (1976). * * *

80. Logan v. Zimmerman Brush Co., 455 U.S. 422, 432 (1982).

not destroy the interests it creates, at least prospectively. But the Court has never so argued. Under the Court's decisions legislatures are free to enact precatory statutes, statutes that contain no rules of decision, retroactive statutes, statutes that lack any methods of enforcement, statutes creating absolute immunities, and otherwise to have vacuous "entitlements." To use some invented numbers, If states may elect ten percent reliability in enforcement (the amount of adherence to a precatory statute), why can they not elect ninety percent (the amount obtainable from rudimentary procedures)? Why, in other words, is the expedient of enfeebling a statutory entitlement by providing "deficient" procedures out of bounds? The Court's cases contain no answers to this question because they are not consistent. There is no single view that could be respected in the name of stare decisis.

To the extent the Court supplies any explanation, it lies in the formula from the *Eldridge* decision. The formula exalts instrumental objectives. The goal of due process is to hold as low as possible the sum of two costs: the costs created by erroneous decisions, including false positives and false negatives, and the costs of administering the procedures. Holding this sum to a minimum maximizes society's wealth, and the gains may be shared among all affected persons. This, however, produces a puzzle. If the goal of the *Eldridge* formula is the maximization of society's wealth, why did the legislature not enact the preferable procedures in the first place? The legislative and executive branches have access to information about the costs and error rates produced by particular procedures. They are well aware that the accuracy of decisions may be improved by adopting more elaborate procedures. That they choose not to use these procedures is strong evidence that their costs outweigh their benefits.

Some might object that the legislative and executive branches do not make impartial decisions in this respect—that is, they are not well-motivated. Given interest group politics, their choices about the types of procedures to employ in decisions might be the result of political compromise rather than any desire to maximize society's well-being. This surely is true for many, perhaps most, statutes, but so what? The observation is equally true for substantive rules. The statute books are full of rules having little purpose other than to transfer wealth from one group to another. The regulation of taxicabs and the subsidy to tobacco farmers and northeast railroads are the rule, not the exception. Even statutes with some essential purpose other than wealth transfers will be influenced in some fashion by interest group politics.

The role of interest groups does not make legislators ill-motivated in a constitutional sense. It does not involve race, sex, or another forbidden ground of decision. Interest group statutes are upheld all the time, on the flimsiest of pretexts. And if the Constitution permits interest group politics to sway decisions and influence the goals of legislation, what principled objection can there be to legislators' achieving part of the preference for an interest group through choice of procedural rules? (One answer, that procedural rules are less visible, will not do; there are lots of poorly perceived substantive rules.)

This discussion overstates the importance of interest group politics in the choice of procedures. Even when the statute affects "weak" groups, there is little reason to think that the procedural rules will be selected on the basis of some animus against those groups that distorts the legislature's ability to make choices that enhance social well-being. Welfare benefits provide an example. Poor people have shown sufficient political power to obtain a welfare system. We know from the existence of the benefits that they have overcome whatever reticence or hostility exists, and they have obtained transfers in their favor. If they (and their altruistic allies) use their power to obtain $X in money transfers and no elaborate procedures, why should anyone be entitled to complain? A claimant disappointed at the outcome of his own application would have a legitimate gripe only if due process created a personal right not to be the victim of a mistake. But the Court's recent cases are clear that due process does not create any personal right to escape the consequences of blunders. The *Eldridge* criteria focus on the welfare of the statutory beneficiaries as a group, and the Court treats errors in individual cases as a cost but not as an independent violation of the guarantee.

* * *

Substance and process are intimately related. The procedures one uses determine how much substance is achieved, and by whom. Procedural rules usually are just a measure of how much the substantive entitlements are worth, of what we are willing to sacrifice to see a given goal attained. The body that creates a substantive rule is the logical judge of how much should be spent to avoid errors in the process of disposing of claims to that right. The substantive rule itself is best seen as a promised benefit coupled with a promised rate of mistake: the legislature sets up an $X\%$ probability that a person will receive a certain boon. The Court cannot logically be reticent about revising the substantive rules but unabashed about rewriting the procedures to be followed in administering those rules. * * *

All of this means that the Court's due process cases are incoherent unless the Court has its own view of substance. The Court must be devising procedures that vindicate the Justices' views of the relative importance of different substantive entitlements, rather than legislators' views. Substantive and procedural due process turn out not to be so different. Yet the Justices leave loopholes for legislators: by abolishing private remedies or substantive standards altogether, they may escape the implications of the Justices' substantive preferences.

B. The Noninstrumental Justifications

Scholars have suggested noninstrumental justifications for the Court's decisions. They suggest that process may be valuable in itself, and not for the benefits it bestows indirectly. There are two lines of noninstrumental justification, dignitary justifications and governmental structure justifications.

1. *Dignity.* Several have argued that process is valuable in itself because it treats each person as an equal, entitled to respect and autonomy, rather than as an object.[91] Such dignitary considerations are exceptionally important to many people. Nonetheless, an argument about the value of process for its own sake is not substantially different from an argument about the value of property, another kind of personal interest. Property in law is the right, within defined limits, to dominion over things and therefore to structure one's relation with others. Without property there is no autonomy and little dignity; property is thus an aspect of personal liberty. Yet the Court permits the legislature the broadest possible scope in the regulation of property and, derivatively, of dignity. The argument linking due process with dignity thus carries no force unless its proponent can show why the Constitution removes decisions about the appropriate level of dignity from the legislature only when claims to hearings are involved but otherwise allows the legislature full control.

* * *

[Neither historical analysis nor stare decisis supports the dignitary analysis.] All that is left * * * is a play on the analysis of *Carolene Products.*[96] It may be possible to depict dignitary considerations as fundamental values slighted by majoritarian processes. * * * [But] [t]here is simply no reason to suppose that process values are slighted by legislatures.

There is no logical reason why legislatures would underestimate the value of process. Process and substance are of a piece. Legislators frequently are lawyers or other specialists in process, not quick to forget their training (or the interests of their friends, also process providers). Process is not historically disfavored. Statutes overflow with process, sometimes to the point of choking the ability of executives to act. Consider for a moment the difficulty a supervisor faces in firing a secretary under the civil service laws. And there is no apparent relationship between the amount of process provided by law and the favor (or disfavor) legislators show for the affected people. Murderers are not an especially favored class, yet statutes provided elaborate procedural protections for murder cases long before the Court entered the due process fray. It can take a decade or more to deport an illegal alien, all because of procedural rules, created by statute, exceeding constitutional requirements. On the other hand, summary procedures

---

91. *E.g.,* L. Tribe, [American Constitutional Law 538–41 (1978)]; Laycock, [*Due Process and Separation of Powers: The Effort to Make the Due Process Clause Nonjusticiable,* 60 Tex. L.Rev. 875 (1982)]; Mashaw, [*Administrative Due Process: The Quest for a Dignitary Theory,* 61 B.U.L. Rev. 885 (1981)]; Michelman, [*Formal and*

Associational Aims in Procedural Due Process, in NOMOS XVIII: Due Process 126 (J.R. Pennock & J. Chapman eds. 1977)].

* * *

96. United States v. Carolene Products Co., 304 U.S. 144, 152–53 n. 4 (1938).

under the Social Security Act principally affect lifetime wage earners, not the poor.

Hearings for claimants are a form of in-kind benefit. It is a commonplace observation that in-kind benefits (including food, housing, and other nonmoney transfers, as well as hearings) are worth less to the recipients than it costs society to provide them. Some of the difference between the cost of the benefits and their value to the recipients is simply lost to society; some of the difference is captured by those who render the benefits. It is not irrational for those affected by a program to spurn elaborate hearings and demand more concrete benefits instead. They may prefer money, which can be turned into other things, to dignity, which cannot be. The important consideration is that if people potentially eligible under the substantive terms of a statute value hearings at more than the cost of providing them, they will clamor for hearings even at the cost of lower money benefits. The contents of the legislation are the best available evidence about the value the affected people place on hearings. Surely it should come as no surprise that the usual proponents of hearings in welfare cases are middle- and upper-class lawyers, professors, and judges—the class from which bureaucrats, administrative law judges, and other process providers come.

2. *Governmental structure.* Professors Stewart and Sunstein have identified another constellation of functions served by hearings.[99] Judicial insistence on procedures might, for example, compel Congress to be more candid in identifying all dimensions of the entitlements it creates, or to deliver on its promises, or to reduce the extent of delegation to agencies. In other words, it would promote the Rule of Law, in which determinate standards rather than potentially capricious bureaucrats establish entitlements. Although these functions have instrumental overtones—less delegation might be thought "better" legislation—they are usually seen as valuable in themselves.

These are weak arguments, as Stewart and Sunstein concede. The objective of "honest" legislation is more threatened by precatory laws, by "rights" without remedies, than by deficient procedures. The objection to delegation is much more forceful when the legislature passes statutes containing no substantive rules than when it enacts rules but does not provide for particularly accurate administration. These laws most subject their beneficiaries to the whims of ill-motivated bureaucrats.

The Stewart and Sunstein arguments sound odd as matters of due process. Governmental structure for the federal branches was settled by Articles I and II, not by the Bill of Rights. The nondelegation doctrine is a name without a doctrine. Improperly motivated decisions are controlled by doctrines other than due process. There is no general

---

99. Stewart & Sunstein, *Public Programs and Private Rights,* 95 Harv.L.Rev. 1193, 1258–63 (1982).

rule that Congress must legislate so clearly that people with grade school educations can follow; if it wants to use roundabout methods of stating its purpose, so be it. And states may delegate as they please; administrative agencies or judges may enact state laws.

Stewart and Sunstein maintain that the Court's control over process is justified only when (*a*) necessary to force Congress to make a clear statement of its aims or (*b*) necessary to enforce favored substantive rights, among which they would include welfare. Part *a* of the test is unsupportable for state governments, and even for Congress it puts the Court in the position of holding a very clear law (say, one providing that there shall be no process for firing a federal employee) unconstitutional because Congress has not been clear enough in its total package. A rule of this sort, unjustified by history or precedent, also gives the Court almost unlimited power. Any law, taken in its entirety, is unclear in some respect. Part *b* of the test, however, just returns us to a proposition presented several times before: there is not much difference between substance and process, and therefore the Court's substance-process dichotomy is unsupportable.

RODNEY A. SMOLLA, THE REEMERGENCE OF THE RIGHT–PRIVILEGE DISTINCTION IN CONSTITUTIONAL LAW: THE PRICE OF PROTESTING TOO MUCH

35 Stan.L.Rev. 69, 69–82, 102, 105–20 (1982).

The "right-privilege" distinction is a constitutional doctrine that scholars and Supreme Court opinions have long been declaring dead. Like the prematurely rumored death of Mark Twain, however, reports of the demise of the privilege doctrine have been greatly exaggerated. Since the nineteenth century, the doctrine has shown an uncanny ability to reconstitute itself in spite of the best efforts of scholars and jurists to bury it. In the last decade it has reemerged in the procedural due process area under the guise of "entitlement" theory to become one of the dominant themes of the Burger Court.

The Burger Court has applied the entitlement concept with increasing rigidity, thereby substantially circumscribing the range of interests to which constitutional due process safeguards apply. As the Court has stepped up the Draconian efficiency of entitlement theory, it has borrowed heavily from both the formal method and the underlying values that have historically sustained the privilege doctrine. At the same time, however, the Court has steadfastly clung to the fiction that the privilege doctrine has been fully and finally repudiated. The almost schizophrenic tendency of the Court to simultaneously disclaim the doctrine by name and resort to the concept in practice exists against a backdrop of almost universal scholarly hostility toward both the privilege and entitlement doctrines. Seldom have the Court and academe so completely talked past each other.

* * *

I. THE RIGHT–PRIVILEGE DISTINCTION

The privilege doctrine is grounded in a dichotomy between "rights" (interests enjoyed "as a matter of right") and mere "privileges" (interests created by the grace of the state and dependent for their existence on the state's sufferance). Privileges can be primarily economic interests, such as public jobs, welfare benefits, or licenses, or primarily noneconomic interests, such as early release from imprisonment through pardon or parole, or permission for an alien to enter the country. According to the doctrine, governmentally created "privileges" may be initially given to recipients on the condition that they surrender or curtail the exercise of constitutional freedoms that they would otherwise enjoy. Further, those privileges may be denied to or withdrawn from recipients without affording them the procedural due process protections that would normally attach to the denial or the taking of "rights."

The entitlement doctrine is a specific application of the right-privilege concept in the context of procedural due process. The entitlement doctrine proceeds from literalist fidelity to the due process clauses of the fifth and fourteenth amendments, which guarantee due process of law only when an individual is deprived of "life, liberty or property." Individuals are entitled to this procedural protection only if they can demonstrate that a vested right or "entitlement" to an interest in "life," "liberty," or "property" is at stake. When the interest involved is state-created rather than preexisting—for example, when the interest is a welfare check or a pardon rather than personal property or the liberty of someone not in lawful custody—the individual is entitled to due process protection only if the state has made the interest a formally protected "entitlement." Such entitlements do not stem from the Constitution, but from nonconstitutional sources, such as statutes or contracts. Furthermore, under the most extreme form of entitlement theory, the nonconstitutional source of law that creates the interest may also determine what procedural protections surround the interest. This would mean that, in a fundamental sense, the procedures attached to interests in largess *are* the interests in largess, and that when a recipient accepts a public benefit he necessarily acquiesces in whatever level of procedural safeguards the legislature has built into the benefit.

In the earlier stages of the development of the entitlement doctrine, the Court avoided the forbidden terminology of "right" and "privilege." Ironically, in *Board of Regents v. Roth,*[13] one of the seminal cases in the development of the entitlement concept, the Court denounced the right-privilege doctrine as a "wooden distinction" that had been "fully and finally rejected."[14] In more recent cases, however, the Court has almost completely dropped all pretense of having abandoned the distinction. * * *

---

13. 408 U.S. 564 (1972).   **14.** *Id.* at 571.

The most basic rationale behind the privilege and entitlement doctrines is that a legal system must acknowledge a distinction between interests that are legally protected and interests that are not. Thus, Professor Kenneth Culp Davis argues that in one fundamental sense the distinction between entitlement and nonentitlement—the distinction between right and privilege—is implicit in the very existence of a legal system.[19]

A second theme underlying entitlement theory comes from the view that government largess is public charity. Just as the right-privilege distinction raised to constitutional dimension the almost homespun notion that the recipient of a gift must accept it with the strings that the giver has attached, the entitlement doctrine states that the recipient of a governmentally created interest must take the interest on the terms offered. One of those terms is the level of procedural protection that the government has decided to include as part of the entitlement "package."

A third major force behind the entitlement doctrine is the idea that a recipient of an interest in largess may contractually agree to accept limited procedural protection for the interest as part of the bargain out of which the interest is created. The contract analogy draws largely from the same values that favor freedom of contract in bargains between parties in the private sector. It finds additional support as far back as the assumption in social contract theory that rules implemented by consent are inherently less onerous than rules imposed by fiat.

A fourth underlying element, one that is a close corollary of the freedom of contract notion, is the idea that government should have greater latitude in its dealings with individuals when it acts as the proprietor of the public business rather than as the pandemic regulator. The proprietary-regulatory distinction, by assuming that restrictions are less necessary when government acts essentially as a private entity administering its internal business, frees government in that context from certain restrictions that would apply to it when it acts as a governing entity.

Clearly the strongest motive force behind entitlement theory, however, is deference to majoritarian sovereignty. In its most extreme form entitlement doctrine rejects the existence of a dichotomy between "substantive" and "procedural" aspects of an interest in largess. It is

19. "A legal system cannot exist without a distinction between a 'right' and 'no right'." 2 K. Davis, [Administrative Law Treatise § 11:4, at 350 (2d ed. 1979).] Yet notwithstanding the logic of this distinction, Davis argues that "[h]uman activities produce interests that ought not to be treated as 'rights' but that still may deserve some sort of legal protection in some circumstances." Id. § 11:4, at 350–51. The principle proposed by Davis is that whenever government officers "impose a grievous loss on any person, due process requires not less than whatever procedural protection is justified by a cost-benefit analysis." Id. at 399. Of course, at least for the time being, the Court has rejected "grievous loss" as a trigger for due process protection. See, e.g., Jago v. Van Curen, 102 S.Ct. 31, 33 (1981) ("we have previously reject[ed] . . . the notion that any grievous loss visited upon a person by the state is sufficient to invoke the procedural protection of the Due Process Clause") (emphasis in original).

possible to treat the creation of a welfare program or a parole system as purely political affairs, as matters of legislative choice beyond the pale of judicial review, while nonetheless arguing that minimum procedural integrity in the administration of those programs is a matter of constitutional right. Entitlement theory in its purest form repudiates that division, and proceeds instead on the assumption that the procedural accoutrements that accompany an interest in largess are among the defining characteristics of the interest itself. Under this theory the level of procedural protection that surrounds a government job, for example, is a political expression of the importance of the job to the body politic; as such it is as much a matter of legislative prerogative as the level of salary assigned to that class of job holder.

II. REEVALUATING THE EVOLUTION OF THE ENTITLEMENT DOCTRINE

A. The Right–Nonright Distinction

* * *

* * * The orthodox view is that *Goldberg* [*v. Kelly,*[33]] was the high water mark for procedural protection for interests in largess, and thus the paradigmatic example of properly applied unitary analysis. That orthodoxy similarly regards *Goldberg* as one of the critical cases in the Court's rejection of the privilege doctrine. Ironically, however, *Goldberg* presaged the development of the entitlement concept, and formed the evolutionary link between the right-privilege cases that preceded it and the entitlement cases that followed.

In *Goldberg,* the Court held that a welfare recipient must be afforded an evidentiary hearing prior to the termination of benefits. Justice Brennan, writing for the Court, confronted the right-privilege distinction with the oft-quoted statement that "[i]t may be realistic today to regard welfare entitlements as more like 'property' than a 'gratuity.' Much of the existing wealth in this country takes the form of rights that do not fall within traditional common-law concepts of property."[36] Although Justice Brennan ostensibly rejected the right-privilege distinction, in actuality he perpetuated the dichotomy that lay at the heart of the privilege doctrine by retaining the operative distinction between vested and nonvested interests.

Justice Brennan's comparison of welfare assistance to property was influenced by the work of Charles Reich. Reich's 1964 article, *The New Property,*[37] cited by Justice Brennan,[38] traced the emergence of public benefits as a major source of wealth in contemporary American society. Reich had argued that in light of the "vast, imperial scale" on which government spews forth its jobs, welfare assistance, services, contracts, franchises, and licenses, interests in those government-created sources of wealth should be protected by the same sorts of procedural safe-

---

33. 397 U.S. 254 (1970) [relocated footnote].

36. *Id.* at 262 n. 8.

37. Reich, *The New Property,* 73 Yale L.J. 733 (1964).

38. 397 U.S. at 262 n. 8.

guards that had always attached to more conventional forms of property.[39]

The "new property" concept provided a way of extending procedural due process protection to public employment, welfare assistance, contracts, and licenses, that would be consistent with the constitutional text. The right-privilege distinction would no longer work as the stock response for defeating claims for procedural protection in largess, because largess could now be included within the rubric of right rather than of privilege. Like one's home, car, or bank account, one's government job or welfare check could be labeled property, and with that label safely attached, procedural due process protection seemed secure.

In retrospect, after the years that have elapsed since the new property idea was first proposed, one can make the harsh judgment that *Goldberg,* by its use of the new property metaphor, unwittingly abetted the development of the entitlement doctrine. * * *

* * *

By resorting to the new property concept to generate increased procedural protection for public sector interests, the Court inevitably placed extreme definitional pressure on the term property. That pressure naturally bred preoccupation with distinguishing between interests that had vested and interests that had not. Reich himself spoke of the need for entitlements to be "vested." [54] The basic distinction between "right" and "privilege," if understood as connoting no more than a distinction between "right" and "nonright," is implicit in the term property; it is impossible to speak of property without conjuring up notions of ownership and dominion. In writing as a philosopher of welfare rather than as a legal technician, Reich wrote for the wrong audience; even the Warren Court was not willing to mechanistically transform principles of welfare philosophy into constitutional rules. Thus, in *Roth,* the Court began to tie due process analysis to notions of vested interests; it drew on the common law of property and contracts to define the interests that would qualify for the protection of the due process clause.

* * *

IV. LIMITATIONS ON ENTITLEMENT THEORY

There are indications that the Court is slowly moving toward limiting the harsher elements of entitlement thinking, even if it is not embracing any free-floating right to minimally fair procedures that transcend entitlements. While the Court probably always will permit governments the power to create jobs in which employees are terminable at will, it probably never will permit welfare administrators to terminate payments at their whim and pleasure or school superintendents to expel students without explanation—even if these practices are explicitly authorized by legislation. It is unlikely that there will ever be vigorous judicial scrutiny of all procedural standards for administer-

---

39. Reich, *supra* note 37, at 783–87.   **54.** Reich, *supra* note 37, at 785.

ing the public largess. But given the major competing values that exist in this sphere of constitutional law, some constraint on the excesses of entitlement theory is inevitable.

* * *

B. Equal Protection and Rationality

* * *

The rational basis standard under the equal protection test seems to require some "reason" in all government action. Government, the argument would go, has no interest in refusing to disclose its reasons for official action unless those reasons are impermissible. Although we talk about capricious action as if officials made decisions through random rolls of mental dice, the truth is that some reason, however spontaneous or ill-conceived, always exists. Since no public official ever really acts "for no reason," what we really mean when we talk of permitting officials to act for no reason is that they need not explain to anyone what their reasons are. As Justice Marshall stated in his *Roth* dissent, "it is not burdensome to give reasons when reasons exist. . . . It is only where the government acts improperly that procedural due process is truly burdensome." [141] Thus, under this argument, the only government "interest" served by allowing the state to fire employees at its "will and pleasure" is the preservation of license to act improperly.

The argument overstates the case, however, since the rational basis equal protection test has always been lenient enough to sustain certain administrative schemes that condone official silence. In certain situations the government may very well be able to articulate a rational basis for allowing administrative officials to exercise discretion without having to explain their actions. Despite initial appearances, unexplained and detrimental administrative actions may not violate the elemental equal protection injunction that persons similarly situated be similarly treated.

If, as far as they can be measured, the performances of two police officers are identical, the equal protection clause would seem to require that they receive identical treatment. If they are to receive different treatment, the burden should be on the government to explain why they are different. If the police chief is free to fire one and retain the other, and is obliged to tell the dismissed officer nothing more than "you're fired but I'm not going to tell you why," equal protection appears to be rendered illusory. Yet, in one sense the officers were treated alike—they were both given jobs in which the axe could fall unannounced and unexplained. It is not the administrative decision to act without explanation in any given case that must be defended with a legitimate state interest, but the systemic decision to allow certain administrators the license to act without explanation.

---

141. Board of Regents v. Roth, 408 U.S. at 591 (Marshall, J., dissenting).

C. Zimmerman Brush

[*Logan v. Zimmerman Brush Co.*,[a] indicates that the Court is moving towards a "rationality requirement." In that case, the Supreme Court of Illinois had held that Logan's employment discrimination complaint had to be dismissed because the Illinois Fair Employment Practices Commission had failed to hold a hearing within the 120–day period required by law (even though Logan had filed his claim in a timely manner). The U.S. Supreme Court reversed, holding that Illinois had deprived Logan of a property interest (the discrimination cause of action) without due process.]

* * *

The importance of *Zimmerman* * * * is that a majority of Justices recognized that regardless of whether or not the state had created a "property" interest—i.e., an "entitlement" that cannot be removed except "for cause"—the state's attempt to permit administrators to act *with or without cause* may sometimes be so devoid of rational justification that it violates equal protection. Under the Court's analysis, the very existence of some programs, in effect, creates "entitlements" triggering minimum procedural protection, even if the legislature has attempted to create the program without procedural protection. To be *internally* rational, certain government programs must by their mere existence be entitlement programs, and further, to be internally rational some entitlement programs must carry minimum procedural safeguards against the taint of official subjectivity.

D. The Contractual Element in Government–Created Largess

Under the Court's *Zimmerman Brush* analysis, the enjoyment of government largess cannot be conditioned upon the fulfillment of procedures that are devoid of a rational basis. But, one must be careful not to read *Zimmerman* too broadly, for it does *not* stand for the proposition that all legislative classifications vesting "will and pleasure" discretion in public officials are constitutionally irrational. The fledgling rights recognized in *Zimmerman* become pressed to their limits when the very meaning of the term "arbitrary" is made part of the debate * * *

Certainly this is dangerous business; a powerful government might, as Justice Sutherland once warned, compel the surrender of all constitutional rights by taking advantage of recipients in an economically or politically weak bargaining position.[163] But when the contractual relationship between the state and the individual is free of such coercive taint, there is no obvious injustice or arbitrariness in holding the individual bound by the *procedural* strings that were voluntarily accepted. Some rights may be inalienable in some situations, just as some bargains are illegal despite mutual and uncoerced assent; but as long as courts retain their normal power to police bargains and careful-

---

a. 455 U.S. 422 (1982).

163. *See* Frost v. Railroad Comm'n of California, 271 U.S. 583, 593–94 (1926).

ly scrutinize the contractual process, the lack of meaningful procedural recourse for an individual can surely be the legitimate object of an enforceable bargain. A government without strong procedural protection for public benefits is less civilized than it ought to be, but it is not unconstitutional.

* * *

E. Contractual Element as a Rational Basis

* * *

All conditions placed on government largess must meet the minimum rationality requirement of *Zimmerman Brush*. The contractual element in the receipt of government benefits is relevant to the analysis because it may itself provide the rational basis for a condition. For example, when the government shifts into its proprietary capacity, it must compete with the private sector for the same workers. These employees will decide whether to accept private sector or government jobs based on the relative benefits offered, including salary as well as procedural and substantive job security. If equal protection is construed to require that government employees receive certain procedural rights before their jobs are terminated, the government will have less money available to offer as salaries, and thus will be at a competitive disadvantage with private employers who can make the allocation between salaries and procedural protection according to the wishes of employees. Thus, competition in the job market provides a rational basis for government to create positions without procedural protection. Government employment at will is not unconscionable because free market competition can be trusted to give employees the leverage to extract from government whatever additional procedural guarantees the political and economic marketplace will bear. Since such conditions do not offend basic notions of fairness in contractual bargains when measured against even the most modern sensibilities of contract law, they should not be regarded as irrational for the purposes of the fourteenth amendment.

* * *

While government employees can extract procedural protections because of competition in the job market, there is an effective government monopoly over the dispensation of benefits such as education and welfare. Since these recipients of public largess lack the bargaining power enjoyed by prospective public sector employees, they cannot be said to have contracted away their right to procedural protection. In contract law terms, these are analogous to contracts of adhesion. Just as a modern common law court will strike down one-sided agreements that fail to give one party a fair quantum of remedy for breach—on the theory that illusory remedies have "failed of their essential purpose"— courts as a matter of constitutional law must strike down administrative programs in which the lack of procedural protection is internally inconsistent with the declared purpose of the program itself. The "contractual element" fails to provide a rational basis defense in such cases because the contractual element does not really exist.

To put the matter in Justice Rehnquist's own terms, the Court itself should take the bitter with the sweet. To the extent that the contractual element in public largess supplies a rational basis for diminished procedural protection, the absence of equal bargaining power should force the government to justify procedural limitations on other grounds.

*   *   *

F. Other Rational Bases for Diminished Procedural Protection

The contractual element in government largess is not the only conceivable rational basis for allowing officials to terminate or deny government benefits without giving reasons. In fact, there are areas in which we routinely allow government officials to exercise absolute and arbitrary discretion because it facilitates the smooth implementation of government policy. [Examples include the Supreme Court's practices regarding writs of certiorari and the President's authority to dismiss top advisors without a hearing or a statement of reasons.] *   *   *

*   *   *

In dealing with the ultimate recipients of government benefit programs, such as welfare and public school education, however, a rational basis for not extending some minimal procedural protections is difficult to imagine. Such systems generally operate with the use of relatively simple, objective qualifying criteria. In many such programs, all persons who meet these criteria are automatically "entitled" to participate. There is no rational basis for granting the administrator of these types of programs the unfettered discretion to cut off persons who meet the objective qualifications. Since, unlike in the employment context, the very purpose of public schooling or welfare is to satisfy the needs of those who qualify for the program, there is no conceivable basis for denying or terminating their benefits "at will."

Where subjective administrative judgment should play no role, recipients should be entitled to at least a statement of reasons before benefits are denied or terminated. Administrative silence in such situations can serve no permissible purpose, and thus seems far more likely to be a means for covering up a motivation outside the scope of the statutory criteria for the benefit. The lesson of *Zimmerman Brush* is that when no plausible explanation of administrative arbitrariness exists other than the government's wish to conceal its failure to follow its own declared principles of entitlement, the procedural scheme must be struck down.

JERRY L. MASHAW, THE SUPREME COURT'S DUE PROCESS CALCULUS FOR ADMINISTRATIVE ADJUDICATION IN *MATHEWS v. ELDRIDGE*: THREE FACTORS IN SEARCH OF A THEORY OF VALUE

44 U.Chi.L.Rev. 28, 46–59 (1976).

[In *Mathews v. Eldridge*,[a] the Supreme Court rejected Eldridge's claim that he was entitled, under the Due Process Clause, to a hearing before his Social Security disability benefits could be terminated. The Court announced a three-part balancing test for determining the constitutionally requisite elements of adjudicatory procedure; the calculus considers (1) the private interest at stake, (2) the risk of an erroneous deprivation of the private interest through the procedures used and the probable value of additional procedural safeguards, and (3) the Government's interest, including the fiscal and administrative burdens that additional procedures would entail.]

A Value-Sensitive Approach to the Eldridge Analysis of Due Process

The Supreme Court's analysis in *Eldridge* is not informed by systematic attention to any theory of the values underlying due process review. The approach is implicitly utilitarian but incomplete, and the Court overlooks alternative theories that might have yielded fruitful inquiry. This section attempts, first, to articulate the limits of the Court's utilitarian approach, both in *Eldridge* and as a general schema for evaluating administrative procedures, and second, to indicate the strengths and weaknesses of three alternative theories—individual dignity, equality, and tradition. These theories, at the level of abstraction here presented, require little critical justification: they are widely held, respond to strong currents in the philosophic literature concerning law, politics, and ethics, and are supported either implicitly or explicitly by the Supreme Court's due process jurisprudence.

A. Utilitarianism

Utility theory suggests that the purpose of decisional procedures—like that of social action generally—is to maximize social welfare. Indeed, the three-factor analysis enunciated in *Eldridge* appears to be a type of utilitarian, social welfare function. That function first takes into account the social value at stake in a legitimate private claim; it discounts that value by the probability that it will be preserved through the available administrative procedures, and it then subtracts from that discounted value the social cost of introducing additional procedures. When combined with the institutional posture of judicial self-restraint, utility theory can be said to yield the following plausible decision-rule: "Void procedures for lack of due process only when

a. 424 U.S. 319 (1976).

alternative procedures would so substantially increase social welfare that their rejection seems irrational."

The utilitarian calculus is not, however, without difficulties. The *Eldridge* Court conceives of the values of procedure too narrowly: it views the sole purpose of procedural protections as enhancing accuracy, and thus limits its calculus to the benefits or costs that flow from correct or incorrect decisions. No attention is paid to "process values" that might inhere in oral proceedings or to the demoralization costs that may result from the grant-withdrawal-grant-withdrawal sequence to which claimants like Eldridge are subjected. Perhaps more important, as the Court seeks to make sense of a calculus in which accuracy is the sole goal of procedure, it tends erroneously to characterize disability hearings as concerned almost exclusively with medical impairment and thus concludes that such hearings involve only medical evidence, whose reliability would be little enhanced by oral procedure. As applied by the *Eldridge* Court the utilitarian calculus tends, as cost-benefit analyses typically do, to "dwarf soft variables" and to ignore complexities and ambiguities.

The problem with a utilitarian calculus is not merely that the Court may define the relevant costs and benefits too narrowly. However broadly conceived, the calculus asks unanswerable questions. For example, what is the social value, and the social cost, of continuing disability payments until after an oral hearing for persons initially determined to be ineligible? Answers to those questions require a technique for measuring the social value and social cost of government income transfers, but no such technique exists. Even if such formidable tasks of social accounting could be accomplished, the effectiveness of oral hearings in forestalling the losses that result from erroneous terminations would remain uncertain. In the face of these pervasive indeterminacies the *Eldridge* Court was forced to retreat to a presumption of constitutionality.

Finally, it is not clear that the utilitarian balancing analysis asks the constitutionally relevant questions. The due process clause is one of those Bill of Rights protections meant to insure individual liberty in the face of contrary collective action. Therefore, a collective legislative or administrative decision about procedure, one arguably reflecting the intensity of the contending social values and representing an optimum position from the contemporary social perspective, cannot answer the constitutional question of whether due process has been accorded. A balancing analysis that would have the Court merely redetermine the question of social utility is similarly inadequate. There is no reason to believe that the Court has superior competence or legitimacy as a utilitarian balancer except as it performs its peculiar institutional role of insuring that libertarian values are considered in the calculus of decision.

Several alternative perspectives on the values served by due process pervade the Court's jurisprudence, and may provide a principled basis for due process analysis. These perspectives can usually be incorporated into a broadly defined utilitarian formula and are therefore not necessarily antiutilitarian. But they are best treated separately because they tend to generate inquiries that are different from a strictly utilitarian approach.

B.   INDIVIDUAL DIGNITY

The increasingly secular, scientific, and collectivist character of the modern American state reinforces our propensity to define fairness in the formal, and apparently neutral language of social utility. Assertions of "natural" or "inalienable" rights seem, by contrast, somewhat embarrassing. Their ancestry, and therefore their moral force, are increasingly uncertain.[65] Moreover, their role in the history of the due process clause makes us apprehensive about their eventual reach. It takes no peculiar acuity to see that the tension in procedural due process cases is the same as that in the now discredited substantive due process jurisprudence—a tension between the efficacy of the state and the individual's right to freedom from coercion or socially imposed disadvantage.

Yet the popular moral presupposition of individual dignity, and its political counterpart, self-determination, persist. State coercion must be legitimized, not only by acceptable substantive policies, but also by political processes that respond to a democratic morality's demand for participation in decisions affecting individual and group interests. At the level of individual administrative decisions this demand appears in both the layman's and the lawyer's language as the right to a "hearing" or "to be heard," normally meaning orally and in person. To accord an individual less when his property or status is at stake requires justification, not only because he might contribute to accurate determinations, but also because a lack of personal participation causes alienation and a loss of that dignity and self-respect that society properly deems independently valuable.[68]

The obvious difficulty with a dignitary theory of procedural due process lies in defining operational limits on the procedural claims it fosters. In its purest form the theory would suggest that decisions affecting individual interests should be made only through procedures acceptable to the person affected. This purely subjective standard of procedural due process cannot be adopted: an individual's claim to a "nonalienating" procedure is not ranked ahead of all other social values.

The available techniques for limiting the procedural claims elicited by the dignitary theory, however, either appear arbitrary or render the theory wholly inoperative. One technique is to curtail the class of substantive claims in which individuals can be said to have a right to

65. *See generally* Woodward, *The Limits of Legal Realism: An Historical Perspective,* 54 Va.L.Rev. 689 (1968).

68. *See generally* Summers, *Evaluating and Improving Legal Processes—A Plea for "Process Values,"* 60 Cornell L.Rev. 1 (1974).

what they consider an acceptable procedure. The "life, liberty, or property" language of the due process clause suggests such a limitation, but experience with this classification of interests has been disappointing. Any standard premised simply on pre-existing legal rights renders a claimant's request for due process, as such, either unnecessary or hopeless. Another technique for confining the dignitary theory is to define "nonalienating" procedure as any procedure that is formulated democratically. The troublesome effect of this limitation is that no procedures that are legislatively authorized can be said to encroach on individual dignity.

Notwithstanding its difficulties, the dignitary theory of due process might have contributed significantly to the *Eldridge* analysis. The questions of procedural "acceptability" which the theory poses may initially seem vacuous or at best intuitive, but they suggest a broader sensitivity than the utilitarian factor analysis to the nature of governmental decisions. Whereas the utilitarian approach seems to require an estimate of the quantitative value of the claim, the dignitary approach suggests that the Court develop a qualitative appraisal of the type of administrative decision involved. While the disability decision in *Eldridge* may be narrowly characterized as a decision about the receipt of money payments, it may also be considered from various qualitative perspectives which seem pertinent in view of the general structure of the American income-support system.

That system suggests that a disability decision is a judgment of considerable social significance, and one that the claimant should rightly perceive as having a substantial moral content. The major cash income-support programs determine eligibility, not only on the basis of simple insufficiency of income, but also, or exclusively, on the basis of a series of excuses for partial or total nonparticipation in the work force: agedness, childhood, family responsibility, injury, disability. A grant under any of these programs is an official, if sometimes grudging, stamp of approval of the claimant's status as a partially disabled worker or nonworker. It proclaims, in effect, that those who obtain it have encountered one of the politically legitimate hazards to self-sufficiency in a market economy. The recipients, therefore, are entitled to society's support. Conversely, the denial of an income-maintenance claim implies that the claim is socially illegitimate, and the claimant, however impecunious, is not excused from normal work force status.

These moral and status dimensions of the disability decision indicate that there is more at stake in disability claims than temporary loss of income.[73] They also tend to put the disability decision in a framework that leads away from the superficial conclusion that disability

73. The *Eldridge* Court, in distinguishing *Goldberg* [*v. Kelly*, 397 U.S. 254 (1970),] largely on the ground that terminated welfare recipients were more desperate financially than terminated disability recipients, thus ignored a very substantial similarity. * * * The potential for feelings of demoralization, rejection, or simple righteous indignation seems essentially the same in both types of cases.

decisions are a routine matter of evaluating medical evidence. Decisions with substantial "moral worth" connotations are generally expected to be highly individualized and attentive to subjective evidence. The adjudication of such issues on the basis of documents submitted largely by third parties and by adjudicators who have never confronted the claimant seems inappropriate. Instead, a court approaching an analysis of the disability claims process from the dignitary perspective might emphasize those aspects of disability decisions that focus on a particular claimant's vocational characteristics, his unique response to his medical condition, and the ultimate predictive judgment of whether the claimant should be able to work.

C. EQUALITY

Justice in a formal philosophical sense is often defined as equality of treatment. In the realm of adjudicatory procedure, a widely recognized aspect of procedural fairness is equality of opportunity to be heard. Indeed, insofar as adjudicatory procedure is perceived to be adversarial and dispute resolving, the degree to which procedures facilitate equal opportunities for the adversaries to influence the decision may be the most important criterion by which fairness is evaluated.

Equality of opportunity is not, however, an exhaustive measure of procedural due process. While equality would seem to require an unbiased decision maker and identical opportunities to present evidence and argument, it has little to say concerning the manner in which evidence and argument are presented. A hearing participant might claim, for example, that oral proceedings, including cross-examination, would illuminate murky aspects of the case or produce a truer disclosure of facts; but if this participant's adversary or other participants are not accorded these procedural rights, he can hardly claim unequal treatment. Similarly, objection to the use of material obtained outside the record, but not from a party, is at most remotely connected with equality of access. A procedure that divested the directly affected parties of all control over the process of shaping issues and developing evidence, indeed that never informed the parties that it had begun, would be "unequal" only if institutionally biased.[77] Yet such a procedure would widely be perceived as "unfair."

Notions of equality can nevertheless significantly inform the evaluation of any administrative process. One question we might ask is whether an investigative procedure is designed in a fashion that systematically excludes or undervalues evidence that would tend to support the position of a particular class of parties. If so, those parties might have a plausible claim that the procedure treated them unequally. Similarly, in a large-scale inquisitorial process involving many adjudicators, the question that should be posed is whether like cases

---

77. *See, e.g.,* F. Kafka, The Trial (3d ed. 1956). Kafka gained many of his impressions of administrative processes as a bu- reaucrat in an agency dispensing disability benefits. M. Brod, Franz Kafka 79–84 (1970).

receive like attention and like evidentiary development so that the influence of such arbitrary factors as location [is] minimized. In order to take such equality issues into account, we need only to broaden our due process horizons to include elements of procedural fairness beyond those traditionally associated with adversary proceedings. These two inquiries might have been pursued fruitfully in *Eldridge*. First, is the state agency system of decision making, which is based on documents, particularly disadvantageous for certain classes of claimants? There is some tentative evidence that it is.[78] Cases such as *Eldridge* involving muscular or skeletal disorders, neurological problems, and multiple impairments, including psychological overlays, are widely believed to be both particularly difficult, due to the subjectivity of the evidence, and particularly prone to be reversed after oral hearing.

Second, does the inquisitorial process at the state agency level tend to treat like cases alike? If the GAO's study[79] is indicative, the answer is decidedly no. According to that study, many, perhaps half, of the decisions are made on the basis of records that other adjudicators consider so inadequate that a decision could not be rendered. The relevance of such state agency variance to Eldridge's claim is twofold: first, it suggests that state agency determinations are unreliable and that further development at the hearing stage might substantially enhance their reliability; alternatively, it may suggest that the hierarchical or bureaucratic model of decision making, with overhead control for consistency, does not accurately describe the Social Security disability system. And if consistency is not feasible under this system, perhaps the more compelling standard for evaluating the system is the dignitary value of individualized judgment, which * * * implies claimant participation.

D. TRADITION OR EVOLUTION

Judicial reasoning, including reasoning about procedural due process, is frequently and self-consciously based on custom or precedent. In part, reliance on tradition or "authority" is a court's institutional defense against illegitimacy in a political democracy. But tradition serves other values, not the least of which are predictability and economy of effort. More importantly, the inherently conservative technique of analogy to custom and precedent seems essential to the evolutionary development and the preservation of the legal system. Traditional procedures are legitimate not only because they represent a set of continuous expectations, but because the body politic has survived their use.

78. *See* W. Popkin, Counsel in the Welfare State: A Statistical and Legal Analysis of the Role of Representation in Administrative Decision-Making Based on a Study of Five Disability Programs 34, 52–53, 59–61 (1975). (This is a draft report to the Administrative Conference Committee on Grant and Benefit Programs. It has not been approved by the Committee or the Conference and represents only the view of its author.)

79. [Staff of Subcomm. on Social Security of The House Comm. on Ways and Means, 94th Cong., 2d Sess., Disability Insurance—Legislative Issue Paper (Comm.Print. 1976).]

The use of tradition as a guide to fundamental fairness is vulnerable, of course, to objection. Since social and economic forces are dynamic, the processes and structures that proved functional in one period will not necessarily serve effectively in the next. Indeed, evolutionary development may as often end in the extinction of a species as in adaptation and survival. For this reason alone tradition can serve only as a partial guide to judgment.

Furthermore, it may be argued that reasoning by analogy from traditional procedures does not actually provide a perspective on the values served by due process. Rather, it is a decisional technique that requires a specification of the purposes of procedural rules merely in order that the decision maker may choose from among a range of authorities or customs the particular authority or custom most analogous to the procedures being evaluated.

This objection to tradition as a theory of justification is weighty, but not devastating. What is asserted by an organic or evolutionary theory is that *the purposes of legal rules cannot be fully known*. Put more cogently, while procedural rules, like other legal rules, should presumably contribute to the maintenance of an effective social order, we cannot expect to know precisely how they do so and what the long-term effects of changes or revisions might be. Our constitutional stance should therefore be preservative and incremental, building carefully, by analogy, upon traditional modes of operation. So viewed, the justification "we have always done it that way" is not so much a retreat from reasoned and purposive decision making as a profound acknowledgment of the limits of instrumental rationality.

Viewed from a traditionalist's perspective, the Supreme Court's opinion in *Eldridge* may be said to rely on the traditional proposition that property interests may be divested temporarily without hearing, provided a subsequent opportunity for contest is afforded. *Goldberg v. Kelly* is deemed an exceptional case, from which *Eldridge* is distinguished.

Like the Court's utilitarian analysis, this general traditionalist method seems incomplete. If the premise of that method is that traditional modes of operation are to provide guidelines, then the Court should have immediately characterized the legal issue in order to select the appropriate guidelines. But given the Court's quite sensible position that administrative functions are to be evaluated individually, how was that characterization to proceed? Presumably, disability payments fall within the general domain of social welfare claims—a domain that is also treated in the *Goldberg* decision. Assuming, however, that the Court properly distinguished *Goldberg*, analogical analysis is aborted because no other Supreme Court decision pertaining to social welfare claims seems apt. Nor could it discover guiding authority in prior administrative practice, which is based on the now discredited notion that social welfare benefits are subject to discretionary divestiture. What the *Eldridge* Court needed, then, was a more general way of thinking about the termination of property interests that might apply both to traditional and to novel forms of property.

The beginnings of such an approach might be found in Justice Black's dissent in *Goldberg*,[82] where he analogized the position of a welfare recipient to the traditional position of a creditor when his debtor refuses further performance. Normally, in that situation, the creditor is left with the inconvenience of forgoing receipt of performance while he seeks legal enforcement of an obligation that may or may not remain due. The majority opinion's implicit response to the analogy is that a welfare recipient is in a special position: he literally cannot wait because he depends upon the state's performance for survival. Given this special circumstance, the Court concludes, the traditional bearer of the risk of erroneous (or otherwise illicit) non-performance has a constitutional right to shift that risk to the state, pending hearing. Given this reading of *Goldberg*, the *Eldridge* opinion may be interpreted as concluding simply that the special *Goldberg* circumstances did not obtain. Therefore, the traditional allocation of the risk was acceptable.

Analyzing *Goldberg* and *Eldridge* by analogy to traditional contract-default remedies is valuable because it discourages the superficial classification of welfare recipients as immediately desperate and of disability recipients as having alternative resources. A court in equity faced with an analogous issue—a request for a temporary restraining order or preliminary injunction to insure performance by an obligor—would look to the particular circumstances of the case to determine whether extraordinary remedies were justified. In so doing, the court would take into account the peculiar hardship to the plaintiff of nonperformance pending a trial, the likelihood that he might prevail on the merits, and the burden on the defendant of requiring maintenance of the status quo. The Social Security Administration, as a matter of due process of law, might sensibly be required to do the same—or at least to explain its inability to do so.

A court pursuing an analysis based on traditional contract-default remedies should also focus on the limitations of that analogy. Contract remedies presume a competitive market in which alternative obligors are available. This presumption of the availability of alternatives undergirds traditional judicial reluctance to require specific performance pending trial, or indeed after trial. The party relying on state support is in a quite different position. His market alternatives have previously been determined to be foreclosed, and his attachment to a particular income-maintenance scheme suggests that others are at best not comparable, and at worst unavailable. While this difference between contract and income-maintenance claims may not be a sufficient reason for reversing the usual allocation of the risk of error pending a full hearing in all cases, it comes close to presenting an a fortiori case

82. Goldberg v. Kelly, 397 U.S. 254, 271
(Black, J., dissenting).

for requiring that the individual income-maintenance claimant, like the contract creditor, be allowed to establish (perhaps by affidavit) that his is such a case.

* * *

The preceding discussion has emphasized the way that explicit attention to a range of values underlying due process of law might have led the *Eldridge* Court down analytic paths different from those that appear in Justice Powell's opinion. The discussion has largely ignored, however, arguments that would justify the result that the Court reached in terms of the alternative value theories here advanced. Those arguments are now set forth.

First, focus on the dignitary aspects of the disability decision can hardly compel the conclusion that an oral hearing is a constitutional necessity prior to the termination of benefits when a full hearing is available later. Knowledge that an oral hearing will be available at some point should certainly lessen disaffection and alienation. Indeed, Eldridge seemed secure in the knowledge that a just procedure was available. His desire to avoid taking a corrective appeal should not blind us to the support of dignitary values that the de novo appeal provides.

Second, arguments premised on equality do not necessarily carry the day for the proponent of prior hearings. The Social Security Administration's attempt to routinize and make consistent hundreds of thousands of decisions in a nationwide income-maintenance program can be criticized both for its failures in its own terms and for its tendency to ignore the way that disability decisions impinge upon perceptions of individual moral worth. On balance, however, the program that Congress enacted contains criteria that suggest a desire for both consistency and individualization. No adjudicatory process can avoid tradeoffs between the pursuit of one or the other of these goals. Thus a procedural structure incorporating (1) decisions by a single state agency based on a documentary record and subject to hierarchical quality review, followed by (2) appeal to de novo oral proceedings before independent administrative law judges, is hardly an irrational approach to the necessary compromise between consistency and individualization.

Explicit and systematic attention to the values served by a demand for due process nevertheless remains highly informative in *Eldridge* and in general. The use of analogy to traditional procedures might have helped rationalize and systematize a concern for the "desperation" of claimants that seems as impoverished in *Eldridge* as it seems profligate in *Goldberg;* and the absence in *Eldridge* of traditionalist, dignitary, or egalitarian considerations regarding the disability adjudication process permitted the Court to overlook questions of both fact and value—questions that, on reflection, seem important. The structure provided by the Court's three factors is an inadequate guide for analysis because its neutrality leaves it empty of suggestive value perspectives.

Furthermore, an attempt by the Court to articulate a set of values that informs due process decision making might provide it with an acceptable judicial posture from which to review administrative procedures. The *Goldberg* decision's approach to prescribing due process—specification of the attributes of adjudicatory hearings by analogy to judicial trial—makes the Court resemble an administrative engineer with an outdated professional education. It is at once intrusive and ineffectual. Retreating from this stance, the *Eldridge* Court relies on the administrator's good faith—an equally troublesome posture in a political system that depends heavily on judicial review for the protection of countermajoritarian values.

The path to a more appropriate and successful judicial role may lie in giving greater attention to the elaboration of the due process implications of the values that have been discussed. If the Court provided a structure of values within which procedures would be reviewed, it could then demand that administrators justify their processes in terms of the degree to which they support the elaborated value structure. The Court would have to be satisfied that the administrator had carefully considered the effects of his chosen procedures on the relevant constitutional values and had made reasonable judgments concerning those effects.

A decision that an administrator had not met that standard would not result in the prescription of a particular adjudicatory technique as a constitutional, and thereafter virtually immutable, necessity; but rather in a remand to the administrator. In meeting the Court's objections, the administrator (or legislature) might properly choose between specific amendment and a complete overhaul of the administrative process. Perhaps more importantly, under a due process approach that emphasized value rather than technique, neither the administrator in constructing and justifying his processes, nor the Court in reviewing them, would be limited to the increasingly sterile discussion of whether this or that particular aspect of trial-type procedure is absolutely essential to due process of law.

BIBLIOGRAPHY

The New Due Process: Entitlement Theory and Beyond

DUE PROCESS—NOMOS XVIII (J.R. Pennock & J. Chapman, eds. 1977).

Handler, *Controlling Official Behavior in Welfare Administration*, 54 Calif.L.Rev. 479 (1966).

Laycock, *Due Process and Separation of Powers: The Effort to Make the Due Process Clause Nonjusticiable*, 60 Tex.L.Rev. 875 (1982).

Mashaw, *Administrative Due Process: The Quest for a Dignitary Theory*, 61 B.U.L.Rev. 885 (1981).

Monaghan, *Of "Liberty" and "Property,"* 62 Cornell L.Rev. 401 (1977).

O'Neil, *Of Justice Delayed and Justice Denied: The Welfare Prior Hearing Cases,* 1970 Sup.Ct.Rev. 161.

Rabin, *Job Security and Due Process: Monitoring Administrative Discretion Through a Reasons Requirement,* 44 U.Chi.L.Rev. 60 (1976).

Reich, *The New Property,* 73 Yale L.J. 733 (1964).

Reich, *Individual Rights and Social Welfare: The Emerging Legal Issues,* 74 Yale L.J. 1245 (1965).

Rendleman, *The New Due Process: Rights and Remedies,* 63 Ky.L.J. 531 (1975).

Rubin, *Due Process and the Administrative State,* 72 Calif. 1044 (1984).

Simon, *Liberty and Property in the Supreme Court: A Defense of Roth and Perry,* 71 Calif.L.Rev. 146 (1983).

Symposium—*Procedural Due Process: Liberty and Justice,* 39 U.Fla.L. Rev. 217–581 (1987).

Terrell, *"Property," "Due Process," and the Distinction Between Definition and Theory in Legal Analysis,* 70 Geo.L.J. 861 (1982).

Tribe, *Structural Due Process,* 10 Harv.Civ.Lib.–Civ.Rights L.Rev. 269 (1975).

Tushnet, *The Newer Property: Suggestions for the Revival of Substantive Due Process,* 1975 Sup.Ct.Rev. 261.

Van Alstyne, *The Demise of the Right–Privilege Distinction in Constitutional Law,* 81 Harv.L.Rev. 1439 (1968).

Wilkinson, *Goss v. Lopez: The Supreme Court as School Superintendent,* 1975 Sup.Ct.Rev. 25.

Williams, *Liberty and Property: The Problem of Government Benefits,* 12 J.Legal Studies 3 (1983).

What Process Is Due

Davis, *The Requirement of a Trial-type Hearing,* 70 Harv.L.Rev. 193 (1956).

Friendly, *"Some Kind of a Hearing,"* 123 U.Pa.L.Rev. 1267 (1975).

Kadish, *Methodology and Criteria in Due Process Adjudication—A Survey and Criticism,* 66 Yale L.J. 319 (1957).

Mashaw, *The Management Side of Due Process: Some Theoretical and Litigation Notes on the Assurance of Accuracy, Fairness, and Timeliness in the Adjudication of Social Welfare Claims,* 59 Cornell L.Rev. 772 (1974).

Redish & Marshall, *Adjudicatory Independence and the Values of Procedural Due Process,* 95 Yale L.J. 455 (1986).

Saphire, *Specifying Due Process Values: Toward A More Responsive Approach to Procedural Protection,* 127 U.Pa.L.Rev. 111 (1978).

Summers, *Evaluating and Improving Legal Processes—A Plea for Process Values*, 60 Cornell L.Rev. 1 (1974).

Verkuil, *A Study of Informal Adjudication Procedures*, 43 U.Chi.L.Rev. 739 (1976).

Chapter VI

EQUALITY AND RACE

The next three Chapters are designed to explore several controversial themes concerning the Constitution's guarantee of equality. The Equal Protection Clause declares that "No State shall . . . deny to any person within its jurisdiction the equal protection of the laws." As the materials on interpretation in Chapter II suggest, there may be more than one approach to understanding those few words.

One way of interpreting the Clause might be: "The laws shall treat all persons alike." But there is surely no constitutional harm in denying drivers' licenses to persons under 16. People are different in many ways, and the law can take account of some of those differences. One problem in reading the Equal Protection Clause is deciding what differences matter. *Who* must be treated alike?

We might instead restate the Clause this way: "People who are alike (in whatever way matters) shall be treated alike by the laws." But what does it mean to be treated alike? A welfare program may treat the poor alike by giving each person what he needs—the difference between his income and some minimum standard of living. Here the end result is "equal." A medical assistance program like Medicaid may treat the poor alike by giving everyone 14 days of free medical care. (This may be less than some need to be cured.) Here the stipend is "equal." A program for granting broadcast licenses (or drafting soldiers) may treat all persons alike by picking the winners (or losers) at random. Here the process gives each person an opportunity that is "equal." Thus another problem in reading the Equal Protection Clause is deciding what *equal* protection means.

As a general matter, courts do not look too hard at legislative decisions about classification and similar treatment.[1] But there is general agreement that assuring equal treatment to blacks is a value that lies at the core of the Equal Protection Clause. Scholars tend to theorize about equal protection by generalizing from the case of blacks.

1. New York City Transit Authority v. Beazer, 440 U.S. 568, 99 S.Ct. 1355, 59 L.Ed.2d 587 (1979).

But what are the salient features of that case? What counts, for example, as equal treatment on the basis of race? Must we make no distinctions based on race? Why, for that matter, is treatment of blacks a core value of the Clause? Because that was the Framers' intent? Because there is something special about racial discrimination? Because blacks are an oppressed group in American society? Because the political process does not work for them? Getting the theory right on these questions is of the greatest importance if we are to get it right in other cases. The readings in this Chapter present a number of different answers.

Raoul Berger argues that race matters because those who wrote the Fourteenth Amendment intended it to. But he believes that they intended the Equal Protection Clause to produce much less in the way of equal treatment than we usually suppose. It was, he contends, no more than a constitutional confirmation of the 1866 Civil Rights Act. Given the racism of Republicans and Democrats alike, Berger finds it unthinkable that Congress would have desired to go further. Michael Perry argues that even if Berger is correct, cases interpreting the Equal Protection Clause "radiate the principle that no person is by virtue of race morally inferior to another." Perry's principle forbids all, not just some, unequal treatment of nonwhites. The reason is that the government should not attach negative significance to traits indicating nothing about a person's moral status.

Paul Brest and Owen Fiss both start from the premise that racial classifications produce special harm. But they disagree about whether we should focus on individuals or on groups in assessing the harm the Clause forbids. Brest seeks to explain the intuitive appeal of an antidiscrimination principle concerned with individual harm. He then addresses a difficult problem for devotees of that principle: what to do with laws that make no discriminatory classification but have a disparate racial impact. Fiss responds that the antidiscrimination principle, because of its focus on individual harm and the lawmaking process, cannot deal satisfactorily with the problem of disparate impact. He proposes instead that we read into the Equal Protection Clause a group-disadvantaging principle. Such a principle might, for example, invalidate civil service job tests simply because blacks failed in disproportionately high numbers.

Charles Lawrence offers a different solution to the problem of disparate impact. Many effects that we treat as innocent may result from unconscious racism, a problem that is more like a disease than a crime. It is a mistake to insist on a showing of individual responsibility before addressing these effects. But the law need not go as far as Fiss suggests in order to combat them. We can accommodate the problem of unconscious racism within the framework of a "stigma" theory like Brest's or a "process" theory like Ely's.

John Hart Ely and Bruce Ackerman disagree about whether the rule of equality is concerned with process or with some more substantive value. Ely believes that the Equal Protection Clause should be used to perfect the democratic process. As Justice Stone said in *United States v. Carolene Products Co.,*[2] "prejudice against discrete and insular minorities" can cause the political process to malfunction. Racial classifications that disadvantage minorities are a signal that that has happened.

Ackerman responds that the process-oriented approach of *Carolene Products* fails on all counts. It ignores anonymous and diffuse minorities (homosexuals and women), who are less able to protect themselves politically than discrete and insular minorities (blacks). More fundamentally, despite its focus on process and its claim to value-neutrality, it ends by imposing substantive values on the political branches of government.

RAOUL BERGER, GOVERNMENT BY JUDICIARY

Pp. 10–14, 22–24, 27, 30–31, 169–172, 176 (1977).

BACKGROUND

The key to an understanding of the Fourteenth Amendment is that the North was shot through with Negrophobia, that the Republicans, except for a minority of extremists, were swayed by the racism that gripped their constituents rather than by abolitionist ideology. At the inception of their crusade the abolitionists peered up at an almost unscalable cliff. Charles Sumner, destined to become a leading spokesman for extreme abolitionist views, wrote in 1834, upon his first sight of slaves, "My worst preconception of their appearance and their ignorance did not fall as low as their actual stupidity . . . They appear to be nothing more than moving masses of flesh unendowed with anything of intelligence above the brutes." Tocqueville's impression in 1831–32 was equally abysmal. He noticed that in the North, "the prejudice which repels the negroes seems to increase in proportion as they are emancipated," that prejudice "appears to be stronger in the States which have abolished slavery, than in those where it still exists."

Little wonder that the abolitionist campaign was greeted with loathing! In 1837 Elijah Lovejoy, an abolitionist editor, was murdered by an Illinois mob. How shallow was the impress of the abolitionist campaign on such feelings is graphically revealed in a Lincoln incident. A delegation of Negro leaders had called on him at the White House, and he told them,

> There is an unwillingness on the part of our people, harsh as it may be, for you free colored people to remain with us . . . [E]ven when you cease to be slaves, you are far removed from being placed on an equality with the white man . . . I cannot alter it if I would. It is a fact.

2. 304 U.S. 144, 152 n. 4, 58 S.Ct. 778, 783 n. 4, 82 L.Ed. 1234 (1938).

Fear of Negro invasion—that the emancipated slaves would flock north in droves—alarmed the North.   The letters and diaries of Union soldiers, [C. Vann] Woodward notes, reveal an "enormous amount of antipathy towards Negroes"; popular convictions "were not prepared to sustain" a commitment to equality.   Racism, David Donald remarks, "ran deep in the North," and the suggestion that "Negroes should be treated as equals to white men woke some of the deepest and ugliest fears in the American mind."

One need not look beyond the confines of the debates in the 39th Congress to find abundant confirmation.   Time and again Republicans took account of race prejudice as an inescapable fact.   George W. Julian of Indiana referred to the "proverbial hatred" of Negroes, Senator Henry S. Lane of Indiana to the "almost ineradicable prejudice," Shelby M. Cullom of Illinois to the "morbid prejudice," Senator William M. Stewart of Nevada to the "nearly insurmountable" prejudice, James F. Wilson of Iowa to the "iron-cased prejudice" against blacks.   These were Republicans, sympathetic to emancipation and the protection of civil rights.   Then there were the Democratic racists who unashamedly proclaimed that the Union should remain a "white man's" government. In the words of Senator Garrett Davis of Kentucky, "The white race . . . will be proprietors of the land, and the blacks its cultivators; such is their destiny."   Let it be regarded as political propaganda, and, as the noted British historiographer Sir Herbert Butterfield states, it "does at least presume an audience—perhaps a 'public opinion'—which is judged to be susceptible to the kinds of arguments and considerations set before it."   Consider, too, that the Indiana Constitution of 1851 excluded Negroes from the State, as did Oregon, that a substantial number of Northern States recently had rejected Negro suffrage, that others maintained segregated schools.   It is against this backdrop that we must measure claims that the framers of the Fourteenth Amendment swallowed abolitionist ideology hook, line, and sinker.

*   *   *

THE CIVIL RIGHTS ACT OF 1866

The meaning and scope of the Fourteenth Amendment are greatly illuminated by the debates in the 39th Congress on the antecedent Civil Rights Act of 1866.   As Charles Fairman stated, "over and over in this debate [on the Amendment] the correspondence between Section One of the Amendment and the Civil Rights Act is noted.   The provisions of the one are treated as though they were essentially identical with those of the other."   George R. Latham of West Virginia, for example, stated that "the 'civil rights bill' which is now a law . . . covers exactly the same ground as this amendment."   In fact, the Amendment was designed to "*constitutionalize*" the Act, that is, to "embody" it in the Constitution so as to remove doubt as to its constitutionality and to place it beyond the power of a later Congress to repeal.   An ardent advocate of an abolitionist reading of the Amendment, Howard Jay Graham, stated that "virtually every speaker in the debates on the

Fourteenth Amendment—Republican and Democrat alike—said or agreed that the Amendment was designed to embody or incorporate the Civil Rights Act."

Section 1 of the Civil Rights Bill provided in pertinent part,

That there shall be *no discrimination in civil* rights or immunities . . . on account of race . . . but the inhabitants of every race . . . shall have the *same* right to make and enforce contracts, to sue, be parties, and give evidence, to inherit, purchase, lease, sell, hold and convey real and personal property, and to full and *equal benefit* of all laws and proceedings for the *security* of person and property, and shall be subject to *like* punishment . . . and no other.[14]

* * *

The explanations of the Civil Rights Bill by the respective committee chairmen made its limited objectives entirely clear. Speaking to "civil rights and immunities," House Chairman Wilson asked,

What do these terms mean? Do they mean that in all things, civil, social, political, all citizens, without distinction of race or color, shall be equal? By no means can they be so construed . . . Nor do they mean that all citizens shall sit on juries, or that their children shall attend the same schools. These are not civil rights and immunities. Well, what is the meaning? What are civil rights? I understand civil rights to be simply the absolute rights of individuals, such as "The right of personal security, the right of personal liberty, and the right to acquire and enjoy property." * * *

* * *

* * * [Senator Lyman] Trumbull [of Illinois] stated that the Bill "has nothing to do with the right of suffrage, or any other political rights." When Senator Willard Saulsbury, a Democrat of Delaware, sought specifically to except "the right to vote," Trumbull replied: "that is a political privilege, not a civil right. This bill relates to civil rights only." And he reiterated that the Bill "carefully avoided conferring or interfering with political rights or privileges of any kind." The views of Trumbull and Wilson were shared by fellow Republicans. The "only effect" of the Bill, said Senator Henderson, was to give the blacks the enumerated rights. "These measures did not pretend to confer upon the negro the suffrage. They left each State to determine the question for itself." Senator Sherman said the bill "defines what are the incidents of freedom, and says that these men must be protected in certain rights, and so careful is its language that it goes on and defines those rights, the rights to sue and be sued [etc.] . . . and other universal incidents of freedom." [Martin] Thayer [of Pennsylvania] stressed that the bill did not "extend the right of suffrage," that suffrage was not a "fundamental right." That the purpose of the bill was to *prevent discrimination with respect to enumerated, fundamental not political or social rights,* was also stated in one form or another by

14. [Cong. Globe, 39th Cong., 1st Sess. 474 (1866) (emphasis added).]

Cook and Moulton of Illinois, Hubbell, Lawrence, and Shellabarger of Ohio, and Windom of Minnesota.

*   *   *

WHAT WAS EQUAL PROTECTION TO PROTECT?

The Civil Rights Act * * * secured to blacks the *same* right to contract, to hold property, and to sue, as whites enjoyed, and the "*equal benefit of all laws for security of person and property.*" "Political rights" were excluded. In describing these aims the framers interchangeably referred to "equality," "equality before the law," and "equal protection" (but always in the circumscribed context of the rights enumerated in the Bill), so that it is reasonable to infer that the framers regarded these terms as synonymous. What is required, said Moulton of Illinois, is "that each State shall provide for equality before the law, equal protection to life, liberty, and property, equal right to sue and be sued." A leading Radical, Samuel Shellabarger of Ohio, said, of the Civil Rights Bill, "whatever rights *as to each of these enumerated* civil (not political) matters the State may confer upon one race . . . shall be held by all races in equality . . . It secures . . . *equality of protection in those enumerated civil rights* which the States may deem proper to confer upon any races." So it was understood by Senator Hendricks, an Indiana Democrat: "To recognize the civil rights of the colored people as equal to the civil rights of the white people, I understand to be as far as Senators desire to go; in the language of the Senator from Massachusetts [Sumner] to place all men upon an equality before the law; and that is proposed in regard to their civil rights." He objected that "in the State of Indiana we do not recognize the civil equality of the races." When Andrew Johnson combed the Bill for objections and vetoed it, he noted that § 1 "contains an enumeration of the rights to be enjoyed" and that "perfect equality" was sought with respect to "these enumerated rights." Thomas T. Davis, a New York Republican, expressed a widely shared feeling in stating, Negroes "must be made equal before the law, and be permitted to enjoy life, liberty, and the pursuit of happiness [property]," but he was against "the establishment of perfect equality between the colored and the white race of the South." While James W. Patterson of New Hampshire was "opposed to any law discriminating against [blacks] in the security and protection of life, liberty, person and property," "beyond this," he stated, "I am not prepared to go," explicitly rejecting "political and social equality." Windom declared that the Civil Rights Bill conferred an "equal right, nothing more . . . to make and enforce contracts," and so on, but no "social privileges." Thus, the concept of "equal protection" had its roots in the Civil Rights Bill and was conceived to be limited to the enumerated rights.

What reason is there to conclude that when the words "equal protection of the laws" were embodied in the Amendment they were freighted with a new cargo of meaning—unlimited equality across the board? The evidence points the other way. In an early version of the

Amendment, provision was made for both "the same political rights and privileges and . . . equal protection in the enjoyment of life, liberty and property, an indication that "equal protection" did not include "political rights and privileges," but was confined to "life, liberty, or property." [John] Bingham [of Ohio] proposed a substitute, H.R. No. 63, that would empower Congress "to secure . . . all privileges and immunities . . . (Art. IV, Sec. 2); and . . . equal protection in the rights of life, liberty and property (5th Amendment)." "Political rights and privileges" had disappeared; in its place was "privileges and immunities." Neither "privileges and immunities," nor its antecedent, "civil rights" had included "political privileges." Bingham explained that his proposal was aimed at "confiscation statutes . . . statutes of unjust imprisonment" of the "rebel states," the objects of the Civil Rights Bill. * * *

Among the statements indicating that § 1 was considered to embody the objectives of the Civil Rights Act is that of Latham of West Virginia: "The 'civil rights bill,' which is now a law . . . covers exactly the same ground as this amendment." [Thaddeus] Stevens [of Pennsylvania] explained that the Amendment

> allows Congress to correct the unjust legislation of the States *so far* that the law which operates upon one shall operate *equally* upon all. Whatever law punishes a white man for a crime shall punish the black man precisely in the same way . . . Whatever law protects the white man shall afford *equal protection* to the black man. Whatever means of redress is afforded to one shall be afforded to all. Whatever law allows the white man to testify in court shall allow the man of color to do the same. These are great advantages over their present [Black] codes . . . I need not enumerate these partial and oppressive laws . . . Your civil rights bill secures the same thing. * * *

* * *

But, it may be asked, does not the differentiation in § 1 between "due process" protection of "life, liberty, and property" and "equal protection of the laws" indicate that "equal protection" was now divorced from the earlier limitation to "life, liberty, and property." Nothing in the debates indicates such a purpose. "Equal protection of the laws" expressed the central object of the framers: to prevent *statutory* discrimination with respect to the rights enumerated in the Civil Rights Act. That purpose had been loosely expressed in Bingham's earlier formulation: "equal protection in the rights of life, liberty, and property," which he mistakenly identified with the "5th Amendment." Possibly some more perceptive lawyer restored the words "life, liberty, and property" to their Fifth Amendment association with due process, thus insuring access to the courts. At the same time, the established association of due process with judicial procedure made it necessary to block what Stevens denominated "partial and oppressive laws," a purpose succinctly expressed by "equal protection of the laws" to which reference had been made during the debate on the Civil Rights Bill.

A number of scholars have offered critical reviews of Berger's historical research and interpretive conclusions.[3] Historian Eric Foner argues that to reduce the aims of framers of the Fourteenth Amendment to invalidation of the Black Codes and validation of the Civil Rights Act of 1866 "is to misconstrue the difference between a statute and a constitutional amendment." The Fourteenth Amendment was a "broad [statement] of principle, giving constitutional form to the resolution of a national cris[i]s, and permanently altering American nationality":

> [Even moderate Republicans] understood Reconstruction as a dynamic process, in which phrases like "privileges and immunities" were subject to changing interpretation. They preferred to allow both Congress and the federal courts maximum flexibility in implementing the Amendment's provisions and combatting the multitude of injustices that confronted blacks in many parts of the South. * * *
>
> * * * [I]t is abundantly clear that Republicans wished to give constitutional sanction to states' obligation to respect such key provisions [of the Bill of Rights] as freedom of speech, the right to bear arms, trial by impartial jury, and protection against cruel and unusual punishment and unreasonable search and seizure. The Freedmen's Bureau had already taken steps to protect these rights, and the Amendment was deemed necessary, in part, precisely because every one of them was being systematically violated in the South in 1866.[4]

MICHAEL J. PERRY, MODERN EQUAL PROTECTION: A CONCEPTUALIZATION AND APPRAISAL

79 Colum.L.Rev. 1023, 1025–1032 (1979).

I. THE ORIGINAL UNDERSTANDING

* * *

To understand the text of the fourteenth amendment, a document written more than a century ago, it is necessary to understand the period in which it was written. Raoul Berger, in his recent historical inquiry into the original understanding of the fourteenth amendment,[11] presents a substantially compelling reconstruction of what the amendment meant to its framers. Berger rightly insists that in ascertaining the original understanding of the amendment, we must remember

---

3. *See, e.g.,* Soifer, *Review Essay—Protecting Civil Rights: A Critique of Raoul Berger's History,* 54 N.Y.U.L.Rev. 651, 657 (1979); Kutler, *Raoul Berger's Fourteenth Amendment: A History or Ahistorical?,* 6 Hast.Const.L.Q. 511 (1979); Murphy, *Book Review—Constitutional Interpretation:* *The Art of Historian, Magician or Statesman?,* 87 Yale L.J. 1752 (1978).

4. E. Foner, Reconstruction 257–259 (1988).

11. R. Berger, Government by Judiciary: The Transformation Of The Fourteenth Amendment (1977).

"that the North was shot through with Negrophobia, that the Republicans, except for a minority of extremists, were swayed by the racism that gripped their constituents rather than by abolitionist ideology." Consequently, the framers did not intend the fourteenth amendment to serve as a charter for the political and social equality of the freed race. Rather, concludes Berger, section one of the amendment was intended only to constitutionalize—and thereby place "beyond the power of a later Congress to repeal"—the specific protections of the Civil Rights Act of 1866. The Civil Rights Act had been designed to protect freedmen in the South from discrimination with respect to certain enumerated rights without which the abolition of slavery was thought largely meaningless. * * *

As originally understood, the privileges or immunities clause—"the central provision of the Amendment's § 1"—forbade every state to deny to any of its residents on the basis of race any "fundamental" right the state granted to its residents generally. The sorts of rights—"fundamental" rights—to which the clause, following the 1866 Act, had reference were rights pertaining to the physical security of one's person, freedom of movement, and capacity to make contracts and to acquire, hold, and transfer chattels and land—*i.e.,* "life, liberty, and property" in the original sense. The equal protection clause forbade enactment or enforcement of laws denying on the basis of race any fundamental right granted residents generally; the due process clause forbade denial on the basis of race of any judicial protections afforded residents generally for the security of their fundamental rights. Given the import of the privileges or immunities clause, the equal protection and due process clauses were, in a strict sense, superfluous. But then, as Professor Karst has noted, the framers made "no serious effort to differentiate the functions of the various clauses." [23] The framers of the fourteenth amendment simply assumed what anyone in their place would have assumed: that every state granted to its residents generally certain fundamental rights—"life, liberty, and property"—and certain avenues for the protection of those rights—"due process." Under the amendment, every state was obligated to extend those same, but only those same, rights and protections to all residents without regard to race.

Thus, the original understanding of the equal protection clause—actually, of section one in its entirety—was that it forbade every state to discriminate against any of its residents on the basis of race *with respect to certain sorts of rights* (and the protection of those rights)—those pertaining to physical security, freedom of movement, and capacity to contract and own property. Of course, by contemporary lights the original understanding of equal protection is exceedingly narrow. The modern principle of equal protection, however, is an "elaboration" of

23. Karst, [*The Supreme Court, 1976 Term—Foreword: Equal Citizenship Under*   *the Fourteenth Amendment,* 91 Harv.L. Rev. 1, 15 (1977).]

this original understanding, developed over the course of nearly a century of Supreme Court decisions. * * *

II. THE PARADIGM: RACIAL DISCRIMINATION

A. Toward a Broader Understanding

In 1880, in *Strauder v. West Virginia*,[25] the Supreme Court sustained the first claim of racial discrimination to come before it. The Court reversed the conviction of a black man who contended that his trial by a jury on which, under state statute, only white males were eligible to serve violated the fourteenth amendment. It seems clear that the Court was substantially faithful to the original understanding of the amendment: the statutory exclusion of blacks from juries, as the Court emphasized, denied to blacks a principal judicial protection of life and liberty granted to residents generally.[26]

But in *Strauder* the Court said something suggestive of a broader understanding of the amendment:

> The very fact that colored people are singled out and expressly denied by a statute all right to participate in the administration of the law, as jurors, because of their color, though they are citizens, and may be in other respects fully qualified, is practically a brand upon them, affixed by the law, an assertion of their *inferiority,* and a stimulant to that race prejudice which is an impediment to securing to individuals of the race that equal justice which the law aims to secure to all others.

This language suggests that *any* law constituting "a brand upon [blacks], . . . an assertion of their inferiority, . . . a stimulant to . . . race prejudice" is offensive to the amendment, *whether or not* the law denies a right, or a judicial protection of a right, pertaining to physical security, freedom of movement, or capacity to contract or own property. * * *

Sixteen years after *Strauder,* the Supreme Court decided the infamous *Plessy v. Ferguson.*[29] There the Court rejected a constitutional attack on a Louisiana statute requiring racially segregated accommodations on passenger trains and making it a crime for any passenger to go "into a coach or compartment to which by race he does not belong." In a prophetic dissent, the first Justice Harlan observed what was indispu-

---

25. 100 U.S. 303 (1880).

26. Raoul Berger would presumably take issue with me here. Berger, who insists that § 1 of the fourteenth amendment was intended to have *exactly* the same scope as the Civil Rights Act of 1866, quotes several sponsors of the Act to the effect that the Act would not grant blacks the right to serve on juries. * * * However, it is not unreasonable, after comparing the general language of § 1 of the amendment to the more specific language of the Act, to think that the framers meant to constitutionalize not only the particular rights enumerated in the Act, but also

rights of the sort enumerated there. As Berger himself acknowledges, § 1 was intended to prohibit racial discrimination not merely with respect to the definition of rights pertaining to "life, liberty, and property" in the narrow, original sense, but also with respect to judicial protections of those rights. * * * And certainly one such "judicial" protection, as the Court in *Strauder* took pains to emphasize, is having members of one's own race, especially when that race is the object of vilification, legally competent to serve on one's criminal jury.

29. 163 U.S. 537 (1896).

table—that the statute was predicated on the view that "colored citizens are so inferior and degraded that they cannot be allowed to sit in public coaches occupied by white citizens." * * *

In sustaining the statute, however, the majority did not invoke the narrow original understanding of the equal protection clause. Far from rejecting Harlan's contention that *any* law predicated on the view that nonwhites are by virtue of race inferior offends equal protection, the majority, in making the wholly implausible argument that the statute was not predicated on the supposed inferiority of nonwhites, implicitly embraced his premise:

> Laws permitting, and even requiring, [the] separation [of the races] in places where they are liable to be brought into contact do not necessarily imply the *inferiority* of either race to the other. . . . [T]he underlying fallacy of the plaintiff's argument . . . [is] the assumption that the enforced separation of the two races stamps the colored race with a badge of inferiority. If this be so, it is not by reason of anything found in the act, but solely because the colored race chooses to put that construction upon it.

Thus, early on, the Supreme Court moved, if only in its rhetoric, beyond the original understanding of equal protection toward a broader understanding, one embracing the principle that *any* law predicated on the view that one person is by virtue of race *inferior* to another offends equal protection. It was not until *Brown v. Board of Education* [35] that the Court was able, or willing, to enforce this broader understanding. *Brown* and the subsequent per curiam opinions disestablishing, with a simple citation to *Brown*, segregated beaches, buses, golf courses, and parks, plainly stand as the major vindication of the principle, implicit in the Court's thinking as early as *Strauder* and *Plessy*, that state action predicated on the supposed moral inferiority of a particular racial group is unjust. *Loving v. Virginia*, [37] in which the Court struck down an antimiscegenation law, represents another significant vindication of this principle. * * *

What precisely is this broader understanding of equal protection? What is the central guiding principle of decisions such as *Brown* and *Loving?* It is a notion of the moral equality of the races—the principle that no person is morally inferior to another by virtue of race. Because race is not a factor indicating anything about the moral worth of persons, race is morally irrelevant to state laws and policies. Therefore, state action predicated on the view that one person is by virtue of race inferior to another offends equal protection.

I should clarify at the outset the special sense in which I use this terminology. To say that one person is the moral equal of another is to say that the former is no less worthy or deserving than the latter of respect, concern, opportunity for self-fulfillment, and the like, and no more deserving of subordination to or domination by others. Even if one accepts that no person is morally inferior to another by virtue of

35. 347 U.S. 483 (1954).   37. 388 U.S. 1 (1967).

race, obviously not every person is the moral equal, in the sense indicated, of every other person. The extent of the respect, concern, and the like that one person accords another is conventionally a function of the extent to which the former approves, disapproves, or regards with indifference the latter's choices and activities, his or her self-definition. Regrettably, the extent of the respect and concern that we accord another person is sometimes also a function of the extent to which we approve or disapprove that person's status, not as an individual, but as a depersonalized abstraction—"black," for example, or "woman." It is, of course, our evolving sense of the justice—indeed, the rationality—vel non of this latter sort of consideration as a basis for evaluating the moral worth of another that informs the ongoing development of equal protection doctrine. This conception of equal protection as embodying a principle of moral equality does not rely on the notion, recently put forth by Ronald Dworkin and amplified by others, that every person is entitled to "equal concern and respect." [42] The distinct notion on which it does rely is this: although not every person is the moral equal of every other person, there are some traits and factors—of which race is the paradigmatic example—by virtue of which no person ought to be deemed morally inferior to any other person.

Whether the Supreme Court's elaboration of the original understanding of the equal protection clause is a persuasive one is not a particularly difficult question. The fourteenth amendment constitutionalized the proposition that it is unjust (or, if it makes a difference, wrong) to deny to nonwhites certain rights—those pertaining to physical security, freedom of movement, or capacity to contract or own property—granted to residents generally. Why is it unjust? Two different reasons might be given. First, it might be unjust because those rights are so important—i.e., "fundamental"—that *even* nonwhites, though not so fully human or equal in moral worth to whites that they should enjoy the same legal status as whites in all respects, should nonetheless enjoy these rights. Second, it might be unjust because to deny these rights on the basis of race, as the Court in

---

42. See R. Dworkin, Taking Rights Seriously 266–78 (1977) * * *. To the extent Dworkin's notion is simply a way of saying that all persons are entitled to be regarded *as persons*, that is, "as human beings who are capable of forming and acting on intelligent conceptions of how their lives should be lived," and "who are capable of suffering and frustration," * * * I have no quarrel with the notion, but I do not rely on it. In fact, in my view the notion is entirely too meager to be of much service in equal protection cases.

At times I wonder whether Dworkin's notion doesn't have a more ambitious thrust, or at least lend itself to misunderstanding. For example, Dworkin says that "the right to *treatment as an equal* . . . is the right . . . to be treated with the *same* respect and concern *as anyone else*." * * * Surely "same" does not mean "same degree of." After all, the claim that every person, no matter what his or her self-definition, is entitled to the same degree of respect, concern, and the like as anyone else—that Hitler, for example, is entitled to the same degree of respect, etc., as Mahatma Ghandi—is wholly implausible. Such a claim, which no one so far as I am aware has made, denies the fundamental insight that the principal function of moral evaluation—of granting or withholding respect, concern, and the like—is to encourage choices and activities deemed beneficial and to discourage those deemed harmful.

Strauder indicated, is to assert the *moral inferiority* of the aggrieved racial minority. Although some of those responsible for the fourteenth amendment, perhaps many, would have given the first reason and rejected the second, others would have given, and certainly most persons today would give, the second reason in support and explanation of the proposition. Although it once was taken seriously, the first reason is not taken seriously now. But, if it is unjust to deny certain rights on the basis of race because to do so is to assert the moral inferiority of the racial minority whose rights are denied, then to discriminate against nonwhites with respect to legal status in any respect must be unjust as well, because such discrimination is an assertion of moral inferiority, a denial of human equality. In this sense, the equal protection clause—or more precisely, the proposition that the clause constitutionalized—can fairly be taken to radiate the principle that no person is by virtue of race morally inferior to another, a principle under which not merely some but all hostile discriminations against nonwhites are unjust. Thus, the principle of *Brown* and *Loving,* that any law or other state action predicated on the supposed moral inferiority of a particular racial group is unjust, is a persuasive, even compelling, elaboration of the equal protection clause.

PAUL BREST, IN DEFENSE OF THE ANTIDISCRIMINATION PRINCIPLE

90 Harv.L.Rev. 1, 5–10, 22–26, 28–29, 31, 33, 43–52 (1976).

By the "antidiscrimination principle" I mean the general principle disfavoring classifications and other decisions and practices that depend on the race (or ethnic origin) of the parties affected.

*   *   *

I. THE ANTIDISCRIMINATION PRINCIPLE

The antidiscrimination principle rests on fundamental moral values that are widely shared in our society. Although the text and legislative history of laws that incorporate this principle can inform our understanding of it, the principle itself is at least as likely to inform our interpretations of the laws. This is especially true with respect to the equal protection clause of the fourteenth amendment. The text and history of the clause are vague and ambiguous and cannot, in any event, infuse the antidiscrimination principle with moral force or justify its extension to novel circumstances and new beneficiaries. Therefore, the argument of this section does not ultimately turn on authority, but on whether it comports with the reader's reflective understanding of the antidiscrimination principle.

Stated most simply, the antidiscrimination principle disfavors race-dependent decisions and conduct—at least when they selectively disadvantage the members of a minority group. By race-dependent, I mean decisions and conduct (hereafter, simply decisions) that would have been different but for the race of those benefited or disadvantaged by them. Race-dependent decisions may take several forms, including overt racial classifications on the face of statutes and covert decisions by officials.

A. Rationales for the Antidiscrimination Principle

The antidiscrimination principle guards against certain defects in the *process* by which race-dependent decisions are made and also against certain harmful *results* of race-dependent decisions. Restricting the principle to a unitary purpose vitiates its moral force and requires the use of sophisticated reasoning to explain applications that seem self-evident.

1. Defects of Process.—The antidiscrimination principle is designed to prevent both irrational and unfair infliction of injury.

Race-dependent decisions are irrational insofar as they reflect the assumption that members of one race are less worthy than other people. Not all such decisions are necessarily irrational, however. For example, if black laborers tend to be absent from work more often than their white counterparts—for whatever reason—it is not irrational for an employer to prefer white applicants for the job. If Americans of Japanese ancestry were more prone to disloyalty than Caucasians during World War II, it was not irrational for the United States government to take special precautions against sabotage and espionage by them. Regulations and decisions based on statistical generalizations are commonplace in all developed societies and essential to their functioning. And it is often rational for decisionmakers to rely on weak and even dubious generalizations. Consider, for example, a fire department's or airline's policy against employing overweight personnel, based on the rather slight probability that they will suffer a heart attack while on duty.

In short, the mere fact that most blacks are industrious and most Japanese–Americans loyal does not make the employer's or the Government's decision irrational. Indeed, if all race-dependent decisions were irrational, there would be no need for an antidiscrimination principle, for it would suffice to apply the widely held moral, constitutional, and practical principle that forbids treating persons irrationally. The antidiscrimination principle fills a special need because—as even a glance at history indicates—race-dependent decisions that are rational and purport to be based solely on legitimate considerations are likely in fact to rest on assumptions of the differential worth of racial groups or on the related phenomenon of racially selective sympathy and indifference.

Mr. Justice Black focused on the first of these dangers in *Korematsu v. United States*,[33] the case in which the Government sought to justify its policy of interning Japanese–Americans, and in which the Court first enunciated the modern "suspect classification" doctrine. He wrote for the majority:

33. 323 U.S. 214 (1944).

[A]ll legal restrictions which curtail the civil rights of a single racial group are immediately suspect. . . . [C]ourts must subject them to the most rigid scrutiny. Pressing public necessity may sometimes justify the existence of such restrictions; racial antagonism never can.

Mr. Justice Black chose the word "suspect" advisedly. For, although a court often cannot ascertain the true motives underlying a decision, our history and traditions provide strong reasons to suspect that racial classifications ultimately rest on assumptions of the differential worth of racial groups. These racial value judgments appear in forms besides "racial antagonism"—for example in paternalistic assumptions of racial inferiority.

By the phenomenon of racially selective sympathy and indifference I mean the unconscious failure to extend to a minority the same recognition of humanity, and hence the same sympathy and care, given as a matter of course to one's own group.

Although racially selective sympathy and indifference (hereafter, just indifference) is an inevitable consequence of attributing intrinsic value to membership in a racial group, it may also result from a desire to enhance our own power and esteem by enhancing the power and esteem of members of groups to which we belong. And it may also result—often unconsciously—from our tendency to sympathize most readily with those who seem most like ourselves. Whatever its cause, decisions that reflect this phenomenon, like those reflecting overt racial hostility, are unfair; for by hypothesis, they are decisions disadvantaging minority persons that would not be made under the identical circumstances if they disadvantaged members of the dominant group. The unequal treatment could be justified only if one group were in fact more worthy than the other. This justification failing, such treatment violates the cardinal rule of fairness—the Golden Rule.

2. *Harmful Results.*—A second and independent rationale for the antidiscrimination principle is the prevention of the harms which may result from race-dependent decisions. Often, the most obvious harm is the denial of the opportunity to secure a desired benefit—a job, a night's lodging at a motel, a vote. But this does not completely describe the consequences of race-dependent decisionmaking. Decisions based on assumptions of intrinsic worth and selective indifference inflict psychological injury by stigmatizing their victims as inferior. Moreover, because acts of discrimination tend to occur in pervasive patterns, their victims suffer especially frustrating, cumulative and debilitating injuries.

* * *

Recognition of the stigmatic injury inflicted by discrimination explains applications of the antidiscrimination principle where the material harm seems slight or problematic. For example, it fully explains the harmfulness of de jure school segregation without the need to invoke controversial social science evidence concerning the effects of segregation on achievement, interracial attitudes, and the like, and thus explains the Supreme Court's casual extension of *Brown* [*v. Board of Education*] to prohibit the segregation of public beaches, parks, golf courses and buses. It also explains how present practices that are racially neutral may nonetheless perpetuate the harms of past de jure segregation.

Racial generalizations usually inflict psychic injury whether or not they are in fact premised on assumptions of differential moral worth. Although all of us recognize that institutional decisions must depend on generalizations based on objective characteristics of persons and things rather than on individualized judgments, we nonetheless tend to feel unfairly treated when disadvantaged by a generalization that is not true as applied to us. Generalizations based on immutable personal traits such as race or sex are especially frustrating because we can do nothing to escape their operation. These generalizations are still more pernicious, for they are often premised on the supposed correlation between the inherited characteristic and the undesirable voluntary behavior of those who possess the characteristic—for example, blacks are less industrious, trustworthy or clean than whites. Because the behavior is voluntary, and hence the proper object of moral condemnation, individuals as to whom the generalization is inaccurate may justifiably feel that the decisionmaker has passed moral judgment on them.

The psychological injury inflicted by generalizations based on race is compounded by the frustrating and cumulative nature of their material injuries. Racial generalizations are pervasive and have traditionally operated in the same direction—to the disadvantage of members of the minority group. A person who is denied one opportunity because he or she is short or overweight will find other opportunities, for in our society height and weight do not often serve as the bases for generalizations determining who will receive benefits. By contrast, at least until very recently, a black was not denied *an* opportunity because of his or her race, but denied virtually *all* desirable opportunities. As door after door is shut in one's face, the individual acts of discrimination combine into a systematic and grossly inequitable frustration of opportunity.

* * *

II. RACIALLY DISPROPORTIONATE IMPACT

Race-dependent decisions typically produce a racially disproportionate impact—a disproportion between the number of blacks and whites on the voting rolls, in an employer's work force, on a jury, or in a school. Because race-dependent decisions are so often concealed, racially disproportionate impact has customarily been offered as evidence that ostensibly nondiscriminatory decisions are in fact race-dependent. * * *

* * *

Last Term, in *Washington v. Davis,*[105] an action challenging the verbal ability test required of applicants by the District of Columbia Police Department, the Supreme Court held that * * * only official conduct having a "discriminatory purpose" violates the equal protection clause. * * *

* * *

Davis reflects both the centrality of race-dependence to the equal protection clause and the judicial unmanageability of a general rule requiring an extraordinary justification for practices that produce racially disproportionate effects. The following discussion identifies and evaluates five possible rationales for the disproportionate impact doctrine. The first three are rooted in the antidiscrimination principle and involve remedies for present, past, and future discrimination. I believe that the disproportionate impact doctrine can continue to play a useful role, for courts as well as for legislatures, in enforcing the antidiscrimination principle. The fourth rationale is concerned with remedying "race-specific harms" produced by disproportionate impact. Although legislatures may properly ameliorate race-specific harms, I argue that the Constitution provides no basis for judicial intervention. The fifth rationale embodies a theory that accords moral status to groups and holds that it is intrinsically unjust for one racial group to be appreciably worse off than others. I believe that this theory is fundamentally misconceived and should not serve as the basis of policymaking by any institution.

A. Suspected Race–Dependency

Federal courts have used the disproportionate impact doctrine to avoid the unique difficulties of dealing with discriminatory intent or motive. * * *

* * *

* * * If courts may grant relief only when plaintiffs have made a clear case [of discriminatory motivation] on the record, many instances will remain where race-dependent decisions are strongly suspected but cannot be proved. Although this is not essentially different from the difficulty facing the proponents in most litigation seeking to overturn government policies, it is especially troubling in the race area. The accumulation of suspected but unproved race-dependent conduct, such as decisions to zone out low income housing, may systematically deprive minorities of important benefits. And the very existence of a state of affairs which "everyone knows" is based on racial discrimination but no one will remedy is demoralizing and stigmatic.

The disproportionate impact doctrine thus acts as a safeguard against improper race-dependent decisions. But * * * the doctrine cannot reasonably be applied across the board. If disproportionate impact is to remain a useful device, it must be used selectively and

105. [426 U.S. 229 (1976).]

perhaps be modified to create rebuttable rather than conclusive presumptions of discriminatory intent. * * *

B. The Effects of Past and Remote Discrimination

The effects of discrimination may attenuate over time or be submerged in superseding events. But the injuries inflicted by discrimination can place its victims at a disadvantage in a variety of future endeavors, and discrimination can also perpetuate itself by altering the social environment to harm new generations of victims. Discrimination often works its injuries through practices, not themselves race-dependent, implemented by institutions that have not themselves discriminated. Past and remote discrimination often manifest themselves in racially disproportionate impact, and the antidiscrimination principle may therefore support its amelioration or elimination.

* * *

The causal connection between past discrimination and present states of affairs has * * * received the Court's attention in school segregation litigation. *Green v. County School Board* [156] involved a small Virginia school district which, like many rural areas, was not residentially segregated. The district had only two schools, which were de jure segregated—first pursuant to state law, later by local practice. In 1965, in order to remain eligible for federal financial aid, the school board adopted a "freedom of choice" plan of desegregation, which required each pupil to choose which school to attend each year. After three years under the plan, fifteen percent of the black pupils attended the formerly all-white school; no whites attended the all-black school.

* * *

In *Green* the causal connection between past discrimination and the current racial composition of the schools was as clear as such matters ever can be. It is not plausible, and the school board did not try to argue, that the county school system would have been substantially segregated in 1968 had children never been assigned by race. * * *

* * *

C. Preventing Future Remote Discrimination

The disproportionate absence of minorities from certain positions—whether or not itself the result of racial discrimination—may conduce to discrimination in other areas. Such a link underlies the special legislative and judicial concern to protect the political power of minorities. * * *

The Supreme Court's constitutional doctrine concerning multimember legislative districts seems responsive to [this] concern[.] A 1966 opinion indicated that constitutional problems would arise if "designedly or otherwise, a multi-member constituency apportionment scheme . . . operate[d] to minimize or cancel out the voting strength of racial

---

156. 391 U.S. 430 (1968).

or political elements of the voting population." [201]   In *White v. Regester*,[202] a unanimous Court struck down two multimember districts in Texas, on the ground that black and Mexican-American minorities were effectively excluded from political processes.   Mr. Justice White's opinion assigned plaintiffs a heavy burden, but not one requiring proof of discriminatory intent:

> [I]t is not enough that the racial group allegedly discriminated against has not had legislative seats in proportion to its voting potential.   The plaintiffs' burden is to produce evidence to support findings that the political processes leading to nomination and election were not equally open to participation by the group in question—that its members had less opportunity than did other residents in the district to participate in the political processes and to elect legislators of their choice.[203]

The Court did not imply that the multimember districts had been discriminatorily designed.   It noted, however, that both counties involved had histories of discrimination in the provision of public services and that in one the major political organization had intentionally excluded minorities.

D.   Race–Specific Harms

The disproportionate disadvantage or exclusion, or the segregation, of the members of a racial minority may give rise to individual and social costs produced solely because of the race of the people affected—costs that would not arise from the identical practices if their impact was random with respect to race.   These "race-specific harms" can result from practices that are not race-dependent.

The disproportionate absence of minorities from juries is an example.   The principle that juries should represent a cross-section of the community reflects a belief that jurors from different racial, ethnic, and socioeconomic groups tend to have different viewpoints which affect their perceptions of fact and exercise of discretion, and that the system will function most accurately and fairly if a variety of viewpoints is brought to bear on the decision.   For this reason, although it would be impossible to assure the proportional representation of the many relevant social groups on jury panels, some legislatures and courts have taken measures to assure that salient groups are not systematically underrepresented.   *   *   *

*   *   * [O]ther putative race-specific harms do not violate definite constitutional provisions.   This is true, for example, of the harms that may result from de facto segregation and from the depressed socioeconomic status of certain minorities.

School segregation, whatever its cause, has been said to reduce the self-esteem, aspirations, motivations, and achievement of black children

---

201. Burns v. Richardson, 384 U.S. 73, 88 (1966). In Whitcomb v. Chavis, 403 U.S. 124 (1971), the Court scrutinized, but upheld, multimember districts in Marion County, Indiana.

202. 412 U.S. 755 (1973).

203. *Id.* at 765–66.

and to encourage racial fears, hostility, and prejudice. But although these hypotheses have been tested in hundreds of studies, none has been established or disproved to the satisfaction of disinterested social scientists. * * *

* * *

The existence, degree, and nature of these and most other race-specific harms arguably produced by non-race-dependent practices are seldom self-evident. The independent significance of race, as distinguished from poverty, will likely remain unknown for the immediate future. Assuming, however, that significant race-specific harms do exist, by what authority may they be ameliorated?

Much race-specific harm in contemporary American society may be traceable to present or past violations of the antidiscrimination principle. It seems improbable that most lower-class, isolated, and intradependent minority communities would possess these vulnerable characteristics to nearly the same degree were it not for longstanding and pervasive patterns of discrimination. The antidiscrimination principle provides sufficient authority for ameliorating race-specific harms to the extent that they depend on conditions caused by discrimination.

An institution enjoying more or less plenary policymaking authority may remedy race-specific harms that are *not* traceable to violations of the antidiscrimination principle, just as it may remedy any number of other kinds of injuries wholly unrelated to race. For example, a school board might focus on the special needs of minority children today, and deal with blind and retarded children a decade later—as claims come to its attention through interest groups, social upheavals, personal experience, and the like. But where the very authority of the judiciary is based on its ability to expound and apply general principles, it cannot act on such an ad hoc basis. Apart from the antidiscrimination principle, does there exist a coherent principle that requires remedy of race-specific harms but not other equally severe injuries—a principle, for example, under which a school district must spend X to prevent Y amount of race-specific harm by integrating the schools, but need not spend the same amount of money to prevent the same amount of harm to mentally or physically handicapped children or to white children from impoverished environments?

To be sure, race-specific harms may produce serious individual and social costs. But these costs seem neither different in kind nor of a greater order of magnitude to the individuals affected than many others that might be ameliorated by changing school assignment schemes, employment criteria, and the like. * * *

E. Justice for Racial Groups

The most pernicious feature of racial prejudice and discrimination is their underlying premise that members of some racial groups are less worthy than members of others. The antidiscrimination principle holds that this assumption is fallacious because race has no moral

salience. For administrative purposes, some remedies for racial discrimination are triggered by disproportionate racial impact or treat
persons according to membership in racial groups; but group membership is always a proxy for the individual's right not to be discriminated
against. Similarly, remedies for race-specific harms recognize the
sociological consequences of group identification and affiliation only to
assure justice for individual members.

In contrast to the theories considered so far, some commentators
have suggested that racial groups should be treated as moral entities,
holding rights as groups to distributive and compensatory justice. The
distributive theory assumes the moral permissibility of unequal distri-
butions of welfare among individuals, but holds that it is at least prima
facie unjust for one racial or ethnic group to be substantially worse off
than others. Like many individual-oriented theories of distributive
justice, a group theory is essentially indifferent to the history that led
to the unequal distribution. For example, Owen M. Fiss proposes a
noncompensatory, purely redistributive principle—a "group disadvantaging principle"—that requires relief for any group that constitutes a "perpetual underclass." He argues that "[t]he redistributive
strategy could give expression to an ethical view against caste, one that
would make it undesirable for any social group to occupy a position of
subordination for any extended period of time." [218]   *   *   *

The arguments supporting the theories of group distributive justice
are difficult to discern. Professor Fiss states that his "group disadvantaging principle" is justified primarily by its intuitive correctness:
"visions about how society should be structured may be as irreducible
as visions about how individuals should be treated—for example, with
dignity."   *   *   *

If a society can be said to have an underlying political theory, ours
has not been a theory of organic groups but of liberalism, focusing on
the rights of individuals, including rights of distributive justice. Of
course, we recognize the sociological fact that people desire to affiliate
and associate with others who share common interests or characteristics. The religion and association clauses of the first amendment are
responsive to such desires. But though groups and associations may
benefit incidentally from these guarantees, the amendment is designed
to protect the individual's freedom to associate. We grant rights to
associations or treat them as fictitious persons only to protect the rights
of their individual members and for other instrumental purposes.
Otherwise, the rights of associations and groups are no greater than the
sum of those of their members. Indeed, under our received—albeit
philosophically inadequate—metaphor of the social contract, the state
itself does not enjoy rights greater than those of its citizens.

To say that we generally embrace the liberal tradition is, of course,
no response to the claim that we should modify the theory and restruc-

---

218. [Fiss, *Groups and the Equal Protection Clause,* 5 Phil. & Pub. Aff. 107 (1976).]

ture our institutions accordingly. But without derogating from competing political traditions, they have implications that vie with, if they are not inconsistent with, principles that we hold fundamental—including the antidiscrimination principle, which attributes no moral significance to membership in racial groups, and notions of individual autonomy. Moreover, although the practices of nations—including our own—often fall short of their aspirations, most societies in which power is formally allocated among racial and national groups are strikingly oppressive, unequal, and unstable. In view of all of this, it seems reasonable to place the burden on proponents of a theory of group racial justice to show that it is morally tenable and consistent with other values that we cherish. To my knowledge, this has not yet been done.

Several commentators, who concede that racial groups have no intrinsic moral salience, assert that they acquire moral rights once the members of a group have suffered racial discrimination. * * *

> [T]here need be no contradiction involved in claiming that being black is both morally irrelevant for discriminating against people and morally relevant in discriminating in favour of people to provide reparations. . . . One may hold that people have an obligation to give reparations to groups they have wronged. By using the characteristic of being black as an identifying characteristic to discriminate against people, a person has wronged the group, blacks. He thus has an obligation to make reparations to the group. Since the obligation is to the group, no specific individual has a right to reparation. However, since the group is not an organized one like a state, church, or corporation, the only way to provide reparations to the group is to provide them to members of the group.[225]

A similar view may be implicit in some judicial decisions requiring employers and unions to adopt hiring and admission quotas to compensate for their past discrimination, even though the remedies are not likely to benefit the victims. * * *

* * *

The notion that the treatment of individuals as a group for malign purposes requires their treatment as a group for benign compensatory purposes has the superficial appeal of all such symmetries. But, unless one adopts a notion of group rights such as that examined and rejected above, the fact is that most injuries of discrimination—even indirect or secondary ones—were inflicted on particular persons and only they are entitled to compensation. Where discrimination has undermined the unity or culture of a group, it may be appropriate to characterize the injury as one to the group; but the appropriate remedy then is one that reestablishes the group, an end that is not promoted by the fiction of treating individual members as its agents.

225. Bayles, *Reparations to Wronged Groups*, 33 Analysis 182, 183 (1973).

OWEN M. FISS, GROUPS AND THE EQUAL PROTECTION CLAUSE

5 Phil. & Pub.Aff. 107, 108, 129, 141–142, 144–156 (1976).

One purpose of this essay is simply to underscore the fact that the antidiscrimination principle is not the Equal Protection Clause, that it is nothing more than a mediating principle. I want to bring to an end the identification of the Clause with the antidiscrimination principle. But I also have larger ambitions. I want to suggest that the antidiscrimination principle embodies a very limited conception of equality, one that is highly individualistic and confined to assessing the rationality of means. I also want to outline another mediating principle—the group-disadvantaging principle—one that has as good, if not better, claim to represent the ideal of equality, one that takes a fuller account of social reality, and one that more clearly focuses the issues that must be decided in equal protection cases.

*   *   *

THE LIMITATIONS OF THE ANTIDISCRIMINATION PRINCIPLE

*   *   * The antidiscrimination principle has structural limitations that prevent it from adequately resolving or even addressing certain central claims of equality now being advanced. For these claims the antidiscrimination principle either provides no framework of analysis or, even worse, provides the wrong one. *   *   *

*   *   *

The Problem of Facially Innocent Criteria

*   *   * [One such] problem area arises from state conduct that does in fact discriminate among persons, but not on the basis of a suspect criterion. The discrimination is based on a criterion that seems innocent on its face and yet nonetheless has the effect of disadvantaging blacks (or other minorities). For example, when the state purports to choose employees or college students on the basis of performance on standardized tests, and it turns out that the only persons admitted or hired are white.

As originally conceived[,] *   *   * the antidiscrimination principle promised to evolve a small, finite list of suspect criteria, such as race, religion, national origin, wealth, sex. These would be presumptively impermissible. The great bulk of other criteria may ultimately be deemed arbitrary in some particular instances because of ill-fit, but they would be presumptively valid. For these criteria—which I call *facially innocent*—the mere rational-relation test would suffice, and the probability would be very high that the statute or administrative action incorporating or utilizing such criteria would be sustained.

In some instances the presumption of validity may be dissolved, and the contrary presumption created, through the use of the concept of the *real* criterion. The plaintiffs can charge cheating: while the state says that it is selecting on the basis of an innocent criterion (such as performance on a written test), in truth the selection is being made on the basis of a suspect criterion (race). The substantiation of this charge confronts the plaintiffs with enormous evidentiary burdens. No one can be expected to admit to charges of cheating, and rarely is the result so striking ∗　∗　∗ as to permit only one inference—discrimination on the basis of a suspect criterion. But if the charge could be substantiated (perhaps with an assist from the reallocation of the burdens of proofs when the criterion had almost the same effect as a suspect one), then there would be no problem of using the strict-scrutiny branch of the antidiscrimination principle: the real criterion, as opposed to the stated criterion, is a suspect one, and there the court should insist upon a very tight fit between purpose and criterion. The troublesome cases arise, however, when the charge of cheating cannot be substantiated, where, for example, the court finds that in truth the jobs were allocated or students selected on the basis of academic performance. What then?

∗　∗　∗

A second, and seemingly more modest way of rationalizing the judicial treatment of facially innocent criteria, is to introduce the concept of past discrimination. Strict scrutiny should be given, so the argument runs, to state conduct that perpetuates the effects of earlier conduct (it might be state or private) that was based on the use of a suspect classification. Conduct that perpetuates the effects of past (suspect-criterion) discrimination is as presumptively invalid as the present use of suspect criteria. An objective civil service test is presumptively impermissible whenever it perpetuates the past discrimination of the dual school system (the dual school system put the blacks at a competitive disadvantage and the test perpetuates that disadvantage). The use of geographic proximity is an impermissible criterion of school assignment whenever it perpetuates the past discrimination of the dual school system. The racial assignments of that school system led to the present residential segregation and account for the location and size of the school buildings, and both of these factors in turn explain why the use of geographic proximity as a criterion of assignment results in segregated patterns of school attendance today.

A ban on "the perpetuation of past arbitrary discrimination" looks like a close cousin of the ban on "arbitrary discrimination." But this tie can only be maintained at great expense to important institutional values—those that cluster around the ideal of objectivity, an ideal the antidiscrimination principle is supposed to serve. A true inquiry into past discrimination necessitates evidentiary judgments that are likely to strain the judicial system—consume scarce resources and yield unsatisfying results. It would require the courts to construct causal connections that span significant periods of time, periods greater than those permitted under any general statute of limitations (a common device used to prevent the judiciary from undertaking inquiries where the evidence is likely to be stale, fragmentary, and generally unreliable). The difficulties of these backward-looking inquiries are compounded because the court must invariably deal with aggregate behavior, not just a single transaction; it must determine the causal explanation for the residential patterns of an entire community, or the skill levels of all the black applicants.

* * *

The third move designed to deal with the problem of facially innocent criteria—the introduction of the concept of de facto discrimination (or discriminatory effect)—does not focus on the past. Instead it shifts the trigger for strict scrutiny from the *criterion* of selection to the *result* of the selection process, and the result is stated in terms of a *group* rather than an individual. What triggers the strict scrutiny is not the criterion of selection itself, but rather the result—the fact that a minority group has been especially hurt. (This special hurt is sometimes described as a "differential impact.")

This concept of de facto discrimination also involves a basic modification of the antidiscrimination principle. The trigger is no longer classification, but rather group-impact. * * * The concern with the result reveals to me that what is ultimately at issue is the welfare of certain disadvantaged groups, not just the use of a criterion, and if that is at issue, there is no reason why the judicial intervention on behalf of that group should be limited to an inquiry as to the degree of fit between a criterion and a purpose.

THE GROUP–DISADVANTAGING PRINCIPLE

* * *

In attempting to formulate another theory of equal protection, I have viewed the Clause primarily, but not exclusively, as a protection for blacks. In part, this perspective stems from the original intent—the fact that the Clause was viewed as a means of safeguarding blacks from hostile state action. The Equal Protection Clause (following the circumlocution of the slave-clauses in the antebellum Constitution) uses the word "person," rather than "blacks." The generality of the word chosen to describe those protected enables other groups to invoke its protection; and I am willing to admit that was also probably intended. But this generality of coverage does not preclude a theory of primary reference—that blacks were the intended primary beneficiaries, that it was a concern for their welfare that prompted the Clause.

* * *

Starting from this perspective, a distinctively racial one, it strikes me as odd to build a general interpretation of the Equal Protection Clause * * * on the rejection of the idea that there are natural classes, that is, groups that have an identity and existence wholly apart from the challenged state statute or practice. There are natural classes, or social groups, in American society and blacks are such a group. Blacks are viewed as a group; they view themselves as a group; their identity is in large part determined by membership in the group; their social status is linked to the status of the group; and much of our action, institutional and personal, is based on these perspectives.

I use the term "group" to refer to a social group, and for me, a social group is more than a collection of individuals, all of whom, to use a polar example, happen to arrive at the same street corner at the same moment. A social group, as I use the term, has two other characteristics. (1) It is an *entity* (though not one that has a physical body). This means that the group has a distinct existence apart from its members, and also that it has an identity. It makes sense to talk about the group (at various points of time) and know that you are talking about the same group. You can talk about the group without reference to the particular individuals who happen to be its members at any one moment. (2) There is also a condition of *interdependence*. The identity and well-being of the members of the group and the identity and well-being of the group are linked. Members of the group identify themselves—explain who they are—by reference to their membership in the group; and their well-being or status is in part determined by the well-being or status of the group. * * *

I would be the first to admit that working with the concept of a group is problematic, much more so than working with the concept of an individual or criterion. It is "messy." For example, in some instances, it may be exceedingly difficult to determine whether particular individuals are members of the group; or whether a particular collection of persons constitutes a social group. I will also admit that my definition of a social group, and in particular the condition of interdependence, compounds rather than reduces, these classificatory disputes. But these disputes do not demonstrate the illegitimacy of this category of social entity nor deny the validity or importance of the idea. They only blur the edges. Similarly, the present reality of the social groups should not be obscured by a commitment to the ideal of a "classless society" or the individualistic ethic—the ideal of treating people as individuals rather than as members of groups. Even if the Equal Protection Clause is viewed as the means for furthering or achieving these individualistic ideals (and I am not sure why it should be), there is no reason why the Clause—as an instrument for bringing about the "good society"—must be construed as though it is itself governed by that ideal or why it should be assumed that the "good society" had been achieved in 1868, or is so now.

The conception of blacks as a social group is only the first step in constructing a mediating principle. We must also realize they are a very special type of social group. They have two other characteristics as a group that are critical in understanding the function and reach of the Equal Protection Clause. One is that blacks are very badly off, probably our worst-off class (in terms of material well-being second only to the American Indians), and in addition they have occupied the lowest rung for several centuries. In a sense, they are America's perpetual underclass. It is both of these characteristics—the relative position of the group and the duration of the position—that make efforts to improve the status of the group defensible. This redistribution may be rooted in a theory of compensation—blacks as a group were *put* in that position by others and the redistributive measures are *owed* to the group as a form of compensation. The debt would be viewed as owed by society, once again viewed as a collectivity. But a redistributive strategy need not rest on this idea of compensation, it need not be backward looking (though past discrimination might be relevant for *explaining* the identity and status of blacks as a social group). The redistributive strategy could give expression to an ethical view against caste, one that would make it undesirable for any social group to occupy a position of subordination for any extended period of time. What, it might be asked, is the justification for that vision? I am not certain whether it is appropriate to ask this question, to push the inquiry a step further and search for the justification of that ethic; visions about how society should be structured may be as irreducible as visions about how individuals should be treated—for example, with dignity. But if this second order inquiry is appropriate, a variety of justifications can be offered and they need not incorporate the notion of compensation. Changes in the hierarchical structure of society—the elimination of caste—might be justified as a means of (a) preserving social peace; (b) maintaining the community as a community, that is, as one cohesive whole; or (c) permitting the fullest development of the individual members of the subordinated group who otherwise might look upon the low status of the group as placing a ceiling on their aspirations and achievements.

It is not just the socioeconomic status of blacks as a group that explains their special position in equal protection theory. It is also their political status. The power of blacks in the political arena is severely limited. For the last two centuries the political power of this group was circumscribed in most direct fashion—disenfranchisement. The electoral strength of blacks was not equal to their numbers. That has changed following the massive enfranchisement of the Voting Rights Act of 1965, but structural limitations on the political power of blacks still persist. These limitations arise from three different sources, which can act either alternatively or cumulatively and which, in any event, are all interrelated. One source of weakness is their numbers, the fact that they are a numerical minority; the second is their economic status, their position as the perpetual underclass; and the third is that, as a "discrete and insular" minority, they are the object of "prejudice"—that is, the subject of fear, hatred, and distaste that make it particularly difficult for them to form coalitions with others (such as the white poor) and that make it advantageous for the dominant political parties to hurt them—to use them as a scapegoat.

* * *

Hence, despite recent demographic shifts in several large cities, I think it appropriate to view blacks as a group that is relatively powerless in the political arena and in my judgment that political status of the group justifies a special judicial solicitude on their behalf. When the product of a political process is a law that hurts blacks, the usual countermajoritarian objection to judicial invalidation—the objection that denies those "nine men" the right to substitute their view for that of "the people"—has little force. For the judiciary could be viewed as amplifying the voice of the powerless minority; the judiciary is attempting to rectify the injustice of the political process as a method of adjusting competing claims. The need for this rectification turns on whether the law is deemed one that harms blacks—a judgment that is admittedly hard to make when the perspective becomes a group one, for that requires the aggregation of interests and viewpoints, many of which are in conflict. It is important to emphasize, however, that the need for this rectification does not turn on whether the law embodies a classification, racial or otherwise; it is sufficient if the state law simply has the *effect* of hurting blacks. Nor should the rectification, once triggered by a harmful law, be confined to questions of fit—the judicial responsibility is more extensive than simply one of guarding against the risk of imprecise classifications by the political agencies. The relative powerlessness of blacks also requires that the judiciary strictly scrutinize the choice of ends; for it is just as likely that the interests of blacks as a group will not be adequately taken into account in choosing ends or goals. Maximizing goals such as reducing transportation costs (a goal that might account for the neighborhood-school plan) or having the most brilliant law students (a goal that might account for requiring a [high score] on the LSAT) are constitutionally permissible goals in the sense that there is no substantive constitutional provision (or implied purpose lying behind some provision) that deny them to the state. On the other hand, these maximizing goals are obviously not in any sense constitutionally compelled goals and there is a chance—a most substantial one—that they would not be chosen as *the* goals (without any modification) if the interests of the blacks as a group were adequately taken into account—if the goal-choosers paid sufficient attention to the special needs, desires, and views of this powerless group.

The injustice of the political process must be corrected, and perhaps as a last resort, that task falls to the judiciary. But this claim does not yield any basis for specifying what the corrected process would look like, or what the court should say when it amplifies the voice of the powerless minority. A just political process would be one in which blacks would have "more" of a voice than they in fact do, but not necessarily one in which they would "win." In a sense there is a remedial lacuna; a pure process claim cannot determine substantive outcomes. * * * But this processual theory focusing on the relative powerlessness of blacks in the political arena need not stand alone. The substantive standards can be supplied by the other critical characteristics of this social group—perpetual subordination. The political status of the group justifies the institutional allocations—our willingness to allow those "nine men" to substitute their judgment (about ends as well as means) for that of "the people." The socioeconomic position of the group supplies an additional reason for the judicial activism and also determines the content of the intervention—improvement of the status of that group.

I would therefore argue that blacks should be viewed as having three characteristics that are relevant in the formulation of equal protection theory: (a) they are a social group; (b) the group has been in a position of perpetual subordination; and (c) the political power of the group is severely circumscribed. Blacks are what might be called a specially disadvantaged group, and I would view the Equal Protection Clause as a protection for such groups. Blacks are the prototype of the protected group, but they are not the only group entitled to protection. There are other social groups, even as I have used the term, and if these groups have the same characteristics as blacks—perpetual subordination and circumscribed political power—they should be considered specially disadvantaged and receive the same degree of protection. What the Equal Protection Clause protects is specially disadvantaged groups, not just blacks. A concern for equal treatment and the word "person" appearing in the Clause permit and probably require this generality of coverage.

Some of these specially disadvantaged groups can be defined in terms of characteristics that do not have biological roots and that are not immutable; the Clause might protect certain language groups and aliens. Moreover, in passing upon a claim to be considered a specially disadvantaged group, the court may treat one of the characteristics entitling blacks to that status as a sufficient but not a necessary condition; indeed the court may even develop variable standards of protection—it may tolerate disadvantaging practices that would not be tolerated if the group was a "pure" specially disadvantaged group. Jews or women might be entitled to less protection than American Indians, though nonetheless entitled to some protection. Finally, these judicial judgments may be time-bound. Through the process of assimilation the group may cease to exist, or even if the group continues to retain its identity, its socioeconomic and political positions may so improve so as to bring to an end its status as specially disadvantaged.

All this means that the courts will have some leeway in identifying the groups protected by the Equal Protection Clause. I think, however, it would be a mistake to use this flexibility to extend the protection to what might be considered artificial classes, those created by a classification or criterion embodied in a state practice or statute, for example, those classes created by tax categories (those having incomes between $27,000 and $30,000, or between $8,000 and $10,000) or licensing statutes (the manufacturers of filled milk). By definition those classes do not have an independent social identity and existence, or if they do, the condition of interdependence is lacking. It is difficult, if not impossible, to make an assessment of their socioeconomic status or of their political power (other than that they have just lost a legislative battle). And, if this is true, neither redistribution nor stringent judicial intervention on their behalf can be justified. It is not that such arguments are unpersuasive, but that they are almost unintelligible. Thus, in only one sense should the group-disadvantaging strategy be viewed as conducive to "more equality": it will get more for fewer. It will get more for the specially disadvantaged groups but will not provide any protection for artificial classes, those solely created by statute or a state practice. Of course, this loss may be more formal than real. Artificial classes constitute part of the universe that the antidiscrimination principle *purports* to protect, but in truth almost never does protect given the permissibility of the minimum-scrutiny inquiry.

[In the concluding portion of his article Fiss explains how he would implement his proposal for a group-disadvantaging principle. He admits that it would reach the same results as the antidiscrimination principle in what he calls "first-order" situations—exclusion of blacks from public institutions. The choice of a principle would matter more in "second-order" cases—challenges to the use of facially innocent criteria such as test performance. And in "third-order" cases—preferential treatment—the differences would be most evident. The antidiscrimination principle, with its individualistic character, tends to prohibit such treatment; a focus on disadvantaged groups tends to allow (perhaps even require) it.

[Not every instance of disparate impact is a "second-order" case. A sales tax, because of its diffuse impact, may harm individuals but not aggravate the subordinate status of blacks as a group. But in any true "second-order" case the state practice would be presumptively invalid. The state could overcome the presumption by showing that its practice was necessary to produce a compelling benefit. It could, for example, insist on certain minimum levels of competence for its employees or students.

[In "third-order" cases Fiss's principle would require only a rational basis for preferential policies. The reason is that the Equal Protection Clause is not concerned with fairness (e.g., to individual whites), but with group harm. For the same reason, it would not matter that some individual beneficiaries (e.g. rich blacks) were not victims.]

CHARLES R. LAWRENCE III, THE ID, THE EGO, AND EQUAL PROTECTION: RECKONING WITH UNCONSCIOUS RACISM

39 Stan.L.Rev. 317, 321–323, 328, 331–339, 344–355 (1987).

Much of one's inability to know racial discrimination when one sees it results from a failure to recognize that racism is both a crime and a disease.[15] This failure is compounded by a reluctance to admit that the illness of racism infects almost everyone. Acknowledging and understanding the malignancy are prerequisites to the discovery of an appropriate cure. But the diagnosis is difficult, because our own

---

15. "Immorality" and "criminality" are thought of in terms of blameworthiness. In contrast, Chester Pierce, a black psychiatrist, has described racism as a "public health problem." Pierce, *Psychiatric Problems of Black Minority,* in 2 American Handbook of Psychiatry 512, 513 (G. Caplan 2d ed. 1974). * * *

contamination with the very illness for which a cure is sought impairs our comprehension of the disorder.

* * *

Americans share a common historical and cultural heritage in which racism has played and still plays a dominant role. Because of this shared experience, we also inevitably share many ideas, attitudes, and beliefs that attach significance to an individual's race and induce negative feelings and opinions about nonwhites. To the extent that this cultural belief system has influenced all of us, we are all racists. At the same time, most of us are unaware of our racism. We do not recognize the ways in which our cultural experience has influenced our beliefs about race or the occasions on which those beliefs affect our actions. In other words, a large part of the behavior that produces racial discrimination is influenced by unconscious racial motivation.

There are two explanations for the unconscious nature of our racially discriminatory beliefs and ideas. First, Freudian theory states that the human mind defends itself against the discomfort of guilt by denying or refusing to recognize those ideas, wishes, and beliefs that conflict with what the individual has learned is good or right. While our historical experience has made racism an integral part of our culture, our society has more recently embraced an ideal that rejects racism as immoral. When an individual experiences conflict between racist ideas and the societal ethic that condemns those ideas, the mind excludes his racism from consciousness.

Second, the theory of cognitive psychology states that the culture—including, for example, the media and an individual's parents, peers, and authority figures—transmits certain beliefs and preferences. Because these beliefs are so much a part of the culture, they are not experienced as explicit lessons. Instead, they seem part of the individual's rational ordering of her perceptions of the world. The individual is unaware, for example, that the ubiquitous presence of a cultural stereotype has influenced her perception that blacks are lazy or unintelligent. Because racism is so deeply ingrained in our culture, it is likely to be transmitted by tacit understandings: Even if a child is not told that blacks are inferior, he learns that lesson by observing the behavior of others. These tacit understandings, because they have never been articulated, are less likely to be experienced at a conscious level.

I. "THY SPEECH MAKETH THEE MANIFEST": A PRIMER ON THE UNCONSCIOUS AND RACE

* * *

Psychoanalytic Theory: An Explanation of Racism's Irrationality

The division of the mind into the conscious and the unconscious is the fundamental principle of psychoanalysis. Psychoanalytic theory explains the existence of pathological mental behavior as well as certain otherwise unexplained behavior in healthy people by postulating two powerful mental processes—the primary and the secondary—which govern how the mind works. The primary process, or Id, occurs outside of our awareness. It consists of desires, wishes, and instincts that strive for gratification. It follows its own laws, of which the supreme one is pleasure. The secondary process, or Ego, happens under conscious control and is bound by logic and reason. We use this process to adapt to reality: The Ego is required to respect the demands of reality and to conform to ethical and moral laws. On their way to gratification, the Id impulses must pass through the territory of the Ego where they are criticized, rejected, or modified, often by some defensive measure on the part of the secondary process. Defensive mechanisms such as repression, denial, introjection, projection, reaction formation, sublimation, and reversal resolve the conflicts between the primary and secondary processes by disguising forbidden wishes and making them palatable.

*   *   *

An examination of the beliefs that racially prejudiced people have about out-groups demonstrates their use of * * * mechanisms observed by both Freudian and nonFreudian behavioralists. For example, studies have found that racists hold two types of stereotyped beliefs: They believe the out-group is dirty, lazy, oversexed, and without control of their instincts (a typical accusation against blacks), or they believe the out-group is pushy, ambitious, conniving, and in control of business, money, and industry (a typical accusation against Jews). These two types of accusation correspond to two of the most common types of neurotic conflict: that which arises when an individual cannot master his instinctive drives in a way that fits into rational and socially approved patterns of behavior, and that which arises when an individual cannot live up to the aspirations and standards of his own conscience. Thus, the stereotypical view of blacks implies that their Id, the instinctive part of their psyche, dominates their Ego, the rationally oriented part. The stereotype of the Jew, on the other hand, accuses him of having an overdeveloped Ego. In this way, the racially prejudiced person projects his own conflict into the form of racial stereotypes.

The preoccupation among racially prejudiced people with sexual matters in race relations provides further evidence of this relationship between the unconscious and racism. Taboos against interracial sexual relations, myths concerning the sexual prowess of blacks, and obsessions with racial purity coexist irrationally with a tendency to break these taboos. Again, psychoanalytic theory provides insights: According to Freud, one's sexual identity plays a crucial role in the unending effort to come to terms with oneself. Thus, the prominence of racism's sexual component supports the theory that racial antagonism grows in large part out of an unstable sense of identity.

*   *   *

Thus far we have considered the role the unconscious plays in creating overtly racist attitudes. But how is the unconscious involved when racial prejudice is less apparent—when racial bias is hidden from the prejudiced individual as well as from others? Increasingly, as our culture has rejected racism as immoral and unproductive, this hidden prejudice has become the more prevalent form of racism. The individual's Ego must adapt to a cultural order that views overtly racist attitudes and behavior as unsophisticated, uninformed, and immoral. It must repress or disguise racist ideas when they seek expression.

* * *

A Cognitive Approach to Unconscious Racism

Cognitive psychologists offer a contrasting model for understanding the origin and unconscious nature of racial prejudice. This is essentially a rational model. The cognitivists acknowledge the importance of emotional and motivational factors, but they do not embrace the Freudian belief that instinctive drives dominate individuals' concepts, attitudes, and beliefs. Instead, they view human behavior, including racial prejudice, as growing out of the individual's attempt to understand his relationship with the world (in this case, relations between groups) while at the same time preserving his personal integrity. But while the ultimate goal of the cognitive process is understanding or rationality, many of the critical elements of the process occur outside of the individual's awareness. This is especially true when there is tension between the individual's desire for simplification and the complexity of the real world or conflict between an understanding of a situation that preserves the individual's self-image and one that jeopardizes a positive view of himself.

Cognitivists see the process of "categorization" as one common source of racial and other stereotypes. All humans tend to categorize in order to make sense of experience. Too many events occur daily for us to deal successfully with each one on an individual basis; we must categorize in order to cope. When a category—for example, the category of black person or white person—correlates with a continuous dimension—for example, the range of human intelligence or the propensity to violence—there is a tendency to exaggerate the differences between categories on that dimension and to minimize the differences within each category.

The more important a particular classification of people into groups is to an individual, the more likely she is to distinguish sharply the characteristics of people who belong to the different groups. Here, cognitivists integrate the observations of personality theorists and social psychologists with their own. If an individual is hostile toward a group of people, she has an emotional investment in preserving the differentiations between her own group and the "others." Thus, the preservation of inaccurate judgments about the out-group is self-rewarding. This is particularly so when prejudiced judgments are made in a social context that accepts and encourages negative attitudes toward the out-group. In these cases, the group judgment reinforces and helps maintain the individual judgment about the out-group's lack of worth.

The content of the social categories to which people are assigned is generated over a long period of time within a culture and transmitted to individual members of society by a process cognitivists call "assimilation." Assimilation entails learning and internalizing preferences and evaluations. Individuals learn cultural attitudes and beliefs about race very early in life, at a time when it is difficult to separate the perceptions of one's teacher (usually a parent) from one's own. In other words, one learns about race at a time when one is highly sensitive to the social contexts in which one lives.

*   *   *

Furthermore, because children learn lessons about race at this early stage, most of the lessons are tacit rather than explicit. Children learn not so much through an intellectual understanding of what their parents tell them about race as through an emotional identification with who their parents are and what they see and feel their parents do. Small children will adopt their parents' beliefs because they experience them as their own. If we do learn lessons about race in this way, we are not likely to be aware that the lessons have even taken place. If we are unaware that we have been taught to be afraid of blacks or to think of them as lazy or stupid, then we may not be conscious of our internalization of those feelings and beliefs.

*   *   *

Case studies have demonstrated that an individual who holds stereotyped beliefs about a "target" will remember and interpret past events in the target's life history in ways that bolster and support his stereotyped beliefs and will perceive the target's actual behavior as reconfirming and validating the stereotyped beliefs. While the individual may be aware of the selectively perceived facts that support his categorization or simplified understanding, he will not be aware of the process that has caused him to deselect the facts that do not conform with his rationalization. Thus, racially prejudiced behavior that is actually the product of learned cultural preferences is experienced as a reflection of rational deduction from objective observation, which is nonprejudicial behavior. The decisionmaker who is unaware of the selective perception that has produced her stereotype will not view it as a stereotype. She will believe that her actions are motivated not by racial prejudice but by her attraction or aversion to the attributes she has "observed" in the groups she has favored or disfavored.

*   *   *

II. A TALE OF TWO THEORIES

*   *   *

Two theories have attempted to specify the central function of suspect classification doctrine. The first, the "process defect" theory, sees the judicial intervention occasioned by strict scrutiny of suspect classifications as an appropriate response to distortions in the democratic process. The second theory cites racial stigma as the primary target of suspect classification doctrine. * * * [R]ecognizing the presence of unconscious motive furthers the central rationale of each theory.[115]

The Process Defect Theory

The chief proponent of the process defect theory has been John Ely.[116] He identifies the systematic exclusion of a group from the normal workings of the political process as the harm that heightened judicial scrutiny for suspect classifications seeks to prevent or remedy.

* * *

Motive and intent are at the center of Ely's theory. The function of suspect classification doctrine is to expose unconstitutional motives that may have distorted the process. A statute that classifies by race is strictly scrutinized, because the requirement of "close fit" between end sought and means used will reveal those instances where the actual motive of the legislature was to disadvantage a group simply because of its race.

Under present doctrine, the courts look for Ely's process defect only when the racial classification appears on the face of the statute or when self-conscious racial intent has been proved * * *. But the same process distortions will occur even when the racial prejudice is less apparent. Other groups in the body politic may avoid coalition with blacks without a conscious awareness of their aversion to blacks or of their association of certain characteristics with blacks. They may take stands on issues without realizing that their reasons are, in part, racially oriented. Likewise, the governmental decisionmaker may be unaware that she has devalued the cost of a chosen path, because a group with which she does not identify will bear that cost. Indeed, because of her lack of empathy with the group, she may have never even thought of the cost at all.

Process distortion exists where the unconstitutional motive of racial prejudice has influenced the decision. It matters not that the decisionmaker's motive may lie outside her awareness. For example, in *Village of Arlington Heights v. Metropolitan Housing Development Corp.*,[127] a predominantly white, upper middle class Chicago suburb

---

115. A third substantive theory of equal protection suggests that racial groups should be treated as moral entities with group rights to distributive and compensatory justice. It holds that it is prima facie unjust for one racial or ethnic group to be substantially worse off than another. This "group disadvantaging principle" requires relief for any group that constitutes a "perpetual underclass" and argues that such redistribution would express an ethical view disfavoring caste. *See* Fiss, [*Groups and the Equal Protection Clause*, 5

Phil. & Pub.Aff. 107 (1976)]. This article will not discuss this approach. Fiss' theory is essentially indifferent to the motives and history that have led to unequal distribution and is, therefore, sufficiently sensitive to the correction of disadvantage resulting from unconscious racism without the assistance of my analysis.

116. *See* J. Ely, Democracy and Distrust 135–79 (1980). * * *

127. 429 U.S. 252 (1977).

prevented the construction of a proposed housing development for low and moderate income families by refusing to rezone the projected site to allow multi-family units. The Supreme Court agreed that the decision not to rezone had racially discriminatory effects, but it rejected the black plaintiffs' equal protection claim on the ground that they had "simply failed to carry their burden of proving that discriminatory purpose was a motivating factor in the Village's decision." The Court focused on the lack of any evidence of conscious intent to discriminate on the part of either the city council in enacting the zoning ordinance that restricted use to single family homes or the planning commission in administering the ordinance.

We can envision several possible scenarios that demonstrate the possible process-distorting effects of unconscious racism on a governmental decision like that in *Arlington Heights:*

(1) The city council refused to rezone for the sole purpose of stigmatizing and denying housing to blacks. This case resembles *Plessy v. Ferguson* [131] and *Gomillion v. Lightfoot,* [132] in which the only motives were unconstitutional, and the ordinances were, therefore, per se unconstitutional.

(2) The city claims a legitimate economic or environmental purpose, but evidence shows that it sought to exclude blacks in order to achieve that purpose. This case is the same as a classification by race on the face of a statute for which a legitimate goal is claimed. It is the case Ely describes where blacks are consciously excluded from the political process and devalued in the assessment of costs and benefits. When this self-conscious motive can be proved, the resulting classification is subject to strict scrutiny under existing doctrine.

(3) The purpose of the ordinance was economic—i.e., to keep property values up by keeping poor people out—but the decisionmakers associated poverty with blacks and would have weighed the costs and benefits differently if the poor people they envisioned excluding were elderly white people on social security. This "selective sympathy or indifference" could have occurred at a conscious or unconscious level. It is more than likely that the decisionmakers knew that the poor people they were excluding were black, but they would not be likely to have known that they undervalued the cost to poor people because they thought of them as black rather than white.

(4) A constituency within Arlington Heights—for example, elderly whites—did not actively campaign for the rezoning because of aversion to blacks who might have benefited from it. This occurred despite the fact that this constituency's interest in low income housing would otherwise have outweighed its interest in property values. This inability or unwillingness to apprehend and act upon an overlapping interest is precisely the kind of process distortion through group vilification that Ely describes. It is as likely as not that these elderly voters are

131. 163 U.S. 537 (1896).   **132.** 364 U.S. 339 (1960).

largely unaware of the vilification and resulting aversion that preempted their potential coalition with blacks.

(5) No one in Arlington Heights thought about blacks one way or the other—i.e., it was a fight between environmentalists and developers—but an inadvertent devaluing of black interests caused inattention to the costs blacks would have to bear. If one asked the decisionmakers how they had valued the cost to blacks of the exclusionary zoning, they might have responded, "I never thought of that." This is an example of selective indifference or misapprehension of costs that occurs entirely outside of consciousness.

The process defect theory sees suspect classification doctrine as a roundabout way of uncovering unconstitutional motive by suspecting those classifications that disadvantage groups we know to be the object of widespread vilification. But by only suspecting laws that classify by race on their face or are the result of overtly self-conscious racial motivation, the theory stops an important step short of locating and eliminating the defect it has identified. Where a society has recently adopted a moral ethic that repudiates racial disadvantaging for its own sake, governmental decisionmakers are as likely to repress their racial motives as they are to lie to courts or to attempt after-the-fact rationalizations of classifications that are not racial on their face but that do have disproportionate racial impact. Unconscious aversion to a group that has historically been vilified distorts the political process no less than a conscious decision to place race hatred before politically legitimate goals.

* * *

The Stigma Theory

A second theory posits elimination of racially stigmatizing actions as the central concern of the equal protection clause. Under this theory, racial classifications should be strictly scrutinized when they operate to shame and degrade a class of persons by labeling it as inferior. Stigmatization is the process by which the dominant group in society differentiates itself from others by setting them apart, treating them as less than fully human, denying them acceptance by the organized community, and excluding them from participating in that community as equals. * * *

The prevention of stigma was at the core of the Supreme Court's unanimous declaration in *Brown v. Board of Education* that segregated public schools are inherently unequal. In observing that the segregation of black pupils "generates a feeling of inferiority as to their status in the community," Chief Justice Warren recognized what a majority of the Court had ignored almost sixty years earlier in *Plessy v. Ferguson*: The social meaning of racial segregation in the United States is the designation of a superior and an inferior caste, and segregation proceeds "on the ground that colored citizens are . . . inferior and degraded."

Stigmatizing actions harm the individual in two ways: They inflict psychological injury by assaulting a person's self-respect and human dignity, and they brand the individual with a sign that signals her inferior status to others and designates her as an outcast. The stigma theory recognizes the importance of both self-esteem and the respect of others for participating in society's benefits and responsibilities.

* * *

The injury of stigmatization consists of forcing the injured individual to wear a badge or symbol that degrades him in the eyes of society. But in most cases the symbol is not inherently pejorative. Rather, the message obtains its shameful meaning from the historical and cultural context in which it is used and, ultimately, from the way it is interpreted by those who witness it. Thus the woman who is asked to use a separate public bathroom from her husband is unlikely to be stigmatized by that action: Our society does not ordinarily interpret sex-segregated toilet facilities as designating the inferiority of women. By contrast, the black who is asked to use a different public bathroom from that of a white companion of the same gender is stigmatized. * * * [R]acially segregated bathrooms were an important part of the system of segregation. That system's ideology held not only that blacks were less than fully human but also that they were dirty and impure. Racially segregated bathrooms ensured that blacks would not contaminate the facilities used by whites.

If stigmatizing actions injure by virtue of the meaning society gives them, then it should be apparent that the evil intent of their authors, while perhaps sufficient, is not necessary to the infliction of the injury. For example, a well-meaning if misguided white employer, having observed that her black employees usually sat together at lunch, might build a separate dining room for them with the intent of making them more comfortable. This action would stigmatize her black employees despite her best intentions. Similarly, when the city of Jackson, Mississippi closed its public pools after a federal court ordered it to integrate them, the action stigmatized blacks regardless of whether the government's purpose was racial or economic.

Given that stigma occurs whether there is racial animus or not, the answer to our initial question, "Is knowledge about the intent of the governmental actor significant to the achievement of the equal protection clause's purpose?" would seem an obvious "No." But many of the stigma theory's advocates find themselves in a quandary when faced with the question of how the Court should approach laws that are not apparently "race-dependent" but that result in disparate and stigmatizing effects. * * *

* * * Paul Brest, having persuasively argued the need to eliminate racially disproportionate impact that stigmatizes, cautions that the impact doctrine "cannot reasonably be applied across the board" and urges that the doctrine be used "selectively." [168]   He warns that "remedies for disproportionate impact may impose heavy costs on institutions and individuals, and cannot be tailored narrowly to compensate all those and only those whose present situation is the result of past discrimination."   Brest's reference to the overbreadth of remedies for disproportionate impact adds to the general concern about unduly limiting legislative discretion and the particular concern about the legitimacy of courts imposing costs on "blameless" individuals and conferring benefits on those who have not been directly harmed.

The consideration of unconscious intent responds to both of these concerns.   Identifying stigmatizing actions that were affected by the actor's unconscious racial attitudes achieves two benefits.   First, it significantly decreases the absolute number of impact cases subject to heightened scrutiny without eviscerating the substantive content of the equal protection clause.   The bridge toll, the sales tax, and the filing fee can no longer be numbered among the parade of horribles that Justice White suggested in [*Washington v.*] *Davis.*[171]   At the same time, cases where racially discriminatory impact results directly from past intentional discrimination or from current but unprovable racial animus will be well within judicial reach.   A law does not stigmatize blacks simply because exclusion itself is stigmatizing, and, in this instance, they are disproportionately represented among the excluded group.   Instead, the stigma stems at least in part from society's predisposition to exclude blacks.   The fact that unconscious racial attitudes affected a governmental action is evidence that the racially stigmatizing symbolism preexisted the present impact.

Second, consideration of unconscious motivation provides a neutral principle for judicial intervention—i.e., the identification of a process defect.   This counters the argument made against the impact test that the judiciary has no principled basis for imposing a priority for the removal of racial stigma over other social goods to which the political branch might choose to give preeminence.   In short, stigma often occurs regardless of the intent of those who have engaged in the stigmatizing action.   Thus, it is arguable that under the stigma theory neither conscious nor unconscious intent should be considered, and heightened judicial scrutiny should apply in all cases when governmental action produces a stigmatizing effect.   Nonetheless, recognizing unconscious racism provides a mechanism for effectively responding to continuing race-based inequalities while minimizing the costs of judicial overreaching.

[In the concluding portion of his article Lawrence deals with the most obvious objection to his theory: how courts can identify cases where unconscious racism is operating.   He proposes that we should look not at individual actions but at the 'cultural meaning' of allegedly

---

168.   [Brest, *Foreword: In Defense of the Antidiscrimination Principle,* 90 Harv.L. Rev. 1 (1976).]

171.   [426 U.S. 229, 248 & n. 14 (1976).]

discriminatory acts as the best evidence of the collective unconscious. This test would evaluate governmental conduct to see whether it conveys a symbolic message to which the culture attaches racial significance. If it does, the court should apply heightened scrutiny.

[For example, the building of a wall between white and black communities in *Memphis v. Greene* [a] has a cultural meaning because of the long history of whites separating themselves from blacks as a symbol of superiority. It would not matter that individual members of the city council were unconscious of their failure to empathize with how blacks felt.

[Lawrence stresses that the task of interpreting cultural meaning is not foreign to courts. In Establishment Clause cases the courts decide whether a practice advances religion by asking what meaning we attach to a practice—*e.g.* a Christmas creche. In sex discrimination cases the courts ask whether laws tend to perpetuate a "stereotyped view" of men and women—*e.g.* as breadwinners and homemakers. Lawrence argues that the task he sets for the judiciary in race cases would not be essentially different.]

JOHN HART ELY, FACILITATING THE REPRESENTATION OF MINORITIES

Democracy and Distrust 145–46, 148–61 (1980).

[In the opening part of the chapter from which this selection is drawn Ely argues that the Equal Protection Clause is primarily concerned with the process by which the government allocates various harms and benefits. This means that the constitutionality of any particular allocation will depend in part on why it was undertaken—*i.e.* on the motives of the actors involved. Ely notes, however, that the courts have generally been reluctant to inquire into legislative or administrative motivation.

[Ely then turns to the doctrine of 'suspect classifications.' He contends that the real point of this doctrine is to serve as a handmaiden of motivation analysis.]

The [suspect classification and motivation] doctrines support each other in this way. The goal the classification in issue is likely to fit most closely, obviously, is the goal the legislators actually had in mind. If it can be directly identified and is one that is unconstitutional, all well and good: the classification is unconstitutional. But even if such a confident demonstration of motivation proves impossible, a classification that in fact was unconstitutionally motivated will nonetheless—thanks to the indirect pressure exerted by the suspect-classification doctrine—find itself in serious constitutional difficulty. For an unconstitutional goal obviously cannot be invoked in a statute's defense. That means, where the real goal was unconstitutional, that the goal

a. 451 U.S. 100, 101 S.Ct. 1584, 67 L.Ed.
2d 769 (1981).

that fits the classification best will not be invocable in its defense, and the classification will have to be defended in terms of others to which it relates more tenuously. Where the requirement is simply the Court's standard call for a "rational" relation between classification and goal, that will seldom matter: even if the goal the classification fits best is disabled from invocation, there will likely be other permissible goals whose relation to the classification is sufficiently close to be called rational. The "special scrutiny" that is afforded suspect classifications, however, insists that the classification in issue fit the goal invoked in its defense more closely than any alternative classification would. There is only one goal the classification is likely to fit *that* closely, however, and that is the goal the legislators actually had in mind. If that goal cannot be invoked because it is unconstitutional, the classification will fall. Thus, functionally, special scrutiny, in particular its demand for an essentially perfect fit, turns out to be a way of "flushing out" unconstitutional motivation, one that lacks the proof problems of a more direct inquiry and into the bargain permits courts (and complainants) to be more politic, to invalidate (or attack) something for illicit motivation without having to come right out and say that's what they're doing.

* * *

During the Warren era, the Supreme Court was quite adventurous in expanding the set of suspect classifications beyond the core case of race. Laws classifying to the comparative disadvantage of aliens, persons of "illegitimate" birth, even poor people, were all at one time or another approached as suspect. The Burger Court has also paid lip service to the general idea. In fact Justice Blackmun was the first ever—apart, of course, from Justice Stone's original *Carolene Products* footnote a—to indicate in an Opinion of the Court that "discrete and insular" minorities are entitled to special constitutional protection from the political process. However, the Burger Court's performance on this score has not matched its rhetoric. Since he came on the Court, Justice Rehnquist has been campaigning to reduce the set of suspect classifications to race and "its first cousin," national origin, and his campaign seems to be succeeding. * * *

The reason Justice Rehnquist gives for wanting to cut the list back to race and national origin is one allegedly grounded in original intent, that those are the classifications the framers of the Fourteenth Amendment would have wanted to subject to unusual scrutiny. * * * The justice thinks he sees a family resemblance between national origin and race, but classifications aren't really the same thing as people and it takes a theory to make one classification the "first cousin" of another.

a. In *United States v. Carolene Products*, 304 U.S. 144, 152 n. 4 (1938), Justice Stone suggested in dictum that "prejudice against discrete and insular minorities may be a special condition, which tends seriously to curtail the operation of those political processes ordinarily to be relied upon to protect minorities, and which may call for a correspondingly more searching judicial inquiry."

It's true, only "racelike" classifications should be regarded as suspect, but we have to figure out what "racelike" should mean in this context.

It's probably because Court and commentator alike have failed here, at the level of theory, that Justice Rehnquist is steadily gaining his way. Factors are frequently mentioned in the literature that in an intuitive way do seem to have something to do with the point—and on further analysis we'll see that in oblique ways some of them do—but somehow none is quite capable of convincing us that it *is* the point. Thus, for example, it is often said that the immutability of the classifying trait ought to make a classification suspect. * * * [But] no one has bothered to * * * tell us exactly *why* we should be suspicious of legislatures that classify on the basis of immutable characteristics. Surely one has to feel sorry for a person disabled by something that he or she can't do anything about, but I'm not aware of any reason to suppose that elected officials are unusually unlikely to share that feeling. Moreover, classifications based on physical disability and intelligence are typically accepted as legitimate, even by judges and commentators who assert that immutability is relevant. The explanation, when one is given, is that *those* characteristics (unlike the one the commentator is trying to render suspect) are often relevant to legitimate purposes. At that point there's not much left of the immutability theory, is there?

A number of commentaries, purporting to find support in *Brown v. Board of Education,* argue that classifications disfavoring racial minorities are suspect because they "will usually be perceived as a stigma of inferiority and a badge of opprobrium." This confuses two issues and thus misreads *Brown.* Feelings of opprobrium *are* relevant to determining whether a classification the state claims is "harmless," such as "separate but equal" schooling, in fact inflicts harm on one or the other class. But *Brown* was unusual in that respect: the existence of comparative harm to one of the classes distinguished by a governmental classification is rarely an issue. Neither can the idea be that the presence of stigma is necessary in order to establish some requisite *amount* of harm. That account would make sense if the Court followed the practice of reviewing more strenuously those distinctions that hurt more, which it doesn't. A taxation distinction worth $1,000,000 receives about the same review as one worth $100—that is, virtually none.

An account that seems more to the point, one to which I've alluded several times, is that attributed to Justice Stone's *Carolene Products* footnote and recently paraphrased for the Court * * * by Justice Blackmun: "Aliens as a class are a prime example of a 'discrete and insular' minority . . . for whom . . . heightened judicial solicitude is appropriate . . ." [59] * * * In a sense the complainant in every case speaks for such a group: he wouldn't be in court if the class in which

59. Graham v. Richardson, 403 U.S. 365, 372 (1971).

the legislature had placed him had not been, on at least one occasion, a political minority (they lost), both discrete (they're the ones on the disfavored side of the statutory line) and insular (they couldn't gather enough allies to defeat the legislation). But obviously that isn't what Justice Stone meant. His reference was rather to the sort of "pluralist" wheeling and dealing by which the various minorities that make up our society typically interact to protect their interests, and constituted an attempt to denote those minorities for which such a system of "mutual defense pacts" will prove recurrently unavailing.

* * *

* * * [T]hough the general idea here may be clear enough—courts should protect those who can't protect themselves politically—the justification for it isn't. In a way it is of the essence of democracy to allow the various persons and groups that make up our society to decide which others they wish to combine with in shaping legislation. We are not all the same in all respects, and on certain subjects our interests in fact do differ substantially. There is thus no way to exclude a priori—as the theory as elaborated so far does—the possibility that there may exist groups or interests with which others will refuse to combine politically for perfectly respectable reasons.

An added element is therefore needed, that the minority in question be one that is barred from the pluralist's bazaar, and thus keeps finding itself on the wrong end of the legislature's classifications, for reasons that in some sense are discreditable. Standard renditions of what we think of as the *Carolene Products* approach, such as the one by Justice Blackmun quoted above, do not include this element: "discrete and insular minorities" are simply entitled to "heightened judicial solicitude." Justice Stone's original, however, was richer than this, indicating that *"prejudice against discrete and insular minorities* may be a special condition, which tends to curtail the operation of those political processes ordinarily to be relied upon to protect minorities . . . ." Now "prejudice" is a mushword in its own right, one we shall have to clarify, but it does supply the element that is missing in the usual rendition. For whatever else it may or may not be, prejudice is a lens that distorts reality. We are a nation of minorities and our system thus depends on the ability and willingness of various groups to apprehend those overlapping interests that can bind them into a majority on a given issue; prejudice blinds us to overlapping interests that in fact exist. As Frank Goodman put it so well eight years ago: "Race prejudice divides groups that have much in common (blacks and poor whites) and unites groups (white, rich and poor) that have little else in common than their antagonism for the racial minority. Race prejudice, in short, provides the 'majority of the whole' with that 'common motive to invade the rights of other citizens' that Madison believed improbable in a pluralistic society." [63]

63. Goodman, [*De Facto School Segregation: A Constitutional and Empirical Analysis,* 60 Calif.L.Rev. 275, 315 (1972).]

Switching the principal perspective thus, from the purely political to one that focuses more on the psychology of decision, possesses the additional virtue of relating rather directly to what we found to be the functional significance of a theory of suspect classifications, one of flushing out unconstitutional motivations. "Prejudice" has a lot to do with that; discreteness and insularity don't seem to (except derivatively, to the extent that they are likely to reflect and engender prejudiced behavior). That connection also puts us in a position to begin to specify the meanings of prejudice relevant in this context. If the doctrine of suspect classifications is a roundabout way of uncovering official attempts to inflict inequality for its own sake—to treat a group worse not in the service of some overriding social goal but largely for the sake of simply disadvantaging its members—it would seem to follow that one set of classifications we should treat as suspicious are those that disadvantage groups we know to be the object of widespread vilification, groups we know others (specifically those who control the legislative process) might wish to injure.

Note that the inquiry suggested is not whether there exists *unjustified* widespread hostility toward the group disadvantaged by the official act in issue—that would constitute a straightforward invitation to second-guess the legislative judgment—but simply whether there exists widespread hostility. There is a good deal of discretion in that inquiry too, of course, and courts must be scrupulous not simply to legislate there either. Later on I shall suggest a refinement that should help bridle the inquiry. For the moment, though, it may help to recall that all that labeling a classification "suspect" means functionally is that a prima facie case has been made out and that the inquiry into its suspiciousness should continue. If it turns out directly to pursue a substantial goal (other than the impermissible one of simply disadvantaging those it disadvantages), it will survive. Thus, for example, burglars are certainly a group toward which there is widespread societal hostility, and laws making burglary a crime certainly do comparatively disadvantage burglars. Such laws plainly should survive, however. There is so patently a substantial goal here, that of protecting our homes by penalizing those who break and enter them, and the fit between that goal and the classification is so close, that whatever suspicion such a classification might under other circumstances engender is allayed so immediately it doesn't even have time to register.

Although there is more to be said about what factors properly give rise to suspicion, we have reached a point where the appeal (and limitations) of a reference to the immutability of the classifying characteristic can begin to be put in perspective. A law making burglary a crime is not suspicious—or, if you prefer, the suspicion is immediately allayed—because the goal of making life unpleasant for burglars is immediately translatable into the goal of discouraging people from breaking into our homes. It would not make sense, however, to defend a law disadvantaging blacks on the ground that we are trying to discourage people from being black. The ability to frame the point of a classification harming (or subsidizing) a certain group in terms of a desire to discourage people from joining (or encourage people to join) that group obviously depends on the mutability of the characteristic that forms the basis of classification. We shouldn't go overboard and conclude that classification on the basis of an immutable characteristic is always suspicious: that would follow only if increasing or decreasing the incidence of the classifying characteristic were the only legitimate governmental end. Forbidding blind people to pilot airplanes will do little to encourage eyesight, but such a prohibition will obviously stand nonetheless, since the classification fits perfectly a different goal, one I need hardly argue is important. Immutability thus cannot be the talisman that some have tried to make it, but it isn't entirely irrelevant either, since classifications geared to characteristics it is not within the power of the individual to change will not be amenable to immediate and innocent explanation in terms of altering the classifying characteristic's incidence.

An account mentioned with increasing frequency, and indeed it does seem more to the point, is that classifications rooted in "stereotypes" should be regarded as suspicious. Stated this way, without elaboration, it cannot do. The dictionary tells us that a stereotype is "a fixed or conventional notion or conception, as of a person, group, idea, etc., held by a number of people, and allowing for no individuality . . ." Legislation on the basis of "stereotype" is thus legislation by generalization, the use of a classification believed in statistical terms to be generally valid without leaving room for proof of individual deviation. That, however, is the way legislation ordinarily proceeds, as in most cases it must. * * *

* * * If the concept is to provide us with anything beyond a basis for begging questions, it has to be refined, so as to separate, if you will, the acceptable stereotypes from the unacceptable. The approach that may initially seem most attractive would be to treat as suspicious those stereotypical generalizations to which there exist unusually high numbers or percentages of counterexamples. * * * It won't work, though; generalizations cannot be intelligibly evaluated simply in terms of the number or percentage of false-positives they entail. Sometimes, as in the case of capital punishment, any nontrivial incidence of counterexample would be intolerable. Other times, as where we are trying to keep those susceptible to heart attacks from piloting commercial airliners, a quite high percentage, surely sometimes more than half, is entirely appropriate. A determination of the acceptable incidence of counterexample must therefore involve, at a minimum, a comparison of the costs to those "wrongfully" excluded or included with the costs to the rest of us, sometimes in time and money but often also in increased risk, of trying to tune the system more finely. A mode of review geared to whether the incidence of counterexample is "too high" is thus indistinguishable from the unacceptable theory that courts should

intervene in the name of the Constitution whenever they disagree with the cost-benefit balance the legislature has struck.

* * * The cases where we ought to be suspicious are not those involving a generalization whose incidence of counterexample is "too high," but rather those involving a generalization whose incidence of counterexample is significantly higher than the legislative authority appears to have thought it was. No matter how many considerations may have entered into the cost-benefit balance, a misapprehension regarding the incidence of counterexample (or for that matter the cost of individualized determination) will have distorted the entire decision. Just as we would want reconsidered any important decision that was made under the influence of an erroneous assumption about the relevant facts, so should we here. * * *

The rub comes in how the Court should go about identifying such situations. Just leaving it to their gestalt judgment seems obviously unacceptable, too close to simply handing over an unbridled power of substantive review. (I am not suggesting bad faith here, but a justice whose instinct is to disagree with the legislative cost-benefit balance is likely in all good faith to suppose the legislature "must have" overestimated the statistical validity of the generalization on the basis of which it appears to have acted.) The Court should therefore look not simply to the legislative product here, but to the process that generated it, to see whether it can identify some factor or factors that suggest the likelihood of such legislative misapprehension. * * *

In deciding how much presumptive credit to extend a given generalization in our everyday lives, we would want to know where it came from—who came up with it and whether it is one that serves their interests. This commonsense insight, again tempered with others, seems relevant to the constitutional inquiry as well. The choice between classifying on the basis of a comparative generalization and attempting to come up with a more discriminating formula always involves balancing the increase in fairness that greater individualization will produce against the added costs it will entail. Where the generalization involved is one that serves the interests of the decision-makers, however, certain dangers that are inherent in any balancing process are significantly intensified. Where it tangibly enhances their fortunes, the dangers may be most obvious—on the one hand that the costs of treating others as they are treating themselves are likely to be overestimated, and on the other that the validity of the generalization being proffered as the basis of classification is likely to be overestimated, thus resulting in an underevaluation of the interest in individual fairness. But even where no tangible gain can be identified, there are psychic rewards in self-flattering generalizations. * * *

Thus generalizations to the effect, say, that whites in general are smarter or more industrious than blacks, men more stable emotionally than women, or native-born Americans more patriotic than Americans born elsewhere, are likely to go down pretty easily—and in fact we know they have—with groups whose demography is that of the typical American legislature. Few will suppose there aren't counterexamples, but the overall validity of such a generalization is likely to be quite readily accepted. By seizing upon the positive myths about the groups to which they belong and the negative myths about those to which they don't, or for that matter the realities respecting some or most members of the two classes, legislators, like the rest of us, are likely to assume too readily that not many of "them" will be unfairly deprived, nor many of "us" unfairly benefited, by a classification of this type. Generalizations of the opposite sort, which attribute superiority to a group to which most legislators do not belong—say, that blacks are better basketball players or that Jews are better students—are a different matter. A generalization of this sort may occasionally find grudging acceptance, but here we can be sure that the imperfect, statistical nature of the claim will be well appreciated, and in addition that there will be explanations—in both these examples, that it has to do with "the way they are brought up"—that will prevail in the legislature to assure an individualized test or at least that the statutory presumption will be rebuttable. A statutory distinction built on a comparison of the qualifications of optometrists and opticians occupies an in-between position, since neither of the groups being compared is one to which most of the legislators belong. Such a law—and most legislative classifications are of this "they-they" contour—may lack the special safeguard that a self-deprecating generalization seems to provide, but it also lacks the unusual dangers of self-serving generalization and is consequently correctly classified as constitutionally unsuspicious.

We have seen already how the mutability of the classifying characteristic will often render a classification immediately defensible in terms of a legitimate social goal and thus allay any incipient suspicion. We are now in a position to understand how mutability (or something like it) may be relevant in another way as well, one that bears on the likelihood that the decision-maker's ability to generalize will be distorted by his or her perspective. For example it is at least arguable that the facts that all of us once were young, and most expect one day to be fairly old, should neutralize whatever suspicion we might otherwise entertain respecting the multitude of laws (enacted by predominantly middle-aged legislatures) that comparatively advantage those between, say, 21 and 65 vis-à-vis those who are younger or older. It is not quite the same thing as immutability, of course: alienage generally is an escapable condition, so in theory are poverty and perhaps even gender. But nonetheless, and it is this that seems more relevant, most legislators have never been alien, poor, or female. They all were young, though, a fact that may enhance their objectivity about just what the difference entails.

One can empathize without having been there, though, and at this point a reference to discreteness and insularity reasserts its relevance. Though theoretically indefensible in its usual free-standing form, it can quite sensibly augment and qualify an approach geared to the distorting effect of perspective. To render the concept useful, though, we have to recognize and break apart its two components, the political and the social. Political access is surely important, but (so long as it falls short of majority control) it cannot alone protect a group against the first type of prejudice we examined, out-and-out hostility, nor will it even serve effectively to correct the subtler self-aggrandizing biases of the majority. If voices and votes are all we're talking about, prejudices can easily survive (and even on occasion be exacerbated): other groups may just continue to refuse to deal, and the minority in question may just continue to be outvoted. Discreteness and insularity have a social component as well, however—of course the two will often go hand in hand—and it is that component that seems more relevant to the amelioration of cooperation-blocking prejudice. Increased social intercourse is likely not only to diminish the hostility that often accompanies unfamiliarity, but also to rein somewhat our tendency to stereotype in ways that exaggerate the superiority of those groups to which we belong. The more we get to know people who are different in some ways, the more we will begin to appreciate the ways in which they are not, which is the beginning of political cooperation.

BRUCE A. ACKERMAN, BEYOND *CAROLENE PRODUCTS*

98 Harv.L.Rev. 713, 713–715, 717–739 (1985).

I. THE PROMISE OF CAROLENE PRODUCTS

"[P]rejudice against discrete and insular minorities may be a special condition . . . curtail[ing] the operation of those political processes ordinarily to be relied upon to protect minorities, and [so] may call for a correspondingly more searching judicial inquiry." [1]

These famous words, appearing in the otherwise unimportant *Carolene Products* case, came at a moment of extraordinary vulnerability for the Supreme Court. They were written in 1938. The Court was just beginning to dig itself out of the constitutional debris left by its wholesale capitulation to the New Deal a year before. With the decisive triumph of the activist welfare state over the Old Court, an entire world of constitutional meanings, laboriously built up over two generations, had come crashing down upon the Justices' heads. Indeed, the Court had been so politically discredited by its constitutional defense of laissez-faire capitalism that it was hardly obvious whether *any* firm ground remained upon which to rebuild the institution of judicial review. How, then, to begin the work of reconstruction?

* * *

* * * *Carolene* promises relief from the problem of legitimacy raised whenever nine elderly lawyers invalidate the legislative decisions of a majority of our elected representatives. The *Carolene* solution is to seize the high ground of democratic theory and establish that

1. United States v. Carolene Prods. Co., 304 U.S. 144, 152 n. 4 (1938). * * *

the challenged legislation was produced by a profoundly defective process. By demonstrating that the legislative decision itself resulted from an undemocratic procedure, a *Carolene* court hopes to reverse the spin of the countermajoritarian difficulty. For it now may seem that the original legislative decision, not the judicial invalidation, suffers the greater legitimacy deficit.

*   *   *

*   *   * I shall argue, however, that the *Carolene* formula cannot withstand close scrutiny.

*   *   *

To demonstrate the need for doctrinal reorientation, I shall examine separately each of *Carolene's* four operative terms: (1) prejudice, (2) discrete, (3) insular, and (4) minorities. It is by means of these four terms that *Carolene* hopes to identify groups that have been unconstitutionally deprived of their fair share of democratic influence. *   *   *

II. DISCRETE AND INSULAR MINORITIES?

*   *   *

A. The Principle of Minority Acquiescence

*   *   * [M]inorities are *supposed* to lose in a democratic system—even when they want very much to win and even when they think (as they often will) that the majority is deeply wrong in ignoring their just complaints. This principle—call it the principle of minority acquiescence—is absolutely central to democratic theory. Of course, a minority may not be denied its right to participate within a democratic framework. Although it must acquiesce in current legislative decisions, it is fully entitled to use all its political resources to induce a future legislative majority to accede to its demands. But *Carolene* promises minorities more than formal rights: it asserts that they are sometimes entitled to demand substantive victory now, not merely the chance of victory later.

The problem this promise raises is all the more acute because *Carolene* refuses to accept the solution that countless others have embraced. It is easy to solve the problem of majority rule by positing the existence of minority rights that are so fundamental as to trump the value of democratic rule itself. Indeed, as the *Carolene* Court was well aware, it is *too* easy to solve the problem in this way. Faced with the political repudiation of *Lochner's* natural rights jurisprudence, the Court was determined to build another foundation for the protection of minority rights: why not redefine the concept of democracy itself in a way that would support the notion that minorities *do* have a right to win some of the time?

B. The Pluralist Solution

While the courts speak vaguely of "those political processes ordinarily relied upon to protect minorities," generations of American political scientists have filled in the picture of pluralist democracy presupposed by *Carolene's* distinctive argument for minority rights.

According to this familiar view, it is a naive mistake to speak of democracy as if it involved rule by a single, well-defined majority over a coherent and constant minority. Instead, normal American politics is pluralistic: myriad pressure groups, each typically representing a fraction of the population, bargain with one another for mutual support.

Once this picture of pluralistic politics is accepted, the stage has been set for the rehabilitation of *Carolene's* concern with ineffective minorities. We may now find that there is something about certain minority groups—call them *Carolene* or *C*-groups—that makes it especially difficult for them to strike bargains with potential coalition partners. As a consequence, *C*-groups will find themselves in politically ascendant coalitions much less often than will otherwise comparable groups. Over time, then, *C*-groups will achieve less than their "fair share" of influence upon legislation. And it is for this reason, the pluralist concludes, that *Carolene* rightly suggests that judicial protection for *C*-groups can be defended in a manner responsive to the countermajoritarian difficulty afflicting judicial review. By intervening on behalf of *C*-groups, a *Carolene* court merely produces the substantive outcomes that the *C*-group would have obtained through politics if it had not been so systematically disadvantaged in the ongoing process of pluralist bargaining.

*   *   *

*   *   * In the common legal understanding, *Carolene* is generally taken to imply that the same level of strict judicial scrutiny should apply to legislation affecting each and every *C*-group. But the pluralist model cannot justify such a uniform judicial approach.

Consider, for example, an American constituency that includes 12 percent blacks and .5 percent Jehovah's Witnesses among its population. Doubtless, both groups will be encouraged by the pluralist vision of democracy, since it suggests that neither group will inexorably be excluded from the pluralist bazaar. Nonetheless, it should be plain that these two groups have absolutely no reason to find the prospect of pluralist bargaining *equally* gratifying. To the contrary, the fact that blacks greatly outnumber Witnesses is bound to play an important role in any plausible bargaining theory. Thus, even if the two groups could somehow be compensated for their *Carolene* disadvantages, the Witnesses could not reasonably expect to win substantive victories nearly as often as the blacks.

To put the point more generally, a bargaining approach to *Carolene* does not suggest that each *C*-group has a right to be treated identically to all other *C*-groups in the legislative process. Instead, the decisive thought-experiment should involve the comparison of a particular *C*-group with a hypothetical minority that I shall call an unencumbered or *U*-group. In each comparison, the relevant *U*-group should be supposed to contain the same proportion of the population as the *C*-group that invokes the Court's protection; the *U*-group differs, however, in that it is unencumbered by the bargaining disadvantages that unconstitutionally burden the *C*-group. Thus, the *Carolene* question for blacks entails a comparative analysis of the bargaining expectations of a 12 percent minority unencumbered by those structural impediments that unconstitutionally impair blacks' bargaining position in the ongoing pluralist process, while the question for Jehovah's Witnesses involves a comparison with a much smaller *U*-group.

Such thought-experiments will most naturally result in a sliding scale of *Carolene* concern. On one end of the scale are groups consisting of ineffective majorities or very large minorities that find themselves disadvantaged in the political process by some constitutionally impermissible barrier to bargaining. In cases involving these "major minorities," a court can be quite confident that a comparable *U*-group would have a decisive impact on the terms of pluralistic legislation. In the middle of the *Carolene* scale are "middling minorities" in the 10 to 20 percent range. Here there is less reason for a court to expect that a *U*-group of comparable size would radically change the terms of political trade, though its influence would be very substantial in many plausible contexts. And finally, on the other end of the scale, there are groups so small as to elicit little solicitude from courts concerned with correcting the failures of democratic bargaining. When faced with "minor minorities" of .01 percent, for example, a judge might well be unmoved by the enumeration of *Carolene* factors that would generate substantial concern in the case of middling minorities, not to mention major minorities. For the fact is that a *U*-group of .01 percent has little to expect from a democratic political process, unless it is very lucky, or exceptionally adept, in the bargaining process. This point is essential to the responsible elaboration of *Carolene Products*—whose promise, be it recalled, is to permit courts to evade the thrust of the countermajoritarian difficulty by appealing over the heads of real-world legislatures to the hypothetical outcomes of a purified democratic process.

There is, then, an inevitably uneasy relationship between *Carolene*'s pluralist approach to democracy and the judicial protection of minority rights. The tension reaches the breaking point in the proverbial case of a minority of one: when the solitary citizen, having little to expect from pluralist bargaining, challenges the invasion of his fundamental rights by the normal political process.

My aim here, though, is to work out the doctrinal implications of the *Carolene* formula rather than to criticize its foundations. So let us focus our attention upon those groups, ranging from middling minorities to encumbered majorities, whose role in the bargaining process might well have a significant impact on the ongoing stream of legislative decisions. How does *Carolene* propose to determine whether a group suffers from severe enough bargaining disadvantages to merit special protection? In other words, how are we supposed to distinguish a *C*-group from a *U*-group?

III. DISCRETE AND INSULAR MINORITIES?

* * *

* * * Other things being equal, "discreteness and insularity" will normally be a source of enormous bargaining advantage, not disadvantage, for a group engaged in pluralist American politics. Except for special cases, the concerns that underlie *Carolene* should lead judges to protect groups that possess the opposite characteristics from the ones *Carolene* emphasizes—groups that are "anonymous and diffuse" rather than "discrete and insular." It is these groups that both political science and American history indicate are systematically disadvantaged in a pluralist democracy.

A. *The Free–Rider Problem*

To see my point, start with insularity and consider a thought-experiment suggested by the previous argument. Imagine two groups, *I* and *D*, of equal size (say each accounts for 12 percent of the population). The members of one group, the *I*'s, are distributed in an insular way, concentrated in a single massive island within the sea of American life; the *D*'s, on the other hand, are diffused evenly throughout the sea. Is it really so clear that, by virtue of their diffusion throughout American life, the *D*'s will gain systematic advantages over the *I*'s in the normal course of pluralist politics?

Hardly. To begin with the basics, a political interest gains a great advantage if its proponents can form a well-organized lobby to press their cause in the corridors of power. Yet the construction of a pressure group is no easy task. The main obstacle is the familiar free-rider problem. Simply because a person would find his interests advanced by the formation of a pressure group, it does not follow that he will spend his own scarce time and energy on political organization. On the contrary, from each individual's selfish viewpoint, abstaining from interest-group activity is a "heads-I-win-tails-you-lose" proposition. If only a few people adopt the do-nothing strategy, the do-nothings will free-ride on the successful lobbying effort of others. If free-riding becomes pervasive, things will not improve much if a single member of the group adds his money and time to the floundering political effort. Either way, it pays for a selfish person to remain a free rider even if he has a lot to gain from concerted lobbying. For this reason, many interests remain ineffectively organized even in pressure-group America. How, then, does a minority's insularity affect the probability that it will break through the free-rider barrier and achieve organizational effectiveness?

Far from being a patent disadvantage, insularity can help *I*-groups in at least four different ways[.] * * *

First, insularity will help breed sentiments of group solidarity. Given an *I*'s daily immersion in social realities that reaffirm his group identity, the typical *I* will conceive his *I*-ness as something much more than an incidental fact about himself. Instead, *I*-ness will serve as a fundamental feature of self-identity—one that will encourage each I to view the political activities of the group from a perspective that transcends the purely instrumental. Thus, when a black or a Jew gives $25 to the NAACP or the Anti–Defamation League, he is not merely, or even principally, gambling that his small bit of money will perceptibly increase his chance of enjoying the fruits of future lobbying victories. Rather, the contribution is a means by which the donor can symbolize the seriousness of his own commitment to his I-ness. By contributing to the group cause, I demonstrate to myself, as well as others, that I am serious about the values I profess to hold. Here, at last, is one commodity—group identification—that is immune from the free-rider problem: for if I do not give even a few dollars to the group cause, can I plausibly say, even to myself, that I take my I-ness seriously?

But insularity ＊ ＊ ＊ also aids the I-group in a second way by providing it with a new range of social sanctions to impose upon would-be free riders. An I who refuses to contribute to his interest group cannot expect this fact to be kept secret from his fellow I's—news travels fast along the grapevine in an insular community. ＊ ＊ ＊ In contrast, a member of a diffuse D-group need not suffer such severe dislocation in order to avoid the disapproval of his fellow group members. Instead, he may insulate himself from their displeasure by assimilating into the majoritarian mainstream—undoubtedly a costly process, but typically less costly than the social stigma heaped on the free-riding I. ＊ ＊ ＊

B.　Organizational Costs

It follows, then, that the average I is more likely to contribute his time and money to the group cause than is an otherwise comparable D. Yet this conclusion tells only half the story: not only will an I-group receive more resources from its constituency, but I's will also find it cheaper to organize themselves for effective political action. First, the dense communications network generated by insularity dramatically reduces one of the heaviest costs involved in effective political lobbying: the cost of communicating with a mass membership. To get its messages out to its constituency, an insular political group can often avail itself of the communications channels already established by the group's churches, businesses, or labor unions. In contrast, a D-group must somehow locate and reach people who interact with one another much less frequently and who have fewer channels already established for the cheap transmission of D-group concerns.

Second, the organic character of insular life greatly reduces the costs of selecting credible political leaders. The I-group can draw upon a pool of people who have already earned the respect of their fellow I's in other communal contexts: ministers and rabbis, successful lawyers, businessmen, union leaders. In contrast, even if D-group members manage to overcome the communications barrier, they must often take the risk of selecting political leaders who have not been tested and observed in other leadership settings.

C. Insularity and Congressional Influence

* * *

We have reached a point, however, where it is necessary to introduce an explicitly geographic concept of insularity into the discussion—for the simple reason that geography is of the first importance in assessing a group's influence within the American political system. For present purposes, it will suffice to restrict our speculations to two simple geographic alternatives. On the one hand, our sociologically insular minority might also be geographically insular: concentrated in a relatively small number of places in the United States. On the other hand, geographic insularity might not accompany sociological insularity. Indeed, at the limit, the *I*-group might be evenly spread over the fifty states and 435 congressional districts. For heuristic purposes, let us begin with the alternative that is empirically less common, but analytically more tractable. Suppose that an *I*-group is distributed in a geographically diffuse way: if it contains 12 percent of the national population, it accounts for 12 percent of each congressional district. Now compare this geographically diffuse *I*-group with a *D*-group that is both sociologically and geographically diffuse. Other things being equal, which group is more likely to succeed in influencing Congressmen?

The previous analysis suggests that the *I*-group will probably have greater influence. Such a group is more likely to form a political lobby peopled by credible leaders who remain in close touch with the insular constituency they represent. When such lobbyists threaten a Congressman with electoral retribution, they can expect a respectful hearing. * * * In short, even if the *I*-group is distributed evenly throughout the nation, it has a greater ability to exert political influence through the ultimate currency of democratic politics: votes on election day.

This conclusion is reinforced when we turn to the more realistic case in which the middling *I*-group is distributed very unevenly throughout the country. In this scenario, a middling minority could reasonably expect to be a local majority—or at least a decisive voting bloc—in 20 to 30 congressional districts. For the representatives of these districts, the support of the *I*-group amounts to nothing less than the stuff of political survival. In fact, for all our *Carolene* talk about the powerlessness of insular groups, we are perfectly aware of the enormous power such voting blocs have in American politics. The story of the protective tariff is, I suppose, the classic illustration of insularity's power in American history. Over the past half-century, we have been treated to an enormous number of welfare-state variations on the theme of insularity by the farm bloc, the steel lobby, the auto lobby, and others too numerous to mention. In this standard scenario of pluralistic politics, it is precisely the diffuse character of the majority forced to pay the bill for tariffs, agricultural subsidies, and the like, that allows strategically located Congressmen to deliver the goods to their well-organized local constituents. Given these familiar stories, it is really quite remarkable to hear lawyers profess concern that insular interests have too little influence in Congress. Instead, the American system typically deprives *diffuse* groups of their rightful say over the course of legislative policy. If there is anything to *Carolene Products,* then, it cannot be a minority's insularity, taken by itself—something more must be involved.

IV. DISCRETE AND INSULAR MINORITIES?

Could that something be the "discreteness" of a *Carolene* minority?

I begin with a question because it is not obvious whether most constitutional lawyers endow the word "discrete" with independent significance in their understanding of the *Carolene* doctrine. Nonetheless, we can conceive the term in a way that adds something important to the overall formula. I propose to define a minority as "discrete" when its members are marked out in ways that make it relatively easy for others to identify them. For instance, there is nothing a black woman may plausibly do to hide the fact that she is black or female. Like it or not, she will have to deal with the social expectations and stereotypes generated by her evident group characteristics. In contrast, other minorities are socially defined in ways that give individual members the chance to avoid easy identification. A homosexual, for example, can keep her sexual preference a very private affair and thereby avoid much of the public opprobrium attached to her minority status. It is for this reason that I shall call homosexuals, and groups like them, "anonymous" minorities and contrast them with "discrete" minorities of the kind paradigmatically exemplified by blacks.

* * *

Carolene takes a straightforward position on this question. In its view, discreteness is a political liability. Once again, however, * * * this is not obvious. * * *

* * * If you are a black in America today, you know there is no way you can avoid the impact of the larger public's views about the significance of blackness. Because exit is not possible, there is only one way to do something about disadvantageous racial stereotypes: complain about them. Among efficacious forms of complaint, the possibility of organized political action will surely rank high.

This is not to say, of course, that individual blacks, or members of other discrete minorities, will necessarily lend their support to interest-group activity. They may, instead, succumb to the temptations of free-riding and thus deprive the group of vital political resources. But even if discreteness is no cure-all for selfishness, it does free a minority from the organizational problem confronting an anonymous group of comparable size. To see my point, compare the problem faced by black political organizers with the one confronting organizers of the homosexual community. As a member of an anonymous group, each homosexual can seek to minimize the personal harm due to prejudice by keeping his or her sexual preference a tightly held secret. Although this is hardly a fully satisfactory response, secrecy does enable homosexuals to "exit" from prejudice in a way that blacks cannot. This means that a homosexual group must confront an organizational problem that does not arise for its black counterpart: somehow the group must induce each anonymous homosexual to reveal his or her sexual preference to the larger public and to bear the private costs this public declaration may involve.

＊　＊　＊ So it would seem that *Carolene Products* is wrong again: a court concerned with pluralist bargaining power should be more, not less, attentive to the claims of anonymous minorities than to those of discrete ones.

V.   PREJUDICE

But surely it is time to stop playing *Hamlet* without the Prince. The whole point of *Carolene*'s concern with "discrete and insular minorities" cannot be understood, I am sure you are thinking, without grasping the final term of the formula: prejudice. Indeed, it has been one of my aims to provoke precisely this reaction. By detailing all the ways discrete and insular minorities gain political advantage over diffuse and anonymous groups, I have meant to emphasize how heavy a burden the idea of prejudice must carry in the overall argument for *Carolene Products.* The burden is of two kinds: one empirical, the other conceptual. To take them one at a time, I shall defer all problems involved in conceptualizing prejudice so that we may first focus upon the empirical side of the matter.

A.   Questions of Fact

Carolene's empirical inadequacy stems from its underinclusive conception of the impact of prejudice upon American society. It is easy to identify groups in the population that are not discrete and insular but that are nonetheless the victims of prejudice, as that term is commonly understood. Thus, the fact that homosexuals are a relatively anonymous minority has not saved the group from severe prejudice. Nor is sexism a nonproblem merely because women are a diffuse, if discrete, majority. Prejudice is generated by a bewildering variety of social conditions. Although some *Carolene* minorities are seriously victimized, they are not the only ones stigmatized; nor is it obvious that all *Carolene* minorities are stigmatized more grievously than any other non-*Carolene* group. Why should the concern with "prejudice" justify *Carolene*'s narrow fixation upon "discrete and insular" minorities?

The answer seemed easy in a world in which members of the paradigmatic *Carolene* minority group—blacks—were effectively barred from voting and political participation. Something is better than nothing: whatever the organizational problems engendered by anonymity and diffuseness, surely they are not nearly so devastating as total disenfranchisement. As we turn toward the future, however, it is far less clear that such selective perception makes constitutional sense. Nonetheless, I shall give *Carolene* the benefit of the doubt by sketching a "pariah" model of the political process in which *Carolene*'s emphasis on the fate of discrete and insular minorities will still seem empirically plausible. As we move beyond the pariah model, however, anonymous or diffuse minorities will increasingly emerge as the groups that can raise the most serious complaints of pluralist disempowerment.

1. *The Pariah Model.*—Assume a polity in which middling minorities—in the 10 to 20 percent range—attain majority status in a significant number of congressional districts because of the way their insularity interacts with the geographic biases of the American political system. Nonetheless, the minority representatives these groups elect are entirely ineffective in Congress—because all remaining Congressmen refuse to bargain with them in any way. * * *

Sound implausible? * * * Yet it is only by indulging in something like these strong empirical assumptions that *Carolene* can claim that the effects of prejudice *plainly* outweigh the political advantages enjoyed by minorities that are discrete and insular.

2. *Beyond the Pariah Model.*—Once we deny the general empirical validity of the pariah model, our assessment of the political impact of a discrete and insular group will invariably be more complex. * * *

* * * I turn to a very different approach to *Carolene* presented by John Hart Ely in his important work, *Democracy and Distrust.* Among its many virtues, the book explicitly recognizes that the conventional *Carolene* wisdom about the powerlessness of discrete and insular minorities is "in need of some reexamination." Yet Dean Ely does not attempt the interest-group analysis that has thus far engaged our energies. Instead, he relies exclusively on a social-psychological approach to the legislative process. On his view, the critical thing about prejudice is the way it allows legislators to stereotype "discrete and insular" minorities. It is this legislative propensity to divide the world into "we-they" categories that, according to Ely, lies at the core of *Carolene*'s concern: "we" legislators will both overestimate the dangers posed by the "they" group and underestimate its similarities to the "we" group. As a consequence, legislation that disadvantages "they" groups will be based on an intolerably distorted perception of social reality.

Even if we were to accept a "we-they" view of legislative psychology, Ely's failure to recognize the limits of the pariah model serves as an independent ground for questioning his conclusions. Quite simply, our efforts in bargaining theory have led us to expect that "middling minorities" of the "discrete and insular" kind will elect a significant number of Representatives—say 20 to 25—who are extremely responsive to their interests. As long as these politicians are not treated like pariahs, they can become a potent legislative force—trading votes with other legislators to further the objectives of their own constituents. * * * This is more than diffuse or anonymous minorities can expect: *their* representatives may not even *be* at the bargaining table. As soon as he moves beyond the narrow confines of the pariah model, Dean Ely cannot rehabilitate *Carolene*'s exclusive focus on discrete and insular minorities through "we-they" psychology alone.

Dean Ely seems aware of all this. Although *Democracy and Distrust* does not contain a fully developed analysis of minority legislative power, it does hint at an approach different from the one I advance here. Dean Ely suggests that minority politicians may suffer from a distinctive psychological affliction: while other Congressmen act on "we-they" prejudices in favor of their own constituents, minority politicians may accept the very stereotypes they should be challenging. If this point were conceded, Ely's argument would take on a self-sealing quality: no matter how actively minority representatives participated in the bargaining process, they would only reinforce, and never challenge, prevailing prejudices.

Dean Ely shows great restraint in dealing with this suggestion of minority "false consciousness." While he says that "[t]he general idea is one that in some contexts has merit," his book does not, in fact, spend very much space defending and elaborating it. I believe, moreover, that an appeal to "false consciousness" cannot be elaborated in a way that makes constitutional sense.

The first question to ask about "false consciousness" is an empirical one: will the rising generation of minority politicians in fact passively accept debasing stereotypes? I see no reason to project such a grim image upon our future. To the contrary, the classic prejudices are under vigorous challenge by powerful voices emerging from a broad range of discrete and insular communities. * * *

The second question is: even if some social psychologist could "prove" the existence of false consciousness, should the Supreme Court transform this social phenomenon into an assumption of constitutional law? We are dealing here not with an academic scientific inquiry, but with a question of institutional relationships. In branding minority politicians as victims of "false consciousness" on the pages of the *United States Reports,* the Supreme Court would be consigning them to a peculiarly demeaning constitutional status. Henceforth, they—and they alone—would be deemed constitutionally incapable of discharging the representative functions of democratically elected legislators. Such a declaration would make a mockery of *Carolene*'s promise. Rather than attempting to approximate the results of a perfect pluralist democracy, the Court would be protecting minority rights by emphatically impugning the capacity of these very same minorities to engage in democratic politics at all.

* * *

B. Questions of Value

But *Carolene*'s failure to recognize the political predicament of anonymous or diffuse groups that are victims of prejudice is only half the problem; the other half is more conceptual, but no less troubling.

The idea of "prejudice" is simply unequal to the task assigned it within the overall *Carolene* analysis. Recall that *Carolene*'s promise is a form of argument that allows a court to say that it is purifying the democratic process rather than imposing its own substantive values upon the political branches. And yet it is just this process orientation that is at risk when a *Carolene* court undertakes to identify the prejudices that entitle a group to special protection from the vagaries of pluralist politics. One person's "prejudice" is, notoriously, another's "principle." How, then, do we identify a group for *Carolene* protection without performing the substantive analysis of constitutional values that *Carolene* hopes to avoid?

The kind of answer required is clear enough. To redeem *Carolene*'s promise, the judicial identification of a prejudice cannot depend upon the substance of the suspect view, but must turn on the way in which legislators come to hold their belief. The process-oriented argument goes something like this: although each of us cannot always expect to convince our legislators, we can at least insist that they treat our claims with respect. At the very least, they should thoughtfully consider our moral and empirical arguments, rejecting them only after conscientiously deciding that they are inconsistent with the public interest. If a group fails to receive this treatment, it suffers a special wrong, one quite distinct from its substantive treatment on the merits. And it is this purely processual kind of prejudice that constitutes the grievance *Carolene* courts may endeavor to remedy without engaging in the suspect task of prescribing substantive values.

* * *

Let me propose a test case. Imagine that, after reading Herbert Wechsler's famous essay,[47] a group of conservative legalists becomes sincerely convinced that *Brown v. Board of Education* could not in fact be based on neutral principles and so does not deserve its place as a cornerstone of our constitutional law. Acting on this conviction, the group begins a campaign advocating a constitutional amendment to repeal *Brown* and generates some modest interest among conservatives across the country. Arriving in Washington, D.C., with their legal process arguments elaborately developed, the group proceeds to the lobbies of Congress. How do you think the group would be received? Would most Representatives be willing and able to confront the Wechslerian arguments with a thoughtful defense of our constitutional commitment to equality? Or would they respond in a *processually* prejudiced fashion—peremptorily brushing aside the Wechslerians' arguments with a catch-phrase or two that fails to join issue?

This is, in principle, an empirical question—though, like many others, it will never get a good empirical answer. Nonetheless, if my study of politics has taught me anything, I would not expect the agitating Wechslerians to receive a processually unprejudiced response

---

47. Wechsler, *Toward Neutral Principles of Constitutional Law,* 73 Harv.L.Rev. 1 (1959).

on Capitol Hill. As far as I can tell, any large representative assembly will contain a bewildering variety of human types—from the elaborately thoughtful to the superficially unquestioning. It is simply self-congratulatory to suppose that the members of our own persuasion have reached their convictions in a deeply reflective way, whereas those espousing opinions we hate are superficial. Instead, a thoughtful judge can expect to find an abundance of stereotype-mongers and knee-jerks on *all* sides of *every* important issue—as well as many who have struggled their way to more considered judgments. Given the complexity of the human comedy, a judge is bound on a fool's errand if he imagines that the good guys and bad guys of American politics can be neatly classified according to the seriousness with which they have considered opposing points of view. Processual prejudice is a pervasive problem in the American political system.

But if this is right, *Carolene* cannot justify its concern with discrete and insular minorities without calling on judges to engage in a very different kind of judgment, one dealing with the *substance* of racial and religious prejudice. In doing so, the judge need not try to play the elaborate psychological and political guessing game required to assess the extent to which a statute is the product of a prejudiced refusal to give a respectful hearing to disfavored interests and opinions. Instead, she proceeds to a more familiar judicial inquiry into the nature of the substantive reasons that might plausibly justify the legislature's assertion of authority. If the only plausible reasons for the statute's enactment offend substantive constitutional principles, the groups aggrieved by the statute are declared victims of "prejudice"; if not, not. Although this judicial inquiry into the rational foundations of a statute may sometimes require a focused inquiry into the data available to, or even the subjective opinions of, particular public officials, the critical legal question is of a very different kind: why are the political principles endorsed by some groups judicially recognized as vindicating the constitutionality of a statute, while others are viewed as inadmissible "prejudices" delegitimating a statute's claim to constitutionality?

If *Carolene* somehow hoped to find a shortcut around this substantive inquiry into constitutional values, its journey was fated to fail from the outset. The difference between the things we call "prejudice" and the things we call "principle" is in the end a substantive moral difference. And if the courts are authorized to protect the victims of certain "prejudices," it can only be because the Constitution has placed certain normative judgments beyond the pale of legitimacy.

BIBLIOGRAPHY

Equal Protection Theory

Cohen, *Is Equal Protection Like Oakland? Equality as a Surrogate for Other Rights*, 59 Tul.L.Rev. 884 (1985).

D'Amato, *Is Equality a Totally Empty Idea?*, 81 Mich.L.Rev. 600 (1983).

Frank & Munro, *The Original Understanding of "Equal Protection of the Laws",* 1972 Wash.U.L.Q. 421.

Michelman, *On Protecting the Poor Through the Fourteenth Amendment,* 83 Harv.L.Rev. 7 (1969).

Miller, *The True Story of Carolene Products,* 1987 Sup.Ct.Rev. 397.

Pennock, J. & Chapman, J., 9 NOMOS: EQUALITY (1967).

Simons, *Overinclusion and Underinclusion: A New Model,* 36 U.C. L.A.L.Rev. 447 (1989).

Sunstein, *Public Values, Private Interests, and the Equal Protection Clause,* 1982 Sup.Ct.Rev. 127.

Tussman & tenBroek, *The Equal Protection of the Laws,* 37 Calif.L.Rev. 341 (1949).

Westen, *The Empty Idea of Equality,* 95 Harv.L.Rev. 537 (1982).

Wilkinson, *The Supreme Court, The Equal Protection Clause, and the Three Faces of Constitutional Equality,* 61 Va.L.Rev. 945 (1975).

Race and the Constitution

Bell, D., AND WE ARE NOT SAVED (1987).

Bell, D., RACE, RACISM AND AMERICAN LAW (2d ed. 1980).

Bickel, *The Original Understanding and the Segregation Decision,* 69 Harv.L.Rev. 1 (1955).

Cover, R., JUSTICE ACCUSED (1975).

Crenshaw, *Race, Reform, and Retrenchment: Transformation and Legitimation in Antidiscrimination Law,* 101 Harv.L.Rev. 1331 (1988).

Dimond, *The Anti-Caste Principle—Toward a Constitutional Standard for Review of Race Cases,* 30 Wayne L.Rev. 1 (1983).

Fairman, C., RECONSTRUCTION AND REUNION, 1864–88, Part I (1971); Part II (1987).

Franklin, J., FROM SLAVERY TO FREEDOM (3d ed. 1967).

Freeman, *Legitimizing Racial Discrimination Through Antidiscrimination Law: A Critical Review of Supreme Court Doctrine,* 62 Minn.L.Rev. 1049 (1978).

Higginbotham, A., IN THE MATTER OF COLOR (1978).

Hyman, H. & Wiecek, W., EQUAL JUSTICE UNDER LAW: CONSTITUTIONAL DEVELOPMENT, 1835–1875 (1982).

Kaczorowski, *Revolutionary Constitutionalism in the Era of the Civil War and Reconstruction,* 61 N.Y.U.L.Rev. 863 (1986).

McNeil, G., GROUNDWORK: CHARLES HAMILTON HOUSTON AND THE STRUGGLE FOR CIVIL RIGHTS (1983).

Oberst, *The Strange Career of Plessy v. Ferguson,* 15 Ariz.L.Rev. 389 (1973).

Robinson, D., SLAVERY IN THE STRUCTURE OF AMERICAN POLITICS, 1765–1820 (1971).

Schmidt, *Principle and Prejudice: The Supreme Court and Race in the Progressive Era. Part I: The Heyday of Jim Crow*, 82 Colum.L.Rev. 444 (1982).

Soifer, *Protecting Civil Rights: A Critique of Raoul Berger's History*, 54 N.Y.U.L.Rev. 651 (1979).

Strauss, *The Myth of Colorblindness*, 1986 Sup.Ct.Rev. 99.

Swisher, C., THE TANEY PERIOD, 1835–64 (1974).

Symposium, *We the People: A Celebration of the Bicentennial of the United States Constitution*, 30 Howard L.J. 915 (1987).

Woodward, C., THE STRANGE CAREER OF JIM CROW (1955).

School Desegregation

Bell, ed., SHADES OF BROWN: NEW PERSPECTIVES ON SCHOOL DESEGREGATION (1980).

Bell, Brown v. Board of Education *and the Interest-Convergence Dilemma*, 93 Harv.L.Rev. 518 (1980).

Black, *The Lawfulness of the Segregation Decisions*, 69 Yale L.J. 421 (1960).

Chang, *The Bus Stops Here: Defining the Constitutional Right of Equal Educational Opportunity and an Appropriate Remedial Process*, 63 B.U.L.Rev. 1 (1983).

Devins, *School Desegregation Law in the 1980's: The Courts' Abandonment of* Brown v. Board of Education, 26 Wm. & Mary L.Rev. 7 (1984).

Fiss, *School Desegregation: The Uncertain Path of the Law*, 4 Phil. & Pub.Aff. 3 (1974).

Fiss, *The Fate of an Idea Whose Time Has Come: Antidiscrimination Law in the Second Decade after* Brown v. Board of Education, 41 U.Chi.L.Rev. 742 (1974).

Gewirtz, *Remedies and Resistance*, 92 Yale L.J. 585 (1983).

Goodman, *De Facto School Segregation: A Constitutional and Empirical Analysis*, 60 Calif.L.Rev. 275 (1972).

Graglia, L., DISASTER BY DECREE (1976).

Kirp, D., JUST SCHOOLS (1982).

Kitch, *The Return of Color-Consciousness to the Constitution: Weber, Dayton, and Columbus*, 1979 Sup.Ct.Rev. 1.

Kluger, R., SIMPLE JUSTICE (1975).

Landsberg, *The Desegregated School System and the Retrogression Plan*, 48 La.L.Rev. 789 (1988).

Liebman, *Desegregation Politics: "All–Out" School Desegregation Explained*, 90 Colum.L.Rev. 1463 (1990).

Note, *The Courts, HEW, and Southern School Desegregation*, 77 Yale L.J. 321 (1967).

Shane, *School Desegregation Remedies and the Fair Governance of Schools*, 132 U.Pa.L.Rev. 1041 (1984).

Tushnet, M., THE NAACP'S LEGAL STRATEGY AGAINST SEGREGATED EDUCATION, 1925–1950 (1987).

Wilkinson, J., FROM BROWN TO BAKKE (1979).

Chapter VII

EQUALITY AND GENDER

Since the early 1970's, the Supreme Court has subjected governmental actions that discriminate on the basis of gender to "heightened scrutiny"—a standard somewhere between the strict scrutiny applied to racial classifications and the rationality review applied to most economic and social legislation. This "middle tier" standard evidences the Court's view that although gender classifications are generally troubling, there may be legitimate reasons for governmental actions that take gender into account.

The readings in this Chapter seek to explore the theoretical issues that lie behind the legal doctrine. Are gender classifications as invidious as racial classifications? Does "gender equality" mean a gender-blind legal system? Or should the Equal Protection Clause tolerate gender-based laws that reflect existing differences between the sexes? Are such differences natural (biological) or are they socially created?

Richard Wasserstrom's article sets the stage for analyzing these questions by asking what role gender might play in an ideal society. He suggests that the arguments for taking gender into account based on biological and social differences are not as strong as is normally supposed.

Suzanna Sherry offers grounds for questioning Wasserstrom's assimilationist model. She examines recent feminist scholarship that suggests that women's moral development and sense of self may differ from men's. Sherry argues that law has been distorted by its reliance on a masculine perspective (that emphasizes autonomy, objectivity, and rights) and its exclusion of a feminine perspective (that would emphasize connection, subjectivity, and responsibility).

The next three excerpts examine the theoretical justifications for constitutional doctrine respecting gender discrimination. John Hart Ely contends that recently enacted gender-based classifications should not be subjected to strict judicial scrutiny.

Wendy Williams analyzes the extent to which current cultural understandings of gender roles may set limits on the work that the Equal Protection Clause can do for gender equality. She argues that the legal strategy of some feminists stressing differences and supporting programs that afford special treatment to women may unwittingly reflect and reinforce traditional cultural notions about the role of women.

Catharine MacKinnon sketches two models of sex discrimination law. The prevailing approach, she asserts, is based on the familiar idea that equality means treating likes alike and unlikes unalike. MacKinnon argues that this "sameness/difference approach" is inadequate because it sets up maleness as the standard against which sameness and difference are to be measured, and it supports dominance of women by approving of distinctions based on differences between the sexes. She proposes a "dominance approach" to gender discrimination which would recognize sex inequalities as matters of imposed status, as the subordination of women to men.

RICHARD A. WASSERSTROM, RACISM AND SEXISM

Philosophy and Social Issues 23–43 (1980).

*   *   * [W]hat would the good or just society make of an individual's race or sex, and to what degree, if at all, would racial and sexual distinctions ever properly be taken into account there?   *   *   *

*   *   *

[O]ne conception of a nonracist society is that which is captured by what I shall call the assimilationist ideal: a nonracist society would be one in which the race of an individual would be the functional equivalent of the eye color of individuals in our society today.[25] In our society no basic political rights and obligations are determined on the basis of eye color. No important institutional benefits and burdens are connected with eye color. Indeed, except for the mildest sort of aesthetic preferences, a person would be thought odd who even made private, social decisions by taking eye color into account.   *   *   *

What is a good deal less familiar is an analogous conception of the good society in respect to sexual differentiation—one in which an individual's sex were to become a comparably unimportant characteristic. An assimilationist society in respect to sex would be one in which an individual's sex was of no more significance *   *   * than is eye color today. There would be no analogue to transsexuality, and, while physiological or anatomical sex differences would remain, they would possess only the kind and degree of significance that today attaches to the physiologically distinct eye colors persons possess.

*   *   *

*   *   * [I]t must be acknowledged that to make the assimilationist ideal a reality in respect to sex would involve more profound and

---

25. There is a danger in calling this ideal the "assimilationist" ideal. That term often suggests the idea of incorporating oneself, one's values, and the like into the dominant group and its practices and values. No part of that idea is meant to be captured by my use of the term. Mine is a stipulative definition.

fundamental revisions of our institutions and our attitudes than would be the case in respect to race. On the institutional level we would, for instance, have to alter significantly our practices concerning marriage. If a nonsexist society is a society in which one's sex is no more significant than eye color in our society today, then laws which require the persons who are getting married to be of different sexes would clearly be sexist laws.

More importantly, given the significance of role differentiation and ideas about the psychological differences in temperament that are tied to sexual identity, the assimilationist ideal would be incompatible with all psychological and sex-role differentiation. That is to say, in such a society the ideology of the society would contain no proposition asserting the inevitable or essential attributes of masculinity or feminity; it would never encourage or discourage the ideas of sisterhood or brotherhood; and it would be unintelligible to talk about the virtues or the disabilities of being a woman or a man. In addition, such a society would not have any norms concerning the appropriateness of different social behavior depending upon whether one were male or female. There would be no conception of the existence of a set of social tasks that were more appropriately undertaken or performed by males or by females. And there would be no expectation that the family was composed of one adult male and one adult female, rather than, say, just two adults—if two adults seemed the appropriate number. To put it simply, in the assimilationist society in respect to sex, persons would not be socialized so as to see or understand themselves or others as essentially or significantly who they were or what their lives would be like because they were either male or female. And no political rights or social institutions, practices, and norms would mark the physiological differences between males and females as important.

Were sex like eye color, these kinds of distinctions would make no sense. Just as the normal, typical adult is virtually oblivious to the eye color of other persons for all significant interpersonal relationships, so, too, the normal, typical adult in this kind of nonsexist society would be equally as indifferent to the sexual, physiological differences of other persons for all significant interpersonal relationships. Bisexuality, not heterosexuality or homosexuality, would be the typical intimate, sexual relationship in the ideal society that was assimilationist in respect to sex.

To acknowledge that things would be very different is, of course, hardly to concede that they would thereby be undesirable—or desirable for that matter. But still, the problem is, perhaps, with the assimilationist ideal. And the assimilationist ideal is certainly not the only possible, plausible ideal.

There is, for instance, another one that is closely related to, but distinguishable from that of the assimilationist ideal. It can be understood by considering how religion rather than eye color tends to be thought about in our culture today and incorporated within social life today. If the good society were to match the present state of affairs in respect to one's religious identity, rather than the present state of affairs in respect to one's eye color, the two societies would be different, but not very greatly so. In neither would we find that the allocation of basic political rights and duties ever took an individual's religion into account. And there would be a comparable indifference to religion even in respect to most important institutional benefits and burdens— for example, access to employment in the desirable vocations, the opportunity to live where one wished to live, and the like. Nonetheless, in the good society in which religious differences were to some degree socially relevant, it would be deemed appropriate to have some institutions (typically those which are connected in an intimate way with these religions) which did in a variety of ways properly take the religion of members of the society into account. For example, it would be thought both permissible and appropriate for members of a religious group to join together in collective associations which have religious, educational, and social dimensions, and when it came to the employment of persons who were to be centrally engaged in the operation of those religious institutions (priests, rabbis and ministers, for example), it would be unobjectionable and appropriate explicitly to take the religion of job applicants into account. On the individual, interpersonal level, it might also be thought natural and possibly even admirable, were persons to some significant degree to select their associates, friends, and mates on the basis of their religious orientation. So there is another possible and plausible ideal of what the good society would look like in respect to a particular characteristic in which differences based upon that characteristic would be to some degree maintained in some aspects of institutional and interpersonal life. The diversity of the religious beliefs of individuals would be reflected in the society's institutional and ideological fabric in a way in which the diversity of eye color would not be in the assimilationist society. The picture is a more complex, somewhat less easily describable one than that of the assimilationist ideal.

* * *

What opponents of assimilationism and proponents of schemes of strong sexual differentiation seize upon is that sexual difference appears to be a naturally occurring category of obvious and inevitable relevance for the construction of any plausible conception of the nature of the good society. The problems with this way of thinking are twofold. To begin with, a careful and thorough analysis of the social realities would reveal, I believe, that it is the socially created sexual differences which constitute most of our conception of sex differences and which tend in fact to matter the most in the way we live our lives as persons of one sex or the other. For, it is, I think, sex-role differentiation and socialization, not the physiological and related biological differences—if there are any—that make men and women as different as they are from each other, and it is these same sex-role-created differences which are invoked to justify the necessity or the desirability of most sexual differentiation proposed to be maintained at any of the levels of social arrangements and practices described earlier.

It is important, however, not to attach any greater weight than is absolutely necessary to the truth or falsity of this causal claim about the source of the degree of sexual distinctions that exist in our or other cultures. For what is significant, although seldom recognized, is the fact that the answer to that question almost never goes very far in settling the question of what the good society should look like in respect to any particular characteristic of individuals. And the answer certainly does not go as far as many persons appear to believe it does to settle that question of the nature of the good society.

Let us suppose that there are what can be called "naturally occurring" sexual differences and even that they are of such a nature that they are in some sense of direct prima facie social relevance. It is essential to see that this would by no means settle the question of whether in the good society sex should or should not be as minimally significant as eye color. Even if there are major or substantial biological differences between men and women that are in this sense "natural" rather than socially created, this does not determine the question of what the good society can and should make of these differences— without, that is, begging the question by including within the meaning of "major" or "substantial" or "natural" the idea that these are things that ought to be retained, emphasized, or otherwise normally taken into account. It is not easy to see why, without begging the question, it should be thought that this fact, if it is a fact, settles the question adversely to anything like the assimilationist ideal. Persons might think that truths of this sort about nature or biology do affect, if not settle, the question of what the good society should look like for at least two different reasons.

In the first place, they might think the differences are of such a character that they substantially affect what would be *possible* within a good society of human persons. Just as the fact that humans are mortal necessarily limits the features of any possible good society, so, they might argue, the fact that males and females are physiologically or biologically different limits in the same way the features of any possible good society.

In the second place, they might think the differences are of such a character that they are relevant to the question of what would be *desirable* in the good society. That is to say, they might not think that the differences determine or affect to a substantial degree what is possible, but only that the differences are appropriately taken into account in any rational construction of an ideal social existence.

The second reason seems to be a good deal more plausible than the first. For there appear to be very few, if any, respects in which the ineradicable, naturally occurring differences between males and females *must* be taken into account. The industrial revolution has certainly made any of the general differences in strength between the sexes capable of being ignored by the good society sexes capable of being ignored by the good society for virtually all significant human activities. And even if it were true that women are naturally better suited than men to care for and nurture children, it is also surely the case that men can be taught to care for and nurture children well. Indeed, the one natural or biological fact that seems *required* to be taken into account is the fact that reproduction of the human species requires that the fetus develop *in utero* for a period of months. Sexual intercourse is not necessary, for artificial insemination is available. Neither marriage nor the nuclear family is necessary either for conception or child rearing. Given the present state of medical knowledge and what might be termed the natural realities of female pregnancy, it is difficult to see why any important institutional or interpersonal arrangements are constrained to take the existing biological differences as to the phenomenon of *in utero* pregnancy into account.

But to say all this is still to leave it a wholly open question to what degree the good society *ought* to build upon any ineradicable biological differences, or to create ones in order to construct institutions and sex roles which would thereby maintain a substantial degree of sexual differentiation. The way to answer that question is to consider and assess the arguments for and against doing so. What is significant is the fact that many of the arguments for doing so are less persuasive than they appear to be upon the initial statement of this possibility.

It might be argued, for instance, that the fact of menstruation could be used as a premise upon which to base the case for importantly different social roles for females than for males. But this could only plausibly be proposed if two things were true: first, that menstruation would be debilitating to women and hence relevant to social role even in a culture which did not teach women to view menstruation as a sign of uncleanliness or as a curse; and, second, that the way in which menstruation necessarily affected some or all women was in fact necessarily related in an important way to the role in question. But even if both of these were true, it would still be an open question whether any sexual differentiation ought to be built upon these facts. The society could still elect to develop institutions that would nullify the effect of these natural differences and it would still be an open question whether it ought to do so. Suppose, for example, what seems implausible—that some or all women will not be able to perform a particular task while menstruating, e.g., guard the border of a country. It would be possible, even easy, if the society wanted to, to arrange for substitute guards for the women who were incapacitated. We know that persons are not good guards when they are sleepy, and we make arrangements so that persons alternate guard duty to avoid fatigue. The same could be done for menstruating women, even given the implausibly strong assumptions about menstruation.

The point that is involved here is a very general one that has application in contexts having nothing to do with the desirability or undesirability of maintaining substantial sexual differentiation. It has to do with the fact that humans possess the ability to alter their natural and social environment in distinctive, dramatic, and unique ways. * * *

* * *

There are, though, several other arguments based upon nature, or the idea of the "natural" that also must be considered and assessed. First, it might be argued that if a way of doing something is natural, then it ought to be done that way. Here, what may be meant by "natural" is that this way of doing the thing is the way it would be done if culture did not direct or teach us to do it differently. It is not clear, however, that this sense of "natural" is wholly intelligible; it supposes that we can meaningfully talk about how humans would behave in the absence of culture. And few if any humans have ever lived in such a state. Moreover, even if this is an intelligible notion, the proposal that the natural way to behave is somehow the appropriate or desirable way to behave is strikingly implausible. It is, for example, almost surely natural, in this sense of "natural," that humans would eat their food with their hands, except for the fact that they are, almost always, socialized to eat food differently. Yet, the fact that humans would naturally eat this way, does not seem in any respect to be a reason for believing that that is thereby the desirable or appropriate way to eat food. And the same is equally true of any number of other distinctively human ways of behaving.

Second, someone might argue that substantial sexual differentiation is natural not in the sense that it is biologically determined nor in the sense that it would occur but for the effects of culture, but rather in the sense that substantial sexual differentiation is a virtually universal phenomenon in human culture. By itself, this claim of virtual universality, even if accurate, does not directly establish anything about the desirability or undesirability of any particular ideal. But it can be made into an argument by the addition of the proposition that where there is a widespread, virtually universal social practice or institution, there is probably some good or important purpose served by the practice or institution. Hence, given the fact of substantial sex-role differentiation in all, or almost all, cultures, there is on this view some reason to think that substantial sex-role differentiation serves some important purpose for and in human society.

This is an argument, but it is hard to see what is attractive about it. The premise which turns the fact of sex-role differentiation into any kind of a strong reason for sex-role differentiation is the premise of conservatism. And it is no more or less convincing here than elsewhere. There are any number of practices or institutions that are typical and yet upon reflection seem without significant social purpose. Slavery was once such an institution; war perhaps still is.

More to the point, perhaps, the concept of "purpose" is ambiguous. It can mean in a descriptive sense "plays some role" or "is causally relevant." Or, it can mean in a prescriptive sense "does something desirable" or "has some useful function." If "purpose" is used descriptively in the conservative premise, then the argument says nothing about the continued desirability of sex-role differentiation of the assimilationist ideal. If "purpose" is used prescriptively in the conservative premise, then there is no reason to think that premise is true.

To put it another way, the question that seems fundamentally to be at issue is whether it is desirable to have a society in which sex-role differences are to be retained in the way and to the degree they are today—or even at all. The straightforward way to think about the question is to ask what would be good and what would be bad about a society in which sex functioned like eye color does in our society; or alternatively, what would be good and what would be bad about a society in which sex functioned in the way in which religious identity does today; or alternatively, what would be good and what would be bad about a society in which sex functioned in the way in which it does today. We can imagine what such societies would look like and how they might work. It is hard to see how thinking about answers to this question is substantially advanced by reference to what has typically or always been the case. If it is true, for instance, that the sex-role-differentiated societies that have existed have tended to concentrate power and authority in the hands of males, have developed institutions and ideologies that have perpetuated that concentration, and have restricted and prevented women from living the kinds of lives that persons ought to be able to live for themselves, then this, it seems to me, says far more about what may be wrong with any strongly nonassimilationist ideal than does the conservative premise say what may be right about any strongly nonassimilationist ideal.

* * *

* * * [It remains an open question] whether a society in which sex functioned in the way in which eye color does (a strictly assimilationist society in respect to sex) would be better or worse than one in which sex functioned in the way in which religious identity does in our society (a nonoppressive, more diversified or pluralistic one). For it might be argued that especially in the case of sex and even in the case of race much would be gained and nothing would be lost if the ideal society in respect to these characteristics succeeded in preserving in a nonoppressive fashion the attractive differences between males and females and the comparably attractive differences among ethnic groups. Such a society, it might be claimed, would be less bland, less homogeneous and richer in virtue of its variety.

I do not think there is any easy way to settle this question, but I do think the attractiveness of the appeal to diversity, when sex or race are concerned, is less alluring than is often supposed. The difficulty is in part one of specifying what will be preserved and what will not, and in part one of preventing the reappearance of the type of systemic dominance and subservience that produces the injustice of oppression. Suppose, for example, that it were suggested that there are aspects of being male and aspects of being female that are equally attractive and hence desirable to maintain and perpetuate: the kind of empathy that is associated with women and the kind of self-control associated with men. It does not matter what the characteristic is, the problem is one of seeing why the characteristic should be tied by the social institutions to the sex of the individuals of the society. If the characteristics are genuinely ones that all individuals ought to be encouraged to display in the appropriate circumstances, then the social institutions and ideology ought to endeavor to foster them in all individuals. If it is good for everyone to be somewhat empathetic all of the time or especially empathetic in some circumstances, or good for everyone to have a certain degree of self-control all of the time or a great deal in some circumstances, then there is no reason to preserve institutions which distribute these psychological attributes along sexual lines. And the same is true for many, if not all, vocations, activities, and ways of living. If some, but not all persons would find a life devoted to child rearing genuinely satisfying, it is good, surely, that that option be open to them. Once again, though, it is difficult to see the argument for implicitly or explicitly encouraging, teaching, or assigning to women, as opposed to men, that life simply in virtue of their sex. Thus, while substantial diversity in individual characteristics, attitudes, and ways of life is no doubt an admirable, even important feature of the good society, what remains uncertain is the necessity or the desirability of continuing to link attributes or behaviors such as these to the race or sex of individuals. And for the reasons I have tried to articulate there are significant moral arguments against any conception of the good society in which such connections are pursued and nourished in the systemic fashion required by the existence and maintenance of sex roles.

SUZANNA SHERRY, CIVIC VIRTUE AND THE FEMININE VOICE IN CONSTITUTIONAL ADJUDICATION

72 Va.L.Rev. 543, 580–91 (1986).

New studies in a variety of academic disciplines suggest that women in fact may have a unique perspective, a world-view that differs in significant respects from that of men. Feminist scholars in such diverse fields as philosophy, history, sociology, art, and anthropology have identified peculiarly feminine perspectives in those disciplines.[167]

---

167. See R. Morgan, The Anatomy of Freedom: Feminism, Physics and Global Politics (1982); N. Noddings, [Caring: A Feminine Approach to Ethics and Moral Education (1984)]; E. Showalter, A Literature of Their Own (1977); P. Spacks, The Female Imagination (1975); Blecki, Feminist Literary Criticism: An Introduction, *in* Feminist Literary Criticism: A Symposium 1 (K. Bordan & F. Rinn eds. 1974); Harding & Hintikka, Introduction, *in* Discovering Reality: Feminist Perspectives on Epistemology, Metaphysics, Methodology, and Philosophy of Science ix (S. Harding & M. Hintikka eds. 1983); O'Brien, Feminist Theory and Dialectical Logic, *in* Feminist Theory: A Critique of Ideology 99 (N. Keohane, M. Rosaldo, & B. Gelpi eds. 1982);

Recent work in psychology and in literary theory is particularly illuminating. Psychological studies suggest that women's moral development and concept of self may differ from those of men. Feminist literary theory suggests that women's writing differs from men's in ways that reflect a radically different perspective. Despite the independence of the research and the differences in both topics of investigation and terms of description, the feminine perspective identified in each of these fields is, at its core, a single, common approach. That approach is captured in the tension between women's primary concern with intimacy or connection and men's primary focus on separation or autonomy.[168]

This difference between men and women may influence the manner in which they think about, write about, and practice their disciplines. Thus, it is probable that women's unique perspective on law and jurisprudence, as a function of their different world-view, extends well beyond areas traditionally seen as affecting women, and in fact encompasses all legal issues. Just as women's writing on all subjects—not just on intimacy, domesticity, or women's place in society—reflects a different cast, women's views on the law in general may provide insights and approaches that are less natural to, and therefore less available to, male lawyers and judges.

This different approach to the law makes women a potentially innovative force in the legal community. Because women have been excluded from the mainstream of legal authority and legal change, the legal system, like moral, political, and philosophical discourse, has become "a set of cultural and symbolic forms that view human experience from the distorted and one-sided perspective of a single gender." [170] This is not to suggest merely that the legal structure ignores or minimizes significant gender differences, but rather that because women have been excluded from shaping our legal structure in general,

Garfunkel, The Improvised Self: Sex Differences in Artistic Identity (Dissertation, Dep't of Psych. & Soc. Rel., Harv. Univ., 1984); Goodman, Women's Studies: The Debate Continues, N.Y. Times Magazine, Apr. 22, 1984, at 39; Kolbert, Scientific Ideas: Women's vs. Men's, N.Y. Times, Oct. 17, 1985, at C1, col. 1; Goleman, Psychology Is Revising Its View of Women, N.Y. Times, Mar. 20, 1984, at C1, col. 1.

168. The most persuasive explanation for the differences between men and women is based on differences between boys' and girls' development of an ego or sense of self. Ego development occurs while the child is still quite young and is therefore significantly influenced by the child's primary caretaker. Because, in general, girls are raised by a primary caretaker of the same gender and boys are raised by a primary caretaker of the opposite gender, girls reaffirm their early attachments while boys repudiate them.

Thus, women come to see themselves as fundamentally connected and men see themselves as fundamentally detached. See N. Chodorow, [The Reproduction of Mothering: Psychoanalysis and the Sociology of Gender 166–68 (1978)]; C. Gilligan, [In A Different Voice: Psychological Theory and Women's Development 5–23 (1982).] Other explanations for the differences between men and women include the socialization process, the mother's varying reaction to sons and daughters, and biological differences. See, e.g., E. Erikson, Identity, Youth and Crisis (1968); E. Janeway, Man's World, Woman's Place: A Study in Social Mythology (1971); J. Miller, Toward a New Psychology of Women (1976); Flax, The Conflict Between Nurturance and Autonomy in Mother–Daughter Relationships and Within Feminism, Fem. Stud., June 1978, at 171.

170. O'Brien, supra note 167, at 99.
  *   *   *

that structure reflects a distorted view of the tension between autonomy and connection and between the individual and society.

What sort of distortion has the masculine paradigm introduced into our legal system? Feminist scholars identify three primary dichotomies between men's and women's thinking: while women emphasize connection, subjectivity, and responsibility, men emphasize autonomy, objectivity, and rights. * * *

* * *

A brief caveat is in order. First, I am not contending that gender-based differences are universal, only that they are likely enough that the historical exclusion of women from the shaping of the legal system has had a profound impact, which cannot be reversed—or, to a large extent, even recognized—until women begin to participate in that enterprise. Second, I am not limiting my analysis to a feminist perspective: feminists have a particular political agenda that may or may not be shared by all women (and is shared by some men). Rather, this is an analysis of a feminine perspective that encompasses aspects of personality and relationship to the world that have nothing to do with one's political preferences. Finally, I am not suggesting that the feminine perspective is any better than the masculine perspective, just that it is different. The incorporation of a new perspective need not imply a hierarchical ranking; I am arguing merely that the law has been distorted by its one-sided focus and that the feminine perspective described here represents a move toward correcting that distortion. * * *

B. CONNECTION AND AUTOMOMY

* * * [T]he feminine perspective views individuals primarily as interconnected members of a community. Nancy Chodorow and Carol Gilligan, in groundbreaking studies on the development of self and morality, have concluded that women tend to have a more intersubjective sense of self than men and that the feminine perspective is therefore more other-directed.[174] Other studies tend to confirm this finding.[175] The essential difference between the male and female perspectives [is that] "[t]he basic feminine sense of self is connected to the world, the basic masculine sense of self is separate." [176] Women thus tend to see others as extensions of themselves rather than as outsiders or competitors.

Gilligan suggests that Kohlberg's description of a morally mature person—a "rational individual aware of values and rights prior to social contracts" who adopts "universal principles of justice," including "re-

---

174. See N. Chodorow, supra note 168; C. Gilligan, supra note 168. * * *

175. For example, even at a very young age, female children tend to be more dependent on and reluctant to leave their mothers. See Goldberg & Lewis, Play Behavior in the Year–Old Infant: Early Sex Difference, 40 Child Dev. 21 (1969); Messer & Lewis, Social Class and Sex Differences in the Attachment and Play Behavior of the Year–Old Infant, 18 Merrill–Palmer Q. Behav. & Dev. 295 (1972).

176. N. Chodorow, supra note 168, at 169 * * *.

spect for the dignity of human beings as individual persons" [178]— instead describes a masculine morality.[179] That masculine perspective embodies the individualism inherent in the modern paradigm. The parallel between the classical paradigm and feminine morality, by contrast, is clearly illustrated by Gilligan's quotation of a typical female response to a moral dilemma:

> By yourself, there is little sense to things. It is like the sound of one hand clapping, the sound of one man or one woman, there is something lacking. *It is the collective that is important to me,* and that collective is based on certain guiding principles, one of which is that *everybody belongs to it,* and that you all come from it. You have to love someone else, because while you may not like them, you are inseparable from them. In a way, it is like loving your right hand. *They are part of you; that other person is part of that giant collection of people that you are connected to.*[180]

Women's emphasis on connection also suggests that the cliche that women are more cooperative and less competitive than men may have some basis in fact. Historically, women have tended to achieve their goals communally; from quilting bees to consciousness-raising sessions, women have banded together rather than striving individually. There are analogous differences between the organization and ideology underlying women's traditional dominion, the family, and men's traditional arena, the marketplace: as Frances Olsen notes, the market is based on an individualist ethic and the family on an altruistic ethic.[182]

Some of the most intriguing evidence of a feminine perspective comes from the field of literary criticism, where feminist critics are discovering characteristic differences in both style and substance between male and female authors. In seeking to identify this "uniquely female literary consciousness," [183] they are discovering indications of a similar tension between autonomy and connection. Male writers typically portray individuals as existing prior to and divorced from society. The male metaphor, and the male travail, is individualist. In contrast, women writers are less apt to focus on purely individual heroism. Unlike the archetypal masculine "coming of age" novel, the developing feminine counterpart describes women's maturation in the context of a group of women, the definition of one "self" from among many "selves[.]" * * *

Feminist literary critics are also beginning to identify some characteristically feminine styles, which also suggest an intersubjective per-

---

178. Kohlberg, Moral Stages and Moralization: The Cognitive–Developmental Approach, *in* Moral Development and Behavior: Theory, Research, and Social Issues 34–35 (T. Lickona ed. 1976) (describing the post-conventional level).

179. See C. Gilligan, supra note 168, at 18–22.

180. Id. at 160 (some emphasis in original, some added).

182. Olsen, The Family and the Market: A Study of Ideology and Legal Reform, 96 Harv.L.Rev. 1497, 1505 (1983)[.] * * *

183. Showalter, Introduction, *in* The New Feminist Criticism: Essays on Women, Literature, and Theory 6 (E. Showalter ed. 1985) * * *.

spective. For example, women writers more frequently use a technique of rotating a novel's perspective from one character to another.[186] This technique is often criticized by male critics, and it may be that women authors are more receptive to the technique because they are better able to perceive not only the relations among characters but also those between themselves and the characters they create. They almost literally "become" their characters (male and female) for the same reason that their intersubjective perspective keeps them from fully separating themselves from others. Males, on the other hand, with their emphasis on autonomy, see the technique as a violation of the ideal of separation.

C. CONTEXTUALITY AND ABSTRACTION

Scholarship in literature and psychology also suggests that women are more contextual and men more abstract. Piaget, for example, found that girls playing children's games tend to treat the rules of the game as less fixed and more flexible than do boys and that girls are more likely to stop a game altogether—thus preserving friendships—if a dispute arises. For boys, development and application of fixed, abstract rules is almost as important as the object of the game itself.[188] Again, Kohlberg's description of moral development (i.e., the development of the masculine perspective) stresses a progression from context-bound judgments to abstract moral principles. Women, on the other hand, in responding to moral dilemmas, tend instead to look to circumstances rather than to abstractions: the right moral response depends on the context.[190]

This concept of feminine reliance on context is borne out in some empirical experiments. For example, the greater familiarity of even young boys with universal principles is well illustrated by a simple experiment in which boys and girls were shown pictures of everyday objects and asked to group related objects:

> [B]oys tend to bracket together objects (or pictures of objects) whose intrinsic characteristics are similar, whereas girls weight more heavily the functional and relational characteristics of the entities to be compared. For instance, boys frequently bracketed together such entities as a truck, a car, and an ambulance, while girls bracketed such entities as a doctor, a hospital bed, and an ambulance.[191]

The boys focused on the abstraction of "locomotion," seeing the objects as independent units, while the girls emphasized instead the concrete

186. See, e.g., Mellown, Character and Themes in the Novels of Jean Rhys, *in* Contemporary Women Novelists: A Collection of Critical Essays 118, 130 (P. Spacks ed. 1977).

188. See J. Piaget, The Moral Judgment of The Child 82 (1965); see also Lever, Sex Differences in the Games Children Play, 23 Social Probs. 478 (1976) (similar findings).

190. See C. Gilligan, supra note 168, at 38.

191. Hintikka & Hintikka, How Can Language Be Sexist? *in* Discovering Reality: Feminist Perspectives on Epistemology, Metaphysics, Methodology, and Philosophy of Science 139, 145 (S. Harding & M. Hintikka eds. 1983) (footnote omitted).

relationships among objects. Other studies confirm that males of all ages are better able to separate discrete objects from their backgrounds and relationships than are females. Males are said to be less field-dependent; that is, they have a greater "ability to overcome the influence of an embedding context."[193]

Moreover, current controversies in philosophy tend to break down along gender lines. Despite exceptions, male philosophers often endorse more abstract and less contextual theories. For example, mainstream discussions of virtue tend to assume that virtues are abstract qualities. Committing murder under dangerous circumstances, though a criminal act, may still constitute an instance of the virtue of courage. Philippa Foot, on the other hand, suggests that virtues are contextual, not abstract: the virtue of courage is exhibited only under circumstances where the act itself can be considered courageous.[194]

* * *

Literary criticism also recognizes the difference between the abstraction of men and the concreteness of women. One critic has suggested, for example, that George Eliot's *Mill on the Floss* illustrates the tension between the male notion of universal maxims and the female unwillingness to differentiate the universal from its particular applications.[199] Women's writing has also been characterized (and criticized) as less linear and unified and more fluid than men's; [200] this again suggests a focus on context rather than on abstract rules of progression. Even feminine literary criticism is more contextual: Elaine Showalter has suggested that one characteristic of feminist criticism is the rejection of (masculine) objective, non-experiential critical theories.[201]

D. RESPONSIBILITY AND RIGHTS

Until recently, the archetypal developmental continuum of individual moral sensibility was believed to be an orderly progression from self-centeredness through other-centeredness to the development of logical, independent, universal principles—rights—that depend neither on one's own needs nor on what others believe is right.[202] Although

193. J. Sherman, On the Psychology of Women: A Survey of Empirical Studies 21 (1971) * * *.

194. See P. Foot, [Virtues and Vices and Other Essays in Moral Philosophy 15–17 (1978).]

199. Jacobus, The Question of Language: Men of Maxims and *The Mill on the Floss, in* Writing and Sexual Difference 37, 42 (E. Abel ed. 1982). Jacobus contrasts Eliot's remark, in her novel, that "the man of maxims is the popular representative of the minds that are guided in their moral judgment solely by general rules," with the view of the central charac-

ter, Maggie Tulliver—" 'to lace ourselves up in formulas is to ignore the special circumstances that mark the individual lot.' " Id. (quoting G. Eliot, Mill on the Floss 628 (A. Byatt ed. 1979)).

200. Gardiner, On Female Identity and Writing By Women, *in* Writing and Sexual Difference 177, 185 (E. Abel ed. 1982); Jacobus, supra note 199, at 39–40.

201. Showalter, Feminist Criticism in the Wilderness, supra note 183, at 244.

202. See L. Kohlberg, The Philosophy of Moral Development (1981); Kohlberg, supra note 178.

this progression mirrors male moral development, it fails to reflect the moral growth pattern of women.[203]

Gender-based differences in moral structure, long seen as evidence of women's moral immaturity,[204] may in fact be evidence of a feminine morality that differs in its emphasis from that of males. In her study of moral development, Carol Gilligan found that women tend to view a moral problem as "a problem of care and responsibility in relationships rather than as one of rights and rules." [205] When faced with the moral dilemma of whether a man should steal a drug he cannot afford to save his dying wife, Gilligan found that, while men struggle with the conflicting rights of the parties, women focus on the druggist's "moral obligation to show compassion," [206] "not on the conflict of rights but on the failure of response." [207] Although men and women may agree that the man ought to steal the drug, men justify it in terms of a resolution between conflicting rights of husband and druggist, and women in terms of the need for more compassion by the druggist in the face of the husband's compassion for his wife.[208] Whether personal or political, the moral structure of "mature" males reflects a paradigm of independent rights, while that of females emphasizes relational responsibilities.

JOHN HART ELY, FACILITATING THE REPRESENTATION OF MINORITIES

Democracy and Distrust 164–70 (1980).

[In this section, Ely considers whether gender-based classifications that disadvantage women should be subject to close judicial scrutiny. We have reprinted Ely's general approach to equal protection in Chapter VI. Recall that he suggests that strict scrutiny is appropriate when there is good reason to suspect that the political process that produced the statute was tainted—either because of ill-will towards the disadvantaged group ("first degree prejudice") or because the legislature is likely to have overestimated the accuracy of the generalization upon which the classification is based ("second degree prejudice").]

The case of women is timely and complicated. Instances of first-degree prejudice are obviously rare, but just as obviously exaggerated stereotyping—typically to the effect that women are unsuited to the work of the world and therefore belong at home—has long been rampant throughout the male population and consequently in our almost exclusively male legislatures in particular. It may all be in apparent good humor, even perceived as protective, but it has cost women dearly. Absent a strong demonstration of mitigating factors, therefore, we would have to treat gender-based classifications that act to the disadvantage of women as suspicious. If the stereotyping has

203. See C. Gilligan, supra note 168, at 18–22.

204. See L. Kohlberg, supra note 202
* * *.

205. C. Gilligan, supra note 168, at 73.

206. Id. at 54 (quoting a subject of Gilligan's study).

207. Id.

208. See, e.g., id. at 29.

been clear, however, so has the noninsularity of the group affected. The degree of contact between men and women could hardly be greater, and neither, of course, are women "in the closet" as homosexuals historically have been. Finally, lest you think I missed it, women have about half the votes, apparently more. As if it weren't enough that they're not discrete and insular, they're not even a minority!

Despite that seeming avalanche of rebuttal, there remains something that seems right in the claim that women have been operating at an unfair disadvantage in the political process, though it's tricky pinning down just what gives rise to that intuition. It is tempting to observe that although women may be a majority, they haven't in any real sense *consented* to the various instances of gender-based legislation. Voters, female and male alike, are typically confronted not with single-issue referenda but rather with packages of attitudes, packages we call candidates. Most women are not injured in any direct way by laws that classify on the basis of sex—depriving women, say, of the opportunity to tend bar, guard railroad crossings, or administer estates—and the fact that they help elect representatives who are unprepared to repeal such laws may mean only that there are other issues about which they feel more strongly. This may indeed be so, but the argument changes the rules. Once we start to shift from a focus on whether something is blocking the opportunity to correct the stereotype reflected in the legislation, to one that attempts to explain why those who have that opportunity have chosen to pursue other goals instead, we begin to lose our way, to permit our disagreement with the substantive merits of the legislation to take the place of what is *constitutionally* relevant, an inability to do anything about it. That answer triggers a more promising inquiry, though—whether it is fair to say that women have "chosen" not to avail themselves of their opportunities either by voting or by personally influencing those men with whom they come in contact, to correct the exaggerated stereotype that many men hold and on the basis of which they have often legislated. A major reason for lack of action on either of these fronts, or so at least it can plausibly be argued, has been that many women have *accepted* the overdrawn stereotype and thus have seen nothing to "correct" by vote or personal persuasion, and by their example may even have acted so as to reinforce it. That could, of course, imply that it wasn't so exaggerated a stereotype after all, but it could mean something else too, that our society, including the women in it, has been so pervasively dominated by men that women quite understandably have accepted men's stereotypes, of women as well as on other subjects.

The general idea is one that in some contexts has merit. A sufficiently pervasive prejudice can block its own correction not simply by keeping its victims "in the closet" but also by convincing even them of its correctness. In *Castaneda v. Partida,* decided in 1977, the Court held that a prima facie case of intentional discrimination against Mexican–Americans in the selection of grand jurors was not constitutionally affected by the fact that Mexican–Americans enjoyed "governing majority" status in the county involved. Concurring, Justice Marshall gave the reason why: "Social scientists agree that members of minority groups frequently respond to discrimination and prejudice by attempting to disassociate themselves from the group, even to the point of adopting the majority's negative attitudes towards the minority." [96] Nor does this insight seem relevant only to numerical minorities: slaves outnumbered masters in the antebellum South, and outnumbered whites generally in some states, but that apparently didn't keep many of them from assimilating much of the mythology used to legitimate their enslavement.

To apply all this to the situation of women in America in 1980, however, is to strain a metaphor past the breaking point. It is true that women do not generally operate as a very cohesive political force, banding together to elect candidates pledged to the "woman's point of view." Constitutional suspiciousness should turn on evidence of blocked access, however, not on the fact that elections are coming out "wrong." There is an infinity of groups that do not act as such in the political marketplace, but we don't automatically infer that they have a "slave mentality." The cause, more often, is that (sensibly or not) the people involved are not in agreement over the significance of their shared characteristic. Thus in assessing suspiciousness it cannot be enough simply to note that a group does not function as a political bloc. A further reference to the surrounding conditions must be had, to see if there are systemic bars (and I'm obviously not suggesting they need be official ones) to access. On that score it seems important that today discussion about the appropriate "place" of women is common among both women and men, and between the sexes as well. The very stereotypes that gave rise to laws "protecting" women by barring them from various activities are under daily and publicized attack, and are the subject of equally spirited defense. (That the common stereotypes are so openly described and debated, as they are not in the case of racial minorities, is itself some evidence of the comparatively free and nonthreatening nature of the interchange.) Given such open discussion of the traditional stereotypes, the claim that the numerical majority is being "dominated," that women are in effect "slaves" who have no realistic choice but to assimilate the stereotypes, is one it has become impossible to maintain except at the most inflated rhetorical level. It also renders the broader argument self-contradictory, since to make such a claim in the context of the current debate one must at least implicitly grant the validity of the stereotype, that women are in effect mental infants who will believe anything men tell them to believe. Many women do seem to prefer the old stereotype to the new liberation. You and I may think that's a mistaken choice. But once we begin regarding serious disagreement with a choice as proof that those who

96. 430 U.S. 483, 503 (1977) (Marshall, J., concurring), citing G. Allport, [The Nature of Prejudice 150–53 (1954).] * * *

made it aren't in control of their minds, we've torn up the rulebook and made substantive wrongheadedness the test of unconstitutionality.

However, most laws classifying by sex weren't passed this morning or even the day before yesterday: in fact it is rare to see a gender-based classification enacted since the New Deal. In general women couldn't even *vote* until the Nineteenth Amendment was ratified in 1920, and most of these laws probably predate even that: they should be invalidated. Throughout this discussion, however, I have been concerned with factors more subtle than the lack of a vote, and it can at least be argued that until quite recently there persisted throughout America's female population a "*Castaneda*-like" acceptance of the prejudices of males, unventilated by more than token airing of their validity. Given what appropriately makes a classification suspicious, it is not necessarily a unitary question whether discrimination against a certain group should be so regarded, and the case of women seems one where the date of enactment should be important. It surely seems more helpful than anything the Court has come up with on the question of whether those who passed the law in issue were proceeding on the basis of an "archaic and overbroad generalization" or whether, say, they were genuinely trying to protect women from certain physical risks to which in statistical terms they are unusually subject, realized there were counterexamples and estimated their incidence about right, but nonetheless felt the costs of identifying the exceptions were simply too high. * * * Direct attempts to judge whether a given law was generated by an overdrawn stereotype can be dangerously subjective since the face of the statute will inevitably be consistent with either of these descriptions of the decision process, and the legislative history will inevitably be partial and subject to manipulation. The date of passage seems a somewhat more solid datum, one that can at least begin to anchor the judicial inquiry. That's an aside, however, since the date of passage seems unquestionably relevant to what our analysis has suggested is a more promising approach to the question of suspiciousness—one geared to the existence of official or unofficial blocks on the opportunities of those the law disadvantages to counter by argument or example the overdrawn stereotypes we might, from the demography of the decision-making body, otherwise suspect were operative.

The case of women can be further put in perspective by exploring what should follow from a judicial determination that the suspiciousness of a given classification has not been allayed and that it therefore is unconstitutional. Here too the answer is not unitary: we have looked at several indicia of suspiciousness, and their remedial implications differ. Where a law is suspect because of what I have been calling first-degree prejudice, or indeed where it has been infected by a subtler form of stereotyping under conditions where the negatively affected group was barred from effective access at the time of passage *and still is*, the only appropriate remedy is to void the classification and insist—if the legislature wishes to continue to classify—on a different, generally more finely tuned, test of qualification. The obvious alternative to this is to have the judiciary restrike the substantive balance, attempting not to let the prejudices that apparently influenced the legislature play a part, and invalidate the classification only if in some sense it still ends up unacceptable on its merits. You will not be surprised to learn that I regard that approach as quite inappropriate. We can cite occasions on which our judiciary has displayed a lesser susceptibility to bare-knuckled first-degree prejudice than our elected officials, but we also can cite some where it hasn't. Moreover, instances of such prejudice, for reasons it is not necessary to review, are almost invariably instances of self-serving comparison as well. Judges tend to belong to the same broad categories as legislators—most of them, for example, are white heterosexual males comfortably above the poverty line—and there isn't any reason to suppose that they are immune to the usual temptations to self-aggrandizing generalization. When in a given situation you can't be trusted to generalize and I can't be trusted to generalize, the answer, if possible, is not to generalize, which suggests that the Supreme Court has chosen wisely in insisting generally that a classification whose suspiciousness has not been allayed simply cannot be employed. Where in fact it was largely the product of a simple desire to disadvantage those disqualified, it probably will just be abandoned, which seems a desirable outcome. Where, however, a classification of some sort does seem necessary (though the one the legislature employed was constitutionally unacceptable), the remedy of flat-out disallowance will impose costs in both time and money, as it will generally necessitate a somewhat more individualized test of qualification. However, legislatures often incur those costs voluntarily, and courts on other occasions have forced them to do so where constitutionally protected interests will be threatened by an imperfectly fitting classification. The unusual dangers of distortion in situations of self-aggrandizing generalization seem also to demand that we bear the increased costs of more individualized justice.

A case like that of women, where access was blocked in the past but can't responsibly be said to be so any longer, seems different in a way that suggests that a less drastic remedy may be appropriate. In cases of first-degree prejudice, or self-serving stereotyping where the access of the disadvantaged group remains blocked, the alternative of "remanding" the question to the political processes for a "second look" would not be acceptable: we don't give a case back to a rigged jury. Here, however, such a "second look" approach seems to make sense. Technically the Court's judgment would be the same in all situations of unallayed suspiciousness: "due process of lawmaking" having been denied, the law that emerged would have to be declared unconstitutional. The difference would emerge in the event—unlikely, precisely because access is no longer blocked—that the legislature after such a declaration of unconstitutionality reconsidered and repassed the same or a similar law. The fact that due process of lawmaking was denied in 1908 or even in 1939 needn't imply that it was in 1982 as well, and consequently the new law should be upheld as constitutional. In fact I may be wrong in supposing that because women now are in a position to protect themselves they will, that we are thus unlikely to see in the future the sort of official gender discrimination that has marked our past. But if women don't protect themselves from sex discrimination in the future, it won't be because they can't. It will rather be because for one reason or another—substantive disagreement or more likely the assignment of a low priority to the issue—they don't choose to. Many of us may condemn such a choice as benighted on the merits, but that is not a constitutional argument.

WENDY W. WILLIAMS, THE EQUALITY CRISIS: SOME REFLECTIONS ON CULTURE, COURTS, AND FEMINISM

7 Women's Rights Law Rept'r 175, 176–200 (1982).

My thesis is that we (feminists) are at a crisis point in our evaluation of equality and women and that perhaps one of the reasons for the crisis is that, having dealt with the easy cases, we (feminists and courts) are now trying to cope with issues that touch the hidden nerves of our most profoundly embedded cultural values.

I will first set the stage for discussion with a brief history of women, equality, and the Supreme Court; second, I will examine what I believe to be evidence that the Supreme Court has, unbeknownst to itself, foundered upon the culturally instilled limits of its ability to dismantle male preserves; and third, I will speculate that there is also a female preserve, functioning as a hidden hand not only for the courts but for feminists as well, and that this unacknowledged influence may be causing problems for feminist legal theorists.

I. A BRIEF HISTORY OF GENDER EQUALITY AND THE SUPREME COURT

Just before the American Revolution, Blackstone, in the course of his comprehensive commentary on the common law, set forth the fiction that informed and guided the treatment of married women in the English law courts. When a woman married, her legal identity merged into that of her husband; she was civilly dead. She couldn't sue, be sued, enter into contracts, make wills, keep her own earnings, control her own property. She could not even protect her own physical integrity—her husband had the right to chastise her (although only with a switch no bigger than his thumb), restrain her freedom, and impose sexual intercourse upon her against her will.

Beginning in the middle of the nineteenth century, the most severe civil disabilities were removed in this country by state married women's property acts. Blackstone's unities fiction was for the most part replaced by a theory that recognized women's legal personhood but which assigned her a place before the law different and distinct from that of her husband. This was the theory of the separate spheres of men and women, under which the husband was the couple's representative in the public world and its breadwinner; the wife was the center of the private world of the family. Because it endowed women with a place, role, and importance of their own, the doctrine of the separate spheres was an advance over the spousal unities doctrine. At the same time, however, it preserved and promoted the dominance of male over female. The public world of men was governed by law while the private world of women was outside the law, and man was free to exercise his prerogatives as he chose.

*   *   *

The separate spheres ideology was repudiated by the Supreme Court only [recently]. The engine of destruction was, as a technical matter, the more rigorous standard of review that the Court began applying to sex discrimination cases beginning in 1971.[20] By 1976 the Court was requiring that sex-based classifications bear a "substantial" relationship to an "important" governmental purpose.[21] This standard, announced in Craig v. Boren, was not as strong as that used in race cases, but it was certainly a far cry from the rational basis standard that had traditionally been applied to sex-based classifications.

As a practical matter, what the Court did was strike down sex-based classifications that were premised on the old breadwinner-home-maker, master-dependent dichotomy inherent in the separate spheres ideology. Thus, the Supreme Court insisted that women wage earners receive the same benefits for their families under military,[23] social security,[24] welfare,[25] and worker's compensation[26] programs as did male wage earners; that men receive the same child care allowance when their spouses died as women did;[27] that the female children of divorce be entitled to support for the same length of time as male children, so that they too could get the education necessary for life in the public world;[28] that the duty of support through alimony not be visited exclusively on husbands;[29] that wives as well as husbands participate in the management of the community property;[30] and that wives as well as husbands be eligible to administer their deceased relatives' estates.[31]

All this happened in the little more than a decade that has elapsed since 1971. The achievement is not an insubstantial one. Yet it also seems to me that in part what the Supreme Court did was simply to recognize that the real world outside the courtroom had already changed. Woman were in fact no longer chiefly housewife-dependents.

20. In Reed v. Reed, 404 U.S. 71, 75 (1971)[.] * * *

21. Craig v. Boren, 429 U.S. 190, 197 (1976). * * *

23. Frontiero v. Richardson, 411 U.S. 677 (1973).

24. Califano v. Goldfarb, 430 U.S. 199 (1977).

25. Califano v. Westcott, 443 U.S. 76 (1979).

26. Wengler v. Druggists Mutual Insurance Co., 446 U.S. 142 (1980).

27. Weinberger v. Wiesenfeld, 420 U.S. 636 (1975).

28. Stanton v. Stanton, 421 U.S. 7 (1975).

29. Orr v. Orr, 440 U.S. 268 (1979).

30. Kirschberg v. Feenstra, 450 U.S. 455 (1981).

31. Reed v. Reed, 404 U.S. 71 (1971).

The family wage no longer existed; for a vast number of two-parent families, two wage earners were an economic necessity. In addition, many families were headed by a single parent. It behooved the Court to account for this new reality and it did so by recognizing that the breadwinner-homemaker dichotomy was an outmoded stereotype.

II. MEN'S CULTURE: AGGRESSOR IN WAR AND SEX

Of course, not all of the Supreme Court cases involved the breadwinner-homemaker stereotype. The other cases can be grouped in several ways; for my purposes I will place them in two groups. One group is composed of the remedial or compensatory discrimination cases—the cases in which a statute treats women differently and better than men for the purpose of redressing past unequal treatment.[35] The other group, the focus of this paper, consists of the cases that don't really seem to fit into any neat category but share a common quality. Unlike the cases discussed above, they do not deal with laws that rest on an economic model of the family that no longer predominates; rather, they concern themselves with other, perhaps more basic, sex-role arrangements. They are what I would call, simply, the "hard" cases, and for the most part, they are cases in which a sex-based classification was upheld by the Court.[36] There are a number of ways one could characterize and analyze them. I want to view them from one of those possible perspectives, namely, what they tell us about the state of our culture with respect to the equality of men and women. What do they say about the cultural limits of the equality principle?

In the 1980–81 Term the Supreme Court decided three sex-discrimination cases. One was *Kirshberg v. Feenstra*,[37] a case which struck down the Louisiana statute that gave husbands total control over the couple's property. That, to my mind, was an easy case. It falls within the line of cases I have already described which dismantle the old

---

35. *See, e.g.,* Kahn v. Shevin, 416 U.S. 351 (1974) (Florida statute granting widows but not widowers property tax exemption constitutional because intended to assist sex financially most affected by spousal loss) and Califano v. Webster, 430 U.S. 313 (1977) (Social Security Act section creating benefit calculation formula more favorable to women than men held constitutional because intended to compensate women for wage discrimination). * * *

36. *See, e.g.,* Schlesinger v. Ballard, 419 U.S. 498 (1975) (Court upheld (5–4) law that results in discharge of male officers if twice passed over for promotion, but guarantees female officers 13–year tenure before discharge for lack of promotion); Rostker v. Goldberg, 453 U.S. 57 (1981); Michael M. v. Superior Court, 450 U.S. 464 (1981); Dothard v. Rawlinson, 443 U.S. 321 (1977); Geduldig v. Aiello, 417 U.S. 484 (1974); General Electric Corp. v. Gilbert, 429 U.S. 125 (1976); Nashville Gas Co. v.

Satty, 434 U.S. 136 (1977). All of these cases were authored either by Justice Stewart or by Justice Rehnquist.

Another case that belongs in this category, even though the gender-based classification was struck down, is the 5–4 decision in Caban v. Mohammed, 441 U.S. 380 (1979). In that case the Court held that a state statute that gave an unwed mother but not an unwed father the right to veto the adoption of her or his child violated the equal protection clause. The Court carefully limited its holding to adoptions of older children who had established a relationship with the father, leaving open the possibility, strongly argued by the dissent, that there were differences between mothers and fathers that would justify a different outcome with respect to the adoption of very young children. * * *

37. 450 U.S. 455 (1981).

separate spheres ideology. The other two cases were *Rostker v. Gold-berg*,[38] the case which upheld the male-only draft registration law, and *Michael M. v. Superior Court*,[39] the case upholding the California statutory rape law. They are prime candidates for my hard-cases category.

Justice Rehnquist wrote the opinion of the Court in both *Rostker* and *Michael M.* In *Rostker,* the draft registration case, his reasoning was a simple syllogism. The purpose of the registration, he said, is to identify the draft pool. The purpose of the draft is to provide combat troops. Women are excluded from combat. Thus, men and women are not similarly situated with respect to the draft, and it is therefore constitutional to register males only. Of course, the problem with his syllogism was that one of the premises—that the purpose of the draft is exclusively to raise combat troops—was and is demonstrably false, but the manipulation of the facts of that case is not what I mean to focus on here.

In *Michael M.*, a 17½–year–old–man and a 16½–year–old woman had sexual intercourse. The 17½–year–old man was prosecuted under California's statutory rape law, which made such intercourse criminal for the man but not the woman. Rehnquist, for a plurality of the Court, accepted the utterly dubious proposition put forward by the State of California that the purpose of the statutory rape statute was to prevent teenage pregnancies. The difference in treatment under the statute is justified, he said, because men and women are not similarly situated with respect to this purpose. Because the young woman is exposed to the risk of pregnancy, she is deterred from sexual inter-course by that risk. The young man, lacking such a natural deterrent, needs a legal deterrent, which the criminal statute provides.

I think that perhaps the outcomes of these two cases—in which the sex-based statutes were upheld—were foregone conclusions and that the only question, before they were decided, was *how* the court would rationalize the outcome. This is perhaps more obvious in the draft case than the statutory rape case, but applies, I think, to both. Let me explain.

Suppose you could step outside our culture, rise above its minutiae, and look at its great contours. Having done so, speculate for a moment about where society might draw the line and refuse to proceed further with gender equality. What does our culture identify as quintessential-ly masculine? Where is the locus of traditional masculine pride and self-identity? What can we identify in men's cultural experience that most divides it from women's cultural experience? Surely, one rather indisputable answer to that question is "war": physical combat and its modern equivalents. (One could also answer that preoccupation with contact sports is such a difference, but that is, perhaps, just a subset of physical combat.)

38. 453 U.S. 57 (1981).   **39.** 450 U.S. 464 (1981).

Not surprisingly, the Court in *Rostker* didn't come right out and say "We've reached our cultural limits." Yet I did not find it insignificant that even the Justices who dissented on the constitutionality of the draft registration law seemed to concede the constitutionality of excluding women from combat. When Congress considered whether women should be drafted, it was much more forthright about its reasons and those reasons support my thesis. The Senate Armed Services Committee Report states:

> [T]he starting point for any discussion of the appropriateness of registering women for the draft is the question of the proper role of women in combat. The principle that women should not intentionally and routinely engage in combat *is fundamental, and enjoys wide support among our people.*

In addition, the committee expressed three specific reasons for excluding women from combat. First, registering women for assignment to combat "would leave the actual performance of sexually mixed units as an experiment to be conducted in war with unknown risk—a risk that the committee finds militarily unwarranted and dangerous." Second, any attempt to assign women to combat could "affect the national resolve at the time of mobilization." Third, drafting women would "place unprecedented strains on family life." The committee envisioned a young mother being drafted leaving a young father home to care for the family and concluded, "The committee is strongly of the view that such a result . . . is unwise and unacceptable to a large majority of our people." To translate, Congress was worried that (1) sexually mixed units would not be able to function—perhaps because of sex in the foxhole? (2) if women were assigned to combat, the nation might be reluctant to go to war, presumably because the specter of women fighting would deter a protective and chivalrous populace; and (3) the idea that mom could go into battle and dad keep the home fires burning is simply beyond the cultural pale. In short, current notions of acceptable limits on sex-role behavior would be surpassed by putting women into combat.

But what about statutory rape? Not such a clear case, you say. I disagree. Buried perhaps a bit deeper in our collective psyches but no less powerful and perhaps even more fundamental than our definition of man as aggressor in war is man as aggressor in sex. The original statutory rape laws were quite explicitly based on this view. Then, as is true even today, men were considered the natural and proper initiators of sex. In the face of male sexual initiative, women could do one of two things, yield or veto, "consent" or decline. What normal women did not, *should* not, do was to initiate sexual contact, to be the sexual aggressor. The premise underlying statutory rape laws was that young women's chastity was precious and their naivete enormous. Their inability knowingly to consent to sexual intercourse meant that they required protection by laws which made their consent irrelevant but punished and deterred the "aggressive" male.

The Court's opinion, I believe, is implicitly based on stereotypes concerning male sexual aggression and female sexual passivity, despite Justice Rehnquist's express denial of that possibility. His recitation of the facts of the case sets the stage for the sexual gender-role pigeon-holding that follows: "After being struck in the face for rebuffing petitioner's advances, Sharon," we are told, "*submitted* to sexual intercourse with petitioner." Although, in theory, coercion and consent are relevant only to the crime of rape, not to statutory rape, we are thus provided with the details of this particular statutory rape case, details which cast Michael and Sharon as prototypes of the sexually aggressive male and the passive female.

But it is Rehnquist's description of the lower court opinion that most clearly reveals sex role assumptions that lead first the California high court and then the United States Supreme Court to uphold the legislation. He says, "Because *males alone* can 'physiologically cause the result which the law properly seeks to avoid' [pregnancy], the [California Supreme Court] further held that the gender classification was readily justified as a means of identifying *offender* and *victim*." [65] The statement is remarkable for two (related) reasons. The first and most dramatic is the strangeness of the biological concept upon which it is based. Do the justices still believe that each sperm carries a homunculus—a tiny person—who need only be planted in the woman in order to grow? Are they ignorant of ova? Or has sex-role ideology simply outweighed scientific fact? Since no one has believed in homunculi for at least a century, it must be the latter. Driven by the stereotype of male as aggressor/offender and woman as passive victim, even the facts of conception are transformed to fit the image.

The second is the characterization of man and woman as "offender" and "victim." Statutory rape is, in criminal law terms, a clear instance of a victimless crime, since all parties are, by definition, voluntary participants. In what sense, then, can Rehnquist assert that the woman is victim and the man offender? One begins to get an inkling when, later, the Justice explains that the statutory rape law is "protective" legislation: "The statute here protects women from sexual intercourse at an age when those consequences are particularly severe." His preconceptions become manifest when, finally, Rehnquist on one occasion calls the statute a "rape" statute—by omitting the word "statutory" inadvertently exposing his hidden assumptions and underlining the belief structure which the very title of the crime, "statutory rape," lays bare.

What is even more interesting to me than the Court's resolution of these cases is the problem they cause for feminist analysis. The notion that men are frequently the sexual aggressors and that the law ought to be able to take that reality into account in very concrete ways is hardly one that feminists could reject out of hand (I'm thinking here of sexual harassment and forcible rape, among other things): it is there-

---

65. 450 U.S. at 467 (emphasis added).

fore an area, like the others I'm about to discuss, in which we need to pay special attention to our impulses lest we inadvertently support and give credence to the very social constructs and behaviors we so earnestly mean to oppose. Should we, for example, defend traditional rape laws on the ground that rape, defined by law as penetration by the penis of the vagina, is a sexual offense the psychological and social consequences of which are so unique, severe, and rooted in age-old power relationships between the sexes that a gender-neutral law would fail in important ways to deal with the world as it really is? Or should we insist that equality theory requires that we reorganize our understanding of sexual crime, that unwanted sexual intrusion of types other than male-female sexual intercourse can similarly violate and humiliate the victim, and that legislation which defines sexual offenses in gender-neutral terms, because it resists our segregationist urges, and affirms our common humanity, is therefore what feminists should support? These are not easy questions, but they must be answered if feminist lawyers are to press a coherent theory of equality upon the courts in these hard cases.

As for *Rostker v. Goldberg,* the conflicts among feminists were overtly expressed. Some of us felt it essential that we support the notion that a single-sex draft was unconstitutional;[76] others felt that feminists should not take such a position. These latter groups explicitly contrasted the female ethic of nurturance and life-giving with a male ethic of aggression and militarism and asserted that if we argued to the Court that single-sex registration is unconstitutional we would be betraying ourselves and supporting what we find least acceptable about the male world.[77]

To me, this latter argument quite overtly taps qualities that the culture has ascribed to woman-as-childrearer and converts them to a normative value statement, one with which it is easy for us to sympathize. This is one of the circumstances in which the feeling that "I

76. See briefs *amici curiae* of the National Organization for Women, and of a group including Women's Equity Action League, Business and Professional Women, and others, in Rostker v. Goldberg, 453 U.S. 57 (1981).

77. *See, e.g., A Feminist Opposition to the Draft* (New Haven, Connecticut, 1980) (authors unidentified) in C. Mackinnon, Sexuality and Legality: Toward a Feminist Theory of the State 151–57 (unpublished materials for a course taught at the Stanford Law School, Fall 1980). At the outset, the author(s) state:

> We need at the beginning to differentiate between two kinds of feminism. The one seeks to assimilate women into the traditional institutions of male society. This is the feminism of a small elite. There is another, more broadly based feminism, and this feminism carries with

it a fundamental critique of the structure of power in this country.

> The one kind of feminism would see the draft as a sign that we have reached equality, or as an opportunity for reaching equality. We consider this to be an extremely narrow notion of equality. We must place the draft in a wider context and see it as an instrument of American policy. The draft, then, is not the only, nor even the primary issue. The real question is what the foreign and domestic policy of this country is, and whether we can assent to it. For a number of reasons we cannot.

Among other grounds for withholding assent, the author or authors "reject the war reflex as an instance of male hysteria; in its essence, feminism is opposed to violence." *Id.* at 151.

want what he's got but I don't want to be what he's had to be in order to get it" comes quickly to the surface. But I also believe that the reflexive response based on these deeper cultural senses leads us to untenable positions.

The single-sex laws upheld in *Michael M.* and *Rostker* ultimately do damage to women. For one thing, they absolve women of personal responsibility in the name of protection. There is a sense in which women have been victims of physical aggression in part because they have not been permitted to act as anything but victims. For another, do we not acquire a greater right to claim our share from society if we too share its ultimate jeopardies? To me, *Rostker* never posed the question of whether women should be forced as men now are to fight wars, but whether we, like them, must take the responsibility for deciding whether or not to fight, whether or not to bear the cost of risking our lives, on the one hand, or resisting in the name of peace, on the other. And do we not, by insisting upon our differences at these crucial junctures, promote and reinforce the us-them dichotomy that permits the Rehnquists and the Stewarts to resolve matters of great importance and complexity by the simplistic, reflexive assertion that men and women "are simply not similarly situated?"

III. WOMEN'S CULTURE: MOTHER OF HUMANITY

We have looked briefly at the male side of the cultural equation. What are the cultural limits on women's side? Step outside the culture again and speculate. If we find limits and conflicts surrounding the male role as aggressor in war and sex, what will be the trouble spots at the opposite pole? What does the culture identify as quintessentially female? Where does our pride and self-identity lie? Most probably, I think, somewhere in the realm of behaviors and concerns surrounding maternity.

I would expect the following areas to be the places where the move toward equality of the sexes might come into collision with cultural limits, both in judicial opinions and in ourselves: treatment of maternity in the workplace, the tender years presumption, and joint custody of children upon divorce. The issues surrounding pregnancy and maternity are the most difficult from a theoretical point of view and for that reason may be the best illustration of the conflict I am trying to explore.

* * *

Once the Supreme Court took on the task of dismantling the statutory structure built upon the separate spheres ideology, it had to face the question of how to treat pregnancy itself. Pregnancy was, after all, the centerpiece, the linchpin, the essential feature of women's separate sphere. The stereotypes, the generalizations, the role expectations were at their zenith when a woman became pregnant. Gender equality would not be possible, one would think, unless the Court was willing to examine, at least as closely as other gender-related rulemaking, those prescriptions concerning pregnancy itself. On the other hand, the capacity to bear a child is a crucial, indeed definitional, difference between women and men. While it is obvious that the sexes can be treated equally with respect to characteristics that they share, how would it be possible to apply the equality principle to a characteristic unique to women?

So what did the Court do? It drew the line at pregnancy. *Of course* it would take a more critical look at sex discrimination than it had in the past—but, it said, discrimination on the basis of pregnancy is not sex discrimination. Now here was a simple but decisive strategy for avoiding the doctrinal discomfort that inclusion of pregnancy within the magic circle of stricter review would bring with it. By placing pregnancy altogether outside that class of phenomena labeled sex discrimination, the Court need not apply to classifications related to pregnancy the level of scrutiny it had already reserved, in cases such as *Reed v. Reed* and *Frontiero v. Richardson,* for gender classifications. Pregnancy classifications would henceforth be subject only to the most casual review.

The position was revealed for the first time in 1974 in *Geduldig v. Aiello,* [86] a case challenging under the equal protection clause exclusion of pregnancy-related disabilities from coverage by an otherwise comprehensive state disability insurance program. The Court explained, in a footnote, that pregnancy classifications were not sex-based but were, instead, classifications based upon a physical condition and should be treated accordingly[.]

* * *

The second time the Supreme Court said pregnancy discrimination is not sex discrimination was in *General Electric Company v. Gilbert,*[88] decided in 1976. *Gilbert* presented the same basic facts—exclusion of pregnancy-related disabilities from a comprehensive disability program—but this case was brought under Title VII rather than the equal protection clause. The Court nonetheless relied on *Geduldig,* saying that when Congress prohibited "sex discrimination," it didn't mean to include within the definition of that term pregnancy discrimination.

There was, however, an additional theory available in *Gilbert* because it was a Title VII case that was not available in the equal protection case. That theory was that if an employer's rule has a disparate *effect* on women, even though there is no intent to discriminate, it might also violate Title VII. And did the Court find that the exclusion of pregnancy-related disabilities had a disparate effect on women? It did not. Men and women, said Justice Rehnquist, received coverage for the disabilities they had in common. Pregnancy was an *extra* disability, since only women suffered it. To compensate women for it would give them more than men got. So here there was no disparate effect—the exclusion of pregnancy merely insured the basic equality of the program.

86. 417 U.S. 484.   **88.** 429 U.S. 125.

The remarkable thing about this statement, like Rehnquist's later assertion in *Michael M.* that only men can "cause" pregnancy, is its peculiarly blinkered male vision.   After all, men received coverage under General Electric's disability program for disabilities they did not have in common with women, including disabilities linked to exclusively male aspects of the human anatomy.   Thus, the only sense in which one can understand pregnancy to be "extra" is in some reverse–Freudian psychological fashion.   Under Freud's interpretation, women were viewed by both sexes as inadequate men (men *minus*) because they lacked penises.   In Rehnquist's view, woman is now man *plus*, because she shares all his physical characteristics except that she also gets pregnant.   Under either of these extravagantly skewed views of the sexes, however, man is the measure against which the anatomical features of woman are counted and assigned value, and when the addition or subtraction is complete, woman comes out behind.

The corollary to *Gilbert* appeared in *Nashville Gas Co. v. Satty,* [94] decided in 1977.   There the Court finally found a pregnancy rule that violated Title VII.   The rule's chief characteristic was its gratuitously punitive effect.   It provided that a woman returning from maternity leave lost all of the seniority she acquired *prior* to her leave.   Here, said Rehnquist, we have a case where women are not seeking extra benefits for pregnancy.   Here's a case where a woman, now back at work and no longer pregnant, has actually had something taken away from her—her pre-pregnancy seniority—and she therefore suffers a burden that men don't have to bear.   This rule therefore has a disproportionate impact on women.

Roughly translated, *Gilbert* and *Satty* read together seemed to stand for the proposition that insofar as a rule deprives a woman of benefits for actual pregnancy, that rule is lawful under Title VII.   If, on the other hand, it denies her benefits she had earned while not pregnant (and hence like a man) and now seeks to use upon return to her non-pregnant (male-like) status, it has a disproportionate effect on women and is not lawful.

In summary, then, the Court seems to be of the view that discrimination on the basis of pregnancy isn't sex discrimination.   The Court achieves this by, on the one hand, disregarding the "ineluctable link" between gender and pregnancy, treating pregnancy as just another physical condition that the employer or state can manipulate on any arguably rational basis, and on the other hand, using woman's special place in "the scheme of human existence" as a basis for treating her claim to benefits available to other disabled workers as a claim not to equal benefits but to extra benefits, not to equal treatment but to special treatment.   The equality principle, according to the Court, cannot be bent to such ends.

In reaction to *Gilbert* and, to a lesser extent, to *Satty.* Congress amended the definitions section of Title VII to provide that discrimina-

94. 434 U.S. 136 (1977).

tion on the basis of pregnancy, childbirth, and related medical conditions was, for purposes of the Act, sex discrimination. The amendment, called the Pregnancy Discrimination Act (PDA),[99] required a rather radical change in approach to the pregnancy issue from that adopted by the Court. In effect, Title VII creates a general presumption that men and women are alike in all relevant respects and casts the burden on the employer to show otherwise in any particular case. The PDA, likewise, rejects the presumption that pregnancy is so unique that special rules concerning it are to be treated as prima facie reasonable. It substitutes the contrary presumption that pregnancy, at least in the workplace context, is like other physical conditions which may affect workers. As with gender classifications in general, it places the burden of establishing pregnancy's uniqueness in any given instance on the employer. The amendment itself specifies how this is to be done:

> [W]omen affected by pregnancy, childbirth, or related medical conditions shall be treated the same for all employment-related purposes, including receipt of benefits under fringe benefit programs, as other persons not so affected but similar in their ability or inability to work. . . .

Under the PDA, employers cannot treat pregnancy less favorably than other potentially disabling conditions, but neither can they treat it more favorably. And therein lies the crisis.

At the time the PDA was passed, all feminist groups supported it. Special treatment of pregnancy in the workplace had always been synonymous with unfavorable treatment; the rules generally had the effect of forcing women out of the work force and back into the home when they became pregnant. By treating pregnancy discrimination as sex discrimination, the PDA required that pregnant women be treated as well as other wage earners who became disabled. The degree to which this assisted women depended on the generosity of their particular employers' sick leave or disability policy, but anything at all was better than what most pregnant women had had before.

The conflict within the feminist community arose because some states had passed legislation which, instead of placing pregnant women at a disadvantage, gave them certain positive protections. Montana, for example, passed a law forbidding employers to fire women who became pregnant and requiring them to give such women reasonable maternity leave.[a] The Miller–Wohl Company, an employer in that state, had a particularly ungenerous sick leave policy. Employees were entitled to *no* sick leave in their first year of employment and five days per year thereafter. On August 1, 1979, the company hired a pregnant woman who missed four or five days over the course of the following three weeks because of morning sickness. The company fired her. She

99. 42 U.S.C. § 2000e(k) (Supp. IV 1980).

a. This article was written before the Supreme Court's decision in *California Federal Savings & Loan Ass'n v. Guerra,* 479 U.S. 272 (1987), which held that a California statute requiring employers to provide leave and reinstatement to women disabled by pregnancy was neither inconsistent with nor pre-empted by the PDA.

asserted her rights under the Montana statute. The company sought declaratory relief in federal court, claiming that Montana's special treatment statute was contrary to the equality principle mandated by the PDA and was therefore invalid under the supremacy clause of the constitution.

Feminists split over the validity of the Montana statute. Some of us felt that the statute was, indeed, incompatible with the philosophy of the PDA. Others of us argued that the PDA was passed to *help* pregnant women, which was also the objective of the Montana statute. Underneath are very different views of what women's equality means; the dispute is therefore one of great significance for feminists.

The Montana statute *was* meant to help pregnant women. It was passed with the best of intentions. The philosophy underlying it is that pregnancy is central to a woman's family role and that the law should take special account of pregnancy to protect that role for the working wife. And those who supported the statute can assert with great plausibility that pregnancy is a problem that men don't have, an extra source of workplace disability, and that women workers cannot adequately be protected if pregnancy is not taken into account in special ways.[110] They might also add that procreation plays a special role in human life, is viewed as a fundamental right by our society, and therefore is appropriately singled out on social policy grounds. The instinct to treat pregnancy as a special case is deeply imbedded in our culture, indeed in every culture. It seems natural, and *right,* to treat it that way.

Yet, at a deeper level, the Supreme Court in cases like *Gilbert,* and the feminists who seek special recognition for pregnancy, are starting from the same basic assumption, namely, that women have a special place in the scheme of human existence when it comes to maternity. Of course, one's view of how that basic assumption cuts is shaped by one's perspective. What businessmen, Supreme Court Justices, and feminists make of it is predictably quite different. But the same doctrinal approach that permits pregnancy to be treated *worse* than other disabilities is the same one that will allow the state constitutional freedom to create special *benefits* for pregnant women. The equality approach to pregnancy (such as that embodied in the PDA) necessarily creates not only the desired floor under the pregnant woman's rights

---

110. Some commentators have argued that treating the unique capabilities of women in a special way is not equivalent to granting special, inequitable favors to women. Perhaps the finest articulation of that view is the following passage:

Uniqueness is a 'trap' only in terms of an analysis such as that generated in *Geduldig v. Aiello,* which assumes that maleness is the norm. 'Unique' does not necessarily mean uniquely handicapped. . . . To account for pregnan-

cy and breastfeeding is . . . to treat women as equals by respecting the female gender and by ceasing to impose upon women a bifurcated existence; it is to reject antiquated classifications and to restore to women the opportunity to live a continuous life, integrated with respect to career and procreation just as are the lives of men.

Scales. *Towards a Feminist Jurisprudence.* 56 Ind. L.J. 375, 435–36 (1981). * * *

but also the ceiling which the *Miller–Wohl* case threw into relief. If we can't have it both ways, we need to think carefully about which way we want to have it.

My own feeling is that, for all its problems, the equality approach is the better one. The special treatment model has great costs. First, as discussed above, is the reality that conceptualizing pregnancy as a special case permits unfavorable as well as favorable treatment of pregnancy. Our history provides too many illustrations of the former to allow us to be sanguine about the wisdom of urging special treatment.

Second, treating pregnancy as a special case divides us in ways that I believe are destructive in a particular political sense as well as a more general sense. On what basis can we fairly assert, for example, that the pregnant woman fired by Miller–Wohl deserved to keep her job when any other worker who got sick for any other reason did not? Creating special privileges of the Montana type has, as one consequence, the effect of shifting attention away from the employer's inadequate sick leave policy or the state's failure to provide important protections to all workers and focusing it upon the unfairness of protecting one class of worker and not others.

Third, as our experience with single-sex protective legislation earlier in this century demonstrated, what appear to be special "protections" for women often turn out to be, at best, a double-edged sword. It seems likely, for example, that the employer who wants to avoid the inconveniences and costs of special protective measures will find reasons not to hire women of childbearing age in the first place.[115]

Fourth, to the extent the state (or employers as proxies for the state) can lay claim to an interest in women's special procreational capacity for "the future well-being of the race," as *Muller v. Oregon* put it in 1908, our freedom of choice about the direction of our lives is more limited than that of men in significant ways. This danger is hardly a theoretical one today. The Supreme Court has recently shown an increased willingness to permit restrictions on abortion in deference to the state's interest in the "potential life" of the fetus, and private employers are adopting policies of exclusion of women of childbearing capacity in order to protect fetuses from exposure to possibly hazardous substances in the workplace.

More fundamentally, though, this issue, like the others I discussed earlier, has everything to do with how, in the long run, we want to define women's and men's places and roles in society.

Implicit in the PDA approach to maternity issues is a stance toward parenthood and work that is decidedly different from that embodied in the special-treatment approach to pregnancy. For many years, the prototype of the enlightened employer maternity policy was

---

115. Title VII does not permit such practices. As a practical matter, however, proof of such motivations is difficult. Ac- tions based on a class sufficiently large to illuminate the hidden motivation are prohibitively expensive and complex.

one which provided for a mandatory unpaid leave of absence for the woman employee commencing four or five months before and extending for as long as six months after childbirth. Such maternity leaves were firmly premised on that aspect of the separate spheres ideology which assigned motherhood as woman's special duty and prerogative; employers believed that women should be treated as severed from the labor force from the time their pregnancies became apparent until their children emerged from infancy. Maternity leave was always based upon cultural constructs and ideologies rather than upon biological necessity, upon role expectations rather than irreducible differences between the sexes.

The PDA also has significant ideological content. It makes the prototypical maternity leave policy just described illegal. In its stead, as discussed above, is a requirement that the employer extend to women disabled by pregnancy the same disability or sick leave available to other workers. If the employer chooses to extend the leave time beyond the disability period, it must make such leaves available to male as well as to female parents. Title VII requires sex neutrality with respect to employment practices directed at parents. It does not permit the employer to base policies on the separate spheres ideology. Accordingly, the employer must devise its policies in such a way that women and men can, if they choose, structure the allocation of family responsibilities in a more egalitarian fashion. It forecloses the assumption that women are necessarily and inevitably destined to carry the dual burden of homemaker and wage earner.

Statutes such as the Montana statute challenged in the *Miller–Wohl* case are rooted in the philosophy that women have a special and different role and deserve special and different treatment. Feminists can plausibly and forcibly claim that such laws are desirable and appropriate because they reflect the material reality of women's lives. We can lay claim to such accommodations based on the different pattern of our lives, our commitment to children, our cultural destiny. We can even resort to arguments based on biological imperatives and expect that at least some members of the Supreme Court might lend a sympathetic ear. Justice Stevens suggested one such approach in a footnote to his dissent in *Caban v. Mohammed*,[124] a case invalidating a law that granted to unwed mothers but denied to unwed fathers the right to withhold consent to adoption of their children. He observed:

> [T]here is some sociological and anthropological research indicating that by virtue of the symbiotic relationship between mother and child during pregnancy and the initial contact between mother and child directly after birth a physical and psychological bond immediately develops between the two that is not then present between the infant and the father or any other person. [Citations omitted.]

Justice Stevens' seductive bit of science is useful for making my point, although other illustrations might do as well. Many women who

124.   441 U.S. 380 (1979).

have gone through childbirth have experienced the extraordinary sense of connection to their newborn that the literature calls "bonding." It may be, as some have contended, that the monolithic role women have so long played has been triggered and sustained by this phenomenon, that the effect of this bonding has made it emotionally possible for women to submit to the stringent limitations imposed by law and culture upon the scope and nature of their aspirations and endeavors. On the other hand, it seems entirely possible that the concept of exclusive mother-infant bonding—the latest variation on "maternal instinct"—is a social construct designed to serve ideological ends.

Less than a century ago, doctors and scientists were generally of the view that a woman's intellect, her capacity for education, for reasoning, for public undertakings, was biologically limited. While men were governed by their intellect, women were controlled by their uteruses. No reputable scientist or doctor would make such claims today. But if women are now understood to share with men a capacity for intellectual development, is it not also possible that mother-infant bonding is, likewise, only half the story? What Justice Stevens overlooks is the evidence of the capacity of fathers (the exploration of whose nurturing potential is as new as their opportunity actively to participate in the birth of their children) to "bond" as well.

Again, the question is, are we clinging, without really reflecting upon it, to culturally dictated notions that underestimate the flexibility and potential of human beings of both sexes and which limit us as a class and as individuals?

IV: CONCLUSION: CONFRONTING YIN AND YANG

The human creature seems to be constructed in such a way as to be largely culture bound. We should not, therefore, be surprised that the creaky old justices on the Supreme Court and we somewhat less creaky feminists sometimes—perhaps often—respond to the same basic characterizations of male and female—although, unquestionably, the justices tend sometimes to do different things with those basic characterizations than feminists would do. At this point, we need to think as deeply as we can about what we want the future of women and men to be. Do we want equality of the sexes—or do we want justice for two kinds of human beings who are fundamentally different? If we gain equality, will we lose the special sense of kinship that grows out of experiences central to our lives and not shared by the other sex? Are feminists defending a separate women's culture while trying to break down the barriers created by men's separate culture? Could we, even if we wanted to, maintain the one while claiming our place within the other? *Michael M.*, which yokes assumptions about male sexual aggression with the conclusion that the sexes are not similarly situated because of women's pregnancy, and the Senate report on the all-male draft, which suggests that what sends men to war and leaves women at home is a fundamental trade-off by which men are assigned to battle and women to child rearing, should give us pause. I for one suspect a deep but sometimes nearly invisible set of complementaries, a yin-yang of sex-role assumptions and assignments so complex and inter-related that we cannot successfully dismantle any of it without seriously exploring the possibility of dismantling it all. The "hard cases"—cases like *Michael M., Rostker, Gilbert, Geduldig, Caban*—give us an opportunity to re-think our basic assumptions about women and men, assumptions some-times buried beneath our consciousness. They allow us to ask afresh who we are, what we want, and if we are willing to begin to create a new order of things.

CATHARINE A. MacKINNON, DIFFERENCE AND DOMINANCE: ON SEX DISCRIMINATION
FEMINISM UNMODIFIED: DISCOURSES ON LIFE AND LAW, ch. 2 (1987).

What is a gender question a question of? What is an inequality question a question of? These two questions underlie applications of the equality principle to issues of gender, but they are seldom explicitly asked. I think it speaks to the way gender has structured thought and perception that mainstream legal and moral theory tacitly gives the same answer to them both: these are questions of sameness and difference. The mainstream doctrine of the law of sex discrimination that results is, in my view, largely responsible for the fact that sex equality law has been so utterly ineffective at getting women what we need and are socially prevented from having on the basis of a condition of birth: a chance at productive lives of reasonable physical security, self-expression, individuation, and minimal respect and dignity. Here I expose the sameness/difference theory of sex equality, briefly show how it dominates sex discrimination law and policy and underlies its discontents, and propose an alternative that might do something.

            .   .   .

According to the approach to sex equality that has dominated politics, law, and social perception, equality is an equivalence, not a distinction, and sex is a distinction. The legal mandate of equal treatment—which is both a systemic norm and a specific legal doc-trine—becomes a matter of treating likes alike and unlikes unlike; and the sexes are defined as such by their mutual unlikeness. Put another way, gender is socially constructed as difference epistemologically; sex discrimination law bounds gender equality by difference doctrinally. A built-in tension exists between this concept of equality, which presup-poses sameness, and this concept of sex, which presupposes difference. Sex equality thus becomes a contradiction in terms, something of an oxymoron, which may suggest why we are having such a difficult time getting it.

Upon further scrutiny, two alternate paths to equality for women emerge within this dominant approach, paths that roughly follow the lines of this tension. The leading one is: be the same as men. This path is termed gender neutrality doctrinally and the single standard philosophically. It is testimony to how substance gets itself up as form in law that this rule is considered formal equality. Because this approach mirrors the ideology of the social world, it is considered abstract, meaning transparent of substance; also for this reason it is considered not only to be *the* standard, but *a* standard at all. It is so far the leading rule that the words "equal to" are code for, equivalent to, the words "the same as"—referent for both unspecified.

To women who want equality yet find that you are different, the doctrine provides an alternate route: be different from men. This equal recognition of difference is termed the special benefit rule or special protection rule legally, the double standard philosophically. It is in rather bad odor. Like pregnancy, which always calls it up, it is something of a doctrinal embarrassment. Considered an exception to true equality and not really a rule of law at all, this is the one place where the law of sex discrimination admits it is recognizing something substantive. Together with the Bona Fide Occupational Qualification (BFOQ), the unique physical characteristic exception under ERA policy, compensatory legislation, and sex-conscious relief in particular litigation, affirmative action is thought to live here.

The philosophy underlying the difference approach is that sex is a difference, a division, a distinction, beneath which lies a stratum of human commonality, sameness. The moral thrust of the sameness branch of the doctrine is to make normative rules conform to this empirical reality by granting women access to what men have access to: to the extent that women are no different from men, we deserve what they have. The differences branch, which is generally seen as patronizing but necessary to avoid absurdity, exists to value or compensate women for what we are or have become distinctively as women (by which is meant, unlike men) under existing conditions.

My concern is not with which of these paths to sex equality is preferable in the long run or more appropriate to any particular issue, although most discourse on sex discrimination revolves about these questions as if that were all there is. My point is logically prior: to treat issues of sex equality as issues of sameness and difference *is to take a particular approach.* I call this the difference approach because it is obsessed with the sex difference. The main theme in the fugue is "we're the same, we're the same, we're the same." The counterpoint theme (in a higher register) is "but we're different, but we're different, but we're different." Its underlying story is: on the first day, difference was; on the second day, a division was created upon it; on the third day, irrational instances of dominance arose. Division may be rational or irrational. Dominance either seems or is justified. Difference *is.*

There is a politics to this. Concealed is the substantive way in which man has become the measure of all things. Under the sameness standard, women are measured according to our correspondence with man, our equality judged by our proximity to his measure. Under the difference standard, we are measured according to our lack of correspondence with him, our womanhood judged by our distance from his measure. Gender neutrality is thus simply the male standard, and the special protection rule is simply the female standard, but do not be deceived: masculinity, or maleness, is the referent for both. Think about it like those anatomy models in medical school. A male body is the human body; all those extra things women have are studied in ob/gyn. It truly is a situation in which more is less. Approaching sex discrimination in this way—as if sex questions are difference questions and equality questions are sameness questions—provides two ways for the law to hold women to a male standard and call that sex equality.

*   *   *

Having been very hard on the difference answer to sex equality questions, I should say that it takes up a very important problem: how to get women access to everything we have been excluded from, while also valuing everything that women are or have been allowed to become or have developed as a consequence of our struggle either not to be excluded from most of life's pursuits or to be taken seriously under the terms that have been permitted to be our terms. It negotiates what we have managed in relation to men. Legally articulated as the need to conform normative standards to existing reality, the strongest doctrinal expression of its sameness idea would prohibit taking gender into account in any way.

Its guiding impulse is: we're as good as you. Anything you can do, we can do. Just get out of the way. I have to confess a sincere affection for this approach. It has gotten women some access to employment and education, the public pursuits, including academic, professional, and blue-collar work; the military; and more than nominal access to athletics. It has moved to change the dead ends that were all we were seen as good for and has altered what passed for women's lack of physical training, which was really serious training in passivity and enforced weakness. It makes you want to cry sometimes to know that it has had to be a mission for many women just to be permitted to do the work of this society, to have the dignity of doing jobs a lot of other people don't even want to do.

*   *   *

*   *   * As applied, the sameness standard has mostly gotten men the benefit of those few things women have historically had—for all the good they did us. Almost every sex discrimination case that has been won at the Supreme Court level has been brought by a man. Under the rule of gender neutrality, the law of custody and divorce has been transformed, giving men an equal chance at custody of children and at alimony. Men often look like better "parents" under gender-neutral rules like level of income and presence of nuclear family, because men make more money and (as they say) initiate the building of family units. In effect, they get preferred because society advantages them before they get into court, and law is prohibited from taking that preference into account because that would mean taking gender into account. The group realities that make women more in need of alimony are not permitted to matter, because only individual factors, gender-neutrally considered, may matter. So the fact that women will live their lives, as individuals, as members of the group women, with women's chances in a sex-discriminatory society, may not count, or else it is sex discrimination. The equality principle in this guise mobilizes the idea that the way to get things for women is to get them for men. Men have gotten them. Have women? We still have not got equal pay, or equal work, far less equal pay for equal work, and we are close to losing separate enclaves like women's schools through this approach.

Here is why. In reality, which this approach is not long on because it is liberal idealism talking to itself, virtually every quality that distinguishes men from women is already affirmatively compensated in this society. Men's physiology defines most sports, their needs define auto and health insurance coverage, their socially designed biographies define workplace expectations and successful career patterns, their perspectives and concerns define quality in scholarship, their experiences and obsessions define merit, their objectification of life defines art, their military service defines citizenship, their presence defines family, their inability to get along with each other—their wars and rulerships—defines history, their image defines god, and their genitals define sex. For each of their differences from women, what amounts to an affirmative action plan is in effect, otherwise known as the structure and values of American society. But whenever women are, by this standard, "different" from men and insist on not having it held against us, whenever a difference is used to keep us second class and we refuse to smile about it, equality law has a paradigm trauma and it's crisis time for the doctrine.

What this doctrine has apparently meant by sex inequality is not what happens to us. The law of sex discrimination that has resulted seems to be looking only for those ways women are kept down that have *not* wrapped themselves up as a difference—whether original, imposed, or imagined. Start with original: what to do about the fact that women actually have an ability men still lack, gestating children in utero. Pregnancy therefore is a difference. Difference doctrine says it is sex discrimination to give women what we need, because only women need it. It is not sex discrimination not to give women what we need because then only women will not get what we need.[18] Move into imposed: what to do about the fact that most women are segregated into low-paying jobs where there are no men. Suspecting that the structure of the marketplace will be entirely subverted if comparable worth is put into effect, difference doctrine says that because there is

18. This is a reference to the issues raised by several recent cases which consider whether states' attempts to compensate pregnancy leaves and to secure jobs on return constitute sex discrimination. California Federal Savings and Loan Assn. v. Guerra, 758 F.2d 390 (9th Cir.1985), [*aff'd*, 479 U.S. 272 (1987)]; *see also* Miller–Wohl v. Commissioner of Labor, 515 F.Supp. 1264 (D.Montana 1981), *vacated and dismissed*, 685 F.2d 1088 (9th Cir.1982). The position argued in "Difference and Dominance" here suggests that if these benefits are prohibited under Title VII, Title VII is unconstitutional under the equal protection clause.

no man to set a standard from which women's treatment is a deviation, there is no sex discrimination here, only sex difference. Never mind that there is no man to compare with because no man would do that job if he had a choice, and of course he has because he is a man, so he won't.

Now move into the so-called subtle reaches of the imposed category, the de facto area. Most jobs in fact require that the person, gender neutral, who is qualified for them will be someone who is not the primary caretaker of a preschool child. Pointing out that this raises a concern of sex in a society in which women are expected to care for the children is taken as day one of taking gender into account in the structuring of jobs. To do that would violate the rule against not noticing situated differences based on gender, so it never emerges that day one of taking gender into account was the day the job was structured with the expectation that its occupant would have no child care responsibilities. Imaginary sex differences—such as between male and female applicants to administer estates or between males aging and dying and females aging and dying—I will concede, the doctrine can handle.

I will also concede that there are many differences between women and men. I mean, can you imagine elevating one half of a population and denigrating the other half and producing a population in which everyone is the same? What the sameness standard fails to notice is that men's differences from women are equal to women's differences from men. There is an *equality* there. Yet the sexes are not socially equal. The difference approach misses the fact that hierarchy of power produces real as well as fantasied differences, differences that are also inequalities. What is missing in the difference approach is what Aristotle missed in his empiricist notion that equality means treating likes alike and unlikes unlike, and nobody has questioned it since. Why should you have to be the same as a man to get what a man gets simply because he is one? Why does maleness provide an original entitlement, not questioned on the basis of *its* gender, so that it is women—women who want to make a case of unequal treatment in a world men have made in their image (this is really the part Aristotle missed)—who have to show in effect that they are men in every relevant respect, unfortunately mistaken for women on the basis of an accident of birth?

The women that gender neutrality benefits, and there are some, show the suppositions of this approach in highest relief. They are mostly women who have been able to construct a biography that somewhat approximates the male norm, at least on paper. They are the qualified, the least of sex discrimination's victims. When they are denied a man's chance, it looks the most like sex bias. The more unequal society gets, the fewer such women are permitted to exist. Therefore, the more unequal society gets, the *less* likely the difference doctrine is to be able to do anything about it, because unequal power

(G. & A.) Const'l Reader 2d Ed.—15

creates both the appearance and the reality of sex differences along the same lines as it creates its sex inequalities.

The special benefits side of the difference approach has not compensated for the differential of being second class. The special benefits rule is the only place in mainstream equality doctrine where you get to identify as a woman and not have that mean giving up all claim to equal treatment—but it comes close. Under its double standard, women who stand to inherit something when their husbands die have gotten the exclusion of a small percentage of the inheritance tax, to the tune of Justice Douglas waxing eloquent about the difficulties of all women's economic situation.[22] If we're going to be stigmatized as different, it would be nice if the compensation would fit the disparity. Women have also gotten three more years than men get before we have to be advanced or kicked out of the military hierarchy, as compensation for being precluded from combat, the usual way to advance.[23] Women have also gotten excluded from contact jobs in male-only prisons because we might get raped, the Court taking the viewpoint of the reasonable rapist on women's employment opportunities.[24] We also get protected out of jobs because of our fertility. The reason is that the job has health hazards, and somebody who might be a real person some day and therefore could sue—that is, a fetus—might be hurt if women, who apparently are not real persons and therefore can't sue either for the hazard to our health or for the lost employment opportunity, are given jobs that subject our bodies to possible harm. Excluding women is always an option if equality feels in tension with the pursuit itself. They never seem to think of excluding men. Take combat. Somehow it takes the glory out of the foxhole, the buddiness out of the trenches, to imagine us out there. You get the feeling they might rather end the draft, they might even rather not fight wars at all than have to do it with us.

The double standard of these rules doesn't give women the dignity of the single standard; it also does not (as the differences standard does) suppress the gender of its referent, which is, of course, the female gender. I must also confess some affection for this standard. The work of Carol Gilligan on gender differences in moral reasoning [27] gives it a lot of dignity, more than it has ever had, more, frankly, than I thought it ever could have. But she achieves for moral reasoning what the special protection rule achieves in law: the affirmative rather than the negative valuation of that which has accurately distinguished women from men, by making it seem as though those attributes, with their consequences, really are somehow ours, rather than what male supremacy has attributed to us for its own use. For women to affirm

22. Kahn v. Shevin, 416 U.S. 351, 353 (1974).

23. Schlesinger v. Ballard, 419 U.S. 498 (1975).

24. Dothard v. Rawlinson, 433 U.S. 321 (1977); *see also* Michael M. v. Sonoma County Superior Court, 450 U.S. 464 (1981).

27. Carol Gilligan, *In a Different Voice* (1982).

difference, when difference means dominance, as it does with gender, means to affirm the qualities and characteristics of powerlessness.

Women have done good things, and it is a good thing to affirm them. I think quilts are art. I think women have a history. I think we create culture. I also know that we have not only been excluded from making what has been considered art; our artifacts have been excluded from setting the standards by which art is art. Women have a history all right, but it is a history both of what was and of what was not allowed to be. So I am critical of affirming what we have been, which necessarily is what we have been permitted, as if it is women's, ours, possessive. As if equality, in spite of everything, already ineluctably exists.

I am getting hard on this and am about to get harder on it. I do not think that the way women reason morally is morality "in a different voice." I think it is morality in a higher register, in the feminine voice. Women value care because men have valued us according to the care we give them, and we could probably use some. Women think in relational terms because our existence is defined in relation to men. Further, when you are powerless, you don't just speak differently. A lot, you don't speak. Your speech is not just differently articulated, it is silenced. Eliminated, gone. You aren't just deprived of a language with which to articulate your distinctiveness, although you are; you are deprived of a life out of which articulation might come. Not being heard is not just a function of lack of recognition, not just that no one knows how to listen to you, although it is that; it is also silence of the deep kind, the silence of being prevented from having anything to say. Sometimes it is permanent. All I am saying is that the damage of sexism is real, and reifying that into differences is an insult to our possibilities.

So long as these issues are framed this way, demands for equality will always appear to be asking to have it both ways: the same when we are the same, different when we are different. But this is the way men have it: equal and different too. They have it the same as women when they are the same and want it, and different from women when they are different and want to be, which usually they do. Equal and different too would only be parity. But under male supremacy, while being told we get it both ways, both the specialness of the pedestal and an even chance at the race, the ability to be a woman and a person, too, few women get much benefit of either.

* * *

There is an alternative approach, one that threads its way through existing law and expresses, I think, the reason equality law exists in the first place. It provides a second answer, a dissident answer in law and philosophy, to both the equality question and the gender question. In this approach, an equality question is a question of the distribution of power. Gender is also a question of power, specifically of male supremacy and female subordination. The question of equality, from the standpoint of what it is going to take to get it, is at root a question of hierarchy, which—as power succeeds in constructing social perception and social reality—derivatively becomes a categorical distinction, a difference. Here, on the first day that matters, dominance was achieved, probably by force. By the second day, division along the same lines had to be relatively firmly in place. On the third day, if not sooner, differences were demarcated, together with social systems to exaggerate them in perception and in fact, because the systematically differential delivery of benefits and deprivations required making no mistake about who was who. Comparatively speaking, man has been resting ever since. Gender might not even code as difference, might not mean distinction epistemologically, were it not for its consequences for social power.

I call this the dominance approach, and it is the ground I have been standing on in criticizing mainstream law. The goal of this dissident approach is not to make legal categories trace and trap the way things are. It is not to make rules that fit reality. It is critical of reality. Its task is not to formulate abstract standards that will produce determinate outcomes in particular cases. Its project is more substantive, more jurisprudential than formulaic, which is why it is difficult for the mainstream discourse to dignify it as an approach to doctrine or to imagine it as a rule of law at all. It proposes to expose that which women have had little choice but to be confined to, in order to change it.

The dominance approach centers on the most sex-differential abuses of women as a gender, abuses that sex equality law in its difference garb could not confront. It is based on a reality about which little of a systematic nature was known before 1970, a reality that calls for a new conception of the problem of sex inequality. This new information includes not only the extent and intractability of sex segregation into poverty, which has been known before, but the range of issues termed violence against women, which has not been. It combines women's material desperation, through being relegated to categories of jobs that pay nil, with the massive amount of rape and attempted rape—44 percent of all women—about which virtually nothing is done; [30] the sexual assault of children—38 percent of girls and 10 percent of boys—which is apparently endemic to the patriarchal family; [31] the battery of women that is systematic in one quarter to one third of our homes; [32] prostitution, women's fundamental economic

---

30. Diana Russell and Nancy Howell, "The Prevalence of Rape in the United States Revisited," 8 *Signs: Journal of Women in Culture and Society* 689 (1983) (44 percent of women in 930 households were victims of rape or attempted rape at some time in their lives).

31. Diana Russell, "The Incidence and Prevalence of Intrafamilial and Extrafamilial Sexual Abuse of Female Children," 7 *Child Abuse & Neglect: The International Journal* 133 (1983).

32. R. Emerson Dobash and Russell Dobash, *Violence against Wives: A Case against the Patriarchy* (1979); Bruno v. Codd, 90 Misc.2d 1047, 396 N.Y.S.2d 974 (Sup.Ct.1977), *rev'd*, 64 A.D.2d 582, 407 N.Y.S.2d 165 (1st Dep't 1978), *aff'd* 47 N.Y.2d 582, 393 N.E.2d 976, 419 N.Y.S.2d 901 (1979).

condition, what we do when all else fails, and for many women in this country, all else fails often; and pornography, an industry that traffics in female flesh, making sex inequality into sex to the tune of eight billion dollars a year in profits largely to organized crime.

These experiences have been silenced out of the difference definition of sex equality largely because they happen almost exclusively to women. Understand: for this reason, they are considered *not* to raise sex equality issues. Because this treatment is done almost uniquely to women, it is implicitly treated as a difference, the sex difference, when in fact it is the socially situated subjection of women. The whole point of women's social relegation to inferiority as a gender is that for the most part these things aren't done to men. Men are not paid half of what women are paid for doing the same work on the basis of their equal difference. Everything they touch does not turn valueless because they touched it. When they are hit, a person has been assaulted. When they are sexually violated, it is not simply tolerated or found entertaining or defended as the necessary structure of the family, the price of civilization, or a constitutional right.

Does this differential describe the sex difference? Maybe so. It does describe the systematic relegation of an entire group of people to a condition of inferiority and attribute it to their nature. If this differential were biological, maybe biological intervention would have to be considered. If it were evolutionary, perhaps men would have to evolve differently. Because I think it is political, I think its politics construct the deep structure of society. Men who do not rape women have nothing wrong with their hormones. Men who are made sick by pornography and do not eroticize their revulsion are not under-evolved. This social status in which we can be used and abused and trivialized and humiliated and bought and sold and passed around and patted on the head and put in place and told to smile so that we look as though we're enjoying it all is not what some of us have in mind as sex equality.

This second approach—which is not abstract, which is at odds with socially imposed reality and therefore does not look like a standard according to the standard for standards—became the implicit model for racial justice applied by the courts during the sixties. It has since eroded with the erosion of judicial commitment to racial equality. It was based on the realization that the condition of Blacks in particular was not fundamentally a matter of rational or irrational differentiation on the basis of race but was fundamentally a matter of white supremacy, under which racial differences became invidious as a consequence. To consider gender in this way, observe again that men are as different from women as women are from men, but socially the sexes are not equally powerful. To be on the top of a hierarchy is certainly different from being on the bottom, but that is an obfuscatingly neutralized way of putting it, as a hierarchy is a great deal more than that. If gender were merely a question of difference, sex inequality would be a problem of mere sexism, of mistaken differentiation, of inaccurate categorization of individuals. This is what the difference approach thinks it is and is therefore sensitive to. But if gender is an inequality first, constructed as a socially relevant differentiation in order to keep that inequality in place, then sex inequality questions are questions of systematic dominance, of male supremacy, which is not at all abstract and is anything but a mistake.

If differentiation into classifications, in itself, is discrimination, as it is in difference doctrine, the use of law to change group-based social inequalities becomes problematic, even contradictory. This is because the group whose situation is to be changed must necessarily be legally identified and delineated, yet to do so is considered in fundamental tension with the guarantee against legally sanctioned inequality. If differentiation is discrimination, affirmative action, and any legal change in social inequality, is discrimination—but the existing social differentiations which constitute the inequality are not? This is only to say that, in the view that equates differentiation with discrimination, changing an unequal status quo is discrimination, but allowing it to exist is not.

Looking at the difference approach and the dominance approach from each other's point of view clarifies some otherwise confusing tensions in sex equality debates. From the point of view of the dominance approach, it becomes clear that the difference approach adopts the point of view of male supremacy on the status of the sexes. Simply by treating the status quo as "the standard," it invisibly and uncritically accepts the arrangements under male supremacy. In this sense, the difference approach is masculinist, although it can be expressed in a female voice. The dominance approach, in that it sees the inequalities of the social world from the standpoint of the subordination of women to men, is feminist.

If you look through the lens of the difference approach at the world as the dominance approach imagines it—that is, if you try to see real inequality through a lens that has difficulty seeing an inequality as an inequality if it also appears as a difference—you see demands for change in the distribution of power as demands for special protection. This is because the only tools that the difference paradigm offers to comprehend disparity equate the recognition of a gender line with an admission of lack of entitlement to equality under law. Since equality questions are primarily confronted in this approach as matters of empirical fit—that is, as matters of accurately shaping legal rules (implicitly modeled on the standard men set) to the way the world is (also implicitly modeled on the standard men set)—any existing differences must be negated to merit equal treatment. For ethnicity as well as for gender, it is basic to mainstream discrimination doctrine to preclude any true diversity among equals or true equality within diversity.

To the difference approach, it further follows that any attempt to change the way the world actually is looks like a moral question requiring a separate judgment of how things ought to be. This approach imagines asking the following disinterested question that can be answered neutrally as to groups: against the weight of empirical difference, should we treat some as the equals of others, even when they may not be entitled to it because they are not up to standard? Because this construction of the problem is part of what the dominance approach unmasks, it does not arise with the dominance approach, which therefore does not see its own foundations as moral. If sex inequalities are approached as matters of imposed status, which are in need of change if a legal mandate of equality means anything at all, the question whether women should be treated unequally means simply whether women should be treated as less. When it is exposed as a naked power question, there is no separable question of what ought to be. The only real question is what is and is not a gender question. Once no amount of difference justifies treating women as subhuman, eliminating that is what equality law is for. In this shift of paradigms, equality propositions become no longer propositions of good and evil, but of power and powerlessness, no more disinterested in their origins or neutral in their arrival at conclusions than are the problems they address.

* * *

To summarize the argument: seeing sex equality questions as matters of reasonable or unreasonable classification is part of the way male dominance is expressed in law. If you follow my shift in perspective from gender as difference to gender as dominance, gender changes from a distinction that is presumptively valid to a detriment that is presumptively suspect. The difference approach tries to map reality; the dominance approach tries to challenge and change it. In the dominance approach, sex discrimination stops being a question of morality and starts being a question of politics.

You can tell if sameness is your standard for equality if my critique of hierarchy looks like a request for special protection in disguise. It's not. It envisions a change that would make possible a simple equal chance for the first time. To define the reality of sex as difference and the warrant of equality as sameness is wrong on both counts. Sex, in nature, is not a bipolarity; it is a continuum. In society it is made into a bipolarity. Once this is done, to require that one be the same as those who set the standard—those which one is already socially defined as different from—simply means that sex equality is conceptually designed never to be achieved. Those who most need equal treatment will be the least similar, socially, to those whose situation sets the standard as against which one's entitlement to be equally treated is measured. Doctrinally speaking, the deepest problems of sex inequality will not find women "similarly situated" to men. Far less will practices of sex inequality require that acts be intentionally discriminatory. All that is required is that the status quo be maintained. As a strategy for maintaining social power first structure reality unequally, then require that entitlement to alter it be grounded on a lack of distinction in situation; first structure perception so that different equals inferior, then require that discrimination be activated by evil minds who *know* they are treating equals as less.

I say, give women equal power in social life. Let what we say matter, then we will discourse on questions of morality. Take your foot off our necks, then we will hear in what tongue women speak. So long as sex equality is limited by sex difference, whether you like it or don't like it, whether you value it or seek to negate it, whether you stake it out as a grounds for feminism or occupy it as the terrain of misogyny, women will be born, degraded, and die. We would settle for that equal protection of the laws under which one would be born, live, and die, in a country where protection is not a dirty word and equality is not a special privilege.

BIBLIOGRAPHY

Feminist Jurisprudence

DuBois, Dunlap, Gilligan, MacKinnon & Menkel–Meadow, *Feminist Discourse, Moral Values, and the Law—A Conversation,* 34 Buff.L. Rev. 11 (1985).

Finley, *Transcending Equality Theory: A Way Out of the Maternity and the Workplace Debate,* 86 Colum.L.Rev. 1118 (1986).

Gibson, *Childbearing and Childrearing: Feminists and Reform,* 73 Va. L.Rev. 1145 (1987).

Littleton, *Reconstructing Sexual Equality,* 75 Cal.L.Rev. 1279 (1987).

Littleton, *Equality and Feminist Legal Theory,* 48 U.Pitt.L.Rev. 1043 (1987).

MacKinnon, *Feminism, Marxism, Method, and the State: An Agenda for Theory,* 7 Signs 515 (1982).

MacKinnon, *Feminism, Marxism, Method, and the State: Toward Feminist Jurisprudence,* 8 Signs 635 (1983).

Minow, *The Supreme Court 1986 Term—Foreword: Justice Engendered,* 101 Harv.L.Rev. 10 (1987).

Olsen, *Statutory Rape: A Feminist Critique of Rights Analysis,* 63 Tex. L.Rev. 387 (1984).

Olsen, *The Family and the Market: A Study of Ideology and Legal Reform,* 96 Harv.L.Rev. 1497 (1983).

Rhode, JUSTICE AND GENDER: SEX DISCRIMINATION AND THE LAW (1989).

Rifkin, *Toward a Theory of Law and Patriarchy,* 3 Harv.Women's L.J. 83 (1980).

Scales, *Towards a Feminist Jurisprudence,* 56 Ind.L.J. 375 (1981).

Scales, *The Emergence of a Feminist Jurisprudence: An Essay*, 95 Yale L.J. 1371 (1986).

Sunstein, *Feminism and Legal Theory* [review of MacKinnon, FEMINISM UNMODIFIED], 101 Harv.L.Rev. 826 (1988).

Symposium, *Feminist Jurisprudence*, 24 Ga.L.Rev. 759–1044 (1990).

Taub & Schneider, Perspectives on Women's Subordination and the Role of Law, in THE POLITICS OF LAW 117 (D. Kairys ed. 1982).

West, *Jurisprudence and Gender*, 55 U.Chi.L.Rev. 1 (1988).

West, *The Difference in Women's Hedonic Lives: A Phenomenological Critique of Feminist Legal Theory*, 3 Wisc.Women's L.J. 81 (1987).

Whitman, *Law and Sex* [review of MacKinnon, FEMINISM UNMODIFIED], 86 Mich.L.Rev. 1388 (1988).

Wishik, *To Question Everything: The Inquiries of Feminist Jurisprudence*, 1 Berkeley Women's L.J. 64 (1985).

E. Wolgast, EQUALITY AND THE RIGHTS OF WOMEN (1980).

Gender and the Constitution

Brown, Emerson, Falk & Freedman, *The Equal Rights Amendment: A Constitutional Basis for Equal Rights for Women*, 80 Yale L.J. 871 (1971).

Colker, *Anti–Subordination Above All: Sex, Race, and Equal Protection*, 61 N.Y.U.L.Rev. 1003 (1986).

Freedman, *Sex Equality, Sex Differences, and the Supreme Court*, 92 Yale L.J. 913 (1983).

Ginsburg, *Gender and the Constitution*, 44 U.Cin.L.Rev. 1 (1975).

Karst, *Woman's Constitution*, 1984 Duke L.J. 447.

Kay, *Models of Equality*, 1985 U.Ill.L.Rev. 39.

D. Kirp, M. Yudof, & M. Franks, GENDER JUSTICE (1986).

Law, *Rethinking Sex and the Constitution*, 132 U.Pa.L.Rev. 955 (1984).

Maltz, Sex Discrimination in the Supreme Court—*A Comment on Sex Equality, Sex Differences, and the Supreme Court*, 1985 Duke L.J. 177.

Wildman, *The Legitimation of Sex Discrimination: A Critical Response to Supreme Court Jurisprudence*, 63 Or.L.Rev. 265 (1984).

Sex Discrimination and the Law

Becker, *Prince Charming: Abstract Equality*, 1987 Sup.Ct.Rev. 201.

Dowd, *Maternity Leave: Taking Sex Differences into Account*, 54 Ford. L.Rev. 699 (1986).

Estrich, *Rape*, 95 Yale L.J. 1087 (1986).

Frug, *Securing Job Equality for Women: Labor Market Hostility to Working Mothers*, 59 B.U.L.Rev. 55 (1979).

Krieger & Cooney, *The Miller–Wohl Controversy: Equal Treatment, Positive Action and the Meaning of Women's Equality,* 13 Golden Gate U.L.Rev. 513 (1983).

Law, *Women, Work, Welfare, and the Preservation of Patriarchy,* 131 U.Pa.L.Rev. 1249 (1983).

C. MacKinnon, SEXUAL HARASSMENT OF WORKING WOMEN: A CASE STUDY OF SEX DISCRIMINATION (1979).

Powers, *Sex Segregation and the Ambivalent Directions of Sex Discrimination Law,* 1979 Wisc.L.Rev. 55.

Taub, *Keeping Women in their Place: Stereotyping Per Se as a Form of Employment Discrimination,* 21 B.C.L.Rev. 345 (1980).

Taub, *Review of MacKinnon,* SEXUAL HARASSMENT OF WORKING WOMEN, 80 Colum.L.Rev. 1686 (1980).

Williams, *Equality's Riddle: Pregnancy and the Equal Treatment/ Special Treatment Debate,* 13 N.Y.U.Rev.L. & Soc.Change 325 (1985).

Chapter VIII

AFFIRMATIVE ACTION

The materials in Chapter VI argue that governmental action that discriminates against racial minorities should be subjected to close judicial scrutiny under the Fourteenth Amendment. What do the justifications provided—the moral irrelevance of race, the stigma imposed on individuals or groups, the political powerlessness of blacks— say about governmental programs established to *benefit* racial minorities? This, of course, is the constitutional question raised by "affirmative action."

The readings in this Chapter analyze the affirmative action debate from a number of different angles.

Kent Greenawalt identifies and evaluates the major justifications for preferential admissions policies to public educational institutions— policies that were at issue in the *DeFunis*[1] and *Bakke*[2] cases. He concludes that affirmative action programs aimed at ameliorating racial stereotypes and compensating for injuries caused by present discrimination and the continuing effects of past discrimination may withstand constitutional scrutiny.

Richard Posner criticizes the theoretical and policy justifications offered by Greenawalt in favor of affirmative action. He argues that the Fourteenth Amendment ought to be read to prohibit the distribution of benefits and costs on the basis of race. Accordingly, affirmative action programs can not be constitutionally sustained.

Morris Abram shares Posner's view that "color-blindness" ought to be the prevailing principle in antidiscrimination law. He contends that the civil rights movement has become dominated by "social engineers" who support affirmative action programs as a way to achieve equality of results. Abrams would return civil rights law to its earlier commitment to equality of opportunity (the "fair shake" principle).

Laurence Tribe and Randall Kennedy disagree with Posner and Abram. Tribe argues that a colorblind standard is not consistent with

1. DeFunis v. Odegaard, 416 U.S. 312, 94 S.Ct. 1704, 40 L.Ed.2d 164 (1974).

2. Regents of the Univ. of Calif. v. Bakke, 438 U.S. 265, 98 S.Ct. 2733, 57 L.Ed.2d 750 (1978).

the original intent of the Fourteenth Amendment nor is it compelled by *Brown v. Board of Education* or considerations of the proper role of the judiciary in a democratic society. Kennedy examines the impact that affirmative action has had on blacks and the nation. He responds to recent claims that affirmative action policies have resulted in harming the racial groups they were established to benefit.

Kathleen Sullivan, writing before the Supreme Court's decision in *City of Richmond v. J.A. Croson Co.,*[3] concludes that the Court has approved affirmative action programs only as "precise penance for the specific sins of [past] discrimination." She criticizes this approach and suggests that "forward-looking" justifications do a better job than current doctrine at answering claims that affirmative action programs unfairly harm innocent individuals and produce windfalls to non-victims.

Charles Fried and Patricia Williams comment on the Court's most recent affirmative action case, *Metro Broadcasting, Inc. v. FCC.*[4] Fried asserts that the majority was wrong to reject a "liberal, individualistic" understanding of equal protection, and that the Court's "group-rights" perspective led it to adopt a standard of review that insufficiently scrutinizes race-based policies. Williams supports the Court's decision, arguing that it provides a vehicle for a better understanding of the significance of and necessity for group claims within our legal system. *Metro Broadcasting* is an important case, she suggests, because it affirms "the desirability of diversity in all aspects of our economy and of multiculturalism in our lives."

KENT GREENAWALT, JUDICIAL SCRUTINY OF "BENIGN" RACIAL PREFERENCE IN LAW SCHOOL ADMISSIONS

75 Colum.L.Rev. 559, 579–94 (1975).

[In the preceding section of this article, Greenawalt argues that "the courts should neither treat benign racial classifications as invalid per se nor subject them to a mere rationality test. They should ascertain if benign classifications are supported by an interest that is substantial, but should not require that the interest be undeniably urgent and paramount. They should give particularly intense scrutiny to whether a nonracial approach or a more narrowly tailored racial classification could promote the substantial interest about as well and at tolerable administrative expense."]

II. CONSTITUTIONAL EVALUATION OF JUSTIFICATIONS FOR PREFERENTIAL ADMISSIONS POLICIES

* * *

A. *Redress for Unwarranted Injury*

One justification for preferential admissions policies is that they redress unjust discrimination that blacks have suffered.

---

3. 488 U.S. 469 (1989).

4. ___ U.S. ___, 110 S.Ct. 2997, 111 L.Ed.2d 445 (1990).

1. *Compensatory and Distributive Justice.* In his analysis, Professor Nickel makes use of the Aristotelian distinction between compensatory justice and distributive justice, between making a person whole for losses he has unjustly suffered and giving him the position in society he "deserves." [114] Though it may be difficult to draw a precise line between these two kinds of claims, in many contexts the distinction is clear. The newly elected public official who argues that he should be paid more makes a claim of distributive justice on society's resources. A rich alcoholic "bum" who returns to society after ten years in jail on an unjust conviction and who is presently at least as well off as he would be if he had never been convicted has a claim of compensatory justice for the pain he has suffered. In the context of preferential programs for blacks, the distinction largely collapses in practice. The claim for distributive justice, like that for compensatory justice, rests on assertions of past injustice. If blacks had never been peculiarly subject to social injustice, there might be no constitutionally adequate reason to treat them as a "class" for determining if society's benefits are justly distributed. If it just happened that few blacks had inherent aptitude for law or an interest in being lawyers, the minute percentage of black lawyers would not reflect any distributive injustice. The main reason why a claim of distributive justice has force is that it is assumed that more blacks would now enjoy high positions if their race had not been held back by social injustice. If preferential benefits were subject to precise calculation, it is possible that claims for compensation would support greater benefits than distributive claims; but for purposes of constitutional law the distinction between claims of compensatory and distributive justice is so slender that in this context we may treat them together as claims for redress of injustices.

2. *Injustices the Government May Constitutionally Redress.* The government's duty to redress injustices is clearest when the government itself causes an injury that is illegal at the time it is caused, but its power to rectify injustice is hardly limited to these situations. It may compensate for injustices that it caused, say by the laws of slavery, that were legal at the time they were inflicted; and it may compensate for injustices suffered at the hands of private individuals, whether or not those injustices amount to a general social practice. It may, in fact, "compensate" for losses that are not the fault of either the government or other individuals, as when it establishes special relief programs for earthquake and flood victims.

The Supreme Court's approval of racial classifications to correct de jure segregation [117] demonstrates that the government's interest in assuring redress of specific instances of illegal discrimination is great enough to justify some use of racial criteria. Since the government has the power to redress illegal discrimination indirectly as well as directly, and to redress injustices other than illegal discrimination, the person

---

114. Nickel, *Preferential Policies in Hiring and Admissions: A Jurisprudential Approach,* 75 Colum.L.Rev. 534 (1975).

* * * [Relocated footnote.]

117. Swann v. Charlotte–Mecklenburg County, 402 U.S. 1 (1971).

who claims that reliance on racial classifications in preferential admissions policies is impermissible must argue that the government's interest here is less important than when it corrects illegal segregation, or that the particular hardships imposed by racially based preferential policies are unacceptable methods for redressing those injustices.

3. *Preferential Admissions and Social Injustice.* "Equal protection of the laws" would not have been denied to impoverished whites if in 1868 a state had made free land available to ex-slaves. If, instead, the state had made land available to all black adults within its borders, on the theory that few, if any, blacks had not suffered the effects of slavery or other state discriminations unique to blacks, it is hard to believe a court would have, or should have, found the program to be unconstitutional because all blacks and no whites were eligible for its benefits.

The constitutionality of modern programs to redress injustices to blacks is not as immediately apparent. I shall put aside for the moment the problem that the "burden" of many of these programs falls on excluded applicants, and assume that, as with the hypothetical grant of land, the burden falls on society generally. One or more of the three following theories might be used in support of a preference for a modern young black: (1) that he has been directly subjected to compensable discrimination; (2) that he has suffered the effects of discrimination against his forebears; or (3) that he should be compensated because of a special relationship to his forebears, whether or not he has suffered from wrongs done to them. We may deal briefly with the third possible theory as based on a dubious moral claim unlikely to be relied on extensively by thoughtful proponents of preferential admissions. Compensation to immediate survivors for harm done to others may have a place in the law of tort, since survival of actions helps to deter and penalize wrongful behavior and to compensate near kin for incalculable losses. Compensation to survivors may also be appropriate when a wrong is done to an ongoing entity like an Indian tribe, or when the perpetrators of a horrendous wrong wish to "purge" their guilt by compensating persons who have a significant relationship to the victims.[119] But when the perpetrators and victims of social injustice are both dead, it is hard to explain why the government should prefer those who happen to be descendants of the victims, unless they have been affected by the injustice. Because two much stronger arguments exist for redressing injustices to blacks we need not explore this one further.

Since widespread discrimination against blacks continues in the United States, it is plausible to suppose that most young blacks have suffered from it in various ways and that government redress is appropriate. But a preferential policy designed for that purpose that includes all blacks and excludes all whites now has much more serious

---

119. An example would be German reparations to Israel for wrongs done to European Jews.

defects of underinclusiveness and overinclusiveness than it would have had if adopted in 1868. It is not clear that most blacks suffer injustices significantly different in character from those inflicted on some whites. And some young blacks are members of families recently arrived from other countries, or of families so well situated that they have not been sharply touched by discrimination. One might try to answer the charge of overinclusiveness with the suggestion that discrimination against blacks is so pervasive that it has touched, or will touch, all blacks significantly. A more general response to the charge of imprecise classification would be that proof of discrimination is too uncertain to be handled administratively, and, further, that it would be undesirable for law schools to decide how much discrimination individual applicants have suffered. This is a close point, but I believe that law schools could assess reasonably well whether particular members of non-preferred groups had suffered injustices similar to those imposed generally on the preferred group, and whether certain members of the preferred group had not suffered such injustices. I therefore think it doubtful that the fourteenth amendment should be interpreted to allow a straight racial preference where the only justification tendered is compensation to those directly injured by discrimination.

Benefits to young blacks may also be urged, however, on the ground that they continue to suffer the effects of discrimination against their parents and more distant forebears. Blacks victimized by discrimination have suffered educational, vocational, economic and psychological harms. Their ability to confer benefits on their children has been sharply impaired. No identifiable group of whites suffered injustice as extreme as that imposed on blacks under the American version of slavery. Not only were they deprived of virtually every kind of social good enjoyed by free men, they were also largely stripped of their culture. It would have taken several generations to wipe out the effects of slavery even if its end had meant instantaneous equal treatment. In fact, further systematic discrimination has perpetuated those effects. Most young blacks are undoubtedly still disadvantaged because of the direct effects of slavery and systematic racial discrimination against post-emancipation generations, and thus they have suffered from racial discrimination even if they have not all been personally subjected to racial bias.

It can be debated whether the young black has a greater claim on society's resources than a young white whose predecessors were equally ill-educated and destitute because they were persecuted in some other country or were lazy drunkards; but it is tenable to believe that a society has a special reason to eliminate the hardships stemming from its own injustices, and that this responsibility can survive the death of oppressors and direct victims, as long as ascertainable persons continue to suffer those hardships. This is not to say that rectifying the effects of injustice on subsequent generations is a typically desirable policy; it usually is not. It is only to say that a decision justified on that basis would not be evidently unsound.

If a reason for preference is to ameliorate the effects on this generation of injustice caused to past generations, then the use of an explicitly racial classification instead of a more individualized alternative is easier to defend than if the focus is on injustice to this generation. As to possible underinclusiveness, few whites have suffered from injustices like those inflicted on blacks by slavery and systematic discrimination, and the effects of any such injustices would be virtually impossible to trace.

Nor could possible overinclusiveness be cured by a study of black family histories to disqualify those few young blacks, if any, who may actually have benefited from slavery and the general discrimination against blacks. Neither this compensatory justification nor administrative necessity, however, would reach recent black immigrants from other countries.

We still have not faced the question whether the purpose of compensation is weighty enough to sustain a racial classification. It may be urged that society should be forward-looking in its policies, that society has survived intact despite the general failure to give government redress for injustices, and that a policy of compensation is of debatable wisdom and certainly does not reflect any paramount state interest. Proponents of preference can argue that social justice is among the most important aims of a social order, and that redress for blacks is both just and needed to relieve a sharp sense of injustice that most blacks feel. The need for redress may not be of undeniable urgency but the reasons that support compensation for most blacks reflect substantial government interests; if those reasons are accepted by legislators or administrators against competing arguments, they should be viewed by courts as important enough to sustain compensatory programs for blacks.

*   *   *

*   *   * [One] objection to preferential admissions policies *   *   * is the limited size of the class on whom the "burden" falls, and this is an objection that can be raised with respect to all the justifications given for preferential policies, not only the "compensatory" ones.

Unless a state expands facilities in order to accept more blacks, the burden of preferential admissions policies falls squarely on excluded white applicants, not the people who have practiced discrimination or even society as a whole. That the burden of preferential policies falls on a few individuals rather than on society at large or the educational institution granting the preference may be a reason for closer judicial scrutiny of the preference, but it is not of major constitutional relevance. No white has a vested interest in a legal education. A white with high test scores and grades from an intellectual city family would have no substantial constitutional claim if he were denied admission to a state law school that decided to admit some "less qualified" applicants who had grown up on farms. Since applicants are vulnerable to being excluded in pursuit of any one of a number of possible policies, no special constitutional difficulty is caused because the burden of racial preference falls on them. Moreover, insofar as it makes sense to assume that without discrimination many more blacks would qualify without preference, a state might assume that borderline whites who are admitted in the absence of preferential policies are indirectly "benefiting" from discrimination of which they are completely innocent. If they are excluded because of preferential policies, they may be put in the position they would have been in if the discrimination had never occurred. Expansion of facilities and resources is not always a sensible option, or an option the relevant institution has the power to choose. While there may be some injustice in casting the burden of preference on excluded whites, the need to make certain kinds of very important benefits the subject of compensation renders that unfortunate effect constitutionally acceptable.

B. Preferential Admissions and Qualifications

A different kind of argument made for preferential admissions is that ordinary admissions procedures inadequately reflect the qualifications of minority group members. * * *

1. *Qualifications for Law School Performance.* It is asserted that the law school aptitude tests and college grades do not adequately indicate the probable law school performance of blacks.[138] Of course, exact predictions of performance are impossible, and even for white students predictions based on tests and grades do not correlate neatly with actual performance, but this argument assumes that these predictions are sufficiently reliable to be a weighty factor in the admissions of whites. The contention is, however, that blacks are special because the law school aptitude tests are culturally biased and college grades also do not reflect the potential of those who are culturally disadvantaged.

One problem with this argument is that predictions of law school performance based on tests and grades are not significantly less accurate for black applicants than for other applicants. Perhaps the test is "culturally biased," but so also may be the law school program and the practice of law, in the sense that they call for skills and attitudes developed in the dominant culture. Insofar as tests and grades are especially inaccurate predictors for most blacks, plainly this is not a result of race pure and simple. Presumably these standards of likely performance are not culturally biased for blacks who have well-educated parents and whose predominant contacts at home and school have been with whites. And the standards may very well be culturally biased for poor whites who were educated in culturally disadvantaged settings and whose predominant contacts have been with poor blacks. If there are special reasons why tests and grades do not accurately predict law school performance for those from particular cultural backgrounds, it would not be very difficult administratively to make

138. See the testimony of the President of the University of Washington quoted in the state supreme court opinion in *DeFunis,* 82 Wash.2d 11, 40, 507 P.2d 1169, 1174 (1973), *vacated as moot,* 416 U.S. 312 (1974).

special exceptions from ordinary standards for whites from those backgrounds and not to make the exceptions for blacks who are not from those backgrounds. Given the constitutional presumption against racial classification, this more particularized approach should be required as a less onerous alternative.

Another reason why this qualifications argument cannot support existing preferential policies is that whatever special dispensation might be given to blacks because of the special inaccuracy of the usual bases for prediction of law school performance, no one can doubt that most law schools have gone far beyond that in their policies. They are admitting blacks who they are reasonably sure will not do as well in law school as white applicants denied admission.

2. *General Qualifications for the Legal Profession.* Only some of the skills lawyers need are tested in law school. Thus, there is a gap between qualifications for law school performance and qualifications for legal practice. As difficult as it may be to identify the skills needed for good lawyering, a state law school could properly decide to admit those who would make better lawyers in preference to those who would make better law students. Perhaps there is some correlation between being black and having qualifications for legal practice that will not be reflected in law school performance. Persons without educational advantages are much less likely to suffer with respect to some qualities lawyers need than with respect to the analytic precision and skill in written communication so important for law school success. And deficiencies in writing and analytical skills are much more likely to be overcome in the course of an entire career than in the three years of law school itself. Nevertheless, as with predicting law school performance, racial classification is much too imprecise a means if the underlying justification for preference is an attempt to gauge more accurately the general qualifications lawyers require.

3. *Job Placement and Qualifications.* Legal education fills a social need. Some legal jobs may be judged socially more important than others, and a state law school might decide to admit some "less qualified" students who are particularly likely to do socially valuable work in preference to "better qualified" applicants less likely to do such work. Again, even if one assumes that there is some correlation between being black and being likely to do socially valuable work, such as work for the poor and otherwise disadvantaged, it would be feasible administratively to make much "finer" guesses about an applicant's likely job orientation, based on his specific background, his previous activities and his expressed reasons for wishing to go to law school.

4. *Ability to Work With Blacks.* It can be argued that black lawyers are more likely to represent black people effectively because they can win their trust and understand them better. Commonality of background, vocabulary and attitude can be helpful for a lawyer's representation of his client. Of course, a rich white lawyer may do a superb job of representing a poor black defendant; and when a major

legal issue is sharply presented, an expert lawyer's personal background makes little difference. But personal background may become much more important when one is counseling clients or trying to learn their story.

* * *

This "special qualifications" argument is the only form of the "qualifications" argument for preferences on explicitly racial lines that is plausibly consistent with the fourteenth amendment; my own conclusion is that even racial preferences based on this rationale should not withstand an equal protection attack. Racial identity is, at most, one small aspect of effective representation. A more talented white lawyer will usually represent blacks better than a less talented black one. Moreover, many black lawyers will find themselves in jobs where they rarely represent black clients, so a general racial preference benefits many applicants for whom this argument will prove to be irrelevant. I believe that the fourteenth amendment policy against such racial classifications is stronger in terms of this argument than with respect to the compensation argument, because a governmental assumption that black lawyers can represent blacks more effectively impliedly endorses racial ways of thought much more than a governmental assumption that blacks deserve compensation. It suggests that private citizens should take race into account in their dealings with lawyers. As Justice Douglas urged in his *DeFunis* dissent: "The purpose of the University of Washington cannot be to produce Black lawyers for Blacks, Polish lawyers for Poles, Jewish lawyers for Jews, Irish lawyers for the Irish." [148] Perhaps if law schools made a more particularized effort to determine which applicants would be most likely to work on behalf of disadvantaged groups, they could take into account the possibility that black lawyers may be more effective in helping disadvantaged blacks than white lawyers. Perhaps also this special qualifications argument, as well as the other qualifications arguments, can give slight added weight to the state's other interests in a general racial preference in admissions, but the qualifications arguments, separately or together, are not sufficient by themselves to sustain such a preference against constitutional attack.

C. *Preferential Admissions and the Values of Diversity and the Amelioration of Attitudes that Hinder Equality of Opportunity*

Some arguments for preferential policies are based on claimed benefits to the general society if there are more black students in law school and black members of the bar.

1. *The Integrated Law School.* As the Supreme Court pointed out many years ago,[150] * * * one of the values of a legal education is the exposure to persons of diverse backgrounds and points of view. One might add that the benefits of diversity in the student body accrue to

---

148. 416 U.S. at 341–42.

150. Sweatt v. Painter, 339 U.S. 629, 634 (1950).

the faculty as well as the students. In order to enrich the education of all its students, a state law school may admit persons with unusual experience, say former school teachers or policemen, in preference to those who are slightly more "qualified" but who lack the special experience.[153] Regrettable though it may be, race is a crucially important aspect of most people's experience; a white student who has never talked seriously with blacks will be unlikely to understand many very important things about life in the United States. While increasing understanding, such contacts may also eliminate or blur racial stereotypes that can inhibit one's effective functioning as a lawyer, judge, or administrator. If the diversity sought is diversity of racial experience, then obviously a preference in racial terms is precisely tailored to the aim.

If preferences are necessary to get a significant number of blacks into law school, the interest in a racially diversified student body is substantial enough to justify preferences for some blacks, since race is now such an important determinant of social perceptions, and so many problems with which lawyers and officials deal concern race. But it should not be assumed that because some preferential representation of a group is permitted to encourage diversity, members of that group can be admitted on a preferential basis until they constitute the same percentage of the student body as their percentage of the general population. It is not certain, for example, that relevant communication between blacks and whites will be much greater if the student body is ten per cent black than if it is five per cent black. Of course, it may be unfair to impose on a small number of blacks the responsibility to communicate the "black experience" to a large number of whites, but a law school justifying its preferential policies in terms of law school diversity should make some effort to decide how widely applicable racial preferences should be to achieve adequate diversity.

The proper degree of judicial review of a policy supported by a diversity justification is very difficult to determine, because it is much harder for judges to second-guess decisions about how much diversity is needed and how it can best be achieved than it is for them to deal with the questions of administrability of alternative standards raised by some compensation and qualifications arguments. It is hard even to conceive of the "evidence" a school might give to support a particular percentage of black representation. Nevertheless, given the general undesirability of racial classifications and the potential broad sweep of diversity arguments, it would be a mistake for the courts to accept a diversity claim as justifying whatever number of preferential admissions law schools choose to make. The courts should at least require a reasoned explanation by administrators of why they believe the actual number of preferences given will yield the desired diversity.

153. Many institutions admit students from distant regions of the country on a preferential basis, in part to expose students to others from diverse regional backgrounds.

2. *The Amelioration of Racial Stereotypes.* Past discrimination has made it very hard for blacks to become professionals. The widespread assumption that blacks are more suited for menial jobs has affected the attitudes of whites toward blacks and the attitude of blacks toward themselves. If young blacks are to aspire to, and work toward, high vocational positions, it is important for them to see that significant numbers of persons with whom they identify are in those positions. And the perception of blacks in those positions will do much to vitiate possible feelings of racial inferiority among a much wider group of blacks. If whites are going to accept blacks as equal, not only as a matter of religious or political philosophy but also on the intuitive level that so influences actual social relations, it is important that they deal with blacks as equals in the performance of social responsibilities.

A special reason why it is important to have black lawyers is that many lawyers become legislators and high administrators. Both blacks and whites need to see blacks in positions of community leadership, as well as to have a black perspective brought directly to bear on the resolution of many community problems.

Increasing the number of blacks in high vocational positions and as community leaders will not only raise the aspirations of young blacks and dissipate white racial stereotypes, but may also ameliorate some stereotypes blacks have about whites. No longer will it be so easy to distinguish "them" (the white power structure) from "us" (the black oppressed), because "them" will include many blacks. Other blacks will come more easily to see the constraints under which those with power operate and will abandon any oversimplified notion that those in responsible positions are invariably "oppressors."

Given the pervasiveness of racial stereotypes in this society and their destructive effect on the quality of life, their dissolution is undoubtedly a proper public purpose. It may be a public purpose that draws implicit support from the thirteenth and fourteenth amendments. The persistence of negative stereotypes about blacks can be argued to be an "incident" of slavery in the extended sense of a debilitating effect of slavery and also an "incident" in the narrower sense of a feature that accompanied slavery itself and continues to disadvantage blacks. As it has developed, the concept of equal protection in the fourteenth amendment implicitly condemns stereotypes based on race and class. It would be a denial of equal protection for the government purposefully to foster such stereotypes, and while attacking them may not be required, it is consistent with the spirit of the amendment.

If the purpose of preferential policies is to reduce racial stereotypes, then, of course, the racial classification fits its purpose exactly. So long as the superbly educated son of a black Senator or the recent immigrant from Africa are identified as relevantly "black" by whites and other blacks, then this purpose of the preferential policy is served by admitting them.

Opponents of preferential policies argue that racial preferences will be unnecessary and even unhelpful in eliminating stereotypes, that the opening up of opportunities to blacks without preference will produce, as it has for many immigrant groups, enough professionals in a generation or two to undercut racial stereotypes, and that admission preferences for blacks will actually confirm stereotypes.[164] I find neither contention persuasive enough to reject preferential policies; certainly neither is so evidently correct that a court should hold that a decision in favor of preferences is unsound. The average quality of black law students has increased quickly since the first years of preference, perhaps in part because law schools are now admitting many blacks who were admitted on a preferential basis to the best colleges. Most black law school graduates perform competently, and whatever "gap" may remain at graduation from a given school between some of them and most white students is likely to be reduced during their careers. The "negative" stereotypes fostered by preferential admissions will be far outweighed by the positive effect of having blacks in important professional positions. The answer to the contention that preferences are unnecessary is twofold. Given the systematic historic discrimination against blacks and the more subtle and pervasive discriminatory attitudes that still exist and are particularly hard to eradicate because of the visibility of racial differences, genuine equality for blacks without preference may take much more than one or two generations. Second, the damage done to blacks by racial stereotypes now is so serious that any program that gives hope of altering stereotypes quickly is to be preferred to one that will work only over a longer term.

Whether the state's interest is put as the long run amelioration of racial stereotypes or the reasonably quick amelioration of these stereotypes, it is important enough to support preferential admissions policies. Whether these policies are "necessary" to achieve these results may be debatable, but the debate is not one that can comfortably be resolved by the judiciary. Legislative or administrative judgments of the need for preferential policies should be accepted; and so long as the gap between the percentage of black professionals and the percentage of blacks in the population remains enormous, this justification for racial preferences will support almost any breadth of application for the preference.

The amelioration of racial stereotypes and compensation of blacks for injuries caused by present discrimination and the lingering effects of past injustices, are the two justifications that are adequate to support outright racial preferences as extensive as those now being employed in many law schools.

---

164. The argument is that if whites think blacks are in positions because of preference, or they find the blacks they deal with to be less qualified than most whites, then racial stereotypes will be strengthened rather than reduced. *See* Graglia, [*Special Admission of the "Culturally Deprived" to Law School*, 119 U.Pa.L. Rev. 351, 355 (1970).]

RICHARD A. POSNER, THE DeFUNIS CASE AND THE CONSTITUTIONALITY OF PREFERENTIAL TREATMENT OF RACIAL MINORITIES
1974 Sup.Ct.Rev. 1, 7–12, 15–25.

II. THE REASONABLENESS OF REVERSE DISCRIMINATION

B. Race as a Surrogate for Other, Nonracial Characteristics

A frequently suggested basis for preferential treatment is the desire to increase the diversity of the student body in the hope of thereby enhancing the quality of the students' educational experience.
* * *

For a diversity argument to be convincing, it must identify a differentiating factor that is relevant to the educational experience. It would make no sense to argue that in selecting the entering first-year class a law school should strive for diversity in the height of the students, or in their weight, pulchritude, posture, depth of voice, or blood pressure, or that it should give a preference to (or disfavor) albinos, or people with freckles or double chins. Diversity in these superficial physical respects contributes nothing of value to the legal education of the students. Race *per se*—that is, race completely divorced from certain characteristics that may be strongly correlated with, but do not inevitably accompany, it—is also, and in a similar sense, irrelevant to diversity. There are black people (and Chicanos, Filipinos, etc.) who differ only in the most superficial physical characteristics from whites—who have the same tastes, manners, experiences, aptitudes, and aspirations as the whites with whom one might compare them (here, white law school applicants). To give such people preferential treatment to the end of increasing the diversity of the student body would be equivalent to giving preferential treatment to albinos—were it not that race is frequently correlated with other attributes that are arguably relevant to meaningful diversity, and albinism is not. The average black applicant for admission is more likely than the average white to have known poverty and prejudice first hand, and his experience, communicated to his fellow students (and teachers) both inside and outside of the classroom, might enrich the educational process.

Race in this analysis is simply a proxy for a set of other attributes—relevant to the educational process—with which race, itself irrelevant to the process, happens to be correlated. The use of a racial proxy in making admissions decisions will produce some inaccuracy— blacks will be admitted who lack the attributes that contribute to genuine diversity—but this cost of using a racial proxy may be less than the cost, which is saved, of having to investigate the actual characteristics of each applicant.

The difficulty with this approach is that it closely resembles and could be viewed as imparting legitimacy to the case for regarding discrimination against racial minorities as a proper, because (generally) efficient, form of conduct. There are several possible explanations for the presence of racial and ethnic discrimination. One is sheer irrationality; another is exploitation; another the desire to limit competition. But it may be that most discrimination in today's America can be explained simply by the cost of information. Suppose that a particular racial or ethnic identity is correlated with characteristics that are widely disliked for reasons not patently exploitive, anticompetitive, or irrational. A substantial proportion of the members of the group in question may be loud, or poor, or hostile, or irresponsible, or poorly educated, or dangerously irascible, or ill-mannered, or have different tastes, values, and work habits from our own, or speak an unintelligible patois.[24] To be averse to association (in housing, recreation, schooling, or employment) with an individual because he possessed such a characteristic would not ordinarily be regarded as a sign of prejudice. To be "prejudiced" means, rather, to ascribe to the members of a group defined by a racial or similarly arbitrary characteristic[25] attributes typically or frequently possessed by members of the group without pausing to consider whether the individual member in question has that characteristic—sometimes without being willing even to consider evidence that he does not. The extreme bigot applies an irrebuttable presumption that every member of the group has the characteristic that he dislikes. The moderate bigot applies a rebuttable presumption to the same effect—and all of us are at least moderate bigots in some areas of life.

The history of this country contains examples of the unreasoning type of racial and ethnic prejudice, of exploitive discrimination—illustrated by the treatment of the American Indian in the nineteenth century and by the enslavement of the black—and of the anticompetitive sort as well (*e.g.*, exclusion of women from various occupations). But, today at least, it may be that most prejudice and discrimination are a product of the cost of making individual distinctions within racial and ethnic groups. This is a type of economically efficient conduct similar to a consumer's reluctance to try a new brand or more generally, to carry the process of searching for products beyond the point where the cost of searching is equal to its benefit in enabling a better purchase to be made. It is perfectly rational for an individual to support the exclusion of Armenians, or Jews, or blacks from his club if his experience, whether first or second hand, is that most or very many members of these groups do not have the characteristics that he likes in

---

24. The proportion of the racial or ethnic group who actually possess the disfavored characteristic may, of course, be exaggerated, since obtaining accurate information about the characteristics of the average member of the group may be costly too.

25. An "arbitrary characteristic" in this sense is one whose only significance is as a proxy for some other characteristic. To dislike short people because one finds them repulsive is not prejudice; to dislike short people because one thinks that short people tend to have aggressive personalities is an example of prejudice, assuming that not all short people in fact possess such personalities.

a social (or business) acquaintance and there is no scarcity of eligible applicants from other groups.

To say that discrimination is often a rational and efficient form of behavior is not to say that it is socially or ethically desirable. "Efficient" must never be confused with "good" or "right." Moreover, there is an important distinction to be drawn between private discrimination and discrimination that is compelled, practiced, or encouraged by the government, or that is practiced by a monopolist. But I am not interested in the normative basis of antidiscrimination policy. My purpose in noting that much discrimination may be applicable in terms of the costs of information is, rather, to suggest a doubt about the merits of the diversity justification for treating racial minorities preferentially. That justification, it will be recalled, rests on the correlation between racial identity and the possession of characteristics that promote meaningful diversity, and implicitly, therefore, on the cost of ascertaining whether a particular member of the racial group actually possesses the desired characteristic. Could not a policy against hostile discrimination be undermined by a program of benevolent discrimination rooted in the same habit of mind—that of using race or ethnic origin to establish a presumption, in the case of a racially preferential admissions program a conclusive one, that the individual possesses some other attribute as well, that is, some educationally relevant characteristic such as a background of deprivation or a cultural difference? The danger is underscored by the fact that the hostile and the well-disposed discriminators seem to be treating race as a proxy for the same set of characteristics. The characteristics that university admissions officers associate with "black" are the distinctive cultural attributes of many black people who have grown up in an urban slum or in the rural South, and these are the same characteristics that the white bigot ascribes to every black, although he uses a different terminology (*e.g.*, "lazy" rather than "unmotivated").

I am not making the familiar argument that the member of the favored minority is humiliated by being singled out for preferential treatment. He may or may not be. My point is rather that the use of a racial characteristic to establish a presumption that the individual also possesses other, and socially relevant, characteristics exemplifies, encourages, and legitimizes the mode of thought and behavior that underlies most prejudice and bigotry in modern America.

* * *

I have dwelled * * * on the diversity argument for preferential treatment because it is the one argument that seems at first glance not racialistic at all. The argument is not that one race should be preferred over another but that a racial preference will benefit all members of the student body, regardless of race, by enriching the educational experience. Yet if one looks a little more closely at the argument it turns out to rest on a premise fundamentally inconsistent with that of a policy against hostile discrimination, for such a policy, if it is to be effective, requires rejection of administrative convenience as a justification for using racial criteria to allocate benefits or impose burdens.

C. Racial Proportional Representation

Where * * * a racial preference is based squarely on a desire to increase the proportion of lawyers of a particular race, it is no longer possible to argue about whether the preference is a form of racial discrimination and it is more difficult to find a justification based on educational purposes, or for that matter on anything else. Four principal reasons are offered for attempting to achieve at least approximately proportional racial representation in the legal profession: (1) making amends for past discrimination against the minority group; (2) putting the group where it would have been but for the handicaps imposed on its members by past discrimination; (3) improving the level of professional service received by the group; and (4) encouraging the aspirations of its members by the provision of suitable "role models." None of these four reasons would be any more persuasive to an objective observer than the sorts of arguments that could be offered for discriminating against racial minorities.

1. The members of the minority group who receive preferential treatment will often be those who have not been the victims of discrimination while the nonminority people excluded because of the preferences are unlikely to have perpetrated, or to have in any demonstrable sense benefited from,[32] the discrimination. Indian reparations may be a distinct case, based on treaty (equivalent to contractual) obligations enforceable by the heirs of the original beneficiaries against the government; also distinguishable, though in my opinion only tenuously, is the use of racial quotas as part of a decree to remedy unlawful discrimination.[33]

---

32. One could spend many profitless hours discussing whether [a white applicant to law school] is better or worse off as the result of the history of racial discrimination in this country. Perhaps he is better off because, but for a history of discrimination, there would be a larger pool of qualified black applicants for a law school education. Perhaps he is worse off because, but for the history of discrimination, fewer blacks (and members of other minorities) would be interested in becoming lawyers. Perhaps if there had never been discrimination against blacks, there would never have been slavery in the United States, and without slavery, it is possible, indeed probable, that the black population in the United States would be insignificant, in which event—perhaps—the real income of whites would be higher.

33. As for example in Swann v. Charlotte–Mecklenburg Bd. of Educ., 402 U.S. 1 (1971). These decisions are difficult to justify because the people adversely affected by the decree are in general different from those who discriminated unlawfully. The remedy does not run against the wrongdoer. A more acceptable remedy would be damages. The costs of a decree imposing a racial quota in a labor market are borne primarily by the white workers (I distinguish the case where the source of the discrimination is the workers themselves or the union representing them) or, in the case of educational discrimination, by children bused to distant or inferior schools. The cost of a damage award, in contrast, would be borne primarily by the owners of the discriminating firm or the taxpayers of the discriminating school district.

In discussions of black reparations, an analogy is frequently drawn to the payment of substantial reparations by Germany to the State of Israel in compensation for Nazi Germany's extermination of millions of European Jews. Among the distinguishing features is the fact that the cost of the German reparations was borne by

2. Many groups are underrepresented in various occupations for reasons of taste, opportunity, or aptitude unrelated to discrimination. There is no basis for a presumption that but for past discrimination, * * * minorities * * * would supply [a percentage] of the nation's lawyers [proportionate to their representation in the general population.]

3. There is no evidence of which I am aware that a substantial number or proportion of minority-group law school graduates will seek in their professional careers to serve the special needs of their minority group rather than follow the normal patterns of professional advancement.

4. The "role model" argument is similarly *ad hoc* and conjectural. So long as a significant number of members of a minority group enter the legal profession and succeed in it (one of the Justices of the Supreme Court is black, after all), others will know that it is not closed to them. There is no basis for requiring proportional representation.

The reasons advanced for proportional representation are unimpressive. But more disturbing than the lack of solid intellectual foundations are the implications of the underrepresentation approach for the overall structure of society. The ultimate logic of underrepresentation is that the percentage of members of each minority racial and ethnic group in each desirable occupation, and in each level of achievement within the occupation, should be raised to equality with its percentage of the total population (either of the entire nation or, in some versions, of some region or local area). The proponents of proportional representation do not as yet urge adoption of the standard of perfect equality, but there seems to be no logical stopping point short of it within the structure of their argument. This is true despite their soothing assurance that affirmative action is required only in a period of transition to a society in which, all vestiges of discrimination having been eliminated by affirmative action, society can resume a policy of color-blindness. If, as seems more likely than not, occupational preferences and abilities are not randomly distributed across all racial and ethnic groups, then governmental intervention in the labor markets (and in the educational process insofar as it affects occupational choice and success) will have to continue forever if proportional equality in the desirable occupations is to be secured. Consistently implemented, this sort of intervention would, by profoundly distorting the allocation of

the German taxpaying public as a whole, rather than by university students, schoolchildren, and members of the working class, who are being asked in this country to subsidize certain racial minorities. But the more important difference is in the degree of felt guilt. If the United States had recently exterminated several millions of blacks, we might be willing to give several billion dollars to some African state that had been established as a refuge for perse- cuted blacks. Some people believe that the American treatment of the black has been comparable in its enormity to Hitler's treatment of the Jews; for them the analogy to German reparations to Israel may be a compelling one. To evaluate such a belief will require more careful studies along the lines of Fogel & Engerman, Time on the Cross: The Economics of American Negro Slavery (1974).

labor and by driving a wedge between individual merit and economic and professional success, greatly undermine the system of incentives on which a free society depends.

* * *

III. THE CONSTITUTIONAL ISSUE

A. *Previous Approaches*

Twenty-eight *amicus curiae* briefs were submitted to the Supreme Court in the *DeFunis* case,[a] and most of them, rather than provide the Court with additional information not available in the record of the case, discuss points of constitutional doctrine. Yet the variety of constitutional arguments in the multitude of briefs is not great. The briefs supporting DeFunis's position point to the undeniable fact that he was treated less favorably than he would have been if he had been a member of one of the four favored racial groups and argue from this fact that he was a victim of racial discrimination, an unconstitutional form of state action. The opposing briefs argue that racial discrimination is unlawful only when invidious and that DeFunis's treatment carried no implication that being a nonmember of one of the favored groups—*i.e.*, being a white—connotes a despised or inferior status.

Neither argument is persuasive in the form expressed. Discrimination against whites, who constitute the vast majority of our population and who never before (in this country) have, as a group, been subjected to discrimination, is not patently the same phenomenon as the sorts of discrimination involved in previous equal-protection cases involving members of racial or ethnic minorities, or women. But neither is it tenable to argue that discrimination is bad only when the circumstances of its adoption or expression connote invidiousness, exploitation, or hostility, or seek to place a stamp of inferiority on the victims of the discrimination. Suppose that New York City adopted an ordinance (supported by the Jewish members of the City Council) limiting the percentage of Jews who could be teachers in the New York City public school system, and the ordinance was based on a finding that Jews are so able that no merit-based principle of selection could keep them from dominating the school system, but that the resulting concentration of Jews in the public schools had exacerbated racial tensions and had, indeed, promoted anti-Semitism. It is difficult to believe that such an ordinance would or should be upheld against a constitutional challenge, albeit one could argue (though not, in my opinion, persuasively) that the ordinance was not "invidious," since it was premised not on the inferiority of the Jews but indeed on the reverse, and even that the ordinance was in the Jews' best interest.

A distinct argument for the constitutionality of discrimination in favor of minority groups has been made in a recent article by Professor Ely. He argues, along lines similar to those suggested earlier, that a

---

a. *DeFunis v. Odegaard,* 416 U.S. 312 (1974) (holding moot a challenge to the University of Washington Law School's special admissions program for Blacks, Chicanos, American Indians, and Filipinos).

policy of discrimination, favorable or unfavorable, might be adopted simply because the costs of individualized treatment were thought to exceed its benefits, but that when members of one racial group—such as the white majority of a state legislature—are appraising the costs and benefits of a proposed discrimination against another racial group the comparison is apt to be distorted by conscious or unconscious racial hostility.[37] Hence, he argues, discrimination against a racial minority should be suspect under the Fourteenth Amendment, but discrimination in favor of a minority should not be since it does not involve any danger of majority exploitation of a minority.

There are two fundamental objections to this argument. One—that it misconceives the nature of the political process—I defer for the moment. The other is that it provides a mode of justifying discrimination against racial minorities. Professor Ely accepts the legitimacy of comparing the costs of discriminating against the members of a racial or ethnic minority with the benefits from thereby avoiding the need to make individual distinctions. He only wants assurance that the balance will be accurately struck. He is suspicious that the majority will fail to take adequate account of the costs, or will exaggerate the benefits, of the discriminatory measure, but this suspicion only warrants that the reviewing court satisfy itself that the legislature has in fact assessed the costs and benefits of the discrimination accurately. Suppose the Post Office were able to demonstrate convincingly that blacks had, on average, inferior aptitudes to whites for supervisory positions, that the costs to the postal system of inadequate supervisors were very great, and that the costs of conducting the inquiries necessary to ascertain whether an individual black had the requisite aptitudes were also great in relation to the probability of discovering qualified blacks. It would seem to follow from Ely's analysis that the Post Office could adopt a rule barring blacks from supervisory positions. By condemning only inefficient discriminations, Ely reduces the scope of the Equal Protection Clause to triviality, if I am correct in arguing that most discrimination in contemporary society is caused by the costs of information rather than by irrationality, exploitation, or the suppression of competition.

B. Toward an Objective Constitutional Principle

In order to determine the constitutionality of racially preferential admissions policies, it is first necessary to derive from the Equal Protection Clause some rule, or principle, or standard for applying the constitutional formula (that no state may "deny to any person within its jurisdiction the equal protection of the laws") to racial discrimination. *   *   *

*   *   *

37. Ely, [*The Constitutionality of Reverse Racial Discrimination,* 41 U.Chi.L. Rev. 723,] 729, 732–33 (1974).

[The task] is to derive from the specific purposes of the constitutional framers a rule that, while sufficiently general to avoid constant recourse to the amendment process, is sufficiently precise and objective to limit a judge's exercise of personal whim and preference. The rule I derive on this basis is that the distribution of benefits and costs by government on racial or ethnic grounds is impermissible. Even though it is frequently efficient to sort people by race or ethnic origin, because racial or ethnic identity may be a good proxy for functional classifications, efficiency is rejected as a basis for governmental action in this context. The government is required to incur the additional costs of determining the individual applicant's fitness to hold a particular job, or patronize a particular facility, or be admitted to one of its educational institutions. To permit discrimination to be justified on efficiency grounds, as would Professor Ely, would not only thwart the purpose of the Equal Protection Clause by allowing much, perhaps most, discrimination to continue, but it would give the judges the power to pick and choose among discriminatory measures on the basis of personal values, for the weighing of the relevant costs and benefits would of necessity be largely subjective.

* * *

It remains to consider whether an exception to the rule forbidding discrimination on racial or ethnic grounds can be recognized where the discrimination can be said to be in favor of a racial or ethnic minority, and the race discriminated against is the white race. The exception is inadmissible, because it requires the court not only to consider whether there is discrimination but to decide whether the discrimination harms or hurts a particular racial group, and to weigh the competing claims of different racial groups, and the additional inquiries rob the principle of its precision and objectivity. The Court had no good evidence before it in the *Brown* case that segregated education in fact harmed blacks. The questions critical to the point were not even asked: Would blacks have fared better under a system of no public education (assuming that whites would prefer such a system to integrated public education)? Under a system where students were sorted by IQ? By family income? In later cases the Court stopped asking whether segregation actually hurt the blacks. (Today, of course, some blacks favor segregation.) The antidiscrimination principle is not only more objective, but more compelling, when it is divorced from empirical inquiries into the effects of particular forms of discrimination on the affected groups. The necessary inquiries are intractable and would leave the field open to slippery conjecture. * * * [A] plausible argument could be made that various forms of discrimination nominally against Jews might actually advance the interests of the Jews as a whole, for example by reducing their prominence and visibility in certain areas where the conspicuousness of the Jews may stimulate anti-Semitism. Similar arguments could be made for various forms of conceivably well-intentioned discrimination against blacks (such as "benign" housing quotas, or limitations on the migration of blacks from southern to northern states). The Supreme

Court would reject such arguments, but not because they are substantially less compelling than the arguments it accepts when it upholds the constitutionality of governmental action. The arguments about the proper characterization of discrimination nominally in favor of racial minorities have a similar elusiveness. Is the position of the whites in this country so unassailable that they cannot be harmed by racial quotas? Or is the impact of such quotas likely to be concentrated on particular, and perhaps vulnerable, subgroups within the white majority? Do racial quotas actually help the minorities intended to be benefited, or harm them by impairing their self-esteem or legitimating stereotypical thinking about race? Are whites entitled to claim minority status when they are a minority within the political subdivision that enacted the measure discriminating against whites? If so, then by parity of reasoning would blacks lack standing to complain about an ordinance discriminating against them enacted by Newark, New Jersey, or Washington, D.C., or other cities in which blacks are a majority of the population eligible to vote? If these are litigable issues, we do not have a constitutional principle but merely a directive that the judges uphold those forms of racial and ethnic discrimination which accord with their personal values.

LAURENCE H. TRIBE, "IN WHAT VISION OF THE CONSTITUTION MUST THE LAW BE COLOR–BLIND?"

20 John Marshall L.Rev. 201 (1986).

* * * [M]y focus today will be on the affirmative action controversy as a window into the constitutional and judicial vision—the philosophy of constitutional meaning and judicial role—of those who deem race-specific preferences for minorities to be presumptively invalid, subject only to a narrow exception for judicial relief to identified victims of proven race discrimination. I will call these the "race neutralists." My question is: Why do the race neutralists set themselves against the view, expressed by Justice Blackmun in his separate *Bakke* opinion, that "to get beyond racism, we must first take account of race . . . [a]nd . . . to treat some persons equally, we must . . . treat them differently." [7] In other words, what constitutional sources or theories can the race neutralists invoke?

To begin with, the race neutralists might invoke the notion that *all* racial classifications, the supposedly benign no less than the overtly malign, are "inherently suspect." Now that broad notion itself has a somewhat suspect source: it was given its first explicit articulation in the justly infamous 1944 decision—*Korematsu v. United States* [8]—upholding our government's forced relocation of Japanese–American citizens to concentration camps. Before announcing its result in *Koremat-*

---

7. Regents of Univ. of Cal. v. Bakke, 438 U.S. 265, 407 (1978) (Blackmun, J., separate opinion).

8. 323 U.S. 214 (1944).

su, the Supreme Court proclaimed that *"all* legal restrictions which curtail the civil rights of a single racial group are immediately suspect. . . . Courts must subject them to the most rigid scrutiny." [9]   It is noteworthy that the Court was speaking there of restricting "civil rights," and *not* of allocating state-created opportunities for individual advancement.   More important still, even in *Korematsu* the Supreme Court held that the *point* of strict scrutiny for racial classifications is to detect whether they reflect "[p]ressing public necessity" or merely "racial antagonism." [10]   Racial antagonism, of course, is hardly the motive of today's minority set-aside programs.

Seeking a sounder source than *Korematsu,* the race neutralists often recur to the first Justice Harlan's dissent in *Plessy v. Ferguson.*[11] Indeed, Solicitor General Charles Fried's argument in *Wygant v. Jackson Board of Education* leans heavily on *Plessy.*[12]   The Solicitor General says: "Whether a Plessy is ejected from a railroad coach because he is one-eighth black or laid-off because he is seven-eighths white, the concrete wrong to him is much the same." [13]   That may seem counterintuitive, however.   For those "wrongs" are *not* self-evidently the same: the actual wrong to Mr. Plessy was a denigration of his moral worth, a perpetuation of slavery, and a reinforcement of his political exclusion; none of this, certainly, can be said of the hypothesized converse harm. Nonetheless, the race neutralists always offer the obligatory quotation from Justice Harlan: "Our Constitution is color-blind."   Those who quote the elder Justice Harlan with such abandon should consider the context of the preceding five sentences in that justly famous dissent:

> The white race deems itself to be the dominant race in this country. *And so it is,* in prestige, in achievements, in education, in wealth and in power.   So, I doubt not, it will continue to be for all time, if it remains true to its great heritage and holds fast to the principles of constitutional liberty.   But in view of the Constitution, in the eye of the law, there is in this country no superior, dominant, ruling class of citizens.   There is no caste here.   Our Constitution is colorblind. . . .[15]

Perhaps it is anachronistic and even unfair to stress too heavily the manifest racism in Justice Harlan's full statement.   But even for this late nineteenth-century proponent of white dominance, the color-blind ideal, it turns out, was only shorthand for the concept that the Fourteenth Amendment prevents our law from enshrining and perpetuating white supremacy.   To say that this particular vice is shared, automatically or presumptively, by race-specific minority set-asides strikes many as far-fetched.

9. *Id.* at 216 (emphasis added).

10. *Id.*

11. 163 U.S. 537 (1896).

12. See Brief of the United States as Amicus Curiae Supporting Petitioners, Wy-

gant v. Jackson Bd. of Educ., 106 S.Ct. 1842 (1986).

13. *Id.* at 21.

15. [163 U.S. at 559 (Harlan, J., dissenting) (emphasis added).]

So the question remains unanswered: *Why* would anyone equate laying off a white Plessy to make room for a black worker, and ejecting a black Plessy from a railroad coach to maintain white supremacy?

The race neutralists' reply to that question sometimes involves a reference to the "original intention" of the Fourteenth Amendment's Framers.[17] But that argument faces an enormous stumbling block. I am not referring to the often-noted historical fact that those same Framers created a Freedman's Bureau to assist former slaves.[18] As the Solicitor General has pointed out, those pieces of nineteenth century legislation were at least partially, if not exclusively, designed to assist *actual victims* of slavery.[19] I am referring to the fact that we know, with as much certainty as such matters ever permit, that the Framers of the Fourteenth Amendment did not think "equal protection of the laws" made *all* racial distinctions in law unconstitutional; they did not intend, for example, to outlaw racially segregated public schools.[20] It involves quite a stretch, then, to take their original intentions as an argument that all race-specific distinctions, even those designed to facilitate practical equality, are either automatically or presumptively unconstitutional.

The necessary response of the race neutralists is, of course, that the Supreme Court was right in *Brown v. Board of Education*—and that the 1954 Court saw the "original intention" more clearly than its 1896 predecessor, when *Brown* rightly held that *all* official distinctions by race are presumptively unconstitutional. But *did* it so hold? That is only the most sweeping and "activist" of at least several equally plausible readings of *Brown*. I will focus upon two such readings, identified as "*Brown* –A" and "*Brown* –B."

Brown –A says that, more than a century after the Civil War, *all* race distinctions must now be banned as inherently "unequal;" in light of modern and more enlightened "values," courts must create a general Fourteenth Amendment right never to be disadvantaged by law on account of one's race, even if this *is* a right the Fourteenth Amendment's authors would not have endorsed.

Brown –B says the Fourteenth Amendment's command of "equal protection of the laws" was *always* intended, at its most basic level, to

17. *E.g.*, Reynolds, *Individualism v. Group Rights: The Legacy of Brown*, 93 Yale L.J. 995, 997 (1984) ("History faithfully records that the purpose of the [Thirteenth, Fourteenth and Fifteenth] Amendments was to end forever a system which determined legal rights, measured status, and allocated opportunities on the basis of race, and to erect in its place a regime of race neutrality."). *Compare* Bork, *Original Intent and the Constitution*, 7 Humanities 22 (1986) *with* Tribe, *The Holy Grail of Original Intent, id.* at 23.

18. *See* Schnapper, *Affirmative Action and the Legislative History of the Four-*

teenth Amendment, 71 Va.L.Rev. 753, 761, 772–73 (1985) (in practice, under the 1865 Act, most of the Bureau's programs applied only to black freedmen; in addition, the 1866 Act contained explicitly race-conscious measures).

19. Brief of the United States as Amicus Curiae Supporting Petitioners at 14–15, Wygant v. Jackson Bd. of Educ., 106 S.Ct. 1842 (1986).

20. *See* Bickel, *The Original Understanding and the Segregation Decision*, 69 Harv.L.Rev. 1, 56 (1955).

ban the use of law to subjugate a racial group; we now see, as the 1896 Court did not, that racial segregation by law in public schools and other public facilities in fact subjugated blacks, despite its appearance of symmetry and equality, because it stood for white supremacy and therefore denied the minority "equal protection." Thus we are creating no *new* basic right the Fourteenth Amendment's authors would have rejected; it is not the law that has changed but only our relevant perceptions and understandings.

On the face of it, *Brown* –B seems a more modest, less radical and less strained interpretation than *Brown* –A. Especially when a national, state or local representative body adopts an affirmative action program fully consistent with *Brown* –B, striking that program down as a violation of *Brown* –A seems hard to square with judicial deference to political majorities absent a textually or historically clear constitutional prohibition.

The difficulty deepens when instrumental reasons are added to support the race-neutral position: arguments that racism and race resentments will be exacerbated, and racial stereotypes perpetuated, unless we demand that government be race-blind are properly addressed to political bodies. For if government's actions violate no constitutional command, why are not arguments about their long-term effects best left to the political process?

I can think of only one constitutional command that the race neutralists might invoke to fill this gap and justify their choice of *Brown* –A: a command that law and government must not restrict *any* innocent individual's "liberty," broadly enough defined to include job opportunities and the like, even when such a restriction is justified by a desire to protect others who are equally innocent. And to deprive someone of a benefit, or to impose a burden, merely because of that person's race (and not because of what that specific individual did wrong) violates this command no less when the deprived individual is white than when she is black. But before anyone gravitates to this view, let me make this observation: when the government exercises its power to single out wholly innocent individuals by taking their "private property . . . for public use," the race neutralists do not object that only the *guilty* should ever have to make such focused sacrifices. Indeed, they often *endorse* such property takings outside the affirmative action context—so long as the "innocents" who have been required to make special sacrifices receive "just compensation" for their losses. In assessing the constitutionality and wisdom of affirmative action plans that impose similarly concrete and personalized costs on "innocent" white individuals—losses of seniority, for example—facing questions of just compensation would offer the race neutralists a more moderate alternative to the extremism of *Brown* –A.

So I end with a genuine puzzle: the race neutralists do not in fact put themselves forward, in other respects, as constitutional radicals. First, they purport to respect the historical intentions of the Framers, insofar as those intentions are knowable. Second, they regard basic constitutional norms as alterable only by constitutional amendment, and not by act of judicial improvization. Third, they advocate deference to political majorities when a constitutional prohibition is at best arguable rather than clear. And fourth, they are reluctant to have courts fashion new rights by generalizing, even with the help of the Ninth Amendment, beyond the Constitution's text. Yet on all four of these dimensions, the race neutralists—the constitutional opponents of affirmative action—seem to look the other way.

What has yet to be produced, then, is a cogent explanation of *why* judicial modesty and constitutional strict construction should be abandoned when the subject is affirmative action for racial minorities.

MORRIS B. ABRAM *, AFFIRMATIVE ACTION: FAIR SHAKERS AND SOCIAL ENGINEERS
99 Harv.L.Rev. 1312, 1312–23 (1986).

I. INTRODUCTION

* * *

Between the mid–1940s and the mid–1960s, the civil rights movement grew into a broad coalition united by moral principle and a shared vision of an American society without racial discrimination but with equal opportunity for all. The overarching political goal of this movement was equality—an equality to be reached by the elimination of discriminatory barriers that denied the individual the opportunity to exercise his franchise effectively, to compete for housing and employment, and to use public accommodations. Government, civil rights advocates agreed, was responsible for ensuring that each individual had access to all spheres of public activity—social, economic, and political—regardless of race, sex, or ethnic origin. Because this original vision of the civil rights movement was concerned with equality of *opportunity* and a fair shake for individuals, I will label its advocates "fair shakers." [2]

The fair shakers were soon challenged, however, by a radically different vision of civil rights. During the late 1960s, the civil rights community began to splinter and, certainly by the mid–1970s, much of its leadership had become preoccupied with equality of *results*. Those who focused on this type of equality attributed socioeconomic or political inequalities between minorities and whites, men and women, the disabled and the unimpaired, to discrimination—past and present. Absent discrimination, these result-oriented leaders claimed, all groups would be represented in the institutions and occupations of society roughly in proportion to their representation in the population. These leaders continue to believe that the only way to measure equality is in terms of such representation, and that it is the government's role to

* Former partner, Paul, Weiss, Rifkind, Wharton & Garrison; presently United States Ambassador to the European Office of the United Nations.

2. I am indebted to Professor James Blumstein of the Vanderbilt University School of Law for suggesting this term.

bring about proportional representation in short order. Because this new vision of the civil rights movement requires the attainment of predetermined ends, rather than the abolition of barriers to fair participation, I will call its adherents "social engineers."

*   *   *

II. FAIR SHAKERS AND SOCIAL ENGINEERS

The fair shake principle is part of a long and respected American legal tradition. It was the force underlying the antislavery amendments to the Constitution, the series of laws passed in the wake of the Civil War that afforded protection of contract and property rights, and the guarantees of equality of opportunity in voting, employment, use of public accommodations, and housing in the mid–1960s. It was in accord with fair shake principles that Congress enacted the Voting Rights Act of 1965 to stymie the effort of states such as Georgia to devalue the minority franchise—a form of racial preference for whites.

*   *   *

Because groups—black, white, Hispanic, male, and female—do not necessarily have the same distribution of, among other characteristics, skills, interest, motivation, and age, a fair shake system may not produce proportional representation across occupations and professions, and certainly not at any given time. This uneven distribution, however, is not necessarily the result of discrimination. Thomas Sowell has shown through comparative studies of ethnic group performance that discrimination alone cannot explain these ethnic groups' varying levels of achievement. Groups such as the Japanese, Chinese, and West Indian blacks have fared very well in American society despite racial bias against these groups.[12]

Moreover, although it is true that concern for qualifications has sometimes masked a purposeful intent to exclude individuals on the basis of race or other invidious criteria, the mere fact that some meritocratic devices have the result of excluding proportionally higher numbers of minorities does not in itself demonstrate that minorities are not getting a fair shake. And the fair shake principle, unlike the norm of proportional representation, is perfectly consistent with our meritocratic view of the relevant differences between individuals—a view through which our society rewards the individual for attainment and avoids patronage and spoils systems.

Yet many of those who opposed the use of social engineering to perpetuate segregation now depart from the fair shake model and actively advocate social engineering to achieve proportional representation. They now insist on a presumption that unequal results are due to intentional discrimination. For them, the franchise is not a right to participate equally in the electoral process but a right to the election of a "fair share" of minority representatives. Although no civil rights

---

12. See T. Sowell, [The Economics and Politics of Race: An International Perspective (1983)].

leader has dared to suggest weighted ballots for blacks, it is now part of civil rights gospel that blacks must not only vote but that we must draw district lines to ensure that blacks are elected. To my mind, these "piece-of-the-action" concerns depart from the civil rights movement's earlier advocacy of fair participation and return us to the spoils system that the early movement worked so hard to displace.

But today's social engineers, dissatisfied with the results of the fair shake model, invoke a new conception of justice. In their view, justice is less an individual's claim to equality before the law—an idea at the heart of our liberal tradition—than a particular distribution of social, economic, and political power among groups. This new conception of justice necessarily repudiates the ideal of the rule of law—a law that "would treat people equally, but . . . not seek to make them equal." [17] And to achieve this newly announced goal of group justice, the social engineers proclaim that it is necessary to abandon color-blindness.

* * *

These social engineers call their plan for allocating social goods by race "affirmative action." But the term as they use it departs radically from the original intent of affirmative action—to give minorities a fair shake. Executive Order 11,246, for example, far from calling the merit system into question, attempted only to eliminate the institutional and informational barriers that stand in the way of the minority individual's ability to compete *equally* with others for jobs and promotions. * * *

* * *

The social engineers' approach to affirmative action is without support in our Constitution and civil rights laws. These revisionists would have us read the equal protection clause of the Constitution and the racially neutral language of civil rights legislation so as to grant preferences for groups that they designate as "subjugated." They advance this argument in the face of the plain English of the text and a legislative history that contradicts their contentions. As Justice Douglas has observed:

> The Equal Protection Clause commands the elimination of racial barriers, not their creation in order to satisfy our theory as to how society ought to be organized. . . . So far as race is concerned, *any* state-sponsored preference to one race over another . . . is in my view "invidious" and violative of the Equal Protection Clause.[25]

And Professor Alexander Bickel agreed:

> The lesson of the great decisions of the Supreme Court and the lesson of contemporary history have been the same for at least a generation: discrimination on the basis of race is illegal, immoral, unconstitutional, inherently wrong, and destructive of democratic society. . . . Hav-

17. D. Bell, *Liberalism in the Postindustrial Society,* in The Winding Passage: Essays and Sociological Journeys 1960–1980, at 228, 230–231 (1980) (discussing Hayek).

25. DeFunis v. Odegaard, 416 U.S. 312, 342 (1972) (Douglas, J., dissenting) (emphasis added).

ing found support in the Constitution for equality, [proponents of racial preferences] now claim support for inequality under the same Constitution.[26]

Without doing violence to the principles of equality before the law and neutral decisionmaking, we simply cannot interpret our laws to support both color-blindness for some citizens and color-consciousness for others.

* * *

* * * The social engineers' vision of affirmative action is, for all intents and purposes, a quota system. Though they usually repudiate the idea of "quotas" and insist on characterizing their preferred remedies as "goals and timetables," the effects of numerous enforcement actions and lawsuits brought by government agencies and civil rights groups belie the social engineers' characterization. These actions have effectively transformed goals into quotas by putting the burden on the employer to rebut the presumption of discrimination if the employer fails to meet its minority hiring goals. Failure to meet the goals—even if established solely by reference to population proportionality—raises a presumption of discrimination that the hapless employer can only overturn after great effort, expense, and public embarrassment.

Moreover, even beyond the practical effects of legal presumptions, there is ultimately little theoretical difference between the goals and timetables the social engineers favor, and the quotas they purport to eschew. For to what end are these goals and timetables established if not to be achieved? And what is their basis unless it be that justice requires the allocation of social goods according to race?

* * *

The social engineers' approach also fails to confront the problem of *who decides* what groups are sufficiently disadvantaged to deserve special treatment. They offer no mechanism for neutral decisionmaking on this critical issue. America is a highly pluralistic and heterogeneous society that has had to expand continuously in order to accommodate different elements; many discrete groups have suffered discrimination here. Consequently, a major problem with addressing discrimination through race-conscious laws is the balancing of historical experiences. How and by whom shall the varying grievances of different groups be weighed and judged in order to decide what varying levels of compensation society should pay?

In the absence of any neutral decisionmaking mechanisms, the attempt to end discrimination through color-conscious remedies must inevitably degenerate into a crude political struggle between groups seeking favored status. Once we have abandoned the principles of fair procedure, equal opportunity, and individual rights in favor of the advancement of a particular group, we have opened wide the door to future abuses of all kinds. * * *

26. A. Bickel, The Morality of Consent 133 (1975).

* * *

Further, the social engineers invite us to view people as statistics; they submerge personality, effort, and character under the blanket concerns of race, sex and ethnicity. In an already divided society, this approach results in a new set of classifications: those who got where they are by merit; those who were leveraged into position by race or gender preferences; those who do not owe their position to such engineering but are viewed as the recipients of preferences by others (and themselves) and are thus stigmatized; and finally those who originally earned their position without any favoritism but were displaced solely because of race, gender or ethnicity. In such a divided system, no one really wins.

Indeed, the social engineers' approach exacerbates divisions within society by implicitly assuming that white males—even the millions who have never finished high school—are the undeserving beneficiaries of special privileges at the expense of all others. * * *

Perhaps the most ironic weakness of the social engineers' redistributive approach is that it fails to help those particular members of disadvantaged groups who are most in need of assistance. Blanket orders which blindly benefit groups defined by race, sex or ethnicity—especially when many members of such groups are prospering nicely—are an extremely crude and costly solution for social problems. While civil rights lobbyists frequently bolster their charge of continuing discrimination by pointing to the existence of the black underclass, many of their proposals can hardly have the effect of helping the millions of ghetto teenagers who lack the most basic entry level skills.

RANDALL KENNEDY, PERSUASION AND DISTRUST: A COMMENT ON THE AFFIRMATIVE ACTION DEBATE

99 Harv.L.Rev. 1327, 1329–1334 (1986).

I. THE EFFICACY AND LAWFULNESS OF AFFIRMATIVE ACTION

A. The Case for Affirmative Action

Affirmative action has strikingly benefitted blacks as a group and the nation as a whole. It has enabled blacks to attain occupational and educational advancement in numbers and at a pace that would otherwise have been impossible. These breakthroughs engender self-perpetuating benefits: the accumulation of valuable experience, the expansion of a professional class able to pass its material advantages and elevated aspirations to subsequent generations, the eradication of debilitating stereotypes, and the inclusion of black participants in the making of consequential decisions affecting black interests. Without affirmative action, continued access for black applicants to college and professional education would be drastically narrowed. To insist, for example, upon the total exclusion of racial factors in admission decisions, especially at elite institutions, would mean classes of college, professional and graduate students that are virtually devoid of Negro representation.

Furthermore, the benefits of affirmative action redound not only to blacks but to the nation as a whole. For example, the virtual absence of black police even in overwhelmingly black areas helped spark the ghetto rebellions of the 1960s. The integration of police forces through strong affirmative action measures has often led to better relations between minority communities and the police, a result that improves public safety for all. Positive externalities have accompanied affirmative action programs in other contexts as well, most importantly by teaching whites that blacks, too, are capable of handling responsibility, dispensing knowledge, and applying valued skills.

B. The Claim That Affirmative Action Harms Blacks

In the face of arguments in favor of affirmative action, opponents of the policy frequently reply that it actually harms its ostensible beneficiaries. Various interrelated claims undergird the argument that affirmative action is detrimental to the Negro. The most weighty claim is that preferential treatment exacerbates racial resentments, entrenches racial divisiveness, and thereby undermines the consensus necessary for effective reform. The problem with this view is that intense white resentment has accompanied every effort to undo racial subordination no matter how careful the attempt to anticipate and mollify the reaction. The Supreme Court, for example, tried mightily to preempt white resistance to school desegregation by directing that it be implemented with "all deliberate speed." This attempt, however, to defuse white resistance may well have caused the opposite effect and, in any event, doomed from the outset the constitutional rights of a generation of black school children. Given the apparent inevitability of white resistance and the uncertain efficacy of containment, proponents of racial justice should be wary of allowing fear of white backlash to limit the range of reforms pursued. This admonition is particularly appropriate with respect to affirmative action insofar as it creates vital opportunities the value of which likely outweigh their cost in social friction. A second part of the argument that affirmative action hurts blacks is the claim that it stigmatizes them by implying that they simply cannot compete on an equal basis with whites. Moreover, the pall cast by preferential treatment is feared to be pervasive, hovering over blacks who have attained positions without the aid of affirmative action as well as over those who have been accorded preferential treatment. I do not doubt that affirmative action causes some stigmatizing effect. It is unrealistic to think, however, that affirmative action causes most white disparagement of the abilities of blacks.[13]   Such

---

13. The stigma problem, moreover, is mainly an affliction besetting elite occupations. There are a great many jobs, generally those requiring relatively little specialized training, to which the problem of stigma is largely irrelevant. After all, when an occupation requires no more than on-the-job training, there is little reason to suspect that blacks who have undergone such training are any less qualified than their white counterparts.

disparagement, buttressed for decades by the rigid exclusion of blacks from educational and employment opportunities, is precisely what engendered the explosive crisis to which affirmative action is a response. Although it is widely assumed that "qualified" blacks are now in great demand, with virtually unlimited possibilities for recognition, blacks continue to encounter prejudice that ignores or minimizes their talent. In the end, the uncertain extent to which affirmative action diminishes the accomplishments of blacks must be balanced against the stigmatization that occurs when blacks are virtually absent from important institutions in the society. The presence of blacks across the broad spectrum of institutional settings upsets conventional stereotypes about the place of the Negro and acculturates the public to the idea that blacks can and must participate in all areas of our national life. This positive result of affirmative action outweighs any stigma that the policy causes.

A third part of the argument against affirmative action is the claim that it saps the internal morale of blacks. It renders them vulnerable to a dispiriting anxiety that they have not truly earned whatever positions or honors they have attained. Moreover, it causes some blacks to lower their own expectations of themselves. Having grown accustomed to the extra boost provided by preferential treatment, some blacks simply do not try as hard as they otherwise would. There is considerable power to this claim; unaided accomplishment does give rise to a special pride felt by both the individual achiever and her community. But the suggestion that affirmative action plays a major role in undermining the internal morale of the black community is erroneous.

Although I am unaware of any systematic evidence on the self-image of beneficiaries of affirmative action, my own strong impression is that black beneficiaries do not see their attainments as tainted or undeserved—and for good reason. First, they correctly view affirmative action as rather modest compensation for the long period of racial subordination suffered by blacks as a group. Thus they do not feel that they have been merely *given* a preference; rather, they see affirmative discrimination as a form of social justice. Second, and more importantly, many black beneficiaries of affirmative action view claims of meritocracy with skepticism. They recognize that in many instances the objection that affirmative action represents a deviation from meritocratic standards is little more than disappointed nostalgia for a golden age that never really existed. Overt exclusion of blacks from public and private institutions of education and employment was one massive affront to meritocratic pretensions. Moreover, a longstanding and pervasive feature of our society is the importance of a wide range of nonobjective, nonmeritocratic factors influencing the distribution of opportunity. The significance of personal associations and informal networks is what gives durability and resonance to the adage, "It's not *what* you know, it's *who* you know." * * *

Finally, and most importantly, many beneficiaries of affirmative action recognize the thoroughly political—which is to say contestable—nature of "merit"; they realize that it is a malleable concept, determined not by immanent, preexisting standards but rather by the perceived needs of society. Inasmuch as the elevation of blacks addresses pressing social needs, they rightly insist that considering a black's race as part of the bundle of traits that constitute "merit" is entirely appropriate.

A final and related objection to affirmative action is that it frequently aids those blacks who need it least and who can least plausibly claim to suffer the vestiges of past discrimination—the offspring of black middle-class parents seeking preferential treatment in admission to elite universities and black entrepreneurs seeking guaranteed set-asides for minority contractors on projects supported by the federal government. This objection too is unpersuasive. First, it ignores the large extent to which affirmative action has pried open opportunities for blue-collar black workers. Second, it assumes that affirmative action should be provided only to the most deprived strata of the black community or to those who can best document their victimization. In many circumstances, however, affirmative action has developed from the premise that special aid should be given to strategically important sectors of the black community—for example, those with the threshold ability to integrate the professions. Third, although affirmative action has primarily benefitted the black middle class, that is no reason to condemn preferential treatment. All that fact indicates is the necessity for additional social intervention to address unmet needs in those sectors of the black community left untouched by affirmative action. One thing that proponents of affirmative action have neglected to emphasize strongly enough is that affirmative discrimination is but part—indeed a rather small part—of the needed response to the appalling crisis besetting black communities. What is so remarkable—and ominous—about the affirmative action debate is that so modest a reform calls forth such powerful resistance.

KATHLEEN M. SULLIVAN, SINS OF DISCRIMINATION: LAST TERM'S AFFIRMATIVE ACTION CASES

100 Harv.L.Rev. 78, 78–80, 91–97 (1986).

Few issues are more starkly divisive in our politics than affirmative action: its opponents wage an all-out war on preferential treatment for blacks, invoking a norm of "color-blindness"; its advocates insist that the norm of equality requires increased black representation in our social institutions now. Yet every time a showdown over the issue has seemed inevitable in the Supreme Court, both sides have been left still standing when the shooting has stopped. Some affirmative action measures have been voted up and some down, but through it all, the Supreme Court has permitted no decisive victory to either side, nor dealt either side a decisive defeat.

Last Term's affirmative action cases were no different. The Court struck down one workplace affirmative action plan[1] and upheld two others.[2] And as the dust settled over the three cases, once again both sides claimed to have won.[3]

* * *

Linking the three cases was the opposition to each plan expressed by the Solicitor General's office, which had supported affirmative action plans in cases arising during previous administrations. In each case, the brief for the United States argued that the challenged affirmative action was invalid because it preferred individuals who were not proven "victims" of past discrimination. The Court rejected this argument, finding "victim"-specificity neither a constitutional limitation on the affirmative action governments may devise,[17] nor a statutory limitation on the affirmative action courts adjudicating title VII lawsuits may order.[18]

This Comment argues that the Court has approved affirmative action only as precise penance for the specific sins of racism a government, union, or employer has committed in the past. Not surprisingly, this approach has invited claims, such as the Solicitor General's last Term, that nonsinners—white workers "innocent" of their bosses' or union leadership's past discrimination—should not pay for "the sins of others of their own race,"[19] nor should nonvictims benefit from their sacrifice. The Court has never answered these claims from within a sin-based paradigm, as it might have either by viewing the category of black "victims" of past discrimination expansively, or by discounting claims of white "innocence." But neither has the Court ever broken

---

1. Wygant v. Jackson Bd. of Educ., 106 S.Ct. 1842, 1846 (1986).

2. Local 28, Sheet Metal Workers' Int'l Ass'n v. Equal Employment Opportunity Commission, 106 S.Ct. 3019, 3031 (1986); Local No. 93, Int's Ass'n of Firefighters v. City of Cleveland, 106 S.Ct. 3063, 3072 (1986).

3. Although *Wygant* struck down an affirmative action plan, civil rights advocates claimed that the case broadly " 'approved the use of affirmative action goals.' " N.Y. Times, May 20, 1986, at A20, col. 4 (quoting attorney Barry Goldstein of the NAACP Legal Defense and Education Fund). And although *Sheet Metal Workers* and *Firefighters* upheld affirmative action plans, the Solicitor General, who had filed briefs in both cases urging that the plans be struck down, claimed a limited victory nonetheless: " 'We have said that race-conscious remedies which are not victim-specific are never permissible,' [Solicitor General] Fried explained. 'The Court has

said: "Not never, but hardly ever." ' " N.Y. Times, July 3, 1986, at B9, col. I.

17. *See Wygant,* 106 S.Ct. at 1853 (O'Connor, J., concurring in part and concurring in the judgment) (interpreting the Court to have "agreed that a[n affirmative action] plan need not be limited to remedying of specific instances of identified discrimination" in order to be constitutional).

18. *See Sheet Metal Workers,* 106 S.Ct. at 3054 (plurality opinion) ("[S]ix members of the Court agree that a district court may, in appropriate circumstances, order preferential relief benefitting individuals who are not the actual victims of discrimination as a remedy for violations of Title VII. . . ."); *Firefighters,* 106 S.Ct. at 3072.

19. Fullilove v. Klutznick, 448 U.S. 448, 530 n. 12 (1980) (Stewart, J., dissenting), *quoted in* Brief for the United States as Amicus Curiae Supporting Petitioners at 27, *Wygant* (No. 84–1340).

out of sin-based rationales to elaborate a paradigm that would look forward rather than back, justifying affirmative action as the architecture of a racially integrated future.

III. The Problem With Sin

Casting affirmative action as penance for particular sins of discrimination, as the Court has done, has appeal at first glance. Limiting affirmative action to those who have specifically wronged blacks or other racial minorities in the past steers neatly between two courses: that all must pay or none. It rejects any notion that the original sin of American slavery so taints everyone in our current society that no defense to affirmative action could ever be raised. But it likewise rejects the notion that all must be equally absolved. Only some—those who have themselves been guilty of race discrimination—may be permitted the *mea culpa* of voluntary affirmative action, or be prescribed such measures as penance by a court.

Visiting affirmative duties to integrate only upon past wrongdoers also makes racial preferences seem more like corrective or retributive justice than like social engineering. It thus helps to rebut charges that racial balancing has become an end in itself. If just any employer were free to become an avenging angel, using affirmative action to right a diffuse and generalized history of racism in society at large, the racial composition resulting in that employer's workplace might appear arbitrary. But if the employer discriminated in the past, its extension of preferential treatment to blacks now can be understood as simply creating a racial balance that might have existed anyway, but for the discrimination.

Making sins of past discrimination the justification for affirmative action, however, dooms affirmative action to further challenge even while legitimating it. As a practical matter, it subjects affirmative action plans to potentially protracted litigation over the "factual predicate" for adopting them: how much past discrimination is enough? And having to ask that question may deter implementation of voluntary affirmative action at all. To admit guilt for past discrimination is against employers' and unions' self-interest, and indeed, may invite race discrimination lawsuits by nonwhites; the Court recognized as much last Term in declining to require that an employer or union adopting affirmative action make "formal findings" of its own past discrimination.[96] Even without formal findings, however, the task of self-judgment and self-condemnation in *any* form casts a chill over efforts to implement affirmative action voluntarily.

More fundamentally, viewing affirmative action as penance for past discrimination invites claims that the focus on that discrimination should be sharper. True, viewing affirmative action that way saves it from the charge that it aims only at racially balanced *results* by making

---

96. [*Wygant,* 106 S.Ct.] at 1863 (Marshall, J., joined by Brennan & Blackmun, JJ., dissenting); *see id.* at 1853 (O'Connor, J., concurring in part and concurring in the judgment) * * *.

it seem instead a matter of corrective or retributive justice, compensating for or punishing earlier racial wrongs. But because corrective justice focuses on victims, and retributive justice on wrongdoers, predicating affirmative action on past sins of discrimination invites claims that neither nonvictims should benefit, nor nonsinners pay. In making such claims last Term, therefore, the Solicitor General's office was in a sense just taking the Court at its word.

The Solicitor General's argument that nonvictims should not benefit from affirmative action was one of sweeping breadth. It amounted to an all-out assault on goals and timetables for the inclusion of nonwhites—whether imposed by a court in a title VII action or adopted voluntarily. For under such goals and timetables, it is nearly always the case that nonwhites against whom a government, employer, or union has not directly discriminated may gain entry or promotion ahead of otherwise better or comparably situated whites. Under the Solicitor General's approach, however, such benefits would be forbidden, and only specific "victims" permitted to displace whites.

The Court rejected that argument last Term without meeting it head-on. It might have done so by adhering to a model of corrective justice while broadening the concept of who has been "victimized" by past discrimination, a solution often urged by defenders of affirmative action. It might have held that because American racism has left blacks an underclass, still systematically disadvantaged as a group compared with whites, no black is not a "victim" of past discrimination. Under such an approach, all blacks are appropriate beneficiaries of affirmative action's "compensation." No opinion last Term, however, chose such a route.[98]

Instead, the Court rejected the "victims-only" argument by suggesting that by "remedy" it meant something other than "compensation" to past victims at all. Affirmative action was portrayed as just one more means of ensuring that discrimination is purged from a particular employer's or union's ways. For example, Justice Brennan wrote for the plurality in *Sheet Metal Workers* that cease-and-desist orders and make-whole relief may be enough to stop discrimination "[i]n most cases," but not all.[99] "In some instances," he wrote, employers' and unions' racist recalcitrance is so great that "it may be necessary to require the employer or union to take affirmative steps to end discrimination. . . ."[100] By describing a quota as merely an adminis-

---

98. The opinion of Justices Brennan, White, Marshall, and Blackmun in *Bakke* had adumbrated such a broad definition of past race discrimination's victims. *See* Regents of the Univ. of Cal. v. Bakke, 438 U.S. 265, 370–71 (1978) (opinion of Brennan, White, Marshall & Blackmun, JJ.) (identifying the underrepresentation of blacks in the medical profession as the "consequence of a background of deliberate, purposeful discrimination against minorities *in education and in society general-*

ly" (emphasis added)). But that approach never gained ascendancy in the Court, as was evident in the plurality's rejection of "societal discrimination" as a predicate for affirmative action in *Wygant*. *See* 106 S.Ct. at 1847–48 (plurality opinion).

99. 106 S.Ct. at 3036.

100. *Id.; see id.* at 3056 (Powell, J., concurring in part and concurring in the judgment) (viewing the 29.23% membership goal as but "a benchmark against

tratively convenient device for measuring a violator's good faith in ceasing discrimination, the Court shifted the focus of correction from compensating victims to reforming sinners. But by suggesting that their sins must be grave to warrant affirmative action, the Court reined in the permissible reach of such reform even as it freed affirmative action from limitation to "victims."

If casting affirmative action as compensation invites protests about windfalls to nonvictims, casting it as punishment invites protests about unfairness to nonsinners. Viewed through the lens of retributive justice, a focus on sin begets claims of innocence. Making an employer or union atone for *its* past discrimination would all be very well, these claims go, but that is not what affirmative action does. For it is not the errant management that "pays" for affirmative action, but "innocent" white workers. And retribution breaks down when aimed at innocent targets. Dead bosses' guilt cannot taint live workers' jobs. Nor are employees or the rank and file responsible for the ongoing racial wrongs that might be committed by their management or union leadership. Therefore, limiting affirmative action to employers or unions guilty of discrimination is not limiting it far enough; it must not harm guiltless white workers.

The Court has never held whites' "innocence" to be an absolute bar to affirmative action that would comparatively disadvantage them. On the contrary, even Justice Powell's opinion in *Wygant* took the Court to be in consensus that, "[a]s part of this Nation's dedication to eradicating racial discrimination, innocent persons may be called upon to bear *some* of the burden of the remedy." [101] And even the briefs filed last Term by the Solicitor General's office presumed that innocent whites could be made to give up job benefits to nonwhites—albeit, they argued, only to nonwhite "victims."

Nor, on the other hand, has the Court ever regarded all white workers as so tainted by American society's past racism—or even the racism of particular employers or unions—that it may discount white claims of "innocence" altogether. The Court might have done just that by ruling that white expectations forged in a discriminatory past are not legitimate, and therefore that affirmative action that defeats those expectations sacrifices no true "innocents." And indeed, the Court has occasionally remarked that whites have reaped windfalls from racism: they would not be where they are but for the prior exclusion of blacks from competition with them.[102] But far more often, the Court has stressed that it takes white claims of innocence seriously—seriously

which [the district court] could measure [the union's] progress in eliminating discriminatory practices").

101. 106 S.Ct. at 1850 (Powell, J., joined by Burger, C.J. & Rehnquist, J.) (emphasis added).

102. *See, e.g.,* Fullilove v. Klutznick, 448 U.S. 448, 485 (1980) (opinion of Burger, C.J.) ("[I]t was within congressional power to act on the assumption that in the past some nonminority businesses may have reaped competitive benefit over the years from the virtual exclusion of minority firms from [public] contracting opportunities.").

enough, at least, to compel consideration of whether remedial purposes could be served with less hardship for whites.[103]

In saying that white "innocence" may count, but only sometimes, the Court shifts from retributive justification of affirmative action to utilitarian balancing of hardships to determine how "punishment" imposed by affirmative action will be distributed—a balancing reflected in formulas such as "no unnecessary trammeling" [104] or "no excessive burden." [105] This suggestion that the social costs and benefits of affirmative action may be judicially weighed and balanced, however, invokes the spectre of social engineering that the Court's sin-based justifications for affirmative action were meant to avoid. It is thus unsurprising that the Court continues to resist making any categorical statements about just how much frustration of white expectations is tolerable.

* * *

The problem with sin as the predicate for affirmative action is thus that it keeps alive protests about windfalls to nonvictims and injustice to innocents. The Court held those protests at bay last Term, but *not* by expanding the concepts of white sin or black injury, as it might well have done. Rather it left behind a doctrine of sin doomed to partial success—a doctrine in search of perpetrators but not of victims, and open still to cries of white innocence.

IV. ALTERNATIVES TO SIN

Public and private employers might choose to implement affirmative action for many reasons other than to purge their own past sins of discrimination. The Jackson school board, for example, said it had done so in part to improve the quality of education in Jackson—whether by improving black students' performance or by dispelling for black and white students alike any idea that white supremacy governs our social institutions. Other employers might advance different forward-looking reasons for affirmative action: improving their services to black constituencies, averting racial tension over the allocation of jobs in a community, or increasing the diversity of a work force, to name but a few examples. Or they might adopt affirmative action simply to eliminate from their operations all de facto embodiment of a system of racial caste. All of these reasons aspire to a racially integrated future, but none reduces to "racial balancing for its own sake."

If such aspirations for the future rather than past sin were the basis for affirmative action, would white claims of "innocence" count for less? They should, for it is easier to show that displacing "innocent" whites is narrowly tailored to goals that turn on integrating institutions now than it is to show that doing so is narrowly tailored to

---

103. *See, e.g., Wygant,* 106 S.Ct. at 1849–52 (opinion of Powell, J.).

104. *See* United Steelworkers v. Weber, 443 U.S. 193, 208 (1979).

105. *See, e.g., Fullilove,* 448 U.S. at 514–15 (Powell, J., concurring) (calculating that a minority preference leaving "96% of contractors" still free "to compete for 99.75% of construction funds" was not a "burden . . . so great that the set-aside must be disapproved").

purging past sins of discrimination that the displaced whites did not themselves "commit." Nor should voluntary affirmative action otherwise give rise to constitutional suspicion in the context of white-dominated institutions in a still white-dominated society. In *Wygant,* for example, it should have been decisive, as the dissenters argued, that the plan to preserve a newly integrated faculty in the Jackson schools was forged by an overwhelmingly white union in collective bargaining with the school board.

Justice Powell's only reply was to declare the right of each white worker against race-based displacement inalienable. Wendy Wygant might waive any claim against the school board's retention of junior black teachers ahead of her, but "[t]hat claim cannot be waived by [her] more senior colleagues"—even by the white workers in the union majority that repeatedly approved Jackson's affirmative action compromise.[111] This proposition, however, can find little basis in equal protection doctrine. Judicial intervention in political processes under the equal protection clause has been justified to limit government from oppressing groups on the basis of race—whether one views such a limit as necessary procedurally to redress the systematic political disempowerment of racial minorities, or substantively to bar results that would provide official reinforcement of white supremacy. Yet Justice Powell would convert this concern for *restraining* government into a doctrine that would bar even the willing extension of benefits to blacks at whites' expense.

Such reasoning might make sense if the white workers who dissent from such collective bargaining outcomes were themselves a systematically disempowered minority, or the victims of racial subordination. But clearly Wendy Wygant was not the latter: as Justice Stevens stated, and no Justice disputed, the white teachers' layoff was "not based on any lack of respect for their race, or on blind habit and stereotype."[114] And Justice Powell's effort to suggest the former[115] lacks force: union membership always entails a kind of social contract to abide by the outcomes of collective bargaining, even when those outcomes are devastating for some, or second best for all. Being junior might make you lose sometimes, but that hardly makes such losses constitutionally suspect.

In the absence of any other strong basis to claim that race can never be a factor in politics or private bargaining, voluntary affirmative action is as defensible as the architecture of a better future as it is as a remedy for sins of discrimination past. And by turning to such forward-looking justification, the Court might more effectively quiet

---

111. *Wygant,* 106 S.Ct. at 1850 n. 8 (opinion of Powell, J.).

114. *Wygant,* 106 S.Ct. at 1870 (Stevens, J., dissenting).

115. *See id.* at 1850 n. 8 (Powell, J., joined by Burger, C.J. & Rehnquist, J.)

(suggesting that "[t]he more senior union members simply had nothing to lose" from a compromise burdening "the most junior union members").

protests about windfalls to nonvictims and injustice to innocents than it has by treating affirmative action as penance for past sins.

CHARLES FRIED *, *METRO BROADCASTING, INC. v. FCC*: TWO CONCEPTS OF EQUALITY

104 Harv.L.Rev. 107–117, 119–121, 123–125 (1990).

Except for the shameful and discredited "separate but equal" doctrine of *Plessy v. Ferguson,* the Supreme Court has always adhered to a liberal, individualistic view of the equal protection guarantee. Until its decision last Term in *Metro Broadcasting, Inc. v. FCC,* the Court had not departed from the view that "[i]t is settled beyond question that the 'rights created by the first section of the Fourteenth Amendment are, by its terms, guaranteed to the individual. The rights established are personal rights.' " [3] The Court took as its premise that "[a]lthough many of the Framers of the Fourteenth Amendment conceived of its primary function as bridging the vast distance between members of the Negro race and the white 'majority,' the Amendment itself was framed in universal terms, without reference to color, ethnic origin, or condition of prior servitude." [4] From this premise, the Court concluded that:

> a more restrictive view of the Equal Protection Clause . . . hold[ing] that discrimination against members of the white 'majority' cannot be suspect if its purpose can be characterized as 'benign' [must be rejected]. . . . It is far too late to argue that the guarantee of equal protection to *all* persons permits the recognition of special wards entitled to a degree of protection greater than that accorded others.[5]

This conviction, expressed in Justice Powell's controlling opinion in *Regents of the University of California v. Bakke,* was reaffirmed by a plurality in *Wygant v. Jackson Board of Education.* And two Terms ago in *City of Richmond v. J.A. Croson Co.,* Justice O'Connor was able to state this position firmly and unequivocally in an opinion for the court.

Two themes underlie this liberal, individualistic conception of equal protection. First, the liberal conception insists on the primacy of individuals, not groups, in our constitutional scheme and views the individual as the object of fundamental rights. Second, it resists a basic separation of the polity into racial groupings from which individuals cannot escape. Such racial balkanization is the opposite of what might be called the common market of the human spirit; balkanization creates, and even celebrates, barriers to trade that in the end impover-

---

* Professor of General Jurisprudence, Harvard Law School. As Solicitor General, Charles Fried authorized the briefs amicus curiae of the United States in the cases that comprised Metro Broadcasting, Inc. v. FCC, 110 S.Ct. 2997 (1990), and was the principal signatory of the government briefs in City of Richmond v. J.A. Croson Co., 109 S.Ct. 706 (1989), and Wygant v.

Jackson Board of Education, 476 U.S. 267 (1986), discussed in this Comment.

3. Regents of the Univ. of Cal. v. Bakke, 438 U.S. 265, 289 (1978) (Powell, J.) (quoting Shelley v. Kraemer, 334 U.S. 1, 22 (1948)).

4. *Id.* at 293 (citation omitted).

5. *Id.* at 294–95 (emphasis in original).

ish the human race. That some degree of separation exists naturally in society is no justification for perpetuating or strengthening it through governmental policy. In keeping with the liberal premise that the public and private spheres are distinct, liberal individualism does not view the existence of discrimination and social segmentation as a sufficient reason to reproduce these in the coercive apparatus of the state.

Standing in sharp contrast to this liberal, individualistic conception of equal protection is the collectivist ("communitarian" or "republican") group-rights conception of equality,[12] generally reflected only in dissents written by Justice Marshall and Justice Brennan.[13] In *Bakke,* for example, Justice Marshall argued:

> It is unnecessary in 20th century America to have individual Negroes demonstrate that they have been victims of racial discrimination; the racism of our society has been so pervasive that none, regardless of wealth or position, has managed to escape its impact. The experience of Negroes in America has been different in kind, not just in degree, from that of other ethnic groups.[14]

The group-rights perspective sees groups—ethnic, cultural, gender—as having a status independent of and even superior to that of individual group members. It assigns a value to the well-being of the group that is similarly independent of and perhaps superior to that of its component members. From this view it follows that governmental policy should measure benefits and burdens in terms of groups and, when equality is the issue, emphasize equality between groups as such.

* * *

The conflict between the liberal, individualistic conception and the collectivist, group-rights conception of equal protection plays out in doctrinal terms through the debate over the proper standard of review for race-based governmental action. The issue is whether government needs a "compelling" justification, one that would overcome "strict scrutiny," whenever it classifies persons by race, or whether a more relaxed standard is appropriate, at least when government favors members of groups seen or designated as disadvantaged. The level of scrutiny is an entirely appropriate, even inevitable doctrinal entail-

12. Under this view, individuals are "constituted" by the groups—including national, ethnic, and religious communities—to which they belong. Sources discussing or exemplifying this outlook include D. Bell, And We Are Not Saved (1987); M. Sandel, Liberalism and the Limits of Justice (1982); Lasch, *The Communitarian Critique of Liberalism,* in Community in America 173 (C. Reynolds & R. Norman eds. 1988); and Lawrence, *The Id, the Ego, and Equal Protection: Reckoning with Unconscious Racism,* 39 Stan.L.Rev. 317 (1987). *Cf.* R. Unger, Knowledge and Politics 236–89 (1975) (positing a theory of political interaction and a vision of "the good" based on "organic group" affiliations); Fiss, *Groups and the Equal Protection Clause,* 5 Phil. & Pub. Aff. 107 (1976) (advocating a group-oriented approach to equal protection).

13. *See* Wygant v. Jackson Bd. of Educ., 476 U.S. 267, 295 (1986) (Marshall, J., dissenting); *Bakke,* 438 U.S. at 324 (Brennan, White, Marshall, and Blackmun, JJ., concurring in the judgment in part and dissenting in part); *id.* at 400 (separate opinion of Marshall, J.).

14. *Bakke,* 438 U.S. at 400 (separate opinion of Marshall, J.).

ment of these contrasting visions. To the individualist, who believes that the equal protection clause requires the government to craft its laws to treat people equally, regardless of race, the government must make a showing of compelling need in order to legislate along racial lines. To the collectivist, for whom equal protection is a command to secure substantive aggregate equality for disadvantaged groups, legislation undertaken in that spirit need not be scrutinized as carefully.

It is impossible to ignore racial differences entirely—pure color-blindness is too extreme a principle.[19] The difficult question is whether government may use race to attack broad social problems and designate as beneficiaries of racial legislation individuals other than the particular persons who have been victimized. Justice Scalia, with a logic that is perhaps more rigorous than practical, argued in *Croson* that it may not. By insisting on victim-specificity, he pointed out, the government remains true to the principle of color-blindness, because government accords benefits to victims as such, not to members of a group against which there has been discrimination. By contrast, the collectivists feel that departing from victim-specificity is the only way to carry out the commands of equal protection. As Justice Blackmun put it in *Bakke*, "[i]n order to get beyond racism, we must first take account of race."

Strict scrutiny and the insistence on a "compelling governmental interest" are the appropriate and usual response of constitutional doctrine when a preeminent moral-political principle is at stake. It is so for limitations of first amendment liberties, and it should be so when government resorts to racial classifications. And although the issue is a close one, I believe strict scrutiny is satisfied by departing from victim-specificity when there is an identified, bigoted wrongdoer and the remedy is narrowly tailored to redress his prior discrimination. Because race is the most divisive and dubious governmental criterion for action, the instinct to resort to race for sentimental or purely political reasons must be vigilantly restrained; the requirement of a demanding and definite showing of direct remediation should be sufficient to provide the necessary discipline.

* * *

In *Metro Broadcasting*, the Court turned away from its past understandings. First, the Court applied a lenient, intermediate level of scrutiny to affirmative action measures approved by Congress and required only that the FCC's racial preferences be substantially related to an important governmental objective. Second, the Court recognized that "diversity," standing alone and unconnected to any remedial purpose, was such an important objective. Finally, the Court took a step that its past vigilance concerning discrimination had never permit-

---

19. If a disease, such as sickle-cell anemia or Tay–Sachs syndrome, overwhelmingly afflicts a particular ethnic group, it would be unreasonable to ignore that fact. If a criminal gang has an exclusive racial composition, it would be fanatical to require the government to ignore this fact in recruiting agents to infiltrate that gang. *See Wygant*, 476 U.S. at 314 (Stevens, J., dissenting). And in remedial circumstances, when a bigot has victimized according to race, race-based remedies seem an inescapable counter-response.

ted: it embraced the notion that some types of racial discrimination are "benign," based on the identity and presumed characteristics of the groups such discrimination is intended to benefit.

The law is now in an unstable condition. The distinctions and arguments offered by the majority to square this decision with the prior cases are so manifestly unsatisfactory that one wonders whether they were put forward quite seriously.

The most serious obfuscation in the opinion is its holding that the FCC's racial preferences should be judged under a standard of intermediate scrutiny. Justice Brennan wrote that a lesser standard of review for "benign" racial discrimination is appropriate when the discrimination is engaged in by Congress. Permission to employ this lenient standard of review is supposed to flow from the decision in *Fullilove v. Klutznick,* which addressed the constitutionality of a congressionally mandated ten percent set-aside for minority businesses in local public works programs receiving federal funds. Justice Brennan relied on *Fullilove* for the proposition that Congress is entitled to deference from the courts when it legislates pursuant to its express constitutional powers and when the expert agencies it has established use their expertise to enact policy. Even allowing for the lack of clarity of Chief Justice Burger's plurality opinion, *Fullilove* hardly authorizes the Court's conclusion in *Metro Broadcasting.*

Fullilove was based primarily on Congress' power under section 5 of the fourteenth amendment. Even assuming that *Metro Broadcasting* also implicated section 5,[41] still there would be no warrant for the Court's application of a lenient standard of review. There is no doubt that section 5 of the fourteenth amendment was meant to add something to the general standard of equal protection set out in the first section. Above all, section 5 makes clear that Congress has a power of legislation to enforce the equal protection command of section 1 against the states, a power that need not depend on the enumeration of its powers in article I, section 8. At the time the amendment was framed—when the power of Congress to reach what might have seemed purely local activities was highly controversial—this surely must have been the crucial consideration. To this function of section 5, which was instrumental in laying the constitutional foundation for the Civil Rights Act and the Voting Rights Act, the *Fullilove* plurality may be taken as proposing another: that section 5 endows Congress with special power to ascertain the facts that make a remedy appropriate, and perhaps also a special power akin to that derived from the necessary and proper clause to establish the remedies tailored to the occasion.

---

41. Justice O'Connor argues convincingly that the policies at issue in *Metro Broadcasting* did not in fact implicate Congress' § 5 power. *See* 110 S.Ct. at 3030–31 (O'Connor, J., dissenting) (arguing that § 5 is implicated only when "Congress . . . act[s] respecting the states").

Regardless of the validity of *Fullilove's* reading of section 5, neither of these special powers of Congress could justify the outcome in *Metro Broadcasting*. The additional deference to which Congress is entitled when acting under its section 5 power amounts to a greater presumption that it has found the facts necessary to prove a constitutional violation and that it has the power to undertake the preferred remedy; deference to congressional fact-finding and remediation in no way alters the substantive standards that determine what does or does not violate the Constitution. * * *

[*Fullilove*] alluded to section 5 only in order to validate Congress' findings concerning the historical record of prior discrimination, not to manipulate the standard of scrutiny under which to evaluate the statute. That "a racial classification is suspect and subject to strict judicial scrutiny" [49] was not in serious doubt. Put another way, Congress is entitled to special deference in selecting the means to a constitutionally permissible end under the equal protection clause, but section 5 does not render an end that would be illegitimate if pursued by other legislative bodies constitutionally acceptable if pursued by Congress.

In the context of *Metro Broadcasting*, this means that the Court would have been well within its rights to show considerable deference to any congressional findings of past discrimination by the government in the broadcasting field and to accept that the precise form of remedy chosen was narrowly tailored to address that discrimination. But congressional and FCC findings concerning diversity, an objective that even the majority does not argue would satisfy the strict scrutiny normally applicable to racial legislation, are simply irrelevant. To argue that section 5 and *Fullilove* could justify a lower standard of substantive review, and thereby transform congressional factual findings into validations of new governmental interests cognizable under the fourteenth amendment, is a disingenuous form of bootstrapping.

Even according Congress the broadest legitimate fact-finding latitude possible, the congressional findings supporting the FCC's distress sale and comparative licensing regimes are inadequate to establish that they were enacted in response to a violation of equal protection. Contrasting Congress' findings in *Metro Broadcasting* with its explicit statements supporting the enactment of the statute at issue in *Fullilove* makes this inadequacy clear. That the construction industry and its corresponding unions had been a locus of vicious, unashamed, and pervasive racism was notorious. Of course nothing of the sort had been, has been, or could be shown about the broadcasting industry. Not lenders, not advertisers, and certainly not the FCC have ever been accused of anything approaching explicitly exclusionary practices. Indeed, the Court specifically denied relying on a purpose to remedy past discrimination by the broadcast industry or the licensing authorities.

---

49. [448 U.S.] at 507 (Powell, J., concurring).

What was clear was the practically nonexistent number of minority owners of broadcast licenses. What was equally clear was that this numerical disparity was the result of economic and social disadvantage—in other words, the societal discrimination which the Court in *Bakke, Wygant,* and *Croson* explicitly held was not a sufficient basis for official racial classification.

The legislative committee materials that announce the factual determination that minority group members own very few broadcast licenses and the conclusion that minority ownership preferences are the only practicable way of increasing diversity in programming that will serve the needs of minority communities are strictly irrelevant unless one already accepts the conclusion of *Metro Broadcasting* that diversity is a permissible goal of race-conscious legislation. And the conclusion that minority ownership preferences will produce diversity is itself questionable. Neither the Congress nor the Court attempted to define what constitutes a minority community or its needs, and neither examined how those needs might be served by a minority broadcaster. We are left with nothing more than the assumption that such racially defined communities exist, that they have distinct needs as to broadcast services, that minority license owners will best discern those racially circumscribed needs, and that minority owners will be more powerfully motivated to serve them once discerned. This is a veritable cascade of non-sequiturs and begged questions.

Fullilove's proposition that Congress has special remedial powers under section 5 is also irrelevant: the issue in *Metro Broadcasting* was not establishing the fact of past discrimination—there was no such fact—and therefore was not determining its appropriate remedy. The issue was the meaning of the substantive constitutional standard itself, the meaning of equal protection. Nothing in *Fullilove* or in common sense suggests that equal protection can mean one thing for the Congress and another thing for every other level and organ of government. Indeed, just this point was at the heart of the Court's morally inevitable, though textually difficult, conclusion in *Bolling v. Sharpe* that the Constitution must not be read to forbid racial segregation by state and local bodies but to allow it if sanctioned by federal enactment. *Bolling* is distinguishable only if we assume what is to be proven: that Congress has wider power to make racial distinctions if it does so in ways judged to be benign. Everything in the Court's jurisprudence until this case seems to assume that if the kind of diversity celebrated by the Court in *Metro Broadcasting* is insufficient to justify legislation by race, but rather constitutes prohibited "discrimination for its own sake," [58] then it should make no difference whether the discrimination is worked by an act of Congress or an ordinance of the Richmond City Council. If the Constitution rejects such a thing as "benign discrimination" and requires a compelling interest to justify all race-conscious

58. Regents of the Univ. of Cal. v. Bakke, 438 U.S. 265, 307 (1978) (Powell, J.).

measures, this must be true across the board.   What the Court has given us is an unstable constitutional regime, one that meets the description of "checkerboard" justice coined by Ronald Dworkin in *Law's Empire*.[60]

* * *

Justice Brennan's defense of applying a lower standard of review to the federal government did not, however, rely solely on Congress' powers to enforce equal protection; indeed, he explicitly asserted that *Fullilove* rested on an "amalgam" of congressional powers and sought to justify the deferential standard of review based on "Congress' institutional competence as the national legislature."   The opinion suggests that one component of this competence is the presumed expertise of administrative agencies.   But this expertise no more justifies lenient constitutional review than does section 5 of the fourteenth amendment.

In the first place, it is questionable whether the FCC brought to bear any expertise upon the affirmative action policies at issue in *Metro Broadcasting*.   The Court's decisions, not only in this case, but also in its previous cases on broadcast regulation, emphasize the expertise of the FCC.   But the minority preference programs formally instituted by the FCC during the Carter administration were not instituted as a result of study by the "expert agency"; rather, they were forced upon the agency by the Court of Appeals for the District of Columbia Circuit.[73]   It was those racial preference programs that the FCC in 1986 proposed to study, now that the broadcasting industry had several years of actual experience under them.   But it was this study by the expert agency that Congress "in no uncertain terms" [74] shut down.   To be sure, Congress may have had an inkling what such a study would conclude, particularly from a Commission whose members had been appointed by President Reagan; however, that is how our system is supposed to work.   The Commission is, after all, an "independent" regulatory agency, which in other contexts is a device favored by Congress when it wants to put a matter beyond executive branch control.

The claim of FCC expertise as applied to these programs is suspect for another reason as well.   What is involved in these cases, as in the minority business enterprise set-aside area generally, is not employment but ownership.   Ownership programs, however, confront discrimination and disadvantage less directly than do other types of programs. The broadcast industry, of course, must comply with the Civil Rights Acts and avoid not only intentional discrimination but also any employment practices that have the effect of unjustifiably denying employment opportunity on the basis of race or gender.   In addition, the FCC has adopted and enforced its own antidiscrimination programs in the industries it regulates.   These legal protections vindicate the rights of individual members of disadvantaged groups to be treated as individu-

60. *See* R. Dworkin, Law's Empire 184 (1986) ("Checkerboard statutes are the most dramatic violations of the ideal of integrity. . . .").

73. *See* TV 9, Inc. v. FCC, 495 F.2d 929, 938 (D.C.Cir.1973), *cert. denied*, 419 U.S. 986 (1974). * * *

74. 110 S.Ct. at 3016 n. 29.

als and to enjoy equal opportunities for employment. By comparison, the FCC's affirmative action programs for additional minority owner- ship of broadcast facilities would likely affect only a small minority elite. * * *

In the end, agency expertise proves no more relevant than section 5 to the very point critically at issue in *Metro Broadcasting*: whether there are race-based conceptions of both community and community needs that are appropriate for constitutional purposes. It would be silly to deny that there are many communities with distinct cultural attributes, and it would be Philistine to deny the richness their diversi- ty lends to national life. But this happy collage takes on a sinister aspect when individuals are compulsorily assigned to groupings and communities, and are penalized or rewarded based on these assign- ments, by the coercive power of the state.

* * *

In *Metro Broadcasting*, the Supreme Court clearly [assumed] that there are race-based conceptions of social interaction that can serve as a legitimate basis for state intervention; this is evident from the Court's belief that some forms of racial discrimination are "benign." By putting the Supreme Court's imprimatur on the idea of "benign discrimination" for the first time—especially without providing an accompanying set of principles that could define "benignity"—*Metro Broadcasting* introduces substantial uncertainty and instability into the law. The dissent characterized the unanalyzed (and therefore unsup- ported) hypotheses that there is such a thing as minority need in broadcasting and that minority ownership will serve that need as issuing from the very kind of racial stereotyping that since *Brown v. Board of Education* the Court has been at pains to condemn. Indeed, there is no form of stereotyping more disturbing than that which assumes that members of racial or ethnic groups exhibit distinct ways of thinking, share particular dispositions, or display common patterns of values and behavior; such stereotyping is hardly "benign." The Court sought to salve the sting of this reasoning by saying that no findings of a distinct minority community interest or capacity to serve it was implied or necessary. Rather, such an interest and special ability to serve this interest may be assumed, so that "in the aggregate" broadcasting diversity will be enhanced. Justice Kennedy in his dis- sent drew the analogy between the Court's hypothesis and South African apartheid, an analogy that attracted Justice Brennan's ire. To be sure, the motivation behind the minority preferences at issue in *Metro Broadcasting* lacks the malice and ugliness of apartheid; it is this that perhaps led the Court to distinguish this race-conscious measure as "benign." Yet this is not a satisfactory response: what is needed is a legal theory to distinguish race-conscious governmental measures—measures that group people by race and assume a coinci- dence of values and interests within such groupings—that are benign from those that are not, a theory based on something better than the Court's "we know it when we see it" intuitions. * * *

The Court's only response to the danger of racial group stereotyping is to reiterate that diversity is an "important" governmental goal and that the FCC's policies are substantially related to that end, thus surviving something only marginally more rigorous than the least demanding standard of constitutional review, the rational basis standard. But this just repeats the problem, by asserting that very little need be shown to justify Congress' recourse to race-based classifications and approximate aggregations of ways of thinking and valuing. To justify the use of a racial category as benign more must be said: for instance, that the historic injustices against African–Americans justify special measures to amplify their presence in all sectors of national life. I am sure that something like that reasoning supports the preferences many people of good will would accord in their private dealings. But in the past, the Court has never embraced this reasoning—only Justice Marshall has done so with clarity.[98]

Reasonable persons can differ about the propriety of this reasoning when private persons—and private institutions—resort to it in their private dealings. But it is understandable that the Court has previously failed to embrace it as a basis for race-conscious governmental measures. The government's monopoly on coercive power, its unique ability to affect the conduct of private actors, its freedom from the equilibrating pressures of market competition, and its duty to represent the entire populace all justify treating its decisions to act in a race-conscious fashion differently from those of private actors. Grounding a theory of benign governmental discrimination in a particular historical injustice, as Justice Marshall argues, would make the equal protection principle of the fourteenth amendment applicable especially or only to the descendants of former slaves. To generalize it beyond African–Americans to Asian–Americans, Native Americans, Spanish-surnamed persons, and, as sometimes happens, Eskimos and Aleuts [99] requires a theory of deprivation that is quite indeterminate and infinitely manipulable. The only way to exclude, for instance, Jews or Italian–Americans is by a kind of casual, anecdotal social engineering that few would want to entrust to government at any level.

Even if a determinate and morally adequate theory could be developed that would identify deprived groups, application of the theory would still be grossly unjust as applied to specific individuals within those groups. Application would almost certainly be both substantially overinclusive and underinclusive, granting significant benefits to many who did not need or deserve them and discriminating against many who badly merited greater solicitude. Furthermore, no matter how racial preferences are structured, the government always would be forced to contend with the unseemly practical difficulties involved in

98. *See* Regents of the Univ. of Cal. v. Bakke, 438 U.S. 265, 395–402 (1978) (separate opinion of Marshall, J.).

99. *See, e.g.,* City of Richmond v. J.A. Croson Co., 109 S.Ct. 706, 713 (1989);

Statement of Policy on Minority Ownership of Broadcasting Facilities, 68 F.C.C.2d 979, 980 n. 8 (1978).

ascertaining whether a given individual does or does not satisfy the "definition" of the eligible race. These problems are inevitable concomitants of the group-rights perspective that Justices Brennan and Marshall have previously espoused in dissent and that *Metro Broadcasting* has finally endowed with some legitimacy as law. If the ultimate concern is for an "aggregate" effect, then situations of, and injustices suffered by, individuals are of secondary importance.

PATRICIA J. WILLIAMS, *METRO BROADCASTING, INC. v. FCC*: REGROUPING IN SINGULAR TIMES
104 Harv.L.Rev. 525–538, 545–546 (1990).

I. THE REAL ISSUES AT STAKE

* * *

Although the majority and the dissenters [in *Metro Broadcasting*] framed the issue in terms of disagreement about the standard of review, their underlying characterizations of the facts and weighing of the evidence were so polarized that the split probably would have remained even had they agreed on this doctrinal issue. The conflict underlying the opinions is revealed by the subtly nuanced and infinitely slippery vocabulary employed by each side. There was a covert adjectival war taking place in *Metro Broadcasting*, in which words were inflated like balloons in order to make the issue of diversity large or trivial, compelling or merely important, natural or momentary, grandly futuristic or of the local past.

The intensity of these divisions is rooted in profound differences in political philosophy about the nature of group identity, individualism, and the role of the market. Justice Brennan's analysis placed issues on a historical continuum that looks backward to our divided and ruthlessly co-optive past and forward to our long-term interest in the cooperative diversification of our airwaves and our lives. The dissenters' insistence, on the other hand, on a "guaranteed" link between diversity in ownership and diversity in programming arises from a highly individualistic notion of discriminatory action in which a court can consider little history beyond the limited confines of an arm's length commercially motivated bargain between neutrally feathered equals.

Similarly, the majority and the dissenters differed in their understandings of the very meaning of "necessity" in their respective descriptions of racial categorization as a means to desired ends. For the dissenters, necessity referred to an abstracted and absolute requirement of racial neutrality in the word of law. For the majority, necessity referred to the historically contextualized objective of media diversity, the achievement of which was constrained by a relative lack of alternative. Beyond that, the starting points of each differed: for the majority, its sense of "narrowly tailoring" race-conscious efforts to eradicate discrimination had as its referential backdrop a larger social context, while for the dissenters, the sense of the menacing, unbounded "enormity" of the very same measures arose out of their singular focus on a methodological individualism.

Finally, although the majority described its measures as "not 'remedial' in the sense of being designed to compensate victims of past governmental or societal discrimination," its reasoning is clearly framed as a corrective for historical conditions that are hardly long buried in the shroud of some long-forgotten past, but whose effects are specifically identifiable and endlessly enumerable. In the dissents, on the other hand, persistent protests about future-oriented remedies divert attention from the fact that the dissenters would not have supported the outcome even if it had involved a remedial scheme for the past. The insistence that the FCC program is " 'generalized' " with " 'no logical stopping point' "—and the concomitant refusal even to entertain any of a host of logical stopping points suggested by the majority—amounts to an insistence on not just a personal or "identifiable" injury, but one with a completely privatized locus.

* * *

In the swirl of all this, I would like to reframe some of the issues from a perspective that does not assume that simply because a problem such as discrimination is "societal" it is irremediable, nor that because a problem is individualized or privatized it is therefore effectively bounded. Whether racial imbalances are called societal or found to be the result of individualized injury, in either case there are overlooked (or underestimated) ways of looking at the problem that could provide both more latitude for courts and a clearer appreciation of the nuanced gradations that characterize judicial responses such as those in *Metro Broadcasting*.

II.   DIVERSITY AND THE RECOGNITION OF GROUPS

Broadcasting diversity is often portrayed as an attempt to propagate special interest markets or to ghettoize audiences into "mass appeal" on the one hand and minority markets on the other. Its implications, however, are more complex; a real notion of diversity includes a concept of multiculturalism. This entails a view of a market in which there are not merely isolated interest groups, of which "mass market" may be one, but in which "mass" accurately reflects the complicated variety of many peoples and connotes "interactive" and "accommodative" rather than "dominant" or even just "majoritarian."

This perspective embodies the historical connotations of the quest for diversity and the underlying intersection of race and culture. In particular, although it is true that there is no guaranteed relation between race and taste in television and radio fare, the seeming simplicity of this statement deserves some qualification. For example, the literal biological truth that blacks (or members of any other racial or ethnic groups) are not born with genetic inclination for "things black" is often used to obscure the fact that "black" (like most racial or ethnic classification) also defines a culture. Blackness as culture (perhaps more easily understood as such in the designation "African–American") usually evokes a shared heritage of language patterns, habits, history, and experience.

Although all the cultures named by the FCC are exceedingly diverse, the most generalized experience is that of battling cultural suppression if not obliteration, as well as discrimination and exclusion from the larger society.[23] If we cannot conclude absolutely that the victims of racial oppression are always the best architects of its cure, we must nevertheless assume that the best insight and inspiration for its amelioration will come from those most immediately and negatively affected. This allowance is not merely a concession in a random contest of cultures; it is a recognition central to the checking and balancing, the fine line of restraint, that distinguishes a fluidly majoritarian society from a singularly tyrannical one.

This notion of blackness, for example, as a culture and the recognition that this culture may be consistently suppressed or denigrated under the guise of neutral "mass" entertainment, may be difficult for people who identify themselves as part of the dominant culture to understand. The parallelism of "whiteness" as culture—or as any kind of unified experience—is not immediately apparent. Although remaining convinced that there is a culture of whiteness in the United States, I appreciate the extent to which its contours are vaguely or even negatively discerned, so that its assertion is most clearly delineated as "not other," and most specifically as "not black." For so many Americans for whom minority cultures are themselves peripheral, I suspect that a realization that a culture of whiteness exists is occasioned only rarely. Perhaps the argument is more easily understood as a matter of ethnic heritage; perhaps it is easier to look at immigrant communities of those whom we now call whites in order to recapture the extent to which acculturation in the United States is assimilationist in a deeply color-coded sense. It is easy to forget, for example, that the first waves of Italian, Portuguese, Greek, Jewish, and Middle–Eastern immigrants to this country were frequently considered non-whites and suffered widespread discrimination.

It is therefore telling to note the degree to which we as Americans celebrate simultaneously our unity as a nation and the Ellis Island tradition of our variety. In the drive to achieve the unity to which our national mythology aspires, we frequently suppress if not undo the richness of our diversity by reconceptualizing any manifestation of it as a kind of unAmerican disunity. I think we do this by consistently, if unconsciously, underestimating ourselves as a distinct national culture and even denying outright the possibility of our power as a consuming, assimilationist force. We tend to universalize the characteristics com-

---

23. I hope that readers will resist the temptation to reduce this struggle to protect one's culture and beliefs into an understanding of all black culture, for example, as merely a "culture of resistance."   To be extremely explicit, battling discrimination, although a generalizable group experience, is not the same as or the whole of what I am calling culture.

monly, if romantically, attributed to middle-class America—individualism, self-interest, self-assertion—so that the very force of our desire to embrace one another becomes an impediment to the necessary recognition that "we" are not the world.

What is also troubling about this tendency is precisely the tendency to universalize individualism. In eliding singular and plural to create an abstract *Über-market-mensch,* we diminish the notion of collectivity as a collection of various overlapping others in favor of a collective *self*—again, a plural singularity—that is both condensed yet general, multiple yet monolithic, self-contained yet presumed representative.

Because the pluralism in our life and laws is so frequently unacknowledged and sometimes even suppressed, it is sometimes hard to see the extent to which we are constantly engaged in not merely discussions among equal individuals, but also complex power struggles of group against group. Recently, for example, I saw a television program in which commentators with important regionless male voices talked about the lack of educational opportunity for black children in inner-city schools. They cited statistics about dropout rates, drugs, crime, teacher apathy, lack of funding, inadequate facilities (particularly for math and science study), low expectations of civic officials and school administrators, and general conditions of hopelessness. At the end of this very depressing summary, the anchor turned to four young teenagers in the studio, all black, all excellent students in a special program designed to encourage inner-city black students with an interest in science. He asked: "We've just heard that black kids aren't very good in math and science; are you here to show us that that's a lie?" The students then proceeded to try to redeem themselves from the great group of the "not very good" by setting themselves apart as ambitious, dedicated, "different" in one sense, yet "just the same as" the majority of all other kids at the same time.

It was unbearable listening to these young people try to answer this question. It put them in an impossible double bind. On the one hand, the invisible norm was the "average" (achieving) white middle-class ideal; although this was never articulated, this is what they had to prove themselves the same as. On the other hand, these were lower class kids who came from tough inner-city neighborhoods where very few of their friends could realistically entertain aspirations to become neurosurgeons or microbiologists. It was this community from which they were being cued to be different. Let me be clear: I am not faulting these young people's aspirations or goals. What concerns me is the way in which not just this commentator, but also society at large forces them and others like them to reconcile their successful status with a covert cultural standard. In a very insidious way, the commentator's question actually limited their alternatives, compromised their function as role models, and prompted explanations of their good fortune that tended to kill their sense of communal affiliation as the only way of permitting the truth of their individualism to remain intact. Although this sort of rhetoric is frequently wrapped in aspirations of racial neutrality, it in fact pits group against individual in a way that is not just racist but classist as well.

Moreover, a question that asks children whether they prove statistics to be "a lie" does not treat statistics as genuinely informative. If the actual conditions of large numbers of people can be proved a lie by the accomplishments of an exemplary few, then statistics only reinforce an exception that proves the rule. They do not represent the likely consequences of social impoverishment; they bear no lessons about the chaotic costs of the last several years of having eliminated from our social commitment the life nets of basic survival. Rather, statistics are reduced to evidence of deserved destitution and chosen despair, the numerical tracking of people who dissemble their purported deprivation.

In another program on the failure of education, the commentator asked, do the parents care enough? "The Parents," he asked. As in "The Blacks." The plural specific. The singular generality. The monolithic multiple. Again, this type of question makes it impossible to acknowledge the complexity of the reality with a simple single answer. Well, yes, some parents care. Well, no, not enough care. Neither of these answers addresses whether "the" parents care; neither of these is as insistently summarizing as the form of the question—do the parents care, yes or no.

I cite these examples because the ability to understand statistics and use them sensibly depends on the ability to understand the difference between information about group behaviors and information that explains individual actions. The Supreme Court in recent cases, perhaps most vividly in *City of Richmond v. J.A. Croson Co.,* has persistently done something with statistical evidence that is very like asking four schoolchildren if they can make into a lie the lost opportunities of countless thousands of others. Richmond had a black population of approximately 50%, yet only 0.67% of public construction expenditures went to minority contractors. The city set a 30% goal in the awarding of its construction contracts to minorities, based on its findings that local, state, and national patterns of discrimination had resulted in all but complete lack of access for minority-owned businesses. The *Croson* majority dismissed these gross underrepresentations of people of color, of blacks in particular, as potentially attributable to their lack of "desire" to be contractors. In other words, the nearly one hundred percent absence of a given population from an extremely lucrative profession was explained away as mere lack of initiative. As long as the glass is 0.67% full. . . .

The dismissiveness of the dissenters' analysis of statistical evidence in *Metro Broadcasting* parallels that of the majority's reasoning in *Croson.* In contrast, one of the remarkable and good things about the majority's decision in *Metro Broadcasting* is that it does not supplant history with individualized hypotheses about free choice, in which each self chooses her destiny even if it is destitution. Rather, the decision takes into account past and present social constraints as realistic infringements on the ability to exercise choice; it puts our destinies on a historical continuum that gives at least as much weight to the possibility that certain minority groups have not had many chances to be in charge of things as to the possibility that they just do not want to or that they just can't. As Congress and the FCC have indicated, we as a society must change if we are not to become permanently divided. Such social necessity not only may have, but must have at least some place in the Court's consideration.

III. DIVERSITY AND BROADCASTING

Given the existence of minority cultures, and not just minority individuals, the attempt by the *Metro Broadcasting* dissenters to disclaim any relation between programming and ownership becomes rooted in paradox. The dissenting opinions contest any relation between the multiculturalism of programming and the racial or ethnic background of station owners. And yet clearly there is *some* relation between programming and the beliefs of an owner. And clearly there is some relation between one's heritage and one's beliefs.

Underlying the dissenters' attempted disavowal of the connection between ownership and broadcasting content is a paradigm in which the class characteristics of good ownership are assumed to transcend racial, ethnic, or other forms of identity. As a friend of mine is fond of saying, middle-class status is nothing more than the inner conquest of any perceived racial or ethnic identity at all. The complete Young Urban Professional (or the accomplished businessperson) is one who has achieved a certain tweedy neutrality of dress, speech, mannerism, and desire. Although there is facetiousness in this depiction, there is certainly nothing too unfamiliar in it: it merely updates and caricatures the model of the rational man who dutifully delays gratification, acts in perfect self-interest, lives with one finger on the pulse of market appetite, patterns a lifestyle upon strong if shifting trends, and under no circumstances wears anything louder than oxblood, loden, or slate.

Ironically, such an identity is not an expression of individuality. It is fashion, a collective aesthetic, a species of mass behavior wrapped in the discourse of self-interest. This deeply embedded notion of the rational market actor is in fact a conformed identity, so normalized that we seem to have lost the ability to see it as such. Nor is this identity really racially or ethnically neutral. For all the brilliant cultural mixtures in art, music, and film that America has given the world, middle- and upper-classness remains deeply steeped in Western European traditions and dominated by strong Protestant values. Ninety-five percent of all corporate executives, including communications executives, are still white males, "a figure that hasn't changed since 1979." [34] * * *

----

34. Mann, *The Shatterproof Ceiling,* Wash. Post, Aug. 17, 1990, at D3, col. 5.

Furthermore, in an era of "infomercials," the media is increasingly used simply to spread (rather than exchange) information about markets (rather than ideas). * * * The degree to which advertising alone purveys and censors information seriously threatens genuine freedom of information. The degree to which the major media, the culture-creators in our society, are owned by very few or are subsidiaries of each other's financial interests, must be confronted as a skewing of the way in which cultural information is collected and distributed.

Thus, executives in the communications industry exercise a power that is not merely concentrated but also propagandistic. They make far-reaching choices in a way that few others in our society can. They project their images of the world out into the world. They do not merely represent, but also recreate themselves and their vision of the world as desirable, salable. What they reproduce is not neutral, not without consequence. To pretend (as we all do from time to time) that film or television, for example, is a neutral vessel, or contentless, mindless, or unpersuasive, is sheer denial. It is, for better and frequently for worse, one of the major forces in the shaping of our national vision, a chief architect of the modern American sense of identity.

Even assuming that profit-seeking behavior explains all or that materialism is itself a kind of culture, if the United States is to be anything more than a loose society of mercenaries—of suppliers and demanders, of vendors and consumers—then it must recognize that other forms of group culture and identity exist. We must respect the dynamic power of these groups and cherish their contributions to our civic lives, rather than pretend they do not exist as a way of avoiding argument about their accommodation. And we must be on guard against either privileging in our law a supposedly neutral "mass" culture that is in fact highly specific and historically contingent or legitimating a supposedly neutral ethic of individualism that is really a corporate group identity, radically constraining any sense of individuality, and silently advancing the claims of that group identity.

This is not to say that all women or blacks or men see the world in the same way or only according to their cultures. I do not believe that a "pure" black or feminist or cultural identity of any sort exists, any more than I think culture is biological. I am arguing against a perceived monolithism of "universal" culture that disguises our overlapping variety and that locates non-whites as "separate," "other," even "separatist" cultures or, as in the context of *Metro Broadcasting*, that argues about whether such cultures even exist.

* * *

* * * Participation in ownership of anything, but most particularly of broadcast stations or other tools of mass communication, is the gateway to our greatest power as Americans. Ownership enables one not merely to sell to others or to offer oneself to the call of the market. It provides the opportunity to propagate oneself in the marketplace of cultural images. Participation in the privileges of ownership thus

involves more than the power to manipulate property itself; it lends an ability to express oneself through property as an instrument of one's interests. We think of freedom of expression as something creative, innovative, each word like a birth of something new and different. But it is also the power to manipulate one's resources to sanction what is not pleasing. The property of the communications industry is all about the production of ideas, images, and cultural representations, but it also selectively silences even as it creates. Like all artistic expression, it is a crafting process of production and negation, in the same way that a painting may involve choices to include yellow and blue while leaving out red and green.

Translating this understanding of ownership into the context of broadcast diversification, the issue becomes not only what is sanctioned, but also who is sanctioning. It is not that minorities live in wholly separate worlds, enclaves walled in by barriers of language, flavors, and music; minorities are not languishing on electronically underserved islands, starving for the rap-marimba beat of a feminist Korean-speaking radio deejay whom only like others can understand. Nevertheless, a feminist Korean deejay is more likely to sanction insulting images of herself and more likely to choose to propagate images of herself that humanize her and her interests.[39] Likewise, it is not that white owners cannot be persuaded not to rerun old *Amos 'n' Andy* shows, in which white actors in blackface portrayed blacks in derogatory if comic ways and which reiterated the exclusive (until recently) image of blacks in the media. Rather, it is that it is much easier—and very likely not even necessary—to persuade Bill Cosby, for example, to choose to run programming that challenges and variegates the perpetual image of blacks as foolish and deviant.

In fact, I think that Bill Cosby's very success—as owner, producer, writer, and actor—in delivering an image of at least a certain middle-class segment of imagistic blackness into the realm of the "normal," rather than the deviant, has run him up against yet an even more complex (if instructive) level of cultural co-optation. As *The Cosby Show's* warm, even smarmy appeal has made it a staple in homes around the country, black cultural inflections that were initially quite conspicuous (speech patterns, the undercurrent of jazz music, the role of Hillman College as the fictional black alma mater of the Huxtables,

39. It is this sanctioning dimension that is so important to the claims of under-represented groups whose interests are not always understood as distinctive or cultural, such as women and gays. Thus, although some have dismissed the potential contributions of women, for example, as limited to programs "geared to the special biological concerns of women—menstruation, childbearing, breastfeeding, menopause, diseases of the female organs," M. Spitzer, Justifying Minority Preferences in Broadcasting 25 (Social Science Working Paper 718, Division of the Humanities and Social Sciences, California Institute of Technology, Mar. 1990) (unpublished manuscript on file at the Harvard Law School Library) (forthcoming 64 S.Cal.L.Rev. (1991)), the very flatness of imagination revealed in this description results, I think, from a general suppression of images of women as anything more than the sum of their parts.

hairstyles ranging from dreadlocks to "high top fades") have become normalized and invisible.

Moreover, the process of normalizing has exaggerated the extent to which the black middle class and white middle class are not merely derivative, but identical, so that *The Cosby Show* has been described as little more than a portrayal of blacks costumed in cultural whiteface. Although this "whitening" of its appeal is refined into the language of "sameness," the process devalues and even robs the program of its black content.

Thus, as black cultural contributions are absorbed into mainstream culture, they actually become seen as exclusively white cultural property, with no sense of the rich multiculturalism actually at work. Ultimately, the minority set-aside policies at issue in *Metro Broadcasting* must address this consuming, unconscious power as well. It is not enough to have one Bill Cosby or two Oprah Winfreys if overall power is so concentrated in one community that it remains inconceivable that power could have any other source.

* * *

V. CONCLUSION

The majority opinion in *Metro Broadcasting* marks an important step toward a recognition of multiculturalism and of the need to take active steps to nurture such diversity. If the holding in this case does not guarantee that minority owners will change programming in any constructive way, it does increase the likelihood. Although the dissenters implicitly insisted on a guarantee that there be some relation, a necessary connection, such a strict guarantee can never be gained without expense to the freedoms provided by the first amendment. Even diversity of employment at other levels than ownership is largely at the will and whimsy of those owners. If cultural diversity is, as even the dissenters acknowledge, an acceptable social goal, then alternative creative means for its encouragement must be employed. That relation is fostered by making more frequent and enhancing the opportunities for minority owners and producers, who are more likely to hire minority writers, sponsor programs designed to serve the needs and interests of minority communities, and, perhaps most importantly, bring multiculturalism to mainstream programming.

Beyond the limited context of broadcasting, what I hope will be enduring about this opinion is the respect it gives to these pronounced social recognitions of the desirability of diversity in all aspects of our economy and of multiculturalism in our lives. A (probably too) concrete illustration may indicate the reconceptualization of equality that is so urgently needed. Imagine a glass half full (or half empty) of blue marbles. Their very hard-edged, discrete, yet identical nature makes it possible for the community of blue marbles to say to one another with perfect consistency both "we are all the same" and, if a few roll away and are lost in a sidewalk grate, "that's just their experience, fate, choice, bad luck." If, on the other hand, one imagines a glass full of soap-bubbles, with shifting permeable boundaries, expanding and contracting in size like a living organism, then it is not possible for the collective bubbles to describe themselves as "all the same." Furthermore, if one of the bubbles bursts, it cannot be isolated as a singular phenomenon. It will be felt as a tremor, a realignment, a reclustering among all.

Marbles and soap-bubbles are my crude way of elucidating competing conceptions of how to guarantee what we call "equal opportunity." One conception envisions that all citizens are equal, with very little variation from life to life or from lifetime to lifetime; even when there is differentiation among some, the remainder are not implicated in any necessary way.

The other conception holds that no one of us is the same and that although we can be grouped according to our similarities, difference and similarity are not exclusive categories but are instead continually evolving. Equal opportunity is not only about assuming the circumstances of hypothetically indistinguishable individuals, but also about accommodating the living, shifting fortunes of those who are very differently situated. What happens to one may be the repercussive history that repeats itself in the futures of us all.

BIBLIOGRAPHY

Bell, *In Defense of Minority Admissions Programs: A Response to Professor Graglia,* 119 U.Pa.L.Rev. 364 (1970).

Blasi, Bakke *as Precedent: Does Mr. Justice Powell Have A Theory?,* 67 Calif.L.Rev. 21 (1979).

Brooks, *The Affirmative Action Issue: Law, Policy and Morality,* 22 Conn.L.Rev. 323 (1990).

Bryden, *On Race and Diversity,* 6 Const.Comm. 383 (1989).

Cohen, *Race and the Constitution, The Nation,* Feb. 8, 1975.

Cohen, *Why Racial Preference is Illegal and Immoral, Commentary,* June 1979, at 40.

Days, *Fullilove,* 96 Yale L.J. 453 (1987).

Devins, *Affirmative Action after Reagan,* 68 Tex.L.Rev. 353 (1989).

Devins, Metro Broadcasting, Inc. v. FCC: *Requiem for a Heavyweight,* 69 Tex.L.Rev. 125 (1990).

Duncan, *The Future of Affirmative Action: A Jurisprudential/Legal Critique,* 17 Harv.C.R.–C.L.L.Rev. 503 (1982).

R. Dworkin, TAKING RIGHTS SERIOUSLY ch. 9 (1977).

Edwards & Zaretsky, *Preferential Remedies for Employment Discrimination,* 74 Mich.L.Rev. 1 (1975).

Ellis, *Victim–Specific Remedies: A Myopic Approach to Discrimination,* 13 N.Y.U.Rev.L. & Soc.Change 575 (1985).

Ely, *The Constitutionality of Reverse Racial Discrimination,* 41 U.Chi.L. Rev. 723 (1974).

EQUALITY AND PREFERENTIAL TREATMENT (M. Cohen, T. Nagel & T. Scanlon eds. 1977).

Fallon, *To Each according to His Ability, From None according to His Race: The Concept of Merit in the Law of Antidiscrimination,* 60 B.U.L.Rev. 815 (1980).

Fallon & Weiler, *Firefighters v. Stotts: Conflicting Models of Racial Justice,* 1984 Sup.Ct.Rev. 1.

R. Fullinwinder, THE REVERSE DISCRIMINATION CONTROVERSY: A MORAL AND LEGAL ANALYSIS (1980).

A. Goldman, JUSTICE AND REVERSE DISCRIMINATION (1979).

Graglia, *Special Admission of the "Culturally Deprived" to Law School,* 119 U.Pa.L.Rev. 351 (1970).

K. Greenawalt, DISCRIMINATION AND REVERSE DISCRIMINATION (1983).

Jones, *The Origins of Affirmative Action,* 21 U.C. Davis L.Rev. 383 (1988).

Kennedy, *A Cultural Pluralist Case for Affirmative Action in Legal Academia,* 1990 Duke L.J. 705.

Matsuda, *Affirmative Action and Legal Knowledge: Planting Seeds in Plowed–Up Ground,* 11 Harv. Women's L.J. 1 (1988).

Meltzer, *The* Weber *Case: The Judicial Abrogation of the Antidiscrimination Standard in Employment,* 47 U.Chi.L.Rev. 423 (1980).

Mishkin, *The Uses of Ambivalence: Reflections on the Supreme Court and the Constitutionality of Affirmative Action,* 131 U.Pa.L.Rev. 907 (1983).

Nickel, *Preferential Policies in Hiring and Admissions: A Jurisprudential Approach,* 75 Colum.L.Rev. 534 or 524 (1975).

O'Neil, *Preferential Admission: Equalizing the Access of Minority Groups to Higher Education,* 80 Yale L.J. 699 (1975).

Peller, *Race Consciousness,* 1990 Duke L.J. 758.

Reynolds, *Individualism vs. Group Rights: The Legacy of Brown,* 93 Yale L.J. 995 (1984).

Rosenfeld, *Affirmative Action, Justice, and Equalities: A Philosophical and Constitutional Appraisal,* 46 Ohio St.L.J. 845 (1985).

Ross, *The Richmond Narratives,* 68 Tex.L.Rev. 381 (1989).

Rutherglen & Ortiz, *Affirmative Action Under the Constitution and Title VII: From Confusion to Convergence,* 35 U.C.L.A. L.Rev. 467 (1988).

Sandalow, *Racial Preferences in Higher Education: Political Responsibility and the Judicial Role,* 42 U.Chi.L.Rev. 653 (1975).

Scalia, *The Disease as Cure,* 1979 Wash.U.L.Q. 147.

Schiff, *Reverse Discrimination Redefined as Equal Protection: Orwellian Nightmare in the Enforcement of Civil Rights Law,* 8 Harv.J.L. & Pub.Pol. 627 (1985).

Schnapper, *Affirmative Action and the Legislative History of the Fourteenth Amendment,* 71 Va.L.Rev. 753 (1985).

Schwartz, *The 1986 and 1987 Affirmative Action Cases: It's All Over But the Shouting,* 86 Mich.L.Rev. 524 (1987).

Sedler, *Beyond Bakke: The Constitution and Redressing the Social History of Racism,* 14 Harv. C.R.–C.L.L.Rev. 133 (1979).

T. Sowell, CIVIL RIGHTS: RHETORIC OR REALITY (1987).

Symposium—*Affirmative Action,* 26 Wayne L.Rev. 1201–1362 (1980).

Symposium—*Affirmative Action,* 72 Iowa L.Rev. 255–85 (1987).

Symposium—*Bakke,* 67 Calif.L.Rev. 1–255 (1979).

Symposium—*Bakke,* 14 Harv.C.L.–C.R.L.Rev. 1–327 (1979).

Symposium—*DeFunis,* 75 Colum.L.Rev. 483–602 (1975).

Symposium—*DeFunis,* 60 Va.L.Rev. 917–1011 (1974).

Van Alstyne, *Rites of Passage: Race, the Supreme Court, and the Constitution,* 46 U.Chi.L.Rev. 775 (1979).

Wasserstrom, *Racism, Sexism and Preferential Treatment: An Approach to the Topics,* 24 U.C.L.A. L.Rev. 581 (1977).

Wright, *Color–Blind Theories and Color–Conscious Remedies,* 47 U.Chi. L.Rev. 213 (1980).

Chapter IX

LIBERTY

It is customary to divide the Constitution's special protections for individuals into two categories—rights and liberties. What makes liberties (like freedom of speech) special is that they entitle a person to *act* in certain ways (to speak). Other rights (like equal protection and the privilege against self-incrimination) promise benefits or forbid harms to essentially passive right-holders. (The only act they perform is the "legal act" of claiming their rights.) [1]

The Constitution guarantees several specific liberties in the First Amendment: freedom of speech, freedom of the press, and the free exercise of religion. These are often taught as a separate course, and are beyond the scope of our subject matter. The Fifth and Fourteenth Amendments also provide that no person shall be deprived of "liberty . . . without due process of law." This brief bit of text conceals several important points. One is that the phrase "due process" has come to mean legislative as well as judicial process. Under some circumstances legislatures are forbidden to pass laws depriving people of liberty. Another is that there are grades of protected liberty. The Supreme Court has said that the term "embrace[s] the right of the citizen to be free in the enjoyment of all his faculties; to be free to use them in all lawful ways[.]" [2] In order to take away most of these liberties the government must have some reason that is not purely arbitrary or vindictive. But there are also a few freedoms picked out by the courts for special protection. In the *Lochner* era this class included freedom of contract. In our time it includes the right of privacy protected in *Roe v. Wade*.

Writings about due process liberty have stressed several important themes. The first is the issue of interpretation. By what criteria of meaning can the courts find substantive protection in a phrase like "due process?" How can they determine that some "liberties" are more important than others? And what makes *the courts* better able to

1. Garvey, *Freedom and Choice in Constitutional Law*, 94 Harv.L.Rev. 1756, 1757–1762 (1981).

2. Allgeyer v. Louisiana, 165 U.S. 578, 589, 17 S.Ct. 427, 431, 41 L.Ed. 832 (1897).

answer these questions than the legislative and executive branches? These issues are the focus of the readings on interpretation in Chapter II.

The readings in this Chapter address a different theme, one of value rather than method: have the courts given right answers and convincing reasons in the controversies about due process liberty? Are the current resolutions likely to be stable and enduring? The readings in Section A ask questions like these about so-called "economic due process." Those in Sections B–D deal with the right to privacy.

A. ECONOMIC DUE PROCESS

Between 1897 [3] and 1937 [4] the Supreme Court held unconstitutional a number of state and federal laws regulating wages, hours, working conditions, prices, market entry, and other business practices. Such laws, the Court often said, took away liberty (freedom of contract) guaranteed by the Due Process Clause. It is now generally agreed that the Court's intervention in these cases was a mistake.

Cass Sunstein's article offers one explanation for why the Court might have made that mistake, and a few reasons why we now see it as erroneous. The Court viewed laws benefiting employees (as in *Lochner v. New York* [5]) as nothing more than ways of favoring employees' interests over employers'. That characterization, if it were accurate, would call into play a rule against naked preferences that Sunstein says figures prominently in constitutional law. But suppose that the legal system was responsible for the employees' problems in the first place. (Suppose the common law helped create and maintain a market in which they fared poorly.) Then it is easier to find a public value, rather than a naked preference, in government intervention.

Richard Posner believes that the Court may have been right after all in many of its economic due process decisions. He uses the example of *New State Ice Co. v. Liebmann* [6] to argue that the Court had a firmer grasp of economics than some of its contemporary critics. Restrictions on business entry, which the Court today tolerates, may in fact be nothing more than naked preferences that injure consumers as well as producers excluded from the market. But not all of the laws struck down during this period excluded entry into occupations. Some were designed to remedy perceived defects in economic bargaining power. *Lochner* itself is an example. Others dealt with business practices like product standards [7] or fee collection. [8] It is worth considering whether arguments like Posner's can be made in support of these statutes.

---

3. *Allgeyer v. Louisiana, supra.*

4. West Coast Hotel Co. v. Parrish, 300 U.S. 379, 57 S.Ct. 578, 81 L.Ed. 703 (1937).

5. 198 U.S. 45, 25 S.Ct. 539, 49 L.Ed. 937 (1905).

6. 285 U.S. 262, 52 S.Ct. 371, 76 L.Ed. 747 (1932).

7. Burns Baking Co. v. Bryan, 264 U.S. 504, 44 S.Ct. 412, 68 L.Ed. 813 (1924) (weight of bread); Weaver v. Palmer Bros. Co., 270 U.S. 402, 46 S.Ct. 320, 70 L.Ed. 654 (1926) (use of "shoddy" in manufacture of bedding).

8. Adams v. Tanner, 244 U.S. 590, 37 S.Ct. 662, 61 L.Ed. 1336 (1917) (fee collec-

Robert McCloskey asks whether the Court has overcompensated for its mistakes in this area. He reviews the various justifications given for distinguishing economic from "personal" rights, and finds them unconvincing. Perhaps the Court should find some half-way house between its former zeal and its present tolerance that will allow it to provide some check on obvious abuses of the legislative process.

CASS R. SUNSTEIN, NAKED PREFERENCES AND THE CONSTITUTION
84 Colum.L.Rev. 1689–1704, 1717–1718 (1984).

One of the most striking facts of modern constitutional law is the overlap—almost the identity—of current tests under many of the most important clauses of the Constitution: the dormant commerce, privileges and immunities, equal protection, due process, contract, and eminent domain clauses. Although these clauses have different historical roots and were originally directed at different problems, they are united by a common theme and focused on a single underlying evil: the distribution of resources or opportunities to one group rather than another solely on the ground that those favored have exercised the raw political power to obtain what they want. I will call this underlying evil a naked preference.

* * *

Because of their common concern with naked preferences, these clauses share a number of features. They are all directed in large part at discrimination [8] based on an impermissible purpose. Effects are relevant, if at all, only to show such a purpose. A number of devices— most prominently, the required showing of some degree of means-ends connection and the identification of a category of impermissible government ends—are applied under all of these clauses to filter out naked preferences.

The prohibition of naked preferences captures a significant theme in the original intent. It is closely related to the central constitutional concern of ensuring against capture of government power by faction.[10] The framers' hostility toward naked preferences was rooted in the fear that government power would be usurped solely to distribute wealth or opportunities to one group or person at the expense of another. The constitutional requirement that something other than a naked preference be shown to justify differential treatment provides a means, admittedly imperfect, of ensuring that government action results from a legitimate effort to promote the public good rather than from a factional takeover. The Court's adherence to this requirement under the various clauses and over long historical periods showing otherwise

tion practices of employment agencies). See generally Wonnell, *Economic Due Process and the Preservation of Competition*, 11 Hastings Const. L.Q. 91 (1983).

8. I use the term "discrimination" throughout this Article to refer to treating one group or individual differently from another. The term need not connote hostility.

10. The Federalist Nos. 10, 51 (J. Madison) are the classic statements * * *.

considerable doctrinal change reflects a striking continuity in general approach.

The prohibition of naked preferences also reflects the Constitution's roots in civil republicanism and accompanying conceptions of civic virtue. The notion that government actions must be responsive to something other than private pressure is associated with the idea that politics is "not the reconciling but the transcending of the different interests of the society in the search for the single common good." Civil republicanism embodies a conception of politics in which preferences are not viewed as private and exogenous. Their selection is the object of the governmental process. The model for this conception of government is the town meeting, where decisions are made during a process of collective self-determination.

In accordance with the original Madisonian understanding, the prohibition is focused on the motivations of legislators, not of their constituents. The prohibition therefore embodies a particular conception of representation. Under that conception, the task of legislators is not to respond to private pressure but instead to select values through deliberation and debate.

* * *

Quite apart from its roots in original intent, the prohibition of naked preferences captures the judicial understanding that the Constitution requires all government action to be justified by reference to some public value. The "reasonableness" constraint of the due process clause is perhaps the most obvious example. The minimum requirement that government decisions be something other than a raw exercise of political power has been embodied in constitutional doctrine under the due process clause before, during, and after the *Lochner* era. The equal protection clause, in its core requirement that classifications be justified by reference to some public value, reflects an identical understanding. The same principle has been embodied in constitutional doctrine under many other clauses as well. The contract and eminent domain clauses, for example, are efforts to apply the general prohibition of naked preferences to several specific instances of government action about which the framers were most concerned.

The notion that government action must be grounded in something other than an exercise of raw political power is in considerable tension with many of the most prominent theories of how government does and should operate. It is especially at odds with pluralism. Naked preferences are common fare in the pluralist conception; interest-group politics invites them.[25] The prohibition of naked preferences, enforced as it is by the courts, stands as a repudiation of theories positing that the judicial role is only to police the processes of representation to

---

25. See R. Dahl, Dilemmas of Pluralist Democracy: Autonomy vs. Control 31–54 (1982); Posner, *The Defunis Case and the* *Constitutionality of Preferential Treatment of Racial Minorities,* 1974 Sup.Ct.Rev. 1, 27–28.

ensure that all affected interest-groups may participate.[26] It presupposes that courts will serve as critics of the pluralist vision, not as adherents striving only to "clear the channels" in preparation for the ensuing political struggle. In this respect, the prohibition of naked preferences reflects a distinctly substantive value and cannot easily be captured in procedural terms. Moreover, it reflects an attractive conception of politics, one that does not understand the political process as simply another sort of market. It is hardly surprising that the prohibition is reflected in many areas of constitutional law.

*   *   *

I. NAKED PREFERENCES AND PUBLIC VALUES: THE FRAMEWORK

It will be useful to begin by distinguishing between two bases for treating one person or group differently from another. The first is a naked preference. When a naked preference is at work, one group or person is treated differently from another solely because of a raw exercise of political power; no broader or more general justification exists. For example, state *A* may treat its own citizens better than those of state *B* —say, by requiring people from state *B* to pay for the use of the local parks—simply because its own citizens have the political power and want better treatment. Or a city may treat blacks worse than whites—say, by denying them welfare benefits—because whites have the power to restrict state largesse to themselves. Or a state may relieve a group of citizens from a contractual obligation, thus benefiting them at the expense of another group of contracting parties, simply because the first group and its allies seized the political power to dispossess the second group of the rights that it previously had.

These examples illustrate a conception of the political process as a mechanism by which self-interested individuals or groups seek to obtain wealth or opportunities at the expense of others. Political ordering is assimilated to market ordering. The public interest is understood as the aggregation of private interests. The task of the legislator is to respond to the pressures imposed by those interests. This conception of the political process reflects a set of values within which any other conception appears mystical, potentially totalitarian, or both.

Contrast with this a conception of a political process in which differential treatment is justified not by reference to raw political power, but to some public value that the differential treatment can be said to serve. A public value can be defined as any justification for government action that goes beyond the exercise of raw political power. For example, a state may impose regulatory requirements on opticians, but not on optometrists, because the methods used by the former group create special risks of deception or overreaching. Or a state may relieve a group of people from a contractual obligation because the contract called for an act—say, the passing on of increased costs to consumers—that violated a public policy demanding that consumers be

26. See J. Ely, Democracy and Distrust (1980).

insulated from some of the dislocations caused by an unregulated marketplace. Or state *A* may treat its own citizens better than those of state *B* —say, by limiting welfare payments to its own citizens—because it wants to restrict social spending to those who in the past have made, or in the future might make, a contribution to state revenues.

These examples reflect a conception of the political process as an effort to select and implement public values. The process is primarily one of collective self-determination, rather than of compromises or trade-offs among preexisting private interests. The role of the representative is to deliberate rather than to respond mechanically to constituent pressures. Politics cannot, in this view, be reduced to the aggregation of private interests. Such interests are not preexisting. They are themselves a product of the political process, whose function is not to choose among preselected values but instead to select values through public deliberation and debate.

 * * * The rest of Part I examines the devices used by the courts to determine which of these poles a particular measure approaches.

A.   The Minimal Requirement

If naked preferences are a legitimate basis for government action, a significant judicial constraint on the exercise of government power is lifted. It is sufficient that a particular group has been able to assemble the raw political power to obtain what it seeks: might makes right. Under some theories of legislation, the whole enterprise of government consists of efforts by various groups to obtain the power to do precisely this. Modern pluralism, for example, depends in large part on the idea that competing groups struggle, in a largely unprincipled fashion, to obtain a share of the pie. If naked preferences are a legitimate basis for government behavior, there is nothing wrong with that.

If naked preferences are forbidden, however, and the government is forced to invoke some public value to justify its conduct, government behavior becomes constrained. The nature and extent of the constraint will depend on several considerations. The first is the content of the category of public values that courts will accept as a legitimate basis for government action. The constraint would be strengthened if, for example, * * * a judicial decision were to prohibit the redistribution of resources through regulation—say, regulation that imposes minimum housing standards for poor tenants—on the ground that redistribution of this sort is a pure transfer of wealth and thus should be assimilated to the category of naked preferences.

The second consideration relates to the devices developed to ensure that public values do in fact account for legislation. If courts are willing to hypothesize a public value as the basis for government action and do not require a close fit between the public value and the measure under review, all or almost all government action will be upheld. By contrast, if courts require a good reason to believe that a naked preference was not in fact at work, many statutes may be invalidated.

* * *

Let us assume that the category of public values has not been limited at all, and that courts will not carefully scrutinize either the process or the outcome to ensure that a public value was actually at work. These assumptions generate what might be called the "weak version" of the prohibition of naked preferences. This version is characterized by two main features. First, there is no category of impermissible ends beyond the prohibition of decisions based solely on raw political power. Second, means-ends scrutiny is deferential because courts will adopt a strong presumption that legislative outcomes can be justified by reference to some public value.

The weak version, thus described, places only a minimal constraint on government action, for it is nearly always possible to justify an action on grounds other than the raw exercise of political power. But because the weak version does require *some* justification that goes beyond raw political power, it cannot be dismissed as a purely formal constraint. It forces those who seek to obtain government assistance to invoke some public value as a basis for assistance. In so doing, the weak version strikes two familiar constitutional themes. By requiring that a public value justify the exercise of government power, it acts as a check on the danger of factional tyranny. Moreover, it reflects the notion that the role of government is not to implement or trade off preexisting private interests, but to select public values.

The weak version accounts for much of modern constitutional doctrine. Rationality review is the prime example. Courts have interpreted the due process and equal protection clauses as imposing the minimal requirement that government action be "reasonable." This corresponds to the core demand of the weak version that government decisions based on the exercise of raw political power be prohibited. Rationality review thus represents a judicial search for some public value by which to justify the measure in question.

Modern rationality review does not seek to rule out a separate category of impermissible government ends; only exercises of raw political power are expressly prohibited. In the *Lochner* era, the Court attempted to create a separate category of impermissible ends, using the libertarian framework of the common law as a theoretical basis. Under that framework, the government's police power was sharply limited, and modern social legislation—for example, maximum hour and minimum wage provisions—appeared not as an effort to promote a public value, but instead as a raw exercise of political power by the beneficiaries of the legislation. But the theoretical basis of the *Lochner* era foundered on a mounting recognition that the market status quo was itself the product of government choices. When private property was viewed as a creation of such choices, efforts to reallocate property rights could be understood as a legitimate effort to promote the public good. In response to this new understanding, the category of impermissible government ends under the due process and equal protection clauses became much narrower.

Modern rationality review is also characterized by extremely deferential means-ends scrutiny. The Supreme Court demands only the weakest link between a public value and the measure in question, and it is sometimes willing to hypothesize legitimate ends not realistically attributable to the enacting legislature. As a result, few statutes fail rationality review. * * *

* * *

B. Beyond the Minimal Requirement

The weak version of the prohibition of naked preferences may account for much of current doctrine; but, as described thus far, it is minimal indeed. It merely requires something other than raw political power to justify an exercise of authority. In most respects, this is a trivial constraint, for almost any decision can be justified by reference to some public value. One might, for example, support preferential treatment of the poor on the ground that they have a special need for public assistance; preferential treatment of the rich might be justified on the ground that it provides incentives for more work and investment. Discrimination in law enforcement against racial minority groups might be justified on the ground that statistics show a propensity to violent crime among their members. Both progressive and regressive taxes would be unobjectionable. Even segregation might be explained on the ground that it is good for whites and blacks alike. Everything, in short, is at least potentially lawful. To develop a more vigorous set of constraints on government, it is necessary to go beyond the weak version described thus far.

* * *

1. *Heightened Scrutiny.*—The first device [used to supplement the prohibition of naked preferences] involves the scope of review of government claims that a public value is being served. "Heightened scrutiny" consists of a careful examination of the government's claim that a public value is in fact the motivating force behind its actions. Here courts find it insufficient, as a basis for a conclusion that a public value is at work, that the measure under review has satisfied all formal requirements and a connection can be hypothesized between it and some public value. Under this approach, a public value is what emerges from a well-functioning political process in which legislators do not respond only to raw political power, and courts will scrutinize the process to ensure that it is in fact well functioning.

Heightened scrutiny involves two principal elements. The first is a requirement that the government show a close connection between the asserted public value and the means that the legislature has chosen to promote it. If a sufficiently close connection cannot be shown, there is reason for skepticism that the asserted value in fact accounted for the legislation.[46]   The second element is a search for less restrictive alternatives—ways in which the government could have promoted the public value without harming the group in question.[47]   The availability of such alternatives also suggests that the public value justification is a facade.

Heightened scrutiny also requires that the government show that it actually considered the public value in enacting the measure in question.[48]   Such a requirement represents a similar effort to ensure that the values on which a statute rests are genuinely public, in the sense that they resulted not from private pressure but from broad deliberation about what the relevant rule should be.   In this respect, the requirements of heightened scrutiny serve as a means, though very tentative and undeveloped, of implementing the republican ideal.

Heightened scrutiny is triggered by a concern that in the circumstances it is especially likely that the measure under review reflects a naked preference.   The most familiar example is review of racial classifications under the equal protection clause.   Review of statutes that discriminate on their face against noncitizens under the privileges and immunities clause falls into the same category.   In both cases, heightened scrutiny is justified by a perception that the groups in question lack the political power to protect themselves against factional tyranny.

By contrast, more relaxed scrutiny—typified by rationality review—reflects a strong presumption that a public value is at work. That presumption is conventionally supported by reference to considerations of judicial competence and legitimacy.[50]   The underlying idea is, first, that courts lack the capacity to review the factual determinations of other branches of government and, second, that vigorous judicial scrutiny of whether a naked preference is at work would be inconsistent with what is taken to be the central constitutional commitment to representative democracy.

2.   *Theory of Impermissible Ends.*—A second device in a more rigorous version of the prohibition, typified by doctrines developed under the due process and equal protection clauses, consists of judicial formulation of a normative theory designed to distinguish between legitimate and illegitimate bases for government action.   The courts attempt to root this normative theory in the text or history of the Constitution.   Under this approach, the weak version of the prohibition of naked preferences is buttressed by a conclusion that a number of

46.   See J. Ely, supra note 26, at 145–48.

47.   See, e.g., Orr v. Orr, 440 U.S. 268, 281–83 (1979) (equal protection); United States Trust Co. v. New Jersey, 431 U.S. 1, 29–31 (1977) (contract clause); Dean Milk Co. v. City of Madison, 340 U.S. 349, 354–56 (1951) (commerce clause).

48.   See, e.g., Fullilove v. Klutznick, 448 U.S. 448, 532, 548–54 (1980) (Stevens, J., dissenting); Califano v. Goldfarb, 430 U.S. 199, 212–17 (1977); Hampton v. Mow Sun Wong, 426 U.S. 88, 103, 114–16 (1976)[.]

50.   See, e.g., Ferguson v. Skrupa, 372 U.S. 726, 730–32 (1963) (due process); South Carolina State Highway Dep't v. Barnwell Bros., 303 U.S. 177, 190–91 (1938) (commerce clause).

ends are illegitimate even if they are not exercises of raw political power in the ordinary sense. This element thus supplements the procedural requirements of heightened scrutiny with a substantive constraint.

During the *Lochner* era, for example, the redistribution of resources from employer to employee was not thought to respond to a public value and was therefore placed in the category of naked preferences. Numerous goals now considered to fall within the realm of public values were not recognized as such, largely because common law conceptions of rights and obligations dominated early public law. If a measure enacted by the government was not a proper exercise of the police power under common law standards, it was impermissible under the due process clause as a naked preference for one group at the expense of another. Identical results occurred under the contract clause. In short, a particular normative theory sharply limited the category of public values.

Under current law, by contrast, all sorts of redistributive measures are permissible. The weak version of the prohibition of naked preferences still applies to such measures, but the normative theory supplementing the weak version has been dramatically altered in a way that has expanded the category of public values to include redistribution. When a normative theory outlaws certain kinds of government action even though such action is not solely an exercise of raw political power, the prohibition of naked preferences has gone well beyond the weak version. To develop a complete theory of the resulting "strong version," it is necessary to identify the expanded category of public values with precision.

The strong version could of course accommodate a wide range of normative theories of government. The *Lochner* era embodied one such theory. Modern equal protection doctrine reflects another: courts do not recognize as public values certain government ends associated with disadvantaging women, aliens, illegitimates, and members of racial minority groups. For example, the government has attempted to justify classifications based on gender on the ground that women participate less frequently or less ably in the labor market. Although justifications of this sort would qualify as public values under the weak version, very good reasons can be advanced for prohibiting them under the strong version. Most important, such justifications may be based on values that are in fact merely reflections of existing power relations.

* * *

The use of these theories of impermissible government ends as an additional source of constraints on government is highly controversial. For one thing, the use of such theories may allow constitutional prohibitions to change dramatically over time as the category of public values expands and contracts—to many, a questionable phenomenon. Moreover, selection of public values is made by the judiciary—an allocation of authority that was sharply criticized during the *Lochner* era and has its share of critics today, at least when selection of the relevant values cannot easily be attributed to the constitutional text and history.

* * *

3. *Rights Constraints.*—The final device involves a category of rights that operate as a shield against certain government actions even when no naked preference has taken place. The Court's recognition of certain fundamental rights, including the right to "privacy," [63] falls in this category of "rights constraints," as did the rights of contract recognized during the *Lochner* era. This approach constrains government action not by assimilating certain justifications to the category of naked preferences, or by concluding that certain ends of government are impermissible, but by invalidating measures even if they are properly motivated under the framework previously described. Rights constraints are sharply distinct from both the weak and the strong versions of the prohibition of naked preferences. Far from making judicial decisions depend on the reasons for government action, such constraints create a shield of private autonomy that operates regardless of the end the government is trying to achieve. In this respect, rights constraints reflect a normative framework altogether different from that underlying the prohibition of naked preferences.

* * *

II. APPLICATIONS: NAKED PREFERENCES AND THE CLAUSES

* * *

D. Due Process Clause

The notion that legislation is unconstitutional if it represents a naked decision to distribute resources to one group rather than to another came through most clearly in the *Lochner* era. In *Mugler v. Kansas*, for example, the Court noted that the test is whether "a statute purporting to have been enacted to protect the public health, the public morals, or the public safety" has a "real or substantial relation to these objects"—the same question the Court now asks under the equal protection clause.

There are, however, several differences between the two clauses. The first relates to what falls within the category of public values. Here the *Lochner* case is itself the best illustration. The statute at issue there prohibited employment in a bakery for more than sixty hours per week or ten hours per day. The question whether the measure fell within the "police power," as understood by the Court, translated into the question whether it involved "the safety, health, morals, and general welfare of the public." In *Lochner*, the Court held that no public value was served. "It seems to us that the real object and purpose were simply to regulate the hours of labor between the master and his employees . . . in a private business, not dangerous in

---

63. See Carey v. Population Serv. Int'l, 431 U.S. 678 (1977); Roe v. Wade, 410 U.S. 113 (1973).

any degree to morals or in any real and substantial degree, to the health of the employees." The same position can be found in many cases.[137]

In this respect, the *Lochner* Court regarded redistribution on an ad hoc basis as an essentially private taking from one person to another, a measure based on raw political power or on the intrinsic desirability of treating the benefited better than the burdened group. A now familiar problem with the *Lochner* reasoning is its perception of the market status quo as natural or preexisting—not as a matter of conscious choice.[138] It was as if the Court did not "see" certain values, generally including redistribution, as legitimate public ends. For this reason, in part, an effort to regulate the hours of labor was considered an impermissible taking from *A* in order to benefit *B*. The decline of the *Lochner* era represented a dramatic broadening of the category of public values. This was brought about by an understanding of how the operation of the private sector is dependent on public choices. Once it became clear that harms produced by the marketplace were also the products of public choices, efforts to alleviate those harms came to be regarded as permissible exercises of government power.

In the post-*Lochner* era, a wide range of justifications count as exercises of the police power and are not treated as naked wealth transfers. The police power is properly used to safeguard the interests of groups or subgroups of workers, of consumers, of the victims of discrimination. There has thus been a shift from the strong to the weak version of the prohibition of naked preferences. One consequence of this development has been to make the line between naked preference and public value quite thin in practice, as we saw earlier in connection with the weak version of the basic prohibition. If protection of the class of statutory beneficiaries is itself seen as a public value, many exercises of raw political power—even if in the service of faction—become automatically justifiable. Current law reflects such perceptions.[139]

The second difference relates to the nature of judicial scrutiny of the state's justifications. In the *Lochner* era, the Court did not merely limit the permissible ends of government, but also demanded a fairly close fit between those ends and enactments attacked as naked wealth transfers. Again, the best example is *Lochner* itself, where the Court found an insufficient connection between protection of the health of bakers and maximum hour legislation. There is no question that the connection would pass modern scrutiny under the rationality test: a legislative judgment that there is a connection between health impair-

137. See, e.g., Adkins v. Children's Hosp., 261 U.S. 525 (1923); Coppage v. Kansas, 236 U.S. 1 (1915); Adair v. United States, 208 U.S. 161 (1908); Allgeyer v. Louisiana, 165 U.S. 578 (1897).

138. See West Coast Hotel Co. v. Parrish, 300 U.S. 379 (1937); Kennedy, *Form*

and Substance in Private Law Adjudication, 89 Harv.L.Rev. 1685, 1746–51 (1976).

139. See, e.g., United States R.R. Retirement Bd. v. Fritz, 449 U.S. 166 (1980); City of New Orleans v. Dukes, 427 U.S. 297 (1976).

ment and workdays of more than ten hours is surely a rational one. Thus, with respect to means-ends scrutiny as well, the *Lochner* era reflected a highly intrusive version of the prohibition of naked preferences. The expansion in legitimate ends under current doctrine has been accompanied by a relaxation in the required means-ends connection, resulting in an extremely weak version of the basic prohibition.

Modern due process doctrine contains at least one holdover from the *Lochner* era. When government action places an undue burden on a fundamental right—most prominently, the right to "privacy"—the action is unconstitutional. In this respect, modern doctrine under the due process clause has gone beyond the weak version of the prohibition of naked preferences. A fundamental right operates as a barrier to government action even if no naked preference is at work. An action may have been properly motivated—in the sense that something other than an exercise of raw political power generated it—but nonetheless be invalid because it invades the realm of personal autonomy.

RICHARD POSNER, ECONOMIC DUE PROCESS
Economic Analysis of Law 589–593 (3rd ed. 1986).

For a period of 50 years ending in the late 1930s, liberty of contract was a key component of due process under the Fifth and Fourteenth Amendments to the Constitution as interpreted by the Supreme Court, and it was the ground on which the Court invalidated, although fitfully, a number of state and federal statutes regulating economic activity. Classical economic theory was thereby elevated to the status of constitutional principle, for the idea that voluntary transactions almost always promote welfare, and regulations that inhibit such transactions almost always reduce it, is a staple of classical theory. * * *

Although long viewed simply as grotesque distortions of constitutional principle, the liberty of contract decisions recently have attracted some staunch advocates as part of a growing revival of interest in classical economic principles. And although there are grave difficulties in reconciling their position with the philosophy of judicial self-restraint or the interest group theory (and reality) of government, the same can be said about the modern emphasis in constitutional law on personal liberties. The arguments for giving greater protection to personal than to economic liberties are superficial. Thus, while it is said that there was no source for a doctrine of liberty of contract in the text or history of the relevant constitutional provisions, the same criticism can be (and has been) made of the Court's decisions in a wide variety of other constitutional areas. It is also said that economic questions are more difficult for courts to decide than questions involving the rights of criminal defendants, political dissidents, or members of racial minorities—yet in fact less is known about those questions than about conventional economic problems. It is said that economic rights are less important than other rights; even if this is so * * *, it does not follow that the Court should give them no protection at all. It is said that the Court's mistake in the liberty of contract cases was to be out of step with dominant public opinion. But this was true only toward the end of the era, and is the reason why the era ended when it did. Moreover, the criticism can easily be turned into a compliment to the Court for its steadfastness in the face of contrary popular opinion. It is also said that the victims of economic controls are businessmen well able to protect themselves without the Court's help, unlike the powerless minorities typically involved in a noneconomic constitutional case. Yet as we are about to see, the brunt of the economic legislation challenged during the liberty of contract era was often borne by politically unorganized groups such as consumers. Nor is it correct that racial and religious minorities are unable to compete effectively in the political arena.

   *   *   * [It is also] commonly believed that the liberty of contract decisions reflected a weak grasp of economics. An early criticism based on this view is found in Justice Brandeis's dissenting opinion in *New State Ice Co. v. Liebmann*.[4] The case involved the constitutionality of a state statute that required anyone who wanted to manufacture and sell ice to obtain a certificate of public convenience and necessity and that provided that a certificate would be denied if existing service was adequate. New State, which had such a certificate, sought to enjoin Liebmann, who did not, from entering the ice business in New State's territory. Liebmann's defense was that the statute was unconstitutional. The Court invalidated the statute for reasons with which most economists would concur:

> Stated succinctly, a private corporation here seeks to prevent a competitor from entering the business of making and selling ice. . . . There is no question now before us of any regulation by the state to protect the consuming public either with respect to conditions of manufacture and distribution or to insure purity of products or to prevent extortion. The control here asserted does not protect against monopoly, but tends to foster it. The aim is not to encourage competition, but to prevent it; not to regulate the business, but to preclude persons from engaging in it. . . . It is not the case of a natural monopoly, or of an enterprise in its nature dependent upon the grant of public privileges. The particular requirement before us was evidently not imposed to prevent a practical monopoly of the business, since its tendency is quite to the contrary.

The Court likened the certification provision to an attempt of one shoemaker, under state authority, "to prevent another shoemaker from making or selling shoes because shoemakers already in that occupation can make and sell all the shoes that are needed."

   Justice Brandeis's economic argument begins with the proposition that the ice business may be "one which lends itself peculiarly to monopoly"; "the business is conducted in local plants with a market narrowly limited in area" because of the weight and perishability of the

4.   285 U.S. 262 (1932).

product. But the fact that a firm has only a local market area does not preclude competition. Brandeis's opinion reveals, moreover, that prior to the passage of the challenged statute there was competition in the ice business in many localities in the state. He argues that "even in those localities the prices of ice were ordinarily uniform," but since, as he stresses elsewhere in his opinion, the product is uniform, one would expect competitive sellers to charge the same price.

*   *   *

No doubt the real purpose of the statute was to foster cartelization of the Oklahoma ice industry. As Brandeis himself curiously emphasizes,

> Trade journals and reports of association meetings of ice manufacturers bear ample witness to the hostility of the industry to such competition, and to its unremitting efforts, through trade associations, informal agreements, combination of delivery systems, and in particular through the consolidation of plants, to protect markets and prices against competition of any character.

He also notes: "the ice industry as a whole in Oklahoma has acquiesced in and accepted the Act and the status which it creates."

In viewing the case as one in which Liebmann's economic rights were pitted against the interests of the poor people of Oklahoma who could not afford refrigerators, Justice Brandeis got it backwards. The right he would have vindicated was the interest of New State Ice and other established ice companies to be free from competition. The people actually wronged by the statute were the poor, who were compelled to pay more for ice; the well-to-do, as Brandeis pointed out, were more likely to have refrigerators.

If the ice business were a natural monopoly, the Brandeis position might be economically defensible, since *   *   * the effort of a natural monopolist to maximize his profits by establishing a monopoly price could lead to a wasteful duplication of facilities. Not only is the premise false, however, but it appears from the latter part of Brandeis's opinion that the natural monopoly language of the earlier part is a makeweight and that he was prepared to embrace the sweeping proposition that ruinous competition is a common phenomenon of economic markets and was a major factor behind the great depression of the 1930s. The case was decided in 1931, and although the Oklahoma statute predated the depression, Brandeis discusses extensively, and with apparent approval, the proposition that the philosophy embodied in the Oklahoma limitation on entry into the ice business might be a remedy of general application to the current economic crisis.

The view of the great depression as rooted in the excesses of competition and curable by reducing competition is discredited *   *   *. Of course, when demand declined during the depression much of the existing industrial capacity, geared as it was to supplying a larger demand, became temporarily excess. But limiting competition would not have increased purchasing power and therefore demand; it would just have impaired the efficiency of economic activity at its reduced level. * * *

Some of the statutes upheld by the Supreme Court in the period when it was guided by liberty of contract notions also were attempts to suppress competition under the guise of promoting the general welfare. In *Muller v. Oregon,*[7] for example, the Court upheld a state statute fixing a maximum work day of 10 hours for women employed in laundries. Unless the state also had a minimum wage law and the wages of women employed in laundries were not significantly higher than the minimum, the statute probably had little effect. Forced to reduce the work day, the employer would compensate by reducing the daily wage. If the employer were prevented from reducing the daily wage, he would treat the statute as having increased the cost of his labor (he gets less output for the same wage) and, under a now-familiar analysis, would adapt by buying a smaller quantity of labor, raising prices, or doing both things. The reduction in employment would harm any workers he laid off who did not have equally good alternative employment opportunities; the increase in prices would harm consumers, and by reducing his output would lead him to further reduce his labor inputs.

Since the Court's repudiation of liberty of contract, it has frequently upheld statutes designed to foster monopoly, such as a state statute that, on grounds of public health, forbade opticians to replace eyeglass frames without a prescription signed by an optometrist or an ophthalmologist [9]—although the statute could have had no purpose other than to increase the incomes of optometrists and ophthalmologists at the expense of opticians and consumers.

ROBERT G. McCLOSKEY, ECONOMIC DUE PROCESS AND THE SUPREME COURT: AN EXHUMATION AND REBURIAL

1962 Sup.Ct.Rev. 34, 45–53.

IV. THE DOUBTFUL DISTINCTION BETWEEN ECONOMIC AND CIVIL RIGHTS

* * *

The arguments for demoting economic rights to their modern lowly constitutional status—lowly when compared with "personal rights"— fall into two categories. First, there is a group of arguments based on judgments about the nature and relative importance of the rights concerned. For example, it is sometimes argued that laws limiting freedom of expression impinge on the human personality more grievously than do laws curbing mere economic liberty, and that the Court is therefore justified in protecting the former more zealously

7. 206 U.S. 412 (1908).

9. See Williamson v. Lee Optical Co., 348 U.S. 438 (1955). For an extreme exam-

ple of the Court's tolerance see Kotch v. Board of River Port Pilot Commrs., 330 U.S. 552 (1947).

than the latter. The individual has, *qua* individual, "the right to be let alone." The right to free choice in the intellectual and spiritual realm is particularly precious to him. A major difficulty with this formulation is that there is the smell of the lamp about it: it may reflect the tastes of the judges and dons who advance it, rather than the real preferences of the commonality of mortals. Judges and professors are talkers both by profession and avocation. It is not surprising that they would view freedom of expression as primary to the free play of their personalities. But most men would probably feel that an economic right, such as freedom of occupation, was at least as vital to them as the right to speak their minds. Mark Twain would surely have felt constrained in the most fundamental sense, if his youthful aspiration to be a river-boat pilot had been frustrated by a State-ordained system of nepotism.[60] Needless to say, no disparagement of freedom of expression is here intended. But its inarguable importance to the human spirit, on the one hand, does not furnish an adequate ground for downgrading all economic rights, on the other.

So much for a purely individual-centered justification for the disparity between economic rights and other civil liberties. Another suggested rationale looks toward the community rather than the separate individuals within it. Progress, it is said, "is to a considerable extent the displacement of error which once held sway as official truth by beliefs which in turn have yielded to other beliefs."[61] To encourage societal progress, it is important then to protect "those liberties of the individual which history has attested as the indispensable conditions of an open as against a closed society," *e.g.,* freedom of expression.

Presumably this "open society" argument would be relevant no matter how the political system was organized—even a benevolent autocracy must tolerate freedom of expression or risk stagnation. But Alexander Meiklejohn has contended that the point takes on an extra dimension when applied to popular government, to democracy as the West understands that term. In any political system, so the argument runs, the ruler must be fully informed if he is to govern well, and he cannot be fully informed when someone else is deciding what ideas he shall be allowed to hear. In a democracy the people are sovereign, and it follows that they and no one else must decide what and whom they will listen to. And it further follows that the Constitution must protect any freedoms that help the people to acquire "the intelligence, integrity, sensitivity, and generous devotion to the general welfare that, in theory, casting a ballot is assumed to express."[63] In short, the special importance of certain civil rights derives from their special relationship to the process of self-government. Other rights, including the economic, can be abridged when the legislature deems abridgment desirable.

---

60. Kotch v. Pilot Commissioners, 330 U.S. 552 (1947).

61. Frankfurter, J., concurring, in Kovacs v. Cooper, 336 U.S. 77 at 95.

63. Meiklejohn, *The First Amendment Is an Absolute,* [1961] Supreme Court Review 245, 255.

Some such reasoning probably underlies the related point implied by Mr. Justice Stone in the first paragraph of his famous "footnote four" [64] and by Mr. Justice Frankfurter in the concluding words of the first flag-salute opinion [65] (though neither would of course have followed Professor Meiklejohn in the absolutist conclusions he drew). Stone suggested that judicial scrutiny would be especially exacting when legislation restricted "those political processes which can ordinarily be expected to bring about repeal of undesirable legislation," and Frankfurter intimated that the crucial question is whether "all the effective means of inducing political changes are left free from interference." These pronouncements may rest partly on Professor Meiklejohn's point that the governors must be fully informed; but they also seem to involve a separable idea: that a majoritarian system must, in the name of both justice and progress, preserve the right of a present minority to make its views the views of the majority. A businessman's price may be controlled by the mandate of a popularly elected legislature, but, if his right to work politically for repeal of the control law is untrammeled, the fundamentals of a just democratic policy are still maintained and so is the fluidity of the sociopolitical order.

The whole "open society" line of argument in its various forms is convincing enough as a justification for protecting the free trade in ideas. If one feels the need to explain why the free speech guarantees are important, these explanations will do pretty well for a start. But they are rather less satisfactory as the basis for a policy of *not* protecting economic freedom, of regarding it as unimportant in a democratic system. For one thing, it is not entirely clear why liberty of economic choice is less indispensable to the "openness" of a society than freedom of expression. Few historians would deny that the growth of entrepreneurial and occupational freedom helped to promote material progress in England in the eighteenth and nineteenth centuries and in America after the Civil War (although they might of course argue that the price paid for this progress was unconscionably high). It is one thing to argue that economic liberty must be subject to rational control in the "public interest"; it is quite another to say in effect that it is not liberty at all and that the proponent of the "open society" can therefore regard it as irrelevant to progress.

As for the "political process" subthemes of the open-society argument—the Meiklejohn–Stone–Frankfurter rationales just described—they too must be queried insofar as they purport to justify a downgrading of economic rights. In fact, their basic difficulty is that, in exalting the freedoms bearing on the political process, they bypass the question of other freedoms altogether. Meiklejohn's arguments for protecting liberty of expression are cogent, but they do not on their face explain why other, "private," rights should be neglected. A decision to protect

---

64. United States v. Carolene Products Co., 304 U.S. 144, 152 (1938).

65. Minersville School Dist. v. Gobitis, 310 U.S. 586, 600 (1940).

Peter does not necessarily involve the decision to abandon Paul.
* * *

If Meiklejohn's argument contains the unexamined assumption that the political is primary and almost exclusive, the "Stone–Frankfurter" point described above contains this and an assumption of its own as well: the majoritarian idea in a peculiarly unqualified form. The notion seems to be that the citizen can have nothing really fundamental to complain about in a law if a free majority has enacted it and if he is protected in his right to agitate for its repeal. But this view ascribes a preponderance to the majority will that has certainly not been acknowledged by the American political tradition. In that tradition, it is not assumed that an unjust law becomes just by virtue of majority approval, not even if the victim has the theoretical right to persuade the majority to change its mind. * * *

Furthermore this argument overlooks a difficulty partly recognized by Stone himself in the *Carolene Products* footnote and invoked by him in the first flag-salute case, the problem of "discrete and insular minorities," *i.e.,* those who have no realistic chance of influencing the majority to rescind the law that does them harm. Stone was speaking specifically of religious, national, or racial minorities, and his suggestion was that prejudice against them might curtail the political processes that would ordinarily be expected to protect their rights. Prejudice against Jehovah's Witnesses for their "queerness" makes repressive governmental action more probable, and precisely because of their queerness they are not likely to be numerous enough or influential enough in any given community so that their weight will be felt in the city council. To speak of their power to defend themselves through political action is to sacrifice their civil rights in the name of an amiable fiction. Yet it is not clear why the thrust of this point should be restricted to ethnic and religious minorities. Perhaps it is true that a prosperous corporation can effectively plead its case at the bar of legislative judgment by resort to publicity and direct lobbying. Economic power may be an adequate surrogate for numerical power; no tears need be shed for helpless General Electric. But the scattered individuals who are denied access to an occupation by State-enforced barriers are about as impotent a minority as can be imagined. The would-be barmaids of Michigan [75] or the would-be plumbers of Illinois have no more chance against the entrenched influence of the established bartenders and master plumbers than the Jehovah's Witnesses had against the prejudices of Minersville School District. In fact the Witnesses may enjoy an advantage, for they are at least cohesive; and other "discrete" minorities, such as racial groups, have occasionally displayed respectable capacities to exert political leverage by virtue of their very discreteness. Not so the isolated economic man who belongs to no identifiable group at all.

75. Goesaert v. Cleary, 335 U.S. 464 (1948).

V. JUDICIAL CAPACITY IN THE REALM OF ECONOMIC REGULATION

*   *   *

Although the policy of abdication cannot be justified in terms of an analysis of the nature and relative unimportance of the rights concerned, there is a second line of thought that merits consideration. Perhaps the decision to leave economic rights to the tender mercy of the legislative power is based on the idea that the Supreme Court is peculiarly ill-equipped to deal with this subject. No one would argue that the right enshrined in Article IV, the guarantee of a republican form of government, is unimportant. Yet the Court has refused to protect it, because of well-founded doubts about judicial competence to make effective judgments in this field. It may be that similar doubts underlie the policy of abdication in the area of economic affairs.

*   *   *

There are, of course, economic subjects so recondite that judicial surveillance of them would be anomalous. The choice between "historical cost" and "replacement cost" as a basis for rate making must be made by the legislature, not because it will always choose well, but because the judiciary lacks the knowledge and expertise for distinguishing good from bad in this area. But this point will carry only as far as its logic will bring it, and there are fields of economic regulation less intricate than the problem of public utility rates. To be sure, even the problems raised in these fields may not be simple. A fair evaluation of Oklahoma's need for its anti-optician law would require the Court to make judgments about a complex matter. But this can be said about most questions that reach the Supreme Court in any field. Our problem is not to identify the issues that present difficulties and then to discard them as improper subjects for judicial review. That would be to abandon judicial review in most of the fields where it is now exercised. Our problem is to determine whether economic statutes always or usually involve such extraordinary difficulties that a modest judiciary must eschew them, even though that same judiciary does claim the competence to judge other, more difficult, issues.

Is it easier for example for the Court to appraise a law empowering a board of censors to ban an "immoral" movie than a law empowering a real estate licensing board to deny a license unless the applicant is of "good moral character"? The two standards would seem to be equally vague and the possibility of arbitrary administrative action would seem to be as menacing in one situation as in the other. *   *   * Is it easier to see that the State corporate registration law in *N.A.A.C.P. v. Alabama* was being used to facilitate private reprisals against Association members than it is to see that State boards of plumbers, barbers, and morticians sometimes use their publicly granted powers to protect the private financial interests of present guild members to the disadvantage of non-members?

The point is *   *   * that [these] issues *   *   * stand on a common level of difficulty and that judicial scrutiny seems as feasible (or unfeasible) for one issue as for the other. And the further, related, point is that there are kinds and kinds of economic subjects and that it is difficult to fashion a generalization that applies to all. Some subjects may be so inscrutable that judicial review cannot fruitfully cope with them; but this is not a justification for avoiding other economic subjects which are no more opaque than the "personal rights" issues that are the standard coinage of judicial discourse these days.

This point likewise applies to the suggestion that the Court, as the relatively weak and non-political branch, simply lacks the power to dictate the economic order, however otherwise competent its members may be. No doubt the Court was presumptuous to imagine, before 1937, that it could hold back such waves as the wage-control movement or the demand for social security. The tide of the welfare state was flowing, and no court could have reversed it. But neither does the judiciary have the practical power to halt any major social developments backed by insistent popular demand. And this would be so whether the development involved economic questions or questions of "personal rights." It was the dimension of the issues in the anti-New Deal cases that made them incongruous for judicial decision, not the mere fact that they were economic in character. No such judicial delusions of grandeur would be implied by enforcement of the requirement that an occupational qualification must be rationally based, or by similar modest applications of substantive due process. The awful will of the sovereign people is not likely to be aroused because the Court has told the morticians of Winnemac that they cannot use State power to maintain a monopoly—or at least no more than it is aroused by other constitutional decisions that issue almost weekly during each Term.

BIBLIOGRAPHY

E. Corwin, LIBERTY AGAINST GOVERNMENT (1948).

Hovenkamp, *The Political Economy of Substantive Due Process,* 40 Stanford L.Rev. 379 (1988).

Miller, *The True Story of Carolene Products,* 1987 Sup.Ct.Rev. 397.

A. Paul, CONSERVATIVE CRISIS AND THE RULE OF LAW (1969).

B. Siegan, ECONOMIC LIBERTIES AND THE CONSTITUTION (1980).

Siegel, *Understanding the Lochner Era: Lessons from the Controversy over Railroad and Utility Rate Regulation,* 70 Va.L.Rev. 187 (1984).

Stigler, *The Theory of Economic Regulation,* 2 Bell J.Econ. & Mgmt.Sci. 3 (1971).

Tarrow, Lochner versus New York: *A Political Analysis,* 5 Lab.Hist. 277 (1964).

Wonnell, *Economic Due Process and the Preservation of Competition,* 11 Hast.Const.L.Q. 91 (1983).

B. ABORTION

In *Griswold v. Connecticut* [1] in 1965 the Supreme Court held that a state law forbidding the use of contraceptives violated the Due Process Clause of the Fourteenth Amendment. The Court did not make clear whether it was protecting a right to prevent conception (a liberty properly speaking—a right to act), or a right to privacy in the Fourth Amendment sense (a protection against government snooping). *Roe v. Wade* [2] eight years later was unequivocal. It held that "the Fourteenth Amendment's concept of personal liberty . . . encompass[ed] a woman's decision whether or not to terminate her pregnancy." Since then the courts have been plagued with issues about the scope of this liberty, not just in abortion cases, but also in cases dealing with other family affairs,[3] homosexual behavior,[4] the provision of medical care,[5] and so on.

The readings in this Section focus on *Roe,* because it is the axis around which these issues revolve. *Roe* has been particularly controversial for two reasons. The first is the difficulty of explaining what makes the freedom to terminate pregnancy a special liberty deserving unusual protection from the courts. The second is the unique quality of the countervailing interest in such cases: the government claims that it is protecting potential (or perhaps actual) human life by restricting abortions.

John Noonan's article asserts that the latter point should be decisive, and that the courts have shied away from confronting it. They have, he argues, dehumanized the unborn child much as nineteenth century courts dehumanized slaves, by treating the idea of a "person" as simply a juridical construct.

Rather than dispute Noonan's assertion, Judith Thomson's famous defense of abortion accepts it as true and asserts that a woman still has a right to decide what shall happen in and to her body. If the fetus is a person it has a right to live, but that is not a right to be kept alive at someone else's expense.

John Hart Ely contends that *Roe* is misguided in identifying the right to have an abortion as a "liberty" deserving of special protection. If it were a weaker liberty (like freedom of contract) it would have to yield to the government's interest in protecting the fetus even if the fetus were *not* a person. Nothing in the text or the framers' thinking identifies the woman's action as special. And Ely argues that in this instance—where women's interests conflict with those of fetuses and

1. 381 U.S. 479, 85 S.Ct. 1678, 14 L.Ed. 2d 510 (1965).

2. 410 U.S. 113, 153, 93 S.Ct. 705, 726, 35 L.Ed.2d 147 (1973).

3. Moore v. East Cleveland, 431 U.S. 494, 97 S.Ct. 1932, 52 L.Ed.2d 531 (1977).

4. Bowers v. Hardwick, 478 U.S. 186, 106 S.Ct. 2841, 92 L.Ed.2d 140 (1986).

5. Cruzan v. Director, Missouri Dept. of Health, ___ U.S. ___, 110 S.Ct. 2841, 111 L.Ed.2d 224 (1990).

not men—the political process can be trusted to reach a satisfactory result.

Catharine MacKinnon is disturbed more by the reasoning than by the result in *Roe*. The Court's decision removes control over abortion from the public sphere and remits it to the private interactions of individual men and women. MacKinnon argues that women cannot protect themselves even in that private sphere (let alone the public arena that Ely trusts) from male oppression. So long as men control sexuality the regime of individual privacy protected by *Roe v. Wade* simply leaves men alone to oppress women one at a time.

JOHN T. NOONAN, JR., THE ROOT AND BRANCH OF *ROE v. WADE*

63 Neb.L.Rev. 668–669, 471–673, 675, 677–679 (1984).

Whoever has the power to define the bearer of constitutional rights has a power that can make nonsense of any particular constitutional right. That this power belongs to the state itself is a point of view associated in jurisprudence with Hans Kelsen. According to Kelsen a person is simply a construct of the law. As he expresses it in *The Pure Theory of Law*, even the apparently natural physical person is a construction of juristic thinking. In this account it appears that just as we personify a corporation for legal purposes so we personify natural physical beings. There are no independent, ontological existences to which we respond as persons. Personhood depends on recognition by the law.[2]

A corollary of that position appears to be what has always seemed to me one of the most terrifying of legal propositions: there is no kind of human behavior that, because of its nature, could not be made into a legal duty corresponding to a legal right. When one thinks of the vast variety of human behavior it is at least startling to think that every variation could be converted into legal duties and legal rights. The proposition becomes terrifying when one thinks of Orwell's *1984* or the actual conduct of the Nazi regime from which Hans Kelsen himself eventually had to flee.

There is one massive phenomenon in the history of our country that might be invoked to support Kelsen's point of view. That phenomenon is the way a very large class of human beings were treated prior to the enactment of the thirteenth and fourteenth amendments. When one looks back at the history of 200 years of slavery in the United States, and looks back at it as a lawyer observing that lawyers had a great deal to do with the classifications that made the phenomenon possible, one realizes that the law, in fact, has been used to create legal rights and legal duties in relation to human behavior that should never have been given a legal form and a legal blessing. To put it bluntly, law was the medium and lawyers were the agents responsible for

---

2. H. Kelsen, The Pure Theory of Law 95 (M. Knight trans. 2nd ed. 1967).

turning one class of human beings into property. The result was that the property laws of the different states made it smooth and easy to transfer ownership of these human beings. The property laws resolved the questions that occurred at those critical junctions where humanity asserted itself either in the birth of a child to a slave or the death of the owner of a slave. The only question left open for argument was whether the human beings classified as property were realty or personalty. In the inheritance cases the slave child was treated like the issue of an animal, compared again and again in legal decisions to the issue of livestock.

Gross characterization of human beings in terms that reduced them to animals, or real estate, or even kitchen utensils now may seem so unbelievable that we all can profess shock and amazement that it was ever done. Eminently respectable lawyers were able to engage in this kind of characterization—among them Thomas Jefferson, who co-authored the slave code of Virginia, and Abraham Lincoln who argued on behalf of a slave owner seeking to recover as his property a woman and her four children who had escaped to the free state of Illinois. Looking at such familiar examples and realizing how commonplace it was for lawyers to engage in this kind of fiction, we learn, I think, that law can operate as a kind of magic. All that is necessary is to permit legal legerdemain to create a mask obliterating the human person being dealt with. Looking at the mask—that is looking at the abstract category created by the law—is not to see the human reality on which the mask is imposed.

* * *

[Consider what happened in] *Scott v. Sanford.* Here the black plaintiff attempted to assert his right to freedom in the federal court. The Supreme Court held that the federal statute that should have made him free was an interference with the property rights guaranteed by the Constitution to his owner. The Court applied the due process clause of the fifth amendment—gratuitously reading into this clause a concept of substantive due process—and held the statute invalid. The property mask dropped over Dred Scott was the means by which the Constitution was brought into play. As James Buchanan, the President at the time, happily put it, the Court had achieved "the final settlement" of the question of slavery in the Territories.[12] It was a final settlement curiously like Adolph Hitler's "final solution" of "the Jewish question" in Germany.

Buchanan's description, of course, was inaccurate. The Supreme Court could not resolve an issue that so fundamentally divided the nation. The legal mask was shattered by the Civil War. The thirteenth and fourteenth amendments were adopted. The legal profession forgot about its participation in molding the mask that made slavery possible. It is only in our time that the analogy seems vital.

12. James Buchanan, *Third Annual Message to Congress,* 4 Papers of the Presidents 3085–86 (J. Richardson ed. 1913).

Kelsen's jurisprudence makes ＊ ＊ ＊ *Dred Scott* a defensible decision: according to it, there is nothing intrinsic in humanity requiring persons to be legally recognized as persons. The relevance of Kelsen's reasoning was acknowledged in a modern case, *Byrn v. New York City Health and Hospital Corporation,*[13] decided a year before the Supreme Court decided *Roe v. Wade.* In *Byrn,* Robert Byrn was appointed guardian *ad litem* of an unborn child and asserted that child's constitutional right not to be aborted. His position was rejected by the majority of the Court of Appeals of New York, speaking through Judge Charles Breitel. Breitel quoted Kelsen explicitly to support his position that it was a policy determination of the state whether legal personality should be recognized or not. It was, Breitel stated, "not true that the legal order corresponds to the natural order." Breitel did not go as far as Kelsen's statement that natural persons were juristic creations— Breitel seemed to assume that there might be natural persons—but he left the recognition of natural persons to the legislature. As New York, at this time, had already enacted a fairly radical abortion law, he held that the legislature had conclusively made the decision that left the unborn child outside the class of recognized humanity.

＊ ＊ ＊

Roe v. Wade itself, decided a year later, was profoundly ambivalent—indeed, to speak bluntly, it was schizoid in its approach to the power of the state to determine who was a person. The opinion was schizoid because the Court wanted to invoke rights that were not dependent on the state—the Court was trying to find a measure by which to invalidate state statutes. The precedents that the Court found to authorize it to act in this area of law were all cases that treated family rights as having a natural basis superior to the law of the state. The cases involved included *Meyer v. Nebraska* and *Pierce v. Society of Sisters,* recognizing a superior right of parents to educate their children; *Skinner v. Oklahoma,* recognizing that a man has a natural right to procreate and so cannot be arbitrarily sterilized by the state; *Loving v. Virginia,* where the natural right to marry was invoked in the course of invalidating a miscegenation statute; and *Griswold v. Connecticut,* where the rights of the married were also asserted, in this case to hold unconstitutional a statute prohibiting the use of contraceptives.

All of these cases rested on the supposition that the family rights being protected were those of persons, and that these persons could not be unmade at will by the state. The natural law fundament of these decisions was camouflaged by their being couched in constitutional language; but the constitutional content was derived from nowhere except the natural law as it had taken shape in the traditions of the United States. At the same time that it invoked such precedents in

---

13. 31 N.Y.2d 194, 286 N.E.2d 887, 335 N.Y.S.2d 390 (1972), *appeal dismissed,* 410 U.S. 940 (1973).

Roe, the Court, when treating of the unborn, felt free to impose its own notions of reality.

In one passage the Court spoke of the unborn before viability as "a theory of life," as though there were competing views as to whether life in fact existed before viability. The implication could also be found that there was no reality there in the womb but merely theories about what was there. The Court seemed to be uncertain itself and to take the position that if it were unsure, nobody else could be sure. In another passage the Court spoke of life in the womb up to birth as "potential life." This description was accurate if it meant there was existing life with a great deal of development yet to come, as one might say a 5–year–old is "potential life" meaning that he or she is only potentially what he or she will be at twenty-five. The Court's description was inaccurate if the Court meant to suggest that what was in the womb was pure potentiality, a zero that could not be protected by law. To judge from the weight the Court gave the being in the womb—found to be protectable in any degree only in the last two months of pregnancy—the Court itself must have viewed the unborn as pure potentiality or a mere theory before viability. The Court's opinion appeared to rest on the assumption that the biological reality could be subordinated or ignored by the sovereign speaking through the Court.

*   *   *

The progeny of *Roe* have confirmed the Kelsenite reading of *Roe* that there is no reality that the sovereign must recognize unless the sovereign, acting through the agency of the Court, decides to recognize it. This view would be psychologically incomprehensible if we did not have the history of the creation of the institution of slavery by judges and lawyers. With that history we can see that intelligent and humane lawyers have been able to apply a similar approach to a whole class of beings that they could see—that they were able to create a mask of legal concepts preventing humanity from being visible. A mask is a little easier to impose when the humanity concealed, being in the womb, is not even visible to the naked eye.

Kelsenite logic permits the judges at the apex of a system to dispense with correspondence to reality. The highest court is then free, within the limits that the society in which it functions will tolerate, to be inventive. It may, as the Supreme Court of the United States has sometimes thought, be constrained by the language of the Constitution and the purposes of its makers. Or, as has also sometimes happened, the Court, viewing itself as the final expounder of the Constitution's meaning, will exercise its inventiveness in creating new constitutional doctrine not dependent on text or purposes. Such doctrine—fantasy in the service of ideology—is "the branch" of *Roe v. Wade.* What then becomes possible was illustrated in 1983 by *Akron v. Akron Center for Reproductive Health.* In this case a whole set of constitutional requirements were created on behalf of the claims of an abortion clinic, named with Orwellian aptness, a center for "reproductive health."

*   *   *

Most strikingly of all, *Akron* held that there could not be a legal requirement that a woman seeking an abortion be informed that the being she wished put to death was a child, that the child was alive, and that the child was human. The Court treated this information as prejudicing the choice of whether to abort or not—as a kind of unfair interference with free choice. The ordinance was bad because it was designed "to influence the woman's informed choice between abortion and childbirth." The holding went beyond the Kelsenite jurisprudential root and any mainline theory of constitutional interpretation. It was, indeed, the invention of a kind of censorship by the Court itself.

*   *   *

A final provision of the Akron ordinance was that "the remains of the unborn child" be "disposed of in a humane and sanitary manner." The Sixth Circuit Court of Appeals found the word "humane" impermissibly vague in a criminal statute.[43] The ordinance could, the court said, mean to "mandate some sort of 'decent burial' of an embryo at the earliest stages of formation. . . ."[44] Justice Powell quoted this analysis and agreed; humane and sanitary burial was beyond the comprehension of a reasonable doctor.

In this conclusion one can observe in the most concrete way the Court's discomfort before reality. The Court cannot uphold a requirement of humane burial without conceding that the being who is to be buried is human. A mask has been placed over this being. Even death cannot remove the mask.

The Court's denial of reality stands in contrast with what Andre Gide has written on the humane burial of an unborn child:

> When morning came, "get rid of that," I said naively to the gardener's wife when she finally came to see how everything was. Could I have supposed that those formless fragments, to which I turning away in disgust was pointing, could I have supposed that in the eyes of the Church they already represented the sacred human being they were being readied to clothe? O mystery of incarnation! Imagine then my stupor when some hours later I saw "it" again. The thing which for me already had no name in any language, now cleaned, adorned, beribboned, laid in a little cradle, awaiting the ritual entombment. Fortunately no one had been aware of the sacrilege I had been about to commit; I had already committed it in thought when I had said get rid of "that." Yes, very happily that ill-considered order had been heard by no one. And, I remained a long time musing before "it." Before that little face with the crushed forehead on which they had carefully hidden the wound. Before this innocent flesh which I, if I had been alone, yielding to my first impulse, would have consigned to the manure heap along with the afterbirth and which religious attentions had just saved from the void. I told no one then of what I felt. Of what I tell here. Was I to think that for a few moments a soul had

---

43. Akron Center for Reproductive Health v. City of Akron, 651 F.2d 1196, 1211 (1981).

44. Id.

inhabited this body? It has its tomb in Couvreville in that cemetery to which I wish not to return. Half a century has passed. I cannot truthfully say that I recall in detail that little face. No. What I remember exactly is my surprise, my sudden emotion, when confronted by its extraordinary beauty.[46]

If the Court could respond to Gide and understand what humane and sanitary burial is, it might also perceive the reality of the extraordinary beauty of each human being put to death in the name of the abortion liberty and concealed from legal recognition by a jurisprudence that substitutes a judge's fiat for the truth.

JUDITH JARVIS THOMSON, A DEFENSE OF ABORTION

1 Phil. & Pub.Aff. 47, 48–62, 65–66 (1971).

I propose ＊ ＊ ＊ that we grant that the fetus is a person from the moment of conception. How does the argument go from here? Something like this, I take it. Every person has a right to life. So the fetus has a right to life. No doubt the mother has a right to decide what shall happen in and to her body; everyone would grant that. But surely a person's right to life is stronger and more stringent than the mother's right to decide what happens in and to her body, and so outweighs it. So the fetus may not be killed; an abortion may not be performed.

It sounds plausible. But now let me ask you to imagine this. You wake up in the morning and find yourself back to back in bed with an unconscious violinist. A famous unconscious violinist. He has been found to have a fatal kidney ailment, and the Society of Music Lovers has canvassed all the available medical records and found that you alone have the right blood type to help. They have therefore kidnapped you, and last night the violinist's circulatory system was plugged into yours, so that your kidneys can be used to extract poisons from his blood as well as your own. The director of the hospital now tells you, "Look, we're sorry the Society of Music Lovers did this to you—we would never have permitted it if we had known. But still, they did it, and the violinist now is plugged into you. To unplug you would be to kill him. But never mind, it's only for nine months. By then he will have recovered from his ailment, and can safely be unplugged from you." Is it morally incumbent on you to accede to this situation? ＊ ＊ ＊

In this case, of course, you were kidnapped; you didn't volunteer for the operation that plugged the violinist into your kidneys. Can those who oppose abortion on the ground I mentioned make an exception for a pregnancy due to rape? Certainly. They can say that persons have a right to life only if they didn't come into existence because of rape; or they can say that all persons have a right to life,

---

46. A. Gide, Last Journals 95 (R. Stookey trans. 1979).

but that some have less of a right to life than others, in particular, that those who came into existence because of rape have less. But these statements have a rather unpleasant sound. Surely the question of whether you have a right to life at all, or how much of it you have, shouldn't turn on the question of whether or not you are the product of a rape. And in fact the people who oppose abortion on the ground I mentioned do not make this distinction, and hence do not make an exception in case of rape.

Some won't even make an exception for a case in which continuation of the pregnancy is likely to shorten the mother's life; they regard abortion as impermissible even to save the mother's life. Such cases are nowadays very rare, and many opponents of abortion do not accept this extreme view. All the same, it is a good place to begin: a number of points of interest come out in respect to it.

1. Let us call the view that abortion is impermissible even to save the mother's life "the extreme view." I want to suggest first that it does not issue from the argument I mentioned earlier without the addition of some fairly powerful premises. Suppose a woman has become pregnant, and now learns that she has a cardiac condition such that she will die if she carries the baby to term. What may be done for her? The fetus, being a person, has a right to life, but as the mother is a person too, so has she a right to life. Presumably they have an equal right to life. How is it supposed to come out that an abortion may not be performed? If mother and child have an equal right to life, shouldn't we perhaps flip a coin? Or should we add to the mother's right to life her right to decide what happens in and to her body, which everybody seems to be ready to grant—the sum of her rights now outweighing the fetus' right to life?

The most familiar argument here is the following. We are told that performing the abortion would be directly killing the child, whereas doing nothing would not be killing the mother, but only letting her die. Moreover, in killing the child, one would be killing an innocent person, for the child has committed no crime, and is not aiming at his mother's death. And then there are a variety of ways in which this might be continued. (1) But as directly killing an innocent person is always and absolutely impermissible, an abortion may not be performed. Or, (2) as directly killing an innocent person is murder, and murder is always and absolutely impermissible, an abortion may not be performed. Or, (3) as one's duty to refrain from directly killing an innocent person is more stringent than one's duty to keep a person from dying, an abortion may not be performed. Or, (4) if one's only options are directly killing an innocent person or letting a person die, one must prefer letting the person die, and thus an abortion may not be performed.

Some people seem to have thought that these are not further premises which must be added if the conclusion is to be reached, but that they follow from the very fact that an innocent person has a right to life. But this seems to me to be a mistake, and perhaps the simplest way to show this is to bring out that while we must certainly grant that innocent persons have a right to life, the theses in (1) through (4) are all false. Take (2), for example. If directly killing an innocent person is murder, and thus is impermissible, then the mother's directly killing the innocent person inside her is murder, and thus is impermissible. But it cannot seriously be thought to be murder if the mother performs an abortion on herself to save her life. It cannot seriously be said that she *must* refrain, that she *must* sit passively by and wait for her death. Let us look again at the case of you and the violinist. There you are, in bed with the violinist, and the director of the hospital says to you, "It's all most distressing, and I deeply sympathize, but you see this is putting an additional strain on your kidneys, and you'll be dead within the month. But you *have* to stay where you are all the same. Because unplugging you would be directly killing an innocent violinist, and that's murder, and that's impermissible." If anything in the world is true, it is that you do not commit murder, you do not do what is impermissible, if you reach around to your back and unplug yourself from that violinist to save your life.

* * *

In sum, a woman surely can defend her life against the threat to it posed by the unborn child, even if doing so involves its death. And this shows not merely that the theses in (1) through (4) are false; it shows also that the extreme view of abortion is false, and so we need not canvass any other possible ways of arriving at it from the argument I mentioned at the outset.

* * *

3. Where the mother's life is not at stake, the argument I mentioned at the outset seems to have a much stronger pull. "Everyone has a right to life, so the unborn person has a right to life." And isn't the child's right to life weightier than anything other than the mother's own right to life, which she might put forward as ground for an abortion?

This argument treats the right to life as if it were unproblematic. It is not, and this seems to me to be precisely the source of the mistake.

For we should now, at long last, ask what it comes to, to have a right to life. In some views having a right to life includes having a right to be given at least the bare minimum one needs for continued life. But suppose that what in fact *is* the bare minimum a man needs for continued life is something he has no right at all to be given? If I am sick unto death, and the only thing that will save my life is the touch of Henry Fonda's cool hand on my fevered brow, then all the same, I have no right to be given the touch of Henry Fonda's cool hand on my fevered brow. It would be frightfully nice of him to fly in from the West Coast to provide it. It would be less nice, though no doubt well meant, if my friends flew out to the West Coast and carried Henry

Fonda back with them. But I have no right at all against anybody that he should do this for me. ＊ ＊ ＊

Some people are rather stricter about the right to life. In their view, it does not include the right to be given anything, but amounts to, and only to, the right not to be killed by anybody. But here a related difficulty arises. If everybody is to refrain from killing that violinist, then everybody must refrain from doing a great many different sorts of things. Everybody must refrain from slitting his throat, everybody must refrain from shooting him—and everybody must refrain from unplugging you from him. But does he have a right against everybody that they shall refrain from unplugging you from him? To refrain from doing this is to allow him to continue to use your kidneys. It could be argued that he has a right against us that *we* should allow him to continue to use your kidneys. That is, while he had no right against us that we should give him the use of your kidneys, it might be argued that he anyway has a right against us that we shall not now intervene and deprive him of the use of your kidneys. I shall come back to third-party interventions later. But certainly the violinist has no right against you that *you* shall allow him to continue to use your kidneys. As I said, if you do allow him to use them, it is a kindness on your part, and not something you owe him.

＊ ＊ ＊

4. There is another way to bring out the difficulty. In the most ordinary sort of case, to deprive someone of what he has a right to is to treat him unjustly. Suppose a boy and his small brother are jointly given a box of chocolates for Christmas. If the older boy takes the box and refuses to give his brother any of the chocolates, he is unjust to him, for the brother has been given a right to half of them. But suppose that, having learned that otherwise it means nine years in bed with that violinist, you unplug yourself from him. You surely are not being unjust to him, for you gave him no right to use your kidneys, and no one else can have given him any such right. But we have to notice that in unplugging yourself, you are killing him; and violinists, like everybody else, have a right to life, and thus in the view we were considering just now, the right not to be killed. So here you do what he supposedly has a right you shall not do, but you do not act unjustly to him in doing it.

The emendation which may be made at this point is this: the right to life consists not in the right not to be killed, but rather in the right not to be killed unjustly. This runs a risk of circularity, but never mind: it would enable us to square the fact that the violinist has a right to life with the fact that you do not act unjustly toward him in unplugging yourself, thereby killing him. For if you do not kill him unjustly, you do not violate his right to life, and so it is no wonder you do him no injustice.

But if this emendation is accepted, the gap in the argument against abortion stares us plainly in the face: it is by no means enough to show that the fetus is a person, and to remind us that all persons have a right to life—we need to be shown also that killing the fetus violates its right to life, i.e., that abortion is unjust killing. And is it?

I suppose we may take it as a datum that in a case of pregnancy due to rape the mother has not given the unborn person a right to the use of her body for food and shelter. Indeed, in what pregnancy could it be supposed that the mother has given the unborn person such a right? It is not as if there were unborn persons drifting about the world, to whom a woman who wants a child says "I invite you in."

But it might be argued that there are other ways one can have acquired a right to the use of another person's body than by having been invited to use it by that person. Suppose a woman voluntarily indulges in intercourse, knowing of the chance it will issue in pregnancy, and then she does become pregnant; is she not in part responsible for the presence, in fact the very existence, of the unborn person inside her? No doubt she did not invite it in. But doesn't her partial responsibility for its being there itself give it a right to the use of her body? If so, then her aborting it would be more like the boy's taking away the chocolates, and less like your unplugging yourself from the violinist—doing so would be depriving it of what it does have a right to, and thus would be doing it an injustice.

And then, too, it might be asked whether or not she can kill it even to save her own life: If she voluntarily called it into existence, how can she now kill it, even in self-defense?

The first thing to be said about this is that it is something new. Opponents of abortion have been so concerned to make out the independence of the fetus, in order to establish that it has a right to life, just as its mother does, that they have tended to overlook the possible support they might gain from making out that the fetus is *dependent* on the mother, in order to establish that she has a special kind of responsibility for it, a responsibility that gives it rights against her which are not possessed by any independent person—such as an ailing violinist who is a stranger to her.

On the other hand, this argument would give the unborn person a right to its mother's body only if her pregnancy resulted from a voluntary act, undertaken in full knowledge of the chance a pregnancy might result from it. It would leave out entirely the unborn person whose existence is due to rape. Pending the availability of some further argument, then, we would be left with the conclusion that unborn persons whose existence is due to rape have no right to the use of their mothers' bodies, and thus that aborting them is not depriving them of anything they have a right to and hence is not unjust killing.

And we should also notice that it is not at all plain that this argument really does go even as far as it purports to. For there are cases and cases, and the details make a difference. If the room is stuffy, and I therefore open a window to air it, and a burglar climbs in, it would be absurd to say, "Ah, now he can stay, she's given him a right to the use of her house—for she is partially responsible for his presence there, having voluntarily done what enabled him to get in, in full knowledge that there are such things as burglars, and that burglars burgle." It would be still more absurd to say this if I had had bars installed outside my windows, precisely to prevent burglars from getting in, and a burglar got in only because of a defect in the bars. It remains equally absurd if we imagine it is not a burglar who climbs in, but an innocent person who blunders or falls in. * * *

It seems to me that the argument we are looking at can establish at most that there are *some* cases in which the unborn person has a right to the use of its mother's body, and therefore *some* cases in which abortion is unjust killing. There is room for much discussion and argument as to precisely which, if any. But I think we should sidestep this issue and leave it open, for at any rate the argument certainly does not establish that all abortion is unjust killing.

5. There is room for yet another argument here, however. We surely must all grant that there may be cases in which it would be morally indecent to detach a person from your body at the cost of his life. Suppose you learn that what the violinist needs is not nine years of your life, but only one hour: all you need do to save his life is to spend one hour in that bed with him. Suppose also that letting him use your kidneys for that one hour would not affect your health in the slightest. Admittedly you were kidnapped. Admittedly you did not give anyone permission to plug him into you. Nevertheless it seems to me plain you *ought* to allow him to use your kidneys for that hour—it would be indecent to refuse.

* * *

Now some people are inclined to use the term "right" in such a way that it follows from the fact that you ought to allow a person to use your body for the hour he needs, that he has a right to use your body for the hour he needs, even though he has not been given that right by any person or act. They may say that it follows also that if you refuse, you act unjustly toward him. This use of the term is perhaps so common that it cannot be called wrong; nevertheless it seems to me to be an unfortunate loosening of what we would do better to keep a tight rein on. Suppose that box of chocolates I mentioned earlier had not been given to both boys jointly, but was given only to the older boy. There he sits, stolidly eating his way through the box, his small brother watching enviously. Here we are likely to say "You ought not to be so mean. You ought to give your brother some of those chocolates." My own view is that it just does not follow from the truth of this that the brother has any right to any of the chocolates. If the boy refuses to give his brother any, he is greedy, stingy, callous—but not unjust. I suppose that the people I have in mind will say it does follow that the brother has a right to some of the chocolates, and thus that the boy does act unjustly if he refuses to give his brother any. But the effect of saying this is to obscure what we should keep distinct, namely the difference between the boy's refusal in this case and the boy's refusal in the earlier case, in which the box was given to both boys jointly, and in which the small brother thus had what was from any point of view clear title to half.

* * *

So my own view is that even though you ought to let the violinist use your kidneys for the one hour he needs, we should not conclude that he has a right to do so—we should say that if you refuse, you are, like the boy who owns all the chocolates and will give none away, self-centered and callous, indecent in fact, but not unjust. And similarly, that even supposing a case in which a woman pregnant due to rape ought to allow the unborn person to use her body for the hour he needs, we should not conclude that he has a right to do so; we should conclude that she is self-centered, callous, indecent, but not unjust, if she refuses. The complaints are no less grave; they are just different. However, there is no need to insist on this point. If anyone does wish to deduce "he has a right" from "you ought," then all the same he must surely grant that there are cases in which it is not morally required of you that you allow that violinist to use your kidneys, and in which he does not have a right to use them, and in which you do not do him an injustice if you refuse. And so also for mother and unborn child. Except in such cases as the unborn person has a right to demand it— and we were leaving open the possibility that there may be such cases—nobody is morally *required* to make large sacrifices, of health, of all other interests and concerns, of all other duties and commitments, for nine years, or even for nine months, in order to keep another person alive.

* * *

8. My argument will be found unsatisfactory on two counts by many of those who want to regard abortion as morally permissible. First, while I do argue that abortion is not impermissible, I do not argue that it is always permissible. There may well be cases in which carrying the child to term requires only Minimally Decent Samaritanism of the mother, and this is a standard we must not fall below. I am inclined to think it a merit of my account precisely that it does *not* give a general yes or a general no. It allows for and supports our sense that, for example, a sick and desperately frightened fourteen-year-old schoolgirl, pregnant due to rape, may *of course* choose abortion, and that any law which rules this out is an insane law. And it also allows for and supports our sense that in other cases resort to abortion is even positively indecent. It would be indecent in the woman to request an abortion, and indecent in a doctor to perform it, if she is in her seventh month, and wants the abortion just to avoid the nuisance of postponing a trip abroad. The very fact that the arguments I have been drawing attention to treat all cases of abortion, or even all cases of abortion in which the mother's life is not at stake, as morally on a par ought to have made them suspect at the outset.

Secondly, while I am arguing for the permissibility of abortion in some cases, I am not arguing for the right to secure the death of the unborn child. It is easy to confuse these two things in that up to a certain point in the life of the fetus it is not able to survive outside the mother's body; hence removing it from her body guarantees its death. But they are importantly different. I have argued that you are not morally required to spend nine months in bed, sustaining the life of that violinist; but to say this is by no means to say that if, when you unplug yourself, there is a miracle and he survives, you then have a right to turn round and slit his throat. You may detach yourself even if this costs him his life; you have no right to be guaranteed his death, by some other means, if unplugging yourself does not kill him. There are some people who will feel dissatisfied by this feature of my argument. A woman may be utterly devastated by the thought of a child, a bit of herself, put out for adoption and never seen or heard of again. She may therefore want not merely that the child be detached from her, but more, that it die. Some opponents of abortion are inclined to regard this as beneath contempt—thereby showing insensitivity to what is surely a powerful source of despair. All the same, I agree that the desire for the child's death is not one which anybody may gratify, should it turn out to be possible to detach the child alive.

JOHN HART ELY, THE WAGES OF CRYING WOLF: A COMMENT ON *ROE v. WADE*

82 Yale L.J. 920, 923–926, 933–939 (1973).

II

Let us not underestimate what is at stake: Having an unwanted child can go a long way toward ruining a woman's life. And at bottom *Roe* signals the Court's judgment that this result cannot be justified by any good that anti-abortion legislation accomplishes. This surely is an understandable conclusion—indeed it is one with which I agree—but ordinarily the Court claims no mandate to second-guess legislative balances, at least not when the Constitution has designated neither of the values in conflict as entitled to special protection. But even assuming it would be a good idea for the Court to assume this function, *Roe* seems a curious place to have begun. Laws prohibiting the use of "soft" drugs or, even more obviously, homosexual acts between consenting adults can stunt "the preferred life styles" of those against whom enforcement is threatened in very serious ways. It is clear such acts harm no one besides the participants, and indeed the case that the participants are harmed is a rather shaky one. Yet such laws survive, on the theory that there exists a societal consensus that the behavior involved is revolting or at any rate immoral. Of course the consensus is not universal but it is sufficient, and this is what is counted crucial, to get the laws passed and keep them on the books. Whether anti-abortion legislation cramps the life style of an unwilling mother more significantly than anti-homosexuality legislation cramps the life style of a homosexual is a close question. But even granting that it does, the *other* side of the balance looks very different. For there is more than simple societal revulsion to support legislation restricting abortion: Abortion ends (or if it makes a difference, prevents) the life of a human being other than the one making the choice.

The Court's response here is simply not adequate. It agrees, indeed it holds, that after the point of viability (a concept it fails to note will become even less clear than it is now as the technology of birth continues to develop) the interest in protecting the fetus is compelling. Exactly why that is the magic moment is not made clear: Viability, as the Court defines it, is achieved some six to twelve weeks after quickening. (Quickening is the point at which the fetus begins discernibly to move independently of the mother and the point that has historically been deemed crucial—to the extent *any* point between conception and birth has been focused on.) But no, it is *viability* that is constitutionally critical: the Court's defense seems to mistake a definition for a syllogism.

> With respect to the State's important and legitimate interest in potential life, the "compelling" point is at viability. This is so because the fetus then presumably has the capacity of meaningful life outside the mother's womb.

With regard to why the state cannot consider this "important and legitimate interest" prior to viability, the opinion is even less satisfactory. The discussion begins sensibly enough: The interest asserted is not necessarily tied to the question whether the fetus is "alive," for whether or not one calls it a living being, it is an entity with the potential for (and indeed the likelihood of) life. But all of arguable relevance that follows are arguments that fetuses (a) are not recognized as "persons in the whole sense" by legal doctrine generally and (b) are not "persons" protected by the Fourteenth Amendment.

To the extent they are not entirely inconclusive, the bodies of doctrine to which the Court adverts respecting the protection of fetuses under general legal doctrine tend to undercut rather than support its conclusion. And the argument that fetuses (unlike, say, corporations) are not "persons" under the Fourteenth Amendment fares little better. The Court notes that most constitutional clauses using the word "persons"—such as the one outlining the qualifications for the Presidency—appear to have been drafted with postnatal beings in mind. (It might have added that most of them were plainly drafted with *adults* in mind, but I suppose that wouldn't have helped.) In addition, "the appellee conceded on reargument that no case can be cited that holds that a fetus is a person within the meaning of the Fourteenth Amendment." (The other legal contexts in which the question could have arisen are not enumerated.)

The canons of construction employed here are perhaps most intriguing when they are contrasted with those invoked to derive the constitutional right to an abortion. But in any event, the argument that fetuses lack constitutional rights is simply irrelevant. For it has never been held or even asserted that the state interest needed to justify forcing a person to refrain from an activity, *whether or not that activity is constitutionally protected,* must implicate either the life or the constitutional rights of another person. Dogs are not "persons in the whole sense" nor have they constitutional rights, but that does not mean the state cannot prohibit killing them: It does not even mean the state cannot prohibit killing them in the exercise of the First Amendment right of political protest. Come to think of it, draft cards aren't persons either.

Thus even assuming the Court ought generally to get into the business of second-guessing legislative balances, it has picked a strange case with which to begin. Its purported evaluation of the balance that produced anti-abortion legislation simply does not meet the issue: That the life plans of the mother must, not simply may, prevail over the state's desire to protect the fetus simply does not follow from the judgment that the fetus is not a person. Beyond all that, however, the Court has no business getting into that business.

III

* * *

* * * In his famous *Carolene Products* footnote, Justice Stone suggested that the interests to which the Court can responsibly give extraordinary constitutional protection include not only those expressed in the Constitution but also those that are unlikely to receive adequate consideration in the political process, specifically the interests of "discrete and insular minorities" unable to form effective political alliances.[84] There can be little doubt that such considerations have influenced the direction, if only occasionally the rhetoric, of the recent Courts. My repeated efforts to convince my students that sex should be treated as a "suspect classification" have convinced me it is no easy matter to state such considerations in a "principled" way. But passing that problem, *Roe* is not an appropriate case for their invocation.

Compared with men, very few women sit in our legislatures, a fact I believe should bear some relevance—even without an Equal Rights Amendment—to the appropriate standard of review for legislation that favors men over women.[85] But *no* fetuses sit in our legislatures. Of

---

84. United States v. Carolene Products Co., 304 U.S. 144, 152 n. 4 (1938).

85. This is not the place for a full treatment of the subject, but the general idea is this: Classifications by sex, like classifications by race, differ from the usual classification—to which the traditional "reasonable generalization" standard is properly applied—in that they rest on "we-they" generalizations as opposed to a "they-they" generalization. Take a familiar example of the usual approach, Williamson v. Lee Optical Co., 348 U.S. 483 (1955). Of course few legislators are opticians. But few are optometrists either. Thus while a decision to distinguish opticians from optometrists will incorporate a stereotypical comparison of two classes of people, it is a comparison of two "they" stereotypes, viz. "They [opticians] are generally inferior to or not so well qualified as *they* [optometrists] are in the following respect(s), which we find sufficient to justify the classification:. . . ." However, legislators traditionally have not only not been black (or female); they have been white (and male). A decision to distinguish blacks from whites (or women from men) will therefore have its roots in a

course they have their champions, but so have women. The two interests have clashed repeatedly in the political arena, and had continued to do so up to the date of the opinion, generating quite a wide variety of accommodations. By the Court's lights virtually all of the legislative accommodations had unduly favored fetuses; by its definition of victory, women had lost. Yet in every legislative balance one of the competing interests loses to some extent; indeed usually, as here, they both do. On some occasions the Constitution throws its weight on the side of one of them, indicating the balance must be restruck. And on others—and this is Justice Stone's suggestion–it is at least arguable that, constitutional directive or not, the Court should throw *its* weight on the side of a minority demanding in court more than it was able to achieve politically. But even assuming this suggestion can be given principled content, it was clearly intended and should be reserved for those interests which, *as compared with the interests to which they have been subordinated,* constitute minorities unusually incapable of protecting themselves. Compared with men, women may constitute such a "minority"; compared with the unborn, they do not. I'm not sure I'd know a discrete and insular minority if I saw one, but confronted with a multiple choice question requiring me to designate (a) women or (b) fetuses as one, I'd expect no credit for the former answer.

Of course a woman's freedom to choose an abortion is part of the "liberty" the Fourteenth Amendment says shall not be denied without due process of law, as indeed is anyone's freedom to do what he wants. But "due process" generally guarantees only that the inhibition be procedurally fair and that it have some "rational" connection—though plausible is probably a better word—with a permissible governmental goal. What is unusual about *Roe* is that the liberty involved is accorded a far more stringent protection, so stringent that a desire to preserve the fetus's existence is unable to overcome it—a protection

comparison between a "we" stereotype and a "they" stereotype, *viz.* "They [blacks or women] are generally inferior to or not so well qualified as *we* [whites or men] are in the following respect(s), which we find sufficient to justify the classification:. . . ."

The choice between classifying on the basis of a comparative generalization and attempting to come up with a more discriminating formula always involves balancing the increase in fairness which greater individualization will produce against the added costs it will entail. It is no startling psychological insight, however, that most of us are delighted to hear and prone to accept comparative characterizations of groups that suggest that the groups to which *we* belong are in some way superior to others. (I would be inclined to exclude most situations where the "we's" used to be "they's," *cf.* Ferguson v. Skrupa, 372 U.S. 726 (1963), and would therefore

agree that the unchangeability of the distinguishing characteristic is indeed relevant, though it is only part of the story.) The danger is therefore greater in we-they situations that we will overestimate the validity of the proposed stereotypical classification by seizing upon the positive myths about our own class and the negative myths about theirs—or indeed the realities respecting some or most members of the two classes—and too readily assuming that virtually the entire membership of the two classes fit the stereotypes and therefore that not many of "them" will be unfairly deprived, nor many of "us" unfairly benefitted, by the proposed classification. In short, I trust your generalizations about the differences between my gang and Wilfred's more than I do your generalizations about the differences between my gang and yours.

more stringent, I think it fair to say, than that the present Court accords the freedom of the press explicitly guaranteed by the First Amendment. What is frightening about *Roe* is that this super-protected right is not inferable from the language of the Constitution, the framers' thinking respecting the specific problem in issue, any general value derivable from the provisions they included, or the nation's governmental structure. Nor is it explainable in terms of the unusual political impotence of the group judicially protected vis-à-vis the interest that legislatively prevailed over it. And that, I believe—the predictable early reaction to *Roe* notwithstanding ("more of the same Warren-type activism")—is a charge that can responsibly be leveled at no other decision of the past twenty years. At times the inferences the Court has drawn from the values the Constitution marks for special protection have been controversial, even shaky, but never before has its sense of an obligation to draw one been so obviously lacking.

IV

Not in the last thirty-five years at any rate. For, as the received learning has it, this sort of thing did happen before, repeatedly. From its 1905 decision in *Lochner v. New York* into the 1930's the Court, frequently though not always under the rubric of "liberty of contract," employed the Due Process Clauses of the Fourteenth and Fifth Amendments to invalidate a good deal of legislation. According to the dissenters at the time and virtually all the commentators since, the Court had simply manufactured a constitutional right out of whole cloth and used it to superimpose its own view of wise social policy on those of the legislatures.   *   *   *

It may be objected that *Lochner et al.* protected the "economic rights" of businessmen whereas *Roe* protects a "human right." It should be noted, however, that not all of the *Lochner* series involved economic regulation; that even those that did resist the "big business" stereotype with which the commentators tend to associate them; and that in some of them the employer's "liberty of contract" claim was joined by the employee, who knew that if he had to be employed on the terms set by the law in question, he could not be employed at all. This is a predicament that is economic to be sure, but is not without its "human" dimension. Similarly "human" seems the predicament of the appellees in the 1970 case of *Dandridge v. Williams,* who challenged the Maryland Welfare Department's practice of limiting AFDC grants to $250 regardless of family size or need.   *   *   * It may be, however—at least it is not the sort of claim one can disprove—that the "right to an abortion," or noneconomic rights generally, accord more closely with "this generation's idealization of America" than the "rights" asserted in either *Lochner* or *Dandridge*. But that attitude, of course, is *precisely* the point of the *Lochner* philosophy, which would grant unusual protection to those "rights" that somehow *seem* most pressing, regardless of whether the Constitution suggests any special solicitude for them. The Constitution has little to say about contract, less about abortion, and those who would speculate about which the framers would have been more likely to protect may not be pleased with the answer. The Court continues to disavow the philosophy of *Lochner.* Yet as Justice Stewart's concurrence admits, it is impossible candidly to regard *Roe* as the product of anything else.

CATHARINE MacKINNON, ROE v. WADE: A STUDY IN MALE IDEOLOGY

Abortion: Moral and Legal Perspectives 45–54 (J. Garfield & P. Hennessey, eds. 1984).

This is a two-part feminist critique of *Roe v. Wade.* First I will situate abortion and the abortion right in the experience of women. The argument is that abortion is inextricable from sexuality, assuming that the feminist analysis of sexuality is our analysis of gender inequality. I will then criticize the doctrinal choice to pursue the abortion right under the law of privacy. The argument is that privacy doctrine reaffirms what the feminist critique of sexuality criticizes: the public/private split. The political and ideological meaning of privacy as a legal doctrine is connected with the concrete consequences of the public/private split for the lives of women. This analysis makes *Harris v. McRae,* in which public funding for abortions was held not required, appear consistent with the larger meaning of *Roe.*

* * *

Most women who seek abortions became pregnant while having sexual intercourse with men. Most did not mean or wish to conceive. In contrast to this fact of women's experience, the abortion debate has centered on separating control over sexuality from control over reproduction, and on separating both from gender. Liberals have supported the availability of the abortion choice as if the woman just happened on the fetus. The political Right imagines that the intercourse which precedes conception is usually voluntary, only to urge abstinence, as if sex were up to women. At the same time, the Right defends male authority, specifically including a wife's duty to submit to sex. Continuing with this logic, many opponents of state funding of abortions, such as supporters of some versions of the Hyde Amendment, would permit funding of abortions when pregnancy results from rape or incest. Thus, they make exceptions for those special occasions during which they presume women did not control sex. From all this I deduce that abortion's proponents and opponents share a tacit assumption that women significantly do control sex.

Feminist investigations suggest otherwise. Sexual intercourse, the most common cause of pregnancy, cannot simply be presumed coequally determined. Feminism has found that women feel compelled to preserve the appearance—which, acted upon, becomes the reality—of male direction of sexual expression, as if it is male initiative itself that we want: it is that which turns us on. Men enforce this. It is much of what men want in a woman. It is what pornography eroticizes and

prostitutes provide.   Rape—that is, intercourse with force that is recognized as force—is adjudicated not according to the power or force that
the man wields, but according to indices of intimacy between the
parties.   The more intimate you are with your accused rapist, the less
likely a court is to find that what happened to you was rape.   Often
indices of intimacy include intercourse itself.   If "no" can be taken as
"yes," how free can "yes" be?

Under these conditions, women often do not use birth control
because of its social meaning, a meaning we did not create.   Using
contraception means acknowledging and planning and taking direction
of intercourse, accepting one's sexual availability, and appearing non-
spontaneous.   It means appearing available to male incursions.   A good
user of contraception is a bad girl.   She can be presumed sexually
available and, among other consequences, raped with relative impunity.
(If you think this isn't true, you should consider rape cases in which the
fact that a woman had a diaphragm in is taken as an indication that
what happened to her was intercourse, not rape.   "Why did you have
your diaphragm in?")   From studies of abortion clinics, women who
repeatedly seek abortions (and now I'm looking at the repeat offenders
high on the list of the Right's villains, their best case for opposing
abortion as female irresponsibility), when asked why, say something
like, "The sex just happened."   Like every night for two and a half
years.   I wonder if a woman can be presumed to control access to her
sexuality if she feels unable to interrupt intercourse to insert a diaphragm;   or worse, cannot even want to, aware that she risks a
pregnancy she knows she does not want.   Do you think she would stop
the man for any other reason, such as, for instance, the real taboo—
lack of desire?   If not, how is sex, hence its consequences, meaningfully
voluntary for women?   Norms of sexual rhythm and romance that are
felt to be interrupted by women's needs are constructed against
women's interests.   Sex doesn't look a whole lot like freedom when it
appears normatively less costly for women to risk an undesired, often
painful, traumatic, dangerous, sometimes illegal, and potentially life-
threatening procedure, than it is to protect oneself in advance.   Yet
abortion policy has never been explicitly approached in the context of
how women get pregnant; that is, as a consequence of intercourse
under conditions of gender inequality; that is, as an issue of forced sex.

Now we come to the law.   In 1973, *Roe v. Wade* found that a
statute that made criminal all abortions except those to save the life of
the mother violated the constitutional right to privacy.   The privacy
right had been previously created as a constitutional principle in a case
that decriminalized the prescription and use of contraceptives.   Note
that courts use the privacy rubric to connect contraception with abortion in a way that parallels what I just did under the sexuality rubric.
In *Roe,* that right to privacy was found "broad enough to encompass a
woman's decision whether or not to terminate her pregnancy."   In *H.L.
v. Matheson,* three justices observed, "In the abortion context, we have
held that the right to privacy shields the woman from undue state

intrusion in and external scrutiny of her very personal choice." [8]   In 1981, the Supreme Court in *Harris v. McRae* decided that this right to privacy did not mean that federal Medicaid programs had to cover medically necessary abortions.   According to the Court, the privacy of the woman's choice was not unconstitutionally burdened by the government supporting her decision to continue, but not her decision to end, a conception.   In support of this conclusion, the Supreme Court stated that "although the government may not place obstacles in the path of a woman's exercise of her freedom of choice, it need not remove those not of its own creation."   It is apparently a very short step from that which the government has a duty *not* to intervene in, to that which it has *no* duty to intervene in.

If regarded as the outer edge of the limitations on government, I think the idea of privacy embodies a tension between precluding public exposure or governmental intrusion on the one hand, and autonomy in the sense of protecting personal self-action on the other.   This is a tension, not just two facets of one whole right.   This tension is resolved in the liberal state by identifying the threshold of the state with its permissible extent of penetration (a term I use advisedly) into a domain that is considered free by definition: the private sphere.   By this move the state secures what has been termed "an inviolable personality" by insuring what has been called "autonomy or control over the intimacies of personal identity."   The state does this by centering its self-restraint on body and home, especially bedroom.   By staying out of marriage and the family, prominently meaning sexuality—that is to say, heterosexuality—from contraception through pornography to the abortion decision, the law of privacy proposes to guarantee individual bodily integrity, personal exercise of moral intelligence, and freedom of intimacy. What it actually does is translate traditional social values into the rhetoric of individual rights as a means of subordinating those rights to specific social imperatives.   In feminist terms, I am arguing that the logic of *Roe* consummated in *Harris* translates the ideology of the private sphere into the individual woman's legal right to privacy as a means of subordinating women's collective needs to the imperatives of male supremacy.

This is my retrospective on *Roe v. Wade*: reproduction is sexual, men control sexuality, and the state supports the interest of men as a group.   *Roe* does not contradict this.   So why was abortion legalized; why were women even imagined to have such a right as privacy?   It is not an accusation of bad faith to answer that the interests of men as a social group converge with the definition of justice embodied in law in what I call the male point of view.   The way the male point of view constructs a social event or legal need will be the way that social event or legal need is framed by state policy.   *   *   *

8.   [450 U.S. 398, 435 (1981) (Marshall, J., dissenting).]

Since Freud, the social problem posed by sexuality has been perceived as the problem of the innate desire for sexual pleasure being repressed by the constraints of civilization. Inequality arises as an issue in this context only in women's repressive socialization to passivity and coolness (so-called frigidity), in women's so-called desexualization, and in the disparate consequences of biology, that is, pregnancy. Who defines what is sexual, what sexuality therefore is, to whom what stimuli are erotic and why, and who defines the conditions under which sexuality is expressed—these issues are not even available for consideration. "Civilization's" answer to these questions instead fuses women's reproductivity with our attributed sexuality in its definition of what a woman is. We are defined as women by the uses to which men put us. In this context it becomes clear why the struggle for reproductive freedom has never included a woman's right to refuse sex. In this notion of sexual liberation, the equality issue has been framed as a struggle for women to have sex with men on the same terms as men: without consequences. In this sense the abortion right has been sought as freedom from the unequal reproductive consequences of sexual expression, with sexuality defined as centered on heterosexual genital intercourse. It has been as if biological organisms, rather than social relations, reproduce the species. But if your concern is not how more people can get more sex, if instead your concern is who defines sexuality—hence pleasure and violation—then the abortion right is situated within a very different problematic: the social and political problematic of the inequality of the sexes. As Susan Sontag said, "Sex itself is not liberating for women. Neither is more sex. . . . The question is, what sexuality shall women be liberated to enjoy?"[13] To be able to address this requires rethinking the problem of sexuality, from the repression of drives by civilization to the oppression of women by men.

Arguments for abortion under the rubric of feminism have rested upon the right to control one's own body—gender neutral. I think that argument has been appealing for the same reasons it is inadequate: Socially, women's bodies have not been ours; we have not controlled their meanings and destinies. Feminists tried to assert that control without risking the pursuit of the idea that something more might be at stake than our bodies, something closer to a net of relations in which we are (at present unescapedly) gendered. Some feminists have noticed that our right to decide has become merged with an overwhelmingly male profession's right not to have his professional judgment second-guessed by the government. But most abortion advocates argue in rigidly and rigorously gender-neutral terms.

Thus, for instance, Judith Jarvis Thomson's argument that an abducted woman had no obligation to be a celebrated violinist's life support system, meant that women have no obligation to support a fetus.[16] Never mind that no woman who needs an abortion—no woman

---

13. Susan Sontag, "The Third World of Women," *Partisan Review* 40 (1973): 188.

16. Judith Jarvis Thomson, "A Defense of Abortion," *Philosophy and Public Affairs* 1 (1971): 47–66.

period—is valued, no potential a woman's life might hold is cherished, like a gender-neutral famous violinist's unencumbered possibilities. Not to mention that in that hypothetical, the underlying parallel to rape—the origin in force, in abduction, that gives the hypothetical its weight while confining its application to instances in which force is recognized as force—is seldom interrogated in the abortion context for its applicability to the normal case. And abortion policy is to apply to the normal case. So we need to talk about sex, specifically about intercourse in relation to rape in relation to conception. By avoiding this issue in the abortion context liberal feminists have obscured the unequal basis on which they are attempting to construct our personhood.

The meaning of abortion in the context of a sexual critique of gender inequality is its promise to women of sex with men on the same terms as promised to men—that is, "without consequences." Under conditions in which women do not control access to our sexuality, this facilitates women's heterosexual availability. In other words, under conditions of gender inequality, sexual liberation in this sense does not free women, it frees male sexual aggression. The availability of abortion thus removes the one remaining legitimized reason that women have had for refusing sex besides the headache. As Andrea Dworkin puts it, analyzing male ideology on abortion: "Getting laid was at stake." [17] The Playboy Foundation has supported abortion rights from day one; it continues to, even with shrinking disposable funds, on a level of priority comparable to its opposition to censorship.

Privacy doctrine is an ideal vehicle for this process. The democratic liberal ideal of the private holds that, so long as the public does not interfere, autonomous individuals interact freely and equally. Conceptually, this private is hermetic. It *means* that which is inaccessible to, unaccountable to, unconstructed by anything beyond itself. By definition, it is not part of or conditioned by anything systematic or outside of it. It is personal, intimate, autonomous, particular, individual, the original source and final outpost of the self, gender neutral. It is, in short, defined by everything that feminism reveals women have never been allowed to be or to have, and everything that women have been equated with and defined in terms of *men's* ability to have. It contradicts the liberal definition of the private to complain in public of inequality within it. In this view, no act of the state contributes to— hence should properly participate in—shaping its internal alignments or distributing its internal forces. Its inviolability by the state, framed as an individual right, presupposes that it is not already an arm of the state. In this scheme, intimacy is implicitly thought to guarantee symmetry of power. Injuries arise in violating the private sphere, not within and by and because of it.

17. Andrea Dworkin, *Right Wing Women* (New York: Perigee, 1983).

*   *   *

In private, consent tends to be presumed. It is true that a showing of coercion voids this presumption. But the problem is getting anything private to be perceived as coercive. Why one would allow force in private—the "why doesn't she leave" question raised to battered women—is a question given its urgency by the social meaning of the private as a sphere of choice. But for women the measure of the intimacy has been the measure of the oppression. This is why feminism has had to explode the private. This is why feminism has seen the personal as the political. The private is public for those for whom the personal is political. In this sense, there is no private, either normatively or empirically. Feminism confronts the fact that women have no privacy to lose or to guarantee. We are not inviolable. Our sexuality is not only violable, it is—hence, we are—seen *in* and *as* our violation. To confront the fact that we have no privacy is to confront the intimate degradation of women as the public order.

In this light, a right to privacy looks like an injury got up as a gift. Freedom from public intervention coexists uneasily with any right which requires social preconditions to be meaningfully delivered. For example, if inequality is socially pervasive and enforced, equality will require intervention, not abdication, to be meaningful. But the right to privacy is not thought to require social change. It is not even thought to require any social preconditions, other than nonintervention by the public. The point for the abortion cases is not that indigency—which was the specific barrier to effective choice in *McRae* —is well within the public power to remedy, nor that the state is hardly exempt in issues of the distribution of wealth. The point is rather that *Roe v. Wade* presumes that government nonintervention into the private sphere promotes a woman's freedom of choice. When the alternative is jail, there is much to be said for this argument. But the *McRae* result sustains the meaning of privacy in *Roe*: women are guaranteed by the public no more than what we can get in private—that is, what we can extract through our intimate associations with men. Women with privileges get rights.

*   *   *

It is not inconsistent, then, that framed as a privacy right a woman's decision to abort would have no claim on public support and would genuinely not be seen as burdened by that deprivation. Privacy conceived as a right from public intervention and disclosure is the opposite of the relief that *McRae* sought for welfare women. State intervention would have provided a choice women did *not* have in private. The women in *McRae,* women whose sexual refusal has counted for particularly little, needed something to make their privacy effective. The logic of the court's response resembles the logic by which women are supposed to consent to sex. Preclude the alternatives, then call the sole remaining option "her choice." The point is that the alternatives are precluded *prior to* the reach of the chosen legal doctrine. They are precluded by conditions of sex, race, and class—the very conditions the privacy frame not only leaves tacit, but which it exists to *guarantee.*

When the law of privacy restricts intrusions into intimacy, it bars change in control over that intimacy. The existing distribution of power and resources within the private sphere will be precisely what the law of privacy exists to protect. Just as pornography is legally protected as individual freedom of expression—without questioning whose freedom and whose expression and at whose expense—abstract privacy protects abstract autonomy, without inquiring into whose freedom of action is being sanctioned, at whose expense. It is probably not coincidence that the very things feminism regards as central to the subjection of women—the very place, the body; the very relations, heterosexual; the very activities, intercourse and reproduction; and the very feelings, intimate—form the core of privacy doctrine's coverage. From this perspective, the legal concept of privacy can and has shielded the place of battery, marital rape, and women's exploited labor; has preserved the central institutions whereby women are *deprived* of identity, autonomy, control and self-definition; and has protected the primary activity through which male supremacy is expressed and enforced.

To fail to recognize the meaning of the private in the ideology and reality of women's subordination by seeking protection behind a right *to* that privacy is to cut women off from collective verification and state support in the same act. I think this has a lot to do with why we can't organize women on the abortion issue. When women are segregated in private, separated from each other, one at a time, a right *to* that privacy isolates us at once from each other and from public recourse. This right to privacy is a right of men "to be let alone" to oppress women one at a time. It embodies and reflects the private sphere's existing definition of womanhood. This instance of liberalism—applied to women as if we *are* persons, gender neutral—reinforces the division between public and private that is *not* gender neutral. It is at once an ideological division that lies about women's shared experience and mystifies the unity among the spheres of women's violation. It is a very material division that keeps the private beyond public redress and depoliticizes women's subjection within it. It keeps some men out of the bedrooms of other men.

BIBLIOGRAPHY

Privacy: In General

Hafen, *The Constitutional Status of Marriage, Kinship, and Sexual Privacy—Balancing the Individual and Social Interests,* 81 Mich.L. Rev. 463 (1983).

Karst, *Freedom of Intimate Association,* 89 Yale L.J. 624 (1980).

Lupu, *Untangling the Strands of the Fourteenth Amendment,* 77 Mich. L.Rev. 981 (1979).

Parent, *Privacy, Morality and the Law,* 12 Phil. & Pub. Aff. 269 (1983).

J. Pennock & J. Chapman, eds., NOMOS XIII: PRIVACY (1971).

Posner, *The Uncertain Protection of Privacy by the Supreme Court,* 1979 Sup.Ct.Rev. 173.

Wellington, *Common Law Rules and Constitutional Double Standards: Some Notes on Adjudication,* 83 Yale L.J. 221 (1973).

Wilkinson & White, *Constitutional Protection for Personal Lifestyles,* 62 Cornell L.Rev. 563 (1977).

Abortion

M. Cohen, T. Nagel, & T. Scanlon, eds., THE RIGHTS AND WRONGS OF ABORTION (1974).

Epstein, *Substantive Due Process by Any Other Name: The Abortion Cases,* 1973 Sup.Ct.Rev. 159.

J. Feinberg, ed., THE PROBLEM OF ABORTION (2d ed. 1984).

Farrell–Smith, *Rights–Conflict, Pregnancy, and Abortion,* in BEYOND DOMINATION 265 (C. Gould ed. 1983).

J. Garfield & P. Hennessey, eds., ABORTION: MORAL AND LEGAL PERSPECTIVES (1984).

M. Glendon, ABORTION AND DIVORCE IN WESTERN LAW (1987).

Heymann & Barzelay, *The Forest and the Trees: Roe v. Wade and its Critics,* 53 B.U.L.Rev. 765 (1973).

Law, *Rethinking Sex and the Constitution,* 132 U.Pa.L.Rev. 955 (1984).

J. Noonan, A PRIVATE CHOICE: ABORTION IN AMERICA IN THE SEVENTIES (1979).

Perry, *Abortion, the Public Morals, and the Police Power: The Ethical Function of Substantive Due Process,* 23 U.C.L.A.L.Rev. 689 (1976).

Regan, *Rewriting Roe v. Wade,* 77 Mich.L.Rev. 1569 (1979).

L. Sumner, ABORTION AND MORAL THEORY (1981).

M. Tooley, ABORTION AND INFANTICIDE (1983).

L. Tribe, ABORTION, THE CLASH OF ABSOLUTES (1990).

C. HOMOSEXUALITY

In *Bowers v. Hardwick* [1] the Supreme Court held that the right to privacy, which earlier cases had found in the Due Process Clause of the Fourteenth Amendment, did not protect homosexual sodomy. Respondent Hardwick, an adult male, had challenged Georgia's criminal sodomy law after he was arrested for committing a sexual act with another adult male in his own bedroom. The Court's brief opinion argued that text, precedent, and tradition did not support Hardwick's claim, and that it was unwilling to override legislative choices without

1. 478 U.S. 186, 106 S.Ct. 2841, 92 L.Ed. 2d 140 (1986).

such authority. Justice Blackmun's dissent asserted, by contrast, that the essential meaning of the right to privacy was the freedom to choose what form one's intimate sexual relationships should take.

Both sides of the Court in *Bowers* take what Michael Sandel calls the "sophisticated" approach to sodomy laws. They assume that the justice of such laws depends, not on a moral judgment about homosexual activity, but on a more general theory about democracy (the majority) or liberty (the dissent). Sandel argues for a more "naive" view. He claims that one cannot successfully defend either prohibition or toleration while bracketing the issue of morality.

Jed Rubenfeld offers an interesting response to Sandel's challenge. He does not argue that homosexual intimacy is a morally valuable practice. But he does say that laws against such behavior are especially harmful. This is not because he accepts Justice Blackmun's "personhood" thesis (the idea that people should be free to define their own identities by making choices about sexual relations). A person's identity, if there is such a thing, is formed by lots of influences besides his own choices. Rubenfeld instead argues that sodomy laws are unconstitutional because they have a pervasive standardizing effect—forcing homosexuals "into a network of social institutions and relations that will occupy their lives to a substantial degree." In that regard they are like laws forbidding private schools and laws whose consequence is compulsory child-bearing.

MICHAEL J. SANDEL, MORAL ARGUMENT AND LIBERAL TOLERATION: ABORTION AND HOMOSEXUALITY

77 Calif.L.Rev. 521–522, 533–534, 536–538 (1989).

People defend laws against * * * homosexual sodomy in two different ways: Some argue that [it is] morally reprehensible and therefore worthy of prohibition; others try to avoid passing judgment on the morality of th[is] practice[], and argue instead that, in a democracy, political majorities have the right to embody in law their moral convictions.

In a similar way, arguments against * * * antisodomy laws take two different forms: Some say the laws are unjust because the practices they prohibit are morally permissible, indeed sometimes desirable; others oppose these laws without reference to the moral status of the practices at issue, and argue instead that individuals have a right to choose for themselves whether to engage in them.

These two styles of argument might be called, respectively, the "naive" and the "sophisticated." The naive view holds that the justice of laws depends on the moral worth of the conduct they prohibit or protect. The sophisticated view holds that the justice of such laws depends not on a substantive moral judgment about the conduct at stake, but instead on a more general theory about the respective claims of majority rule and individual rights, of democracy on the one hand, and liberty on the other.

I shall try in this paper to bring out the truth in the naive view, which I take to be this: The justice (or injustice) of laws against * * * homosexual [practices] depends, at least in part, on the morality (or immorality) of those practices. This is the claim the sophisticated view rejects. In both its majoritarian and its liberal versions, the sophisticated view tries to set aside or "bracket" controversial moral and religious conceptions for purposes of justice. It insists that the justification of laws be neutral among competing visions of the good life.

In practice, of course, these two kinds of argument can be difficult to distinguish. In the debate over cases like * * * *Bowers v. Hardwick*,[3] both camps tend to advance the naive view under cover of the sophisticated. (Such is the prestige of the sophisticated way of arguing.) For example, those who would ban * * * [homosexual activity] out of abhorrence often argue in the name of deference to democracy and judicial restraint. Similarly, those who want permissive laws because they approve of * * * homosexuality often argue in the name of liberal toleration.

This is not to suggest that all instances of the sophisticated argument are disingenuous attempts to promote a substantive moral conviction. Those who argue that law should be neutral among competing conceptions of the good life offer various grounds for their claim, including most prominently the following:

> (1) the *relativist* view says law should not affirm a particular moral conception because all morality is relative, and so there are no moral truths to affirm; (2) the *utilitarian* view argues that government neutrality will, for various reasons, promote the general welfare in the long run; (3) the *voluntarist* view holds that government should be neutral among conceptions of the good life in order to respect the capacity of persons as free citizens or autonomous agents to choose their conceptions for themselves; and (4) the *minimalist,* or pragmatic view says that, because people inevitably disagree about morality and religion, government should bracket these controversies for the sake of political agreement and social cooperation.

In order to bring out the truth in the naive way of arguing, I look to the actual arguments judges and commentators have made in recent cases dealing with * * * homosexuality. Their arguments, unfailingly sophisticated, illustrate the difficulty of bracketing moral judgments for purposes of law. * * *

* * *

THE VOLUNTARIST CASE FOR TOLERATION: HOMOSEXUALITY

The dissenters' argument for toleration in *Bowers v. Hardwick* illustrates the difficulties with the version of liberalism that ties toleration to autonomy rights alone. In refusing to extend the right of

3. 478 U.S. 186 (1986).

privacy to homosexuals, the majority in *Bowers* declared that none of the rights announced in earlier privacy cases resembled the rights homosexuals were seeking: "No connection between family, marriage, or procreation on the one hand and homosexual activity on the other has been demonstrated. . . ." Any reply to the Court's position would have to show some connection between the practices already subject to privacy protection and the homosexual practices not yet protected. What then is the resemblance between heterosexual intimacies on the one hand, and homosexual intimacies on the other, such that both are entitled to a constitutional right of privacy?

This question might be answered in at least two different ways— one voluntarist, the other substantive. The first argues from the autonomy the practices reflect, whereas the second appeals to the human goods the practices realize. The voluntarist answer holds that people should be free to choose their intimate associations for themselves, regardless of the virtue or popularity of the practices they choose so long as they do not harm others. In this view, homosexual relationships resemble the heterosexual relationships the Court has already protected in that all reflect the choices of autonomous selves.

By contrast, the substantive answer claims that much that is valuable in conventional marriage is also present in homosexual unions. In this view, the connection between heterosexual and homosexual relations is not that both result from individual choice but that both realize important human goods. Rather than rely on autonomy alone, this second line of reply articulates the virtues homosexual intimacy may share with heterosexual intimacy, along with any distinctive virtues of its own. It defends homosexual privacy the way *Griswold* defended marital privacy, by arguing that, like marriage, homosexual union may also be "intimate to the degree of being sacred . . . a harmony in living . . . a bilateral loyalty," an association for a "noble . . . purpose." [74]

Of these two possible replies, the dissenters in *Bowers* relied wholly on the first. Rather than protect homosexual intimacies for the human goods they share with intimacies the Court already protects, Justice Blackmun cast the Court's earlier cases in individualist terms, and found their reading applied equally to homosexuality because "much of the richness of a relationship will come from the freedom an individual has to *choose* the form and nature of these intensely personal bonds." At issue was not homosexuality as such but respect for the fact that "different individuals will make different choices" in deciding how to conduct their lives.

* * *

The * * * precedent [offered in *Bowers*] for homosexual rights [was] not *Griswold* but *Stanley v. Georgia*,[84] which upheld the right to possess obscene materials in the privacy of one's home. *Stanley* did not

---

74. The phrases are from Griswold v. Connecticut, 381 U.S. 479, 486 (1965).

84. 394 U.S. 557 (1969).

hold that the obscene films found in the defendant's bedroom served a "noble purpose," only that he had a right to view them in private. The toleration *Stanley* defended was wholly independent of the value or importance of the thing being tolerated.

* * *

The case for toleration that brackets the morality of homosexuality has a powerful appeal. In the face of deep disagreement about values, it seems to ask the least of the contending parties. It offers social peace and respect for rights without the need for moral conversion. Those who view sodomy as sin need not be persuaded to change their minds, only to tolerate those who practice it in private. By insisting only that each respect the freedom of others to live the lives they choose, this toleration promises a basis for political agreement that does not await shared conceptions of morality.

Despite its promise, however, the neutral case for toleration is subject to two related difficulties. First, as a practical matter, it is by no means clear that social cooperation can be secured on the strength of autonomy rights alone, absent some measure of agreement on the moral permissibility of the practices at issue. It may not be accidental that the first practices subject to the right of privacy were accorded constitutional protection in cases that spoke of the sanctity of marriage and procreation. Only later did the Court abstract privacy rights from these practices and protect them without reference to the human goods they were once thought to make possible. This suggests that the voluntarist justification of privacy rights is dependent—politically as well as philosophically—on some measure of agreement that the practices protected are morally permissible.

A second difficulty with the voluntarist case for toleration concerns the quality of respect it secures. * * * [T]he analogy with *Stanley* tolerates homosexuality at the price of demeaning it; it puts homosexual intimacy on a par with obscenity—a base thing that should nonetheless be tolerated so long as it takes place in private. If *Stanley* rather than *Griswold* is the relevant analogy, the interest at stake is bound to be reduced * * * to "sexual gratification." (The only intimate relationship at stake in *Stanley* was between a man and his pornography.)

The majority in *Bowers* exploited this assumption by ridiculing the notion of a "fundamental right to engage in homosexual sodomy." The obvious reply is that *Bowers* is no more about a right to homosexual sodomy than *Griswold* was about a right to heterosexual intercourse. But by refusing to articulate the human goods that homosexual intimacy may share with heterosexual unions, the voluntarist case for toleration forfeits the analogy with *Griswold* and makes the ridicule difficult to refute.

The problem with the neutral case for toleration is the opposite side of its appeal; it leaves wholly unchallenged the adverse views of homosexuality itself. Unless those views can be plausibly addressed, even a Court ruling in their favor is unlikely to win for homosexuals more than a thin and fragile toleration. * * *

                              *   *   *

Admittedly, the tendency to bracket substantive moral questions makes it difficult to argue for toleration in the language of the good. Defining privacy rights by defending the practices privacy protects seems either reckless or quaint; reckless because it rests so much on moral argument, quaint because it recalls the traditional view that ties the case for privacy to the merits of the conduct privacy protects. But as the * * * sodomy case [ ] illustrate[s,] the attempt to bracket moral questions faces difficulties of its own. [It] suggest[s] the truth in the "naive" view, that the justice or injustice of laws against * * * homosexual [practices] may have something to do with the morality or immorality of those practices after all.

JED RUBENFELD, THE RIGHT OF PRIVACY
102 Harv.L.Rev. 737, 783–787 792–794, 797–802 (1989).

METHOD

The methodology heretofore universal in privacy analysis has begun with the question, "What is the state trying to forbid?" The proscribed conduct is then delineated and its significance tested through a pre-established conceptual apparatus: for its role in " 'the concept of ordered liberty,' " its status as a "fundamental" right, its importance to one's identity, or for any other criterion of fundamentality upon which a court can settle. Suppose instead we began by asking not what is being *prohibited,* but what is being *produced.* Suppose we looked not to the negative aspect of the law—the interdiction by which it formally expresses itself—but at its positive aspect: the real effects that conformity with the law produces at the level of everyday lives and social practices.

                              *   *   *

SUBSTANCE

Consider the three principal areas in which the right to privacy has been applied: child-bearing (abortion and contraception), marriage (miscegenation laws, divorce restrictions, and so on), and education of children (*Meyer* [a] and *Pierce* [b]). According to the prevailing method of privacy analysis, certain decisions concerning these matters cannot be proscribed because they are "fundamental." But what is fundamental about these decisions? Are they fundamental in themselves? If, for example, the right to decide whom to marry is inherently fundamental, how is it, for example, that the proscriptions against incestuous and bigamous marriage do not offend it? In fact, a "liberty of fundamental decisions" cannot serve as a constitutional principle any more than could that quite similar quantity—the "liberty of contract"—that

a. Meyer v. Nebraska, 262 U.S. 390   **b.** Pierce v. Society of Sisters, 268 U.S.
(1923).   510 (1925).

animated the *Lochner* jurisprudence. There *is* something fundamental at stake in the privacy decisions, but it is not the proscribed conduct, nor even the freedom of decision—it is not what is being taken away.

The distinctive and singular characteristic of the laws against which the right to privacy has been applied lies in their *productive* or *affirmative* consequences. There are perhaps no legal proscriptions with more profound, more extensive, or more persistent affirmative effects on individual lives than the laws struck down as violations of the right to privacy. Anti-abortion laws, anti-miscegenation laws, and compulsory education laws all involve the forcing of lives into well-defined and highly confined institutional layers. At the simplest, most quotidian level, such laws tend to *take over* the lives of the persons involved: they occupy and preoccupy. They affirmatively and very substantially shape a person's life; they direct a life's development along a particular avenue. These laws do not simply proscribe one act or remove one liberty; they inform the totality of a person's life.

The principle of the right to privacy is not the freedom to do certain, particular acts determined to be fundamental through some ever-progressing normative lens. It is the fundamental freedom not to have one's life too totally determined by a progressively more normalizing state.

Someone might say, I suppose, that anti-abortion or anti-contraception laws do not force women to bear children because women can simply refrain from having sex. Similarly one might say that whites and blacks, confronted by laws forbidding interracial marriage, can simply decline to marry if they do not wish to live with members of their own race.

This is no answer at all. To begin with, it is no answer to the pregnant woman seeking an abortion. More fundamentally, it is no answer because it is merely another attempt to hide behind a factitious focus on the prohibitory aspect of the law. The practical consequence of obeying laws against contraception or interracial marriage is that people become pregnant or marry intraracially. Indeed these laws derive the depth of their affirmative force from the fact that they operate on drives and desires too strong or too subtle for most to resist.

The danger, then, is a particular kind of creeping totalitarianism, an unarmed *occupation* of individuals' lives. That is the danger of which * * * the right to privacy is warning us: a society standardized and normalized, in which lives are too substantially or too rigidly directed. That is the threat posed by state power in our century.

This threat is not unknown to our constitutional jurisprudence. Consider first Justice Jackson's words in *West Virginia State Board of Education v. Barnette*,[187] when, in the midst of the Second World War, the Court struck down a law that required schoolchildren to salute the flag and profess their loyalty to the country:

187. 319 U.S. 624 (1943).

Struggles to coerce uniformity of sentiment in support of some end thought essential to their time and country have been waged by many good as well as by evil men. . . . As first and moderate attempts to attain unity have failed, those bent on its accomplishment must resort to an ever-increasing severity. . . . Ultimate futility of such attempts to compel coherence is the lesson of every such effort from the Roman drive to stamp out Christianity . . . down to the fast failing efforts of our present totalitarian enemies.

* * *

With this image, however, we have left West Virginia's enforced flag-salute far behind. Or rather we have imagined that flag-salute systematized and ramified into numerous aspects of the child's daily life. We have imagined an existence totally informed or occupied, rather than a single act of enforced loyalty. This distinction is critical: it explains why *Barnette* is not, after all, a right-to-privacy case but rather a first amendment case.

Because of the signal role that speech plays in political freedom and because of the express constitutional guarantee, government in this country can hardly forbid or compel citizens to utter a single opinion without violating their rights. By contrast, in privacy cases, the government must go much further before it transgresses a constitutional limit. Consider now the cases of *Meyer* and *Pierce,* which * * * may be considered the true progenitors of the privacy decisions. Like *Barnette, Meyer* and *Pierce* also involved laws pertaining to the education of children—laws suggestive of a nationalism heightened by war. Yet the statutes struck down in *Meyer* and especially *Pierce* differed significantly from that in *Barnette.*

In *Meyer,* the law at issue prohibited the teaching of "modern" foreign languages to elementary schoolchildren. In *Pierce,* the state had prohibited private elementary schooling altogether, requiring all children between the ages of eight and sixteen to attend public schools. In each of these statutes, the state had gone much further in the effort—using Justice Jackson's phrase—to "coerce uniformity" than had West Virginia in enacting its flag-salute law. It is not that a greater degree of coercion was present; I am not referring to the potential consequences of violating the law. To the contrary, it was the potential consequences of *obeying* the law that mattered. The *Meyer* Court saw the state as attempting to "foster a homogeneous people with American ideals." The Court drew in this connection on images from ancient civilization:

For the welfare of his Ideal Commonwealth, Plato suggested a law which would provide: "That the wives of our guardians are to be common, and their children are to be common, and no parent is to know his own child, nor any child his parent. . . . The proper officers will take the offspring of the good parents to the pen or fold, and there they will deposit them with certain nurses who dwell in a separate quarter; but the offspring of the inferior, or of the better when they chance to be deformed, will be put away in some mysterious, unknown place, as they should be." In order to submerge the individual and develop ideal citizens, Sparta assembled the males at seven into barracks and intrusted [sic] their subsequent education and training to official guardians. Although such measures have been deliberately approved by men of great genius, their ideas touching the relation between individual and State were wholly different from those upon which our institutions rest; and it hardly will be affirmed that any legislature could impose such restrictions upon the people of a State without doing violence to both letter and spirit of the Constitution.

* * *

Pierce presented this threat even more starkly because there the state had prohibited all organized elementary education outside the public schools. That the Court was reacting to this threat—and not merely to a deprivation of the "liberty of contract"—cannot be doubted. In language that implicitly derived its force from the same sources on which the Court drew in *Meyer*, the Court struck down the law and held that the "fundamental theory of liberty upon which all governments in this Union repose excludes any general power of the State to *standardize its children*."

This concept of standardization as applied in *Pierce* is critical for our purposes. It includes both quantitative and qualitative components. The law struck down in *Pierce*—like the Platonic or Spartan regimes described by the *Meyer* Court, but unlike *Barnette*'s flag-salute law—had the effect of affirmatively occupying a substantial portion of the material, day-to-day lives of those individuals subject to it. At the same time, this occupation potentially subjected these individuals to a narrowly directed existence: a regimen, a discipline, a curriculum in which the totality of their personhood or identity could be forcefully compressed into a particular mold.

These two elements—the affirmative occupation of one's time and the directedness of this occupation—are crucial in understanding why the mandatory public schooling law in *Pierce* implicated a constitutional concern, now called the right to privacy, even though no explicit constitutional guarantee could be said to forbid it. Privacy takes its stand at the outer boundaries of the legitimate exercise of state power. It is to be invoked only where the government threatens to take over or occupy our lives—to exert its power in some way over the totality of our lives.

In a few, rare instances this "totalitarian" intervention into a person's life may occur as a result of a single legal prohibition. The burden of elaborating a conception of privacy based on an anti-totalitarian principle is to perceive how a single law may operate positively to take over and direct the totality of our lives.

* * *

DISTINCTIONS

[L]aws against abortion, interracial marriage, * * * and private education all involve a peculiar form of obedience that reaches far beyond mere abstention from the particular proscribed act. It is a form of obedience in which the life of the person forced to obey is thereafter substantially filled up and informed by the living, institutional consequences of obedience. The person finds himself in a new and sharply-defined, but also broadly encompassing institutional role. Because of their affirmative direction of individuals' lives, these roles—whether as mother, spouse, student or family member—have profoundly formative effects on identity and character.

This attribute of the laws discussed above distinguishes them from other proscriptions of unquestionable constitutional validity that might otherwise appear to fall within the ambit of the principles elaborated here. Consider laws against murder. Are such laws not "standardizing" in that they compel all of us to be non-murderers? Do they not operate "on our bodies" in that they work by forbidding us, for example, to pick up a knife and use it in a certain way? And do they not "instrumentalize" us by requiring us to serve the state's interests insofar as we are made thereby to refrain from causing harm to society at large?

* * *

Laws against murder foreclose an avenue; they do not harness us to a given seat and direct us down a single, regulated road. This formulation is not so much a conclusion from logic as from practical, material realities. One may always reformulate propositions to state negatives as positives. Refraining from murder, however, does not fill up one's life in the same way as does bearing a child, attending public school, * * * or marrying only within one's race. Forcing a person to do these latter things goes much further in thrusting him into socially defined, particularized practices and institutions.

This distinction between "negative" and "affirmative" effects of legal rules will no doubt be greeted with skepticism. Yet—to repeat the point—the distinction is not a matter of propositional logic; it is essentially normative. Whether the obligation not to murder is called a negative or affirmative duty makes no difference. The question is the degree to which, and the ways in which, the law informs, shapes, directs, and occupies the actual day-to-day activities of the persons concerned. Power may be understood and experienced as a purely prohibitory force acting upon essentially independent individual lives; it may also, however, appear and act as a force producing those lives from the inside.

The same negative-affirmative distinction directly parallels the essential difference between the anti-totalitarian right to privacy elaborated here and the personhood version of that right [espoused by the dissenters in *Bowers v. Hardwick*]. Formulated propositionally, the two principles seem almost like corollaries. The anti-totalitarian right to privacy, it might be said, prevents the state from imposing on individuals a defined identity, whereas the personhood right to privacy ensures that individuals are free to define their own identities. Is the anti-totalitarian theory of privacy nothing more in reality than a restatement of the personhood idea from another angle?

On the contrary: first, when personhood speaks of the "freedom to define oneself," it speaks for the most part of a chimera. We are all so powerfully influenced by the institutions within which we are raised that it is probably impossible, both psychologically and epistemologically, to speak of defining one's own identity. The point is not to save for the individual an abstract and chimerical right of defining himself; the point is to prevent the state from taking over, or taking undue advantage of, those processes by which individuals are defined in order to produce overly standardized, functional citizens.

Second, because personhood concentrates on the fundamentality of the act or decision at stake in a given case—whether to have a child, whom to marry, and so on—it will produce a different analysis and different results from the anti-totalitarian principle. * * *

* * *

There remains a third and final differentiation to be made between personhood and the right to privacy as understood here. To speak of resisting state-imposed identities—as we have done—does not commit privacy to personhood's central premise: that each individual's defining his identity is an act of such value that it is of constitutional importance. Indeed the right to privacy as developed here may suggest a repudiation of personal identity altogether.

The concept of personal identity—that sense of a unitary, atomic self that we all tend to consider ourselves to "have"—is complex and difficult. It has an almost theological or metaphysical aspect, as if one's "identity" were a kind of hypostatic quantity underlying the multiplicity of his vastly different relations in the world and the mutability of his nature over time. * * * This conception of a unitary personal identity has been radically challenged again and again this century in various fields, including psychoanalysis,[217] literature,[218] and—most recently and surprisingly—analytic philosophy.[219] Personhood, reflecting an essentially liberal philosophy, is obliged to embrace and valorize the idea of a unitary personal identity; the right to privacy is not.

* * *

217. One of Freud's great theoretical innovations was his tripartite conception of the mind, in which the ego—the "I" of our apperception—is but one of the three strata of subjectivity within each individual. *See generally* S. Freud, New Introductory Lectures on Psychoanalysis 51–71 (J. Strachey trans. 1965) (describing the ego, the id, and the superego). * * *

218. It is a central theme of Proust's *Remembrance of Things Past* to disabuse us of the illusion of having a singular identity over time, in order (perhaps) for us to regain our past in an even more essential way. *See, e.g.,* 3 M. Proust, Remembrance of Things Past 499 (C. Moncrieff, T. Kilmartin & A. Mayor trans. 1981) [.]
* * *

219. Derek Parfit has made the most powerful arguments within analytic philosophy against the concept of a unitary "I" persisting over time. *See generally* D. Parfit, Reasons and Persons (1984) [.]
* * *

HOMOSEXUALITY

[Let us consider] *Bowers v. Hardwick* in our new terms. * * *
The * * * privacy argument against laws forbidding homosexual sex
cannot be rested on the claim that they deprive certain persons of
something deeply important to them, crucial to their happiness, or even
central to their identity. Nor can such laws be attacked on the ground
that * * * laws must not impose on individuals any majoritarian
values impinging on their autonomy. * * *

Yet laws against homosexual sex have an effect that most laws do
not. They forceably channel certain individuals—supposing the law is
obeyed—into a network of social institutions and relations that will
occupy their lives to a substantial degree.

Most fundamentally, the prohibition against homosexual sex channels individuals' sexual desires into *reproductive* outlets. Although the
prohibition does not, like the law against abortions, produce as an
imminent consequence compulsory child-bearing, it nonetheless forcibly
directs individuals into the pathways of reproductive sexuality, rather
than the socially "unproductive" realm of homosexuality. These pathways are further guided, in our society, into particular institutional
orbits, chief among which are the nuclear family and the constellation
of practices surrounding a heterosexuality that is defined in conscious
contradistinction to homosexuality. Indeed it is difficult to separate
our society's inculcation of a heterosexual identity from the simultane-
ous inculcation of a dichotomized complementarity of roles to be borne
by men and women. Homosexual couples by necessity throw into
question the allocation of specific functions—whether professional, personal, or emotional—between the sexes. It is this aspect of the ban on
homosexuality—its central role in the maintenance of institutionalized
sexual identities and normalized reproductive relations—that have
made its *affirmative* or *formative* consequences, as well as the reaction
against these consequences, so powerful a force in modern society.

* * *

It is no answer to say that an individual interested in homosexual
relations might simply remain celibate. The living force of the law is
at issue, not its logical form, and the real force of anti-homosexual laws,
if obeyed, is that they enlist and redirect physical and emotional desires
that we do not expect people to suppress. Indeed, it is precisely the
propensity of such prohibitions to operate on and put to use an
individual's most elemental bodily faculties that gives the exertion of
power in this area such formative force. We tend to analyze these
proscriptions today in terms of the propriety of punishing people for
homosexual conduct. We tend, in measuring their morality, to form an
image of either the homosexual imprisoned or the homosexual forced to
give up his sexual acts. We ought, however, to give up the image of
"the homosexual" in the first place and measure the law instead in
terms of its creation of heterosexuals (and, in a different way, of

homosexuals too) within the standardized parameters of a state-regulated identity.

It should be emphasized that conceiving of the right to privacy as protecting homosexuality for the reasons just discussed is not at all to convert the right to privacy into a general protection of "sexual intimacy," as Justice Blackmun suggested. The point is this: childbearing, marriage, and the assumption of a specific sexual identity are undertakings that go on for years, define roles, direct activities, operate on or even create intense emotional relations, enlist the body, inform values, and in sum substantially shape the totality of a person's daily life and consciousness. Laws that force such undertakings on individuals may properly be called "totalitarian," and the right to privacy exists to protect against them.

BIBLIOGRAPHY

Arriola, *Sexual Identity and the Constitution: Homosexual Persons as a Discrete and Insular Minority,* 10 Women's Rights L.Rep. 143 (1988).

Conkle, *The Second Death of Substantive Due Process,* 62 Ind.L.J. 215 (1987).

Delgado, *Fact, Norm, and Standard of Review—The Case of Homosexuality,* 10 U.Dayton L.Rev. 575 (1985).

P. Devlin, THE ENFORCEMENT OF MORALS (1965).

R. Dworkin, *Lord Devlin and the Enforcement of Morals,* 75 Yale L.J. 986 (1966).

Goldstein, *History, Homosexuality, and Political Values: Searching for the Hidden Determinants of* Bowers v. Hardwick, 97 Yale L.J. 1073 (1988).

Grey, *Eros, Civilization, and the Burger Court,* 43 L. & Contemp.Probs. 83 (1980).

H.L.A. Hart, LAW, LIBERTY AND MORALITY (1963).

Khan, *The Invasion of Sexual Privacy,* 23 San Diego L.Rev. 957 (1986).

Law, *Homosexuality and the Social Meaning of Gender,* 1988 Wis.L.Rev. 187.

Maroney, Bowers v. Hardwick: *A Case Study in Federalism, Legal Procedure, and Constitutional Interpretation,* 38 Syracuse L.Rev. 1223 (1987).

Note, *Developments in the Law—Sexual Orientation and the Law,* 102 Harv.L.Rev. 1508 (1989).

Richards, *Unnatural Acts and the Constitutional Right to Privacy: A Moral Theory,* 45 Fordham L.Rev. 1281 (1977).

Richards, *Sexual Autonomy and the Constitutional Right to Privacy: A Case Study in Human Rights and the Unwritten Constitution,* 30 Hast.L.J. 957 (1979).

Rivera, *Our Straight–Laced Judges: The Legal Position of Homosexual Persons in the United States,* 30 Hast.L.J. 799 (1979).

Stoddard, Bowers v. Hardwick: *Precedent by Personal Predilection,* 54 U.Chi.L.Rev. 648 (1987).

Sunstein, *Sexual Orientation and the Constitution: A Note on the Relationship Between Due Process and Equal Protection,* 55 U.Chi. L.Rev. 1161 (1988).

Survey on the Constitutional Right to Privacy in the Context of Homosexual Activity, 40 U.Miami L.Rev. 521 (1986).

Symposium, *Sex, Politics, & the Law: Lesbians and Gay Men Take the Offensive,* 14 N.Y.U.Rev. of L. & Soc.Change 891 (1986).

Symposium, *Law, Community, and Moral Reasoning,* 77 Calif.L.Rev. 475 (1989).

Vieira, Hardwick *and the Right of Privacy,* 55 U.Chi.L.Rev. 1181 (1988).

West, *Taking Preferences Seriously,* 64 Tulane L.Rev. 659 (1990).

D. THE RIGHT TO DIE

The right to die is quite a modern issue. When life was shorter people avoided death. Advances in medical science now enable most of us to reach old age. Machines can keep us going as our systems wear out. It is now possible for many people to live (or be kept alive) longer than they might want. Is there a point to prolonging respiration, circulation, or nutrition when a patient is in great pain and will not get better? Or when she is, as the doctors say, in a persistent vegetative state?

There are no simple answers to these questions. And the Constitution might seem an unlikely place to look for them. It comes into play because most people now die in hospitals, and state law regulates the behavior of health care providers. It may require keeping a patient alive longer than she wants, or her family wants her, to be. Does the Constitution impose a limit on what state law can require?

In *Cruzan v. Director, Missouri Dept. of Health,*[1] the Supreme Court addressed that question for the first time. It assumed, though it did not actually decide, that competent people have a constitutional right (a Fourteenth Amendment liberty) to refuse lifesaving treatment. But Cruzan herself was in a persistent vegetative state. The Court held that the state was entitled to require clear and convincing proof of her wishes before withdrawing treatment. Absent such proof, the state was not required to accept the decision of Cruzan's family about the proper course of action.

The most obvious difficulty with talking about Cruzan's constitutional rights is that she herself is not able to exercise them. As John Garvey explains, freedom (Fourteenth Amendment liberty) is a right to

1. ___ U.S. ___, 110 S.Ct. 2841, 111 L.Ed.2d 224 (1990).

act, and perhaps a right to choose. Cruzan could do neither of these things. Garvey argues that we can make sense of her right only if there is a representative to exercise it for her.

Nancy Rhoden draws a different conclusion from the same observation. She suggests that the idea of constitutional rights in this area may be both misguided and counterproductive. It leads, among other things, to difficult standards of proof like the one the Court approved in *Cruzan*. Perhaps we would do better to drop the idea of *rights* and focus instead on how to make the *right* decision.

Ronald Dworkin assumes that the question of rights is settled in Cruzan's favor, and looks at the other side of the balance. What interest does the state have in requiring that she be kept alive when her family opposes that course of action? He concludes that none of the reasons given by the Court is convincing enough to override Cruzan's right to die.

Yale Kamisar, alone among the commentators represented here, argues that it is permissible (and perhaps proper) for the state to keep Cruzan alive. He notes that the law has fairly strict evidentiary requirements governing the disposition of property. Why should it be less demanding on the question of life and death? He also argues that there is a difference between nutrition and hydration (which Cruzan was getting) and medical treatment. Nearly half of the states that have living will laws do not allow people to refuse the former.

JOHN H. GARVEY, FREEDOM AND REPRESENTATION

In D. Meyers, K. Kipnis & C. Murphy, Kindred Matters (1991).

I. FREEDOM

Whenever we speak of freedom as a right we are referring to a relation of four variables. This 'freedom' is always the freedom of some person (X) from some constraint (y) by another person (Y) to do (or refrain from doing) some act (x).   *   *   * [M]y constitutional right to freedom of speech means that I (X) am free from laws or other obstacles (y) imposed by the government (Y) to speak (or remain silent) (x).

*   *   *

Freedoms are different from other rights in this way: the term x always refers to an action. My constitutional rights (freedoms) to speak, worship, and contract allow me to do various things. My rights to counsel and to just compensation, and my privilege against self-incrimination, do not allow me to act in any special way. They promise benefits or forbid harms to me as an essentially passive right-holder. (The only act I perform here is the 'legal act' of claiming my rights.)

In liberal constitutional theory freedoms are also bilateral. Whenever I am free to do x, I am also free to do not-x. My freedom of religion allows me to attend or stay away from church. My freedom of speech lets me speak or remain silent. This means that constitutional freedoms protect choices about certain kinds of actions.

* * *

These features (protection for choices, actions) create the problem I want to address. Some people are unable to make rational decisions about how to act. There is a real problem with saying that these people have a right to be free (to make choices about actions). [I am talking about children, people who are severely retarded, senile, comatose, etc.]

* * *

Everyone agrees that it is OK to help these people out by making some decisions for them. This is a weak version of paternalism. In general terms paternalism is action by one person (R = 'Representative') for the good of another (X), but contrary to X's present desires, and not justified by X's consent.[1] The weak version holds that R may interfere when X is unable to make a rational decision about some action (x), and x involves a risk of harm (or maybe a chance of good).

* * *

II. REPRESENTATION

As I have said, freedoms allow us to make choices about actions: to have children, to speak, to worship, or not to do any of these things. In an obvious way X is not free to do these things when we allow paternalistic intervention. X does not choose for himself; rather, R chooses for him.

Yet there is a derivative sense in speaking of X's freedom under these circumstances. Freedom allows people to be self-governing, and in some cases of paternalism we may say that X is self-governing. The proper metaphor is not a direct democracy but a republic in which X rules through a representative (R).

In a republic the people are self-governing because they choose representatives by consent. That is not possible in most of the paternalistic relations we are concerned with, where R acts for X because X is incompetent to choose. Representatives in these cases are instead chosen because of ties of love and kinship: parents for children, spouses for one another, children for aged parents, etc. The issue we are concerned with is whether that method of selection is the functional equivalent of consent; or if that is asking too much, at least whether their paternalism can be seen as a kind of 'freedom.'

I would argue that the bonds of love and kinship embody all that is good in the relation between representative and represented. Their most important feature is the selfless character of love, which moves R to put X's interests ahead of all other considerations. As motives go that beats the desire for reelection, which is what we count on to make

1. See Brock, *Paternalism and Promoting the Good,* in R. Sartorius, ed., PATERNALISM 237, 238 (1983).

members of Congress consider the interests of their constituents. In addition to love there is the similarity of interests that derives from ties of kinship—what some call 'descriptive' or 'virtual' representation. We frequently rely on this fact to justify the choice of a representative. The Federal Rules of Civil Procedure do so in selecting representatives for class actions. The rules of property law allow siblings to represent the future interests of unborn children. Finally, those who love one another and live together will be best informed about one another's actual needs and preferences.

* * *

III. Freedom and the Representative

When X acts through a representative we can look at his freedom from two angles: (i) X's freedom vis à vis his representative; (ii) X's freedom vis à vis the government. Here I examine (i). There are three different ways of structuring the relation between X and R, and each presents a different issue about X's freedom.

A. Proxy

One way of understanding X's relation with R is most appropriate for decisions made on behalf of the post-competent (people who are senile, irreversibly comatose, etc.) and the temporarily incompetent. In these cases R will often be in a position to exercise a kind of proxy for X, giving consent to things that X would agree to if he were still competent. Sometimes the metaphor of a proxy is exactly right. Suppose I execute a living will (with my wife as executrix) that says I do not wish to be kept alive on a respirator if I should permanently lose my cognitive faculties. When my wife consents to turning off the respirator she simply announces the decision I have already made, just as my proxy at a corporate shareholders' meeting announces my vote. In cases like this R does not even act paternalistically toward X; she is merely his agent. Because X makes his own choices we can say that he is free vis à vis R. X cannot enforce his choice if R acts unfaithfully (since X is incompetent), so there is always a possibility that R can restrict X's freedom. But ties of love and duty constrain R to behave as a faithful agent. And in extreme cases the law may enforce X's proxy.

Suppose, though, that my wife had no living will to rely on. She might then say that I would want the respirator turned off, and that she knew this because she knew my history and personality about as well as her own. We had talked about death and hospitals, about medical costs and what made life worthwhile. And while I had never said in so many words that I didn't want to be kept alive on a respirator she knew what I would say if I could just speak for a moment. In cases like this my consent is hypothetical, not real.

What makes us comfortable with R's decision is not X's consent but the fact that R is guided by X's view of the good. R represents X like a Senator up for reelection. The Senator's votes are not guided by written instructions but by familiarity with the desires of her constituents. They do not actually consent to her actions—it has been five years since they voted for her. But if she wants to be reelected she must try hard to determine what they would say if asked.

Here too it is meaningful to speak of X's freedom vis à vis R, because R's choices on X's behalf are determined by X himself. They seek X's good as X has seen it up to the time of his incompetence. X's freedom again depends on R's faithful performance as an agent. He cannot threaten to discharge her as voters can their Senator. But as I said above, R is bound by other constraints to carry out X's wishes.

B.   Trustee: The Objective View

When we cannot say with any confidence what X would choose, R must act more like a trustee than like a proxy.   *   *   *

[There are two ways of viewing R's actions.]   For lack of better terms I will call them the objective and the subjective approaches. The objective approach allows R to choose for X, and the courts to review R's performance for conformity with a standard like 'best interests' or 'reasonable person.'   *   *   *

The objective approach is most convincing when applied to health care issues: blood transfusions for children,   *   *   * life support systems for sub-competent [*i.e.* retarded] patients (or post-competent patients whose views are unknown). These cases assume that R has a motive (religious scruples, a desire to put down the burden of care) to choose wrongly for X. They also assume that courts can correct R's choice because there are certain primary goods (life, health, the absence of pain) that any rational person would want. In rejecting them, the argument goes, R acts irrationally on X's behalf. The government therefore intervenes to free X from the burden of R's representation.

There are problems, though, with relying on these goods to define X's 'best interests.' People value other things too, some more highly than the 'primary' goods. Suppose that I am hit by a truck and rendered irreversibly comatose. My wife might refuse treatment for me, because she believed that a dignified death and peace of mind for my family were more important for me than prolonged nonsapient life. There is nothing objectively wrong about this choice. A court could not confidently say that she ought to do otherwise. It might say that treatment was a more popular option than the one my wife had chosen. But even if that were true (and I doubt it), it is not a convincing reason for imposing it on me.

*   *   *

C.   Trustee: The Subjective View

Given th[is] difficult[y] I see no alternative in many, perhaps most, cases to having R choose for X what R thinks is good.   *   *   *

If we structure the relation between X and R in this way, then X is not free vis à vis R. R is not guided by X's choices as in proxy cases. *   *   * R simply chooses for X as R thinks best. This loss of freedom is not as serious as some people suppose. If X is [post]-competent he is incapable of acting freely except through a representative. The real question is who his representative should be—[his family] or the state. [His family], because they are tied to him by bonds of love and kinship, are more likely to understand his good * * * and to pursue it for his sake. * * *

IV. FREEDOM AND THE GOVERNMENT

I now want to look at X's freedom vis à vis the government. This is the kind of freedom the Constitution is concerned with. * * * I will conclude that in many cases we can quite sensibly speak about X's 'freedom.' But when the government steps into R's shoes, or when it supervises R's choices according to its own standards, then I think we should say that X is not free.

* * *

[A]. The Government as Representative

As a general matter * * * it is sensible to speak about X's freedom against the government when X is represented by R. But who R is makes a difference. Consider first the situation where X is incompetent and has no R to act for him: * * * the homeless mentally disabled, and similar unfortunates. Because they are incompetent these people cannot act and choose for themselves. Nor can they act and choose through representatives. If people who act through representatives are like self-governing citizens of a republic, these unfortunates are like slaves or aliens. They are not self-governing because they are unrepresented.

In these circumstances it is senseless to talk about freedom as a constitutional right. That freedom is a relation of four variables (X, x, Y, y), but here one variable is absent: such a person cannot do x. A comatose patient who has no family or friends cannot choose to live or die. * * * These people may have a right to considerate treatment, but they are not free.

Suppose though that the government as *parens patriae* steps into the role of R. It may initiate involuntary commitment of the mentally ill, or [provide treatment for abandoned people] in state institutions * * *. It is no condemnation of such treatment to say that it is inconsistent with freedom. These people have no other representative and would not be free in any event. But we must acknowledge that they are not free when the government represents them. There is a sense in which they can then act and choose. But their actions are not free because they are directed by the government. In terms of the symbols we have used (X, x, Y, y) we could say that x is not an independent variable. Rather, $x = y$. * * *

[B]. Government Supervision of Representatives

Suppose, though, that * * * X has [someone] (R) to represent him, and that the government intervenes only to assure that R acts in a way that is objectively good for X. I have already discussed in Part III.B. a number of cases that correspond to this model. In dealing with incompetent patients whose wishes are unclear, the Supreme Court has allowed states to give life-sustaining treatment over the [family's] objection.[2] * * *

What happens in these cases is that X has a representative (R) who is not the government, and R can choose some actions (x) on X's behalf. But the range of choices open to R is restricted to what is objectively good, as defined by a 'best interests' or some similar standard. [Families] may be allowed to do x * * * but forbidden to do not-x: they may opt for continued treatment, * * * but not for death[.] Once again it becomes hard to talk about X's constitutional freedom as a relation of four variables (X, x, Y, y). By controlling R's discretion the government makes choices for X, and once again $x = y$.

* * *

V. CONCLUSION

I have argued that people who cannot act rationally are free in a constitutional sense when they have a representative to choose for them. It is inconsistent with the idea of freedom for the government to act as a representative or to supervise a representative's choices. The Constitution requires, as a general rule, that the government withdraw from these cases. This is not a radical proposition. It simply commits those who are not competent to the care of their families rather than the state.

I do not mean to idealize familial relations beyond the limits that the data support. I recognize, as anyone must, that there are [family members who have no love for one another], and whose choices can be callous, selfish, or downright evil. In such cases we should disqualify [them] as proper representatives and override their choices. In the terminology of the legal rules that we apply to claims about freedom, we would say of such cases that there is a compelling state interest in overriding X's claim to freedom. But that is not inconsistent with my argument. X, though better off, is not free.

NANCY K. RHODEN, LITIGATING LIFE AND DEATH

102 Harv.L.Rev. 375, 380, 384–394 (1988).

A. THE PARADIGM OF THE INCOMPETENT'S "RIGHTS"

* * *

The legal paradigm * * * holds that the justification for stopping treatment for incompetents—self-determination—is the same as for competent patients; it merely must be implemented differently.

---

2. See *Cruzan [v. Director, Missouri Dept. of Health*], 110 S.Ct. [2841,] 2855–2856 [(1990)]. Alternatively, states can decide to give or withhold treatment according to their assessment of the patient's "best interests." *Id.* at 2848–2849; *Matter of Conroy,* 486 A.2d [1209,] 1231 [(N.J.1985)].

Where incompetents are concerned, family members must prove that termination is what the patient would choose. It is easy to see why courts have taken this approach: a constitutional right of families to decide these issues has never been recognized, and without hearkening back to the patient's right to privacy, a decision to terminate treatment, no matter how reasonable, appears to lack legal justification. Nonetheless, this approach creates certain conceptual problems.

B. OBVIOUS LIMITATIONS OF THIS PARADIGM

Even supporters of the incompetent's "right" to choose must recognize that this approach has its limitations. A case that exceeded such limits was *Saikewicz,* in which the issue was whether Mr. Saikewicz, a sixty-seven-year-old, profoundly retarded state hospital patient with leukemia, should be given chemotherapy. Even with the proposed treatment, his prognosis was grim—a thirty to fifty percent chance of a brief remission.[46] The chemotherapy would cause pain, nausea, and vomiting, and because Mr. Saikewicz would not understand its purpose, he might perceive it as torture and would probably have to be restrained. The *Saikewicz* court reached the perfectly reasonable, albeit not uncontroversial, conclusion that even though most people would choose the chemotherapy, the treatment's severe limitations, combined with the patient's inability to understand the reason for the pain, made withholding chemotherapy appropriate. The perceived need for a rights-based justification, however, led the *Saikewicz* court to articulate the following rather remarkable statement of the standard for decision:

> In short, the decision in cases such as this should be that which would be made by the incompetent person, if that person were competent, but taking into account the present and future incompetency of the individual as one of the factors which would necessarily enter into the decision-making process of the competent person.

Criticism of this convoluted counterfactual legal standard abounds, and borders on ridicule. John Arras has called it the "bioethical equivalent of squaring the circle." In *In re Storar,*[51] another court faced with a treatment decision for a profoundly retarded, nonverbal patient said that asking what the patient would want if he could, for a miraculous moment, comprehend his plight, would be like asking, " '[I]f it snowed all summer would it then be winter?' " * * * [T]he miraculously lucid Mr. Saikewicz would not be Mr. Saikewicz at all. He would be someone else entirely—a person who could comprehend complex medical and moral dilemmas. The *Saikewicz* opinion is indeed an apt target for ridicule. It should be noted, however, that this is only because the court was following the judicial inclination to equate incompetents with competents to its logical—if incoherent—extension.

* * *

46. [*Superintendent of Belchertown State School v. Saikewicz,* 373 Mass. 728, 370 N.E.2d 417 (1977).]

51. 52 N.Y.2d 353, 420 N.E.2d 64 (1981).

A proponent of the rights paradigm might respond that, although Mr. Saikewicz lacked capacity to choose, and thus was not exactly like competent or previously competent patients, it is still perfectly sensible to hold that a proxy may exercise Mr. Saikewicz's right of self-determination. After all, because it is generally agreed that all humans have a right to life, if someone were simply proposing to kill Mr. Saikewicz, we would correctly say that a guardian who objected was protecting Mr. Saikewicz's right to life. This response, however, simply does not work in cases like *Saikewicz*. Deciding whether Mr. Saikewicz should have been treated was not as simple as deciding to protect an incompetent's right to life, because the issue posed was one about which reasonable people could differ. The right in question was thus not the right to have one thing or another done, but the right to choose.

   * * * A person can certainly have the right to do something she is incapable of doing successfully—such as sinking every basket she shoots—or at least can have a right to try. Yet it seems very odd, and certainly not helpful, to attribute to her a right to do something for which she lacks all capacity. The quadriplegic's freedom from external restraint against sinking baskets does not give her a meaningful right to sink them. Moreover, it is no solution to hold that a personal right requiring cognitive capacity—like a right of choice—can be exercised for the incompetent by someone else. Such a theory would make it perfectly sensible to claim that my cat has a right to choose where we live, and that I simply exercise it for her, as a caring, responsible proxy. In cases such as *Saikewicz,* it is unavoidable that a proxy must make the choice. Yet it is misleading to justify or characterize that act as proxy implementation of a right to choose, much as it would be misleading to say that a social worker assigned to bring a profoundly retarded person to some church or other is exercising the incompetent's "right" to freedom of religion. In these cases the proxy must simply decide, making the best decision she can.

C. LESS OBVIOUS LIMITATIONS OF THE PARADIGM

Cases involving patients who never had rational, developed value systems into which proxies could delve are, of course, the ones for which the rights-paradigm seems the most implausible. Persons who were never competent are radically and inescapably unlike competent persons. Indeed, later decisions such as *In re Conroy* have admitted that the subjective test may be unworkable for such patients and that decisions made for them cannot be justified by reference to the right of self-determination.[58] The *Conroy* court, however, adhered to the view that, when there is clear proof of a formerly competent patient's probable desires, the subjective test can be seen as implementing the patient's right to self-determination. We must, however, distinguish between a proxy's acting upon a perceived preference and actually implementing an expressed choice.

58. [98 N.J. 321, 486 A.2d 1209 (1985).]

Morally speaking, acting on the basis of even quite clear desires is not the same thing as obeying a living will and implementing the patient's choice. Perhaps an example will make this clear. Inmates on death row have a right to choose what they want to eat for their final dinner. Suppose inmate *A* specifically requests steak, french fries, and a chocolate shake. The prison chef, however, believes that a macrobiotic diet is far more healthful, and brings *A* his tastiest concoction of rice, wheatberries, and tofu. Despite the delicacy of the fare, *A*'s right to choose has been infringed. However, suppose inmate *B*, whose dietary inclinations and execution date are identical to *A*'s, is busy doing other things and forgets to put in his dinner request. Although the chef is well aware of *B*'s preferences, he brings him the macrobiotic dinner as well. The chef has certainly not made the most kind or considerate choice. But has he violated *B*'s rights? It seems not, inasmuch as *B* never explicitly made a choice. Moreover, had the chef brought *B* a juicy steak, we would say that he made a compassionate choice, even the right choice, but not that he satisfied *B*'s rights.

Treatment decisions are no different. The competent person who leaves no clear directives cannot claim a right that her wishes, imagined or extrapolated, be followed. * * * [A] proxy who implements a patient's prior choice exercises the patient's right to choose, whereas one who bases a decision on the patient's preferences does something that cannot be characterized in precisely the same way.

One might ask why this matters. After all, if there is clear proof of the patient's desires * * * a proxy should act upon them, even though her action is not rights-based in the same way as obeying a living will. This is true, but there are several problems with hearkening back to rights and requiring, even if only verbally, clear proof of what the patient would want. The problems all center around the fact that courts require a higher quantum of justification than is typically available, and are led to write opinions that misleadingly imply that such a justification is possible. In so doing, they again downplay the important differences between competent and incompetent patients: formerly competent patients differ from never-competent ones, but if they never expressed a choice, they also differ significantly from competent patients and from formerly competent patients who did make their choices known.

1. The Evidentiary Standard.—The *Conroy* court insisted that the subjective test requires clear proof of a formerly competent patient's desires. Ms. Conroy had made no specific statements about how she wanted to be treated. She had, however, avoided doctors, refused to sign herself into an emergency room, and expressed a desire to die in her own house. Although these facts did not satisfy the subjective test, *Conroy* erected no insuperable barriers to meeting the test when the patient has made no specific statements on the topic. Indeed, not only did the *Conroy* court permit inferences from such things as religious beliefs and prior medical practices, but it also said that Ms. Conroy's guardian should, for example, have investigated her responses to such things as the illnesses and deaths of her sisters and others.

* * * Yet the stringency of the *Conroy* court's evidentiary standard seems fundamentally incompatible with using someone's views about life, the afterlife, and the illnesses of others to prove her intent. By nature, inferences from this type of evidence cannot lead to the clear, unambiguous proof required by the *Conroy* court's subjective test. Ms. Conroy was independent, a trait various decisions have relied on to support their judgments that patients would have chosen to have treatment terminated. But are independent people necessarily less tenacious in clinging to life? And what if the patient was a timorous, dependent soul? Would this clearly imply a preference for nonsentient life? Suppose Claire Conroy had nursed her sisters, sadly mourned their passing, and said she wished they had not died so soon? Would this suggest she wished to linger on in her current state? Alternatively, what if she had called someone's sudden death a blessing? Would this suggest that she would also want to go quickly? Or is viewing another's rapid demise as a blessing simply too far removed from seeing your own death as one? * * * In sum, little other than explicit statements for or against termination seems more than mildly inferential in these cases. It is reassuring to believe that Ms. Conroy would view her life as being as intolerable as those around her saw it. Absent explicit prior statements, however, the problems in applying the subjective standard to formerly competent patients mirror, albeit in a milder form, the problems that arise when the patient was never competent. It seems that the stringent evidentiary standard, although reassuring, is often impossible to meet, even when available evidence points to nontreatment as a perfectly reasonable course of action.

2. *The Need for Proxy Interpretation.*—The problem of proving a patient's intent under *Conroy*'s subjective standard is closely connected to the problem of determining how relatives "know" what the patient would want in the absence of clear prior statements, and how this knowledge is influenced by the relatives' own values and beliefs. I am not expressing skepticism here about a family member's knowledge: the loving wife of forty years who says she *just knows* her husband would not want further treatment is probably right. Yet her knowledge may largely be of an intuitive, nonverbal sort that is difficult to translate into clear proof in a court of law. Moreover, the wife may, quite reasonably, be unable to view her husband as entirely separate from herself, or his interests and values as entirely independent of hers.
* * *

* * *

What all this means is that, although a decision to terminate can be shown to be congruent with the patient's former values and psychological traits, it is unlikely, absent specific statements, that the family can prove to outsiders that these patient characteristics clearly mandate such a choice. Absent prior directives, decisions are not, properly speaking, rights-based. Nor are they likely to be demonstrably "right" to objective third parties unconnected to the patient. To someone who lacks intuitive knowledge of the patient, such a subjective test will seldom go further than yielding answers that seem reasonable, or perhaps more reasonable than the alternatives.

RONALD DWORKIN, THE RIGHT TO DEATH
N.Y.Rev. of Books 14–17 (Jan. 31, 1991).

[In *Cruzan v. Director, Missouri Department of Health* Justice Rehnquist] offered two different, though not clearly distinct, arguments why Missouri has a right to tip the scales in favor of keeping comatose people alive by demanding "clear and convincing" evidence that they had decided they would rather die. His first argument appealed to the best interests of incompetent people. He said that a rule requiring evidence of a formal declaration of a past decision to die, before life support can be terminated, benefits people who have become comatose because it protects them against guardians who abuse their trust, and because a decision not to terminate is always reversible if documented evidence of a formal past decision emerges later. His second argument is very different: it appeals not to the interests of comatose patients but to Missouri's supposed independent interests in keeping such patients alive. * * *

* * *

Rehnquist devotes most of his opinion to the first argument: that the Missouri rule is in the best interests of most of the thousands of people who live in a permanent vegetative state and did not sign living wills when they could. * * *

* * *

[But] the insensate life of the permanently vegetative * * * is not valuable to anyone. Some people, no doubt, would want to be kept alive indefinitely in such a state out of religious convictions: they might think that failing to prolong life as long as possible is insulting to God, for example. But even they do not think that it is in *their* interests to live on; most such people would hope, I think, for an early death in that situation, though one in which everything had been done to prolong life. They would regard an early death as an instance of God's mercy.

* * *

Some of Rehnquist's arguments depend not on the assumption that it is normally in the interests of a permanently comatose person to continue living, but on the equally implausible assumption that continued life in those circumstances is never against such a person's interests. This is the premise of his argument, for example, that it is better to keep a comatose patient alive than to allow her to die, even if the chances of recovery are infinitesimal, because the latter decision is irreversible. He assumes that someone in Nancy Cruzan's position suffers no disadvantage in continuing to live, so that if there is only the barest conceivable possibility of some extraordinary medical discovery in the future, however remote that may seem now, it must be on balance in their interests to continue living as long as possible.

If the only things people worried about, or wanted to avoid, were pain and other unpleasant physical experiences, then of course they would be indifferent about whether, if they became permanently comatose, their bodies continued to live or not. But people care about many other things as well. They worry about their dignity and integrity, and about the view other people have of them, how they are conceived and remembered. Many of them are anxious that their relatives and friends not have to bear the burdens, whether emotional or financial, of keeping them alive. Many are appalled by the thought of resources being wasted on them that might be used for the benefit of other people, who have genuine, conscious lives to lead.

These various concerns explain the horror so many people feel at the idea of existing pointlessly for years as a vegetable. They think that a bare biological existence, with no intelligence or sensibility or sensation, is not a matter of indifference, but something bad for them, something that damages their lives considered as a whole. * * *

* * *

We must therefore turn to Rehnquist's second, much less developed, argument: that Missouri can impose evidentiary requirements, even if that is against Cruzan's interests and those of other permanently incompetent people, in order to protect its own interests in preserving life. * * *

* * *

* * * Of course government is properly concerned with the welfare and well-being of its citizens, and it has the right, for that reason, to try to prevent them from being killed or put at risk of death from disease or accident. But the state's obvious and general concern with its citizen's well-being does not give it a reason to preserve someone's life when his or her welfare would be better served by being permitted to die in dignity. So the state interest that Rehnquist has in mind, as justifying Missouri's otherwise unreasonable evidentiary rule, must be a different, less familiar, one: it must supply a reason for forcing people to accept medical treatment when they or their guardians plausibly think they would be better off dead.

* * *

* * * It might be said that keeping people alive, even when they would be better off dead, helps to protect the community's sense of the importance of life. I agree that society is better and more secure when its members share a sense that human life is sacred, and that no effort should be spared to save lives. People who lack that sense may themselves be more ready to kill, and will be less anxious to make sacrifices to protect the lives of others. That seems to me the most powerful available argument why states should be permitted to outlaw elective abortion of very late-stage fetuses, for example. But it is

extremely implausible that allowing a permanently comatose patient to die, after a solemn proceeding devoted only to her wishes and interests, will in any way erode a community's sense of the importance of life.

So a state cannot justify keeping comatose people alive on the instrumental ground that this is necessary to prevent murder or to encourage people to vote for famine relief. If Rehnquist is right that a state has a legitimate interest in preserving all human life, then this must be in virtue not of any instrumental argument but of the *intrinsic* value of such life, its importance for its own sake. Most people do believe that human life has intrinsic importance, and perhaps Rehnquist thinks it unnecessary either to clarify or to justify that idea. It is unclear, however, that they accept the idea on any ground, or in any sense, that supports his case. For some people, for example, life has intrinsic value because it is a gift of God; they believe, as I said, that it is wrong not to struggle to prolong life, because this is an insult to Him, who alone should decide when life ends. But the Constitution does not allow states to justify policy on grounds of religious doctrine; some more secular account of the intrinsic value of life would be needed to support Rehnquist's second argument.

It will be helpful to distinguish two forms that a more secular version of the claim might take. The first supposes that a human life, in any form or circumstance, is a unique and valuable addition to the universe, so that the stock of value is needlessly diminished when any life is shorter than it might be. That does not seem a convincing view. Even if we think that a conscious, reflective, engaged human life is inherently valuable, we might well doubt that an insensate, vegetative life has any value at all.

The view that all forms of life are inherently valuable is also disqualified for a different reason. On that view we would have as much reason to bring new lives into being, increasing the population, as for prolonging lives already in progress. After all, people who think that great art is inherently valuable have the same reason for encouraging the production of more masterpieces as for preserving art that now exists. But most people who think life has intrinsic significance do not think that they therefore have any general duty to procreate or to encourage procreation. In any case, the Supreme Court's decision in *Griswold,* which is now accepted by almost everyone, holds that the states have no power to prohibit contraception.

People who think that life has intrinsic value or importance, but do not think that this fact offers any reason for increasing the population, understand life's value in a second and more conditional way. They mean, I think, that once a human life has begun it is terribly important that it go well, that it be a good rather than a bad life, a successful rather than a wasted one. Most people accept that human life has inherent importance in that sense. That explains why they try not just to make their lives pleasant but to give them worth and also why it seems a tragedy when people decide, late in life, that they can take neither pride nor satisfaction in the way they have lived. Of course nothing in the idea that life has intrinsic importance in this second sense can justify a policy of keeping permanently comatose people alive. The worth of their lives—the character of the lives they have led—cannot be improved just by keeping the bodies they used to inhabit technically alive. On the contrary, that makes their lives worse, because it is a bad thing, for all the reasons I described earlier, to have one's body medicated, fed, and groomed, as an object of pointless and degrading solicitude, after one's mind is dead. Rehnquist's second argument is therefore a dramatic failure: Missouri's policy is not supported but condemned by the idea that human life is important for its own sake, on the only understanding of that idea that is available in our constitutional system.

YALE KAMISAR, FINAL FRONTIER: LIFE, DEATH, AND LAW: RIGHT TO DIE OR LICENSE TO KILL?

Legal Times 26 (Nov. 13, 1989).

[T]o call Nancy Cruzan's case a matter of the right to die seems strained, if not contrived. The situation is a tragic one. Cruzan has been in a persistent vegetative state since 1983, when, at the age of 25, she was in a severe car accident. Although she is able to breathe on her own, she receives all her nutrition and fluids through a feeding tube inserted into her stomach. When her parents sought to halt this life support, they were rebuffed, first by officials of the Missouri state hospital where Cruzan is a patient and ultimately by the Missouri Supreme Court.

Many would argue that Nancy Cruzan is "better off dead." Others would contend that keeping her alive is a misuse of limited resources—especially at a time of soaring health-care costs. These may be good policy arguments. But policy arguments do not establish a constitutional right. * * *

Nancy Cruzan * * * did not ask to die or consent to her death. Before lapsing into her present condition, she neither made a "living will" nor executed any other directive requesting that she be allowed to die without "medical intervention." Nor did she designate anyone else to make health-care decisions for her.

When she was still a vibrant person, Cruzan once remarked that she did not want to live "as a vegetable." In another conversation, she stated that if she couldn't do things for herself "even halfway, let alone not at all," she "wouldn't want to live that way." To a majority of the Missouri Supreme Court, those remarks were so remote, general, and casual as to be "unreliable for the purpose of establishing her intent." For a guardian to exercise whatever right an incompetent person may have to be free from life support, the court ruled, there must be "clear and convincing evidence" of the incompetent patient's wishes.

No doubt many medical/legal commentators would argue (or already have) that in a case like Cruzan the family decision to pull the feeding tube should be honored. Indeed, a goodly number of other state courts would reach (or already have reached) a different result than did the Missouri Supreme Court. This is not surprising in an exploding, still evolving area of law, morality, ethics, and social judgment.

But the U.S. Supreme Court could not establish a right to die in the Cruzan case without generating other difficult questions: What quantum of proof is needed to support the right to die? What presumptions and burdens of production and persuasion should the Court assign? What should the right mean for the never-competent and the no-longer-competent? What if there is clear and convincing evidence that the patient would prefer to die quickly by lethal injection, rather than slowly by starvation and dehydration? If a person has a constitutional right to die, why doesn't she have the right to choose what she regards as the most "humane" or "dignified" way to die?

On the other hand, the U.S. Supreme Court could uphold the Missouri Supreme Court's decision in Cruzan without restricting other states' authority to permit a different result on similar facts. After all, the Court is not being asked to decide whether someone like Nancy Cruzan has a constitutional right to live (although it would not be surprising if someday someone made that argument). The issue presented is whether a state is constitutionally compelled to allow someone in Cruzan's circumstances to die.

Those who favor letting "hopeless" patients die talk much about "the patient's preference" and the "right of self-determination," about "individual autonomy" and the "right to privacy" and the "right to decide what is to be done with one's person." How meaningful are these words and phrases in a case like Cruzan? Whose preferences are really being advanced, Cruzan's or her family's? Whose right to decide what to do with her person is really involved, Cruzan's or her family's?

* * *

I can hear the argument now: She is being kept alive "against her will." Cruel as it is to say, Cruzan no longer has "a will." And she never clearly explained her desires on life-and-death matters when she did have one.

I can also hear the argument that the only way to honor Cruzan's right to privacy is to let her family exercise it for her. But why start with the premise that someone in her plight still has a right to privacy? If the right exists because there are choices that belong to the individual alone, and the individual did not exercise those choices—and is no longer able to do so—is it not more coherent to say that this right no longer exists?

To be sure, the dissenting Missouri justices maintained that the statements Cruzan made before becoming incompetent do provide sufficient evidence of her wish to be allowed to die in her present condition. Some state courts would agree. Others would go still further and permit life support to be terminated absent any specific evidence of the patient's intent if the family and physician deemed it in the patient's "best interests" to do so.

On the other hand, the highest court of New York * * * would probably side with the majority of the Missouri Supreme Court. Last year, for example, in Matter of Westchester County Medical Center, 531 N.E.2d 607, the New York Court of Appeals underscored its "clear and convincing" standard when it concluded that patient's remarks—before she was struck and silenced by illness—that she would not want to live without dignity or without being able to care for herself did not furnish sufficient proof that she held "a firm and settled commitment to the termination of life support" under the circumstances presented.

Other states are free to adopt a less demanding standard than Missouri or New York. But must they?

Consider the views of Rabbi J. David Bleich, professor of Jewish law and ethics at Yeshiva University's Benjamin N. Cardozo Law School * * *:

"[A] casual comment reflecting an emotional reaction to a dramatic presentation of the negative aspects of prolongation of life does not constitute a reasoned, deliberate choice. Law provides that material possessions may be disposed of only by a written testament executed in a manner designed to assure that the decisions reflected therein reflect deliberation, purpose, and seriousness of intent. Surely, no less a standard should be acceptable for the disposition of one's life."

The question is not whether Professor Bleich is right or wrong. The question is whether a state court (or a state legislature) that shares his view is violating the federal Constitution. Can it seriously be said that it is?

The argument that nothing in the Constitution prevents a state from adopting such a demanding standard is particularly strong, I think, when the death at issue is death by starvation and dehydration. (No one has suggested that Nancy Cruzan ever considered the possibility of dying this way.) According to Mark Siegler, medical professor at the University of Chicago, and Alan Weisbard, executive director of the New Jersey Bioethics Commission, as recently as 1980 the idea that fluids and nutrients might be withdrawn from any patient, even a dying one, "was a notion that would have been repudiated, if not condemned, by most health professionals." But the law has moved quickly since then.

In recent years, the American Medical Association, various medical/legal groups, and some courts have rejected any distinction between the termination of artificial feeding and the cessation of other forms of life-sustaining treatment. But this is still a matter of considerable dispute. Many respected commentators * * * insist that the distinction should be preserved for various reasons: (1) Nutrition and hydration are basic care, not medical treatment; (2) providing such care is an important symbol of our human relatedness and commitment to care; (3) denial of such care poses a serious threat to the doctor/patient and health-care facility/patient relationships; and (4) permitting withdrawal of nutrition and hydration undermines the psychological separation of "killing" from "letting die."

The New York State Task Force on Life and the Law is one of the medical/legal groups that, in a 1987 report, did reject the distinction between artificial nutrition and hydration and other forms of life-sustaining treatment. But for purposes of Cruzan, I think the conclusion the task force reached is less significant than an observation it made along the way: Cases involving decisions about artificial nutrition and hydration "are at the outer edges of our collective social and medical experience." Indeed they are—all the more reason not to constitutionalize them yet.

Although those who balk at terminating artificial nutrition and hydration have not prevailed in bioethics circles recently, they have met with considerable success in legislative halls. Consider this: * * * nearly half of the 39 states that have adopted living-will statutes (including Missouri) specifically exclude artificial nutrition and hydration from the category of life-sustaining treatment that may be refused. In only one state—Utah—does the law provide that a person may give a directive to withdraw or withhold nutrition and hydration in a living will.

If, as the Supreme Court recently told us in Stanford v. Kentucky, 110 S.Ct. 23 (1989), the pattern of enacted laws constitutes "the primary and most reliable indication of consensus," the reluctance of many state legislatures to permit the termination of artificial feeding, even where the patient has executed a living will, poses a significant obstacle to the right to die in cases like Cruzan.

Moreover, the living-will legislation presents a second hurdle. In most states, a living will only becomes operative after its maker has become "terminally ill[.]" [As this term is commonly defined, a patient must be suffering from an irreversible condition that will produce death within a short time *regardless* of medical intervention. If this common definition applies,] Nancy Cruzan is neither dying nor terminally ill. If artificial nutrition and hydration are not stopped, she could live for many years.

Again, I can hear the argument of right-to-die proponents: In this area, the Supreme Court should defer to the medical profession, not to the legislative consensus. Whether life-sustaining treatment should be ended, at least when the family agrees with the doctor, is essentially a medical judgment to be left to the medical community.

I think not. Whether a patient is in a vegetative state and whether a patient's condition is irreversible are medical questions. But whether a patient should live or die is not. Rather, it is a fundamental moral-legal-philosophical-social-political question.

BIBLIOGRAPHY

Beschle, *Autonomous Decisionmaking and Social Choice: Examining the "Right to Die"*, 77 Ky.L.J. 319 (1989).

Buchanan, *The Limits of Proxy Decision–Making*, in R. Sartorious, ed., PATERNALISM 153 (1983).

R. Burt, TAKING CARE OF STRANGERS, ch. 7 (1979).

Burt, *The Ideal of Community in the Work of the President's Commission*, 6 Cardozo L.Rev. 267 (1984).

D. Callahan, SETTING LIMITS: MEDICAL GOALS IN AN AGING SOCIETY (1987).

Emanuel, *A Communal Vision of Care for Incompetent Patients*, 17 Hastings Center Rep. 15 (1987).

Garvey, *Freedom and Choice in Constitutional Law*, 94 Harv.L.Rev. 1756 (1981).

Mayo, *Constitutionalizing the "Right to Die"*, 49 Md.L.Rev. 103 (1990).

A. Meisel, THE RIGHT TO DIE (1989).

Minow, *Beyond State Intervention in the Family: For Baby Jane Doe*, 18 Mich.J.L.Rev. 933 (1985).

Mooney, *Deciding Not To Resuscitate Hospital Patients: Medical and Legal Perspectives*, 1986 U.Ill.L.Rev. 1025.

Note, *Developments in the Law—Medical Technology and the Law*, 103 Harv.L.Rev. 1519 (1990).

Note, *Proxy Decisionmaking for the Terminally Ill: The Virginia Approach*, 70 Va.L.Rev. 1269 (1984).

Note, *Voluntary Active Euthanasia for the Terminally Ill and the Constitutional Right to Privacy*, 69 Cornell L.Rev. 363 (1984).

Rachels, *Active and Passive Euthanasia*, 292 New Eng.J.Med. 78 (1975).

O. Russell, FREEDOM TO DIE (2d ed. 1977).

Schneider, *Rights Discourse and Neonatal Euthanasia*, 76 Calif.L.Rev. 151 (1988).

Symposium, *Privacy and the Family in Medical Decisions*, 23 J.Family L. 173 (1984–85).

The President's Commission for the Study of Ethical Problems in Medicine and Biomedical and Behavioral Research, DECIDING TO FOREGO LIFE–SUSTAINING TREATMENT (1983).

J. Wilson, DEATH BY DECISION (1975).

Wreen, *Breathing a Little Life Into a Distinction*, 46 Phil.Stud. 395 (1984).

†